Joaquin Quiñonero-Candela Ido Dagan
Bernardo Magnini Florence d'Alché-Buc (Eds.)

# Machine Learning Challenges



## Evaluating Predictive Uncertainty Visual Object Classification and Recognizing Textual Entailment

First PASCAL Machine Learning Challenges Workshop, MLCW 2005
Southampton, UK, April 11-13, 2005
Revised Selected Papers

Volume Editors

Joaquin Quiñonero-Candela
Max Planck Institute for Biological Cybernetics
Spemannstr. 38, 72076 Tübingen, Germany
E-mail: joaquin@first.fraunhofer.de

Ido Dagan
Bar Ilan University
Ramat Gan 52900, Israel
E-mail: dagan@macs.biu.ac.il

Bernardo Magnini
ITC-irst, Centro per la Ricerca Scientifica e Tecnologica
Via Sommarive 14, 38050 Povo (Trento), Italy
E-mail: magnini@itc.it

Florence d'Alché-Buc
Université d'Evry-Val d'Essonne
IBISC CNRS FRE 2873 and GENOPOLE
523, Place des terrasses, 91000 Evry, France
E-mail: florence.dalche@ibisc.univ-evry.fr

Library of Congress Control Number: 2006924677

CR Subject Classification (1998): I.2.6-8, I.2.3, I.4-7, F.1, F.2, F.4

LNCS Sublibrary: SL 7 – Artificial Intelligence

ISSN 0302-9743
ISBN-10 3-540-33427-0 Springer Berlin Heidelberg New York
ISBN-13 978-3-540-33427-9 Springer Berlin Heidelberg New York



Springer is a part of Springer Science+Business Media

springer.com


Printed in Germany

Typesetting: Camera-ready by author, data conversion by Scientific Publishing Services, Chennai, India
Printed on acid-free paper SPIN: 11736790 06/3142 5 4 3 2 1 0

# Preface

The first **PASCAL** Machine Learning Challenges Workshop (MLCW 2005) (see, `www.pascal-network.org/Workshops/PC04/`) was held in Southampton, UK, during April 11-13, 2005. This conference was organized by the Challenges programme of the European Network of Excellence PASCAL (Pattern Analysis, Statistical modelling and ComputationAl Learning) in the framework of the IST Programme of the European Community. First annually and now quarterly, the PASCAL Challenges Programme plays the role of selecting and sponsoring challenging tasks, either practical or theoretical. The aim is to raise difficult machine learning questions and to motivate innovative research and development of new approaches. Financial support covers all the work concerning the cleaning and labelling of the data as well as the preparation of evaluation tools for ranking the results. For the first round of the programme, four challenges were selected according to their impact in the machine learning community, supported from summer 2004 to early spring 2005 by PASCAL and finally invited to participate in MLCW 2005 :

- The first challenge, called "Evaluating Predictive Uncertainty", dealt with the fundamental question of assigning a degree of confidence to the outputs of a classifier or a regressor.
- The goal of the second challenge, called "Visual Object Classes", was to recognise objects from a number of visual objects classes in realistic scenes.
- The third challenge task, called "Recognizing Textual Entailment", consisted in recognizing, given two texts fragments, whether the meaning of one text can be inferred (entailed) from the other.
- The fourth challenge was concerned with the assessment of "Machine Learning Methodologies to Extract Implicit Relations from Documents".

Each of these challenges raised noticeable attention in the research community, attracting numerous participants. The idea behind having a unique workshop was to make participants in different challenges exchange and benefit from the research experienced in other challenges. For the workshop, the session chairs made a first selection among submissions leading to 34 oral contributions. This book is concerned with selected proceedings of the first three challenges, providing a large panel of machine learning issues and solutions. A second round of selection was made to extract the 25 contributed chapters that make up this book, resulting in a selection rate of one half for the three considered challenges whose description follows.

*Evaluating Predictive Uncertainty Challenge*
When making decisions based on predictions, it is essential to have a measure of the uncertainty associated to them, or predictive uncertainty. Decisions are of course most often based on a loss function that is to be minimized in expectation. One common approach in machine learning is to assume knowledge of the loss

function, and then train an algorithm that outputs decisions that directly minimize the expected loss. In a realistic setting, however, the loss function might be unknown, or depend on additional factors only determined at a later stage. A system that predicts the presence of calcification from a mammography should also provide information about its uncertainty. Whether to operate or not will depend on the particular patient, as well as on the context in general. If the loss function is unknown, expressing uncertainties becomes crucial. Failing to do so implies throwing information away.

There does not seem to be a universal way of producing good estimates of predictive uncertainty in the machine learning community, nor a consensus on the ways of evaluating them. In part this is caused by deep fundamental differences in methodology (classical statistics, Bayesian inference, statistical learning theory). We decided to organize the Evaluating Predictive Uncertainty Challenge (`http://predict.kyb.tuebingen.mpg.de/`) to allow the different philosophies to compete directly on the empirical battleground. This required us to define losses for probabilistic predictions. Twenty groups of participants competed on two classification and three regression datasets before the submission deadline of December 11, 2004, and a few more after the deadline. We present six contributed chapters to this volume, by all the winners plus authors of other outstanding entries.

*Visual Objects Classes*

The PASCAL Visual Object Classes Challenge ran from February to March 2005 (`http://www.pascal-network.org/challenges/VOC/`). The goal of the challenge was to recognize objects from a number of visual object classes in realistic scenes (i.e., not pre-segmented objects). Although there already exist benchmarks such as the so-called 'Caltech 5' (faces, airplanes, motorbikes, cars rear, spotted cats) and UIUC car side images, largely used by the community of image recognition, it appears now that the developed methods are achieving such good performance that they have effectively saturated on these datasets, and thus the datasets are failing to challenge the next generation of algorithms. Such saturation can arise because the images used do not explore the full range of variability of the imaged visual class. Some dimensions of variability include: clean vs. cluttered background; stereotypical views vs. multiple views (e.g., side views of cars vs. cars from all angles); degree of scale change, amount of occlusion; the presence of multiple objects (of one or multiple classes) in the images.

Given this problem of saturation of performance, the Visual Object Classes Challenge was designed to be more demanding by enhancing some of the dimensions of variability listed above compared to the databases that had been available previously, so as to explore the failure modes of different algorithms. Four object classes were selected: motorbikes, bicycles, cars and people. Twelve teams entered the challenge. This book includes a contributed review chapter about the methods and the results achieved by the participants.

*Recognizing Textual Entailment*
Semantic analysis of language has been addressed traditionally through interpretation into explicitly stipulated meaning representations. Such semantic interpretation turned out to be a very difficult problem, which led researchers to approximate semantic processing at shallow lexical and lexical-syntactic levels. Usually, such approaches were developed in application-specific settings, without having an encompassing application-independent framework for developing and evaluating generic semantic approaches.

The Recognizing Textual Entailment (RTE) challenge was an attempt to form such a generic framework for applied semantic inference in text understanding. The task takes as input a pair of text snippets, called *text* (T) and *hypothesis* (H), and requires determining whether the meaning of T (most likely) entails that of H or not. The view underlying the RTE task is that different natural language processing applications, including question answering, information extraction, (multi-document) summarization, and machine translation, have to address the language variability problem and recognize that a particular target meaning can be inferred from different text variants. The RTE task abstracts this primary inference need, suggesting that many applications would benefit from generic models for textual entailment.

It is worth emphasizing some relevant features of the task, which contributed to its success:

- RTE is interdisciplinary: the task has been addressed with both machine learning and resource-based NLP techniques. It also succeeded to bridge, as a common benchmark, over different application-oriented communities.
- RTE was a really challenging task: RTE-1, in several respects, was a simplification of the complete task (e.g., we did not consider temporal entailment), but it proved to be at the state of the art of text understanding.
- The challenge attracted 17 participatants and made a strong impact in the research community, followed by a related ACL 2005 workshop and a dozen more conference publications later in 2005, which used the publicly available RTE-1 dataset as a standard benchmark.

February 2006

Joaquin Quiñonero-Candela
Ido Dagan
Bernardo Magnini
Florence d'Alché-Buc
MLCW 2005

# Organization

The first (PASCAL) Machine Learning Challenges Workshop (MLCW 2005) was organized by the Challenges programme of the Network of Excellence PASCAL in Southampton, UK, April 11-13, 2005.

## PASCAL Challenges Programme Committee

| | |
|---|---|
| Programme Chairs | Florence d'Alché–Buc (Université d'Evry)<br>Steve Gunn (University of Southampton)<br>Michèle Sebag (Université de Paris XI) |
| Programme committee | Samy Bengio (IDIAP-Martigny)<br>Alex Clark (Royal Holloway, University of London)<br>Walter Daelemans (University of Antwerp)<br>Cyril Goutte (Xerox Research Centre Europe)<br>Steve Gunn (University of Southampton)<br>Klaus-Robert Mueller (Fraunhofer FIRST)<br>John Shawe-Taylor (University of Southampton)<br>Bill Triggs (INRIA)<br>Chris Watkins (Royal Holloway, University of London) |

## Programme Committee of (PASCAL) MLCW 2005

| | |
|---|---|
| Conference Chair | Florence d'Alché–Buc (Université d'Evry)<br>Steve Gunn (University of Southampton) |
| Local Organization | Eileen Simon (University of Southampton) |

**Session Chairs**

| | |
|---|---|
| Evaluating Predictive Uncertainty | Joaquin Quiñonero-Candela (Max Planck Institute for Biological Cybernetics, Fraunhofer FIRST and TU Berlin) |
| Visual Object Classes | Christopher Williams (University of Edinburgh)<br>Andrew Zisserman (University of Oxford) |

| | |
|---|---|
| Recognizing Textual Entailment | Ido Dagan (Bar-Ilan University)<br>Oren Glickman (Bar-Ilan University)<br>Bernardo Magnini (ITC-irst, Istituto per la Ricerca Scientifica e Tecnologica) |
| Evaluating Machine Learning for Information Extraction | Mary Elaine Califf (Illinois State University)<br>Fabio Ciravegna (University of Sheffield)<br>Dayne Freitag (Fair Isaac Corporation)<br>Nicholas Kushmerick (University College Dublin)<br>Neil Ireson (University of Sheffield)<br>Alberto Lavelli (ITC-irst, Istituto per la Ricerca Scientifica e Tecnologica, Povo) |

## Sponsoring Institution

PASCAL (Pattern Analysis, Statistical modelling and ComputationAl Learning): European Network of Excellence, IST Programme of the European Community, grant number IST-2002-506778.

## Acknowledgements

FAB would like to thank cheerfully Steve Gunn and Michèle Sebag for co-managing the Challenges Programme, Eileen Simon for the nice local organization of the workshop at Southampton and John Shawe-Taylor for his support and his coordination of the European Network of Excellence PASCAL.

# Table of Contents

Evaluating Predictive Uncertainty Challenge
*Joaquin Quiñonero-Candela, Carl Edward Rasmussen, Fabian Sinz, Olivier Bousquet, Bernhard Schölkopf* ............................ 1

Classification with Bayesian Neural Networks
*Radford M. Neal* ............................................ 28

A Pragmatic Bayesian Approach to Predictive Uncertainty
*Iain Murray, Edward Snelson* .................................. 33

Many Are Better Than One: Improving Probabilistic Estimates from Decision Trees
*Nitesh V. Chawla* ............................................ 41

Estimating Predictive Variances with Kernel Ridge Regression
*Gavin C. Cawley, Nicola L.C. Talbot, Olivier Chapelle* .............. 56

Competitive Associative Nets and Cross-Validation for Estimating Predictive Uncertainty on Regression Problems
*Shuichi Kurogi, Miho Sawa, Shinya Tanaka* ........................ 78

Lessons Learned in the Challenge: Making Predictions and Scoring Them
*Jukka Kohonen, Jukka Suomela* ................................. 95

The 2005 PASCAL Visual Object Classes Challenge
*Mark Everingham, Andrew Zisserman, Christopher K.I. Williams, Luc Van Gool, Moray Allan, Christopher M. Bishop, Olivier Chapelle, Navneet Dalal, Thomas Deselaers, Gyuri Dorkó, Stefan Duffner, Jan Eichhorn, Jason D.R. Farquhar, Mario Fritz, Christophe Garcia, Tom Griffiths, Frederic Jurie, Daniel Keysers, Markus Koskela, Jorma Laaksonen, Diane Larlus, Bastian Leibe, Hongying Meng, Hermann Ney, Bernt Schiele, Cordelia Schmid, Edgar Seemann, John Shawe-Taylor, Amos Storkey, Sandor Szedmak, Bill Triggs, Ilkay Ulusoy, Ville Viitaniemi, Jianguo Zhang* ................................ 117

The PASCAL Recognising Textual Entailment Challenge
*Ido Dagan, Oren Glickman, Bernardo Magnini* ...................... 177

Using Bleu-like Algorithms for the Automatic Recognition of Entailment
*Diana Pérez, Enrique Alfonseca* ................................ 191

What Syntax Can Contribute in the Entailment Task
*Lucy Vanderwende, William B. Dolan* . . . . . . 205

Combining Lexical Resources with Tree Edit Distance for Recognizing Textual Entailment
*Milen Kouylekov, Bernardo Magnini* . . . . . . 217

Textual Entailment Recognition Based on Dependency Analysis and *WordNet*
*Jesús Herrera, Anselmo Peñas, Felisa Verdejo* . . . . . . 231

Learning Textual Entailment on a Distance Feature Space
*Maria Teresa Pazienza, Marco Pennacchiotti, Fabio Massimo Zanzotto* . . . . . . 240

An Inference Model for Semantic Entailment in Natural Language
*Rodrigo de Salvo Braz, Roxana Girju, Vasin Punyakanok, Dan Roth, Mark Sammons* . . . . . . 261

A Lexical Alignment Model for Probabilistic Textual Entailment
*Oren Glickman, Ido Dagan, Moshe Koppel* . . . . . . 287

Textual Entailment Recognition Using Inversion Transduction Grammars
*Dekai Wu* . . . . . . 299

Evaluating Semantic Evaluations: How RTE Measures Up
*Sam Bayer, John Burger, Lisa Ferro, John Henderson, Lynette Hirschman, Alex Yeh* . . . . . . 309

Partial Predicate Argument Structure Matching for Entailment Determination
*Alina Andreevskaia, Zhuoyan Li, Sabine Bergler* . . . . . . 332

VENSES – A Linguistically-Based System for Semantic Evaluation
*Rodolfo Delmonte, Sara Tonelli, Marco Aldo Piccolino Boniforti, Antonella Bristot* . . . . . . 344

Textual Entailment Recognition Using a Linguistically–Motivated Decision Tree Classifier
*Eamonn Newman, Nicola Stokes, John Dunnion, Joe Carthy* . . . . . . 372

Recognizing Textual Entailment Via Atomic Propositions
*Elena Akhmatova, Diego Mollá* . . . . . . 385

Recognising Textual Entailment with Robust Logical Inference
*Johan Bos, Katja Markert* ........ 404

Applying COGEX to Recognize Textual Entailment
*Daniel Hodges, Christine Clark, Abraham Fowler, Dan Moldovan* ........ 427

Recognizing Textual Entailment: Is Word Similarity Enough?
*Valentin Jijkoun, Maarten de Rijke* ........ 449

**Author Index** ........ 461

# Evaluating Predictive Uncertainty Challenge

Joaquin Quiñonero-Candela[1,2,3], Carl Edward Rasmussen[1], Fabian Sinz[1], Olivier Bousquet[1,4], and Bernhard Schölkopf[1]

[1] Max Planck Institute for Biological Cybernetics, Spemannstr. 38, D-72076 Tübingen, Germany
{carl, fabee, bernhard.schoelkopf}@tuebingen.mpg.de

[2] Fraunhofer FIRST.IDA, Kekuléstr. 7, D-12489 Berlin, Germany
joaquin@first.fraunhofer.de

[3] TU Berlin, SWT, Franklinstr. 28/29, D-10587 Berlin, Germany

[4] Pertinence, 32, rue des Jeûneurs, F-75002 Paris, France
olivier.bousquet@pertinence.com

**Abstract.** This Chapter presents the PASCAL[1] Evaluating Predictive Uncertainty Challenge, introduces the contributed Chapters by the participants who obtained outstanding results, and provides a discussion with some lessons to be learnt. The Challenge was set up to evaluate the ability of Machine Learning algorithms to provide good "probabilistic predictions", rather than just the usual "point predictions" with no measure of uncertainty, in regression and classification problems. Participants had to compete on a number of regression and classification tasks, and were evaluated by both traditional losses that only take into account point predictions and losses we proposed that evaluate the quality of the probabilistic predictions.

## 1 Motivation

Information about the uncertainty of predictions, or *predictive uncertainty*, is essential in decision making. Aware of the traumatic cost of an operation, a surgeon will only decide to operate if there is enough evidence of cancer in the diagnostic. A prediction of the kind "there is 99% probability of cancer" is fundamentally different from "there is 55% probability of cancer", although both could be summarized by the much less informative statement: "there is cancer". An investment bank trying to decide whether to invest or not in a given fund might react differently at the prediction that the fund value will increase by "10%± 1%" than at the prediction that it will increase by "10%± 20%", but it will in any case find any of the two previous predictions way more useful than the point prediction "the expected value increase is 10%". Predictive uncertainties are also used in active learning to select the next training example which will bring most information. Given the enormous cost of experiments

[1] Pattern Analysis, Statistical Modelling and Computational Learning (PASCAL) Network of Excellence, part of the IST Programme of the European Community, IST-2002-506778.

J. Quiñonero-Candela et al. (Eds.): MLCW 2005, LNAI 3944, pp. 1–27, 2006.

with protein binding chips, a drug making company will not bother making experiments whose outcome can be predicted with very low uncertainty.

Decisions are of course most often based on a loss function that is to be minimized in expectation. One common approach in Machine Learning is to assume knowledge of the loss function, and then train an algorithm that outputs decisions that directly minimize the expected loss. In a realistic setting however, the loss function might be unknown, or depend on additional factors only determined at a later stage. A system that predicts the presence of calcification from a mammography should also provide information about its uncertainty. Whether to operate or not will depend on the particular patient, as well as on the context in general. If the loss function is unknown, expressing uncertainties becomes crucial. Failing to do so implies throwing information away.

One particular approach to expressing uncertainty is to treat the unknown quantity of interest ("will it rain?") as a random variable, and make to predictions in the form of probability distributions, also known as *predictive distributions*. We will center our discussion around this specific representation of the uncertainty. But, how to produce reasonable predictive uncertainties? What is a reasonable predictive uncertainty in the first place?

Under the Bayesian paradigm, posterior distributions are obtained on the model parameters, that incorporate both the uncertainty caused by the noise, and by not knowing what the true model is. Integrating over this posterior allows to obtain the posterior distribution on the variables of interest; the predictive distribution arises naturally. Whether the resulting predictive distribution is meaningful depends of course on the necessary prior distribution, and one should be aware of the fact that inappropriate priors can give rise to arbitrarily bad predictive distributions. From a frequentist point of view, this will be the case if the prior is "wrong". From a Bayesian point of view, priors are neither wrong nor right, they express degrees of belief. Inappropriate priors that are too restrictive, in that they discard plausible hypotheses about the origin of the data, are sometimes still used for reasons of convenience, leading to unreasonable predictive uncertainties (Rasmussen and Quiñonero-Candela, 2005). If you believe your prior is reasonable, then the same should hold true for the predictive distribution. However, this distribution is only an updated belief — the extent to which it is in agreement with reality will depend on the extent to which the prior encompasses reality.

It is common in Machine Learning to not consider the full posterior distribution, but to rather concentrate on its mode, also called the Maximum a Posteriori (MAP) approach. The MAP approach being equivalent to maximum penalized likelihood, one could consider that any method based on minimizing a regularized risk functional falls under the MAP umbrella. The MAP approach produces predictions with no measure of the uncertainty associated to them, like "it will rain"; other methods for obtaining predictive uncertainties are then needed, such as Bagging for example (Breiman, 1996). More simplistic approaches would consist in always outputting the same predictive uncertainties, independently of the input, based on an estimate of the overall generalization error. This generalization error can in turn be estimated empirically by cross-validation, or theoretically by means Statistical Learning bounds on the generalization error. This simplistic approach should of course be regarded as a baseline, since any reasonable method that individually estimates predictive uncertainties depending on the input could in principle be superior.

It appears that there might not be an obvious way of producing good estimates of predictive uncertainty in the Machine Learning (or Statistical Learning) community. There is also an apparent lack of consensus on the ways of evaluating predictive uncertainties in the first place. Driven by the urgent feeling that it might be easier to validate the goodness of the different philosophies on the empirical battleground than on the theoretical, we decided to organize the Evaluating Predictive Uncertainty Challenge, with support from the European PASCAL Network of Excellence. The Challenge allowed different Machine Learning approaches to predictive uncertainty in regression and classification to be directly compared on identical datasets.

### 1.1 Organization of This Chapter

We begin by providing an overview and some facts about the Challenge in Sect. 2. We then move on to describing in detail the three main components of the Challenge: 1) in Sect. 3 we define what is meant by probabilistic predictions in regression and in classification, and explain the *format of the predictions* that was required for the Challenge, 2) in Sect. 4 we present the *loss functions* that we proposed for the Challenge, and 3) Section 5 details the five *datasets*, two for classification and three for regression, that we used for the Challenge. In Sect. 6 we present the results obtained by the participants, and in Sect. 7 we focus in more detail on the methods proposed by the six (groups of) participants who contributed a Chapter to this book. The methods presented in these six contributed chapters all achieved outstanding results, and all the dataset winners are represented. Finally, Sect. 8 offers a discussion of results, and some reflection on the many lessons learned from the Challenge.

## 2 An Overview of the Challenge

The Evaluating Predictive Uncertainty Challenge was organized around the following website: http://predict.kyb.tuebingen.mpg.de. The website remains open for reference, and submissions are still possible to allow researchers to evaluate their methods on some benchmark datasets.

The results of the Challenge were first presented at the NIPS 2004 Workshop on Calibration and Probabilistic Prediction in Machine Learning, organized by Greg Grudic and Rich Caruana, and held in Whistler, Canada, on Friday December 17, 2004. The Challenge was then presented in more depth, with contributed talks from some of the participants with best results at the PASCAL Challenges Workshop held in Southampton, UK, on April 11, 2005.

Using the website, participants could download the datasets (described in Sect. 5), and submit their predictions. Immediately after submission, the results obtained where displayed in a table, and sorted according to the loss (given in Sect. 4). Inspired by the NIPS 2003 Feature Selection Challenge (Guyon et al, 2005), we divided the Challenge chronologically into two parts. In the first part the competing algorithms were evaluated on a "validation set", with no limitation on the number of submissions. In the second part, shorter, of duration one week, the validation targets were made available and participants had to make a limited number of final submissions on the "test set". The final ranking of the Challenge was built according to the test performance.

The reason for having a validation set evaluation in the first part is to allow for temporary assessment and comparison of the performance of the different submissions. Simply put, to make the challenge more "fun" and encourage participation by immediately allowing to see how the participants were doing in comparison to others. To discourage participants from trying to guess the validation targets by making very many submissions, the targets associated to the validation set were be made public at the start of the second part of the Challenge, one week before the submission deadline. The participants could then use them to train their algorithms before submitting the test predictions.

Unlike in the NIPS 2003 Feature Selection Challenge (Guyon et al, 2005), participants did not need to submit on every of the five datasets to enter the final ranking. Individual rankings were made for each of the datasets. Indeed, as discussed in Sect. 5, the nature of the datasets was so diverse that one could hardly expect the same algorithm to excel in all of them. Our intention was to evaluate algorithms and methods rather than participants.

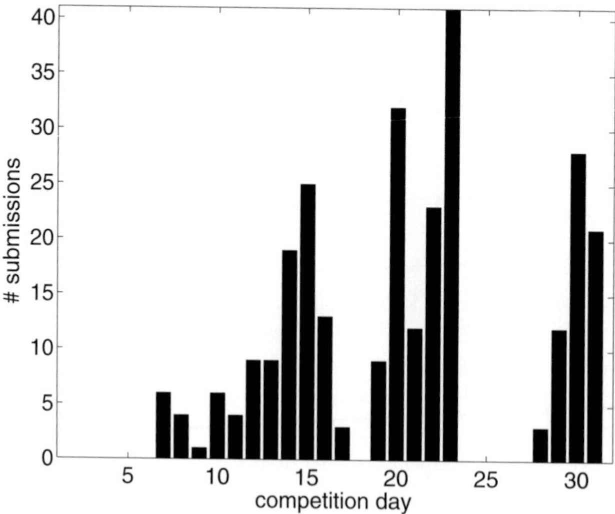


**Fig. 1.** Number of valid submissions on each day of the Challenge. Notice the break between the first and the second phase of the Challenge: the 68 valid test submissions were made on days 28 to 31.

The Challenge ran for 31 days, and attracted 20 groups of participants. A total of 280 submissions were made, of which 68 were "final" submissions on the test set. Figure 1 shows the number of submissions that were made each day of the Challenge.

The website opened for submissions on November 10 2004, and closed on December 10 2004. The second phase of the Challenge, with validation targets available and predictions to be made on the test inputs, started on December 3. The test results were made public on December 11. The website remains open for submission. After the closing deadline, some interesting submissions were made, which we include in the results section. Some of the contributed chapters were also written by participants who made very good post-Challenge submissions.

### 2.1 Design of the Website

When we designed the webpage for the *Evaluating Predictive Uncertainty* Challenge we had two objectives in mind. First, to build it in as flexible a way as possible way in order to be able to do minor changes very easily, like for example including additional losses, even during the competition. The second objective was a high degree of automation, to be able to for example give instant feedback whenever a submission was made. This way the participants were able to compare their preliminary scores with those the other participants.

The webpage consists of two separate parts, *appearance* and *functionality*, that are kept disjoint possible. An overview is given in Fig. 2. The website's appearance, was programmed with the use of PHP and CSS. PHP (*PHP Hypertext Preprocessor*) is a widely used open source script language, specially suited for easy website development, that can be embedded into HTML code. We used it to define the website's global structure on a higher level, that is to dynamically create HTML code. CSS (*cascading style-sheets*) is a simple standard for defining the style of a website. While the website's structure was created by PHP via HTML, CSS was used to define its final look. PHP was also used to implement a part of the website's functionality like managing the `ftp` upload and the interaction with external applications. The remaining functional part was implemented using Python and MySQL. Python is an interpreted, interactive, object-oriented programming language that combines a very clear syntax with a remarkable power. Although it is not open source, it is absolutely free. We used it in the project for mathematical computations, to compute the scores of the submissions, and to verify that the submissions were correctly formatted. MySQL is a key part of LAMP (*Linux, Apache, MySQL, PHP/Perl/Python*) and the world's most popular open source database. We used it to maintain a database of all information relevant to the submissions, as well ad the error scores under the different losses we used.

The appearance of the Challenge website is shown in 3. The structural framework of the website was implemented by the exclusive use of PHP. The structure of the navigation bar is defined in an separate file, used by formatting functions to

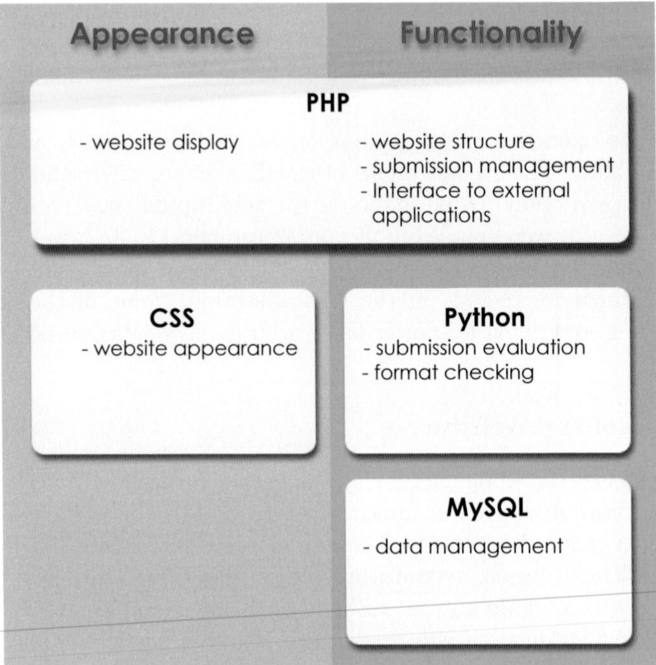


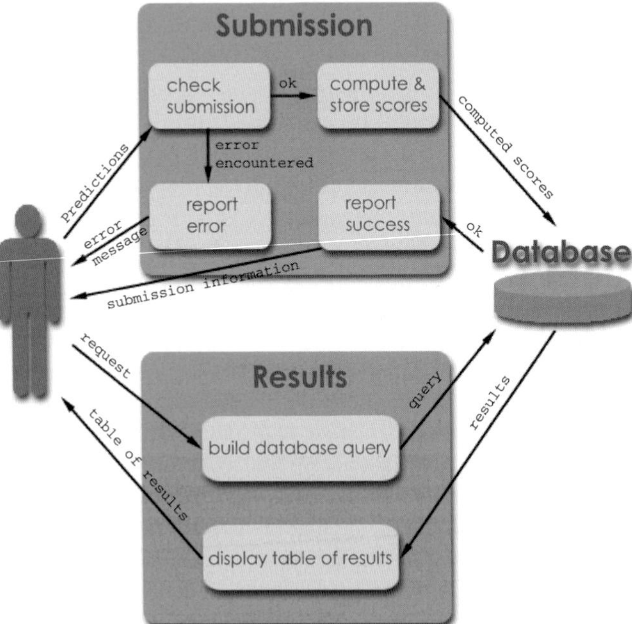


**Fig. 2.** Top: The website's functional units and the programming languages used to implement them. Bottom: Interaction control between user, website and database.

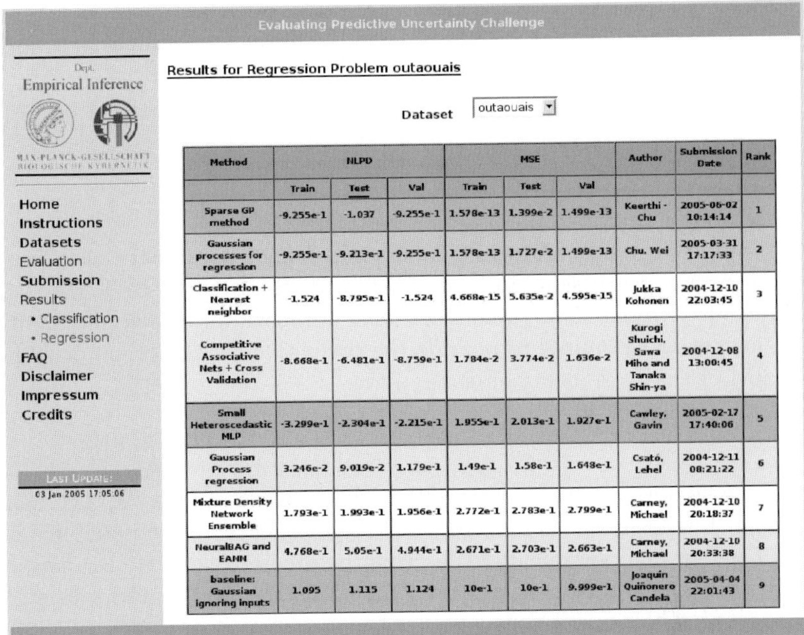


| Method | NLPD | | | MSE | | | Author | Submission Date | Rank |
|---|---|---|---|---|---|---|---|---|---|
| | Train | Test | Val | Train | Test | Val | | | |
| Sparse GP method | -9.255e-1 | -1.037 | -9.255e-1 | 1.578e-13 | 1.399e-2 | 1.499e-13 | Keerthi - Chu | 2005-06-02 10:14:14 | 1 |
| Gaussian processes for regression | -9.255e-1 | -9.213e-1 | -9.255e-1 | 1.578e-13 | 1.727e-2 | 1.499e-13 | Chu, Wei | 2005-03-31 17:17:33 | 2 |
| Classification + Nearest neighbor | -1.524 | -8.795e-1 | -1.524 | 4.668e-15 | 5.635e-2 | 4.595e-15 | Jukka Kohonen | 2004-12-10 22:03:45 | 3 |
| Competitive Associative Nets + Cross Validation | -8.668e-1 | -6.481e-1 | -8.759e-1 | 1.784e-2 | 3.774e-2 | 1.636e-2 | Kurogi Shuichi, Sawa Miho and Tanaka Shin-ya | 2004-12-08 13:00:45 | 4 |
| Small Heteroscedastic MLP | -3.299e-1 | -2.304e-1 | -2.215e-1 | 1.955e-1 | 2.013e-1 | 1.927e-1 | Cawley, Gavin | 2005-02-17 17:40:06 | 5 |
| Gaussian Process regression | 3.246e-2 | 9.019e-2 | 1.179e-1 | 1.49e-1 | 1.58e-1 | 1.648e-1 | Csató, Lehel | 2004-12-11 08:21:22 | 6 |
| Mixture Density Network Ensemble | 1.793e-1 | 1.993e-1 | 1.956e-1 | 2.772e-1 | 2.783e-1 | 2.799e-1 | Carney, Michael | 2004-12-10 20:18:37 | 7 |
| NeuralBAG and EANN | 4.768e-1 | 5.05e-1 | 4.944e-1 | 2.671e-1 | 2.703e-1 | 2.663e-1 | Carney, Michael | 2004-12-10 20:33:38 | 8 |
| baseline: Gaussian ignoring inputs | 1.095 | 1.115 | 1.124 | 10e-1 | 10e-1 | 9.999e-1 | Joaquin Quiñonero Candela | 2005-04-04 22:01:43 | 9 |

**Fig. 3.** Screenshot of the website's result page

determine the actual HTML code. That way new pages can easily be integrated in or removed from the existing website structure. Formatting functions are also used to put together the navigation bar itself, the contents of the different pages and to produce the final HTML code. All this is transparent to the users, all that is sent to them is pure HTML.

**Example Process Flow.** Let us describe the interaction between the different single components given above during the submission of predictions. This is also shown in the right diagram of figure 2. After checking the validity of informations entered by the user into the form of the submission page, the submission is uncompressed into a temporary directory and the format of the prediction files is checked. If errors are found at this stage, they are collected and jointly reported to the user. If no errors are found, the information related to the submission, like the description of the method, the submission time-stamp, the name of the participant, etc, are stored in a MySQL table and the evaluation scores are computed and inserted into the database. After moving the submitted file to a backup directory, a "successful submission" message is given to the user. At this point, the results of this submission are already available from the results table. If the user enters the results page, the evaluation scores for this challenge type and the default dataset are requested from database, sorted according to a default score, formatted by PHP and displayed. The user can change sorting the results according to a different loss, request the descriptions of other submissions, or access the results for a different dataset. Every time she does so, a completely new result table is requested from the database.

## 3 Probabilistic Predictions in Regression and Classification

The two modelling tasks addressed in the Challenge were binary classification and scalar output regression. For classification let the two classes be labelled by "+1" and "-1". Probabilistic predictions were required: for a each test input $\boldsymbol{x}_*$, the participant was required to provide the predictive (or posterior) probability of the label of that case being of class "+1":

$$p(y_* = +1|\boldsymbol{x}_*) \in [0, 1] \ , \qquad p(y_* = -1|\boldsymbol{x}_*) = 1 - p(y_* = +1|\boldsymbol{x}_*) \ . \tag{1}$$

For regression, participants were required to specify the probability density function of the output $y_*$ associated to the test input $\boldsymbol{x}_*$. Two possibilities are offered. The first, simpler one, is to describe the predictive density in a parametric form by means of a Gaussian density function. The predictive mean $m_*$ and variance $v_*$ need to be specified:

$$p(y_*|\boldsymbol{x}_*) \sim \frac{1}{\sqrt{2\pi v_*}} \exp\left(-\frac{\|y_* - m_*\|^2}{2v_*}\right) \ . \tag{2}$$

In some situations more complex predictive densities are appropriate (for example multi-modal). To allow participants to approximately specify any predictive density function we allowed them to describe it by means of any given number $N$ of quantiles $[q_{\alpha_1}, \ldots, q_{\alpha_N}]$ such that:

$$p(y_* < q_{\alpha_j} \,|\, x_*) = \alpha_j \ , \qquad 0 < \alpha_j < 1 \ . \tag{3}$$

Imposing $0 < \alpha_j < 1$ avoids that some regions of the output space be given zero probability, which is unreasonable under the loss we use (see Sect. 4). The remaining probability mass, equal to $\alpha_1 + (1 - \alpha_N)$, is accounted for by two exponential tails of the form $\hat{p}(y|x) \propto \exp(-|y|/b)$.

Figure 4 gives an example of a predictive density being specified by quantiles. The participants need to specify the quantiles and their values. To recover the estimated predictive density $\hat{p}(y_*|x_*)$ from the quantiles, we need to distinguish between three cases:

1. if $q_{\alpha_1} \geq y_* > q_{\alpha_N}$ and $\alpha_i$ and $\alpha_{i+1}$ are such that $q_{\alpha_i} \geq y_* > q_{\alpha_{i+1}}$ then

$$\hat{p}(y_*|\boldsymbol{x}_*) = \frac{\alpha_{i+1} - \alpha_i}{q_{\alpha_{i+1}} - q_{\alpha_i}} \ , \tag{4}$$

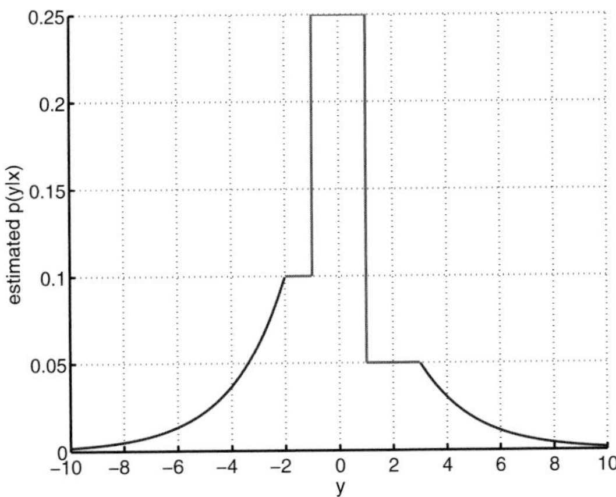


**Fig. 4.** Specifying the predictive density with quantiles. Example where the quantiles $q_{0.2} = -2$, $q_{0.3} = -1$, $q_{0.8} = 1$ and $q_{0.9} = 3$ are specified. The exponential tails guarantee that distribution integrates to 1.

2. if $y < q_{\alpha_1}$ then from the lower exponential tail:

$$\begin{aligned}
\hat{p}(y_*|\boldsymbol{x}_*) &= z_1 \exp\left(-\frac{|y_* - q_{\alpha_1}|}{b_1}\right) , \\
z_1 = \hat{p}(q_{\alpha_1}|\boldsymbol{x}_*) &= \frac{\alpha_2 - \alpha_1}{q_{\alpha_2} - q_{\alpha_1}} , \\
\int_{-\infty}^{q_{\alpha_1}} \hat{p}(q_{\alpha_1}|\boldsymbol{x}_*) &= \alpha_1 \iff b_1 = \frac{\alpha_1}{z_1} .
\end{aligned} \tag{5}$$

3. if $q_{\alpha_N} \geq y$ then from an upper exponential tail:

$$\begin{aligned}
\hat{p}(y_*|\boldsymbol{x}_*) &= z_N \exp\left(-\frac{|y_* - q_{\alpha_N}|}{b_N}\right) , \\
z_N = \hat{p}(q_{\alpha_N}|\boldsymbol{x}_*) &= \frac{\alpha_N - \alpha_{N-1}}{q_{\alpha_N} - q_{\alpha_{N-1}}} , \\
\int_{q_{\alpha_N}}^{\infty} \hat{p}(q_{\alpha_1}|\boldsymbol{x}_*) &= (1 - \alpha_N) \iff b_N = \frac{(1-\alpha_N)}{z_N} .
\end{aligned} \tag{6}$$

In addition to the loss that takes into account the probabilistic nature of the predictions we will also compute the standard mean squared error loss (see Sect. 4). Since we only obtain predictive densities from the participants, we need to compute their mean, which is the optimal point estimator under the squared loss. For the case where quantiles are specified, computing the predictive mean is easily done by computing the following three contributions:

– The contribution of the quantiles to the mean is:

$$m_q = \sum_{i=1}^{N-1} \left[\frac{q_{\alpha_j} + q_{\alpha_{j+1}}}{2}\right] (\alpha_{j+1} - \alpha_j) \tag{7}$$

– The contribution of the lower exponential tail is:

$$m_{lt} = z_1 \int_0^\infty (q_{\alpha_1} - y_*) \exp\left(-\frac{y_*}{b_1}\right) = z_1(q_{\alpha_1} b_1 - {b_1}^2) = \alpha_1(q_{\alpha_1} - \frac{\alpha_1^2}{z_1}) \quad (8)$$

– Similarly, the contribution of the upper exponential tail is:

$$\begin{aligned} m_{ut} &= z_N \int_0^\infty (q_{\alpha_N} + y_*) \exp\left(-\frac{y_*}{b_N}\right) = z_N(q_{\alpha_N} b_N + {b_N}^2) \\ &= (1 - \alpha_N)\left[q_{\alpha_N} + \frac{(1-\alpha_N)^2}{z_N}\right] \end{aligned} \quad (9)$$

The estimate of the mean is obtained by adding up the terms:

$$m = m_q + m_{lt} + m_{ut}. \quad (10)$$

## 4 Loss Functions Proposed

Algorithms that perform well under classical losses, for hard decisions in classification and, scalar predictions in regression, do not necessarily perform well under losses that take into account predictive uncertainties. For this reason, we did evaluate the performance with losses of both natures.

In Sect. 4.1 we describe the losses used for classification, and in Sect. 4.2 those used for regression. We will denote the actual target associated to input $\boldsymbol{x}_i$ by $t_i$. In classification $t_i$ will take the value "+1" or "-1", and in regression a value in $\mathbb{R}$. In Sect. 4.3 we justify the use of losses based on the logarithm for the evaluation of probabilistic predictions.

### 4.1 Losses for Classification

We used three losses for classification. The classic average classification error (relative number of errors, or 0/1 loss), the negative log probability (log loss, or negative cross entropy), and the "lift loss". The final ranking was established according to the log loss, the two other losses being used only for comparison.

**The Average Classification Error**

$$L = \frac{1}{n}\left[\sum_{\{i|t_i=+1\}} \mathbf{1}\{p(y_i = +1|\boldsymbol{x}_i) < 0.5\} + \sum_{\{i|t_i=-1\}} \mathbf{1}\{p(y_i = +1|\boldsymbol{x}_i) \geq 0.5\}\right] \quad (11)$$

where $\mathbf{1}\{z\}$ is an indicator function, equal to 1 if z=true, and to 0 if z=false. This is the classic 0/1 loss, obtained by thresholding the predictive probabilities at 0.5. Its minimum value is 0, obtained when no test (or validation) examples are missclassified; it is otherwise equal to the fraction of missclassified examples relative to the total number of examples.

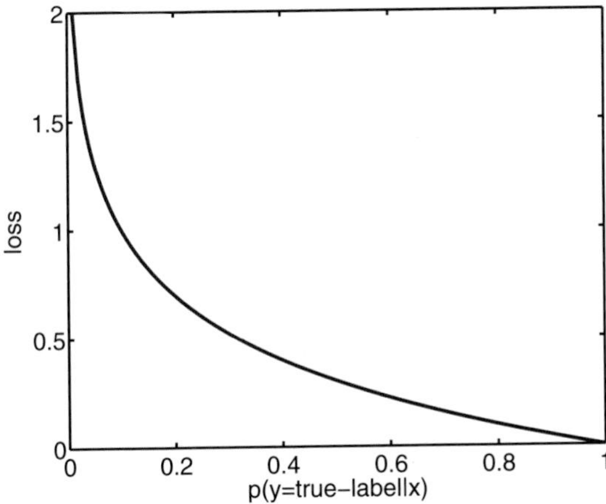


**Fig. 5.** NLP loss when predicting the class of a single test point that actually belongs to class "+1". Observe how the loss goes to infinity as the model becomes increasingly certain that the point belongs to the wrong class.

### The Negative Log Probability (NLP) Loss

$$L = -\frac{1}{n}\left[\sum_{\{i|t_i=+1\}} \log p(y_i = +1|\boldsymbol{x}_i) + \sum_{\{i|t_i=-1\}} \log\left[1 - p(y_i = +1|\boldsymbol{x}_i)\right]\right] \tag{12}$$

Notice that this loss penalizes both over and under-confident predictions. Over-confident predictions can be infinitely penalized, which should discourage predictive probabilities equal to zero or one. Zero is the minimum value of this loss, that could be achieved if one predicted correctly with 100% confidence. If one predicts otherwise, the worse one predicts, the larger the loss. This loss is also referred to as "negative cross-entropy loss". Figure 5 shows NLP loss incurred when predicting the class of a single point $\boldsymbol{x}_i$ that belongs to class "+1". The figure illustrates how the penalty becomes infinite as the predictor becomes increasingly certain that the test point belongs to the wrong class.

An interesting way of using this loss, is to give it relative to that of the random uninformative predictor, that always predicts 0.5. If one takes the difference between the log loss of a given algorithm and that of the random predictor one obtains the average gain in information (in bits if one takes base 2 logarithms).

**The LIFT Loss.** Although we decided not to rely on this loss to rank the submissions, which we ranked according to the log loss instead, we have decided to still explain it here, since it might be useful to some readers for other purposes. The "LIFT loss" is based on the area under the lift loss curve, and is minimum when that area is maximum. We define it in such a way that it is equal to 1 for an average random predictor. As we will explain, the LIFT loss is the area lost

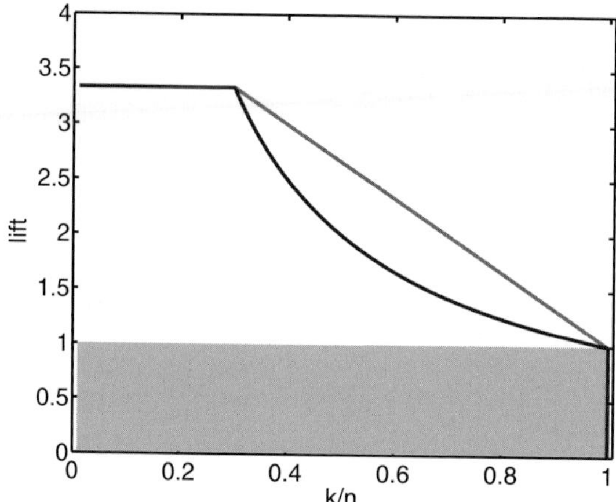


**Fig. 6.** Explaining the LIFT loss. The curve is the lift loss of the ideal predictor, and the line above it is a simple upper bound on it. The shaded region is the area under the average loss curve of a random predictor. The LIFT loss is defined as the ratio between two areas. The numerator is given by the area encompassed by the upper bound lift curve and the lift curve of the predictor being evaluated. The denominator is given by the area encompassed between the upper bound lift curve and that of the average random predictor. In this way the LIFT loss is the area lost relative to the ideal predictor, normalized by the loss of the average random predictor.

to the ideal predictor by the evaluated predictor, normalized by the area lost to the ideal predictor by the average random predictor. The reason why we build a loss based on the area under the lift loss, rather than looking at a particular value of the lift loss is similar to the reason why the area under the Area Under the ROC Curve (AUC) (Hanley and McNeil, 1982) has become a popular loss. In the absence of a specific point at which to evaluate the lift loss, we go for a measure that integrates over all its values.

The lift loss is obtained by first sorting the predictive probabilities with $p_i = p(y_i = +1|x_i)$ for the $n$ test points in decreasing order: $p_{s_1} \geq p_{s_2} \geq \ldots \geq p_{s_n}$. The obtained reordering contained in the $s_i$'s is applied to the test targets, and for $k = 1, \ldots, n$ the lift loss is defined as:

$$l(k/n) = \frac{1}{\bar{n}_+} \frac{1}{k} \sum_{i=1}^{k} \mathbf{1}\{t_{s_i} = +1\} \ , \qquad \bar{n}_+ = \frac{n_+}{n} \ , \tag{13}$$

where $n_+$ is the number of test examples that belong to class "+1". Notice that the lift loss is always, positive, that $l(1) = 1$ and that $l(k/n) \leq 1/\bar{n}_+$.

Figure 6 shows in blue the lift curve for an ideal predictor that would get a perfect ordering. In the figure we have set $\bar{n}_+ = 0.3$. For $0 \leq k/n \leq n_+$, all $y_{s_k}$="+1", and therefore the lift loss is equal to $1/n_+$ (from Eq. 13). For $k/n > n_+$, all $y_{s_k}$="-1" and therefore the lift loss is $l(k/n) = n/k$. The average lift loss of a random predictor is $l(k/n) = 1$ for all $k$. The shaded gray region in the figure represents the area under the average lift loss of such a random predictor, whose surface is equal to 1. In magenta we show a simple linear upper bound to the ideal lift curve, where the $n/k$ decaying part of the ideal loss is replaced by a linear upper bound.

The area under the upper bound curve to the lift loss of the ideal predictor is given by:

$$\mathrm{A_I} = 1 + \frac{1}{2}\left(\frac{1}{\bar{n}_+} - 1\right)(\bar{n}_+ + 1) \;, \tag{14}$$

while the area under the lift loss curve for the predictor we want to evaluate is given by

$$\mathrm{A} = \frac{1}{n}\sum_{k=1}^{n} l(k/n) \;. \tag{15}$$

In order to obtain a loss that is equal to 1 for the average random predictor, we define the LIFT loss as the ratio between the area lost by the predictor being evaluated and the area lost by the average random predictor:

$$L = \frac{\mathrm{A_I} - \mathrm{A}}{\mathrm{A_I} - 1} \tag{16}$$

Notice that $L \gtrapprox 0$ is the minimum loss, $L \approx 1$ is the average loss of a random predictor, and $L > 1$ is worse than random.

### 4.2 Losses for Regression

We used two losses to evaluate performance in the regression tasks. The first is the classic average normalized mean squared error (nMSE), which only takes into account the means of the predictive distributions (these are the optimal point estimates under the nMSE loss). The second loss is the average negative log predictive density (NLPD) of the true targets. We used the NLPD to rank the results of the participants.

**The nMSE Loss**

$$L = \frac{1}{n}\sum_{i=1}^{n} \frac{(t_i - m_i)^2}{\mathrm{var}(t)} \tag{17}$$

where $m_i$ is the mean of the predictive distribution $p(y_i|\boldsymbol{x}_i)$. Observe that we normalize the MSE wrt. to the variance of the true targets: predicting the empirical mean of the training targets, independently of the test input, leads thus to a normalized MSE of close to 1. In practice of course, we don't know the variance of the true test targets, and we simply estimate $\mathrm{var}(t)$ empirically by computing the sample variance of the test targets.

**The NLPD Loss**

$$L = -\frac{1}{n}\sum_{i=1}^{n} \log p(y_i = t_i|\boldsymbol{x}_i) \tag{18}$$

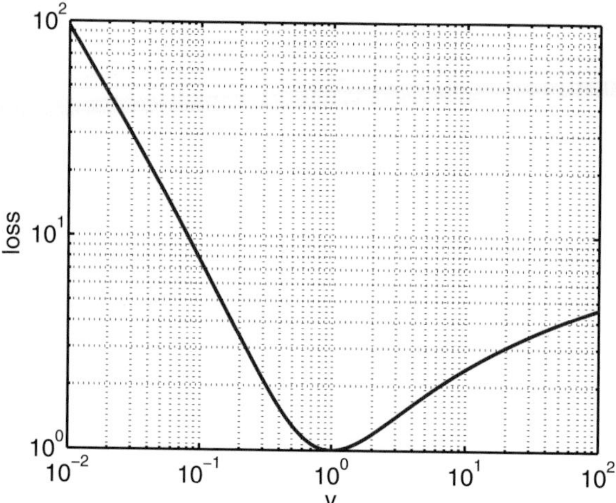


**Fig. 7.** NLPD loss (up to a constant) incurred when predicting at a single point with a Gaussian predictive distribution. In the figure we have fixed $\|t_i - m_i\|^2 = 1$ and show how the loss evolves as we vary the predictive variance $v_i$. The optimal value of the predictive variance is equal to the actual squared error given the predictive mean.

This loss penalizes both over and under-confident predictions. To illustrate this, let us take a closer look at the case of Gaussian predictive distributions. For a predictive distribution with mean $m_i$ and variance $v_i$ the NLPD loss incurred for predicting at input $\boldsymbol{x}_i$ with true associated target $t_i$ is given by:

$$L_i = \frac{1}{2}\left[\log v_i + \frac{(t_i - m_i)^2}{v_i}\right] + c \ , \tag{19}$$

where $c$ is a constant, independent of $m_i$ and $v_i$. Given $m_i$, the optimal value of $v_i$ is $(t_i - m_i)^2$. Figure 7 illustrates the variation of $L_i$ as a function of $v_i$ when $(t_i - m_i)^2 = 1$.

The NLPD loss favours conservative models, that is models that tend to be under-confident rather than over-confident. This is illustrated in Fig. 7, and can be deduced from the fact that logarithms are being used. An interesting way of using the NLPD is to give it relative to the NLPD of a predictor that ignores the inputs and always predicts the same Gaussian predictive distribution, with mean and variance the empirical mean and variance of the training data. This relative NLPD translates into a gain of information with respect to the simple Gaussian predictor described.

### 4.3 Discussion About Losses

Both log losses, NLP and NLPD, have the property of infinitely penalizing wrong predictions made with zero uncertainty. It might be argued that this is too strong a penalty. However, on the one hand if one is to take probabilistic predictions seriously, it might be desirable for consistency to discourage statements made with 100% confidence, that turn out to be wrong. On the other hand, think about the binary classification problem. If $n$ data points are observed, it might seem ambitious to have predictive uncertainties smaller than $1/n$: one has just not observed enough data to be more confident than that! So one obvious technique to avoid infinite penalties in classification would be to replace those predictive probabilities smaller than $1/n$ by $1/n$, and those larger than $1 - 1/n$ by $1 - 1/n$.

In regression, using the NLPD can be dangerous for certain specific types of outputs. Take for example the case where in a regression problem the outputs take values from a (potentially large) finite discrete set. One obvious strategy to minimize the NLPD in that case would be to distribute the available probability mass equally on tiny intervals one around each discrete output value. Since the NLPD only cares about density, the NLPD can be made arbitrarily small by decreasing the width of the intervals. Of course, there are machine precision limitations in practice. In this Challenge we had two datasets, Stereopsis (with outputs very close to discrete) and Gaze (with discrete outputs), where the NLPD could be exploited in this way (see Sect. 5). One way out of this issue would be to limit the minimum interval size when specifying predictive distributions by means of histograms, detailed in Sect. 4.2. The contributed Chapter by Kohonen and Suomela addresses this potential problem with the NLPD, and proposes an alternative loss for probabilistic predictions in regression.

For classification, the mutual information between the true class labels and the predicted class labels is sometimes used as a measure of performance. The mutual information however is an aggregate measure, that only depends on the conditional probabilities of predicting one class given that another class is true. It is totally insensitive to individual predictive probabilities, and therefore useless for our purposes. The Area Under the ROC Curve (AUC) is another common measure of performance, for classifiers that are able to output some number whose magnitude relates to the degree of belief that a point belongs to one class rather than to the other. The AUC score is fully determined by the *ordering* of these scalar predictions, and does not capture anything at all about calibration. In fact, the AUC score ignores the fact that the outputted numbers are probabilities. These are the reasons why we did not used the AUC score in this Challenge.

## 5 Datasets Proposed

We proposed two datasets for classification, and 3 for regression tasks for the Challenge, summarized in Table 1. All datasets are "real world data" in the sense that they were not synthesized nor fabricated, but rather measured or extracted from a real phenomenon.

The Gatineau and Outaouais datasets come from industry, and we are unfortunately not allowed to reveal any details about them. They were kindly donated by Yoshua Bengio, to whom we are very grateful.

**Table 1.** Datasets proposed for the Challenge. dim: input dimension. # Tr, # Val and # Test are respectively the number of training, validation and test cases. SV and ST are respectively the number of submissions during the validation and during the test phase of the Challenge.

| Name | dim | # Tr | # Val | # Test | SV | ST |
|---|---|---|---|---|---|---|
| **Classification** | | | | | | |
| Catalysis | 617 | 873 | 300 | 700 | 44 | 11 |
| Gatineau | 1092 | 3000 | 2176 | 3000 | 52 | 27 |
| **Regression** | | | | | | |
| Stereopsis | 4 | 192 | 300 | 500 | 18 | 8 |
| Gaze | 12 | 150 | 300 | 427 | 50 | 16 |
| Outaouais | 37 | 20000 | 9000 | 20000 | 22 | 5 |

**Catalysis.** This dataset comes from the Yeast Functional Catalog[2], and was kindly prepared by Alexander Zien at the Max Planck Institute for Biological Cybernetics. The binary targets are obtained from assigning the functional categories of all yeast proteins to one of two classes. These two classes roughly correspond to presence (or absence) of catalytic activity. The inputs are gene expression levels of the genes encoding those proteins. The dataset is quite balanced, there are approximately as many positive as negative examples.

**Gatineau.** (Secret data) This is a very unbalanced binary classification dataset, with less than 10% positive examples. The data is also very hard to model, which makes the average classification (0/1 Loss) useless in practice. Models have to compete in terms of their probabilistic predictions.

**Stereopsis.** This dataset was collected at the Max Planck Institute for Biological Cybernetics, for a detailed account see (Sinz et al, 2004). The dataset was obtained by measuring the 3 dimensional location of a pointer attached to a robot arm by means of two high resolution cameras. The resulting 4 dimensional inputs correspond to the two pairs of coordinates on both cameras focal planes. Figure 8 illustrates one particularity of this dataset, that turns out to be of central importance when analyzing the results: when collecting the data, measurements were taken at a set of parallel planes, giving the impression that the variable to be estimated (the depth) was in fact naturally clustered around the discrete set of distances of the planes to the cameras.

**Gaze.** This dataset was also collected at the Max Planck Institute for Biological Cybernetics, with the help of Kienzle to whom we are very grateful. The targets are the pixel value of the horizontal position of a target displayed on a computer monitor. The corresponding 12-dimensional inputs are a set of measurements from head mounted cameras, that focus on markers on the monitor

[2] `http://mips.gsf.de`

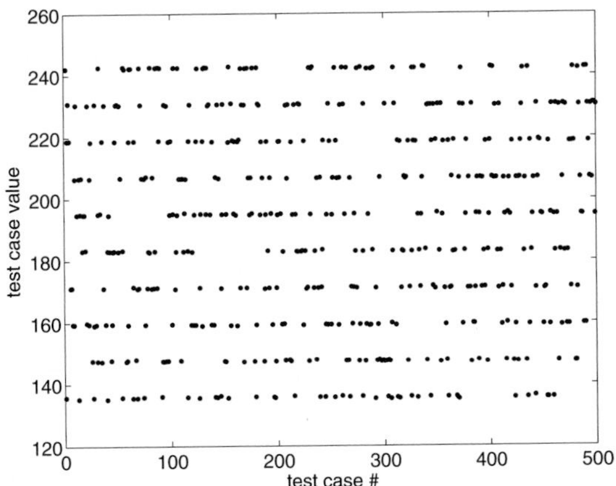


**Fig. 8.** Test targets of the Stereopsis datasets plotted against their index. The targets are clearly clustered around what appears to be 10 discrete values. In fact, there is structure within each "cluster". This discretization is solely an artifact of the way the data was collected, and has nothing to do with its nature.

and estimate the positions of the eyes of the subject looking at the monitor. This experimental setup is prone to severe outliers, since the cameras occasionally loose their calibration. It was indeed the case that there were severe outliers in the data, which the participants had to deal with, as reported in their contributed Chapters in the following. Another strong peculiarity of this dataset was that, being pixel values, the targets were discrete! This was exploited for instance by Kurogi et. al (see their contributed Chapter in this Volume) to "abuse" the NLPD loss. See Sect. 4.3 for a discussion on abusing the NLPD loss. This is just an example of the fact that losses and datasets should not be independent, but rather the opposite, see Sect. 8.

**Outaouais.** (Secret data) This is a regression dataset with very structured inputs, strongly clustered. This was noticed and exploited by Kohonen and Suomela, see Sect. 6.

## 6 Results of the Challenge

We now give the results of the Challenge for each of the datasets, following the order in which we presented them in table 1. We only provide a short list of the best performing entries. The complete tables can be found online, in the Challenge webpage: `http://predict.kyb.tuebingen.mpg.de`. The names of the participants who have contributed a Chapter to this Volume are shown in **bold** characters in the results tables. All dataset winners have contributed a chapter to this volume, in addition to some other participants with best results. The contributed Chapters are presented in Sect. 7.

The entries made before the validation targets were released are marked with a less than sign '<', meaning "before" the final submission period. The entries made after the deadline of December 10th 2004 (post-Challenge entries) are marked with a greater than sign '>', meaning "after". The remaining entries (with no mark) were made after the validation targets were available, and before the submission deadline of December 10th, 2004. The entries made before the validation targets were released only benefited from the training targets, while the final entries benefited both from the training and validation targets. The test targets have never been released, therefore the post-Challenge entries had only the training and validation targets available. Some of the participants who made post-Challenge entries have also contributed invited chapters to this volume.

The results are compared to a baseline method. In classification, the baseline outputs the empirical training class frequencies independently of the inputs. In regression, the baseline is a Gaussian predictive distribution independent of the inputs, with mean and variance equal to the empirical mean and variance of the training targets. In Fig. 9 we present a scatter plot of the entries in the tables, one loss versus the other, for each dataset.

### Catalysis (Classification)

| Method | NLP | 01L | Author |
|---|---|---|---|
| Bayesian NN | 0.2273 | 0.249 | **Neal, R** |
| < Bayesian NN | 0.2289 | 0.257 | **Neal, R** |
| SVM + Platt | 0.2305 | 0.259 | **Chapelle, O** |
| > Bagged R-MLP | 0.2391 | 0.276 | **Cawley, G** |
| > Bayesian Logistic Regression | 0.2401 | 0.274 | **Neal, R** |
| Feat Sel + Rnd Subsp + Dec Trees | 0.2410 | 0.271 | **Chawla, N** |
| Probing SVM | 0.2454 | 0.270 | Zadrozny, B & Langford, J |
| **baseline: class frequencies** | **0.2940** | **0.409** | |

(NLP: average negative log probability, 01L: average zero-one loss)

The winner was Radford Neal with Bayesian Neural Networks. Radford Neal also produced the second best entry, with the same model but learning only from the training targets during the "validation" part of the Challenge, therefore not benefitting from the validation targets. The third best submission is a support vector machine by Olivier Chapelle, that used Platt scaling (Platt, 1999) to produce calibrated probabilistic predictions. There is another support vector machine submission by Zadrozny and Langford, with lower ranking, that used Probing (Langford and Zadrozny, 2005) to obtain probabilistic predictions. Cawley's post-Challenge submission based on neural networks uses Bagging (Breiman, 1996) instead of Bayesian averaging. Bayesian logistic regression, a post-Challenge submission by Radford Neal, outperforms Nitesh Chawla's

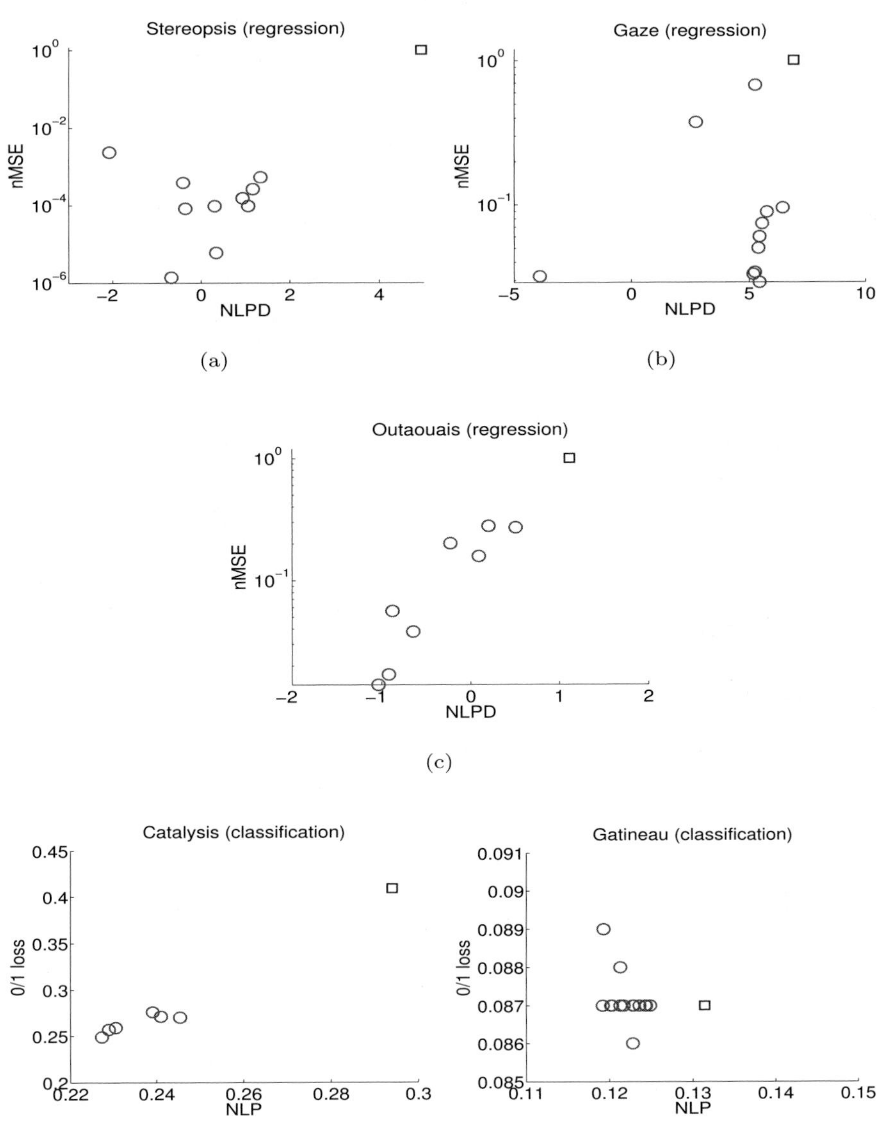


**Fig. 9.** Visualization of results, non-probabilistic loss vs. probabilistic loss. The circles represent the participant's entries, the square the baseline method that ignores the inputs. Top (a-c): Regression, NLPD vs. nMSE. Outaouais is the dataset for which both losses are most highly correlated. For Stereopsis, the entry with lowest NLPD has the highest nMSE, and for Gaze there are a number of submissions with very low nMSE that have a very high NLPD: this might be due to the outliers present in this dataset. Bottom (d-e): Classification, NLP vs. 0/1 Loss. While for Catalysis both losses seem correlated, for Gatineau the 0/1 Loss is vacuous, and the only informative loss is really the NLP.

decision trees, which won the Gatineau dataset. This might be an indication that the performance of these methods is quite dataset dependent.

**Gatineau (Classification)**

| Method | NLP | 01L | Author |
|---|---|---|---|
| Feat Sel + Rnd subsp + Dec Trees | 0.1192 | 0.087 | **Chawla, N** |
| Feat Sel + Bagging + Dec Trees | 0.1193 | 0.089 | **Chawla, N** |
| Bayesian NN | 0.1202 | 0.087 | **Neal, R** |
| < Bayesian NN | 0.1203 | 0.087 | **Neal, R** |
| Simple ANN Ensemble | 0.1213 | 0.088 | Ohlsson, M |
| EDWIN | 0.1213 | 0.087 | Eisele, A |
| > Bayesian Logistic Regression | 0.1216 | 0.088 | **Neal, R** |
| > ANN with L1 penalty | 0.1217 | 0.087 | Delalleau, O |
| > CCR-MLP | 0.1228 | 0.086 | **Cawley, G** |
| Rnd Subsp + Dec Trees | 0.1228 | 0.087 | **Chawla, N** |
| Bagging + Dec Trees | 0.1229 | 0.087 | **Chawla, N** |
| > R-MLP | 0.1236 | 0.087 | **Cawley, G** |
| Probing J48 | 0.1243 | 0.087 | Zadrozny, B & Langford, J |
| > Bagged R-MLP (small) | 0.1244 | 0.087 | **Cawley, G** |
| SVM + Platt | 0.1249 | 0.087 | **Chapelle, O** |
| **baseline: class frequencies** | **0.1314** | **0.087** | |

(NLP: average negative log probability, 01L: average zero-one loss)

The 0/1 loss is not informative for the Gatineau dataset: under this loss, none of the methods beats a baseline classifier that always predicts class '-1'. The dataset is very unbalanced, with about only 9% examples from the less frequent class '+1', which lead most methods to also classify all test examples as members of class '-1'. In this situation probabilistic predictions become of great importance. The contestants managed to perform significantly better than the baseline classifier, which outputs a probability of belonging to class '+1' of 0.087, independently of the input. This probability is equal to the empirical class frequency. The two winning entries, by Nitesh Chawla, correspond to decision trees with feature selection and averaging. For the winner entry averaging consists in randomly sub-sampling the feature space, and for the second best entry in Bagging. Interestingly both ensemble methods give very similar performance. Feature selection appears to be decisive for improving the performance of the decision trees used, as can be seen from the decision tree entries without feature selection. Radford Neal's Bayesian Neural Network achieved the 3rd and 4th best results, when trained on training and validation, and training targets only respectively. Other Neural Networks are represented, in Delalleau and Cawley's post-Challenge entries. Interestingly, SVMs with Platt scaling perform much worse on this dataset than on Catalysis.

**Stereopsis (Regression)**

| Method | NLPD | nMSE | Author |
|---|---|---|---|
| Mixture of Bayesian Neural Nets | -2.077 | 2.38e-3 | **Snelson & Murray** |
| Compet Assoc Nets + Cross Val | -0.669 | 1.39e-6 | **Kurogi, S et al** |
| > Mixt of LOOHKRR Machines | -0.402 | 3.86e-4 | **Cawley, G** |
| > Gaussian Process Regression | -0.351 | 8.25e-5 | **Chapelle, O** |
| > Inflated Var MLP Committee | 0.309 | 9.59e-5 | **Cawley, G** |
| KRR + Regression on the variance | 0.342 | 9.60e-5 | **Chapelle, O** |
| < Hybrid: Neural Net | 0.940 | 1.52e-4 | Lewandowski, A |
| Mixture Density Network Ensemble | 1.171 | 2.62e-4 | Carney, M |
| **baseline: empirical Gaussian** | **4.94** | **1.002** | |
| Modelling the experimental setting | 209.4 | 2.49e-4 | **Kohonen & Suomela** |

(NPLD: negative log predictive density, nMSE: normalized mean squared error)

The winning entry, by Snelson and Murray, had the worst nMSE loss. However, this entry achieved the lowest NLPD by providing multi-modal predictive distributions, which is a natural choice given the clustered nature of the outputs, see Fig. 8. The entry by Kohonen and Suomela scored extremely low under the NLPD loss with unimodal Gaussian predictive distributions, with too small variances. As detailed in their chapter, this might not be a problem as long as the prediction falls within the right cluster. However, a single prediction that fell in the wrong cluster blew the NLPD loss. Excluding that case, Kohonen and Suomela's entry would have ranked first in Stereopsis. In their chapter, Kohonen and Suomela discuss the appropriateness of the NLPD loss. The second best entry, competitive associative networks, achieved a nMSE loss an order of magnitude smaller than the second best. It did not win because it provided under-confident unimodal, Gaussian predictive distributions. Mixtures of leave-one-out heteroscedastic kernel ridge regressors (LOOHKRR) (post-Challenge) was third, with unimodal Gaussian predictive distributions as well.

**Gaze (Regression)**

| Method | NLPD | nMSE | Author |
|---|---|---|---|
| Compet Assoc Nets + Cross Val | -3.907 | 0.032 | **Kurogi, S et al** |
| LLR Regr + Resid Regr + Int Spikes | 2.750 | 0.374 | **Kohonen & Suomela** |
| > LOOHKRR | 5.180 | 0.033 | **Cawley, G** |
| > Heteroscedastic MLP Committee | 5.248 | 0.034 | **Cawley, G** |
| Gaussian Process regression | 5.250 | 0.675 | Csató, L |
| KRR + Regression on the variance | 5.395 | 0.050 | **Chapelle, O** |
| < Neural Net | 5.444 | 0.029 | Lewandowski, A |
| Rand Forest with OB enhancement | 5.445 | 0.060 | Van Matre, B |
| NeuralBAG and EANN | 5.558 | 0.074 | Carney, M |
| Mixture Density Network Ensemble | 5.761 | 0.089 | Carney, M |
| **baseline: empirical Gaussian** | **6.91** | **1.002** | |

The winners, Kurogi et al. with competitive associative networks, achieved a NLPD loss spectacularly lower than that of the second best entry. The authors took advantage of a flaw of the NLPD loss for this dataset. Indeed, the outputs of the Gaze dataset take discrete values. Kurogi et al. provided predictive distributions by means of quantiles, to specify predictive histograms with one bin around each discrete output level. By making the bins small enough, any arbitrarily low value of the NLPD can be achieved. This inappropriateness of the NLPD loss for discrete-valued regression problems was also exploited by the second best entry, although to a lesser extent. More details are given in the chapter contributed by Kohonen and Suomela. The remaining entries did not abuse the NLPD loss. The lowest nMSE loss was achieved by Lewandowski with a neural network to estimate the predictive mean, and another network to estimate the predictive variance. This entry did not achieve excellent predictive uncertainties. It must be noted though, that it did only used the training targets, and not validation targets, for training. The best entry during made before the deadline, that did not abuse the NLPD loss was a Gaussian process by Lehel Csató. Leave-one-out heteroscedastic kernel ridge regression (LOHKRR), a post-Challenge submission, ranked third. This submission provided Gaussian predictive distributions, with one regressor to model the mean, and another to model the variance. A committee of multi-layer perceptrons, also post-Challenge, ranked fourth.

**Outaouais (Regression)**

| Method | NLPD | nMSE | Author |
|---|---|---|---|
| > Sparse GP method | -1.037 | 0.014 | Keerthi & Chu |
| > Gaussian Process regression | -0.921 | 0.017 | Chu, Wei |
| Classification + Nearest Neighbour | -0.880 | 0.056 | **Kohonen, J** |
| Compet Assoc Nets + Cross Val | -0.648 | 0.038 | **Kurogi S et al** |
| > Small Heteroscedastic MLP | -0.230 | 0.201 | **Cawley, G** |
| Gaussian Process regression | 0.090 | 0.158 | Csató, L |
| Mixture Density Network Ensemble | 0.199 | 0.278 | Carney, M |
| NeuralBAG and EANN | 0.505 | 0.270 | Carney, M |
| **baseline: empirical Gaussian** | **1.115** | **1.000** | |

The winning entry before the deadline, by Kohonen and Suomela, was not achieved by any conventional Machine Learning "black box" method, but rather by a "data-mining" approach. Nearest neighbours were used to make predictions. The input space was divided into clusters, and a cluster dependent distribution of the outputs was empirically estimated, for each cluster. Test predictive distributions were subsequently obtained by attributing the test input to one of the clusters. Kohonen and Suomela won in spite of not having the best nMSE score. Competitive associative networks ranked second, achieving the lowest nMSE loss before the submission deadline. It is interesting to see that two post-Challenge submissions outperform all the rest both in terms of nMSE and NLPD loss. These two submissions are based on Gaussian Processes: the winning entry managed to use the entire training set thanks to a sparse approximation, while the second used a full GP trained only on a subset of the training data.

## 7 Presentation of the Invited Chapters

This volume includes six additional contributed chapters, written by participants who achieved outstanding results in the Evaluating Predictive Uncertainty Challenge. All dataset winners and seconds are represented, as well as the authors of some of the post-Challenge submissions. There is high variety in the methods used. In classification, neural networks are used with Bayesian averaging by Radford Neal, and with Bagging by Gavin Cawley. Decision trees are used with Bagging and with random sub-samples of the inputs by Nitesh Chawla. Support vector machines and Gaussian Processes are used by Olivier Chapelle. In regression neural networks are used with Bayesian averaging by Ed Snelson and Iain Murray, and as committees by Gavin Cawley. Competitive associative networks with cross-validation, which can be seen as a gating network of local experts, are used by Shuichi Kurogi, Miho Sawa and Shinya Tanaka. Kernel methods are represented as Gaussian processes, in Olivier Chapelle's submission, and as heteroscedastic leave-one-out kernel ridge regression on the mean and on the variance by Gavin Cawley. Datamining is used in Jukka Kohonen's submission to the Outaouais dataset, where he used nearest neighbours together with a gating classifier. Jukka Kohonen and Jukka Suomela do also provide the single submission that was not made using a "black box" model: for Stereopsis, they deduce from the name of the dataset the physical underlying model of two cameras looking at one object. In their chapter, Jukka Suomela and Jukka Kohonen additionally provide with a discussion on the kind of losses that seem appropriate for evaluating probabilistic predictions.

The contributed Chapters are, in order of appearance in this volume:

**Bayesian Neural Networks**
*Radford M. Neal*
The author describes his use of Bayesian neural networks for the Catalysis and Gatineau datasets. Use was made of the author's publicly available[3] Flexible Bayesian Modelling (FBM) software. Since no information was revealed about the datasets at the time of the competition, the author decided to use vague priors with a complex neural network architecture. The author describes how model complexity is automatically adjusted through Bayesian averaging. In addition, the author comments on his post-Challenge entry, based on Bayesian logistic regression, which achieved a fair performance.

**A Pragmatic Bayesian Approach to Predictive Uncertainty**
*Iain Murray and Ed Snelson*
The authors explain how they used a Bayesian approach tailored to the Stereopsis dataset. First, a probabilistic classifier based on Radford Neal's FBM software

[3] `http://www.cs.utoronto.ca/~radford/fbm.software.html`

serves as a soft gating network, that allows the combination of a mixture of local regression experts, each trained on a cluster of the Stereopsis outputs, see Fig. 8.

**Decision Trees with Feature Selection and Random Subspaces**
*Nitesh V. Chawla*
The author first explains why decision trees are not suited for probabilistic classification when used directly, nor when used with over-simplistic smoothing schemes such as Laplace or m-estimates. He then argues that ensemble methods allow to obtain large improvements in the predictive probabilities from decision trees. He discusses the use of two ensemble methods: random subsets and Bagging. The author also points out the importance that feature selection had for his good results. Finally, a discussion is given on how to improve performance on highly unbalanced datasets, such as Gatineau.

**Heteroscedastic Kernel Regression Methods**
*Gavin Cawley, Nicola Talbot and Olivier Chapelle*
The approach proposed in this work is to directly model the predictive distribution. For regression, a Gaussian predictive distribution is chosen. Its mean and variance are explicitly modelled separately by kernel ridge regression, and learning is achieved by assuming that the loss is the NLPD, and directly minimizing it. A leave-one-out scheme is used to avoid biased variance estimates.

**Competitive Associative Nets and Cross-Validation for Estimating Predictive Uncertainty on Regression Problems**
*Shuichi Kurogi, Miho Sawa and Shinya Tanaka*
Competitive associative nets (CANs) are presented. These are piece-wise linear approximations to non-linear functions. The input space is divided into a Voronoi tessellation, with a linear model associated to each region. For the Stereopsis and Outaouais datasets, Gaussian predictive distributions were provided, where the means were directly obtained from CANs trained to minimize the leave-one-out mean squared error. The variances were then estimated within the Voronoi regions by means of K-fold cross-validation. For the Gaze dataset, the authors took advantage of the discrete outputs to abuse the NLPD. The authors specified the predictive distribution by means of quantiles, and concentrated all the mass around tiny intervals centered around the integer output values.

**Lessons Learned in the Challenge: Making Predictions and Scoring Them**
*Jukka Suomela and Jukka Kohonen*
The authors present their winning entry for the Outaouais dataset: a pragmatic data-mining approach, based on a gating classifier followed by nearest neighbour regression. They also explain how they abused the NLPD loss on the discrete outputs Gaze dataset, in a similar but less extreme way than Kurogi et al. This motivates a very important discussion by the authors, on the more general problem of defining good losses for evaluating probabilistic predictions in regression. The authors propose to use of the continuous ranked probability score (CRPS), which does not suffer from the disadvantages of the NLPD loss.

## 8 Discussion

The wealth of methods successfully used by the participants to the Challenge indicates that there was not a single universally good way of producing good predictive uncertainties. However, averaging was common in many of the best submissions, see Fig. 10 for a qualitative impression in classification. Both classification winners used averaging: Radford Neal used Bayesian averaging of neural networks, and Nitesh Chawla decision trees averaged over random subsets of the inputs. Chawla's bagged decision trees achieved second position. In regression, averaging was used by the winning entry for the Stereopsis dataset with a Bayesian mixture of neural networks. Other successful entries for regression that used averaging include mixtures of kernel ridge regressors, bagged multi-layer perceptrons (MLPs) and committees of MLPs. Leave-one-out cross-validation was also found in many successful entries. It was used for example by Kurogi, Sawa and Tanaka with competitive associative networks (CANs), and by Cawley, Talbot and Chapelle with kernel ridge regression.

In terms of architectures, neural networks had a strong presence, and generally achieved very good results. Other architectures, like decision trees, Gaussian Processes and support vector machines also gave good results. Interestingly, an approach from datamining by Jukka Kohonen won the Outaouais regression dataset, later outperformed by two post-Challenge Gaussian Processes entries.

The Challenge revealed a difficulty inherent to measuring in general. While the goal was to evaluate "honest" predictive uncertainties, in practice the loss

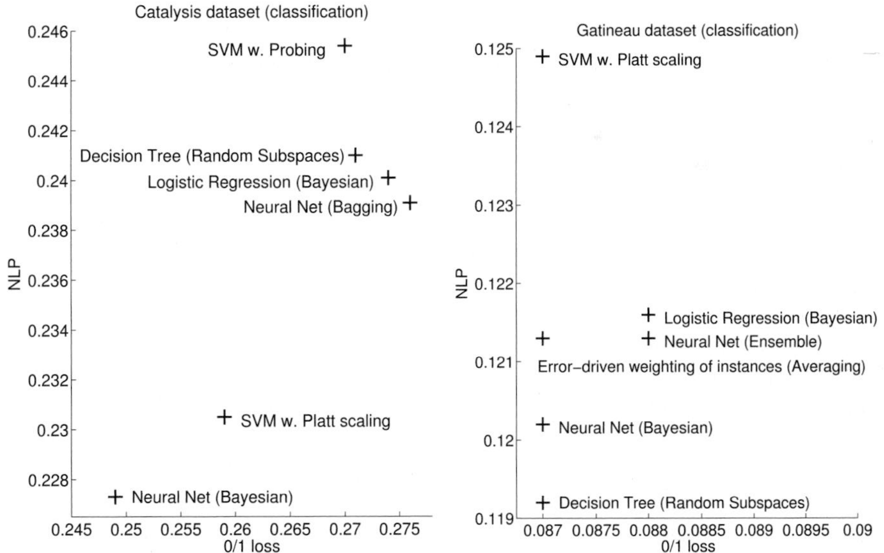


**Fig. 10.** Qualitative display of some classification results: 0/1 loss (average error rate) versus Negative Log Probability (NLP). Whenever averaging was used, the kind of averaging is indicated between brackets.

biased the predictive distributions of the participants. An example of this is the approach of Cawley, Talbot and Chapelle for regression, consisting in providing Gaussian predictive distributions tuned to minimize the NLPD loss. The authors would certainly have provided a different predictive distribution, if a different loss had been used.

The use of the NLPD loss turned out to be clearly inappropriate for the Gaze dataset. The outputs of this dataset take values from a finite discrete set. This encourages a simple strategy to achieve an arbitrarily small loss (the NLPD is unbounded from below). It is enough to specify a predictive histogram, with one bin encompassing each output discrete value. Making the bins narrow enough allows to arbitrarily increase the amount of probability density on the targets, and to therefore attain any arbitrarily small value of the NLPD, the being machine precision. This inadequacy of the NLPD for the Gaze dataset was exploited by two groups of participants, Kurogi, Sawa and Tanaka, and Snelson and Murray, who achieved respectively the best and second best results.

We have seen that the accuracy according to a point-prediction-based loss does not always give the same ranking as a loss which takes uncertainties into account, and that for some datasets like Gatineau, only the loss that evaluates probabilistic predictions is useful. However, it seems that defining good losses for probabilistic predictions is hard, since the losses might encourage strategies that are loss-dependent Maybe one way of encouraging unbiased and "honest" predictive distributions would be to apply several losses that encourage contradictory strategies. Another way could be not to reveal the loss under which predictions will be evaluated.

It would have been very interesting to empirically evaluate in this challenge a very recent paradigm for probabilistic predictions, based on "conformal predictions" (Vovk, Gammerman and Shafer, 2005).Conformal predictors are capable of producing accurate and reliable point predictions, while providing information about their own accuracy and reliability. This work was unfortunately published after the closing deadline of the Evaluating Predictive Uncertainty Challenge. Perhaps future competitions will allow to evaluate its practical utility.

## Acknowledgements

Many thanks to Olivier Chapelle for beta testing, to Yoshua Bengio for providing the Outaouais and Gatineau datasets, and to both for many discussions. Special thanks to Greg Grudic and Rich Caruana for accommodating the presentation of the challenge at the NIPS 2004 Workshop on Calibration and Probabilistic Prediction in Machine Learning.

We thank Alexander Zien for preparing for us the Catalysis dataset, and Wolf Kienzle for the Gaze dataset. We thank Sebastian Stark for his help setting up the mysql database for the Challenge. Many thanks to Jan Loderhose for allowing us to use his php framework as a basis to build ours.

We thank Florence d'Alché-Buc and Steve Gunn for putting together the Southampton PASCAL Challenges Workshop, where this Challenge was also presented and discussed. We are grateful for the support received by the PASCAL European Network of Excellence, IST Programme of the European Community, grant number IST-2002-506778. JQC and CER were partly supported by the German Research Council (DFG) through grant RA 1030/1. This work was partly done while JQC and OB where with the Max Planck Institute for Biological Cybernetics.

## References

Carl Edward Rasmussen and Joaquin Quiñonero-Candela. Healing the relevance vector machine by augmentation. In De Raet and Wrobel, editors, *Proceedings of the 22nd International Conference on Machine Learning*, pages 689–696, ACM Press, 2005.

Leo Breiman. Bagging predictors. *Machine Learning*, 24(2):123–140, 1996.

Isabelle Guyon, Steve Gunn, Asa Ben-Hur, and Gideon Dror. Result analysis of the nips 2003 feature selection challenge. In Lawrence K. Saul, Yair Weiss, and Léon Bottou, editors, *Advances in Neural Information Processing Systems 17*, pages 545–552, Cambridge, Massachussetts, 2005. The MIT Press.

James A. Hanley and Barbara J. McNeil. The meaning and use ofthe Area under a Receiver Operating Characteristic ROC Curve. *Radiology*, 143(1):29–26, 1982.

F. Sinz, J. Quiñonero-Candela, G. H. Bakir, C. E. Rasmussen, and M.O. Franz. Learning depth from stereo. In Carl Edward Rasmussen, Henrich H. Bülthoff, Martin A. Giese, and Bernhard Schölkopf, editors, *Proc. 26 DAGM Pattern Recognition Symposium*, pages 245–252, Heidelberg, Germany, 2004. Springer.

John C. Platt. Probabilistic outputs for support vector machines and comparisons to regularized likelihood methods. In Alexander J. Smola, Peter Bartlett, Bernhard Schölkopf, and Dale Schuurmans, editors, *Advances in Large Margin Classifiers*, pages 61–74, Cambridge, MA, 1999. MIT Press.

John Langford and Bianca Zadrozny. Estimating class membership probabilities using classifier learners. In Robert G. Cowell and Zoubin Ghahramani, editors, *Proceedings of the Tenth International Workshop on Artificial Intelligence and Statistics*, pages 198–205. Society for Artificial Intelligence and Statistics, 2005. (Available electronically at http://www.gatsby.ucl.ac.uk/aistats/).

Vladimir Vovk, Alex Gammerman and Glenn Shafer. Algorithmic Learning in a Random World. New York, 2005. Springer.

# Classification with Bayesian Neural Networks

Radford M. Neal

Dept. of Statistics and Dept. of Computer Science, University of Toronto
radford@stat.utoronto.ca
http://www.cs.utoronto.ca/~radford/

I submitted entries for the two classification problems — "Catalysis" and "Gatineau" — in the Evaluating Predictive Uncertainty Challenge. My entry for Catalysis was the best one; my entry for Gatineau was the third best, behind two similar entries by Nitesh Chawla.

The Catalysis dataset was later revealed to be about predicting a property of yeast proteins from expression levels of the genes encoding them. The nature of the Gatineau dataset has not been revealed, for proprietary reasons. The two datasets are similar in number of input variables that are available for predicting the binary outcome (617 for Catalysis, 1092 for Gatineau). They differ substantially in the number of cases available for training (1173 for Catalysis, 5176 for Gatineau) and in the fractions of cases that are in the two classes (43%/57% for Catalysis, 9%/91% for Gatineau).

For both problems, I used Bayesian neural network models, implemented using Markov chain Monte Carlo methods. This methodology is described in the book based on my thesis (Neal 1996). Lampinen and Vehtari (2001) provide a more recent review and case studies. Markov chain Monte Carlo methods are discussed in a review of mine (Neal 1993), and in a number of other books, such that of Liu (2001).

The software I used is freely available from my web site, as part of my software package for Flexible Bayesian Modeling (I used the version of 2004-11-10). The command scripts I used for this competition are also available from my web site.

Multilayer-perceptron neural networks are flexible models capable of representing a wide class of functions as the parameters (the "weights" and "biases") of the network are varied. For binary classification problems, the real-valued function of the inputs, $f(x)$, defined by the network is used to produce the probability of class 1 for a case with these inputs. I used the logistic function to produce class probabilities, as follows:

$$P(\text{class } 1 \,|\, x) = 1/(1 + \exp(-f(x)) \tag{1}$$

Of the many possible neural network architectures, I chose to use an architecture with two layers of "hidden units", which is flexible enough to efficiently represent quite complex relationships, but which can also behave much like a simpler architecture if that is favoured by the data. The function, $f(x)$, computed by this network can be expressed in terms of functions for units in the first hidden layer, whose values are denoted by $g_k(x)$, for $k = 1, \ldots, G$, and units in the second hidden layer, whose values are denoted by $h_\ell(x)$, for $\ell = 1, \ldots, H$.

J. Quiñonero-Candela et al. (Eds.): MLCW 2005, LNAI 3944, pp. 28–32, 2006.

For a training or test case with input vector $x$, of length $p$, the output of the network can be expressed as follows:

$$f(x) = c + \sum_{l=1}^{H} w_\ell h_\ell(x) \tag{2}$$

$$h_\ell(x) = \tanh\left(b_\ell + \sum_{k=1}^{G} v_{k\ell} g_k(x)\right) \tag{3}$$

$$g_k(x) = \tanh\left(a_k + \sum_{j=1}^{p} u_{jk} x_j\right) \tag{4}$$

The parameters of the network are the "biases", $a_k$, $b_\ell$, and $c$, and the "weights" $u_{jk}$, $v_{k\ell}$, and $w_\ell$. Provided that $G$ and $H$, are fairly large, varying these parameters produces a large variety of functions, $f(x)$, which in turn define a variety of class probability functions.

Traditional neural network training methods select a single "best" set of parameters by minimizing the "error" on the training set. For classification problems, the error is often the sum over all training cases of minus the log probability of the correct class. A "weight decay" penalty proportional to the sum of the squares of the weights is sometimes added. This penalty is a means of avoiding "overfitting", by encouraging small weights, which generally correspond to smoother $f(x)$. The parameters found by minimizing the error plus penalty are then used to make predictions for test cases.

Bayesian training departs from traditional methods in two ways, which together provide a more principled approach to using a complex network while avoiding overfitting. The Bayesian framework also provides a way of automatically determining which input variables are most relevant.

The first difference between traditional and Bayesian training is that Bayesian methods do not use a single set of parameter values to make predictions for test cases. Instead, the predictive probabilities produced by networks with many sets of parameter values are averaged. These sets of parameters are sampled from the "posterior distribution" of network parameters, described below. Since this distribution is extremely complex, Markov chain sampling methods must be used, in which one or more realizations of a Markov chain having the posterior distribution as its asymptotic equilibrium distribution are simulated until they reach a good approximation to this equilibrium distribution. Sets of network parameters from many subsequent iterations of these Markov chains are then used to produce predictions for the test cases.

The second distinctive aspect of Bayesian training is that it uses not only the information in the training data, but also "prior" information regarding the likely values of the parameters. Sometimes, we may have quite specific prior information regarding the class probability function, which translates into information about the parameters of the network. For the challenge problems, however, no information was released about the actual situation until after the competition, so only very general prior information could be used. This is also the situation for some real problems, either because little is known beforehand, or because expressing what is known in suitable mathematical form is too difficult.

The prior information used in Bayesian training takes the form of a "prior" probability density function over the parameters of the network. The information from the data is contained in the "likelihood", which is the probability of the actual classes in the training cases, given the inputs for these training cases, seen as a function of the network parameters. The product of the prior density and the likelihood is (after normalization) the "posterior" probability density function for the parameters. It is from this posterior distribution that we sample parameter values in order to make predictions for test cases, as described above.

Specifying the prior distribution is a crucial part of Bayesian modeling. For the two-layer neural network model used here, one simple option would be to give each parameter a Gaussian distribution with mean zero and some specified standard deviation, with all parameters being independent. Unless we have very specific information about the problem, however, such a prior would be too inflexible. It would fix the likely scales of the weights, and hence the overall magnitude and scale of variation in $f(x)$, even though we don't know enough to say what suitable values for these would be. Accordingly, although Gaussian distributions with mean zero are often used for weights and biases, the standard deviations of these distributions are typically unknown "hyperparameters", which are themselves given prior distributions (usually rather broad ones). The introduction of hyperparameters is an indirect way of making the parameters be dependent in the prior, since they each depend on the hyperparameter controlling their standard deviation. The effect is that, for instance, a large value for $w_1$ tends to go with a large value for $w_2$ as well.

Very general prior information can be incorporated into the model by deciding which groups of parameters will share a hyperparameter controlling their prior standard deviation. Almost always, one would want to use different hyperparameters for the $u_{jk}$, the $v_{k\ell}$, and the $w_\ell$, since they play quite different roles in the network. Dividing the weights into smaller groups can also be useful, however. In particular, we may wish to use a different hyperparameter for the $u_{jk}$ associated with each input, $j$. This allows the Bayesian procedure to "learn" that one input is less relevant than another, by using a smaller hyperparameter for the less relevant input, with the result that the weights associated with that input will also be small. This scheme is known as "Automatic Relevance Determination" (ARD).

For the two classification datasets in the challenge, I used identical network architectures, having two hidden layers, as described above, with $G = 16$ and $H = 8$. The prior distributions used were also almost identical. ARD priors were used for both problems, on the assumption that probably not all of the large number of input variables are highly relevant. Inputs were standardized to have mean zero and standard deviation one, in an attempt (in the absence of real prior information) to equalize the expected effect of a one-unit change in the various inputs. Slightly different priors were used for the ARD hyperparameters for the two datasets, since in preliminary runs the relevance of inputs appeared to be more variable for Gatineau than for Catalysis. This manual adjustment is a substitute for making the variance of the prior for the ARD hyperparameters be a higher-level hyperparameter, which is quite possible, but not implemented in my software package.

The Markov chain Monte Carlo methods used for the two problems were also very similar, with slight differences to tune them to the requirements of the different posterior distributions. For each problem, I did two independent Markov chain sampling runs, each of which took approximately four days on a 3 GHz Pentium machine. I used parameter sets from the latter parts of both runs to make predictions. In the context of a competition, it is natural to do such long runs, since longer runs may give at least slightly better results. However, quite similar results were obtained when using only the first tenth of each run.

For complete details on the priors and Markov chain Monte Carlo methods used, see the scripts available from my web page.

On the Catalysis dataset, my method achieved an average negative log probability over test cases of 0.2273, and a classification error rate of 0.249, better than any other method (the corresponding figures for the next best method were 0.2305 and 0.259). On the Gatineau dataset, my method achieved an average negative log probability over test cases of 0.1202, slightly worse than the best result of 0.1192, achieved by Nitesh Chawla. Both his and my methods predicted the same (more common) class for all test cases. The highest probability for the less frequent class produced by my method was 0.329. The resulting error rate was 0.087, the frequency of the less common class. No method for the Gatineau dataset had an error rate significantly better than this.

After the competition, I submitted predictions found using Bayesian logistic regression — essentially, a neural network with no hidden units — for which the class probabilities are derived using equation (1), but with $f(x)$ given by

$$f(x) = \sum_{j=1}^{p} \beta_j x_j \tag{5}$$

As the prior for $\beta_j$, I used a heavy-tailed $t$ distribution, with 2.5 degrees of freedom for Catalysis and 1.5 degrees of freedom for Gatineau. The width of the $t$ distribution was a hyperparameter. Predictions were made using Markov chain Monte Carlo.

The results using logistic regression were quite good, but not as good as with the neural network model. For Catalysis, the average negative log probability over test cases was 0.2401, and the error rate was 0.2743. This would have been the third-best entry if it had been submitted during the competition. For Gatineau, the average negative log probability over test cases was 0.1216, and the error rate was 0.088. This would have been the sixth-best entry if it had been submitted during the competition. The Bayesian logistic regression model predicted that three of the test cases would be in the less common class; none of these predictions were correct. These mistaken predictions may have been due to the presence of occasional extreme input values in the Gatineau dataset, which can cause a linear logistic model to produce extreme probabilities. The tanh non-linearity in the neural network's hidden units tends to limit the effect of extreme values.

The good results I obtained in this competition demonstrate that Bayesian models using ARD priors can successfully deal with around a thousand inputs, without any preliminary selection of inputs. In entries to an earlier competition focused on feature selection (Neal and Zhang 2006), I dealt with larger numbers of inputs (up to 100,000) by either selecting a smaller number (up to about a thousand), or by reducing dimensionality using Principal Components Analysis. Failure to properly account for varying relevance of inputs may not only reduce classification accuracy, but also distort predictive probabilities — for example, a model that doesn't know that some inputs are irrelevant may produce an under-confident prediction for a test case that differs from the training cases in such an irrelevant input.

Another challenge when dealing with complex problems is deciding what type of model is most appropriate. In this competition, I adopted the strategy of using a single rather flexible model, which can behave in various ways depending on the values found for the hyperparameters. Accordingly, I made only one submission for each dataset (apart from one submission for each in the preliminary phase of the competition, when only the initial portion of the training set, excluding the "validation" cases, was available). This strategy of using the most complex model that is practically feasible (which I also advocated in (Neal 1996)) worked well for these problems.

## Acknowledgements

This work was supported by the Natural Sciences and Engineering Research Council of Canada. I hold a Canada Research Chair in Statistics and Machine Learning.

## References

Lampinen, J. and Vehtari, A. (2001) "Bayesian approach for neural networks — review and case studies", *Neural Networks*, vol. 14, pp. 257-274.

Liu, J. S. (2001) *Monte Carlo Strategies in Scientific Computing*, Springer-Verlag.

Neal, R. M. (1993) *Probabilistic Inference Using Markov Chain Monte Carlo Methods*, Technical Report CRG-TR-93-1, Department of Computer Science, University of Toronto, 144 pages. Available from `http://www.cs.utoronto.ca/~radford/`.

Neal, R. M. (1996) *Bayesian Learning for Neural Networks*, Lecture Notes in Statistics No. 118, Springer-Verlag.

Neal, R. M. and Zhang, J. (2006) "High Dimensional Classification with Bayesian Neural Networks and Dirichlet Diffusion Trees", in I. Guyon, S. Gunn, M. Nikravesh, and L. Zadeh (editors) *Feature Extraction, Foundations and Applications*, Studies in Fuzziness and Soft Computing, Physica-Verlag, Springer.

# A Pragmatic Bayesian Approach to Predictive Uncertainty

Iain Murray and Edward Snelson

Gatsby Computational Neuroscience Unit, University College London,
London WC1N 3AR, UK
{i.murray, snelson}@gatsby.ucl.ac.uk
http://www.gatsby.ucl.ac.uk/

**Abstract.** We describe an approach to regression based on building a probabilistic model with the aid of visualization. The "stereopsis" data set in the predictive uncertainty challenge is used as a case study, for which we constructed a mixture of neural network experts model. We describe both the ideal Bayesian approach and computational shortcuts required to obtain timely results.

## 1 Introduction

We describe our treatment of the "stereopsis" regression data set in the predictive uncertainty challenge. Our aim was to construct an appropriate statistical model of the data, and use Bayesian inference to form the required predictive distributions given the data. Our starting point was some simple exploratory visualization of the data.

The stereopsis data set is very amenable to visualization, as it has only four input dimensions, and structure quickly reveals itself. For example plotting various input dimensions against each other, as in Figure 1(a), shows some clear clustering in the input space. There are 10 distinct branches of points, each with some interesting substructure. Figure 1(b) shows a one dimensional projection of the training inputs plotted against the training outputs. This projection was made by doing a least squares linear fit to the training data, $\hat{\mathbf{w}} = \mathrm{argmin}_{\mathbf{w}} \sum_n (y^{(n)} - \mathbf{w}^\top \mathbf{x}^{(n)})^2$, and plotting the targets $y$ against projected inputs $\hat{\mathbf{w}}^\top \mathbf{x}$. The training outputs also seem to be grouped into 10 discrete clusters, so one might guess that there is a correspondence between the clustering in input space, and the clustering in output space. Further visualization confirmed that this was the case. Zooming in on a cluster in Figure 1(b), it becomes clear that there is also substructure relevant for regression within each output cluster.

When we see obvious structure from simple visualizations like Figure 1, it makes us curious about the data generating process. Are the input points sampled from some natural distribution on the space of possible inputs? In which case we might not worry about generalizing well to input points far away from those already observed. Alternatively the clustering in input and output space may be an artifact of a particular choice of experiments that have been done. Then some new test positions may lie in other parts of the input space outside

J. Quiñonero-Candela et al. (Eds.): MLCW 2005, LNAI 3944, pp. 33–40, 2006.

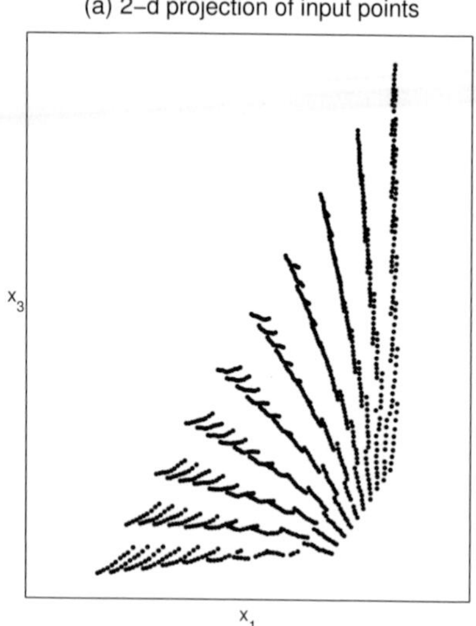


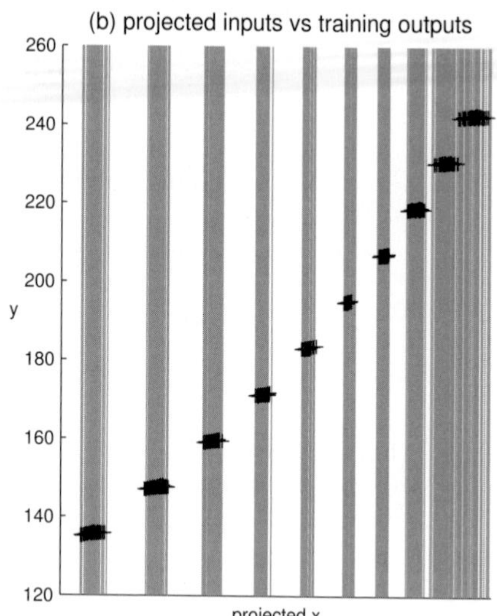


**Fig. 1.** Visualization of stereopsis dataset. (a) The first and third dimensions of the input space are plotted against each other. (b) The training outputs are plotted against $\hat{\mathbf{w}}^\top \mathbf{x}$, the input points projected onto the least squares linear regression weight vector. The test input projections onto the same weight vector are plotted as the vertical lines.

the regions observed in the training data. In which case, we would need to concentrate on building a global model that extrapolates well outside the observed clusters with appropriate uncertainties. In a real world task we would probably have information regarding the locations of future predictions.

Unknown to us, the 'stereopsis' task was to infer the depth of an object from stereo image information [1]. The data were generated by attaching an LED to a robot arm and recording the spatial location via the arm's spatial encoders and the LED image positions on two stereo cameras. The robot arm was then moved in a structured way in different discrete planes of depth whilst data were recorded. With this small amount of information it is clear where the almost discrete nature of the outputs (the depths) comes from, and also the clustering in the inputs. It is also clear that for a model to be useful it must be able to extrapolate away from the training data clusters, as we will need to be able to predict the whole range of depths well.

The nature of a machine learning competition is a little different. The data are presented with no information except a slight clue in the title! Clearly with all the structure visible, we could still make a good guess that this was caused by a certain choice of experimental sampling. We are also given the test inputs; a projection of these is shown in Figure 1(b). From this it seems plausible, as in most machine learning competitions, that the test data have been produced from the same sampling distribution as the training data. Therefore, in order to perform well in the competition it made sense to model the cluster structure. This is described in the next section.

## 2 Mixture of Experts Model

As described above, we based our model on intuitions gained from visualizing the training data and the test input locations. Further visualization of each of the ten clusters in figure 1 showed that the targets seemed to vary smoothly with any linear projection of the input space. We chose to model the targets within each cluster as noisy observations around a smooth function of the input space. To complete the model we defined a conditional distribution for belonging to a particular cluster given its input location. This is a mixture of experts model [2], which we refer to as "$\mathcal{H}$":

$$p(y|x, \theta, \mathcal{H}) \equiv \sum_k p(y|x, \mathbf{w}_k, \mathcal{H}_k) p(k|x, \mathbf{w}_{\text{gate}}, \mathcal{H}_{\text{gate}}), \tag{1}$$

where $k$ indexes the experts and $\theta \equiv \{\mathbf{w}_k, \mathbf{w}_{\text{gate}}\}$ summarizes any free parameters in the models. We wanted flexible models for both the gating model, $\mathcal{H}_{\text{gate}}$, specifying the conditional probability of choosing an expert given input location, and for each expert's regression model $\mathcal{H}_k$. The groups over which the gating model puts a distribution have a clear ordering, see figure 1(b). This makes learning $p(k|x)$ an ordinal regression task, although for simplicity we considered it to be a standard multi-way classification problem. We chose to use neural networks [3] for both the regression and classification problems. Each neural network had a single layer of 15 units; we thought this would be sufficiently flexible while being manageable in the time available. Without further knowledge about the data, any flexible models such as Gaussian processes would have been equally sensible.

Each cluster in the training data only contains a small number of data points that will be useful for training that cluster's regression model $\mathcal{H}_k$. Therefore, there is a danger of over-fitting if we optimized the many parameters of the flexible models we chose. We could have chosen simpler models, but it might have been difficult to capture the non-linear structure we observed within the clusters. It is also possible that careful regularization could avoid over-fitting. Instead we decided to take our model seriously, and as far as possible perform the correct coherent inference given our assumptions; this is achieved by the ideal Bayesian approach.

## 3 Ideal Bayesian Inference

Our target is $p(y|x, D, \mathcal{H})$, the predictive distribution for an output $y$ sampled at a new location $x$ given previously observed data $D$ and our modeling assumptions, $\mathcal{H}$. Our model has many free parameters, $\theta$, corresponding to the weights in the classifier $\mathcal{H}_{\text{gate}}$ and each of the regression neural networks $\mathcal{H}_k$. As $\theta$ are unknown, we must marginalize these out:

$$p(y|x, D, \mathcal{H}) = \int p(y, \theta|x, D, \mathcal{H}) \, \mathrm{d}\theta = \int p(y|x, \theta, \mathcal{H}) p(\theta|D, \mathcal{H}) \, \mathrm{d}\theta. \tag{2}$$

The integrand consists of two parts. The first, $p(y|x, \theta, \mathcal{H})$ from equation (1), describes the predictive distribution given known parameters. The second part is the posterior over parameters from Bayes' rule:

$$p(\theta|D, \mathcal{H}) = \frac{p(D|\theta, \mathcal{H})p(\theta|\mathcal{H})}{p(D|\mathcal{H})} \propto p(D|\theta, \mathcal{H})p(\theta|\mathcal{H}), \tag{3}$$

which requires a prior over parameters $p(\theta|\mathcal{H})$ and a likelihood, which under our i.i.d. model is a product of terms:

$$p(D|\theta, \mathcal{H}) = \prod_n p(y^{(n)}|x^{(n)}, \theta, \mathcal{H}). \tag{4}$$

Each term, specified in (1), involves summing over the latent class assignment $k^{(n)}$. In order to obtain results more quickly we chose to approximate (1) by assuming we knew the class assignments for the training data based on the clusters in figure 1(b). While this is not the ideal procedure, it saved time and seemed a reasonable approximation given how well separated the targets were.

For the prior over parameters $p(\theta|\mathcal{H})$ we used the same hierarchical prior as in the neural network regression and classification examples in Neal's FBM documentation [4]. It is possible that the regression experts $p(y|x, \mathbf{w}_k, \mathcal{H}_k)$ should be related, especially now we know how the data were generated. Therefore it would make sense to introduce a priori correlations between the parameters, $\mathbf{w}_k$, of the experts. We chose not to do this; we assume our experts obtained parameters independently. As a result we probably did not make best use of the data.

The above theory says that the predictive distribution (2) is available without reference to how the input locations $x$ were chosen, or what the predictions will be used for. Normally a loss function would only be necessary if we wanted to use the predictive distribution, eg for making a decision. Then, given the loss function $\mathcal{L}(y_{\text{guess}}, y_{\text{true}})$, which specifies the penalty for predicting $y_{\text{guess}}$ when the test target is $y_{\text{true}}$, we would minimize our expected loss:

$$y_{\text{guess}} = \operatorname{argmin} \int \mathcal{L}(y_{\text{guess}}, y)\ p(y|x, D, \mathcal{H})\ \mathrm{d}y, \tag{5}$$

where again, the predictive distribution is independent of the loss function. In the challenge the loss function depended on the distribution itself and we had to decide which quantiles to report. It turns out that both loss functions used in this challenge, mean squared error (MSE) and negative log predictive density (NLPD) have a consistency property: the expected loss is minimized by reporting the predictive distribution that actually reflects our beliefs.

In practice we will experience computational difficulties. As is often the case, the posterior in (3) has no simple form and the integral in (2) is intractable. A variety of approximate approaches exist. When using an approximation, the predictive distribution that results is, frankly, wrong: it does not correspond to the correct rational inference for combining our model with the data. The seriousness of this problem may depend on the loss function, although we did not use this to guide our approximation.

## 4 Monte Carlo Approximation

Here we present a standard Monte Carlo approach for predictive distributions. The first step is to draw $S$ samples from the posterior distribution over parameters (3). These could be used to approximate the integral in (2):

$$\begin{aligned} p(y|x, D, \mathcal{H}) &= \int p(y|x, \theta, \mathcal{H}) p(\theta|D, \mathcal{H}) \, \mathrm{d}\theta \\ &\approx \sum_{s=1}^{S} p(y|x, \theta^{(s)}, \mathcal{H}), \qquad \theta^{(s)} \sim p(\theta|D, \mathcal{H}). \end{aligned} \tag{6}$$

However, this does not easily give us the quantiles required for reporting the whole distribution. Draws from the predictive distribution, $y^{(s)} \sim p(y|x, D, \mathcal{H})$, will be more useful. These can be obtained by first drawing a set of parameters, $\theta^{(s)} \sim p(\theta|D, \mathcal{H})$, then drawing $y^{(s)} \sim p(y|x, \theta^{(s)}, \mathcal{H})$. Quantiles of the predictive distribution may be approximated by drawing many samples and using the empirical quantiles of the set of samples. For implementational reasons we found approximate quantiles for each expert's distribution $p(y|x, D, \mathcal{H}_k)$ separately, and then combined these distributions using the mixing fractions $p(k|x, D, \mathcal{H}_{\mathrm{gate}})$.

All of these sampling procedures are frequentist not Bayesian in nature. They give unbiased procedures, which are correct in the limit of an infinite number of samples under fairly general conditions. If our procedures used independent samples, then the errors in estimators of expectations are usually nearly Gaussian distributed and estimators of quantiles are also well understood as Beta distributed "order statistics".

In this case, independent sampling is intractable. Markov Chain Monte Carlo (MCMC) methods allow drawing correlated samples from $p(\theta|D, \mathcal{H})$ [5]. Also, given a valuable parameter sample, $\theta^{(s)}$, it makes sense to draw multiple samples from $p(y|x, \theta^{(s)}, \mathcal{H})$, which are correlated samples from $p(y|x, D, \mathcal{H})$. Diagnosing the errors from these approximations remains a difficult problem; our approach was pragmatic. We ran a trial run of MCMC using only the training set and checked our results made reasonable predictions on the validation set. We then performed a longer run using both the training and validation sets for our final results. Strictly the Bayesian framework does not need a separate validation set at any stage, but we wished to check that the approximate inference procedure gave sensible results.

All of the above approximations were performed on neural networks with hierarchical priors by Radford Neal's FBM software [4].

## 5 Discussion

We exploited an artificial cluster structure of the stereopsis data, which should not necessarily be done in a real world modeling situation, eg [1]. This suggests some alternative formats for future competitions. Firstly, the standard assumption that the test data should come from the same *input* distribution as the training data could be relaxed. Secondly some information about the data could be given to competitors to guide modeling. This goes somewhat against a common view that a machine learning algorithm should be a general purpose black box. Competitors would need to tailor their methods using the information given about the training and test data generating processes. From this format it may be more difficult to achieve a consensus as to which machine learning algorithm performs best generally, but it may be more realistic, and some useful modeling approaches may come out of it.

These reservations aside, the approach outlined in the previous sections performed well in the competition, although was the mixture of experts approach really necessary? Initially we had tried to construct predictive distributions using only a single, global neural network regression model (we also tried Gaussian processes). Our visualizations indicated that the resulting error bars were too conservative. The added flexibility in the mixture model gave better NLPD scores on the validation set.

The ideal Bayesian approach assumes that all dependence on the data is contained in the likelihood. By looking at the data before constructing our model we were effectively using the data twice and risked over-fitting. As a result it is likely that we would not perform well on points drawn from a different input distribution. Fortunately for us, the competition did not reflect what often happens when a system is deployed: the input distribution changes.

It is unlikely we would have considered the model we used without any visualization. In a real application we would still recommend looking at the data to suggest suitable models. However, choosing one model by hand, as we did, is potentially dangerous. Better would be to consider a range of possibilities as well, eg: other settings for $k$ and some simpler models. Predictions from different models can be combined quantitatively by Bayesian model averaging:

$$p(y|x, D) = \sum_i p(y|x, D, \mathcal{H}_i)p(\mathcal{H}_i|D). \tag{7}$$

This could be more robust than our approach using one model, if the clustering assumptions of our model turned out to be inappropriate for the test set.

Our approach scored an NLPD score considerably higher than other entrants to the competition. We believe the (nearly) Bayesian approach we followed was largely responsible. Firstly when regressing the individual clusters we integrated over uncertainty in the neural net parameters using MCMC, which avoided over-fitting. Secondly we were able to integrate over uncertainty in our classification parameters. This resulted in predictive distributions with ten modes, one for each expert, $\mathcal{H}_k$. Putting probability mass in all of these locations makes us robust to classification errors. If we had chosen to use only one expert for predictions we would risk obtaining an arbitrarily bad NLPD score.

Figure 2 shows on a log scale a typical predictive distribution given a new test input, from our competition submission. One of the experts $\mathcal{H}_k$ is favored over the others; it contributes the sharp spike close to $y = 220$. Notice how the predictions from the experts far from the most probable spike give broader, less certain predictions. This is because the new test input is far from the training inputs for those particular experts. The constant density between the spikes

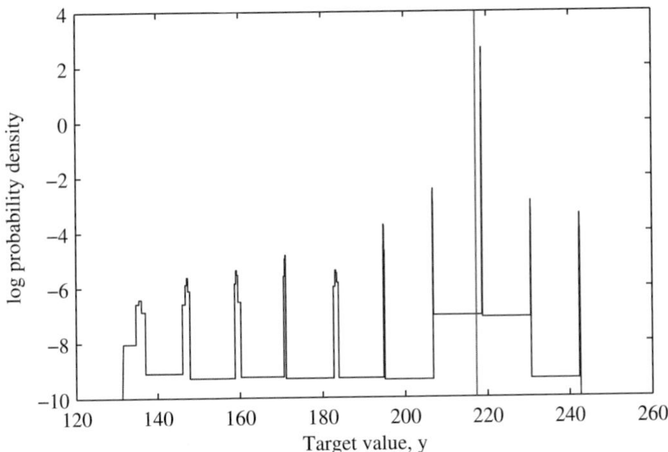


**Fig. 2.** A predictive log probability density constructed from quantiles submitted to the competition by us for a typical point in the test set. The vertical bar shows the corresponding mean of the predictive distribution.

results from an artifact of the way we combined the quantiles from each expert. The tail masses from adjacent experts was spread uniformly across the gap between them. We hoped that such artifacts would have low enough densities not to matter.

Also notice that the mean of the distribution in figure 2 does not coincide with any of the predictive spikes. This happens on most of our test set predictions, resulting in a poor mean squared error score; in fact we scored *last* on MSE score. The mean of a predictive distribution is fairly sensitive to small changes in the probability mass assigned to extreme predictions. In this case, small changes in the distribution of mass amongst the experts, $p(k|x, D, \mathcal{H}_{\text{gate}})$, can have a large effect. We made ourselves robust for NLPD score by placing mass on all modes, but at the expense of poor MSE score. The MSE score would have been most likely much improved if we had done hard classification.

## 6 Conclusions

This case study illustrated some of our opinions on how to construct models that capture predictive uncertainty:

– Visualization helps in understanding data when constructing probabilistic models, especially in the absence of any further domain knowledge.
– Bayesian inference provides a natural framework for finding predictive distributions given modeling assumptions. It can help avoid overfitting when limited data are available.
– Looking at the data before specifying modeling assumptions and using approximations both fall outside the Bayesian framework. By checking on a validation set, we found approximate Bayesian procedures still behaved robustly.

## References

1. Sinz, F., Quiñonero-Candela, J., Bakir, G.H., Rasmussen, C.E., Franz, M.: Learning depth from stereo. In Rasmussen, C.E., Buelthoff, H.H., Giese, M.A., Schoelkopf, B., eds.: Proc. 26th DAGM Symposium, Springer (2004) 245–252
2. Jordan, M.I., Jacobs, R.A.: Hierarchical mixtures of experts and the EM algorithm. Neural Computation **6** (1994) 181–214
3. Neal, R.M.: Bayesian Learning for Neural Networks. Number 118 in Lecture Notes in Statistics. Springer-Verlag, New York (1996)
4. Neal, R.M.: Flexible Bayesian modeling software (FBM). Available through `http://www.cs.toronto.edu/~radford/` (2003)
5. Neal, R.M.: Probabilistic inference using Markov chain Monte Carlo methods. Technical report, Dept. of Computer Science, University of Toronto (1993)

# Many Are Better Than One: Improving Probabilistic Estimates from Decision Trees

Nitesh V. Chawla

Department of Computer Science and Engineering,
University of Notre Dame, Notre Dame, IN 46556
nchawla@cse.nd.edu

**Abstract.** Decision trees, a popular choice for classification, have their limitation in providing probability estimates, requiring smoothing at the leaves. Typically, smoothing methods such as Laplace or m-estimate are applied at the decision tree leaves to overcome the systematic bias introduced by the frequency-based estimates. In this work, we show that an ensemble of decision trees significantly improves the quality of the probability estimates produced at the decision tree leaves. The ensemble overcomes the myopia of the leaf frequency based estimates. We show the effectiveness of the probabilistic decision trees as a part of the Predictive Uncertainty Challenge. We also include three additional highly imbalanced datasets in our study. We show that the ensemble methods significantly improve not only the quality of the probability estimates but also the AUC for the imbalanced datasets.

## 1 Introduction

Inductive learning identifies relationships between the attributes values of training examples and the class of the examples, thus establishing a learned function. Decision trees [BFOS84, Qui87, Qui92] are a popular classifier for inductive inference. Decision trees are trained on examples comprised of a finite number of predicting attributes with class labels and a learned model is established based on tests on these attributes. This learning mechanism approximates discrete valued functions as the target attribute. The type of training examples applicable to decision trees are diverse, and could range from the consumer credit records to medical diagnostics.

Decision trees typically produce crisp classifications, that is the leaves carry decisions for individual classes. However, that is not sufficient for various applications. One can require a score output from a supervised learning method to rank order the instances. For instance, consider the classification of pixels in mammogram images as possibly cancerous [WDB+93]. A typical mammography dataset might contain 98% normal pixels and 2% abnormal pixels. A simple default strategy of guessing the majority class would give a predictive accuracy of 98%. Ideally, a fairly high rate of correct cancerous predictions is required, while allowing for a small to moderate error rate in the majority class. It is more costly to predict a cancerous case as non-cancerous, than otherwise. Thus, a

J. Quiñonero-Candela et al. (Eds.): MLCW 2005, LNAI 3944, pp. 41–55, 2006.

probabilistic estimate or ranking of cancerous cases can be decisive for the practitioner. The cost of further tests can be decreased by thresholding the patients at a particular rank. Secondly, probabilistic estimates can allow one to threshold ranking for class membership at values $< 0.5$. Thus, the classes assigned at the leaves of the decision trees have to be appropriately converted to reliable probabilistic estimates. However, the leaf frequencies can require smoothing to improve the "quality" of the estimates [PD03, PMM+94, SGF95, Bra97]. A classifier is considered to be well-calibrated if the predicted probability approaches the empirical probability as the number of predictions goes to infinity [GF83]. The quality of probability estimates, resulting from decision trees, has not been measured as is proposed in the PASCAL Challenge on Evaluating Predictive Uncertainty.

In this Chapter, we report on our experience in the NIPS 2004 Evaluating Predictive Uncertainty Challenge [QC05].

## 2 Probabilistic Decision Trees with C4.5

A decision tree is essentially in a disjunctive-conjunctive form, wherein each path is a conjunction of the attributes-values and the tree by itself is a disjunction of all these conjunctions. An instance arriving at the root node, takes the branch it matches based on the attribute-value test and moves down the tree following that branch. This continues until a path is established to a leaf node, providing the classification of the instance. If the target attribute is true for the instance, it is called a "true example"; otherwise it is called a 'negative example'. The decision tree learning aims to make "pure" leaves, that is leaves in which all the examples belong to one particular class. This growing procedure of the decision tree becomes its potential weakness for constructing probability estimates.

The leaf estimates, which are a natural calculation from the frequencies at the leaves, can be systematically skewed towards 0 and 1, as the leaves are essentially dominated by one class. For notational purposes, let us consider the confusion matrix given in Figure 1. $TP$ is the number of true positives at the leaf, $FP$ is the number of false positives, and $C$ is the number of classes in the dataset. Typically, the probabilistic (frequency-based) estimate at a decision tree leaf is:

$$P(c|x) = TP/(TP + FP) \tag{1}$$

However, simply using the frequency derived from the correct counts of classes at a leaf might not give sound probabilistic estimates [PD03, ZE01]. A small leaf can potentially give optimistic estimates for classification purposes. For instance, the frequency based estimate will give the same weights to leaves with the following $(TP, FP)$ distributions: $(5, 0)$ and $(50, 0)$. The relative coverage of the leaves and the original class distribution is not taken into consideration. Given the evidence, a probabilistic estimate of 1 for the $(5, 0)$ leaf is not very sound. Smoothing the frequency-based estimates can mitigate the aforementioned problem [PD03].

| | Predicted Negative | Predicted Positive |
|---|---|---|
| Actual Negative | TN | FP |
| Actual Positive | FN | TP |

**Fig. 1.** Confusion matrix

Aiming to perfectly classify the given set of training examples, a decision tree may overfit the training set. Overfitting is typically circumvented by deploying various pruning methodologies. Pruning involves evaluating every node of the decision tree and the subtree it may root, as a potential candidate for removal. A node is converted into a leaf node by assigning the most common classification associated at that node. But pruning deploys methods that typically maximize accuracies. Pruning is equivalent to coalescing different decision regions obtained by thresholding at feature values. This can result in coarser probability estimates at the leaves. While pruning improves the decision tree generalization, it can give poorer estimates as all the examples belonging to a decision tree leaves are given the same estimate. We used C4.5 decision trees for our experiments [Qui92].

### 2.1 Improving Probabilistic Estimates at Leaves

One way of improving the probability estimates given by an unpruned decision tree is to smooth them to make them less extreme. One can smooth these estimated probabilities by using the Laplace estimate [PD03], which can be written as follows:

$$P(c|x)_{Laplace} = (TP + 1)/(TP + FP + C) \tag{2}$$

Laplace estimate introduces a prior probability of $1/C$ for each class. Again considering the two pathological cases of $TP = 5$ and $TP = 50$, the Laplace estimates are 0.86 and 0.98, respectively, which are more reliable given the evidence.

However, Laplace estimates might not be very appropriate for highly imbalanced datasets [ZE01]. In that scenario, it could be useful to incorporate the prior of positive class to smooth the probabilities so that the estimates are shifted towards the minority class base rate ($b$). The m-estimate [Cus93] can be used as follows [ZE01]:

$$P(c|x)_m = (TP + bm)/(TP + FP + m) \tag{3}$$

where $b$ is the base rate or the prior of positive class, and $m$ is the parameter for controlling the shift towards $b$. Zadrozny and Elkan (2001) suggest using $m$, given $b$, such that $bm = 10$.

However, these smoothing estimates also cannot completely mitigate the effect of overfit and overgrown trees. We use ensemble methods to further "smooth" out the probability estimates at the leaves. Each leaf will potentially have a different $P(c|x)$ due to different training set composition. Averaging these estimates will improve the quality of the estimates, as it overcomes the bias introduced by the systematic error caused by having axis-parallel splits. The overfitting will also be countered as the variance component will be reduced by voting or averaging.

# 3 Ensemble Methods

> "To solve really hard problems, we'll have to use several different representations..... It is time to stop arguing over which type of pattern-classification technique is best..... Instead we should work at a higher level of organization and discover how to build managerial systems to exploit the different virtues and evade the different limitations of each of these ways of comparing things. [Min91]"

## 3.1 Random Subspaces

The random subspace method, introduced by Ho [Ho98], randomly selects different feature dimensions and constructs multiple smaller subsets. A classifier is then constructed on each of those subsets, and a combination rule is applied in the end for prediction on the testing set. For each random subspace a decision tree classifier is constructed. The random subspaces are particularly useful when there is a high redundancy in the feature space and for sparse datasets with small sample sizes.

The feature vector, where $m$ is the number of features, can be represented as $X = (x_1, x_2, ..., x_{m-1})$. Then, multiple random subspaces of size $m \times p$ are selected, $k$ times, where $p$ is the size of the randomly selected subspace, $X_p^k\{(x_1, x_2, ..., x_p)|p < (m-1)\}$.

The hyperplanes constructed for each tree will be different, as each tree is essentially constructed from a randomly selected subset of features. The classification can either be done by taking the most popular class attached to the test example or by aggregating the probability estimate computed from each of the subspaces. Each tree has a different representation of the training set (different $P(x|c)$), thus resulting in a different function for $P(c|x)$ at each leaf. The classification assigned by the individual decision trees is effectively invariant for test examples that are different from the training examples in the unselected dimensions. The random subspaces are similar to the uncertainty analyses framework that simulates the distribution of an objective by sampling from the distribution of model inputs, and re-evaluating the objective for each selected set of model inputs.

We let the trees grow fully to get precise estimates, as the averaging would then reduce the overall variance in the estimates. Let $L_j(x)$ indicate the leaf that an example x falls into; let $P(c|L_j(x))$ indicate the probability that an example $x$ belongs to class $c$ at leaf $L_j$; let the number of trees in the ensemble be $K$.

$$\hat{P(c|L_j(x))} = \frac{P(c, L_j(x))}{\sum_{k=1}^{n_c} P(c_k, L_j(x))} \tag{4}$$

$$g_c(x) = \frac{1}{K}\sum_{i=1}^{K} \hat{P(c|L_j(x))} \tag{5}$$

$g_c(x)$ averages over probabilities conditioned on reaching a particular leaf (L). Each leaf is, in essence, defining its own region of probability distribution. Since, the trees are constructed from random subspaces, the regions can be of different shapes and sizes.

The random subspace method can be outlined as follows:

1. For each *k=1,2,..K*
   (a) Select a p dimensional random subspace, $X_p^k$, from $X$.
   (b) Construct the decision classifier, $C_p^k$ using C4.5.
   (c) Smooth the leaf frequencies by Laplace or m-estimate.
2. Aggregate the probability estimates by each of the $C^k$ classifiers. Output $g_c(x)$.

The individual classifiers can be weaker than the aggregate or even the global classifier. Moreover, the subspaces are sampled independently of each other. An aggregation of the same can lead to a reduction in the variance component of the error term, thereby reducing the overall error [DB98, Bre96]. There is a popular argument that diversity among the weak classifiers in an ensemble contributes to the success of the ensemble [KW03, Die00]. Classifiers are considered diverse if they disagree on the kind of errors they make. Diversity is an important aspect of the ensemble techniques — bagging, boosting, and randomization [Die00]. Diversity, thus, is a property of a group of classifiers. The classifiers might be reporting similar accuracies, but be disagreeing on their errors. One can, for example, construct a correlation measure among the rank-orders provided by each of the individual classifiers to get an estimate of diversity. In addition, the random subspace technique also counters the sparsity in the data, as the subspace dimensionality gets smaller but the training set size remains the same.

### 3.2 Bagging

Bagging, [Bre96], has been shown to improve classifier accuracy. Bagging basically aggregates predictions (by voting or averaging) from classifiers learned on multiple bootstraps of data. According to Breiman, bagging exploits the instability in the classifiers [Qui96], since perturbing the training set can produce different classifiers using the same learning algorithm, where the difference is in the resulting predictions on the testing set and the structure of the classifier. For instance, the decision trees learned from bootstraps of data will not only have different representations but can also have disagreements in their predictions. It is desired that the classifiers disagree or be diverse as the averaging or voting their predictions will lead ot a reduction in variance resulting in improved performance.

[Dom97] empirically tested two alternative theories supporting bagging: (1) bagging works because it approximates Bayesian model averaging or (2) it works because it shifts the priors to a more appropriate region in the decision space. The empirical results showed that bagging worked possibly because it counter-acts the inherent simplicity bias of the decision trees. That is, with M different bags, M different classifiers are learned, and together their output is more complex than that of the single learner. Bagging has been shown to aid improvement in the probability estimates [PD03, BK99]. The bagging procedure can be outlined as follows:

1. For each $k$=*1,2,..K*
   (a) Randomly select with replacement 100% of the examples from the training set $X$, to form a subsample $X^k$.
   (b) Construct a decision tree classifier, $C^k$, from $X^k$.
   (c) Smooth the leaf frequencies for each of the $C^k$ classifiers by Laplace or m-estimate.
2. Aggregate the probability estimates by each of the $C^k$ classifiers. Output $g_c(x)$.

## 4 Challenge Entry

The characteristics of the datasets prompted us to look at different stages of modeling. The high dimensionality introduced the sparsity in the feature space. Thus, we wanted to have feature selection as the first stage. As we will see in the subsequent sections, feature selection significantly reduced the number of relevant features to be used for modeling. Moreover, feature selection also curtailed the data sparsity issue. For feature selection we used information gain using entropy based discretization [FK93]. We then selected all the features with information gain greater than 0. We then generated ensembles with bagging and random subspaces using probabilistic decision trees as the base classifiers. Thus, our challenge entry comprised of the following steps. Note that our final best submission was with random subspaces.

1. Feature Selection
2. C4.5 Decision Trees
   - Fully grown and Laplace correction at the leaves
3. Ensembles
   - Random subspaces
   - Bagging

*Challenge Datasets.* The following classification datasets were provided for the Challenge.

1. Catalysis has 617 features and 1,173 examples in the final training set. The testing set has 300 examples.
2. Gatineau has 1,092 features and 5,176 examples in the final training set. It is a highly unbalanced dataset with the positive class comprising only 8.67% of the entire dataset. The testing set has 3000 examples.

### 4.1 Feature Selection Results

As we mentioned, our first step with both the datasets involved feature selection. We noted in our validation study that feature selection significantly improved the performance. Moreover, feature selection was particularly amenable for random subspaces as the feature relevance was now (approximately) uniformly spread. We, thus, selected the following number of features for both the datasets:

- 312 features for catalysis. Thus, almost 50% reduction in the total number of features. Figure 2 shows the information gain of the selected features for the catalysis dataset. There are not very high ranking features. The average information gain is 0.029 with a standard deviation of 0.0120.

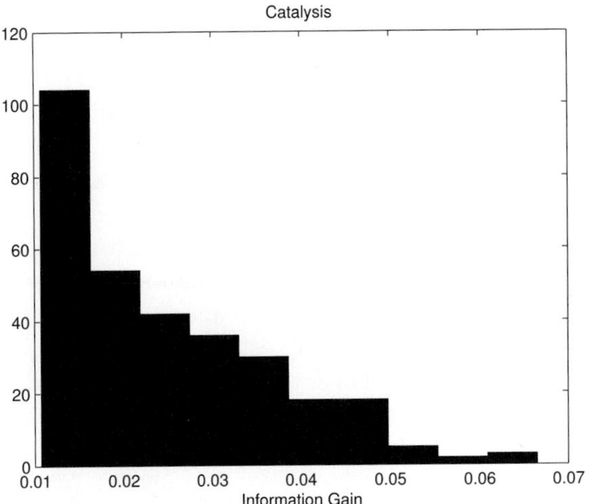


**Fig. 2.** Information Gain of the selected features for the catalysis dataset

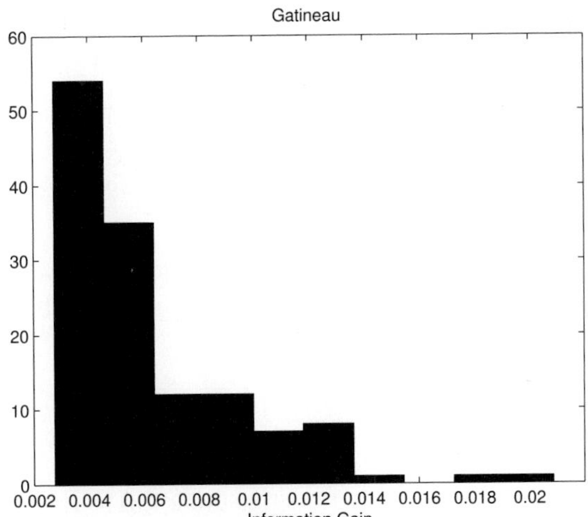


**Fig. 3.** Information Gain of the selected features for the gatineau dataset

– 131 features for gatineau. Thus, only 11% of the total number of features was retained. Figure 3 shows the information gain of the selected features for the gatineau dataset. The information gain of features is even lower for the gatineau dataset. The average information gain is 0.0061 and standard deviation is 0.0034.

### 4.2 Ensembles

After feature selection, we implemented random subspaces by setting $p = 50$ and $p = 25$ for catalysis and gatineau, respectively. We used $K = 30$ decision tree classifiers for both the datasets. We also learned 30 bags each for both the datasets. However, bagging did not improve the performance as much as the random subspaces. We attribute that to the sparsity of the dataset. Tables 1 and 2 show the final results of our entries. It is evident from the Tables that feature selection formed an important element of our entry.

Figures 4 and 5 show the probability distributions achieved after applying the ensemble methods. It is evident from the Figures that the ensemble methods improved the probability mass, and overcame the limitations of skewed probability estimates from the decision tree leaves. The ensembles successfully overcame the bias and variance limitations associated with the decision tree leaves estimates. As expected, the gatineau dataset shows an interesting trend with Laplace smoothing. Gatineau is highly imbalanced, thus the Laplace estimate, which is trying to correct the probability estimate by adding $\frac{1}{C}$ is still being biased towards the minority class. Thus, there is no significant difference between the probability estimates from leaf frequencies and the ones generated from from applying Laplace smoothing. However, the ensembles improve the quality of the

**Table 1.** Challenge Results for the Catalysis dataset. FS: Feature Selection; RS: Random Subspaces. This entry was ranked Fourth at the time of Challenge termination in December, 2004.

| Method | NLP | OIL | LIFT |
|---|---|---|---|
| FS + RS | 2.41e-1 | 2.714e-1 | 2.371e-1 |
| RS | 2.485e-1 | 2.843e-1 | 2.534e-1 |
| FS + Bagging | 2.49e-1 | 3e-1 | 2.565e-1 |
| Bagging | 2.51e-1 | 2.971e-1 | 2.649e-1 |

**Table 2.** Challenge Results for the Gatineau dataset. FS: Feature Selection; RS: Random Subspaces. This entry was ranked First at the time of Challenge termination in December, 2004.

| Method | NLP | OIL | LIFT |
|---|---|---|---|
| FS + RS | 1.192e-1 | 8.7e-2 | 7.408e-1 |
| RS | 1.228e-1 | 8.7e-2 | 7.555e-1 |
| FS + Bagging | 1.193e-1 | 8.867e-2 | 7.311e-1 |
| Bagging | 1.229e-1 | 8.7e-2 | 7.506e-1 |

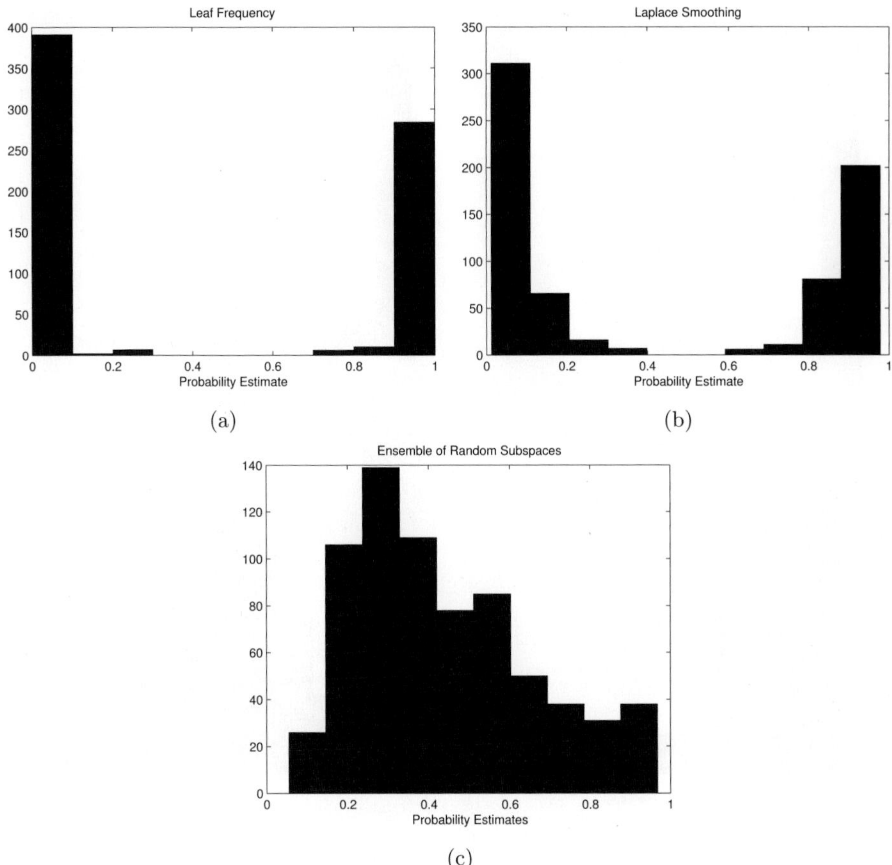


**Fig. 4.** a) Probability Distribution using the leaf frequencies as estimates. b) Probability distribution by smooting leaf frequencies using Laplace estimates. c) Probability Distribution using random subspaces as ensemble methods. The probabilities are $g_c(x)$ that are averaged from the smoothed leaf estimates.

**Table 3.** Post-Challenge Entry. These are our best results so far.

| Dataset | Method | NLP | OIL | LIFT |
|---|---|---|---|---|
| Catalysis | FS + RS | 2.4076e-1 | 2.7e-1 | 2.2874e-1 |
| Gatineau | FS + RS | 1.2475e-1 | 0.87e-1 | 7.4835e-1 |

estimates. Then, we applied m-estimate smoothing by setting the base rate to compensate for the high class imbalance. As one can see, the resulting probability estimates follow a much better distribution.

As the Post-challenge participation, we increased the ensemble size and implemented $m - estimate$ for smoothing the decision tree leaves. This further improved our performance on the gatineau dataset, while maintaining similar performance (marginally better) on the catalysis dataset. Table 3 contains those results.

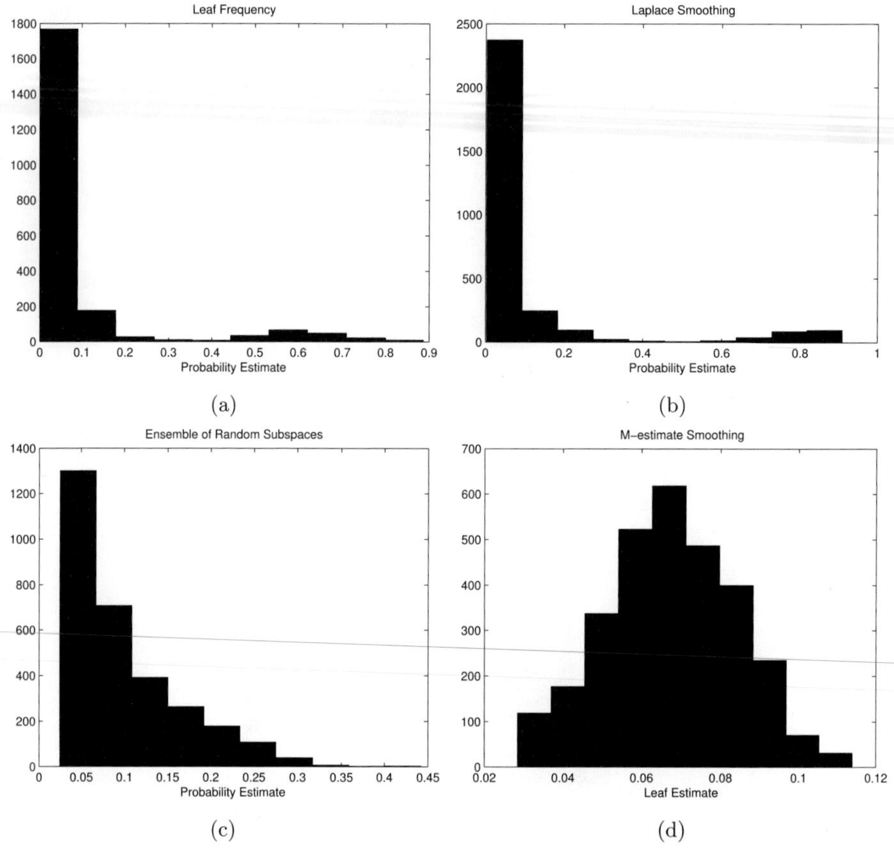


**Fig. 5.** a) Probability distribution using the leaf frequencies as estimates. b) Probability distribution by smooting leaf frequencies using Laplace estimates. c) Probability distribution using random subspaces as ensemble methods. The probabilities are $g_c(x)$ that are averaged from the smoothed leaf estimates. d) Probability Distribution using random subspaces as ensemble methods. The probabilities are $g_c(x)$ that are averaged from the m-estimate smoothed leaf probability estimates.

## 5 Experiments with Imbalanced Datasets

A dataset is imbalanced if the classes are not approximately equally represented [CHKK02, JS02]. There have been attempts to deal with imbalanced datasets in domains such as fraudulent telephone calls [FP96], telecommunications management [ESN96], text classification [LR94, DPHS98, MG99, Coh95] and detection of oil spills in satellite images [KHM98].

Distribution/cost sensitive applications can require a ranking or a probabilistic estimate of the instances. For instance, revisiting our mammography data example, a probabilistic estimate or ranking of cancerous cases can be decisive for the practitioner. The cost of further tests can be decreased by thresholding

**Table 4.** Dataset distribution

| Dataset | Majority Class | Minority Class |
|---|---|---|
| Satimage | 5809 | 626 |
| Mammography | 10923 | 260 |
| Oil | 896 | 41 |

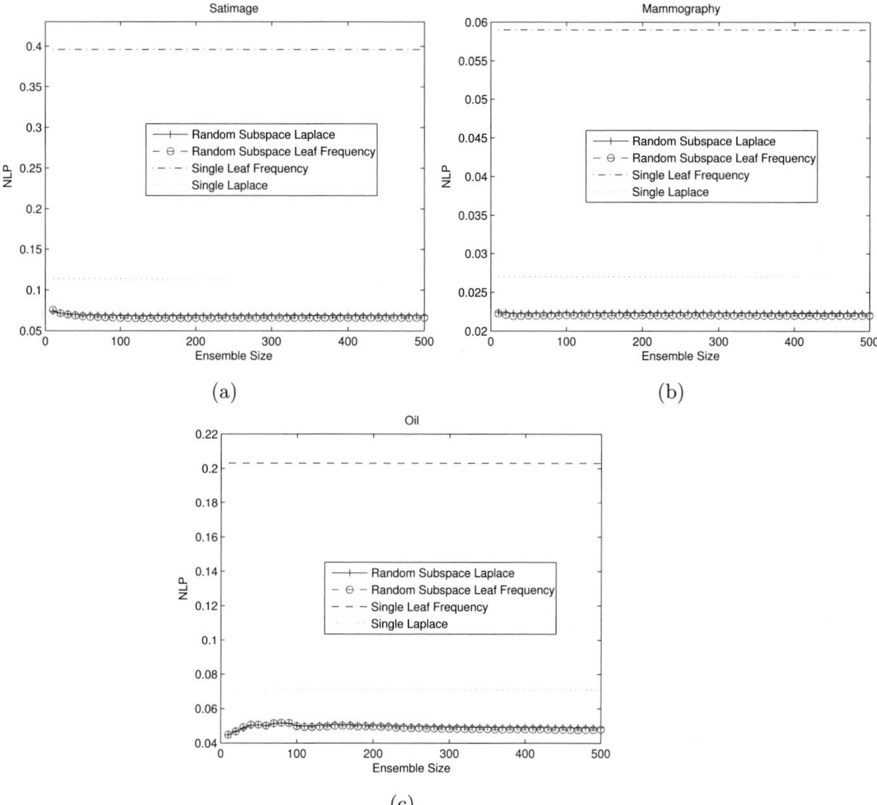


**Fig. 6.** a) NLP as the ensemble size varies for the Satimage dataset. b) NLP as the ensemble size varies for the Mammography dataset. c) NLP as the ensemble size varies for the Oil dataset.

the patients at a particular rank. Secondly, probabilistic estimates can allow one to threshold ranking for class membership at values $< 0.5$. Hence, the classes assigned at the leaves of the decision trees have to be appropriately converted to probabilistic estimates [PD03]. This brings us to another question: *What is the right probabilistic estimate for imbalanced datasets?*

We added the following three imbalanced datasets to our study for empirically evaluating the effect of the smoothing parameters and ensembles. These datasets

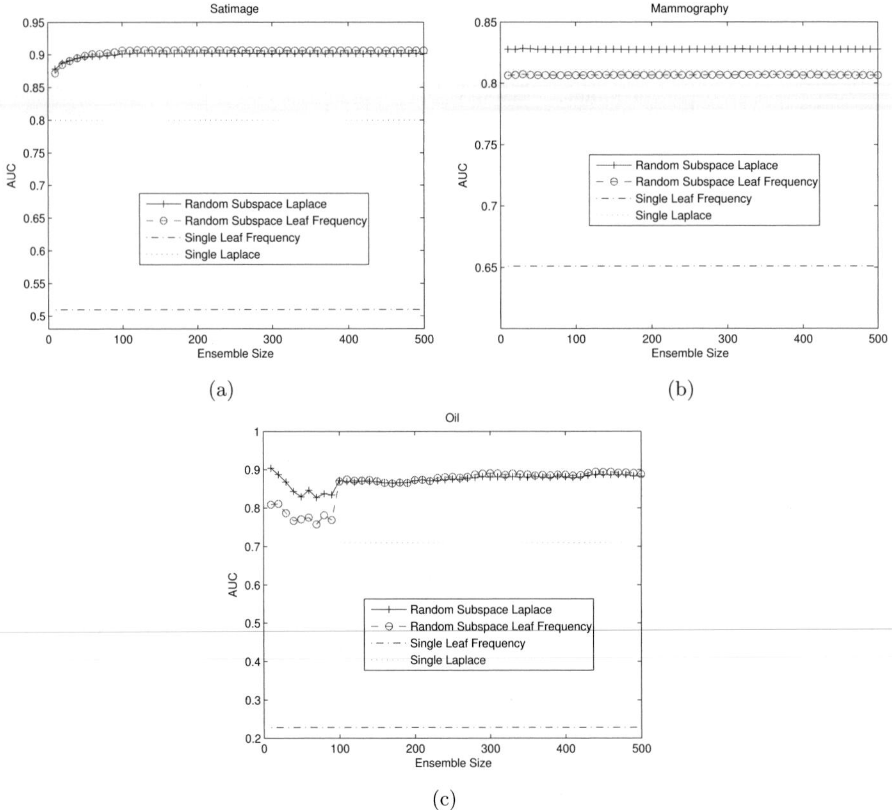


**Fig. 7.** a) AUC as the ensemble size varies for the Satimage dataset. b) AUC as the ensemble size varies for the Mammography dataset. c) AUC as the ensemble size varies for the Oil dataset.

vary extensively in their size and class proportions, thus offering different. Table 4 shows the class distribution.

1. The Satimage dataset [BM98] has 6 classes originally. We chose the smallest class as the minority class and collapsed the rest of the classes into one as was done in [PFK98]. This gave us a skewed 2-class dataset, with 5809 majority class samples and 626 minority class samples.
2. The Oil dataset was provided by Robert Holte [KHM98]. This dataset has 41 oil slick samples and 896 non-oil slick samples.
3. The Mammography dataset [WDB+93] has 11,183 samples with 260 calcifications. If we look at predictive accuracy as a measure of goodness of the classifier for this case, the default accuracy would be 97.68% when every sample is labeled non-calcification. But, it is desirable for the classifier to predict most of the calcifications correctly.

We report the same NLP loss estimate as used in the Challenge. In addition, we also report the Area Under the ROC Curve. The purpose of the AUC is to see if ranking of the exemplars is affected by improving the quality of the probability estimates. Figure 6 shows the trend of NLP as the ensemble size varies. The single tree estimates are much weaker when no smoothing is applied, as one might expect. This is particularly more critical for the imbalanced datasets, when the positive class is more relevant. However, the ensembles are sufficient in overcoming the bias and variance at the leaves without using the Laplace estimate. The same trend is observed for all the three imbalanced datasets.

Figure 7 shows the AUC's for the three datasets. Again, the single tree AUC using leaf frequencies as the probability estimates is very low, which is also affirmed by the high NLP. And the AUC's significantly improve with ensembles and Laplace smoothing. This results show that there is a relationship between the AUC's and the quality of the probability estimates as established by the NLP. Improving the quality of the estimates not only provides a better spread of probabilities but also improves the ranking of exemplars, thus impacting the AUC.

## 6 Summary

We summarized our entry for the NIPS 2004 Evaluating Predictive Uncertainty Challenge. We show that ensembles of decision trees, particularly random subspaces, can generate good probability estimates by smoothing over the leaf frequencies. The ensembles overcome the bias and variance arising from the homogeneous and small decision tree leaves. We show that decision trees are a viable strategy for probability estimates and rank among the best methods reported in the challenge. The ensembles are able to overcome the bias in estimates arising from the axis-parallel splits of decision trees, resulting in smoother estimates. We also saw that the prior smoothing at the leaves using Laplace estimate did not offer much gain with ensembles. However, Laplace smoothing did provide significant improvements over just using leaf frequencies.

We also added three highly imbalanced datasets to our study. We show that the rank-order of the exemplars and the resulting AUC is related to the quality of the probability estimates. For most of the applications requiring imbalanced datasets, the resulting rank-order of examples or $P(Xp > Xn)$ can be very important, where $Xp$ is the positive class example. Thus, having reliable probability estimates is important for an improved rank-ordering.

As a part of ongoing work, we are investigating evolutionary techniques to carefully prune away members of the ensemble that don't contribute to the qualaity of the final probability estimation [SC05]. It is important for the classifiers in an ensemble to assist each other and cancel out their errors, resulting in higher accuracy. If all the classifiers are in complete agreement, then the averaging will not result in any changes in the probability estimates (each estimate will be the same). Thus, we would like to identify the more "collaborative" members of the ensemble, and assign higher weights to their predictions. We can, for example, select those classifiers from the ensemble that particularly optimize on the NLP loss function.

## References


[BFOS84] L. Breiman, J.H. Friedman, R.A. Olshen, and P.J. Stone. *Classification and Regression Trees.* Wadsworth International Group, Belmont, CA, 1984.

[BK99] E. Bauer and R. Kohavi. An empirical comparison of voting classification algorithms: Bagging, boosting and variants. *Machine Learning*, 36(1,2), 1999.

[BM98] C.L. Blake and C.J. Merz. UCI Repository of Machine Learning Databases http://www.ics.uci.edu/~mlearn/~MLRepository.html. Department of Information and Computer Sciences, University of California, Irvine, 1998.

[Bra97] A. P. Bradley. The Use of the Area Under the ROC Curve in the Evaluation of Machine Learning Algorithms. *Pattern Recognition*, 30(6):1145–1159, 1997.

[Bre96] L. Breiman. Bagging predictors. *Machine Learning*, 24(2):123–140, 1996.

[CHKK02] N.V. Chawla, L.O. Hall, Bowyer K.W., and W.P. Kegelmeyer. SMOTE: Synthetic Minority Oversampling TEchnique. *Journal of Artificial Intelligence Research*, 16:321–357, 2002.

[Coh95] W. Cohen. Learning to Classify English Text with ILP Methods. In *Proceedings of the 5th International Workshop on Inductive Logic Programming*, pages 3–24. Department of Computer Science, Katholieke Universiteit Leuven, 1995.

[Cus93] J. Cussents. Bayes and pseudo-bayes estimates of conditional probabilities and their reliabilities. In *Proceedings of European Conference on Machine Learning*, 1993.

[DB98] B. Draper and K. Baek. Bagging in computer vision. In *IEEE International Conference on Computer Vision and Pattern Recognition*, pages 144–149, 1998.

[Die00] T. Dietterich. An empirical comparison of three methods for constructing ensembles of decision trees: bagging, boosting and randomization. *Machine Learning*, 40(2):139 – 157, 2000.

[Dom97] P. Domingos. Why does bagging work? a bayesian account and its implications. In *Proceedings of Third International Conference Knowledge Discovery and Data Mining*, pages 155–158, 1997.

[DPHS98] S. Dumais, J. Platt, D. Heckerman, and M. Sahami. Inductive Learning Algorithms and Representations for Text Categorization. In *Proceedings of the Seventh International Conference on Information and Knowledge Management.*, pages 148–155, 1998.

[ESN96] J. Ezawa, K., M. Singh, and W. Norton, S. Learning Goal Oriented Bayesian Networks for Telecommunications Risk Management. In *Proceedings of the International Conference on Machine Learning, ICML-96*, pages 139–147, Bari, Italy, 1996. Morgan Kauffman.

[FK93] U. Fayyad and R. Kohavi. Multi-interval discretization of continuous-valued attributes for classification learning. In *Proceedings of 13th International Joint Conference on Artificial Intelligence*, pages 1022–1027, 1993.

[FP96] T. Fawcett and F. Provost. Combining Data Mining and Machine Learning for Effective User Profile. In *Proceedings of the 2nd International Conference on Knowledge Discovery and Data Mining*, pages 8–13, Portland, OR, 1996. AAAI.

[GF83] M. De Groot and S. Fienberg. The Comparison and Evaluation of Forecasters. *Statistician*, 32:12 – 22, 1983.

[Ho98] T. K. Ho. The random subspace method for constructing decision trees. *IEEE Transactions on Pattern Analysis and Machine Intelligence*, 20(8):832–844, 1998.

[JS02] N. Japkowicz and S. Stephen. The class imbalance problem: A systematic study. *Intelligent Data Analysis*, 6(5), 2002.

[KHM98] M. Kubat, R. Holte, and S. Matwin. Machine Learning for the Detection of Oil Spills in Satellite Radar Images. *Machine Learning*, 30:195–215, 1998.

[KW03] L. Kuncheva and C. Whitaker. Measures of diversity in classifier ensembles and their relationship with the ensemble accuracy. *Machine Learning*, 51:181–207, 2003.

[LR94] D. Lewis and M. Ringuette. A Comparison of Two Learning Algorithms for Text Categorization. In *Proceedings of SDAIR-94, 3rd Annual Symposium on Document Analysis and Information Retrieval*, pages 81–93, 1994.

[MG99] D. Mladenić and M. Grobelnik. Feature Selection for Unbalanced Class Distribution and Naive Bayes. In *Proceedings of the 16th International Conference on Machine Learning.*, pages 258–267. Morgan Kaufmann, 1999.

[Min91] M. Minsky. Logical versus analogical, symbolic versus connectionist, neat versus scruffy. *AI Magazine*, 12, 1991.

[PD03] F. Provost and P. Domingos. Tree induction for probability-based rankings. *Machine Learning*, 52(3), 2003.

[PFK98] F. Provost, T. Fawcett, and R. Kohavi. The Case Against Accuracy Estimation for Comparing Induction Algorithms. In *Proceedings of the Fifteenth International Conference on Machine Learning*, pages 445–453, Madison, WI, 1998. Morgan Kauffmann.

[PMM+94] M. Pazzani, C. Merz, P. Murphy, K. Ali, T. Hume, and C. Brunk. Reducing misclassification costs. In *Proceedings of the Eleventh International Conference on Machine Learning*, pages 217–215, 1994.

[QC05] Joaquin Quiñonero-Candela. Evaluating Predictive Uncertainty Challenge, 2005. `predict.kyb.tuebingen.mpg.de`.

[Qui87] J.R. Quinlan. Simplifying decision trees. *International Journal of Man Machine Studies, V.27*, pages 227–248, 1987.

[Qui92] J.R. Quinlan. *C4.5: Programs for Machine Learning.* Morgan Kaufmann, San Mateo, CA, 1992.

[Qui96] J. R. Quinlan. Bagging, boosting, and C4.5. In *Proceedings of the Thirteenth National Conference on Artificial Intelligence*, pages 725–730, 1996.

[SC05] J. Sylvester and N. V. Chawla. Evolutionary ensembles: Combining learning agents using genetic algorithms. In *AAAI Workshop on Multiagent Learning*, pages 46–51, 2005.

[SGF95] P. Smyth, A. Gray, and U. Fayyad. Retrofitting decision tree classifiers using kernel density estimation. In *Proceedings of the Twelth International Conference on Machine Learning*, pages 506–514, 1995.

[WDB+93] K. Woods, C. Doss, K. Bowyer, J. Solka, C. Priebe, and P. Kegelmeyer. Comparative Evaluation of Pattern Recognition Techniques for Detection of Microcalcifications in Mammography. *International Journal of Pattern Recognition and Artificial Intelligence*, 7(6):1417–1436, 1993.

[ZE01] B. Zadrozny and C. Elkan. Learning and making decisions when costs and probabilities are both unknown. In *Proceedings of the Seventh International Conference on Knowledge Discovery and Data Mining*, 2001.

# Estimating Predictive Variances with Kernel Ridge Regression

Gavin C. Cawley[1], Nicola L.C. Talbot[1], and Olivier Chapelle[2]

[1] School of Computing Sciences, University of East Anglia, Norwich NR4 7TJ, U.K.
{gcc, nlct}@cmp.uea.ac.uk

[2] Max Plank Institute for Biological Cybernetics, 72076 Tübingen, Germany
olivier.chapelle@teubingen.mpg.de

**Abstract.** In many regression tasks, in addition to an accurate estimate of the conditional mean of the target distribution, an indication of the predictive uncertainty is also required. There are two principal sources of this uncertainty: the noise process contaminating the data and the uncertainty in estimating the model parameters based on a limited sample of training data. Both of them can be summarised in the *predictive variance* which can then be used to give confidence intervals. In this paper, we present various schemes for providing predictive variances for kernel ridge regression, especially in the case of a heteroscedastic regression, where the variance of the noise process contaminating the data is a smooth function of the explanatory variables. The use of leave-one-out cross-validation is shown to eliminate the bias inherent in estimates of the predictive variance. Results obtained on all three regression tasks comprising the predictive uncertainty challenge demonstrate the value of this approach.

## 1 Introduction

The standard framework for regression is the following: Given a training set

$$\mathcal{D} = \{(\boldsymbol{x}_i, y_i)\}_{i=1}^{\ell}, \quad \boldsymbol{x}_i \in \mathcal{X} \subset \mathbb{R}^d, \quad y_i \in \mathbb{R}, \tag{1}$$

the goal is to infer a function $\mu(\boldsymbol{x})$ which predicts the best value (in the least squares sense) of the target function on any test point $\boldsymbol{x}$. However, in some situations, it is also useful to know the confidence of this prediction. For this reason, we also want to infer a function $\sigma(\boldsymbol{x})$ corresponding to the uncertainty of our prediction. For instance, the result of our prediction could be a statement of the form: "with 95% confidence, I think that the target associated with point $\boldsymbol{x}$ is in the interval $[\mu(\boldsymbol{x}) - 2\sigma(\boldsymbol{x}), \mu(\boldsymbol{x}) + 2\sigma(\boldsymbol{x})]$". It is important to note that this uncertainty comes from two independent components:

1. The noise in the data
2. The uncertainty in the estimation of the target function

J. Quiñonero-Candela et al. (Eds.): MLCW 2005, LNAI 3944, pp. 56–77, 2006.

Typically, the first contribution is preponderant when there are a lot of training data, while the second one becomes more important when they are few training data. Let us illustrate this by two extreme examples. First, imagine that $\mathcal{X} = \boldsymbol{x}_0$ and $P(y|\boldsymbol{x}_0)$ is normally distributed with mean 0 and variance $\sigma$. After seeing $\ell$ examples, the empirical mean is near from the true target (0 in this case and the distance is of the order $\frac{\sigma}{\sqrt{\ell}}$). Thus, when $\ell$ is large, we can predict the target value very accurately (i.e. the conditional mean), but because of the noise, we are not so sure about the target associated with an unseen test point. Another extreme example is the following: suppose that we know that there is no noise in the data, but that we are given a test point which is infinitely far away from the other training samples. Then, we are just completely unsure of the conditional mean. In summary, one can say that the uncertainty of the prediction is the sum of two terms:

Uncertainty in the conditional mean + estimated noise level.

In this paper, we will try to estimate this uncertainty directly, by considering that the goal is to infer a function from $\mathcal{X}$ to $\mathbb{R} \times \mathbb{R}^+$, $\boldsymbol{x} \mapsto (\mu(\boldsymbol{x}),\ \sigma(\boldsymbol{x}))$ where the loss associated to a test point $(\boldsymbol{x}, y)$ is

$$\log \sigma^2(\boldsymbol{x}) + \frac{[\mu(\boldsymbol{x}) - y]^2}{\sigma^2(\boldsymbol{x})}. \tag{2}$$

Let us now be more precise by giving the definitions of the following quantities:

**Conditional mean.** This is true mean $E_{y|\boldsymbol{x}} y$ where the expectation is taken with respect to the true data generating process.

**Predictive mean.** We define this quantity as $\mu(\boldsymbol{x})$, the first output of the function being inferred. This is an estimate of the conditional mean given a training set.

**Conditional variance.** We do not define it as the true noise level but in association with a predictive mean as

$$E_{y|\boldsymbol{x}}(y - \mu(\boldsymbol{x}))^2 = (E_{y|\boldsymbol{x}} y - \mu(\boldsymbol{x}))^2 + E_{y|\boldsymbol{x}}(y - E_{y|\boldsymbol{x}} y)^2.$$

**Predictive variance.** Similarly to the predictive mean, this is defined as $\sigma^2(\boldsymbol{x})$, the square of the second output argument of the inferred function.

At this point, we would like to make the following remarks:

- The reason for considering the loss (2) is that it is (up to a constant) the negative log probability of a test point under the Gaussian predictive distribution with mean $\mu(\boldsymbol{x})$ and variance $\sigma^2(\boldsymbol{x})$, as used in [1].
- From the above definitions, the best predictive mean and variance for the loss (2) are the conditional mean and variance.
- The loss might seem arbitrary and from a decision theory point of view, one should consider the loss associated with the action taken based on the prediction $(\mu(\boldsymbol{x}), \sigma(\boldsymbol{x}))$. However, this still seems a reasonable "generic" loss. More generally, it is worth noting that a loss function is always necessary whenever a prediction is required.

– Instead of computing a predictive mean and variance, one could compute a predictive distribution (and the loss would be negative log predictive probability). But estimating a function instead of two real numbers is a more complicated inference problem and for the sake of simplicity, we do not consider it here. Note that in binary classification, the problem is much simpler as there is only real number to estimate, $P(y = 1|\boldsymbol{x})$.

The algorithm we propose in this paper alternates between updates of the predictive mean and of the predictive variance. For fixed $\sigma$, the predictive mean $\mu$ is modelled using an heteroscedastic kernel ridge regression algorithm. Heteroscedastic here just means that the error on a given training point $\boldsymbol{x}_i$ is weighted by $\sigma^{-2}(\boldsymbol{x}_i)$ (cf equation (2)). For fixed $\mu$, a regression is performed on $\log \sigma$ in order to minimise (2). Again a regularised kernel regression algorithm is used for this purpose. Note that for learning the conditional variance, one should not use the same set of training points as the one used to learn the conditional mean since $(\mu(\boldsymbol{x}_i) - y_i)^2$ is not an unbiased estimator of the conditional variance at $\boldsymbol{x}_i$ if this point has been used to learn $\mu$. Instead of a considering a "fresh" training set, we will use the leave-one-out procedure.

The basic algorithm that we use is Kernel Ridge Regression [2]. Considering the strong link of this algorithm with Gaussian Processes [3], the reader might wonder why we do not use this latter to estimate the predictive variances. The two reasons for this are:

1. We consider the more general case of heteroscedastic noise (i.e. whose variance depends on the input location).
2. We aim at showing that predictive variances can be calculated in a *non Bayesian* framework. However, we do not pretend that this approach is superior to the Bayesian approach. One of our main motivation is to answer the usual Bayesian criticism that standard non Bayesian methods do not provide predictive variances.

## 2 Kernel Ridge Regression

Kernel ridge regression (KRR) [2], or equivalently the least-squares support vector machine (LS-SVM) [4] provides perhaps the most basic form of kernel learning method. Given labelled training data (1), the kernel ridge regression method constructs a linear model $\mu(\boldsymbol{x}) = \boldsymbol{w} \cdot \boldsymbol{\phi}(\boldsymbol{x}) + b$ in a fixed feature space $\mathcal{F}$ given by a fixed transformation of the input space, $\boldsymbol{\phi}(\boldsymbol{x}) : \mathcal{X} \to \mathcal{F}$. However, rather than specifying $\mathcal{F}$ directly, it is induced by a positive-definite kernel function [5] $\mathcal{K} : \mathcal{X} \times \mathcal{X} \to \mathbb{R}$, which defines the inner product between vectors evaluated in $\mathcal{F}$, i.e. $\mathcal{K}(\boldsymbol{x}, \boldsymbol{x}') = \boldsymbol{\phi}(\boldsymbol{x}) \cdot \boldsymbol{\phi}(\boldsymbol{x}')$. Kernel functions typically used in kernel learning methods include the spherical or isotropic Gaussian radial basis function (RBF) kernel,

$$\mathcal{K}(\boldsymbol{x}, \boldsymbol{x}') = \exp\left\{-\kappa \|\boldsymbol{x} - \boldsymbol{x}'\|^2\right\} \tag{3}$$

where $\kappa$ is a kernel parameter, controlling the locality of the kernel, and the anisotropic Gaussian RBF kernel,

$$\mathcal{K}(\boldsymbol{x}, \boldsymbol{x}') = \exp\left\{-\sum_{i=1}^{d} \kappa_i \left[x_i - x_i'\right]^2\right\} \tag{4}$$

which includes separate scale parameters, $\boldsymbol{\kappa} = (\kappa_1, \kappa_2, \ldots, \kappa_d)$, for each input dimension. The "kernel trick" allows us to create powerful linear models in high, or even infinite-dimensional feature spaces, using only finite dimensional quantities, such as the kernel or Gram matrix, $\boldsymbol{K} = [k_{ij} = \mathcal{K}(\boldsymbol{x}_i, \boldsymbol{x}_j)]_{i,j=1}^{\ell}$ (for a more detailed introduction to kernel learning methods, see [6, 7]). The kernel ridge regression method assumes that the data represent realisations of the output of some deterministic process that have been corrupted by additive Gaussian noise with zero mean and fixed variance, i.e.

$$y_i = \mu(\boldsymbol{x}_i) + \varepsilon_i, \qquad \text{where} \qquad \varepsilon_i \sim \mathcal{N}(0,\ \sigma^2), \qquad \forall\, i \in \{1, 2, \ldots, \ell\}.$$

As in conventional linear ridge regression [8], the optimal model parameters $(\boldsymbol{w}, b)$ are determined by minimising a regularised loss function representing the penalised negative log-likelihood of the data,

$$\frac{1}{2}\gamma||\boldsymbol{w}||^2 + \sum_{i=1}^{\ell} \left[\mu(\boldsymbol{x}_i) - y_i\right]^2.$$

The parameter $\gamma$ can either be interpreted as a regularisation parameter or as an inverse noise variance. As shown in a more general setting in Section 3, the optimal $\boldsymbol{w}$ can be expressed as $\boldsymbol{w} = \sum_{i=1}^{\ell} \alpha_i \phi(\boldsymbol{x}_i)$, where $\boldsymbol{\alpha}$ is found by solving the following linear system,

$$\begin{bmatrix} \boldsymbol{K} + \gamma \boldsymbol{I} & \boldsymbol{1} \\ \boldsymbol{1}^\top & 0 \end{bmatrix} \begin{bmatrix} \boldsymbol{\alpha} \\ b \end{bmatrix} \begin{bmatrix} \boldsymbol{y} \\ 0 \end{bmatrix}.$$

## 2.1 A Simple Model for Heteroscedastic Data

The kernel ridge regression model assumes the target data represent realisations of a deterministic system that have been corrupted by a Gaussian noise process with zero mean and constant (homoscedastic) variance. This is unrealistic in some practical applications, where the variance of the noise process is likely to be dependent in some way on the explanatory variables. For example, in environmental applications, the variability in the intensity of sunlight reaching ground level is more variable in Spring, Summer and Autumn as, at least in the United Kingdom, the Winter sky is predominantly overcast. A less restrictive approach is based on the assumption of a heteroscedastic, where the variance of the Gaussian noise is made a function of the explanatory variables. It is well known that for a model trained to minimise the squared error, the output approximates the conditional mean of the target data. Therefore, if we then train a second kernel ridge regression model to predict the squared residuals of the first, the output of the second model will be an estimate of the conditional mean of the squared residuals, i.e. the conditional variance of the target distribution.

This method was suggested in the case of multi-layer perceptron networks (see e.g. [9]) by Satchwell [10] and applied to the problem of automotive engine calibration by Lowe and Zapart [11].

There are two problems with this method: the first one is that the squared residual is not an estimate of the conditional variance. Indeed, imagine that some over-fitting occurred while modelling the conditional mean: the squared residuals can then be very small not reflecting the true conditional variance. The second problem is that while modelling the conditional mean, the amount of regularisation is the same over all the space, while intuitively, one would like to regularise more in noisy regions. The first problem will be addressed in section 5 and the second one in the following section.

## 3 Heteroscedastic Kernel Ridge Regression

A more natural method of modelling heteroscedastic data fits the models of the predictive mean and predictive variance, or equivalently the predictive standard deviation, simultaneously, using a likelihood function corresponding to a Gaussian noise process with data-dependant variance, i.e.

$$p(\mathcal{D}|\boldsymbol{w}) = \prod_{i=1}^{\ell} \frac{1}{\sqrt{2\pi}\sigma(\boldsymbol{x}_i)} \exp\left\{ -\frac{[\mu(\boldsymbol{x}_i) - y_i]^2}{2\sigma^2(\boldsymbol{x}_i)} \right\}$$

where $\boldsymbol{w}$ represents the parameters of the combined model. A linear model of the conditional mean, $\mu(\boldsymbol{x}) = \boldsymbol{w}^\mu \cdot \boldsymbol{\phi}^\mu(\boldsymbol{x}) + b^\mu$ is then constructed in a feature space $\mathcal{F}^\mu$ corresponding to a positive definite kernel $\mathcal{K}^\mu(\boldsymbol{x}, \boldsymbol{x}') = \boldsymbol{\phi}^\mu(\boldsymbol{x}) \cdot \boldsymbol{\phi}^\mu(\boldsymbol{x}')$. Similarly, the standard deviation being a strictly positive quantity, a linear model of the logarithm of the predictive standard deviation, $\log \sigma(\boldsymbol{x}) = \boldsymbol{w}^\sigma \cdot \boldsymbol{\phi}^\sigma(\boldsymbol{x}) + b^\sigma$ is constructed in a second feature space, $\mathcal{F}^\sigma$, induced by a second positive-definite kernel $\mathcal{K}^\sigma(\boldsymbol{x}, \boldsymbol{x}') = \boldsymbol{\phi}^\sigma(\boldsymbol{x}) \cdot \boldsymbol{\phi}^\sigma(\boldsymbol{x}')$. The optimal model parameters, $(\boldsymbol{w}^\mu, b^\mu . \boldsymbol{w}^\sigma, b^\sigma)$, are determined by minimising a penalised negative log-likelihood objective function,

$$L = \frac{1}{2}\gamma^\mu \|\boldsymbol{w}^\mu\|^2 + \frac{1}{2}\gamma^\sigma \|\boldsymbol{w}^\sigma\|^2 + \frac{1}{2}\sum_{i=1}^{\ell} \left\{ \log \sigma(\boldsymbol{x}_i) + \frac{[\mu(\boldsymbol{x}_i) - y_i]^2}{2\sigma^2(\boldsymbol{x}_i)} \right\}, \tag{5}$$

with regularisation parameters, $\gamma^\mu$ and $\gamma^\sigma$, providing individual control over the complexities of the models of the predictive mean and standard deviation respectively (c.f. [12, 13]). Note that (5) is the regularised objective function associated with the loss (2). The use of a heteroscedastic loss leads to an important interaction between the data misfit and regularisation terms comprising the objective function : The squared error term is now weighted according to the estimated local variance of the data. As a result, the influence of the regularisation term is now increased in areas of high predictive variance. This is in agreement with our intuition that more flexible models are more easily justified where amplitude of the noise contaminating the data is low and meaningful variations in the underlying deterministic system we hope to model are obscured to a lesser degree. The $\log \sigma(\boldsymbol{x}_i)$ term penalises unduly high predictive standard deviations. It should be noted that it is possible for the negative log-likelihood term in (5) to go to minus infinity if the predictive variance goes to zero and $\mu(\boldsymbol{x}_i) = y_i$. One could circumvent this problem by adopting a suitable prior on $b^\sigma$, to indicate that we do not believe in very small predictive variances. However, this might not be enough and a more principled solution is presented in section 5. From a theoretical point of view, it is known that the ERM principle is consistent [14], so it might seem surprising that the minimiser of (5) would not yield functions giving a good test error (2), as the number of points goes to infinity. The reason why ERM could fail here is that the *loss is unbounded* and thus the convergence results about ERM do not apply.

A straight-forward extension of the representer theorem [15, 16, 17] indicates that the minimiser of this objective function can be expressed in the form of a pair of kernel expansions: For the model of the predictive mean,

$$\boldsymbol{w}^\mu = \sum_{i=1}^{\ell} \alpha_i^\mu \boldsymbol{\phi}^\mu(\boldsymbol{x}_i) \qquad \Longrightarrow \qquad \mu(\boldsymbol{x}) = \sum_{i=1}^{\ell} \alpha_i^\mu \mathcal{K}^\mu(\boldsymbol{x}_i, \boldsymbol{x}) + b^\mu,$$

and similarly for the model of the predictive standard deviation,

$$\boldsymbol{w}^\sigma = \sum_{i=1}^{\ell} \alpha_i^\sigma \boldsymbol{\phi}^\sigma(\boldsymbol{x}_i) \qquad \Longrightarrow \qquad \log \sigma(\boldsymbol{x}) = \sum_{i=1}^{\ell} \alpha_i^\sigma \mathcal{K}^\sigma(\boldsymbol{x}_i, \boldsymbol{x}) + b^\sigma.$$

The resulting model is termed a heteroscedastic kernel ridge regression (HKRR) machine [18, 17] (see also [19]). An efficient iterative training algorithm for this model alternates between updates of the model of the predictive mean and updates of the model of the predictive standard deviation.

### 3.1 Updating the Predictive Mean

Ignoring any terms in the objective function (5) that do not involve $\boldsymbol{w}^\mu$ or $b^\mu$, a simplified cost function is obtained, which is used to update the parameters of the model of the predictive mean, $\mu(\boldsymbol{x}_i)$,

$$L^\mu = \frac{1}{2}\gamma^\mu \|\boldsymbol{w}^\mu\|^2 + \frac{1}{2}\sum_{i=1}^{\ell} \lambda_i \left[\mu(\boldsymbol{x}_i) - y_i\right]^2 \tag{6}$$

where $\lambda_i^{-1} = 2\sigma^2(\boldsymbol{x}_i)$. This is essentially equivalent to the cost function for a weighted least-squares support vector machine (LS-SVM) [4]. Minimising (6) can be recast in the form of a constrained optimisation problem,

$$\min \mathcal{J} = \frac{1}{2}\|\boldsymbol{w}\|^2 + \frac{1}{2\gamma^\mu}\sum_{i=1}^{\ell} \lambda_i \varepsilon_i^2 \tag{7}$$

subject to

$$y_i = \boldsymbol{w}^\mu \cdot \boldsymbol{\phi}^\mu(\boldsymbol{x}_i) + b^\mu + \varepsilon_i, \qquad \forall\, i \in \{1, 2, \ldots, \ell\}, \tag{8}$$

The Lagrangian for this optimisation problem gives the unconstrained minimisation problem,

$$\mathcal{L} = \frac{1}{2}\|\boldsymbol{w}^\mu\|^2 + \frac{1}{2\gamma^\mu}\sum_{i=1}^{\ell}\lambda_i\varepsilon_i^2 - \sum_{i=1}^{\ell}\alpha_k^\mu\left\{\boldsymbol{w}^\mu\cdot\boldsymbol{\phi}^\mu(\boldsymbol{x}_i) + b^\mu + \varepsilon_i - y_i\right\}, \quad (9)$$

where $\boldsymbol{\alpha}^\mu = (\alpha_1^\mu, \alpha_2^\mu, \ldots, \alpha_\ell^\mu) \in \mathbb{R}^\ell$ is a vector of Lagrange multipliers.

$$\frac{\partial\mathcal{L}}{\partial\boldsymbol{w}^\mu} = \boldsymbol{0} \implies \boldsymbol{w}^\mu = \sum_{i=1}^{\ell}\alpha_i^\mu\boldsymbol{\phi}^\mu(\boldsymbol{x}_i) \quad (10)$$

$$\frac{\partial\mathcal{L}}{\partial b^\mu} = 0 \implies \sum_{i=1}^{\ell}\alpha_i^\mu = 0 \quad (11)$$

$$\frac{\partial\mathcal{L}}{\partial\varepsilon_i} = 0 \implies \alpha_i^\mu = \frac{\lambda_i\varepsilon_i}{\gamma^\mu}, \quad \forall_i \in \{1, 2, \ldots, \ell\} \quad (12)$$

Using (10) and (12) to eliminate $\boldsymbol{w}$ and $\boldsymbol{\varepsilon} = (\varepsilon_1, \varepsilon_2, \ldots, \varepsilon_\ell)$, from (9), we find that

$$\sum_{j=1}^{\ell}\alpha_j^\mu\boldsymbol{\phi}^\mu(\boldsymbol{x}_j)\cdot\boldsymbol{\phi}^\mu(\boldsymbol{x}_i) + b^\mu + \frac{\gamma^\mu\alpha_i^\mu}{\lambda_i} = y_i \qquad \forall\, i \in \{1, 2, \ldots, \ell\} \quad (13)$$

Noting that $\mathcal{K}^\mu(\boldsymbol{x}, \boldsymbol{x}') = \boldsymbol{\phi}^\mu(\boldsymbol{x})\cdot\boldsymbol{\phi}^\mu(\boldsymbol{x}')$, the system of linear equations can be written more concisely in matrix form as

$$\begin{bmatrix}\boldsymbol{K}^\mu + \gamma^\mu\boldsymbol{Z} & \boldsymbol{1} \\ \boldsymbol{1}^T & 0\end{bmatrix}\begin{bmatrix}\boldsymbol{\alpha}^\mu \\ b\end{bmatrix}\begin{bmatrix}\boldsymbol{y} \\ 0\end{bmatrix},$$

where $\boldsymbol{K}^\mu = \left[k_{ij}^\mu = \mathcal{K}^\mu(\boldsymbol{x}_i, \boldsymbol{x}_j)\right]_{i,j=1}^{\ell}$ and $\boldsymbol{Z} = \mathrm{diag}\{\lambda_1^{-1}, \lambda_2^{-1}, \ldots, \lambda_\ell^{-1}\}$. The parameters for the model of the predictive mean can then be obtained with a computational complexity of $\mathcal{O}(\ell^3)$ operations.

### 3.2 Updating the Predictive Standard Deviation

Similarly, neglecting terms in the objective function (5) that do not involve $\boldsymbol{w}^\sigma$ or $b^\sigma$, a simplified cost function is obtained, which is used to update the parameters of the model of the predictive standard deviation, $\sigma(\boldsymbol{x}_i)$, dividing through by $\gamma^\sigma$,

$$L^\sigma = \frac{1}{2}\|\boldsymbol{w}^\sigma\|^2 + \frac{1}{2\gamma^\sigma}\sum_{i=1}^{\ell}\left[z_i + \xi_i\exp\{-2z_i\}\right], \quad (14)$$

where $\xi_i = \frac{1}{2}\left[\mu(\boldsymbol{x}_i) - y_i\right]^2$ and $z_i = \log\sigma(\boldsymbol{x}_i)$. The reason for this latter re-parametrisation is that (14) yields an *unbounded* and *convex* optimisation problem.

A closed form expression for the minimum of this objective function is not apparent, and so it is minimised via an iteratively re-weighted least-squares

(IRWLS) procedure [20], which is effectively equivalent to a Newton's method. Indeed, at each iteration, a quadratic approximation of the objective function around the solution is performed and this quadratic approximation is minimised analytically, yielding an updated solution. Consider the negative log-likelihood for a single training pattern,

$$l_i = z_i + \xi_i \exp\{-2z_i\},$$

with first and second derivatives, with respect to $z_i$, given by

$$\frac{\partial l_i}{\partial z_i} = 1 - 2\xi_i \exp\{-2z_i\} \qquad \text{and} \qquad \frac{\partial^2 l_i}{\partial z_i^2} = 4\xi_i \exp\{-2z_i\}.$$

As we are interested only in minimising the negative log-likelihood, we substitute a weighted least-squares criterion, providing a local approximation of $l_i$ only up to some arbitrary constant, $C$, i.e.

$$q_i = \beta_i[\eta_i - z_i]^2 \approx l_i + C,$$

Clearly, we require the gradient and curvature of $q_i$ and $l_i$, with respect to $z_i$, to be identical, and therefore

$$\frac{\partial^2 q_i}{\partial z_i^2} = \frac{\partial^2 l_i}{\partial z_i^2} \implies \beta_i = 2\xi_i \exp\{-2z_i\},$$
$$\frac{\partial q_i}{\partial z_i} = \frac{\partial l_i}{\partial z_i} \implies \eta_i = z_i - \frac{1}{2\beta_i} + \frac{1}{2}.$$

The original objective function (14) for the model of the predictive standard deviation, can then be solved iteratively by alternating between updates of $\boldsymbol{\alpha}^\sigma$ and $b^\sigma$ via a regularised weighted least-squares loss function,

$$\widetilde{L}^\sigma = \frac{1}{2}\|\boldsymbol{w}\|^2 + \frac{1}{2\gamma^\sigma}\sum_{i=1}^{\ell} \beta_i[\eta_i - z_i]^2, \tag{15}$$

and updates of the weighting coefficients, $\boldsymbol{\beta} = (\beta_1, \beta_2, \ldots, \beta_\ell)$, and targets, $\boldsymbol{\eta} = (\eta_1, \eta_2, \ldots, \eta_\ell)$, according to,

$$\beta_i = 4\xi_i \exp\{-2z_i\} \qquad \text{and} \qquad \eta_i = z_i - \frac{2}{\beta_i} + \frac{1}{2}. \tag{16}$$

The weighted least-squares problem (15) can also be solved via a system of linear equations, with a computational complexity of $\mathcal{O}(\ell^3)$ operations, using the methods described in section 3.1.

## 4 Model Selection

While efficient optimisation algorithms exist for the optimisation problems defining the primary model parameters for kernel machines, generalisation performance is also dependent on the values of a small set of hyper-parameters, in this case the regularisation and kernel parameters. The search for "good" values of these hyper-parameters is an activity known as model selection. A common model selection strategy seeks to minimise a cross-validation [21] estimate of some appropriate performance statistic, such as the mean squared error or negative log-likelihood. The $k$-fold cross-validation procedure partitions the available data into $k$ disjoint subsets of approximately equal size. A series of $k$ models are then fitted, each using a different combination of $k-1$ subsets. The model selection criterion (2) is then evaluated for each model, in each case using the subset of the data not used in fitting that model. The $k$-fold cross-validation estimate of the model selection criterion is then taken to be the mean of the criterion on the "test" data for each model. The most extreme form of cross-validation, in which each partition consists of a single pattern, is known as leave-one-out cross-validation [22].

## 5 Unbiased Estimation of the Predictive Variance

Maximum likelihood estimates of variance, whether homoscedastic or heteroscedastic are known to be biased. If over-fitting is present in the model of the predictive mean, then the apparent variance of training data is reduced as the model attempts to "explain" the realisation of the random noise process corrupting the data to some degree. This will cause any estimate of the conditional variance based on the predictive mean to be unrealistically low. For this reason, the conditional variance should be estimated using training samples which have not been used to estimate the conditional mean. In this study, we use instead a leave-one-out cross-validation estimate for the predictive variance. As a result, the model of the predictive variance is effectively fitted on data that has not been used to fit the model of the predictive mean, where in principle no over-fitting can have occurred and so the bias in the predictive variance is eliminated. This approach is equally valid for estimating the constant variance of a conventional kernel ridge regression model, for estimates of predictive variance made by a second kernel ridge regression model, or for the joint model of predictive mean and variance implemented by the heteroscedastic kernel ridge regression model. Fortunately, this approach is computationally feasible, as leave-one-out cross-validation can be performed efficiently in closed form for kernel learning methods minimising a (weighted) least-squares cost function [23].

### 5.1 Efficient Leave-One-Out Cross-Validation of Kernel Models

Consider a linear regression model $\hat{y}(\boldsymbol{x}) = \boldsymbol{w} \cdot \boldsymbol{\phi}(\boldsymbol{x}) + b$ constructed in a feature space induced by a positive definite kernel, where the parameters $(\boldsymbol{w}, b)$ are given by the minimiser of a regularised weighted least-squares objective function,

$$L = \sum_{i=1}^{\ell} \lambda_i \left[ y_i - \boldsymbol{w} \cdot \boldsymbol{\phi}(\boldsymbol{x}_i) - b \right]^2 + \gamma \|\boldsymbol{w}\|^2.$$

The parameters of the resulting kernel expansion, $\hat{\boldsymbol{y}}(\boldsymbol{x}) = \sum_{i=1}^{\ell} \alpha_i \mathcal{K}(\boldsymbol{x}_i, \boldsymbol{x}) + b$, are given by the solution of a system of linear equations,

$$\begin{bmatrix} \boldsymbol{K} + \gamma \boldsymbol{\Lambda} & \boldsymbol{1} \\ \boldsymbol{1}^T & 0 \end{bmatrix} \begin{bmatrix} \boldsymbol{\alpha} \\ b \end{bmatrix} = \begin{bmatrix} \boldsymbol{y} \\ 0 \end{bmatrix}$$

where $\boldsymbol{\Lambda} = \text{diag}\left\{\lambda_1^{-1}, \lambda_2^{-1}, \ldots, \lambda_\ell^{-1}\right\}$. Let $\boldsymbol{H}$ represent the "hat" matrix, which maps the targets onto the model outputs, i.e. $\hat{\boldsymbol{y}} = \boldsymbol{H}\boldsymbol{y}$, such that

$$\boldsymbol{H} = [h_{ij}]_{i,j=1}^{\ell} = [\boldsymbol{K}\ \boldsymbol{1}] \begin{bmatrix} \boldsymbol{K} + \gamma \boldsymbol{\Lambda} & \boldsymbol{1} \\ \boldsymbol{1}^T & 0 \end{bmatrix}^{-1} \tag{17}$$

For the sake of notational convenience, let $\hat{y}_j = \hat{y}(\boldsymbol{x}_j)$. During each iteration of the leave-one-out cross-validation procedure, a regression model is fitted using all but one of the available patterns. Let $\hat{y}_j^{(-i)}$ represent the output of the model for the $j^{\text{th}}$ pattern during the $i^{\text{th}}$ iteration of the leave-one-out procedure and $\hat{\boldsymbol{y}}^{(-i)} = \left(\hat{y}_1^{(-i)}, \hat{y}_2^{(-i)}, \ldots, \hat{y}_\ell^{(-i)}\right)$. Note that given any training set and the corresponding learned model, if one adds a point in the training set with target equal to the output predicted by the model, the model will not change since the cost function will not be increased by this new point. Here, given the training set with the point $\boldsymbol{x}_i$ left out, the predicted output are by definition $\hat{\boldsymbol{y}}^{(-i)}$ and they will not change if the point $\boldsymbol{x}_i$ is added with target $\hat{y}_i^{(-i)}$

$$\hat{\boldsymbol{y}}^{(-i)} = \boldsymbol{H}\boldsymbol{y}^*, \qquad \text{where} \qquad y_j^* = \begin{cases} y_j & \text{if } j \neq i \\ \hat{y}_j^{(-i)} & \text{if } j = i \end{cases}. \tag{18}$$

Subtracting $y_i$ from both sides of the $i^{\text{th}}$ equation in the system of linear equations (18),

$$\begin{aligned} \hat{y}_i^{(-i)} - y_i &= \sum_{j=1}^{\ell} h_{ij} y_j^* - y_i \\ &= \sum_{j \neq i} h_{ij} y_j + h_{ii} \hat{y}_i^{(-i)} - y_i \\ &= \sum_{j=1}^{\ell} h_{ij} y_j - y_i + h_{ii} \left\{\hat{y}_i^{(-i)} - y_i\right\} \\ &= \hat{y}_i - y_i + h_{ii} \left\{\hat{y}_i^{(-i)} - y_i\right\} \end{aligned}$$

This may be rearranged in order to obtain a closed form expression for the the residual for the $i^{\text{th}}$ training pattern during the $i^{\text{th}}$ iteration of the leave-one-out cross-validation procedure, $e_i^{-i}$, in terms of the residual for a model trained on the entire dataset for that pattern, $e_i$, and the $i^{\text{th}}$ element of the principal diagonal of the hat matrix, $h_{ii}$,

$$e_i^{(-i)} = y_i - \hat{y}_i^{(-i)} = \frac{y_i - \hat{y}_i}{1 - h_{ii}} = \frac{e_i}{1 - h_{ii}} \tag{19}$$

Note that the diagonal elements of the hat matrix lie in the range $[0,\ 1]$, and so the residuals under leave-one-out cross-validation can never be smaller in magnitude than the residuals for a model trained on the entire dataset. Therefore any estimate of predictive variance based on leave-one-out cross-validation will also be greater than the estimate based on the output of a model trained on the entire dataset, thereby reducing, if not actually eliminating, the known conservative bias in the latter. Another derivation of the leave-one-out error is given in Appendix A.

### 5.2 Experimental Demonstration

In this section we use a synthetic regression problem, taken from Williams [13], in which the true predictive standard deviation is known exactly, to demonstrate

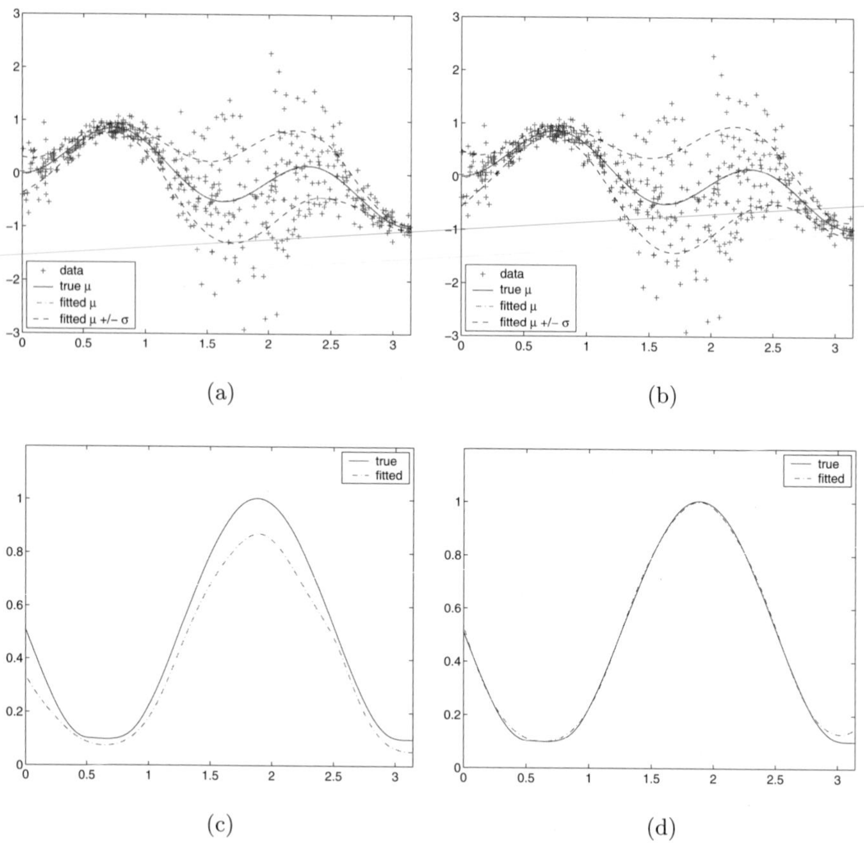


**Fig. 1.** Arithmetic mean of the estimate of the predictive mean and ± one standard deviation credible interval for (a) simple heteroscedastic kernel ridge regression (HKRR) and (b) leave-one-out heteroscedastic kernel ridge regression (LOOHKRR) models for a synthetic regression problem, (c) and (d) display the corresponding means of the estimated predictive standard deviation for the HKRR and LOOHKRR models respectively. All graphs show average results computed over 1000 randomly generated datasets (see text for details).

that the leave-one-out heteroscedastic kernel ridge regression (LOOHKRR) model provides almost unbiased estimates of the predictive standard deviation. The univariate input patterns, $x$, are drawn from a uniform distribution on the interval $(0,\ \pi)$; the corresponding targets, $y$, are drawn from a univariate Normal distribution with mean and variance that vary smoothly with $x$:

$$x \sim \mathcal{U}(0, \pi), \quad \text{and} \quad y \sim \mathcal{N}\left(\sin\left\{\frac{5x}{2}\right\}\sin\left\{\frac{3x}{2}\right\}, \frac{1}{100} + \frac{1}{4}\left[1 - \sin\left\{\frac{5x}{2}\right\}\right]^2\right).$$

Figure 1, parts (a) and (b), show the arithmetic mean of the predictive mean and $\pm$ one standard deviation credible interval for simple and leave-one-out heteroscedastic kernel ridge regression models respectively, over 1000 randomly generated realisations of the dataset, of 64 patterns each. A radial basis function kernel was used, with width parameter, $\kappa = 2$, for both the model of the predictive mean and the model of the predictive standard deviation, the regularisation parameters were set as follows: $\gamma^\mu = \gamma^\sigma = 1$ (the hyper-parameters we deliberately chosen to allow some over-fitting in the model of the predictive mean). In both cases the fitted mean is, on average, in good agreement with the true mean. Figure 1, parts (c) and (d), show the arithmetic mean of the predictive standard deviation for the simple and leave-one-out heteroscedastic kernel ridge regression models. The simple heteroscedastic kernel ridge regression model, on average, consistently under-estimates the conditional standard deviation, and so the predicted credible intervals are optimistically narrow. The mean predictive standard deviation for the leave-one-out heteroscedastic kernel ridge regression model is very close to the true value. This suggests that the estimation of the predictive standard deviation is essentially unbiased as the expected value is approximately equal to the true value.

## 6 Gaussian Process Models

Gaussian Processes (GP) for regression [3] are powerful non parametric probabilistic models. They makes use of a prior covariance matrix of the targets $\boldsymbol{y}$ which has the form

$$K_{ij} = a(\mathcal{K}(\boldsymbol{x}_i, \boldsymbol{x}_j) + \gamma\delta_{ij}),$$

where $\mathcal{K}$ is any kernel function (for instance, the one defined in equation (3)), $a$ is the *amplitude* parameter and $\gamma$ is the *noise to signal ratio* parameter. Those parameters, as well as the hyper-parameters of the kernel are found by minimising the negative log *evidence*

$$\log\det \boldsymbol{K} + \boldsymbol{y}^\top \boldsymbol{K}^{-1}\boldsymbol{y}. \tag{20}$$

Note that $a$ can be found in closed form,

$$a = \frac{\boldsymbol{y}^\top \boldsymbol{K}_{a=1}^{-1}\boldsymbol{y}}{n}.$$

The mean prediction is the same as in homoscedastic kernel ridge regression (without bias),

$$\mu(\boldsymbol{x}) = \boldsymbol{k}^\top(\boldsymbol{x})\boldsymbol{K}^{-1}\boldsymbol{y},$$

with $\boldsymbol{k}^\top(\boldsymbol{x}) = a(\mathcal{K}(\boldsymbol{x}_1, \boldsymbol{x}), \ldots, \mathcal{K}(\boldsymbol{x}_n, \boldsymbol{x}))$. The difference between kernel ridge regression and Gaussian Processes is that GP give a natural estimation of the predictive uncertainty as:

$$\sigma^2(\boldsymbol{x}) = a\gamma + a\mathcal{K}(\boldsymbol{x}, \boldsymbol{x}) - \boldsymbol{k}^\top(\boldsymbol{x})\boldsymbol{K}^{-1}\boldsymbol{k}(\boldsymbol{x}). \tag{21}$$

Note that the first term is constant and is the estimated noise level. The sum of the two others corresponds to the uncertainty in the mean prediction: for instance, it is large when the test point is far away from the training data.

Let us compare the leave-one-out predictive variances given by our method and by GP. For GP, if we let the point $i$ out of the training set, its predictive variance will be:

$$a(K_{ii} - K_{\overline{i}i}^\top (K_{\overline{i}\overline{i}})^{-1} K_{\overline{i}i}) = \frac{a}{K_{ii}^{-1}} = \frac{y^\top K^{-1} y}{n K_{ii}^{-1}}, \tag{22}$$

where $K_{\overline{i}\overline{i}}$ is the matrix $K$ with the $i$-th column and row removed. This is not completely exact as one should recompute $a$ once the point $i$ is out of the training set. But usually, values of hyper-parameters are not really affected by the leave-one-out procedure. For our method, the leave-one-out error on the point $i$ is given by

$$\left( \frac{[K^{-1}y]_i}{K_{ii}^{-1}} \right)^2. \tag{23}$$

We can see that the two expressions are similar, but the GP takes the data less into account (the numerator is constant). This is not surprising, as in general, Bayesian methods rely more on the prior and less on the data. This yields near optimal predictions when the prior correctly reflects our knowledge of the problem, but can be suboptimal when there is prior mismatch. We will illustrate this point by the following toy problem. We want to model the step function on $[-1, 1]$, $f(t) = 1$ if $t > 0$, 0 otherwise. For this purpose, we used the Gaussian kernel (3). Note that this kernel is not the best suited for this task because it is smooth and stationary whereas the target function is not. The kernel width $\kappa$ and the ridge $\gamma$ have been optimised by minimising the negative log evidence (20). 100 points $x_i$ have been chosen uniformly spaced in the interval $[-1, 1]$ and the targets have been corrupted with a Gaussian noise of standard deviation 0.1. The data and the mean prediction (which is the same for GP and kernel ridge regression) are plotted in the left of figure 2.

Given a test point $x$ and the mean prediction $\mu(x)$, the "optimal" predictive variance (which we actually defined in the introduction as the conditional variance) is obtained by minimising the loss (2) and is

$$\sigma^2(x) = E_{y|x}(\mu(x) - y)^2 = (\mu(x) - f(x))^2 + \text{noise variance},$$

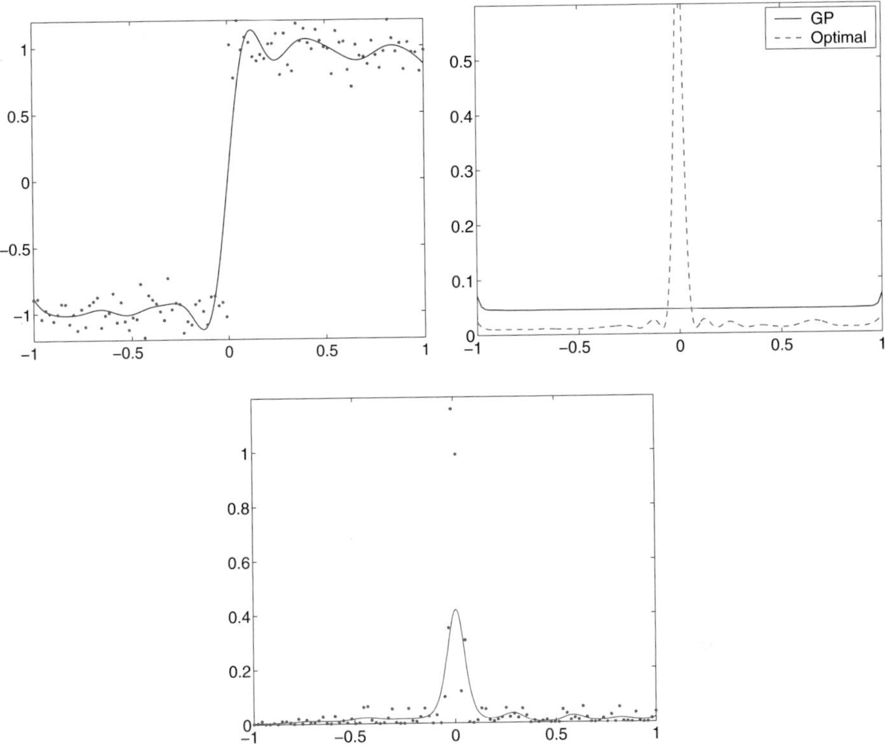


**Fig. 2.** Step function toy problem. *Left*: Training points and mean prediction. *Right:* GP predictive variance and the "optimal" one (given the mean). *Bottom*: Leave-one-out errors and the resulting predictive variance learned by the proposed method.

where $f(x)$ is the (unknown) target function. In our toy problem, we know the target function and the noise variance, so we can compute this optimal predictive uncertainty, as shown in the right of figure 2. We can see that this "optimal" predictive variance is very large around 0. This is because the mean prediction is not very good in this region and ideally, the predictive variance needs to be increased in regions where the mean prediction is far form the target function. However, when the kernel function used by the GP is stationary and the points are equally spaced, the predictive variance (21) given by the GP is almost constant, as shown in the right of figure 2: in this case, it is unable to see that the predictive variance should be increased around 0. The leave-one-out errors are plotted as dots in the bottom of figure 2. The first observation is that the misfit around 0 is well captured. However, the variance of the leave-one-out errors in the flat regions is high. This is directly related to the noise in the targets. For instance, it can happen that "by chance", the leave-one-out error on a given point is almost 0; but that does not mean that we are necessarily sure of the value of the function at this point. That is the reason why we have to perform a regression for the predictive variance (cf section 3.2). For this toy problem, we took the same kernel and regularisation parameter as used for the mean prediction and minimised (14), with $\xi_i$ being the leave-one-out error on $x_i$. The estimated predicted variance is plotted at the bottom of figure 2. For this toy problem, the average negative log likelihoods (2) computed on a large test set are: -3.17 for the "optimal", -2.93 for our method and -2.3 for the GP. We would like to point out that in most real world examples, GP give reasonable predictive variances. This toy problem is just an illustration of what can happen in the case of a "prior mismatch" and how a non Bayesian method can overcome this difficulty.

As an aside, it is interesting to note that even if the leave-one-out predictive variance (22) for GP and the leave-one-out error (23) can be quite different, their *average* should be similar, as they are both estimate of the test error. On our toy problem, they were respectively 0.0447 and 0.0459, while the test error was 0.0359. We can try to see this similarity from an analytical point of view. First note that the gradient of (20) with respect to the ridge parameter should be 0, yielding

$$\text{trace } K^{-1} = \frac{1}{a}\sum [K^{-1}y]_i^2.$$

So the mean of (22) can be rewritten as

$$\frac{1}{n}\sum \frac{1}{K_{ii}^{-1}} \frac{\sum [K^{-1}y]_i^2}{\sum K_{ii}^{-1}},$$

which is very similar to the mean of (23),

$$\frac{1}{n}\sum \left(\frac{[K^{-1}y]_i}{K_{ii}^{-1}}\right)^2,$$

if the variance of the $K_{ii}^{-1}$ is small.

## 7 Results for Challenge Benchmark Datasets

In this section, we detail results obtained on the three non-linear regression benchmark problems considered by the predictive uncertainty challenge, namely `gaze`, `stereopsis` and `Outaouais`. The methods that we considered are the following:

**KRR.** Conventional kernel ridge regression with fixed variance prediction based on the training set MSE.

**KRR + LOO.** Conventional kernel ridge regression with fixed variance prediction based on the leave-one-out estimate of the MSE.

**KRR + KRR.** Conventional kernel ridge regression with predictive variance via kernel ridge regression on the residuals over the training set.

**KRR + LOO + KRR.** Conventional kernel ridge regression with predictive variance via kernel ridge regression on the leave-one-out residuals.

**HKRR.** Heteroscedastic kernel ridge regression.

**LOOHKRR.** Heteroscedastic kernel ridge regression with unbiased estimation of the predictive variance. This is the method described in this paper.

### 7.1 Gaze

Table 1 shows the negative logarithm of the predictive density (NLPD) and mean squared error (MSE) for various kernel ridge regression-based models over training, validation and test partitions of the `gaze` benchmark dataset. A visual inspection of the data revealed that columns 3 and 4 of the validation and test partitions contained a small number of outliers (large negative values well outside the range of values observed in the training data). These outliers were "repaired" via a simple missing data imputation procedure based on linear regression. An isotropic Gaussian radial basis function kernels were used throughout, with model selection based on minimisation of the the 10-fold cross-validation estimate of the MSE (for standard kernel ridge regression models) or NLPD (for the heteroscedastic kernel ridge regression models). The use of leave-one-out cross-validation in fitting the model of the predictive variance also provides demonstrably better performance, with the KRR+LOO and KRR+LOO+KRR outperforming the KRR, and KRR+KRR models respectively. The very poor performance of the KRR+KRR model provides a graphic example of the dangers associated with the unrealistically low estimates of predictive variance provided by existing approaches. In the case of the HKRR and LOOHKRR models, the NLPD is lower for the HKRR model because it provides a better model of the conditional mean. It should be noted, however, that the differences in test set NLPD between models, with the exception of the KRR and KRR+KRR, are generally very small and unlikely to be really meaningful.

**Table 1.** Performance of various models, based on kernel ridge regression, on the `gaze` dataset, in terms of mean squared error (MSE) and negative log predictive density (NLPD) over the training and validation partitions

| Mean description | Train Set NLPD | Valid Set NLPD | Test Set NLPD | Train Set MSE | Valid Set MSE | Test Set MSE |
|---|---|---|---|---|---|---|
| KRR | 4.723 | 5.776 | 5.8172 | 0.01165 | 0.03654 | 0.04029 |
| KRR+LOO | 4.912 | 5.292 | 5.3077 | 0.01165 | 0.03653 | 0.04029 |
| KRR+KRR | 5.003 | 12.119 | 7.6011 | 0.01165 | 0.03653 | 0.04029 |
| KRR+LOO+KRR | 4.857 | 5.282 | 5.2951 | 0.01165 | 0.03653 | 0.04029 |
| HKRR | 5.119 | 5.248 | 5.2650 | 0.02574 | 0.03272 | 0.03607 |
| LOOHKRR | 4.881 | 5.305 | 5.3214 | 0.01159 | 0.03677 | 0.04051 |

### 7.2 Stereopsis

Table 2 shows the negative logarithm of the predictive density (NLPD) and mean squared error (MSE) for various kernel ridge regression models over training, validation and test partitions of of the `stereopsis` benchmark dataset. An anisotropic Gaussian radial basis function kernels and model selection based on validation set NLPD are used throughout. The labels for the first six models

**Table 2.** Performance of various models, based on kernel ridge regression, on the stereopsis dataset, in terms of mean squared error (MSE) and negative log predictive density (NLPD) over the training and validation partitions. Two values of the NLPD for the test set are given; the first gives the NLPD computed over the entire test set, the second excludes the problematic pattern #162.

| Model description | Train Set NLPD | Valid Set NLPD | Test Set NLPD 1 | Test Set NLPD 2 | Train Set MSE | Valid Set MSE | Test Set MSE |
|---|---|---|---|---|---|---|---|
| KRR | -0.5930 | +0.0241 | +1.8742 | -0.1124 | $1.464\times10^5$ | $3.481\times10^5$ | $3.095\times10^5$ |
| KRR+LOO | -0.4917 | -0.1889 | +0.7189 | -0.2559 | $1.464\times10^5$ | $3.481\times10^5$ | $3.095\times10^5$ |
| KRR+KRR | -0.6194 | +0.0620 | +1.4088 | -0.0805 | $1.464\times10^5$ | $3.481\times10^5$ | $3.095\times10^5$ |
| KRR+LOO+KRR | -0.5835 | -0.2459 | +0.4924 | -0.2718 | $1.464\times10^5$ | $3.481\times10^5$ | $3.095\times10^5$ |
| HKRR | -0.3940 | -0.2061 | +1.6928 | -0.1306 | $2.176\times10^5$ | $3.041\times10^5$ | $3.369\times10^5$ |
| LOOHKRR | -0.4813 | -0.1798 | +2.8873 | -0.0803 | $1.725\times10^5$ | $2.599\times10^5$ | $2.860\times10^5$ |
| KRR + Quant. Var. | -0.2726 | -0.0872 | +0.2626 | -0.1238 | $1.288\times10^5$ | $3.892\times10^5$ | $3.447\times10^5$ |
| KRR Mixture | -2.3967 | -1.5538 | +121.00 | -1.6173 | $0.025\times10^5$ | $0.169\times10^5$ | $1.681\times10^5$ |

are as described for the gaze dataset. An investigation of the test data revealed that the negative log-likelihood for one of the test patterns dominated the contribution from the other patterns, as shown in Figure 3 (a). An advantage of generating a predictive distribution, rather than a single point prediction, is that it is possible to detect potential outliers in the test data (i.e. observations that cannot be reconciled with an otherwise accurate model of the data). If we choose to interpret the results as indicating, for instance a data entry error, and delete pattern number 162, the resulting test-set NLPD statistics are much more closely in accord with the corresponding validation set statistics. Looking at the data in more detail, we can see that the test targets are clustered into 10 relatively compact clusters. Pattern #162 belongs to the cluster of values lying between 150 and 170, Figure 3 (b). Figure 3 (c) the projection of points with targets lying between 150 and 170 onto the first two principal components of the corresponding input features (excluding pattern #162). This shows that the input features for pattern #162 are atypical of patterns with a target of $\approx 160$. Figure 3 (d) shows the results obtained using simple linear regression on all patterns belonging to this cluster, excluding pattern #162 (blue circles). It can be seen that there is a reasonably strong correlation between the predicted and true target values. The prediction of this model on pattern #162 predicts a much lower target value, suggesting that the relationship between target and input features for pattern #162 is different than that for the rest of the cluster. The predicted targets for a KRR model based on the entire training partition are also shown (green $\times$ and black square). Again the model predicts a target significantly lower than the given target value. This suggests the model may well be correct in assigning a very low likelihood to pattern #162.

The results for the stereopsis dataset are more equivocal than those for the gaze dataset. Again, a modest improvement in validation and test set NLPD is obtained through the use of leave-one-out cross-validation in fitting the model of the conditional variance, in the case of KRR/KRR+LOO and KRR+KRR/

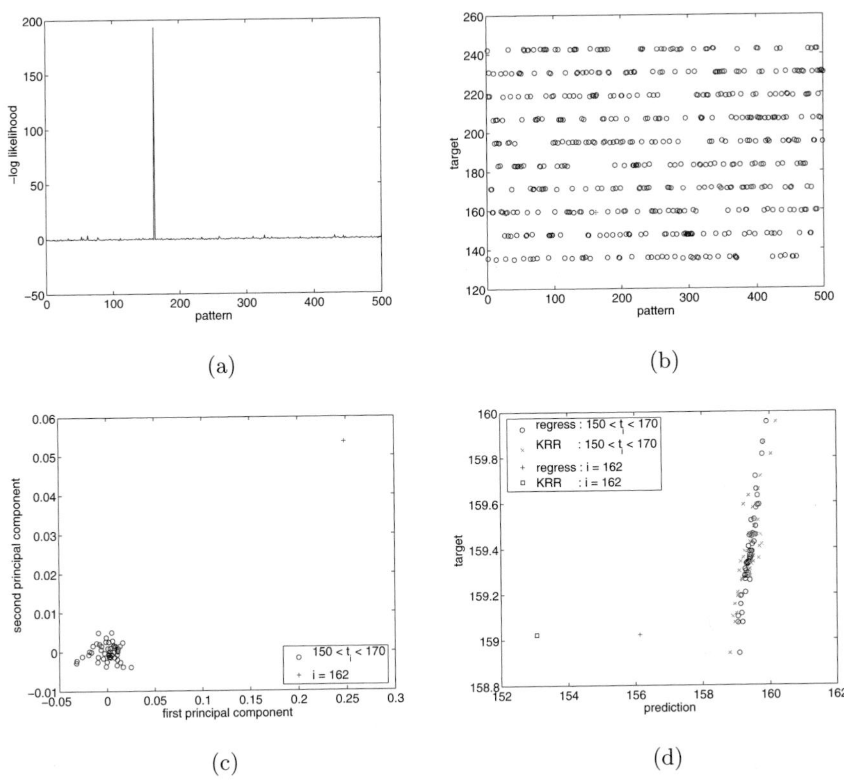


**Fig. 3.** Analysis of `stereopsis` dataset: (a) The negative log-likelihood is dominated by the contribution from pattern #162. (b) Illustration of the discrete nature of the test targets. (c) Plot of the projection of points with targets lying between 150 and 170 onto the first two principal components of the corresponding input features. (d) Regression results demonstrate that pattern #162 is clearly an outlier.

KRR+LOO+KRR models. However in this case, both HKRR and LOOHKRR models perform poorly. This may be because the data were not collected randomly across the pattern space and this complicates the regularisation of the model.

The last two rows of Table 2 relate to further experiments inspired by the solution of Snelson and Murray, who noticed that the targets for this dataset were strongly clustered into ten compact groups. The KRR + Quant. Var. model adopted a KRR model of the predictive mean, and then estimated the constant variance separately for each cluster. The KRR mixture model used a KRR model to estimate the predictive mean of the target distribution and one of a set of ten KRR models used to estimate the predictive variance within each cluster, depending on the estimate of the predictive mean. The KRR Mixture model clearly provides a substantial improvement in the achievable validation set NLPD. However the clustering of the target values was later revealed to be an artifact of the data collection process, and so this improvement is essentially meaningless as this approach would not be feasible in operation.

### 7.3 Outaouais

The `outaouais` dataset is the largest of the challenge benchmarks, and is too large (20,000 training patterns and 37 features) to easily apply kernel learning methods directly. We therefore modelled this dataset using a multi-layer perceptron network (e.g. [9]), with a heteroscedastic loss function [13] similar to that used in training the heteroscedastic kernel ridge regression model. Bayesian regularisation with a Laplace prior [24] was used to avoid over-fitting the training data and to identify and prune redundant connections. It is interesting to note that this, rather dated, technique performed quite creditably, as shown in Table 3.

**Table 3.** Performance of various models on the `outaouais` dataset, in terms of mean squared error (MSE) and negative log predictive density (NLPD) over the training, validation and test partitions. All the numbers are multiplied by 100.

| Model description | Train NLPD | Test NLPD | Valid NLPD | Train MSE | Test MSE | Valid MSE |
|---|---|---|---|---|---|---|
| Gaussian process | -92.55 | -92.13 | -92.55 | 0 | 1.727 | 0 |
| Classification + NN | -152.4 | -87.95 | -152.4 | 0 | 5.635 | 0 |
| CAN + CV | -86.68 | -64.81 | -87.59 | 1.784 | 3.774 | 1.636 |
| Heteroscedastic MLP | -32.99 | -23.04 | -22.15 | 19.55 | 20.13 | 19.27 |
| Gaussian Process | 3.246 | 9.019 | 11.79 | 14.9 | 15.8 | 16.48 |
| MDN Ensemble | 17.93 | 19.93 | 19.56 | 27.72 | 27.83 | 27.99 |
| NeuralBAG/EANN | 47.68 | 50.5 | 49.44 | 26.71 | 27.03 | 26.63 |
| baseline | 109.5 | 111.5 | 112.4 | 10 | 10 | 10 |

## 8 Conclusions

In this paper, we have shown that the assumption of a *heteroscedastic* (input dependent) noise structure can improve the performance of kernel learning methods for non-linear regression problems. The resulting estimate of the predictive variance provides a useful estimate of the uncertainty inherent in the usual estimate of the predictive mean. We have also demonstrated that leave-one-out cross-validation, which can be implemented very efficiently in closed form for a variety of kernel learning algorithms, can be used to overcome the bias inherent in (penalised) maximum likelihood estimates of predictive variance. It would be interesting to compare the leave-one-out cross-validation method investigated here with the Bayesian scheme proposed by Bishop and Qazaz [25], which instead marginalises over the estimate of the predictive mean in fitting the model of the predictive variance, or the Gaussian process treatment of Goldberg *et al.* [26].

## References

1. Quiñonero-Candela, J.: Evaluating Predictive Uncertainty Challenge (2005) predict.kyb.tuebingen.mpg.de.
2. Saunders, C., Gammerman, A., Vovk, V.: Ridge regression learning algorithm in dual variables. In: Proc., 15th Int. Conf. on Machine Learning, Madison, WI (1998) 515–521
3. Williams, C., Rasmussen, C.: Gaussian Processes for Regression. In Touretzky, D.S., Mozer, M.C., Hasselmo, M.E., eds.: Advances in Neural Information Processing Systems, NIPS. Volume 8., MIT Press (1995)
4. Suykens, J.A.K., De Brabanter, J., Lukas, L., Vanderwalle, J.: Weighted least squares support vector machines : robustness and sparse approximation. Neurocomputing **48** (2002) 85–105
5. Mercer, J.: Functions of positive and negative type and their connection with the theory of integral equations. Philosophical Transactions of the Royal Society of London, A **209** (1909) 415–446
6. Cristianini, N., Shawe-Taylor, J.: An Introduction to Support Vector Machines (and other kernel-based learning methods). Cambridge University Press, Cambridge, U.K. (2000)
7. Schölkopf, B., Smola, A.J.: Learning with kernels - support vector machines, regularization, optimization and beyond. MIT Press, Cambridge, MA (2002)
8. Hoerl, A.E., Kennard, R.W.: Ridge regression: Biased estimation for nonorthogonal problems. Technometrics **12** (1970) 55–67
9. Bishop, C.M.: Neural Networks for Pattern Recognition. Oxford University Press (1995)
10. Satchwell, C.: Finding error bars (the easy way). Neural Computing Applications Forum **5** (1994)
11. Lowe, D., Zapart, C.: Point-wise confidence interval estimation by neural networks: A comparative study based on automotive engine calibration. Neural Computing and Applications **8** (1999) 77–85
12. Nix, D.A., Weigend, A.S.: Estimating the mean and variance of the target probability distribution. In: Proceedings of the IEEE International Conference on Neural Networks. Volume 1., Orlando, FL (1994) 55–60
13. Williams, P.M.: Using neural networks to model conditional multivariate densities. Neural Computation **8** (1996) 843–854
14. Vapnik, V.: Statistical Learning Theory. John Wiley & Sons (1998)
15. Kimeldorf, G.S., Wahba, G.: Some results on Tchebycheffian spline functions. Journal of Mathematical Analysis and Applications **33** (1971) 82–95
16. Schölkopf, B., Herbrich, R., Smola, A.J.: A generalised representer theorem. In: Proceedings of the Fourteenth International Conference on Computational Learning Theory, Amsterdam, the Netherlands (2001) 416–426
17. Cawley, G.C., Talbot, N.L.C., Foxall, R.J., Dorling, S.R., Mandic, D.P.: Heteroscedastic kernel ridge regression. Neurocomputing **57** (2004) 105–124
18. Foxall, R.J., Cawley, G.C., Talbot, N.L.C., Dorling, S.R., Mandic, D.P.: Heteroscedastic regularised kernel regression for prediction of episodes of poor air quality. In: Proceedings of the European Symposium on Artificial Neural Networks (ESANN-2002), Bruges, Belgium (2002) 19–24
19. Yuan, M., Wahba, G.: Doubly penalized likelihood estimator in heteroscedastic regression. Statistics and Probability Letters **69** (2004) 11–20

20. Nabney, I.T.: Efficient training of RBF networks for classification. In: Proceedings of the Ninth International Conference on Artificial Neural Networks. Volume 1., Edinburgh, United Kingdom (1999) 210–215
21. Stone, M.: Cross-validatory choice and assessment of statistical predictions. Journal of the Royal Statistical Society, B **36** (1974) 111–147
22. Luntz, A., Brailovsky, V.: On estimation of characters obtained in statistical procedure of recognition (in Russian). Techicheskaya Kibernetica **3** (1969)
23. Cawley, G.C., Talbot, N.L.C.: Efficient leave-one-out cross-validation of kernel Fisher discriminant classifiers. Pattern Recognition **36** (2003) 2585–2592
24. Williams, P.M.: Bayesian regularization and pruning using a Laplace prior. Neural Computation **7** (1995) 117–143
25. Bishop, C.M., Qazaz, C.S.: Bayesian inference of noise levels in regression. In von der Malsburg, C., von Seelen, W., Vorbrüggen, J.C., Sendhoff, B., eds.: Proceedings of the International Conference on Artificial Neural Networks (ICANN-96). Volume 1112 of Lecture Notes in Computer Science., Bochum, Germany, Springer (1996) 59–64
26. Goldberg, P.W., Williams, C.K.I., Bishop, C.M.: Regression with input-dependent noise : A Gaussian process treatment. In Jordan, M., Kearns, M., Solla, S., eds.: Advances in Neural Information Processing Systems. Volume 10. MIT Press (1998) 493–499

## Appendix A: An Alternative Derivation of the Leave-One-Out Error

We present here an other derivation of (19). Suppose that the point $\boldsymbol{x}_1$ is taken out of the training set. Let $\boldsymbol{\alpha}^{(-1)}$ and $b^{(-1)}$ the parameters found by kernel ridge regression and let us write the following block matrix decomposition:

$$\begin{bmatrix} \boldsymbol{K} + \gamma \boldsymbol{\Lambda} & \mathbf{1} \\ \mathbf{1}^T & 0 \end{bmatrix} = \begin{bmatrix} m_{11} & \boldsymbol{m_1}^\top \\ \boldsymbol{m_1} & \boldsymbol{M_1} \end{bmatrix} \equiv \boldsymbol{M}$$

Then

$$\begin{bmatrix} \boldsymbol{\alpha}^{(-1)} \\ b^{(-1)} \end{bmatrix} = \boldsymbol{M_1}^{-1} [y_2 \dots y_n \; 0]^\top$$

And

$$\begin{aligned} \hat{y}_1^{(-1)} &= \boldsymbol{m_1}^\top [\boldsymbol{\alpha}^{(-1)} \; b^{(-1)}]^\top \\ &= \boldsymbol{m_1}^\top \boldsymbol{M_1}^{-1} [y_2 \dots y_n \; 0]^\top \\ &= \boldsymbol{m_1}^\top \boldsymbol{M_1}^{-1} [\boldsymbol{m_1} \; \boldsymbol{M_1}][\boldsymbol{\alpha} \; b]^\top \\ &= \boldsymbol{m_1}^\top \boldsymbol{M_1}^{-1} \boldsymbol{m_1} \, \alpha_1 + \boldsymbol{m_1}^\top [\alpha_2 \cdots \alpha_n \; b]^\top \end{aligned}$$

On the other hand, the first row of the vector equality $\boldsymbol{M}[\boldsymbol{\alpha} \; b]^\top = \boldsymbol{y}$ gives $y_1 = m_{11}\alpha_1 + \boldsymbol{m_1}^\top [\alpha_2 \cdots \alpha_n \; b]^\top$. And thus we get

$$\begin{aligned} y_1 - \hat{y}_1^{(-1)} &= \alpha_1 (m_{11} - \boldsymbol{m_1}^\top \boldsymbol{M_1}^{-1} \boldsymbol{m_1}) \\ &= \frac{\alpha_1}{(\boldsymbol{M}^{-1})_{11}} \end{aligned} \tag{24}$$

The last equality comes from block matrix inversion (also known as Schur complement). Thus computing the leave-one-out error only requires the inversion of the matrix $\boldsymbol{M}$ (and this matrix has been previously inverted to find the coefficients $\boldsymbol{\alpha}$ and $b$ of the kernel ridge regression algorithm).

This result is the same as (19). Indeed, the denominator $1 - h_{ii}$ is the $i$-th diagonal element of

$$I - \begin{bmatrix} \boldsymbol{K} & \mathbf{1} \\ \mathbf{1}^\top & 0 \end{bmatrix} \boldsymbol{M}^{-1} = \left( \boldsymbol{M} - \begin{bmatrix} \boldsymbol{K} & \mathbf{1} \\ \mathbf{1}^\top & 0 \end{bmatrix} \right) \boldsymbol{M}^{-1} = \gamma \boldsymbol{\Lambda} \boldsymbol{M}^{-1}.$$

The first equality comes from the definition of $\boldsymbol{H}$ (17). Finally, combining with (12) (with $\lambda_i = \lambda_i$ and $\gamma^\mu = \gamma$), we get

$$\frac{e_i}{1 - h_{ii}} = \frac{e_i \lambda_i}{\gamma (\boldsymbol{M}^{-1})_{ii}} = \frac{\alpha_i}{(\boldsymbol{M}^{-i})_{ii}}.$$

Note that even though (19) and (24) are equal, the latter might be more numerically stable when $\gamma$ is very small: indeed, in this case $h_{ii} \approx 1$.

# Competitive Associative Nets and Cross-Validation for Estimating Predictive Uncertainty on Regression Problems

Shuichi Kurogi, Miho Sawa, and Shinya Tanaka

Kyushu Institute of Technology, Kitakyushu Fukuoka 8048550, Japan
kuro@cntl.kyutech.ac.jp

**Abstract.** This article describes the competitive associative net called CAN2 and cross-validation which we have used for making prediction and estimating predictive uncertainty on the regression problems at the Evaluating Predictive Uncertainty Challenge. The CAN2 with an efficient batch learning method for reducing empirical (training) error is combined with cross-validation for making prediction (generalization) error small and estimating predictive distribution accurately. From an analogy of Bayesian learning, a stochastic analysis is derived to indicate a validity of our method.

## 1 Introduction

This article describes the method which we have used for making prediction error small and estimating predictive uncertainty accurately on the regression problems at the Evaluating Predictive Uncertainty Challenge held as a part of NIPS 2004 Workshop on Calibration and Probabilistic Prediction in Machine Learning [1]. In the Challenge, the participants can use any learning method for predicting target values and estimating the accuracy of the predictions (or model uncertainty), and then the results are ranked by negative log probability density (NLPD) while normalized mean squared error (MSE) is also evaluated.

Our first decision was to use our competitive associative net called CAN2. The CAN2 uses competitive and associative schemes [2, 3] for learning efficient piecewise linear approximations to nonlinear functions. This approach has been shown effective in several areas such as function approximation, control, rainfall estimation and time series predictions [7, 8, 9, 10, 11]. We believe the success of the CAN2 lies in a combination of the following properties: Firstly the learning methods are simple and efficient: a gradient method for competitive learning and recursive least squares for associative learning. Secondly an exploration heuristic based on an "asymptotic optimality" criterion (see appendix) helps overcome local minima problems with the gradient method.

For achieving smaller NLPD, we had better estimate the uncertainty for each target value as accurately as possible, where the Bayesian learning scheme is one of the methods to deal with this task theoretically and practically [4, 5, 6]. Although several implementations of the Bayesian scheme using conventional feed forward neural networks have been developed so far, we had not been ready

J. Quiñonero-Candela et al. (Eds.): MLCW 2005, LNAI 3944, pp. 78–94, 2006.

to incorporate the CAN2 into the Bayesian paradigm, which will be for our future work. Instead of the Bayesian scheme, we had utilized cross-validation [12, 13, 14, 15] for estimating the distribution of predictions obtained by means of the CAN2, where the Voronoi regions for piecewise linear approximation by the CAN2 are utilized for estimating the variance from region to region in the input space, while the effectiveness of this method was not so clear but we are going to make a stochastic analysis in this article.

Further, we had put an effort to achieving smaller prediction error or smaller MSE for test data, because the estimation of predictive distribution can be divided into estimating the mean value of predictive distribution and then obtaining error distribution, where the performance of the former can be measured by the MSE for test data. So, our method for reducing NLPD consists of reducing the prediction error first and then estimating the error distribution. Since the learning algorithm of the CAN2 is for minimizing empirical (training) error, we had utilized cross-validation for making prediction (generalization) error small as well as estimating predictive distribution accurately. The validity of the method is also stochastically analyzed in this article.

In the next section, we show the CAN2 as a predictor, and then present and examine the cross-validation method for reducing prediction error and estimating predictive uncertainty, where we try to show the validity of the present method by mean of stochastic approach. In Sec. **3**, the procedure and the strategies for obtaining small NLPD as well as small MSE on the regression problems at the Challenge are summarized.

## 2 CAN2 and Cross-Validation for Making Predictions and Estimating Predictive Uncertainty

In order to focus on estimating predictive uncertainty, we first show the CAN2 for making predictions briefly, and then explain and examine cross-validation for estimating predictive uncertainty. See appendix for the batch learning method of the CAN2 for reducing empirical (training) error.

### 2.1 CAN2 for Making Predictions

Suppose there is an input-output system which is fed by a $k$-dimensional vector $\boldsymbol{x}_j \triangleq (x_{j1}, x_{j2}, \cdots, x_{jk})^T \in \mathbb{R}^{k\times 1}$ and outputs a scalar $y_j \in \mathbb{R}$ for $j = 1, 2, \cdots$ as follows;

$$y_j \triangleq f(\boldsymbol{x}_j) + d_j, \tag{1}$$

where $f(\cdot)$ is a nonlinear function, $d_j$ is zero-mean noise with the variance $\sigma_d^2$.

A CAN2 has $N$ units (see Fig. 1). The $i$th unit has a weight vector $\boldsymbol{w}_i \triangleq (w_{i1}, \cdots, w_{ik})^T \in \mathbb{R}^{k\times 1}$ and an associative matrix (or a row vector) $\boldsymbol{M}_i \triangleq (M_{i0}, M_{i1}, \cdots, M_{ik}) \in \mathbb{R}^{1\times(k+1)}$ for $i \in I = \{1, 2, \cdots, N\}$. The CAN2 approximates the above function $f(\boldsymbol{x})$ by

$$\widehat{y} \triangleq \widehat{f}(\boldsymbol{x}) \triangleq \widetilde{y}_c \triangleq \boldsymbol{M}_c \widetilde{\boldsymbol{x}}, \tag{2}$$

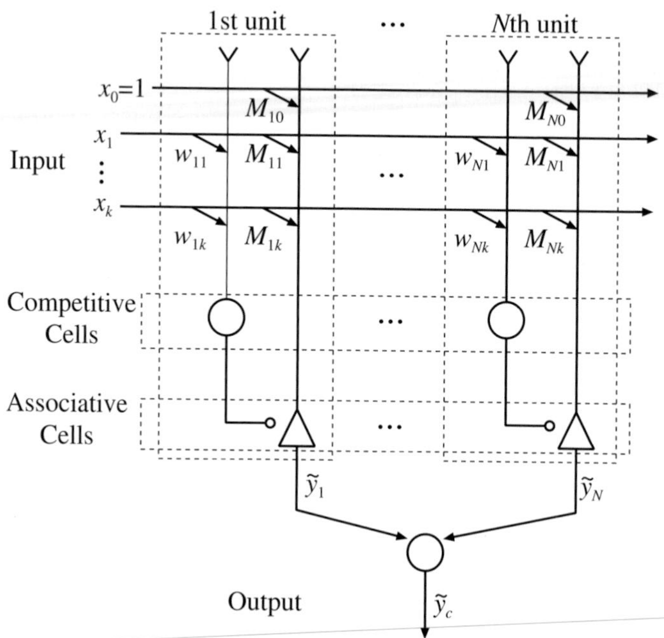


**Fig. 1.** Schematic diagram of the CAN2

where $\widetilde{\boldsymbol{x}} \triangleq (1, \boldsymbol{x}^T)^T \in \mathbb{R}^{(k+1)\times 1}$ denotes the (extended) input vector to the CAN2 and $\widetilde{y}_c = \boldsymbol{M}_c\widetilde{\boldsymbol{x}}$ is the output value of the $c$th unit of the CAN2, and the $c$th unit has the weight vector $\boldsymbol{w}_c$ closest to the input vector $\boldsymbol{x}$, or

$$c \triangleq c(\boldsymbol{x}) \triangleq \underset{i \in I}{\operatorname{argmin}} \|\boldsymbol{x} - \boldsymbol{w}_i\|. \tag{3}$$

The above function approximation partitions the input space $V = \mathbb{R}^k$ into the Voronoi (or Dirichlet) regions

$$V_i \triangleq \{\boldsymbol{x} \mid i = \underset{j \in I}{\operatorname{argmin}} \|\boldsymbol{x} - \boldsymbol{w}_j\|\}, \tag{4}$$

for $i \in I$, and performs piecewise linear approximation of the function $f(\boldsymbol{x})$.

Note that the CAN2 has been introduced for utilizing competitive and associative schemes, on which there are differences to other similar methods. For example, the method of local linear models [16] uses linear models obtained from $K$-nearest neighbors of input vectors while the CAN2 utilizes linear models (associative memories) optimized by the learning involving competitive and associative schemes. The CAN2 may be viewed as a mixture-of-experts model that utilizes linear models as experts and competitive scheme as gating. Although the MARS (multivariate adaptive regression splines) model [17] as a mixture-of-experts model executes continuous piecewise linear approximation, the CAN2 executes discontinuous one intending for optimizing each linear model in the corresponding Voronoi region.

### 2.2 Cross-Validation and the Loss for Tuning Parameter Values

Since the learning method of the CAN2 is for reducing empirical error, we use cross-validation described below for reducing prediction error by means of tuning the parameter values of the CAN2.

Let $D^n = \{(\boldsymbol{x}_j, y_j) \mid j = 1, 2, \cdots, n\}$ be a given training dataset, and assume $\boldsymbol{x}_i \in D^n$ for $i = 1, 2, \cdots, n$ are i.i.d. (independently and identically distributed) in the population. Let $D^m$ be a dataset consisting of $m$ data sampled from $D^n$, and a predictor (a learning machine, or the CAN2 for us) with parameter values denoted by $\theta$ learns $D^m$ and approximates the target value $y_j$ by $\widehat{y}_j = \widehat{f}(\boldsymbol{x}_j) = \widehat{f}(\boldsymbol{x}_j; D^m, \theta)$ corresponding to an input vector $\boldsymbol{x}_j$. Then, we define the mean squared error loss given by

$$L(D^l; D^m, D^n, \theta) \triangleq \frac{1}{l} \sum_{j=1}^{l} \left\| y_j - \widehat{f}(\boldsymbol{x}_j; D^m, \theta) \right\|^2, \tag{5}$$

where $D^l = \{(\boldsymbol{x}_{\rho(i)}, y_{\rho(i)}) \mid i = 1, 2, \cdots, l\}$ indicates a dataset sampled with a certain sequence $\rho(i)$ from the population.

$K$-fold cross-validation, a.k.a. $V$-fold or multifold cross-validation, is described as follows; let $D_j^{n/K}$ for $j = 1, 2, \cdots, K$ be the datasets called folds which partition $D^n$ with almost the same size, where $n/K$ is not always the integer but we use this expression for simplicity. Then, the loss is given by

$$L_{CV(K)} \triangleq \frac{1}{K} \sum_{j=1}^{K} L\left(D_j^{n/K}; D^n \backslash D_j^{n/K}, D^n, \theta\right). \tag{6}$$

When $K = n$ as a special case, $K$-fold cross-validation is called leave-one-out cross-validation whose loss, therefore, is given by

$$L_{LOOCV} \triangleq L_{CV(n)} = \frac{1}{n} \sum_{j=1}^{n} L\left(\boldsymbol{d}_j; D^n \backslash \boldsymbol{d}_j, D^n, \theta\right), \tag{7}$$

where $\boldsymbol{d}_j = (\boldsymbol{x}_j, y_j) \in D^n$. Note that, for the Challenge, we simply had selected the parameter values $\theta^*$ of the predictor (or the CAN2) which had minimized the above loss.

### 2.3 Stochastic Feature of Cross-Validation Applied to Regression Problems

We here would like to make a stochastic interpretation of cross-validation for examining the validity of our strategies which we have used for the Challenge; first, we suppose the target value $y_j$ and the prediction $\widehat{f}(\boldsymbol{x}_j) = \widehat{f}(\boldsymbol{x}_j, D^n, \theta)$ have the relation given by the Gaussian function,

$$p(y_j \mid \boldsymbol{x}_j, D^n, \theta) \triangleq \frac{1}{\sqrt{2\pi}\sigma} \exp\left(-\frac{\|y_j - \widehat{f}(\boldsymbol{x}_j)\|^2}{2\sigma^2}\right) \tag{8}$$

Then, the mean squared error loss for a dataset $D^l = \{(\boldsymbol{x}_{\rho(i)}, y_{\rho(i)}) \mid i = 1, 2, \cdots, l\}$ sampled from the population is derived as

$$
\begin{aligned}
L(D^l; D^n, D^n, \theta) &\triangleq \frac{1}{l}\sum_{j=1}^{l} \|y_{\rho(j)} - \widehat{f}(\boldsymbol{x}_{\rho(j)})\|^2 \\
&= 2\sigma^2 \left[ -\frac{1}{l}\sum_{j=1}^{l} \log p(y_{\rho(j)} \mid \boldsymbol{x}_{\rho(j)}, D^n, \theta) - \log(\sqrt{2\pi}\sigma) \right] \\
&\simeq 2\sigma^2 \left[ -\int\!\!\int \log p(y \mid \boldsymbol{x}, D^n, \theta) q(y|\boldsymbol{x}) q(\boldsymbol{x}) d\boldsymbol{x} dy - \log(\sqrt{2\pi}\sigma) \right] \\
&= 2\sigma^2 \left[ \int KL(q(y|\boldsymbol{x}) \| p(y|\boldsymbol{x}, D^n, \theta)) q(\boldsymbol{x}) d\boldsymbol{x} + c \right] \qquad (9)
\end{aligned}
$$

where $q(\boldsymbol{x})$ and $q(y|\boldsymbol{x})$ indicate the population probabilities,

$$KL(q(y|\boldsymbol{x}) \parallel p(y|\boldsymbol{x}, D^n, \theta)) \triangleq \int q(y|\boldsymbol{x}) \log \frac{q(y|\boldsymbol{x})}{p(y|\boldsymbol{x}, D^n, \theta)} dy \qquad (10)$$

is the Kullback distance between $q(y|\boldsymbol{x})$ and $p(y|\boldsymbol{x}, D^n, \theta)$ for each $\boldsymbol{x}$, and

$$c \triangleq -\int\!\!\int q(y|\boldsymbol{x}) \log(q(y|\boldsymbol{x})) q(\boldsymbol{x}) d\boldsymbol{x} dy - \log(\sqrt{2\pi}\sigma) \qquad (11)$$

is a constant independent to $D^n$ and $\theta$. Here, note that $L(D^l; D^n, D^n, \theta)$ indicates the training (empirical) error when $D^l$ is the training dataset $D^n$, and the generalization (prediction) error when $D^l$ is independent to $D^n$, where however in many cases the generalization error is evaluated over $D^l$ with no datum in $D^n$, which is also assumed by the cross-validation methods. Thus, the loss of $K$-fold cross-validation is written stochastically as

$$L_{CV(K)} \simeq 2\sigma^2 \left[ \frac{1}{K}\sum_{j=1}^{K} \int_{X_j^{n/K}} KL(q(y|\boldsymbol{x}) \| p(y|\boldsymbol{x}, D^n \backslash D_j^{n/K}, \theta_j)) q(\boldsymbol{x}) d\boldsymbol{x} + c \right], \qquad (12)$$

where $X_j^{n/K}$ is the region which involves $\boldsymbol{x}$ of $(\boldsymbol{x}, y) \in D_j^{n/K}$. When $D^n$ is large enough for every $D^n \backslash D_j^{n/K}$ to involve sufficient number of data so that the predictor (the CAN2) can approximate the function to be learned sufficiently, then the predictive distribution by the predictor which has learned $D^n \backslash D_j^{n/K}$ is supposed to be almost the same for all $j$, and we can write

$$
\begin{aligned}
L_{CV(K)} &\simeq 2\sigma^2 \left[ \frac{1}{K}\sum_{j=1}^{K} \int_{X_j^{n/K}} KL(q(y|\boldsymbol{x}) \| p(y|\boldsymbol{x}, D^{n-n/K}, \theta)) q(\boldsymbol{x}) d\boldsymbol{x} + c \right] \\
&\simeq 2\sigma^2 \left[ \int KL(q(y|\boldsymbol{x}) \| p(y|\boldsymbol{x}, D^{n-n/K}, \theta)) q(\boldsymbol{x}) d\boldsymbol{x} + c \right], \qquad (13)
\end{aligned}
$$

where we suppose that the data in $D_j^{n/K}$ are independent to $D^{n-n/K}$ because the data in $D^n$ are i.i.d and that $X_j^{n/K}$ for all $j$ covers all input space because $D^n = \cup_j D_j^{n/K}$. On the other hand, the generalization loss over the population is represented as

$$L_{gen} \triangleq 2\sigma^2 \left[ \int KL(q(y|\boldsymbol{x}) \| p(y|\boldsymbol{x}, D^n, \theta)) q(\boldsymbol{x}) d\boldsymbol{x} + c \right]. \tag{14}$$

Thus, from the above two equations, we can see that a large $K$ ($\leq n$), especially the maximum value $K = n$ or leave-one-out cross-validation, is desirable for estimating the generalization loss $L_{gen}$ by the cross-validation loss $L_{CV(K)}$. However, this result is obtained when $D^n$ is sufficiently large, otherwise $L_{CV(K)}$ may involve bias and variance from the generalization loss much more. In fact, it is often noted that the loss of leave-one-out cross-validation has low bias but sometimes involves high variance [15].

Actually, at the Challenge, we have applied leave-one-out cross-validation to stereopsis and gaze datasets because the change of the loss is smooth and unimodal for the change of parameter values (especially the number of units) of the CAN2 so that we can select the parameter value which minimizes the loss. However, we have used $K = 20$-fold cross-validation for outaouais dataset, because the size of the dataset is very large (20,000) and a large $K$ takes a huge computational cost. Here, we show that the above assumption that $D^n$ is sufficiently large for deriving Eq.(13) is consistent with the following data obtained. Namely, for the stereopsis training dataset ($n = 192$), the number of units selected for approximating the function to be learned is $N = 6$ for lower resolution and $N = 16$ for higher resolution (see below for multi resolution prediction for stereopsis dataset), which indicates $n/N = 32$ and 12 data on average are available for training each $k = 4$ dimensional linear model (associative memory), which seems to indicate that $D^n$ is sufficiently large. For the gaze training dataset ($n = 150$), the selected number of units is $N = 3$, and then $n/N = 50$ seems sufficiently larger than $k = 12$. For the outaouais training dataset ($n = 20000$), the selected number is $N = 330$ and then $n/N = 60.6$ seems to be sufficiently larger than $k = 37$ (practically $k = 32$ because we have almost neglected five elements; see below for details). Thus, it is supposed that the cross-validation loss is almost the same as the generalization loss, and then the prediction $\widehat{f}(\boldsymbol{x})$ is almost the same as the mean value of the predictive distribution.

### 2.4 Estimation of Predictive Uncertainty

There are two methods to submit predictive uncertainty at the Challenge, one is the mean and the variance of the Gaussian distribution and the other is the set of quantiles that describe the predictive distribution. We have used the former for stereopsis and outaouais datasets, and the latter for gaze dataset as follows.

**Estimating Gaussian Distribution.** We set the mean value of the Gaussian distribution by the prediction by the CAN2 after tuning the parameter values by

$K$-fold cross-validation described above ($K = n = 192$ for stereopsis and $K = 20$ for outaouais). We had estimated the predictive gaussian variance for each $\widehat{y}_j$ as follows; by means of $K$-fold cross-validation, the variance of predictions for $\boldsymbol{x}$ in the Voronoi region $V_i$ can be estimated by the mean square error for the validation dataset $D_j^{n/K}$ $(j = 1, 2, \cdots, K)$ given by

$$\widehat{\sigma}_i^2(\boldsymbol{x}) \triangleq \frac{\sum_{j=1}^{K} \sum_{\boldsymbol{x}_l \in V_i \cap X_j^{n/K}} \|y_l - \widehat{f}(\boldsymbol{x}_l)\|^2}{\sum_{\boldsymbol{x}_l \in V_i} 1}. \tag{15}$$

In order to clarify this estimation, we suppose $q(y|\boldsymbol{x}) = p(y|\boldsymbol{x}, D^{n-n/K}, \theta^*) = (1/(\sqrt{2\pi}\sigma_{Ki})) \exp(-\|y - \widehat{f}(\boldsymbol{x})\|^2/(2(\sigma_{Ki})^2))$, and derive a stochastic expression as

$$\begin{aligned}\widehat{\sigma}_i^2(\boldsymbol{x}) &\simeq 2\left(\sigma_{Ki}\right)^2 \left[-\int\!\!\int_{V_i} \log p(y \mid \boldsymbol{x}, D^{n-n/K}, \theta^*) q(y|\boldsymbol{x}) q(\boldsymbol{x}) d\boldsymbol{x} dy - \log(\sqrt{2\pi}\sigma)\right] \\ &\equiv \left(\sigma_{Ki}\right)^2, \end{aligned} \tag{16}$$

where $\theta^*$ indicates the parameter values of the CAN2 which has minimized the cross-validation loss $L_{CV(K)}$. Although this estimation had been applied to the predictive variance which we have submitted for steraopsis and outaouais datasets, a meaning of this estimation is that the estimated variance is the one for the training dataset $D^{n-n/K}$ and we may had better use different $K$ as described in the next section which we had applied to gaze dataset.

**Estimating Quantiles Describing Distribution.** Since the target values of gaze dataset are integer, the quantiles describing the discreet distribution instead of using the gaussian variance was supposed to improve the NLPD, and we had put an effort to estimate precise predictive distribution. First of all, we have to care that gaze dataset involves outliers or input vectors far from the cluster of other input vectors (see Fig. 2). However, the distribution of all data is supposed to be not affected by the outliers so much because they are not so many. Only the treatment we had done for such outliers is that if the input vector $\boldsymbol{x}_j$ has negative $x_{j3}$ or $x_{j4}$ we describe its distribution by the gaussian variance with the value 4500 which is identified by cross-validation, while the distribution of other data are described by the quantiles obtained as follows.

For obtaining predictive distribution, we first calculate the sum of distributions of prediction error obtained via $K$-fold cross-validations for several $K$, namely we had estimated the predictive distribution by

$$\widehat{p}(e|D^n) \triangleq \frac{1}{C} \sum_{K \in J_K} \sum_{j=1}^{K} \sum_{\boldsymbol{x} \in X_j^{n/K}} p(e|\boldsymbol{x}, D^n \backslash D_j^{n/K}, \theta^*) \tag{17}$$

where $e$ indicates the prediction error $e = \widehat{f}(\boldsymbol{x}) - y$, $C$ is the constant for normalizing $\widehat{p}(e|D^n)$ and $J_K$ is a set of $K$ of $K$-fold cross-validation, and we actually

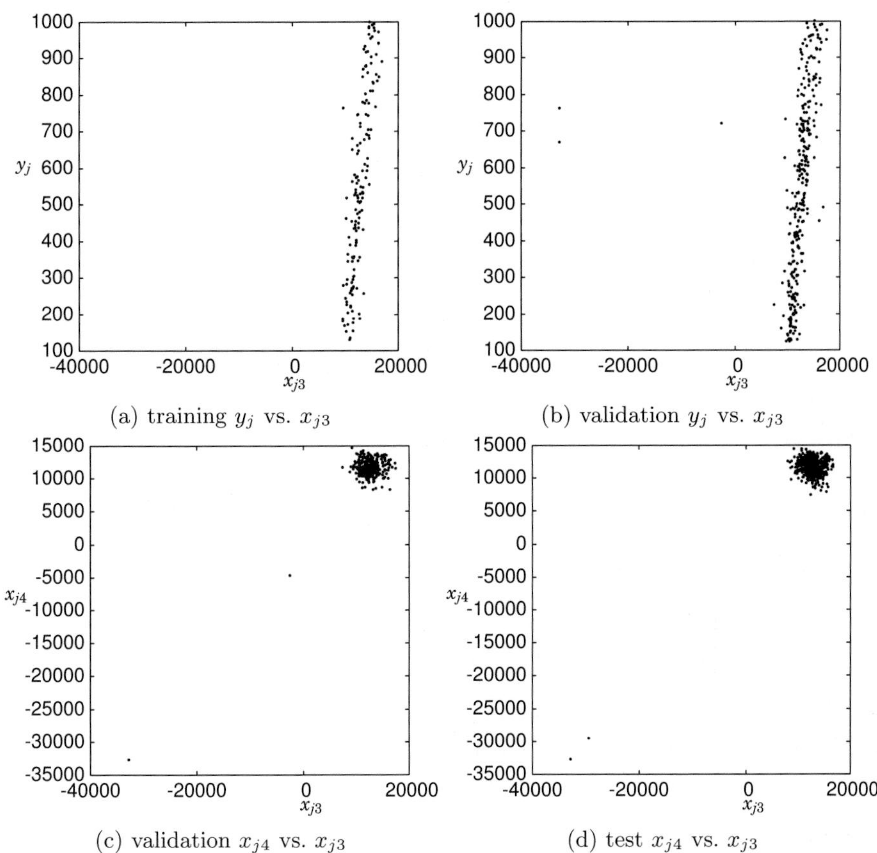


(a) training $y_j$ vs. $x_{j3}$

(b) validation $y_j$ vs. $x_{j3}$

(c) validation $x_{j4}$ vs. $x_{j3}$

(d) test $x_{j4}$ vs. $x_{j3}$

**Fig. 2.** Outliers of gaze dataset

had used $J_K = \{2, 3, 4, 5, 6, 7, 8, 9, 10, 11, 12, 13, 15, 16, 18, 21, 25, 30, 50, 75, 150\}$ for the submission. Here, note that we at first used the distribution obtained only via $J_K = \{K = n = 150\}$ or leave-one-out cross-validation, with which we could not have small NLPD owing supposedly that the number of data is not large enough to approximate the distribution to be obtained (see Fig. 3(a), where $\widetilde{p}(e|D^n)$ is the quantized $\widehat{p}(e|D^n)$ introduced below). Further, if we use all integer values from $K = 2$ to 150, the result had not been so different and it takes a huge computational cost. Note that this method is ad hoc, but we try to make an interpretation in the next section. Next, we calculate the predictive distribution for the input data $\boldsymbol{x}$ given by

$$\widehat{p}(y|\boldsymbol{x}, D^n) \triangleq \widehat{p}(\widehat{f}(\boldsymbol{x}) + e|\boldsymbol{x}, D^n). \tag{18}$$

Finally, since the target values of gaze dataset are integer, it is ideal to express the distribution by $\widetilde{p}(y|D^n) = \sum_m \widehat{p}(y|\boldsymbol{x}, D^n)\delta(y - m)$ with the Dirac delta

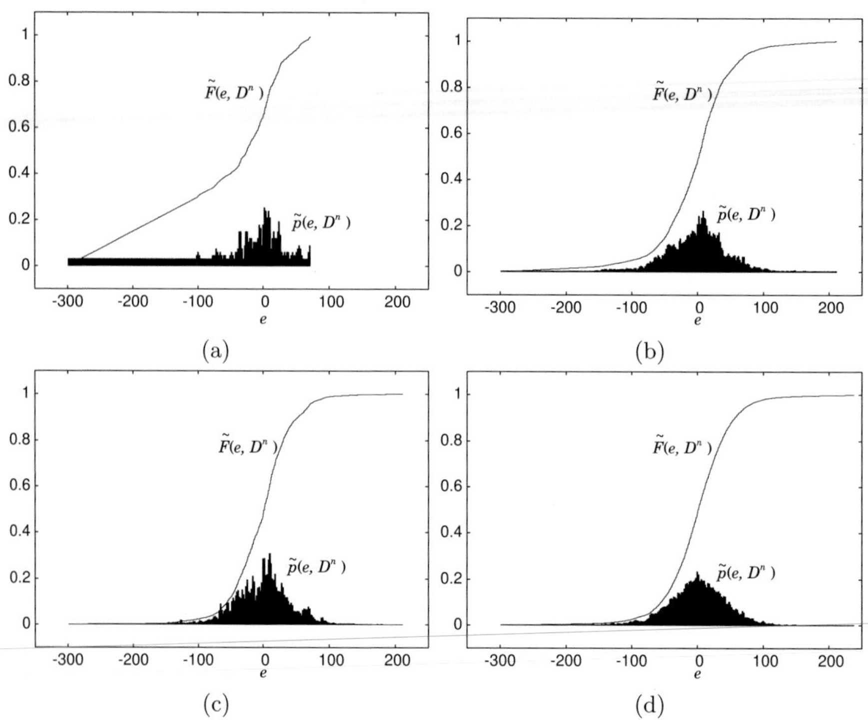


**Fig. 3.** Estimated distribution of prediction error $\widetilde{p}(e|D^n)$ and the cumulative distribution $\widetilde{F}(e|D^n) = \int_{-\infty}^{e} \widetilde{p}(z, D^n)dz$. The distribution is the sum of the prediction error distributions obtained by $K$-fold cross-validation for $K \in J_K$ and (a) $J_K = \{150\}$, (b) $J_K = \{2, 3, 4, 5, 6, 7, 8, 9, 10, 11, 12, 13, 15, 16, 18, 21, 25, 30, 50, 75, 150\}$, (c) $J_K$ consisting of all integers from 2 to 150, which are obtained with the given training dataset($n = 150$). (d) is of $J_K = \{2, 3, 4, 5, 6, 7, 8, 9, 10, 11, 12, 13, 15, 16, 18, 21, 25, 30, 50, 75, 150, 200, 300, 450\}$ for the dataset ($n = 450$) consisting of the training data ($n = 150$) and validation data ($n = 300$). See text for details.

function $\delta(y)$, which however cannot be dealt with by the evaluation program "eval.py" [1] thus we approximate the distribution as

$$\widetilde{p}(y|\boldsymbol{x}, D^n) \triangleq \frac{1}{\widetilde{C}} \sum_{m=m_{\min}}^{m_{\max}} \widehat{p}(y|\boldsymbol{x}, D^n) d_T(y - m) \tag{19}$$

where $\widetilde{C}$ is the constant for normalizing $\widetilde{p}(y|\boldsymbol{x}, D^n)$,

$$d_T(y) \triangleq \begin{cases} 1 \text{ if } |y| \leq T \\ 0 \text{ otherwise} \end{cases} \tag{20}$$

is the pulse function with $T$ (we have used $T = 5.5 \times 10^{-5}$).

[1] The evaluation program "eval.py" is the python program that has been provided from the web page[1].

**Stochastic Analysis of the Method.** Although the aim of the above method is for estimating the predictive distribution of $p(y|\boldsymbol{x}, D^n)$, it is not so clear whether $\widehat{p}(y|\boldsymbol{x}, D^n)$ in Eq.(19) adequately estimates $p(y|\boldsymbol{x}, D^n)$ or not. In order to clarify it, suppose that $D^n$ is large enough for every $D^n \backslash D_j^{n/K}$ to involve sufficient number of data for approximating the function to be learned, then for every $K$ and $j$ the predictive distribution by the predictor which learns $D^n \backslash D_j^{n/K}$ is supposed to be almost the same as the predictive distribution to be obtained $p(y|\boldsymbol{x}, D^n)$. Thus, for obtaining the distribution over the input space, the error distribution

$$\widehat{p}(e|D^{n-n/K}) \triangleq \sum_{j=1}^{K} \sum_{\boldsymbol{x} \in X_j^{n/K}} p(e|\boldsymbol{x}, D^n \backslash D_j^{n/K}, \theta^*) \tag{21}$$

for all $K$ and the normalized sum

$$\widehat{p}(e|D^n) \equiv \frac{1}{C} \sum_{K \in J_K} \widehat{p}(e|D^{n-n/K}) \tag{22}$$

are also suppose to be almost the same as the predictive error distribution to be obtained. Thus, $\widehat{p}(y|\boldsymbol{x}, D^n) = \widehat{p}(\widehat{f}(\boldsymbol{x}) + e|\boldsymbol{x}, D^n)$ is supposed to estimate $p(y|\boldsymbol{x}, D^n)$.

The validity of the above interpretation seems to depend on the supposition that $D^n$ is large enough for every $D_j^{n-n/K}$ to involve sufficient number of data for approximating the function to be learned. Since the optimized number of units of the CAN2 is $N = 3$ for gaze training dataset $D^n = D^{150}$, a unit is supposed to learn $(n - n/K)/N = 25$ to $49.7$ training data on average for $K = 2$ to $150$, which seems sufficient for learning by the $k = 12$ dimensional linear model(or associative matrix). Thus, it is considered that the above method works. Actually, we have had the best NLPD for gaze dataset at the Challenge.

It is embarrassing, but we here have to note that the submitted predictions had been generated with the dataset with $n = 450$ consisting of the training data ($n = 150$) and the validation data ($n = 300$) although the submitted distribution had been produced via the original training data ($n = 150$) as described above, which means that we should have submitted the distribution calculated with the combined training dataset with $n = 450$, then the numerical values described above are slightly changed as follows; the optimized number of units is $N = 6$, so that the average number of data for a unit, $(n - n/K)/N$, ranges from 37.5 ($K = 2$) to 74.8 ($K = 450$) which is much sufficient enough for learning by the $k = 12$ dimensional linear model. Thus, the distribution of prediction error with $J_K = \{2, 3, 4, 5, 6, 7, 8, 9, 10, 11, 12, 13, 15, 16, 18, 21, 25, 30, 50, 75, 150, 200, 300, 450\}$ (see Fig. 3(d)) is smoother than Fig. 3(b) submitted. With this distribution, we may be able to make the NLPD smaller.

# 3 Procedure and Strategies for Solving Regression Problems at the Challenge

Here, we summarize the procedure and the strategies for achieving small MSE and then small NLPD in solving regression problems at the Challenge.

**Step 1.** Tune roughly the scale of every element of input vectors so that all elements may distribute equally on the input space as much as possible, or actually, for the $l$th element of input vectors $\boldsymbol{x}_j = (x_{j1}, \cdots, x_{jl}, \cdots, x_{jk})^T$ ($j = 1, 2, \cdots, n$), tune $a_l$ and $b_l$ of the linear transformation $x_{jl} := a_l x_{jl} + b_l$. These parameters will be tuned precisely at the cross-validation step shown below. Further, we have tuned $b_l$ as well as $a_l$ so that all the data (training, valid and test) will be in the unit hyper-cube.

*Example.* An example of the original and tuned distributions is shown in Fig. 4, where the tuned one is obtained after the cross-validation shown below. From this figure, the original distribution for $x_{j2}$ seems sparse relatively to the distribution for $x_{j1}$ and the difference seems to be reduced in the tuned distribution.

**Step 2.** When the target values seem to take only discrete values, identify the values, and let the predictor (learning machine) output only such discrete values.

*Example.* The target values of gaze dataset take only integer values, and those of stereopsis dataset seem to cluster around the discrete values $y = 11.8561m + 123.818$ for $m = 1, 2, \cdots$ (see Fig. 5), while we will apply multi-resolution prediction for stereopsis dataset as shown in Step 4 described bellow.

**Step 3.** Apply $K$-fold cross-validation to tune the parameters of the learning machine so that the mean square error loss $L_{CV(K)}$ become smaller. The parameters $a_l$ and $b_l$ for scaling the $l$th element are also tuned precisely here. As

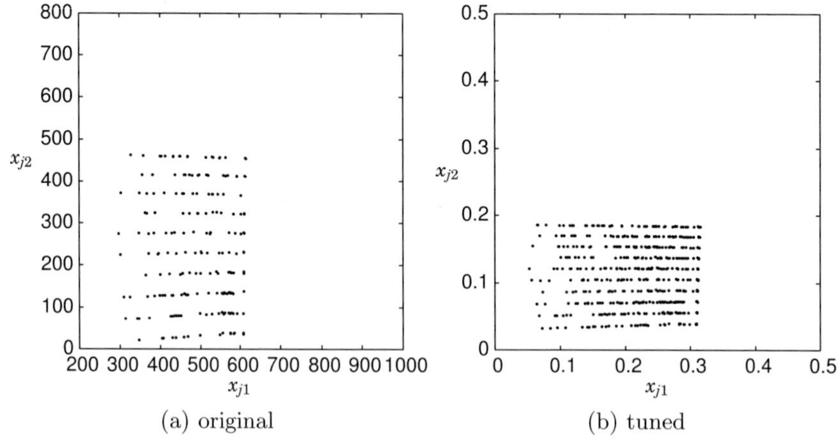


(a) original (b) tuned

**Fig. 4.** Distribution of the original and tuned $x_{j1}$ and $x_{j2}$ for stereopsis training data

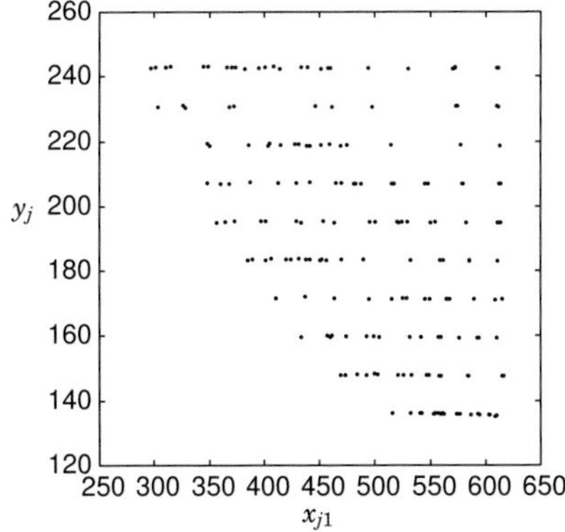


**Fig. 5.** The chunks of target values $y_j$ of stereopsis training data

mentioned before, we have used leave-one-out cross-validation or $K = n$ for stereopsis ($n = 192$), and gaze ($n = 150$) datasets, and $K = 20$ for outaouais dataset.

*Example.* For outaouais dataset, $a_l$ for $l = 25, 32, 33, 34$ and 36 have been set very small so that those elements have been neglected. We do not tune $a_l$ for stereopsis and gaze datasets so much because the result looks like to have achieved a sufficient level.

**Step 4.** When the output values of the predictor have been restricted as described in Step 2, store the loss $L_{CV(K)}$, say $L^1_{CV(K)}$, and every prediction error $e(\boldsymbol{x}_j) = y_j - \widehat{f}(\boldsymbol{x}_j; D^n \backslash D^{n/K}_{l(j)}, \theta^*)$ $(j = 1, 2, \cdots, n)$ obtained via the cross-validation with the optimal parameter $\theta^*$, say $\theta^{1*}$, where $D^{n/K}_{l(j)}$ indicates the fold which includes $\boldsymbol{x}_j$. Further, train $e(\boldsymbol{x}_j)$ $(j = 1, 2, \cdots, n)$ as target values of input vectors $\boldsymbol{x}_j$ via cross-validation, and obtain the loss $L_{CV(K)}$, say $L^2_{CV(K)}$, for the prediction of $e(\boldsymbol{x}_j)$. When $L^2_{CV(K)}$ with optimized parameter values, say $\theta^{2*}$, is smaller than $L^1_{CV(K)}$ we make the final predictions given by $\widehat{y}_j = \widehat{f}(\boldsymbol{x}_j; D^n, \theta^{1*}) + \widehat{f}(\boldsymbol{x}_j; D^n, \theta^{2*})$, which we say multi-resolution prediction. Otherwise we make the final predictions given by $\widehat{y}_j = \widehat{f}(\boldsymbol{x}_j; D^n, \theta^{1*})$.

*Example.* The loss $L^2_{CV(K)}$ had been smaller than $L^1_{CV(K)}$ not for gaze but for stereopsis dataset, so that we execute the multi-resolution prediction for stereopsis dataset.

**Step 5.** Obtain the predictive variance of the Gaussian distribution or the predictive quantile distribution as described in Sec. **2.4**.

## 4 Conclusion

We have described the CAN2 and cross-validation which we have used for making prediction error small and estimating predictive distribution accurately on the regression problems at Evaluating Predictive Uncertainty Challenge. We have also shown stochastic analysis of the method for estimating predictive uncertainty from an analogy of the Bayesian learning theory. Although we have obtained good score at the Challenge with the same procedure and strateges applied to all of the three regression problems, it is clarified in this article that our method largely depends on the supposition that given training dataset is sufficiently large. Thus, in order to improve the present method for dealing with smaller datasets, it may be useful and possible to incorporate Bayesian scheme which uses variable learning machines for generating predictive distribution while cross-validation uses variable datasets smaller than given training dataset.

The authors would like to thank the organizers who have promoted this Challenge, from which we could have obtained various information on prediction problems and we could improved our method by means of solving the problems. Finally, we would like to note that our works on the CAN2 are partially supported by the Grant-in-Aid for Scientific Research (B) 16300070 of the Japanese Ministry of Education, Science, Sports and Culture.

## References

1. `http://predict.kyb.tuebingen.mpg.de/pages/home.php`
2. T. Kohonen: Associative Memory, *Springer Verlag* (1977)
3. D. E. Rumelhart and D. Zipser: A feature discovery by competitive learning, ed. D. E. Rumelhart, J. L. McClelland and the PDP Research Group: Parallel Distributed Processing, The MIT Press, Cambridge, vol.1, 151–193 (1986)
4. P. Mueller and D. R. Insua: Issues in Bayesian analysis of neural network models, Neural Computation, 10, 571–592 (1995)
5. J. M. Bernardo and A. D. M. Smith: Bayesian Theory, New York, John Wiley (1994)
6. `http://www.cs.toronto.edu/~radford/fbm.software.html`
7. S. Kurogi, M. Tou and S. Terada: Rainfall estimation using competitive associative net, Proc. of 2001 IEICE General Conference (in Japanese), vol.SD-1, 260–261 (2001)
8. S. Kurogi: Asymptotic optimality of competitive associative nets for their learning in function approximation, Proc. of the 9th International Conference on Neural Information Processing, vol. 1, 507–511, (2002)
9. S. Kurogi: Asymptotic optimality of competitive associative nets and its application to incremental learning of nonlinear functions, Trans. of IEICE D-II (in Japanese), vol. J86-D-II no. 2, 184–194 (2003)
10. S. Kurogi, T. Ueno and M. Sawa: A batch learning method for competitive associative net and its application to function approximation, Proc. of SCI2004, no.V, 24–28 (2004)
11. S. Kurogi, T. Ueno and M. Sawa: Batch learning competitive associative net and its application to time series prediction, Proc. of IJCNN 2004, International Joint Conference on Neural Networks, Budapest (Hungary), CD-ROM, (25-29 July 2004)
12. B. Efron :Estimating the error rate of a prediction rule: improvement on cross-validation, Journal of the American Statistical Association, 78(382), 316-331 (1983)
13. R. Kohavi: A study of cross-validation and bootstrap for accuracy estimation and model selection. Proc. of the Fourteenth International Conference 18 on Artificial Intelligence (IJCAI), 1137–1143, San Mateo, CA, Morgan Kaufmann (1995)

14. B. Efron and R. Tbshirani: Improvements on cross-validation: the .632+ bootstrap method, Journal of the American Statistical Association, 92, 548–560 (1997)
15. A. Elisseeff and M. Pontil: Leave-one-out error and stability of learning algorithms with applications, in : Advances in Learning Theory: Methods, Models and Applications, NATO Advanced Study Institute on Learning Theory and Practice, 111-130 (2002)
16. J.D.Farmer and J.J.Sidorowich: Predicting chaotic time series. Phys. Rev.Lett., 59:845–848 (1987)
17. J.H.Friedman: Multivariate adaptive regression splines. Ann Stat, 19, 1-50 (1991)
18. M.I.Jordan and R.A.Jacobs: Hierarchical mixtures of experts and the EM algorithm. Neural Computation, 6:181–214 (1994)


## Appendix: Batch Learning Method for the CAN2

The batch learning method that we have used for the Challenge is supposed to have contributed to solving the problems effectively and efficiently because its performance in learning finite number of training data has been shown higher than online learning method for the CAN2[11]. Here, we summarize the method as follows, where several parts are modified from [11] and constant values specified for the Challenge are presented; let us denote the training set of input-output data by $D \triangleq \{(\boldsymbol{x}_j, y_j = f(\boldsymbol{x}_j) + d_j) \mid j \in J \triangleq \{1, 2, \cdots, n\}\}$, the set of input vectors by $X \triangleq \{\boldsymbol{x}_j \mid j \in J\}$, and the set of output values by $Y \triangleq \{y_j \mid j \in J\}$. The learning of the CAN2 is designed for minimizing the energy or the mean square error given by

$$E \triangleq \frac{1}{n} \sum_{i \in I} \sum_{\boldsymbol{x} \in X_i} \|e(\boldsymbol{x})\|^2 = \sum_{i \in I} E_i, \tag{23}$$

by means of modifying $\boldsymbol{w}_i$ and $\boldsymbol{M}_i$ for $i = 1, 2, \cdots, N$, where $e(\boldsymbol{x}) \triangleq \widehat{f}(\boldsymbol{x}) - f(\boldsymbol{x}) \triangleq \boldsymbol{M}_{c(\boldsymbol{x})}\widetilde{\boldsymbol{x}} - f(\boldsymbol{x})$ is the training (empirical) error, $X_i = \{\boldsymbol{x} \in X \cap V_i\}$ is the set of training input vectors in the Voronoi region $V_i$, and $E_i \triangleq (1/n)\sum_{\boldsymbol{x} \in X_i} \|e(\boldsymbol{x})\|^2$ is the energy of the region.

This minimization problem is a nonlinear one, and we repeat the optimization iteration consisting of a batch modification of $\boldsymbol{w}_i$ for all $i \in I$, and a batch modification of $\boldsymbol{M}_i$ for all $i \in I$, followed by reinitialization, as follows.

**Modification of Weight Vectors.** Provided that $\boldsymbol{M}_i$ $(i \in I)$ are constant, we can optimize $\boldsymbol{w}_i$ via the following gradient method; let the boundary of a Voronoi region $V_i$ and the adjacent $V_l$ with the width $W_\theta$ $(< 1;$ we have used $0.2)$ be

$$W_{il} \triangleq \left\{ \boldsymbol{x} \;\middle|\; \boldsymbol{x} \in X_i \cup X_l \quad \text{and} \quad \frac{\left|(2\boldsymbol{x} - \boldsymbol{w}_i - \boldsymbol{w}_l)^T(\boldsymbol{w}_i - \boldsymbol{w}_l)\right|}{\|\boldsymbol{w}_i - \boldsymbol{w}_l\|^2} \le W_\theta \right\}. \tag{24}$$

When a training vector $\boldsymbol{x}$ is in $W_{il}$ and moves from $V_i$ to $V_l$ (or from $V_l$ to $V_i$) owing to the change of $\boldsymbol{w}_i$ by $\Delta\boldsymbol{w}_i$, the energy $E$ increases by $(1/n)(e_i^2(\boldsymbol{x}) - e_l^2(\boldsymbol{x})) \times s$ where $s \triangleq \mathrm{sign}(\Delta\boldsymbol{w}_i^T(\boldsymbol{x} - \boldsymbol{w}_i))$, while $E$ does not change when $\boldsymbol{x} \in V_i$

and $s = 1$ or $\boldsymbol{x} \in V_l$ and $s = -1$. Thus, the increase of $E$ is discontinuous, but it can be stochastically approximated by

$$\Delta E \simeq \frac{1}{2n} \Delta \boldsymbol{w}_i^T \boldsymbol{\xi}_i, \tag{25}$$

where

$$\boldsymbol{\xi}_i \triangleq \sum_{l \in A_i} \sum_{\boldsymbol{x} \in W_{il}} (e_i^2(\boldsymbol{x}) - e_l^2(\boldsymbol{x})) \frac{\boldsymbol{x} - \boldsymbol{w}_i}{||\boldsymbol{x} - \boldsymbol{w}_i||}, \tag{26}$$

and $A_i$ is the index set of $V_l$ adjacent to $V_i$. Thus, in order to decrease $E$, we modify the weight vectors as $\Delta \boldsymbol{w}_i = -\gamma \boldsymbol{\xi}_i$, or

$$\boldsymbol{w}_i := \boldsymbol{w}_i - \gamma \boldsymbol{\xi}_i \tag{27}$$

for $i \in I$, where $:=$ indicates the substitution. We use the learning rate

$$\gamma \triangleq \frac{\gamma_0}{1 + t/t_0} \frac{d_x}{d_\xi}, \tag{28}$$

where $\gamma_0$ ($< 1$; we have used 0.05) is a positive constant, $t$ ($= 0, 1, 2, \cdots$) indicates global time or the number of batch modification having done so far, and $t_0$ is a constant. For all cases in solving the regression problems of the Challenge, we have used $t_0 = 5$, and $t$ is terminated at 100 until when the training (empirical) error had converged in all cases. Note that the part $t/t_0$ is augmented from [11] for faster convergence. The parameter $d_x$ is the maximum width between the elements $x_{jl}$ of $\boldsymbol{x}_j$ as follows

$$d_x \triangleq \max_{l=1,\cdots,k} \left( \max_{\substack{i \in J \\ j \in J}} |x_{il} - x_{jl}| \right), \tag{29}$$

and $d_\xi$ is the maximum value of the element $\xi_{il}$ of $\boldsymbol{\xi}_i$ as follows,

$$d_\xi \triangleq \max_{l=1,\cdots,k} \max_{i \in I} \xi_{il}. \tag{30}$$

Thus, $\gamma = (\gamma_0/(1 + t/t_0))(d_x/d_\xi)$ guarantees that the absolute value of the element of weight change, $|\Delta w_{ij}| = |\gamma \xi_{ij}|$, is less than the maximum span of the elements of input vectors, $d_x = \max_{l,i,j} |x_{il} - x_{jl}|$ multiplied by $(\gamma_0/(1 + t/t_0))$.

All initial weight vectors $\boldsymbol{w}_i$ ($i \in I$) are set by the vectors selected randomly from the training input vectors $\boldsymbol{x}_j$ ($j \in J$) at only the first batch learning iteration.

**Modification of Associative Matrices.** Provided that the weight vectors $\boldsymbol{w}_i$ ($i \in I$) are constant, the nonlinear problem of minimizing $E = \sum_{i \in I} E_i$ becomes a linear one to minimize

$$E_i = \frac{1}{n} ||\boldsymbol{M}_i \widetilde{\boldsymbol{X}}_i - \boldsymbol{Y}_i||^2 \tag{31}$$

for each $i$, and the solution is given by $\boldsymbol{M}_i = \boldsymbol{Y}_i \widetilde{\boldsymbol{X}}_i^+$, where $\widetilde{\boldsymbol{X}}_i^+$ is the generalized inverse of the matrix $\widetilde{\boldsymbol{X}}_i \in \mathbb{R}^{(k+1)\times n_i}$ which consists of $\widetilde{\boldsymbol{x}} = (1, \boldsymbol{x}^T)^T$ for all $\boldsymbol{x} \in X_i$, and $\boldsymbol{Y}_i \in \mathbb{R}^{1\times n_i}$ is the matrix consisting of $y = f(\boldsymbol{x}) + d$ for all $\boldsymbol{x} \in X_i$. In order to avoid the situation where $n_i$ or the number of the vectors in $X_i$ is so small that the approximation error may become large, we do not use the unit with $n_i = 0$ for modifying $\boldsymbol{w}_i$ and $\boldsymbol{M}_i$ and calculating the output of the CAN2 until the reinitialization (see below) is triggered. Further, for $X_i$ with $n_i \geq 1$, we compensate training vectors near $V_i$ up to a certain number $n_\theta$ (we have used 3 for all cases), or search the training vectors in

$$B_i \triangleq \{\boldsymbol{x}_j \,|\boldsymbol{x}_j \in X \backslash X_i, \|\boldsymbol{x}_j - \boldsymbol{w}_i\| \leq \|\boldsymbol{x}_l - \boldsymbol{w}_i\| \text{ for } \boldsymbol{x}_l \in X \backslash B_i, |B_i| = n_\theta - n_i\}, \tag{32}$$

where $|B_i|$ is the number of the vectors in $B_i$, and then set $X_i := X_i \cup B_i$ for calculating $\boldsymbol{M}_i = \boldsymbol{Y}_i \widetilde{\boldsymbol{X}}_i^+$. Further, for stable learning performance accompanied with modifying $\boldsymbol{w}_i$ ($i \in I$), we do not directly calculate $\boldsymbol{M}_i = \boldsymbol{Y}_i \widetilde{\boldsymbol{X}}_i^+$, but apply the following RLS (recursive least square) method,

$$\boldsymbol{M}_i := \boldsymbol{M}_i + \frac{(y - \boldsymbol{M}_i \widetilde{\boldsymbol{x}})\, \widetilde{\boldsymbol{x}}^T \boldsymbol{\Psi}_i}{1 + \widetilde{\boldsymbol{x}}^T \boldsymbol{\Psi}_i \widetilde{\boldsymbol{x}}}, \tag{33}$$

where $\boldsymbol{\Psi}_i \in \mathbb{R}^{(k+1)\times(k+1)}$ is also updated as

$$\boldsymbol{\Psi}_i := \boldsymbol{\Psi}_i - \frac{\boldsymbol{\Psi}_i \widetilde{\boldsymbol{x}} \widetilde{\boldsymbol{x}}^T \boldsymbol{\Psi}_i}{1 + \widetilde{\boldsymbol{x}}^T \boldsymbol{\Psi}_i \widetilde{\boldsymbol{x}}}, \tag{34}$$

and the above two updates are applied for all $\boldsymbol{x} \in X_i$ and the corresponding $y \in Y_i$ for all $i \in I$ once at each batch iteration. Further, at only the first batch iteration, we set the initial values to the matrices as $\boldsymbol{M}_i = \boldsymbol{O}$ and $\boldsymbol{\Psi}_i = \boldsymbol{I}/\epsilon$, respectively, where $\boldsymbol{O}$ and $\boldsymbol{I}$ are the null (zero) and unit matrices, respectively, and $\epsilon$ is a small constant (we have used $\epsilon := 10^{-4}$).

**Reinitialization.** The gradient method for modifying $\boldsymbol{w}_i$ shown above has the local minima problem. To overcome the problem, the condition called asymptotic optimality for a large number of weight vectors has been derived and the online learning methods embedding this condition are shown effective [8, 9]. Here, we also embed it to the present batch learning, as follows; first suppose there are many input data and weight vectors, and let the energy be given by

$$E = \sum_{i\in I} \int_{V_i} \|e_i(\boldsymbol{x})\|^2 p(\boldsymbol{x}) d\boldsymbol{x} = \sum_{i\in I} E_i, \tag{35}$$

where $p(\boldsymbol{x})$ is the probability density function of the training data $\boldsymbol{x}$. Further, suppose the area of $V_i$ is small and $p(\boldsymbol{x})$ is approximated by a constant $p_i$ in each $V_i$, and $f(\boldsymbol{x})$ is the function of class $C^2$, then we have

$$\begin{aligned} E = \sum_{i\in I} E_i = & \sum_{i\in I} (C_i p_i v_i^{1+4/k} + \sigma_2^2 p_i v_i) \\ \geq & N^{-4/k} \|C(\boldsymbol{x}) p(\boldsymbol{x})\|_{\frac{1}{1+4/k}} + \sigma_d^2, \end{aligned} \tag{36}$$

where $C_i \triangleq C(\boldsymbol{w}_i)$ is called quantization coefficient which represents the complexity of $f(\boldsymbol{x})$ at $\boldsymbol{x}=\boldsymbol{w}_i$ (see [8, 9] for details). And $\|g(\boldsymbol{x})\|_\alpha = \left(\int_V |g(\boldsymbol{x})|^\alpha d\boldsymbol{x}\right)^{1/\alpha}$, $\|C(\boldsymbol{x})p(\boldsymbol{x})\|_{\frac{1}{1+4/k}}$ is constant for the given $f(\boldsymbol{x})$ and $p(\boldsymbol{x})$. Further, the right hand side of Eq.(36) is the minimum of $E$ and the equality holds iff

$$\alpha_i \triangleq C_i p_i v_i^{1+4/k} = \text{constant for all } i \in I. \tag{37}$$

This equation represents the condition of asymptotic optimality, which can be used as follows.

From Eq.(23), Eq.(36) and Eq.(37), the square error $S_i$ of the $i$th unit is given by

$$S_i \triangleq \sum_{\boldsymbol{x}\in X_i} \|e(\boldsymbol{x})\|^2 \simeq n\alpha_i + \sigma_d^2 n_i. \tag{38}$$

On the other hand, when there is a region $V_i$ where $f(\boldsymbol{x})$ is approximated by a linear function which may be achieved with many weight vectors, then $C_i$ and $\alpha_i$ are 0, and we can estimate the variance of the noise $d_i$ by

$$\widehat{\sigma}_d^2 := \min\{S_i/n_i \mid i \in I \text{ and } n_i \geq \theta_U\}, \tag{39}$$

where $\theta_U$ is a constant much larger than the dimension $k$ of $\boldsymbol{x}$ because $S_i = 0$ for the optimum $\boldsymbol{M}_i$ when $n_i \leq k$ is not appropriate for estimating $\sigma_d^2$. Then, from Eq.(38) and Eq.(39), we can estimate $\alpha_i$ as

$$\widehat{\alpha}_i := \frac{S_i - \widehat{\sigma}_d^2 n_i}{n}. \tag{40}$$

In order to decide whether $\alpha_i$ $(i \in I)$ satisfy the asymptotic optimality of Eq.(37) or not, we use the following condition

$$\frac{\widehat{\alpha}_i}{\langle\widehat{\alpha}_i\rangle} \geq \theta_\alpha \quad \text{and} \quad \frac{H}{\ln(N)} \leq \theta_H, \tag{41}$$

where $\theta_\alpha$ $(> 1;$ we have used 5) and $\theta_H$ $(< 1;$ we have used 0.7) are positive constants, $\langle\widehat{\alpha}_i\rangle$ is the mean of $\widehat{\alpha}_i$, and $H$ is the entropy given by

$$H \triangleq -\sum_{i\in I} \frac{\alpha_i}{\sum_{j\in J}\alpha_j} \ln\left(\frac{\alpha_i}{\sum_{j\in I}\alpha_j}\right). \tag{42}$$

When the above condition in Eq.(41) is fulfilled, we reinitialize the $s(j)$th unit that has the $j$th smallest $\widehat{\alpha}_i$ for all $i \in I$ (the unit with $n_i = 0$ as described above is supposed to have the smallest $\widehat{\alpha}_i = 0$), and move it near to the $b(j)$th unit that satisfies the former inequality in Eq.(41) and have the $j$th biggest $\widehat{\alpha}_i$ for all $i \in I$, as follows

$$\boldsymbol{w}_{s(j)} := \boldsymbol{w}_{b(j)} + \theta_r(\boldsymbol{x}_{c(b(j))} - \boldsymbol{w}_{b(j)}), \tag{43}$$

$$\boldsymbol{M}_{s(j)} := \boldsymbol{M}_{b(j)}, \tag{44}$$

where $\boldsymbol{x}_{c(b(j))}$ is the training vector nearest to $\boldsymbol{w}_{b(j)}$. We use the value $\theta_r = 1.9$, which guarantees that the region $V_{s(j)}$ of the new $\boldsymbol{w}_{s(j)}$ involves at least one training vector $\boldsymbol{x}_{c(b(j))}$.

# Lessons Learned in the Challenge: Making Predictions and Scoring Them

Jukka Kohonen and Jukka Suomela

Helsinki Institute for Information Technology, Basic Research Unit,
Department of Computer Science, P.O. Box 68,
FI-00014 University of Helsinki, Finland
jukka.kohonen@cs.helsinki.fi,
jukka.suomela@cs.helsinki.fi

**Abstract.** In this paper we present lessons learned in the Evaluating Predictive Uncertainty Challenge. We describe the methods we used in regression challenges, including our winning method for the Outaouais data set. We then turn our attention to the more general problem of scoring in probabilistic machine learning challenges. It is widely accepted that scoring rules should be proper in the sense that the true generative distribution has the best expected score; we note that while this is useful, it does not guarantee finding the best methods for practical machine learning tasks. We point out some problems in local scoring rules such as the negative logarithm of predictive density (NLPD), and illustrate with examples that many of these problems can be avoided by a distance-sensitive rule such as the continuous ranked probability score (CRPS).

## 1 Introduction

In this paper we present lessons learned in the *Evaluating Predictive Uncertainty Challenge* (EPUC). The challenge was organised by Joaquin Quiñonero Candela, Carl Edward Rasmussen, and Yoshua Bengio, and the deadline for submission was in December 2004. The challenge consisted of five tasks: two classification tasks (where the targets are discrete, in this case binary), and three regression tasks (where the targets are continuous). We describe the methods we used in the regression tasks, and some lessons to learn from the methods and from the results. We have included our winning method for the 'Outaouais' data set, our abuse of the scoring method in the 'Gaze' data set, as well as our miserable failure with the 'Stereopsis' data set.

Inspired by observations made in the regression tasks, we will turn our attention to the more general problem of *scoring* in probabilistic machine learning challenges. Probabilistic predictions take the form of discrete distributions for classification tasks, and of continuous distributions for regression tasks. Scoring in classification is better understood, especially in the case of binary classification. In this paper, we focus on regression.

Ideally, the scoring function would guide competitors' work: by selfishly maximising their own score they would also work towards a common good in machine learning research and practice. It is widely accepted that scoring rules should be

J. Quiñonero-Candela et al. (Eds.): MLCW 2005, LNAI 3944, pp. 95–116, 2006.

*proper* in the sense that the true generative distribution has the best expected score. We note that while this is useful, it does not guarantee finding the best methods for practical machine learning tasks.

We will discuss what else is required of a scoring rule in addition to properness. We will point out some problems in using *local* scores, which depend only on the predictive density exactly at the true target value. We illustrate with examples that many of these problems can be avoided by using *distance sensitive* scores, which also depend on how much predictive probability mass is placed *near* the true target. As an example of a local rule we will consider the *logarithmic score* and the corresponding loss function, *negative logarithm of predictive density* (NLPD). As an example of a distance sensitive rule we will consider the *continuous ranked probability score* (CRPS).

Finally, we will briefly discuss how one can *represent* continuous predictions. Both in challenges and in practical applications there is obviously a need for a finite representation. We observe that a *sample* can be used as a very simple representation of an arbitrary distribution, provided that one is using a non-local scoring rule such as CRPS.

This paper is organised as follows. In Section 2, we describe the methods we used in the challenge. The general problem of scoring in probabilistic challenges is discussed in Section 3. Section 4 is devoted to discussing what other properties of scoring functions would be useful in addition to properness. Finally, we discuss in Section 5 how one can represent continuous predictions by finite samples. We conclude by proposing experimenting with distance sensitive scoring rules in future probabilistic challenges.

## 2 Selected Regression Methods

In the EPUC challenge, probabilistic predictions were required. Instead of a single *point estimate* of the target value, we were required to predict a probability distribution for each target, expressing how likely we thought each possible value was, given the training data and the known input values for the target.

The predictions were evaluated by using the so called NLPD loss. This loss function, and scoring in general, will be discussed in detail in Sections 3 and 4. For now, it is enough to note that the score was a function of the predicted probability *density* at the location of the true target.

No other information of data sets was given in addition to raw data and the name of the data set. The competitors did not know what kind of phenomenon they were dealing with.

Each data set was divided into three parts: training, validation, and test data. For simplicity, we will usually regard both training and validation data as training data, as this was the setting during the final phase of the challenge.

### 2.1 Outaouais

In the so called 'Outaouais' data set, the amount of data was relatively large. There were 37 input variables, and as many as 29 000 training samples. Some of the input variables contained only discrete values, while some other input dimensions were continuous.

No obvious easy solutions or quick wins were found by visual observation. To gain more information on the data, we tried $k$-nearest-neighbour methods with different values of $k$, different distance metrics, etc. We noticed that very small values of $k$ produced relatively good predictions, while the results with larger neighbourhoods were much worse.

We next focused on 1-nearest-neighbour and studied the data more closely, checking which input variables were typically close to each other for nearest neighbours. We noticed that there seemed to be a surprisingly large number of discrete input variables whose values were often *equal* for a pair of nearest neighbours.

The discrete dimensions were clearly somewhat dependent. Starting with an initial set of possibly dependent discrete dimensions, we formed a collection of input dimensions which could be used to group all data points into classes. As a greedy heuristic, we kept adding dimensions which left much more than one training point in most classes.

The results were surprising. We found a set of 23 dimensions which classified all training input into approximately 3 500 classes, each typically containing 1 to 14 training points. Next we checked if any of these classes occurred in the test data, too. It turned out that both training and test input could be classified into approximately 3 500 classes, each typically containing 13 or 14 points. Almost all classes contained both training and test points. Thus, given a test point we almost always had some training points in the same class.

Next we focused on those classes which contained large numbers of training samples. For each class, the data points looked as if they were time series data. There was one dimension which we identified as "time". Naturally we do not know if the dimension actually represents time. However, having this kind of metaphors to support human thinking proved to be useful.

Fig. 1 shows training points from five different classes. This figure illustrates well typical behaviour in all classes: usually the target values changed slowly with time within each class, but there were also some classes with more variation.

If we had had to just predict the values, we could have fitted a smooth curve within each class. However, in this challenge we needed probabilistic predictions. We had 29 000 training points. Thus we could calculate *empirical* error distributions for *pairs* of samples within one class, conditioned on the discretised distance in the "time" dimension.

In other words, we first answered the following question: If we know that two points, $x_1$ and $x_2$, are in the same class, and the "time" elapsed between measuring $x_1$ and $x_2$ is roughly $T$, what is the expected distribution of the difference of target values $y_1$ and $y_2$?

We created 27 empirical distributions, one for each discretised time difference. Actually only 14 distributions are needed, others are mirror images. Fig. 2 shows histograms of three of these empirical distributions. For comparison, we also show Gaussian distributions with the same mean and the same variance. The empirical

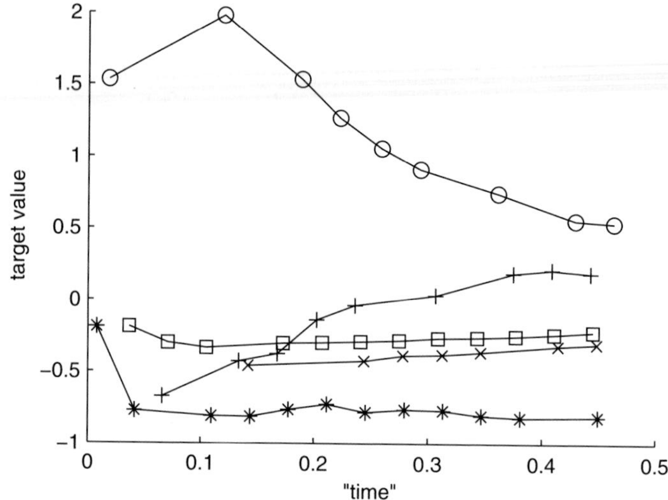


**Fig. 1.** Examples of some classes in the 'Outaouais' data set. Each set of connected dots corresponds to training points in a certain class. From the figure it is obvious that within one class, target values change only slightly in a short time interval.

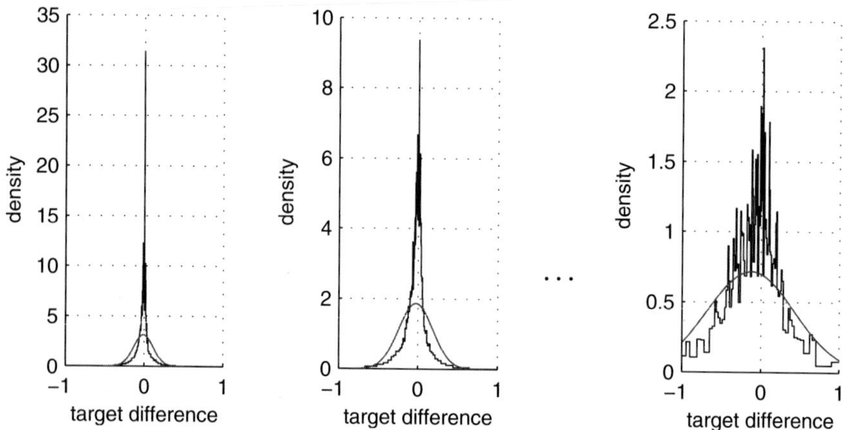


**Fig. 2.** Three precomputed error distributions for the 'Outaouais' data set, contrasted to Gaussians with the same mean and the same variance. The first figure corresponds to the shortest "time" interval (approx. 0.034 units) while the last figure corresponds to the longest "time" interval (approx. $13 \cdot 0.034 = 0.442$ units). Compare with Fig. 1.

distributions are clearly non-Gaussian, and their Pearson kurtoses range from 6 to 22, while a Gaussian would have a kurtosis of 3.

Now we were ready for prediction: For a given test input, we classified it, and picked the nearest neighbour value within the same class, measuring the distance in the "time" dimension. We discretised the distance and took the corresponding empirical error distribution. Then we predicted the target value of the neighbour plus the error distribution. Thus, each prediction had a shape similar to one of the graphs in Fig. 2, shifted horizontally.

Our mean square error (0.056) was worse than what some other competitors had achieved (0.038). However, the NLPD loss was the lowest: -0.88 for us, -0.65 for the second place. Thus, our predictive distributions were more accurate.

If our method is viewed as a dimensionality reduction, one can see that 23 input dimensions (the ones used for classification) were converted into one class identifier; 1 "time" dimension was used as is; and 13 dimensions were discarded. Thus we reduced the dimensionality from 37 to 2 with very simple methods.

There is at least one thing to learn here: surprisingly naive methods may work *if* you can use large amounts of real data to estimate probability distributions. One may also consider whether the construction of training and test data was really compatible with the intended practical application. In practice one might have to make predictions before there are any known samples in the same class. Did we learn the phenomenon or just abuse the construction of the data?

### 2.2 Gaze

In the 'Gaze' data set, input was 12-dimensional, and there were only 450 training and validation samples. Sparsity of the data called for some kind of dimensionality reduction.

We visually inspected the $(x_j, y)$ scatter plots of each input variable $x_i$ versus the target $y$, for $j = 1, \ldots, 12$. Two of the input dimensions, $j = 1$ and $j = 3$, revealed a definite, albeit noisy regression structure (Fig. 3). The other 10 input dimensions appeared less useful for predicting $y$, and were discarded.

In the validation data, a few $x_3$ values were conspicuously low (Fig. 3); likewise in the test data. To avoid huge losses from erroneous regression estimates, we applied a manually chosen outlier detection rule ($x_3 < 0$). The outlying $x_3$ values were simply replaced with the sample mean. The values after this preprocessing step will be denoted $\tilde{x}_3$.

For further reduction of dimensionality, we linearly combined $x_1$ and $\tilde{x}_3$ into one quantity, $z = w_1 x_1 + w_3 \tilde{x}_3$, with $w$ chosen by cross-validation so as to maximise prediction accuracy within the training data.

We now had a one-dimensional regression problem of predicting $y$ from $z$. For this task, we chose a standard regression method, namely local linear regression [1] where the local weights were assigned using a Gaussian kernel.

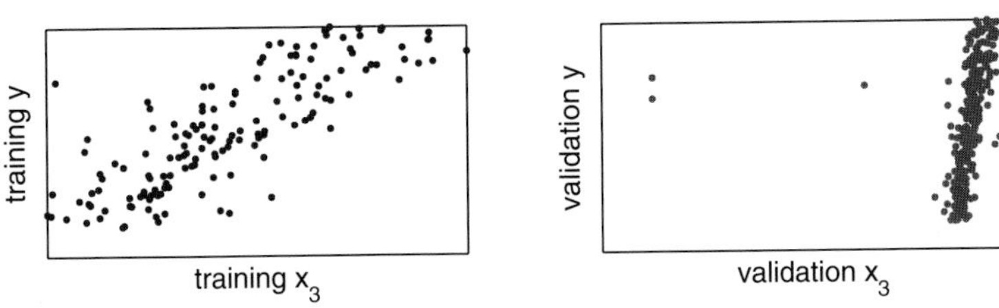


**Fig. 3.** 'Gaze' scatter plots of input variable $x_3$ versus regression target $y$

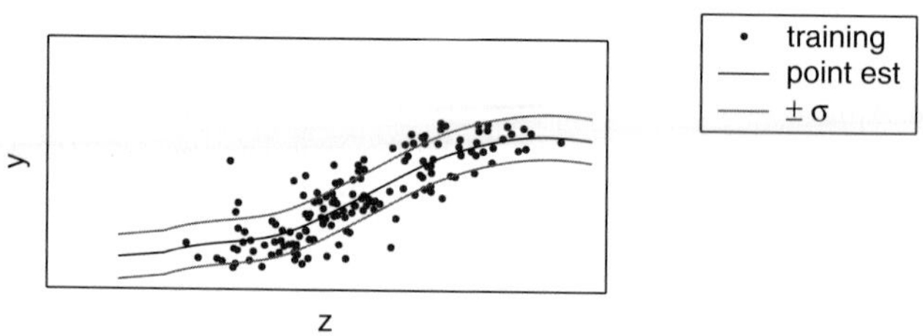


**Fig. 4.** LLR point estimates and standard error bounds for 'Gaze' data

Local linear regression (LLR) provides, for each unknown target, a point estimate $\hat{y}$. For probabilistic prediction, we also need the distribution of the error $\varepsilon = \hat{y} - y$. A standard practice is to estimate its variance with a local or global average of the squared errors for the training data [2]; or more generally, with an arbitrary smoother of the squared errors. After experimenting with different smoothers, we decided that a homoscedastic (i.e. constant-variance) error model with variance $\hat{\sigma}^2 = \sum_{i=1}^{n} (\hat{y} - y)^2 / n$ was accurate enough. Furthermore, the error distribution appeared more or less normal in the training and validation data sets.

Assuming normally distributed errors, we could thus predict $N(\hat{y}_i, \hat{\sigma}^2)$ for target $i$, where $\hat{y}$ is the point estimate from local linear regression, and $\hat{\sigma}^2$ is the global estimate of error variance. Such predictions are illustrated in Fig. 4.

A closer look at the training and validation data revealed that all target values were integers ranging from 122 to 1000. Since arbitrary predictive distributions were allowed, it seemed pointless to assign any significant probability mass to non-integral target values. Doing so could, in fact, be seen as a failure to report a pronounced feature of the target distribution.

Accordingly, we concentrated the predicted probability on the integers. Because the number of quantiles seemed to be limited by allowed file size, we did this only for a part of the distribution. We discretised the predicted Gaussian into 7 equiprobable brackets, delimited by the $i/7$ quantiles for $i = 1, \ldots, 6$. The probability in the central bracket was then mostly reallocated around the integers within the bracket (Fig. 5). Limited only by the floating point precision, the spikes on the integers were $2 \cdot 10^{-13}$ units wide. As a result, each spike could be assigned a very high probability density, about $1.5 \cdot 10^{10}$. If a target indeed coincides with such a spike, we would thus gain a negative logarithmic score of $-\log_2 1.5 \cdot 10^{10} \approx -23$ for that target.

What did we learn from this regression task? The methods we applied were quite standard. The distinctive feature of our second-ranking solution was exploiting the integrality of the targets. It would be fair to say that this was an abuse of the scoring method. On the other hand, *assuming* that the scoring method faithfully represents what kind of prediction is being sought for, one could argue that NLPD essentially mandates that the competitors submit every bit of information they possibly can about the test targets, including the fact that they are precisely on the integers. We will return to this topic in Section 4.

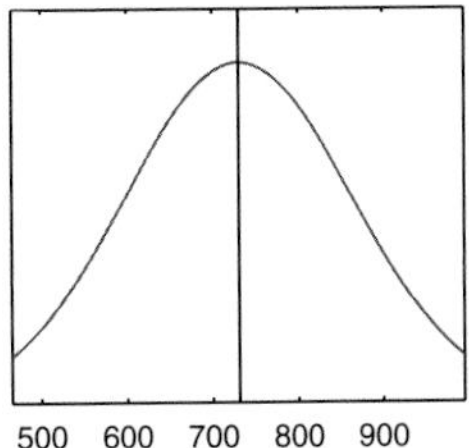

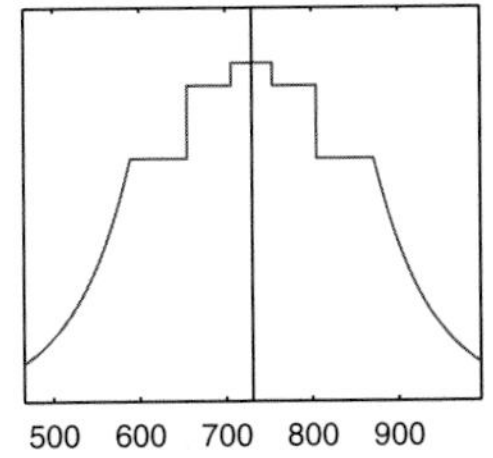

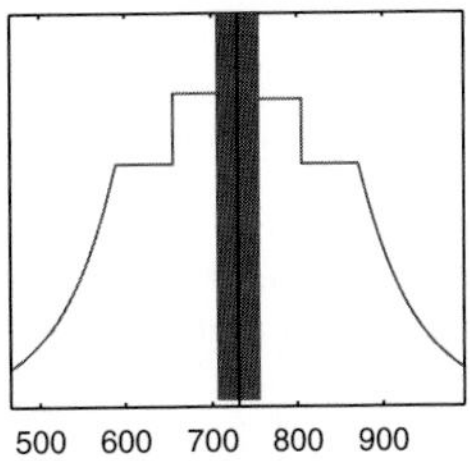


**Fig. 5.** Successive prediction stages for 'Gaze'. Left: The original Gaussian. Centre: Discretised Gaussian. Right: Centre bracket replaced with narrow spikes on integers.

### 2.3 Stereopsis

The 'Stereopsis' data set had only 4 input dimensions. Visual inspection of the data showed clear, regular structure. The name of the set was an additional hint: the word "stereopsis" means stereoscopic vision. Based on studies, we formed a hypothesis of the physical phenomenon that had created the data.

The assumed model was as follows: The input data consists of two coordinate pairs, $(x_1, y_1)$ and $(x_2, y_2)$. Each pair corresponds to the location of the image of a calibration target, as seen by a video camera. The target data corresponds to the distance $z$ between the calibration target and a fixed surface. Both cameras are fixed. The calibration target is moved in a $10 \times 10 \times 10$ grid. The grid is almost parallel to the surface from which distances are measured.

Naturally we had no idea if this model is right. However, having some visual model of the data helps in choosing the methods. Having a model in mind, we proceeded in two phases.

1. We first *classified* the data into 10 distance classes. Each class was supposed to correspond to one $10 \times 10$ surface in the grid. Distances (training target values) within each class are close to each other.
2. Within each class, we fitted a *low-order surface* to the training points.

The first part, classification, seemed trivial. We used a linear transformation to reduce dimensionality to 1, and used 9 threshold values to separate the classes.

In the second part, the physical model guided the selection of the parameterisation of each surface. It turned out that simply mapping the coordinates of one camera, $(x_1, y_1)$, to the polynomial $(1, x_1, y_1, x_1 y_1)$ made it possible to find a highly accurate linear fitting. Higher order terms seemed to cause only over-fitting, while leaving the $x_1 y_1$ term out produced worse results in validation.

This particular polynomial makes sense if we assume that the grid is formed by defining four corner points of each surface and interpolating linearly. Errors due to lens distortions may be large in $x$ and $y$ dimensions, but their effect on almost parallel surfaces in the $z$ dimension are minor.

Given this prediction method, there are two error sources in these predictions. Firstly, there is the possibility of a classification error. However, we assumed that classifications are correct. When the classifier was formed by using only training points, all validation samples were classified correctly and with large margins. This assumption turned out to be a fatal mistake.

Secondly, there is the distance between the surface and the true target. We assumed that this error is primarily contributed by Gaussian noise in measurements. Variance was estimated for each surface by using the training samples. Thus, we submitted simple Gaussian predictions.

The results were a bit disappointing. There was a huge NLPD loss. It turned out that 499 of the 500 test samples were predicted well. 1 of the 500 samples was completely incorrect. This was a classification mistake and one huge loss was enough to ruin the score of the entire prediction. We, obviously, should not have trusted the simple classification method too much.

In addition to that single classification mistake, is there anything one can learn from this effort? If our guess of the model is correct, and the real objective was training a computer vision system to estimate distances, this method is completely useless. However, it did predict almost all test points well. This is due to learning the structure of the calibration process, not due to learning how to calculate the distance from stereo images. The lesson learned: One needs to be careful when choosing the training and validation data. For example, random points in continuous space instead of a grid could have helped here to avoid this problem.

## 3 About Challenges and Scoring

Probabilistic machine learning challenges, such as the EPUC challenge, can give us new empirical information on applying machine learning in practical problems. Ideally, one would gain information on which methods work well in practice. One could also learn more on how to choose the right tool for a given problem, and how to choose parameters. However, as we will see, one needs to be careful when choosing the scoring rules used in the competition.

The quality of a machine learning method can be defined in various ways. We narrow the scope by ignoring issues such as computational complexity. We will focus on how useful the predictions would be in a practical application.

### 3.1 Notation and Terminology

For scoring rules, we use the notation used by Gneiting and Raftery [3]. Let $P$ be the predictive distribution and let $x$ be the true target. A *scoring rule* is any function $S(P, x)$. Given a distribution $Q(x)$, we use $S(P, Q)$ for the expected value of $S(P, x)$ under $Q$, i.e. $S(P, Q) = \int S(P, x)\, Q(x)\, dx$.

If $P$ is a probability distribution, we use $P(x)$ to denote its density function, and $P(X \leq x)$ to denote cumulative density.

### 3.2 Modelling a Challenge

In our model of a competition, training inputs $X = (\mathbf{x}_j)$, training targets $Y = (y_j)$, and test inputs $T = (\mathbf{t}_i)$ are given to competitors while true test targets $U = (u_i)$ are not yet published.

The competition consists of three phases:

1. Each competitor $k \in K$ chooses a machine learning method $f_k$, forms a hypothesis $h_k = f_k(X, Y)$, and use the hypothesis to form a personal probability distribution $Q_{k,i} = h_k(\mathbf{t}_i)$.
2. The competitor chooses a prediction $P_{k,i} = g_k(Q_{k,i})$ by using any function $g_k$. The prediction $P_k = (P_{k,i})$ and a description of the method $(f_k, g_k)$ are reported to the organiser.
3. Each competitor is assigned a score $s_k = \frac{1}{|U|} \sum S(P_{k,i}, u_i)$.

In our model, $f_k$ encodes essentially everything one needs in order to re-use the same method in a new, similar problem. In addition to a machine learning algorithm, it describes all rules the expert used for, say, choosing the right parameters. Evaluating $f_k(X, Y)$ may require not only computer resources but also work by a human expert.

Competitors typically have no a priori knowledge on the phenomenon. Thus a competitor's personal probability distribution, $Q_{k,i}$, is formed solely by using the method $f_k$, as described above.

However, a competitor does not necessarily want to report her honest personal probability distribution. Perhaps her expected personal utility would be maximised by reporting an overconfident prediction. This could be caused either by the peculiar nature of her utility function, or by the general characteristics of the scoring method being applied in the competition. Instead of denying the possibility of such human behaviour, we have added in our model the mapping $g_k$ which the competitor uses for forming her prediction. This model, where the competitors seek to maximise their personal utilities, is in line with Bernardo and Smith's argumentation that "the problem of reporting inferences is essentially a special case of a decision problem" [4, p. 68].

We are explicitly requiring that the methods are revealed. Otherwise there is little one can learn from the results of the competition. However, the score does not depend on the structure of $f_k$. The whole point of these competitions is evaluating methods by their practical results, not by their theoretical merits.

The score does not depend directly on $Q_{k,i}$, either. While the competition organisers could, in principle, use $f_k$ to re-calculate $Q_{k,i}$, the amount of human work involved could be huge. Thus we are left with scoring the reported predictions, $P_{k,i}$.

The EPUC challenge conforms to this model. The requirement of reporting $(f_k, g_k)$ is implemented by asking the winners to present their methods.

### 3.3 Results of a Challenge

Let us assume that the competitor $\tilde{k}$ achieved one of the highest scores. In spite of all limitations mentioned above, we would like to be able to learn something on $f_{\tilde{k}}$. Ideally, $f_{\tilde{k}}$ should now be among the strong candidates for use in similar practical machine learning problems. Obviously, this is not always true, a trivial counterexample is a competition where all participants were novices and all predictions were useless.

Competitors have many degrees of freedom for choosing what to do in the competition. On the other hand, there is relatively little what the organiser of the competition can do in order to affect the quality of the results. Assuming the data sets are fixed, the organiser can only choose the set of competitors $K$ and the scoring rule $S$.

In this paper, we concentrate on the task of choosing the scoring rule. We will not discuss the task of choosing the competitors. However, we briefly note that in order to find good methods $f_k$, the set of competitors should preferably contain a number of leading machine learning experts. On the other hand, participation is voluntary. If the experts notice that the scoring rules of the competition are poorly designed, they may be reluctant to participate. Thus choosing the scoring rules plays a role even in the task of choosing the competitors.

### 3.4 Scoring and Linearity of Utilities

A score as such has little meaning. In this paper, we assume that each competitor has a utility function which depends linearly on her score, $s_k$. This is a strong assumption. It may be hard to implement in a competition. If reputation, fame and publicity are the only prize, typically the winner takes it all.

However, a non-linear dependency makes it hard to analyse competitions. If, for example, only the winning score has a high utility, competitors are encouraged to take a risk with overconfident predictions. A small chance for a winning score would have a better expected utility than a safe medium-level score. In such a setting, the winners could be those who were lucky, not those who used the best methods. Competitors can also be risk-averse; in that case they might choose to play it safe and report underconfident predictions. Both risk-seeking and risk-averse patterns of behaviour have been observed in probability forecasting competitions; see, for example, Sanders [5].

Implementing a linear utility has been studied in the literature. A typical construction involves a single-prize lottery where the winning probabilities are proportional to the scores. See, for example, Smith's construction [6].

### 3.5 Scoring in a Challenge

There is a rich literature on scoring probabilistic predictions, both for discrete probability distributions (classification) and for continuous probability distributions (regression) [7, 8, 9]. Much of the work is related to atmospheric sciences for obvious reasons [5, 10, 11, 12]. In this subsection, we will look at the scoring from the point of view of probabilistic machine learning challenges.

Matheson and Winkler [13] summarise three common uses for scoring rules. First, scoring rules can be used to encourage assessors *make careful assessments*. Second, scoring rules can be used to *keep assessors honest*. Finally, scoring rules can be used to *measure the goodness* of predictions. We will soon see that this list applies well to a machine learning challenge.

The direct requirements for a scoring rule are two-fold:

1. The scoring rule should encourage experts to work seriously in order to find a good method, $f_k$.
2. The final score should reflect how good the method $f_k$ is.

These two requirements correspond directly to two applications on Matheson and Winkler's list: encouraging good assessments and measuring the goodness of predictions.

However, the scores reflect the quality of the method only indirectly. There are two layers of indirection: First, we are scoring $f_k$ by using a sample. The second issue is that we are not scoring the quality of the competitor's personal probability $h_k(\mathbf{t}_i)$ but the quality of her reported probability $g_k(h_k(\mathbf{t}_i))$ for an arbitrary $g_k$.

For the first issue there is little we can do besides using a relatively large and representative test set. By using a sample mean $s_k = \frac{1}{|U|} \sum S(P_{k,i}, u_i)$ we are estimating the expected value of the score and determining the quality of the estimator is standard statistics.

The second issue is more subtle. Ideally we would like to have $g_k(x) = x$ for all $k$. This is needed not only for making it easier to analyse the competition but also for encouraging careful assessments. If the connection between competitors' work and the final score becomes more indirect and complicated, the competitors cannot see where they should focus their attention.

One can naturally ask: why not simply *require* that competitors use the identity function as $g_k$. We were assuming, after all, that competitors report both $f_k$ and $g_k$, and the reported $f_k$ and $g_k$ could be manually checked by a competition organiser, if needed. Unfortunately, competitors could incorporate the mapping $g_k$ in their reported $f_k$ and let $g_k$ be the identity function. Nothing would be gained but the goal of the competition would be missed. The method $f_k$ would no longer be a good way of estimating probabilities, it would only be a way of maximising the score. Its use in practical problems would be limited.

Instead of *requiring*, the competitors should be *encouraged*, by the design of the challenge, to use an identity function as $g_k$. This is what Matheson and Winkler refer to as keeping assessors honest. If the scoring rule is such that for a competitor, the identity function is the best choice of $g_k$ in terms of her expected score, we gain a lot. The competition organiser can announce this fact and the competitors can check it. Now the competitors can concentrate on developing a method to estimate true probabilities of the phenomenon.

A scoring method with this useful property is called *proper*. Focusing on proper scoring rules is similar to focusing on truthful or strategyproof mechanisms in the field of mechanism design.

### 3.6 Proper Scoring Rules

The problem of keeping assessors honest is easily expressed and well understood. See, for example, Gneiting and Raftery [3] for a modern treatment on the subject.

A scoring rule is called *proper* if $S(Q, Q) \geq S(P, Q)$ for all $P$ and $Q$. A scoring rule is *strictly proper* if it is proper and if $S(Q, Q) = S(P, Q)$ only if $Q = P$. If a predictor's personal probability is $Q$, under proper scoring she gains nothing, on average, by predicting anything else than $Q$. Under strictly proper scoring she always loses, on average, by predicting anything else than $Q$.

Proper scoring rules have gained a lot of attention in the literature. There are large families of proper and strictly proper scoring rules [3, 7, 13]. However, properness by itself has only limited use in encouraging careful assessments and measuring the goodness of predictions. Strict properness essentially guarantees that *if* one works hard enough to make a perfect prediction by deducing the true generative distribution, one is expected to gain more than other competitors. However, a useless prediction can achieve *almost* as high a score as the perfect prediction. We will later see examples of this. As a competitor's utility depends both on the score and on the work required, an easy and highly scored solution is inviting. This problem will be reflected also in measuring the goodness of predictions. If competitors were encouraged to focus on highly scored but useless predictions, that is also what the highest scoring methods are expected to be.

In summary, properness is useful, it allows a large variety of alternative scoring rules, and it is not enough by itself. Properness is a good starting point. The next section illustrates what else should be expected from a good scoring rule.

## 4 Beyond Properness

While keeping assessors honest can be formulated and solved in a uniform way for all problems, encouraging careful assessments and measuring the goodness depends on the application. This is intimately tied to the question of how we value the information provided by different kinds of probabilistic predictions.

Scoring rules can be divided into *local* and *non-local* rules. In a local rule [14], the score of a predictive distribution $P$ depends on the predictive density at the true target value only, that is, on $P(x)$. A non-local scoring rule may take into account also other characteristics of the predictive distribution. An interesting class of non-local scoring rules are *distance sensitive* rules [15, 16], which favour predictions that place probability mass *near* the target value, even if not exactly at the target.

It is an intriguing question whether a scoring rule should be local or not. Statistical inference problems may be vaguely divided into "pure inference problems" where the goal is simply to gain information about the targets, and "practical problems" where we seek information in order to solve a particular decision problem. Bernardo [4, 14] states that in a pure inference setting, a local scoring rule should be used. However, in many practical settings there seems to be a need for non-local rules.

In order to help make this discussion more concrete, we introduce two proper scoring rules which have been proposed for scoring continuous predictions: the negative log predictive density (NLPD), which is a local rule, and the continuous ranked probability score (CRPS), which is non-local.

### 4.1 NLPD

NLPD is the scoring function which was used, for example, in the EPUC challenge. NLPD stands for *negative log estimated predictive density.* It is a loss function: large values imply poor performance. To make it compatible with our framework, we derive a scoring function by changing the sign. The result is simply the *logarithmic score* (see, for example, Matheson and Winkler [13]):

$$S_{\text{NLPD}}(P, x) = \log P(x). \tag{1}$$

In this text we will use the terms NLPD score and the logarithmic score interchangeably. Both refer to the scoring function defined in Equation (1).

The NLPD score is obviously local. In fact, under suitable smoothness conditions, it is essentially the *only* proper scoring rule which is also local [14]. If locality is indeed desirable, this is a strong argument in favour of the NLPD.

### 4.2 CRPS

CRPS stands for *continuous ranked probability score.* CRPS is a generalisation of the idea of the *ranked probability score* (RPS), introduced by Epstein [11] for scoring in probabilistic classification.

Epstein observed that existing proper scoring rules did not use the concept of distance. However, the classes may represent, for example, ranges of measurements. In this case the classes are not independent.

Epstein uses weather forecasting as an example: It is assumed that the classes represent consecutive temperature ranges, $A$ predicts (0.1, 0.3, 0.5, 0.1), $B$ predicts (0.5, 0.3, 0.1, 0.1), and the fourth class corresponds to the observed temperature. If the ordering of the classes is ignored, both predictions would obtain the same score.

However, these predictions are not equivalent for a typical *user* of the prediction. Given the prediction $B$, the user would be prepared for much colder weather than given the prediction $A$. Epstein developed this line of thought further to estimate the expected utility of the user of the prediction. For example, given the prediction $B$ above, the user's utility is low as she had to prepare for cold weather while preparation was not needed. With a number of simplifying assumptions, and after normalising the scores, Epstein derived his recommendation for a scoring rule, the ranked probability score. Murphy [17] showed that this score is proper.

In order to simplify notation, let us define a probability distribution function $R_x$ based on the observed value $x$, such that $R_x(X \leq i) = 0$ for all $i < x$, and $R_x(X \leq i) = 1$ for all $i \geq x$. Now we can present RPS as follows:

$$S_{\text{RPS}}(P, x) = 1 - \frac{1}{n-1} \sum_{i=1}^{n-1} (P(X \leq i) - R_x(X \leq i))^2. \tag{2}$$

Here $n$ is the number of classes. We see that the ranked probability score is a linear transform of the *square error* between the predicted and observed *cumulative* distribution functions.

This can be directly generalised to a continuous distribution. Thus we obtain the continuous ranked probability score which was introduced, and proved to be proper, by Matheson and Winkler [13]:

$$S_{\mathrm{CRPS}}(P,x) = -\int (P(X \le u) - R_x(X \le u))^2\, w(u)\, du. \tag{3}$$

Here $w(u)$ is arbitrary weight. NLPD and CRPS scores are illustrated in Fig. 6.

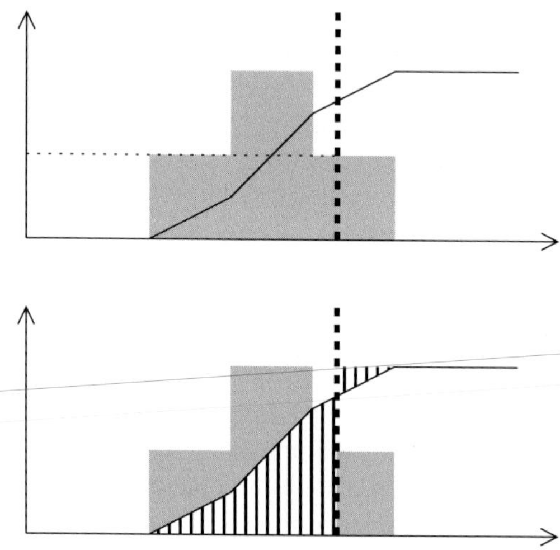

**Fig. 6.** An illustration of the NLPD and CRPS scores. In these figures, grey areas illustrate predicted probability density functions. Solid lines are used to show the corresponding cumulative distribution. Dashed vertical bars show the true target. The first part, (a), shows the NLPD score: it is logarithm of the predicted density near the true target values, as indicated by the horizontal dotted line. The second part, (b), shows the CRPS score: it is the square error between the predicted and observed cumulative distribution functions, the error is illustrated by a vertical striped pattern.

The CRPS is a non-local rule, and in general, it favours predictions that put a lot of probability mass near the target. We will refer to this property as *distance-sensitivity*. Its exact definition varies in the literature; CRPS is sensitive to distance according to Staël von Holstein's "tail sums" definition [15], but not according to Murphy's "symmetric sums" definition [16].

### 4.3 Locality Versus Distance-Sensitivity

Let us now continue the discussion of the relative merits of local and distance sensitive scoring rules. We will here accept the view of Bernardo [14] that statistical inference about an unknown quantity is essentially a decision problem, where one tries to maximise the expected *utility* of information attained by doing inference. A central question is then how to define the utility of information.

Recall the distinction of "pure inference problems" and "practical problems". In a practical problem, the application at hand may dictate a particular scoring function, related to the end utility of making decisions based on partial information. Such a scoring function is quite often non-local.

On the other hand, in a pure inference problem, there is no immediate practical application. One simply wants to gain knowledge about the targets. Bernardo states that in such a setting, one should *maximise the expected gain of information* [4, p. 72]. This leads to requiring a local scoring function, and if also properness and smoothness are desired, essentially choosing the NLPD.

While Bernardo's argument is otherwise compelling, it rests on an important hidden assumption: that if one desires to gain knowledge (about the value of a target quantity), one should then indeed maximise the *amount of information* gained. This implicitly means that all information about the target value is treated as equal in value; for example, that learning the tenth decimal of an unknown quantity is just as valuable as learning its first decimal.

For regression tasks, where the target values are continuous, we find such equivalence rather unnatural even in pure inference; more so if the inference task is in any way related to a practical setting, such as inferring the value of a physical magnitude. This is particularly evident when we consider how probabilistic predictions can be used.

When using a probabilistic prediction, the predicted distribution tells us how likely various undesirable or difficult situations are. Then, the costs of preparing for those situations can be compared to the probabilities and the potential damages in case of no protection. We list here some examples from various fields:

1. Weather prediction: Difficult situations can be, for example, very high or low temperatures, heavy rain, storms, etc. The costs of preparing for those situations can range from carrying an umbrella to cancelling flights.
2. Financial sector: Undesirable situations can be financial risks in investments. Preparing for those situations may involve, for example, bidding a lower price and the possibility of losing a deal.
3. Measuring distances: An undesirable situation can be, for example, a robot colliding with an obstacle. Preparing for that situation might require slowing down and thus spending more time.

In all of these examples, if the undesirable situation did *not* realise, the preparations were done in vain. In that case, all other factors being equal, a prediction which estimated a high risk of an undesirable situation is more costly than a prediction which did not do so.

Furthermore, usually some undesirable situations are more severe than others. The more extreme situations are possible, the more costly preparations we may need to do. Thus, the practical use of a prediction depends on the distance between the true target and the predicted probability mass.

In all examples described above, the concept of distance plays a role: In weather prediction, the practical significance of small and large differences in predicted temperatures was already illustrated in Epstein's [11] example in Section 4.2 above. In financial sector, if an investment was actually highly profitable,

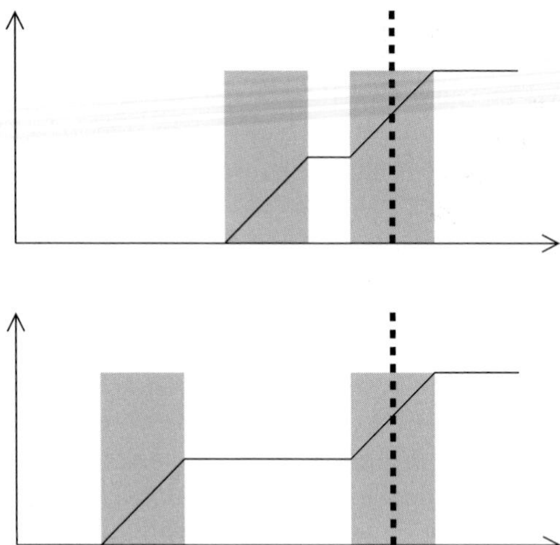

**Fig. 7.** An illustration of the concept of distance. Both predictions, (a) and (b), will gain the same NLPD score, while the CRPS score is much lower in case (b). The CRPS score corresponds well to the practical applicability of the predictions: given the prediction (b), the user of the prediction needs to be prepared for a wide range of different values, making her utility lower.

having a prediction of possible low profits may be relatively harmless while having a prediction of possible large losses may lead into the wrong decision. When measuring distances, if a wall is actually at the distance of 200 cm, predicting a possible obstacle at the distance of 196 cm is typically harmless, while predicting a possible obstacle at 5 cm may make robot navigation much harder.

The concept of distance is commonly used in many non-probabilistic loss functions designed for regression tasks: consider, for example, the square loss. We argue that it should also be taken into account in probabilistic loss functions. Fig. 7 illustrates how the CRPS score takes the distance into account, while the NLPD score ignores it. It should be noted that in this example, both predictions contain exactly the same amount of information, while the practical value of this information differs. In practical applications, not every bit of information is worth the same. We will elaborate this issue further in the next section.

### 4.4 Information Which Is of Little Use

Typically, knowing the finest details of a probability distribution function is of very little use. When predicting a real value in the range $[0, 1]$, accurately predicting the first decimal digit is of much higher practical use than accurately predicting the second (or tenth) decimal digit. This issue is closely related to the concept of distance: knowing the first decimal digit corresponds to a prediction where all probability mass is concentrated in a small range.

Let us assume that $A$ predicts correctly the first decimal digit of the true target (all values with the right 1st digit having the same probability) and $B$ predicts correctly the second decimal digit. Both predictors gain the same amount of information. Furthermore, the NLPD score will be the same for both predictors. However, we can easily see that the CRPS score is much higher for the prediction $A$. Actually, with respect to the CRPS score, the prediction $B$ is not much better than a prediction where nothing is known. This is well in balance with the practice: knowing, say, the second decimal digit of rainfall is typically of no practical use if the more significant digits are uncertain. The user of the prediction would have to be prepared for all kinds of weathers.

In the EPUC challenge, the problem of useless information can be illustrated by the 'Stereopsis' data set. As mentioned above in Section 2.3, one possible approach consists of classifying points to 10 distance classes, and predicting within each class. Our failure could have been avoided by assigning a positive probability for each of these classes, and by giving predictions with 10 narrow Gaussians instead of only 1 narrow Gaussian distribution. This may gain a good NLPD score, yet be of no practical use in a computer vision application.

### 4.5 Point Masses

In practical regression settings, one often encounters the problem of point masses. By this we mean that the predictor has some reason to believe that in an otherwise continuous target domain, there are special values which have a nonzero mass. There are several different sources of this problem.

Fig. 8 illustrates how a predictor may use this information. Part (a) presents the original prediction before information on point masses is used. Part (b) shows how a competitor may slightly modify her prediction to reflect her belief that there are point masses.

The spikes can be made arbitrarily high, and at the same time their probability mass can be made very small simply by limiting their width. Thus adding spikes can leave the predicted density outside the spikes virtually unchanged.

If the true target does not match any of those spikes, neither NLPD nor CRPS score is considerably changed when comparing predictions (a) and (b). Thus, adding spikes is relatively harmless from a competitor's point of view.

However, if the true target indeed happens to match one of the predicted spikes, the NLPD score for prediction (b) is arbitrarily high while the CRPS score for prediction (b) is still essentially the same as for prediction (a). Thus, the NLPD score strongly encourages working towards finding some discrete point masses, while the CRPS score does not reward for it unless the point masses are large enough to considerably change the density function.

If there is at least one match with *any* predicted spike in *any* of the test targets, the NLPD score is dominated by that spike. If the NLPD score is used and any such point masses are found, there is little reason for predictors to make any efforts to model any other aspects of the phenomenon.

Thus, this problem, too, is primarily related to encouraging careful assessments. It seriously affects measuring the goodness of predictions: the existence of such point masses may be trivial and uninteresting, while NLPD score may be dominated by them.

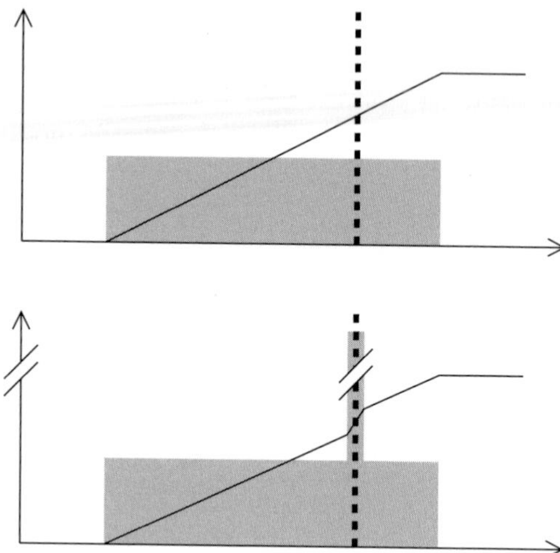

**Fig. 8.** An illustration of the problem of point masses. Part (a) shows the original prediction. Part (b) shows how a competitor may slightly modify her prediction if she has a reason to believe there is a nonzero point mass. The competitor has added an extremely narrow spike in the predicted density function. The probability mass of the spike can be made low, and density everywhere else can be left virtually unchanged.

In practice the format in which the predictions are submitted may not allow arbitrarily high and arbitrarily narrow spikes. For example, the range and precision of IEEE floating point numbers effectively limited this problem in the EPUC challenge. However, such limits are quite unsatisfactory and arbitrary and still allow manipulating scores by using some narrow spikes.

Thus, using *any* local scoring rule which is based on the value of the probability density function at the location of the true target should be avoided in this kind of challenges unless data sets are selected very carefully in order to avoid the problem of point masses. Non-local scoring rules which are based on comparing cumulative distribution functions are better in this respect.

Now we will have a look at some practical examples of point masses. We have three categories of point mass problems. These categories are based on features of the data sets of the EPUC challenge, and thus clearly relevant in the context of probabilistic challenges.

**Known Targets.** The first category is the case of known targets. For example, the first version of the 'Stereopsis' data set in the EPUC challenge accidentally contained some overlap between training and test data. This should not affect the results of the challenge: each competitor has the same knowledge, and the scores of these overlapping known points would simply be an additive constant in final scores. However, for the NLPD score, this additive constant would be infinity, ruining the final scores. For the CRPS score, the constant would be zero.

**Special Values in the Target Domain.** The second category deals with special values in the target domain. For example, the 'Outaouais' training data contained 250 points where the target was exactly zero. Thus, it is likely that also the test data set of comparable size contains some targets that are zero.

Such special values may occur if *missing data* are represented as zeroes. There may also be a natural reason why a continuous physical variable really has a nonzero point mass somewhere, precipitation being a good example [3].

**Discrete Target Domain.** The third category is the case of discrete target domain. The 'Gaze' data set had integral target values. Modifying predictions to reflect this trivial fact improved NLPD scores considerably.

Discrete target values are actually relatively typical in practical applications:

- The target domain may actually be integral; the prediction task might deal with counting some occurrences.
- Financial quantities such as money and shares are almost always expressed with a fixed precision.
- Devices which measure physical quantities usually work with finite precision.

One may argue that at least discrete target domains could be dealt with by interpreting them as classification tasks instead of regression tasks, and by asking for discrete predictions instead of continuous predictions. However, the set of possible values may be large or infinite, making this approach impractical.

## 5 Representing Predictions

One needs a finite representation for continuous probability distributions. A single Gaussian is not flexible enough in order to represent arbitrary predictions.

In the EPUC challenge, the other alternative was a *set of quantiles*, essentially a histogram with exponential tails (see Fig. 5 for an example). Quantiles are flexible but handling quantile predictions in, for example, mathematical software is a bit complicated. One typically needs to handle the histogram part and the tails separately, making program code more complicated and error-prone.

There is a need for simpler ways to represent continuous predictions, both in challenges and in practical applications. One possible idea would be using a *sample*. One could simply draw a finite set of sample values randomly from the predicted distribution and report those.

Naturally, one could then use density estimation to recover an approximation of the original distribution. However, this would not simplify matters at all, and one would also need to specify the parameters used in density estimation. By using suitable scoring methods, there is an easier solution.

One could interpret a finite sample literally as a probability distribution with a finite set of point masses. This is illustrated in Fig. 9. The density function would consist of infinitely high and narrow spikes, while the cumulative distribution function would consist of a finite number of steps.

In most cases, the true target value would not match exactly any point mass. The expected NLPD loss would be infinite. However, the shape of the *cumulative* distribution function would be close to the original distribution. Thus, if one

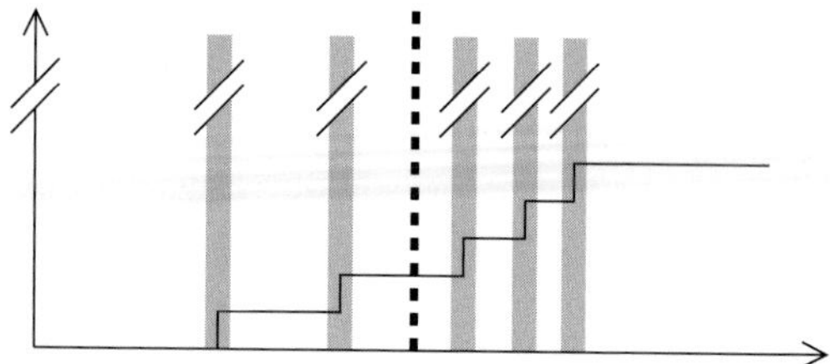

**Fig. 9.** An illustration of using samples to represent predictions. In this example, the prediction was given as a sample of five points. It corresponds to a probability distribution with five spikes.

used the CRPS score, a finite set of sample points would give approximately the same score as a quantile prediction, but with considerably less complexity. A key difference with quantile predictions is that there would be no need to handle tails in any special way. CRPS is well-defined even if the target is outside the range of the sample points.

This line of thought may be also used to guide the selection of the scoring method. Clearly, a finite sample cannot represent accurately all aspects of a continuous distribution, such as the shape of the density function in low-density areas. Such details are not much reflected in the CRPS score, either. If we have a practical problem where the CRPS score can be used, it means that we are not interested in such details, and thus we can use samples to represent predictions. Conversely, if we cannot use a sample, it may be because we *are* interested in such details, and then we probably should not be using CRPS.

While evaluating the CRPS score in equation (3) may be difficult for an arbitrary prediction [3], it is straightforward if a prediction is represented as a finite sample. One may actually interpret this process as a (possibly randomised) approach to approximate numerical integration. By letting the competitors perform sampling, they may use arbitrarily complicated predictions. Scoring will be also fair in the sense that the organiser of the challenge does not need to use any randomised or approximate method when evaluating submitted predictions.

Finite samples arise naturally in the context of *ensemble prediction*. For example, by running a weather model with several slightly perturbed initial conditions we can obtain an ensemble of different point predictions for, say, tomorrow's temperature. Typically the ensemble is then converted into a probability distribution of suitable form. But if predictions are represented as finite samples, no conversion is needed: the ensemble itself can serve as the representative sample.

## 6 Conclusion

In this paper, we reported our methods in the regression tasks of the Evaluating Predictive Uncertainty Challenge. The tasks also demonstrated some pitfalls in using the well-known NLPD score. We analysed the problem of organising a probabilistic machine learning challenge and proposed two possible improvements for future challenges:

1. One can avoid many pitfalls, if one uses a distance-sensitive scoring method such as CRPS.
2. Description and implementation of the scoring methods can be simplified, if predictions are represented as samples.

We accept that NLPD is the method of choice for the tasks it was designed for: truly continuous, pure inference tasks where every bit of information is worth the same. Unfortunately, one often encounters regression tasks that do not conform to this idealised model, even if they appear so on the surface.

CRPS is not the only possible solution. Whether there are other distance-sensitive scoring methods which reflect significantly better the practical value of predictions is still an open question.

We assumed that the competitors' utilities depend linearly on their scores. Further research is needed on this issue. Firstly, one can pay more attention on implementing linear utilities in challenges. Secondly, more research can be done on modelling challenges where the winner takes it all.

## Acknowledgements

We wish to thank the organisers and the PASCAL network for an interesting and thought-provoking challenge.

This work was supported in part by the Academy of Finland, Grant 202203, and by the IST Programme of the European Community, under the PASCAL Network of Excellence, IST-2002-506778. This publication only reflects the authors' views.

## References

1. Hastie, T., Tibshirani, R., Friedman, J.: The Elements of Statistical Learning. Springer-Verlag (2001)
2. Härdle, W.: Applied Nonparametric Regression. Cambridge University Press (1990)
3. Gneiting, T., Raftery, A.E.: Strictly proper scoring rules, prediction, and estimation. Technical Report 463, Department of Statistics, University of Washington (2004)
4. Bernardo, J.M., Smith, A.F.M.: Bayesian Theory. John Wiley & Sons, Inc. (2000)
5. Sanders, F.: The verification of probability forecasts. Journal of Applied Meteorology **6** (1967) 756–761
6. Smith, C.A.B.: Consistency in statistical inference and decision. Journal of the Royal Statistical Society. Series B **23** (1961) 1–37
7. Savage, L.J.: Elicitation of personal probabilities and expectations. Journal of the American Statistical Association **66** (1971) 783–801
8. Winkler, R.L.: Probabilistic prediction: Some experimental results. Journal of the American Statistical Association **66** (1971) 678–685
9. Corradi, V., Swanson, N.R.: Predictive density evaluation. Technical Report 200419, Rutgers University, Department of Economics (2004)
10. Bremnes, J.B.: Probabilistic forecasts of precipitation in terms of quantiles using NWP model output. Monthly Weather Review **132** (2004) 338–347

11. Epstein, E.S.: A scoring system for probability forecasts of ranked categories. Journal of Applied Meteorology **8** (1969) 985–987
12. Hamill, T.M., Wilks, D.S.: A probabilistic forecast contest and the difficulty in assessing short-range forecast uncertainty. Weather and Forecasting **10** (1995) 620–631
13. Matheson, J.E., Winkler, R.L.: Scoring rules for continuous probability distributions. Management Science **22** (1976) 1087–1096
14. Bernardo, J.M.: Expected information as expected utility. The Annals of Statistics **7** (1979) 686–690
15. Staël von Holstein, C.A.S.: A family of strictly proper scoring rules which are sensitive to distance. Journal of Applied Meteorology **9** (1970) 360–364
16. Murphy, A.H.: The ranked probability score and the probability score: A comparison. Monthly Weather Review **98** (1970) 917–924
17. Murphy, A.H.: On the "ranked probability score". Journal of Applied Meteorology **8** (1969) 988–989

# The 2005 PASCAL Visual Object Classes Challenge

Mark Everingham[1], Andrew Zisserman[1], Christopher K.I. Williams[2], Luc Van Gool[3], Moray Allan[2], Christopher M. Bishop[10], Olivier Chapelle[11], Navneet Dalal[8], Thomas Deselaers[4], Gyuri Dorkó[8], Stefan Duffner[6], Jan Eichhorn[11], Jason D.R. Farquhar[12], Mario Fritz[5], Christophe Garcia[6], Tom Griffiths[2], Frederic Jurie[8], Daniel Keysers[4], Markus Koskela[7], Jorma Laaksonen[7], Diane Larlus[8], Bastian Leibe[5], Hongying Meng[12], Hermann Ney[4], Bernt Schiele[5], Cordelia Schmid[8], Edgar Seemann[5], John Shawe-Taylor[12], Amos Storkey[2], Sandor Szedmak[12], Bill Triggs[8], Ilkay Ulusoy[9], Ville Viitaniemi[7], and Jianguo Zhang[8]

[1] University of Oxford, Oxford, UK
[2] University of Edinburgh, Edinburgh, UK
[3] ETH Zentrum, Zurich, Switzerland
[4] RWTH Aachen University, Aachen, Germany
[5] TU-Darmstadt, Darmstadt, Germany
[6] France Télécom, Cesson Sévigné, France
[7] Helsinki University of Technology, Helsinki, Finland
[8] INRIA Rhône-Alpes, Montbonnot, France
[9] Middle East Technical University, Ankara, Turkey
[10] Microsoft Research, Cambridge, UK
[11] Max Planck Institute for Biological Cybernetics, Tübingen, Germany
[12] University of Southampton, Southampton, UK

**Abstract.** The PASCAL Visual Object Classes Challenge ran from February to March 2005. The goal of the challenge was to recognize objects from a number of visual object classes in realistic scenes (i.e. not pre-segmented objects). Four object classes were selected: motorbikes, bicycles, cars and people. Twelve teams entered the challenge. In this chapter we provide details of the datasets, algorithms used by the teams, evaluation criteria, and results achieved.

## 1 Introduction

In recent years there has been a rapid growth in research, and quite some success, in visual recognition of object classes; examples include [1, 5, 10, 14, 18, 28, 39, 43]. Many of these papers have used the same image datasets as [18] in order to compare their performance. The datasets are the so-called 'Caltech 5' (faces, airplanes, motorbikes, cars rear, spotted cats) and UIUC car side images of [1]. The problem is that methods are now achieving such good performance that they have effectively saturated on these datasets, and thus the datasets are failing to challenge the next generation of algorithms. Such saturation can arise because the images used do not explore the full range of variability of the imaged visual

J. Quiñonero-Candela et al. (Eds.): MLCW 2005, LNAI 3944, pp. 117–176, 2006.

class. Some dimensions of variability include: clean vs. cluttered background; stereotypical views vs. multiple views (e.g. side views of cars vs. cars from all angles); degree of scale change, amount of occlusion; the presence of multiple objects (of one or multiple classes) in the images.

Given this problem of saturation of performance, the Visual Object Classes Challenge was designed to be more demanding by enhancing some of the dimensions of variability listed above compared to the databases that had been available previously, so as to explore the failure modes of different algorithms.

The PASCAL[1] Visual Object Classes (VOC) Challenge ran from February to March 2005. A development kit of training and validation data, baseline algorithms, plus evaluation software was made available on 21 February, and the test data was released on 14 March. The deadline for submission of results was 31 March, and a challenge workshop was held in Southampton (UK) on 11 April 2005. Twelve teams entered the challenge and six presented their findings at the workshop. The development kit and test images can be found at the website `http://www.pascal-network.org/challenges/VOC/`.

The structure of the remainder of the chapter is as follows. Section 2 describes the various competitions defined for the challenge. Section 3 describes the datasets provided to participants in the challenge for training and testing. Section 4 defines the *classification* competitions of the challenge and the method of evaluation, and discusses the types of method participants used for classification. Section 5 defines the *detection* competitions of the challenge and the method of evaluation, and discusses the types of method participants used for detection. Section 6 presents descriptions of the methods provided by participants. Section 7 presents the results of the classification competitions, and Section 8 the results for the detection competitions. Section 9 concludes the chapter with discussion of the challenge results, aspects of the challenge raised by participants in the challenge workshop, and prospects for future challenges.

## 2 Challenge

The goal of the challenge was to recognize objects from a number of visual object classes in realistic scenes. Four object classes were selected, namely motorbikes, bicycles, cars, and people. There were two main competitions:

1. Classification: For each of the four classes, predicting the presence/absence of an example of that class in the test image.
2. Detection: Predicting the bounding box and label of each object from the 4 target classes in the test image.

Contestants were permitted to enter either or both of the competitions, and to tackle any or all of the four object classes. The challenge further divided the competitions according to what data was used by the participants for training their systems:

[1] PASCAL stands for pattern analysis, statistical modelling and computational learning. It is the name of an EU Network of Excellence funded under the IST Programme of the European Union.

1. Training using any data excluding the provided test sets.
2. Training using only the data provided for the challenge.

The intention in the first case was to establish just what level of success could currently be achieved on these problems, and by what method. Participants were free to use their own databases of training images which might be much larger than those provided for the challenge, additional annotation of the images such as object parts or reference points, 3D models, etc. Such resources should potentially improve results over using a smaller fixed training set.

In the second case, the intention was to establish which methods were most successful given a specified training set of limited size. This was to allow judgement of which methods generalize best given limited data, and thus might scale better to the problem of recognizing a large number of classes, for which the collection of large data sets becomes an onerous task.

## 3 Image Sets

Two distinct sets of images were provided to participants: a first set containing images both for training and testing, and a second set containing only images for testing.

### 3.1 First Image Set

The first image set was divided into several subsets:

`train`: Training data

`val`: Validation data (suggested). The validation data could be used as additional training data (see below).

`train+val`: The union of `train` and `val`.

`test1`: First test set. This test set was taken from the same distribution of images as the training and validation data, and was expected to provide an 'easier' challenge.

In the preliminary phase of the challenge, the `train` and `val` image sets were released with the development kit. This gave participants the opportunity to try out the code provided in the development kit, including baseline implementations of the classification and detection tasks, and code for evaluating results. The baseline implementations provided used the `train` set for training, and demonstrated use of the evaluation functions on the `val` set. For the challenge proper, the `test1` set was released for evaluating results, to be used for testing alone. Participants were free to use any subset of the `train` and `val` sets for training. Table 1 lists statistics for the first image set.

Examples of images from the first image set containing instances of each object class are shown in Figure 1. Images were taken from the PASCAL image database collection; these were provided by Bastian Leibe & Bernt Schiele

**Table 1.** Statistics of the first image set. The number of images (containing at least one object of the corresponding class) and number of object instances are shown.

| | train | | val | | train+val | | test1 | |
|---|---|---|---|---|---|---|---|---|
| | images | objects | images | objects | images | objects | images | objects |
| **motorbikes** | 107 | 109 | 107 | 108 | 214 | 217 | 216 | 220 |
| **bicycles** | 57 | 63 | 57 | 60 | 114 | 123 | 113 | 123 |
| **people** | 42 | 81 | 42 | 71 | 84 | 152 | 84 | 149 |
| **cars** | 136 | 159 | 136 | 161 | 272 | 320 | 275 | 341 |

**Fig. 1.** Example images from the first image set. From top to bottom: motorbikes, bicycles, people, and cars. The original images are in colour.

(TU-Darmstadt), Shivani Agarwal, Aatif Awan & Dan Roth (University of Illinois at Urbana-Champaign), Rob Fergus & Pietro Perona (California Institute of Technology), Antonio Torralba, Kevin P. Murphy & William T. Freeman

(Massachusetts Institute of Technology), Andreas Opelt & Axel Pinz (Graz University of Technology), and Navneet Dalal & Bill Triggs (INRIA).

The images used in the challenge were manually selected to remove duplicate images, and very similar images taken from video sequences. Subjective judgement of which objects are "recognizable" was made and images containing annotated objects which were deemed unrecognizable were discarded. The subjective judgement required that the object size (in pixels) was sufficiently large, and that the object could be recognized in isolation without the need for "excessive" contextual reasoning e.g. "this blob in the distance must be a car because it is on a road." Images where the annotation was ambiguous were also discarded, for example images of many bicycles in a bike rack for which correct segmentation of the image into individual objects proves impossible even for a human observer.

The images contain objects at a variety of scales and in varying context. Many images feature the object of interest in a "dominant" position, i.e. in the centre of the image, occupying a large area of the image, and against a fairly uniform background. The pose variation in this image set is somewhat limited, for example most motorbikes appear in a "side" view, and most cars in either "side" or "front" views (Figure 1). Pose for the bicycles and people classes is somewhat more variable. Most instances of the objects appear un-occluded in the image, though there are some examples, particularly for people (Figure 1) where only part of the object is visible.

**Annotation.** All the images used in the first image set had already been annotated by contributors of the data to the PASCAL image databases collection. The annotation was not changed for the challenge beyond discarding images for which the annotation was considered incomplete, ambiguous, or erroneous. For each object of interest (e.g. cars), the annotation provides a bounding box (Figure 2a); for some object instances additional annotation is available in the form of a segmentation mask (Figure 2b) specifying which pixels are part of the object.

(a) Bounding box

(b) Segmentation mask

**Fig. 2.** Annotation of objects available for training. (a) all objects are annotated with their bounding boxes. (b) some objects additionally have a pixel segmentation mask.

Each object is labelled with one of the object classes used in the challenge: motorbikes, bicycles, people or cars; in addition, the original PASCAL object class labels were included in the annotation. For some object instances these specify a more detailed label, typically corresponding to a pose of the object e.g. `PAScarSide` and `PAScarRear` respectively identify side and rear views of a car. Participants were free to use this information, for example the group from TU-Darmstadt chose to only train on side views (Section 6.2).

### 3.2 Second Test Set

In the first image set, images from the original pool of data were assigned randomly to training sets (`train+val`) and test set (`test1`). This follows standard practice in the machine learning field in which training and test data are

**Fig. 3.** Example images from the `test2` test set. From top to bottom: motorbikes, bicycles, people, and cars. The original images are in colour. There is greater variability in scale and pose, and more occlusion than the images of `test1` shown in Figure 1.

**Table 2.** Statistics of the `test2` image set. The number of images (containing at least one object of the corresponding class) and number of object instances are shown.

| | `test2` | |
|---|---|---|
| | images | objects |
| **motorbikes** | 202 | 227 |
| **bicycles** | 279 | 399 |
| **people** | 526 | 1038 |
| **cars** | 275 | 381 |

assumed to be drawn from the same distribution. To enable a more difficult set of competitions a second test set (`test2`) was also prepared, intended to give a distribution of images with more variability than the training data. This image set was collected from Google Images specifically for the challenge. Example images from `test2` are shown in Figure 3. The image set is less homogenous than the first image set due to the wide range of different sources from which the images were taken. Some images resembling the composition of those in the first image set were selected, but also images containing greater variation in scale, pose, and level of occlusion. Table 2 lists statistics for the `test2` image set.

### 3.3 Negative Examples

For both training and testing it is necessary to have a pool of *negative* images not containing objects of a particular class. Some other work has used a fixed negative image set of generic "background" images for testing; this risks oversimplifying the task, for example finding images of cars might reasonably be achieved by finding images of roads; if however the negative image set contains many images of roads with *no* cars, the difficulty of the task is made more realistic.

The challenge treated both the classification and detection tasks as a set of *binary* classification/detection problems (Sections 4, 5) e.g. car vs. non-car, and made use of images containing *other* object classes as the negative examples. For example in the *car* detection task, images containing motorbikes (but no cars) were among the negative examples; in the *motorbike* detection task, images containing cars (but no motorbikes) became negative examples. Because the contexts in which the four object classes appear might be considered similar, e.g. cars, motorbikes, bicycles and people may all appear in a street scene, re-use of the images in this way should make for a more realistic (and harder) task.

## 4 Classification Task

The goal in the classification task is to determine whether a given image contains at least one instance of a particular object class. The task was treated as four independent *binary* classification tasks i.e. "does this image contain an object of type $x$?" where $x$ was either motorbike, bicycle, people or cars. Treating the task in this way enables the use of the well-established Receiver Operating Characteristic (ROC) for examining results. Other work has also considered the "forced choice" scenario i.e. "is this an image of a motorbike, a bicycle, a person, or a car?"; this scenario is inapplicable in the context of the challenge since a single image may contain instances of objects from more than one class.

### 4.1 Evaluation of Results

Evaluation of results was performed using ROC curve analysis. This required that participants' methods output a "confidence" for an image, with large values indicating high confidence that the object class of interest is present. Figure 4 shows an example ROC curve, obtained by applying a set of thresholds to the confidence output by a method. On the $x$-axis is plotted the proportion of false positives (how many times a method says the object class is present when it is not); on the $y$-axis is plotted the proportion of true positives (how many times a method says the object class is present when it is). The ROC curve makes it easy to observe the trade-off between the two; some methods may recognize some small proportion of objects very accurately but fail to recognize many, where others may give more balanced performance.

A definitive measure for quantitative evaluation of ROC curves is not possible since, depending on the application, one might wish to place different emphasis on the accuracy of a method at low or high false positive rates. The challenge used two measures to avoid bias: (i) the Equal Error Rate (EER) measures the accuracy at which the number of false positives and false negatives are equal. This measure somewhat emphasizes the behaviour of a method at low false positive rates which might be reasonable for a real-world application; (ii) the Area Under Curve (AUC) measures the total area under the ROC curve. This measure penalizes failures across the whole range of false positives, e.g. a method which recognizes some large proportion of instance with zero error but fails on the remaining portion of the data. In practice, in the experiments, the method judged "best" by each of the two measures was typically the same.

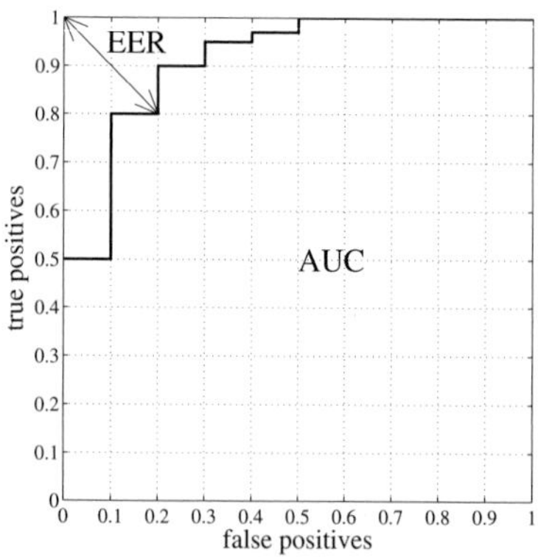


**Fig. 4.** Example Receiver Operating Characteristic (ROC) curve for the *classification* task. The two quantitative measures of performance are illustrated: the Equal Error Rate (EER) and Area Under Curve (AUC).

## 4.2 Competitions and Participation

Four competitions were defined for the classification task, by the choice of training data: provided for the challenge, or the participant's own data; and the test set used: the "easier" `test1` images, or the "harder" `test2` images. Table 3 summarizes the competitions. For each competition, performance on each of the four object classes was evaluated. Participants were free to submit results for any or all of the object classes.

Table 4 lists the participation in competitions 1 and 2, which used the provided `train+val` image set for training. Nine of the twelve participants entered results for these competitions. All but one tackled all object classes (see Section 4.3). Half the participants submitted results for both test sets. No results were submitted for competitions 3 and 4, in which data other than the provided `train+val` image set could be used.

**Table 3.** Competitions for the *classification* task, defined by the choice of training data and test data

| No. | Task | Training data | Test data |
|---|---|---|---|
| 1 | Classification | `train+val` | `test1` |
| 2 | Classification | `train+val` | `test2` |
| 3 | Classification | **not** VOC `test1` or `test2` | `test1` |
| 4 | Classification | **not** VOC `test1` or `test2` | `test2` |

**Table 4.** Participation in *classification* competitions 1 and 2 which used the provided `train+val` image set for training. Bullets indicate participation in the competition for a particular test set and object class.

| | `test1` | | | | `test2` | | | |
|---|---|---|---|---|---|---|---|---|
| | motorbikes | bicycles | people | cars | motorbikes | bicycles | people | cars |
| Aachen | • | • | • | • | • | • | • | • |
| Darmstadt | • | – | – | • | • | – | – | • |
| Edinburgh | • | • | • | • | • | • | • | • |
| FranceTelecom | – | – | – | – | – | – | – | – |
| HUT | • | • | • | • | • | • | • | • |
| INRIA-Dalal | – | – | – | – | – | – | – | – |
| INRIA-Dorko | – | – | – | – | – | – | – | – |
| INRIA-Jurie | • | • | • | • | – | – | – | – |
| INRIA-Zhang | • | • | • | • | • | • | • | • |
| METU | • | • | • | • | – | – | – | – |
| MPITuebingen | • | • | • | • | • | • | • | • |
| Southampton | • | • | • | • | – | – | – | – |

## 4.3 Overview of Classification Methods

Section 6 gives full details of the methods used by participants. The approaches used for the classification task can be broadly divided into four categories:

**Distributions of Local Image Features.** Most participants took the approach of capturing the image content as a distribution over local image features. In these methods a set of vector-valued descriptors capturing local image content is extracted from the image, typically around "interest" points; the image is represented by some form of probability distribution over the set of descriptors. Recognition is carried out by training a classifier to distinguish the distributions for a particular class.

All participants in this category used the SIFT descriptor [32] to represent the appearance of local image regions.

All but one participant (INRIA-Jurie) used "interest point" detection algorithms to define points about which local descriptors were extracted, including the Harris and LoG detectors. Aachen additionally extract descriptors around points on a fixed coarse grid; INRIA-Jurie extracted descriptors around points on a dense grid at multiple scales.

Four participants: Aachen, Edinburgh, INRIA-Jurie, and INRIA-Zhang used a "bag of words" representation. In these methods, local descriptors are assigned a discrete "visual word" from a dictionary obtained by clustering. The image representation is then a histogram over the dictionary, recording either the presence of each word, or the number of times each word occurs in the image.

Two participants MPITuebingen and Southampton used an alternative method based on defining a kernel between sets of extracted features. Both participants used the Bhattacharyya kernel; for Southampton this was defined by a Gaussian distribution in SIFT feature space, while MPITuebingen used a "minor kernel" to lift the calculation into a kernel feature space.

All but two participants in this category used a support vector machine (SVM) classifier. Aachen used a log-linear model trained by iterative scaling; Edinburgh used a functionally equivalent model trained by logistic regression.

**Recognition of Individual Local Features.** METU proposed a method also employing interest point detection and extraction of local features; the SIFT descriptor and colour features were used. In the METU method, rather than examining the entire distribution of local descriptors for an image, a model is learnt which assigns a class probability to *each* local feature; a class is assigned to the image by a noisy-or operation on the class probabilities for each local feature in the image.

**Recognition Based on Segmented Regions.** HUT proposed a method combining features extracted both from the entire image and from regions obtained by an image segmentation algorithm; features included colour, shape and texture descriptors. A number of Self Organizing Maps (SOMs) defined on the different feature spaces were used to classify descriptors obtained from the segmented regions and the whole image, and these results were combined to produce an overall classification.

**Classification by Detection.** Darmstadt adopted the approach of "classification by detection" in which a *detector* for the class of object is applied to the image and the image assigned to the object class if a sufficiently confident detection is found. The method is described more fully in Section 5.3. This approach is of particular interest since it is able to show "why" the object class is assigned to the image, by highlighting the image area thought to be an instance of the object class.

### 4.4 Discussion of Classification Methods

Most participants used "global" methods in which a descriptor of the overall image content is extracted; this leaves the task of deciding which elements of the descriptor are relevant to the object of interest to the classifier. All of these participants used only the class label attached to an image for training, ignoring additional annotation such as the bounding boxes of objects in the image.

One possible advantage of "global" methods is that the image description captures information not only about the object of interest e.g. a car, but also it's context e.g. the road. This contextual information might prove useful in recognizing some object classes; however, the risk is that the system may fail to distinguish the object from the context and thus show poor generalization to other environments, for example recognizing a car in a street vs. in a field.

The approach used by METU uses very *local* information: the classification may be based on a *single* local feature in the image; interestingly, the learning method used here ignores the bounding box information provided. HUT combined global and more local information by computing feature descriptors from both the whole image and segmented regions.

Darmstadt's "classification by detection" approach explicitly ignores all but the object, using bounding boxes or segmentation masks for training, and looking at local evidence for testing; this ensures that the method is modelling the object class of interest rather than statistical regularities in the image background, but may also fail to take advantage of contextual information.

The Darmstadt method is able to give a visual explanation of *why* an image has been classified as containing an object of interest, since it outputs bounding boxes for each object. For some of the other methods (Aachen, Edinburgh, METU, HUT) it might be possible to obtain some kind of labelling of the objects in the image by back-projecting highly-weighted features into the image.

Only two participants explicitly incorporated any geometric information: HUT included shape descriptors of segmented regions in their image representation, and the Darmstadt method uses both local appearance of object parts and their geometric relations. In the global methods, geometric information such as the positions of object parts might be implicitly encoded, but is not transparently represented.

## 5 Detection Task

The goal in the detection task is to detect and localize any instances of a particular object class in an image. Localization was defined as specifying a 'bounding box' rectangle enclosing each object instance in the image. One detection task was run for each class: motorbikes, bicycles, people, and cars.

### 5.1 Evaluation of Results

Evaluation of results was performed using Precsion/Recall (PR) curve analysis. The output required from participants' methods was a set of bounding boxes with corresponding "confidence" values, with large values indicating high confidence that the detection corresponds to an instance of the object class of interest. Figure 5 shows an example PR curve, obtained by applying a set of thresholds to the confidence output by a method. On the $x$-axis is plotted the *recall* (what proportion of object instances in the image set have been detected); on the $y$-axis is plotted the *precision* (what proportion of the detections actually correspond to correct object instances). The PR curve makes it easy to observe the trade-off between the two; some methods may have high precision but low recall, for example detecting a particular view of an object reliably, where other methods may give more balanced performance. Use of Precision/Recall as opposed to the Receiver Operating Characteristic was chosen to provide a standard scale for evaluation which is independent of the algorithmic details of the methods, for example whether a "window scanning" mechanism or other means were used.

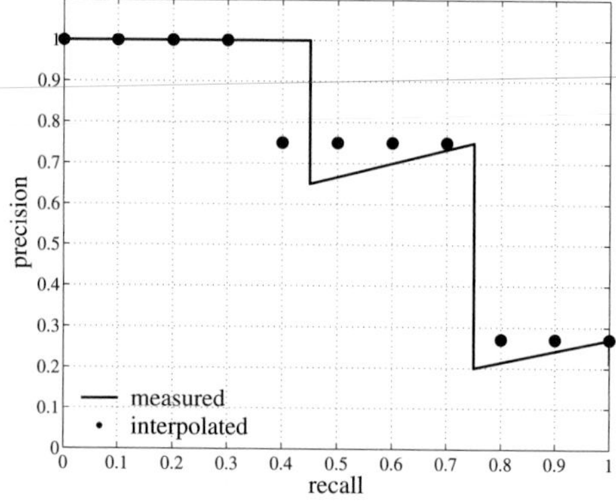


**Fig. 5.** Example Precision/Recall (PR) curve for the *detection* task. The solid line denotes measured performance (perfect precision at zero recall is assumed). The dots indicate the corresponding interpolated precision values used in the average precision (AP) measure.

As in the classification case, a definitive measure for quantitative evaluation of PR curves is not possible, because of the possible requirements for different emphasis at low or high recall. The challenge used the interpolated Average Precision (AP) measure defined by the Text Retrieval Conference (TREC). This measures the mean precision at a set of eleven equally spaced recall levels $[0, 0.1, \ldots, 1]$:

$$AP = \frac{1}{11} \sum_{r \in \{0, 0.1, \ldots, 1\}} p_{interp}(r)$$

The precision at each recall level $r$ is *interpolated* by taking the maximum precision measured for a method for which the corresponding recall exceeds $r$:

$$p_{interp}(r) = \max_{\tilde{r}:\tilde{r}\geq r} p(\tilde{r}) \tag{1}$$

where $p(\tilde{r})$ is the measured precision at recall $\tilde{r}$.

Figure 5 shows the interpolated precision values for the measured curve shown. Use of the interpolated precision ameliorates the effects of different sampling of recall that each method may produce, and reduces the influence of the "saw-tooth" pattern of temporary false detections typical of PR curves. Because the AP measure includes measurements of precision across the full range of recall, it penalizes methods which achieve low total recall (failing to detect some proportion of object instances) as well as those with consistently low precision.

**Evaluation of Bounding Boxes.** Judging each detection output by a method as either a true positive (object) or false positive (non-object) requires comparing the corresponding bounding box predicted by the method with ground truth bounding boxes of objects in the test set. To be considered a correct detection, the area of overlap $a_o$ between the predicted bounding box $B_p$ and ground truth bounding box $B_{gt}$ was required to exceed 50% by the formula

$$a_o = \frac{area(B_p \cap B_{gt})}{area(B_p \cup B_{gt})} \tag{2}$$

The threshold of 50% was set deliberately low to account for inaccuracies in bounding boxes in the ground truth data, for example defining the bounding box for a highly non-convex object, e.g. a side view of a motorbike or a car with an extended radio aerial, is somewhat subjective.

Detections output by a method were assigned to ground truth objects satisfying the overlap criterion in order ranked by the (decreasing) confidence output. Lower-ranked detections of the same object as a higher-ranked detection were considered false positives. The consequence is that methods producing *multiple* detections of a single object would score poorly. All participants included algorithms in their methods to arbitrate between multiple detections.

### 5.2 Competitions and Participation

Four competitions were defined for the detection task, by the choice of training data: provided for the challenge, or the participant's own data; and the test set used: the "easier" `test1` images, or the "harder" `test2` images. Table 5 summarizes the competitions. For each competition, performance on each of the four object classes was evaluated. Participants were free to submit results for any or all of the object classes.

Table 6 lists the participation in competitions 5 and 6, which used the provided `train+val` image set for training. Five of the twelve participants entered results for these competitions. All five of these participants tackled the motorbike class, four the car class, and three the people class. Edinburgh submitted baseline results for all four classes. The concentration on the motorbike and car classes is expected as these are more typical "opaque" objects which have attracted

**Table 5.** Competitions for the *detection* task, defined by the choice of training data and test data

| No. | Task | Training data | Test data |
|---|---|---|---|
| 5 | Detection | `train+val` | `test1` |
| 6 | Detection | `train+val` | `test2` |
| 7 | Detection | **not** VOC `test1` or `test2` | `test1` |
| 8 | Detection | **not** VOC `test1` or `test2` | `test2` |

**Table 6.** Participation in the *detection* task. Bullets indicate participation in the competition for a particular test set and object class.

| | `test1` | | | | `test2` | | | |
|---|---|---|---|---|---|---|---|---|
| | motorbikes | bicycles | people | cars | motorbikes | bicycles | people | cars |
| Aachen | – | – | – | – | – | – | – | – |
| Darmstadt | • | – | – | • | • | – | – | • |
| Edinburgh | • | • | • | • | • | • | • | • |
| FranceTelecom | • | – | – | • | • | – | – | • |
| HUT | – | – | – | – | – | – | – | – |
| INRIA-Dalal | • | – | • | • | • | – | • | • |
| INRIA-Dorko | • | – | • | – | – | – | – | – |
| INRIA-Jurie | – | – | – | – | – | – | – | – |
| INRIA-Zhang | – | – | – | – | – | – | – | – |
| METU | – | – | – | – | – | – | – | – |
| MPITuebingen | – | – | – | – | – | – | – | – |
| Southampton | – | – | – | – | – | – | – | – |

most attention in the object recognition community; recognition of more "wiry" objects (bicycles) or articulated objects (people) has been a recent development.

Only one participant, INRIA-Dalal, submitted results for competitions 7 and 8, in which training data other than that provided for the challenge could be used. This participant submitted results for the people class on both `test1` and `test2` image sets.

### 5.3 Overview of Detection Methods

Section 6 gives full details of the methods used by participants. The approaches used for the detection task can be broadly divided into three categories:

**Configurations of Local Image Features.** Two participants: Darmstadt and INRIA-Dorko used an approach based on local image features. These methods use interest point detectors and local image features represented as "visual words", as used by many of the methods in the classification task. In contrast to the classification task, the detection methods explicitly build a model of the spatial arrangement of the features; detection of the object then requires image features to match the model both in terms of appearance and spatial configuration. The two methods proposed differed in terms of the feature representation: patches of pixels/SIFT descriptors, clustering method for dictionary or "codebook" learning, and voting scheme for detection. Darmstadt used a Minimum Description Length (MDL) method to refine ambiguous detections and an SVM classifier to verify detections. INRIA-Dorko added a measure of discriminative power of each visual word to the voting scheme.

**Window-Based Classifiers.** Two participants: FranceTelecom and INRIA-Dalal used "window-based" methods. In this approach, a fixed sized window is scanned over the image at all pixel positions and multiple scales; for each window, a classifier is applied to label the window as object or non-object, and positively labelled windows are grouped to give detections. FranceTelecom used a Convolutional Neural Network (CNN) classifier which applies a set of successive feature extraction (convolution) and down-sampling operations to the raw input image. INRIA-Dalal used a "histogram of oriented gradient" representation of the image window similar to computing SIFT descriptors around grid points within the window, and an SVM classifier.

**Baseline Methods.** Edinburgh proposed a set of "baseline" detection methods. Confidence in detections was computed either as the prior probability of a class from the training data, or using the classifier trained for the classification task. Several baseline methods for proposing bounding boxes were investigated including simply proposing the bounding box of the entire image, the mean bounding box from the training data, the bounding box of all strong interest points, or bounding boxes based on the "purity" of visual word representations of local features with respect to a class.

## 5.4 Discussion of Detection Methods

There have been two main approaches to object detection in the community: (i) window-based methods, which run a binary classifier over image windows, effectively turning the detection problem into a large number of whole-image classification problems; (ii) parts-based methods, which model objects as a collection of parts in terms of local appearance and spatial configuration. It is valuable that both these approaches were represented in the challenge. The methods proposed differ considerably in their representation of object appearance and geometric information. In the INRIA-Dalal method, a "holistic" representation of primitive local features (edges) is used; the position of features is encoded implicitly with respect to a fixed coordinate system. The FranceTelecom method might be understood as learning the approximate position of local object parts; the convolution operations can be viewed as part detection, and the sub-sampling steps introduce "slack" in the coordinate frame. The Darmstadt and INRIA-Dorko methods *explicitly* decompose the object appearance into local parts and their spatial configuration. It is particularly interesting to see how these methods compare across more rigid objects (cars/motorbikes), and those for which the shape of the object changes considerably (people).

## 6 Participants

Twelve participants took part in the challenge. We include here participants' own descriptions of the methods used.

### 6.1 Aachen

**Participants:** Thomas Deselaers, Daniel Keysers, Hermann Ney
**Affiliation:** RWTH Aachen, Aachen, Germany
**E-mail:** `{deselaers,keysers,ney}@informatik.rwth-aachen.de`
**WWW:** `http://www-i6.informatik.rwth-aachen.de/`

The approach used by the Human Language Technology and Pattern Recognition group of the RWTH Aachen University, Aachen, Germany, to participate in the PASCAL Visual Object Classes Challenge consists of four steps:

1. patch extraction
2. clustering
3. creation of histograms
4. discriminative training and classification

where the first three steps are feature extraction steps and the last is the actual classification step. This approach was first published in [12] and was extended and improved in [13].

The method follows the promising approach of considering objects to be constellations of parts which offers the immediate advantages that occlusions can be handled very well, that the geometrical relationship between parts can be modelled (or neglected), and that one can focus on the discriminative parts of an object. That is, one can focus on the image parts that distinguish a certain object from other objects.

The steps of the method are briefly outlined in the following paragraphs.

**Patch Extraction.** Given an image, we extract square image patches at up to 500 image points. Additionally, 300 points from a uniform grid of $15\times20$ cells that is projected onto the image are used. At each of these points a set of square image patches of varying sizes (in this case $7\times7, 11\times11, 21\times21$, and $31\times31$ pixels) are extracted and scaled to a common size (in this case $15\times15$ pixels).

In contrast to the interest points from the detector, the grid-points can also fall onto very homogeneous areas of the image. This property is on the one hand important for capturing homogeneity in objects which is not found by the interest point detector and on the other hand it captures parts of the background which usually is a good indicator for an object, as in natural image objects are often found in a "natural" environment.

After the patches are extracted and scaled to a common size, a PCA dimensionality reduction is applied to reduce the large dimensionality of the data, keeping 39 coefficients corresponding to the 40 components of largest variance but discarding the first coefficient corresponding to the largest variance. The first coefficient is discarded to achieve a partial brightness invariance. This approach is suitable because the first PCA coefficient usually accounts for global brightness.

**Clustering.** The data are then clustered using a $k$-means style iterative splitting clustering algorithm to obtain a partition of all extracted patches. To do so, first one Gaussian density is estimated which is then iteratively split to obtain more densities. These densities are then re-estimated using $k$-means until convergence is reached and then the next split is done. It has be shown experimentally that results consistently improve up to 4096 clusters but for more than 4096 clusters the improvement is so small that it is not worth the higher computational demands.

**Creation of Histograms.** Once we have the cluster model, we discard all information for each patch except its closest corresponding cluster centre identifier. For the test data, this identifier is determined by evaluating the Euclidean distance to all cluster centres for each patch. Thus, the clustering assigns a cluster $c(x) \in \{1, \ldots C\}$ to each image patch $x$ and allows us to create histograms of cluster frequencies by counting how many of the extracted patches belong to each of the clusters. The histogram representation $h(X)$ with $C$ bins is then determined by counting and normalization such that $h_c(X) = \frac{1}{L_X} \sum_{l=1}^{L_X} \delta(c, c(x_l))$, where $\delta$ denotes the Kronecker delta function, $c(x_l)$ is the closest cluster centre to $x_l$, and $x_l$ is the $l$-th image patch extracted from image $X$, from which a total of $L_X$ patches are extracted.

**Training and Classification.** Having obtained this representation by histograms of image patches, we define a decision rule for the classification of images. The approach based on maximum likelihood of the class-conditional distributions does not take into account the information of competing classes during training. We can use this information by maximizing the class posterior probability $\prod_{k=1}^{K} \prod_{n=1}^{N_k} p(k|X_{kn})$ instead. Assuming a Gaussian density with pooled covariances for the class-conditional distribution, this maximization is equivalent to maximizing the parameters of a log-linear or maximum entropy model

$$p(k|h) = \frac{1}{Z(h)} \exp\left(\alpha_k + \sum_{c=1}^{C} \lambda_{kc} h_c\right),$$

where $Z(h) = \sum_{k=1}^{K} \exp\left(\alpha_k + \sum_{c=1}^{C} \lambda_{kc} h_c\right)$ is the renormalization factor. We use a modified version of generalized iterative scaling. Bayes' decision rule is used for classification.

**Conclusions.** The method performs well for various tasks (e.g. Caltech {airplanes, faces, motorbikes}), was used in the ImageCLEF 2005 Automatic Annotation Task[2] where it performed very well, and also performed well in the PASCAL Visual Object Classes Challenge described in this chapter. An important advantage of this method is that it is possible to visualize those patches

[2] http://ir.shef.ac.uk/imageclef2005/

which are discriminative for a certain class, e.g. in the case of faces it was learned that the most discriminative parts are the eyes.

### 6.2 Darmstadt

**Participants:** Mario Fritz, Bastian Leibe, Edgar Seemann, Bernt Schiele
**Affiliation:** TU-Darmstadt, Darmstadt, Germany
**E-mail:** `mario.fritz@informatik.tu-darmstadt.de`

We submit results on the categories car and motorbike obtained with the *Implicit Shape Model (ISM)* [28] and the *Integrated Representative Discriminant (IRD)* approach [19]. The ISM in itself is an interesting model, as it has recently shown impressive results on challenging object class detections problems [30]. The IRD approach augments the representative ISM by an additional discriminant stage, which improves the precision of the detection system.

**Local Feature Representation.** We use local features as data representation. As scale-invariant interest point detector we use difference-of-Gaussians and as region descriptor we use normalized raw pixel patches. Even though there exist more sophisticated descriptors, we want to point out that due to the rather high resolution of 25×25 pixels the representation is quite discriminant. The high dimensionality of the resulting features is taken care of by the quantization of the feature space via soft-matching to a codebook. More recently [35] [41] we have used more efficient feature representation for the task of object class detection.

**Codebook.** In both approaches, we use a codebook representation as a first generalization step, which is generated by an agglomerative clustering scheme. Up to now, our approaches have only been evaluated on single viewpoints. In order to stay consistent with those experiments, we only selected side views from the training set. This leaves us with 55 car images and 153 motorbike images for building the codebook and learning the model.

**Learning and Evaluating the Model.** The basic idea of the ISM is to represent the appearance of an object by a non-parametric, spatial feature occurrence distribution for each codebook. When using the model for detection, local feature are computed from the test image and afterwards matched to the codebook. Based on these matches, the spatial distributions stored in the ISM can be used to accumulate evidence for object hypothesis characterized by position in the image and size of the object. For a more detailed description - in particular how to achieve scale-invariance - we refer to [29].

**MDL Hypothesis Verification Stage.** As the ISM facilitates the use of segmentation masks for increased performance, we included the provided annotations in the training. Given this information, a pixel-level segmentation can be inferred on the test images. On the one hand this information can be fed back in the recognition loop for interleaved recognition and segmentation [28]. On the other hand, the problem of accepting a subset of ambiguous hypothesis in an image can be formulated as an optimization problem in a MDL framework based on the inferred figure and background probabilities[28]. For both methods submitted to the challenge we make use of the MDL stage.

**SVM with Local Kernel of IRD Approach.** The SVM validation stage is trained on detections and false alarms of the ISM on the whole training set for cars and motorbikes. We want to point out, that both systems work on the same data representation, so that the SVM makes full use of the information provided by the ISM. A hypothesis consists of an inferred position of the object centre in the image, an inferred object scale and a set of features that are consistent with this hypothesis. Based on this information, the SVM is used to eliminate false positives of the representative ISM model during detection. The whole process is illustrated in Figure 6.

Besides the fact, that it is appealing to combine representative and discriminant models from a machine learning point of view, we also profit from the explicit choices of the components: While part of the success of the ISM is a result of its capability for "across instances" learning, the resulting hypothesis can lack global consistency which result in superfluous object parts. By using an SVM with a kernel function of appearance *and* position we enforce a global

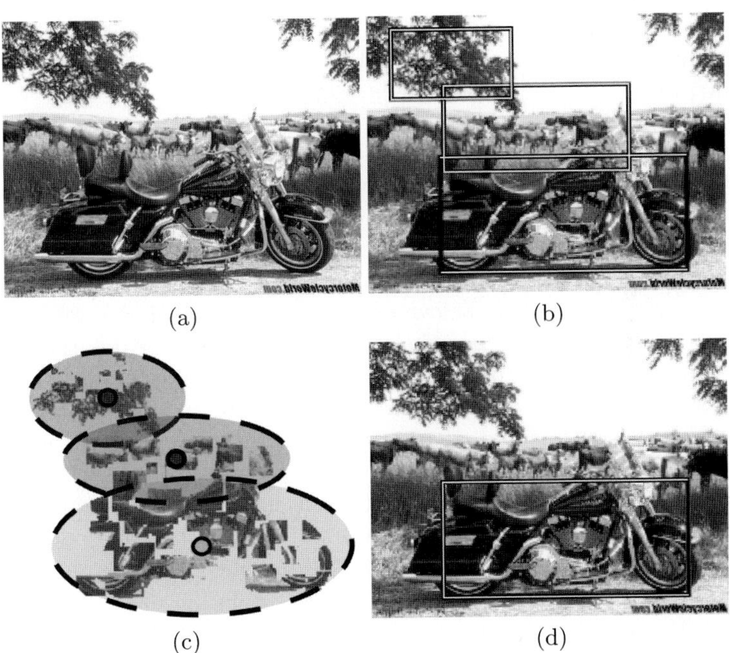


**Fig. 6.** *Darmstadt:* Illustration of the IRD approach. (a) input image; (b) detected hypothesis by the ISM model using a rather low threshold; (c) input to the SVM stage; (d) verified hypothesis.

consistency again. The benefit of enforcing global consistencies were studied in more detail in [30].

**Experiments.** All experiments were performed on the test-sets exactly as specified in the PASCAL challenge. For computational reasons, the test images were rescaled to a uniform width of 400 pixels. We report results on both the object detection and the present/absent classification task. Detection performance is evaluated using the hypothesis bounding boxes returned by the ISM approach. For the classification task, an object-present decision is taken if at least one hypothesis is detected in an image. Since our integrated ISM+SVM approach allows for an additional precision/recall trade-off, we report two performance curves for the detection tasks. One for optimal equal error rate (EER) performance and one for optimized precision (labelled "ISMSVM_2" in the plots).

**Notes on the Results.** The models were exclusively trained on side-views. As the test data also includes multiple viewpoints, 100 % recall is not reachable given the used training scheme. Given that test-set 1 contains only side-views for the motorbikes and approximately 59% side-views for the cars and 39% and 12% for test-set 2 respectively, we detect nearly all side-views with a high level of precision.

### 6.3 Edinburgh

**Participants:** Tom Griffiths, Moray Allan, Amos Storkey, Chris Williams
**Affiliation:** University of Edinburgh, Edinburgh, UK
**E-mail:** moray@sermisy.org

**Experiments.** Our aim in these experiments was to assess the performance that can be obtained using a simple approach based on classifiers and detectors using SIFT representations of interest points. We deliberately did not use state-of-the-art class-specific detectors.

All the systems described below begin by detecting Harris-Affine interest points in images[3] [37]. SIFT representations are then found for the image regions chosen by the interest point detector [32]. The SIFT representations for all the regions chosen in the training data are then clustered using $k$-means. A test image can now be represented as a vector of activations by matching the SIFT representation of its interest point regions against these clusters and counting how many times each cluster was the best match for a region from the test image. This approach was suggested by recent work of Csurka, Dance et al. [10].

All the systems were trained only on the provided training data (`train`), with parameters optimised using the provided validation data (`val`). The test data sets were only used in the final runs of the systems to obtain results for submission. All the detectors described below assume a *single* object of interest per image.

[3] We used code from the Oxford Visual Geometry Group available at http://www.robots.ox.ac.uk/ vgg/research/affine/.

**`Edinburgh_bof` Classifier.** This classifier uses logistic regression[4], based on a 1500-dimensional bag-of-features representation of each image. Interest points were detected using the Harris-Affine region detector and encoded as SIFT descriptors. These were pooled from all images in the training set and clustered using simple $k$-means ($k = 1500$). The 1500-dimensional bag-of-features representation for each image is computed by counting, for each of the 1500 cluster centres, how many regions in the image have no closer cluster centre in SIFT space.

**`Edinburgh_meanbb` Detector.** This naïve approach is intended to act as a baseline result. All images in the test set are assigned the class probability as their confidence level. This class probability is calculated from the class frequency as the number of positive examples of the class in the training set divided by the total number of training images.

All detections are made using the class mean bounding box, scaled according to the size of the image. The class mean bounding box is calculated by finding all the bounding boxes for this class in the training data, and normalising them with respect to the sizes of the images in which they occur, then taking the means of the normalised coordinates.

**`Edinburgh_wholeimage` Detector.** This naïve approach is intended to act as a baseline result. All images in the test set are assigned the class probability as their confidence level. The object bounding box is simply set to the perimeter of the test image.

**`Edinburgh_puritymeanbb` Detector.** We define the 'purity' of a cluster with respect to an object class as the fraction of all the Harris-Affine interest points in the training images for which it is the closest cluster in SIFT space (subject to a maximum distance threshold $t$) that are located within a bounding box for an object of the class.

In detection, the centre of the bounding box is set as the weighted mean of the location of all Harris-Affine interest points in the test image, where the weight of each interest point's location is the purity of its nearest cluster in SIFT space (with respect to the current object class, subject to a maximum distance threshold $t$).

The size and shape of the bounding box for all detections was set to that of the class mean bounding box, scaled according to the size of the image. The class mean bounding box was calculated as for the `Edinburgh_meanbb` method.

Confidences are calculated by the bag-of-features classifier, as described for `Edinburgh_bof`, with the addition of a maximum distance threshold $t$ (so descriptors very far from any cluster do not count).

Throughout, $t$ was set to three times the standard deviation of the distances of all SIFT descriptors from their nearest cluster centre, a value chosen by experiment on the validation data.

---

[4] We used the Netlab logistic regression function, `glm`.

`Edinburgh_siftbb` **Detector.** This detector assigns the confidence levels calculated by the bag-of-features classifier, as described for `Edinburgh_bof`, while bounding boxes are predicted as the tight bounding box of the interest points found in the image by the Harris-Affine detector.

**Discussion.** Our entries consisted of one straightforward 'bag-of-features' approach to classification and four simple approaches to the detection task. In comparison to other entries tackling the classification task, the performance of our bag-of-features classifier was almost always behind that of the competitors. By the area under ROC curve measure (AUC), it achieved only 0.77, 0.72, 0.60 and 0.80 on the four object categories compared with 0.88, 0.82, 0.82 and 0.91 for the next highest competitor in each case. In all but the final category (cars), this meant our entry was the poorest performer.

Following discussions at the challenge workshop, we modified our approach in two small ways and performance improved considerably, to 0.89, 0.87, 0.81 and 0.85. The changes we made were to: 1) train our classifier on the `train+val` data set instead of only the `train` data set; and 2) normalise the bag-of-feature representation vectors. This first modification provided substantially more training data with which to refine the decision boundary of the classifier, leading to a small improvement in performance. The fact that the second modification led to such a significant performance increase suggests it is the *proportions* of the different visual words in the image that are useful for classification rather than their absolute number. This makes sense, as the images (and the objects within them) are commonly of different sizes and hence the number of features representing them varies.

Our approaches to the detection task were intended as simple baselines from which to judge the more complex approaches of the other competitors. Such baselines were widely acknowledged as useful by attendees at the workshop, and serve to highlight the real progress made in tackling this challenging task by the other entries.

### 6.4 FranceTelecom

**Participants:** Christophe Garcia, Stefan Duffner
**Affiliation:** France Télécom division R&D, Cesson Sévigné, France
**E-mail:** `christophe.garcia@francetelecom.com`
**WWW:** `http://www.francetelecom.com/rd/`

The proposed system, called Convolutional Object Finder (COF), is based on a convolutional neural network architecture inspired from our previous work on face detection [20]. It automatically synthesises simple problem-specific feature extractors and classifiers, from a training set of object and non-object patterns, without making any assumptions concerning the features to be extracted or the areas of the object pattern to be analysed. Once trained, for a given object, the COF acts like a fast pipeline of simple convolution and subsampling modules

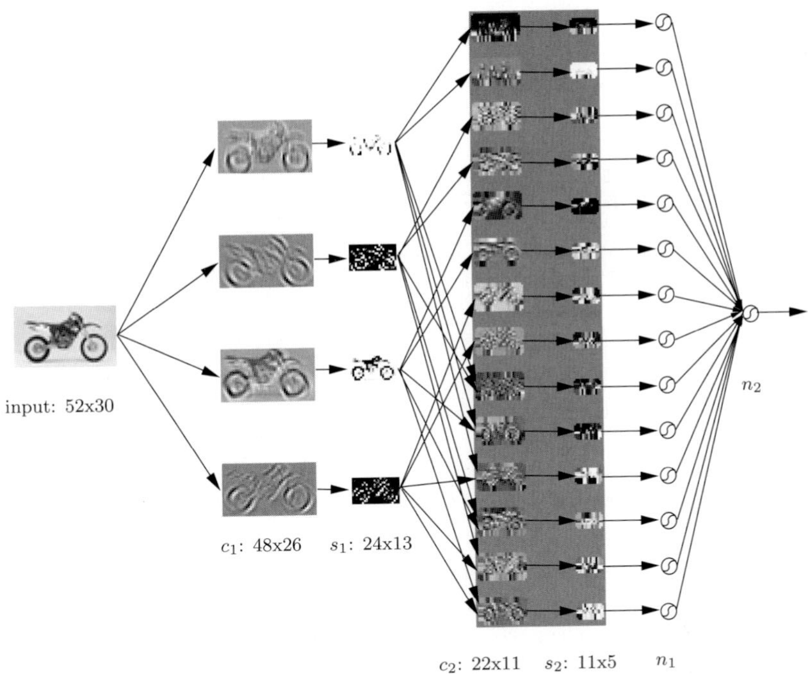


**Fig. 7.** *FranceTelecom:* Architecture of the Convolutional Object Finder (COF) system

that treat the raw input image as a whole, at different scales, without requiring any local pre-processing of the input image (brightness correction, histogram equalisation, etc.).

The COF system consists of six layers, excepting the input plane (retina) that receives an image area of fixed size (52×30 pixels in the case of motorbikes) to be classified as *object* or *non-object* (see Fig.7). Layers $c_1$ through $s_2$ contain a series of planes where successive convolutions and subsampling operations are performed.

These planes are called *feature maps* as they are in charge of extracting and combining a set of appropriate features. Layer $n_1$ contains a number of partially connected sigmoid neurons and layer $n_2$ contains the output unit of the network. These last two layers carry out the classification task using the features extracted in the previous layers.

The neural network is fully trained using a modified version of the backpropagation algorithm, by receiving object and non-object images with target answer $+1$ and $-1$ respectively. The positive training sets (object images) are augmented by virtual examples, generated by slightly rotating, translating and scaling the original object images. In order to reduce the number of false alarms, the set of negative (non-object) examples is iteratively constructed by a bootstrapping procedure. It uses a set of scenery images that do not contain the object to detect, in order to extract non-object image areas that produce a positive output

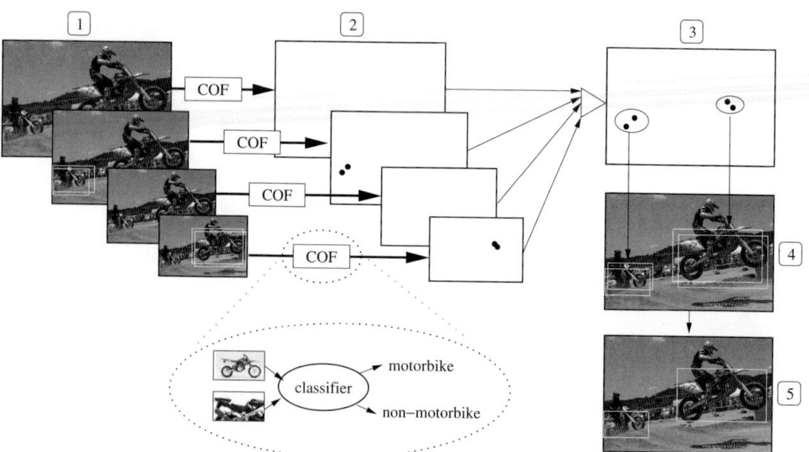


**Fig. 8.** *FranceTelecom:* Different steps of object localisation

value (false alarm) greater than a certain threshold. This threshold is initialised with a high value (e.g. 0.8) and is gradually decreased (until 0.0), throughout the iterative learning process, so that a rough class boundary is quickly found in the first iterations and refined later on.

In order to detect objects at different scales, the COF system is placed into a multi-scale framework as depicted in Fig. 8.

The input image is repeatedly subsampled by a factor of 1.2, resulting in a pyramid of images (step 1). Each image of the pyramid is then filtered by our convolutional network COF (step 2). After this processing step, object candidates (pixels with positive values in the result image) in each scale are mapped back to the input image scale (step 3). They are then grouped according to their proximity in image and scale spaces. Each group of object candidates is fused into a representative object whose centre and size are computed as the centroids of the centres and sizes of the grouped objects, weighted by their individual network responses (step 4). After applying this grouping algorithm, the set of remaining representative object candidates serve as a basis for finer object localisation and false alarm dismissal (step 5). This finer localisation consists of a local search with smaller scale steps in a limited area around each object candidate. In order to remove false alarms, the sum of positive network outputs over the local search space is computed at each candidate position and candidate areas with a value below a certain threshold are rejected.

Experimental results show that the proposed system is very robust with respect to lighting, shape and pose variations as well as noise, occlusions and cluttered background. Moreover, processing is fast and a parallel implementation is straightforward. However, it should be noticed that detection results can be drastically enhanced if a large training set of thousands of object images is made available. As future extensions, we plan to enhance the COF system by allowing a variable aspect ratio for the retina image that will help to cope with highly variable 3D object shapes and poses.

### 6.5 HUT

**Participants:** Ville Viitaniemi, Jorma Laaksonen, Markus Koskela
**Affiliation:** Helsinki University of Technology, Helsinki, Finland
**E-mail:** {ville.viitaniemi,jorma.laaksonen, markus.koskela}@hut.fi

**Overview of the PicSOM System.** For all the experiments we used a similar setup utilising our general purpose content-based image retrieval system named PicSOM [26]. Given a set of positive and negative example images, the system looks through the image collection and returns images most similar to the positive and most dissimilar to the negative examples. The system operates in its interactive mode by the principles of *query by pictorial example* and *relevance feedback*. In these experiments, however, the system was operated in batch mode, as if the user had given relevance feedback on all images in the training set at once.

The basic principle of the PicSOM system is to use Self-Organizing Maps (SOMs), which are two-dimensional artificial neural networks, to organise and index the images of the collection. The SOM orders images so that visually similar images – in the sense of some low-level statistical feature – are mapped to the same or nearby map units in a two-dimensional grid. The PicSOM system inherently uses multiple features, creates a separate index for each of them and uses them all in parallel when selecting the retrieved images. In our current experiments, we used the system to give a qualification value for every image in the test set. That way we could order them in the order of descending similarity to the corresponding set of training images.

The visual features that were used to describe the images were chosen among the ones that were already available in the PicSOM system. These are targeted to the general domain image description, i.e. the feature set was not specialised a priori to the target image classes. The set of available features consisted of:

- MPEG-7 content descriptors ColorLayout, DominantColor, EdgeHistogram, RegionShape and ScalableColor
- average colour in CIE L*a*b* colour space
- first three colour moments in CIE L*a*b* colour space
- Fourier descriptors of object contours
- a texture feature measuring the relative brightness of neighbouring pixels

**Details of the Experimental Procedure.** The PicSOM system was applied to the image classification task using the following procedure:

1. The training set images were projected to the parallel feature SOMs.
2. The distance of the projection of a given test image was locally compared with the nearby projections of positive and negative training images. This was achieved by kernel smoothing the SOM surface field defined by the positive and negative training impulses.
3. The results from the parallel feature SOMs were summed together.

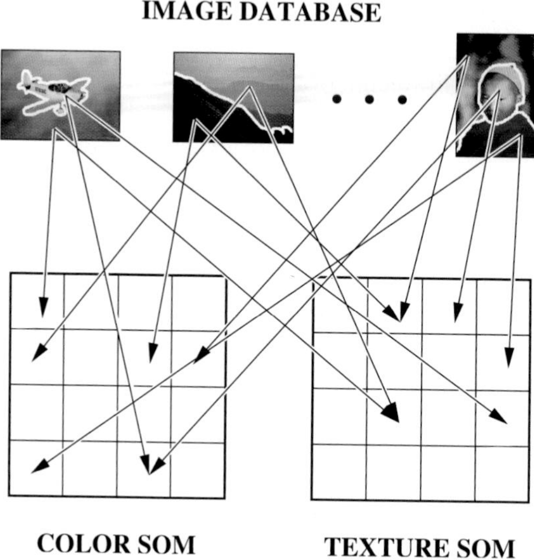


**Fig. 9.** *HUT:* An example of using two parallel SOM indices for segmented images in the PicSOM system. The colour and texture SOMs are trained with image segments and each segment is connected to its best-matching map unit on each SOM.

In the time frame of the VOC challenge, we were not able to utilise the training set annotations beyond the presence/absence information, i.e. the bounding boxes and other additional annotations were not used.

System parameters were tuned using the validation set performance as an optimisation criterion. Feature selection was performed based on the performance in the validation set. As the performance measure we used the area under the ROC curve. All four target classes were processed separately and the optimisations led us to use four different sets of features. We used all four optimised feature sets for all four classes. This resulted in the total of 16 result sets submitted. Other parameters, such as the size of the SOMs, were not optimised. The final results were obtained by using only the union of the provided training and validation data sets in the training of the SOMs in the system.

The training, validation and testing set images were automatically segmented to a few parallel segmentations with predetermined numbers of segments. Visual features were extracted from both the segments and the whole images. Separate SOMs were trained for the segment features and the whole-image features. Figure 9 illustrates the use of the image segments and the parallel SOMs.

### 6.6 INRIA-Dalal

**Participants:** Navneet Dalal, Bill Triggs
**Affiliation:** INRIA Rhône-Alpes, Montbonnot, France
**E-mail:** {navneet.dalal,bill.triggs}@inrialpes.fr

**Introduction.** INRIA participated in eight of the object detection challenges with its Histogram of Oriented Gradient (HOG) object detector: competitions 5 and 6 for classes Motorbike, Car, Person and competitions 7 and 8 for class Person.

In use, the detector scans the image with a detection window at multiple positions and scales, running an object/non-object classifier in each window. Local maxima of "object" score are found, and if the score is above threshold a detection is declared. The classifier is a linear SVM over our HOG feature set, trained using SVM-Light [22, 23].

The Histogram of Oriented Gradient feature set is described in detail in [11]. Here we focus on giving information not available in [11], but briefly, after some optional input normalization, we calculate image gradients at each pixel, use the gradient orientation to select an orientation channel and the gradient magnitude as a weight to vote into it, and accumulate these votes over small local regions called *cells*. Each cell thus contains a weighted gradient orientation histogram. The cells are gathered into somewhat larger spatial *blocks*, and the block's histograms are normalized as a group to provide local illumination invariance. The final descriptor is the concatenated vector of all channels of all cells of all blocks in the detection window. To reduce aliasing, the implementation includes careful spatial and angular interpolation and spatial windowing of the cells within each block. The blocks are usually chosen to overlap so (modulo windowing effects) each cell's histogram appears several times with different normalizations. The window is usually chosen somewhat (10-20%) larger than the object as including context helps recognition.

**Data Preparation.** For training and validation we use the size-normalized object boxes from the positive *train* and *val* sets. The corresponding negatives are sampled randomly from negative images. To allow for context we include an 8 or 16 pixel margin around the image window. Table 7 lists the window sizes and key parameters of each detector.

**HOG Parameter Optimization.** HOG descriptors have a number of parameters to set. This was done using the PASCAL *train* and *val* sets respectively for training and validation. For the window sizes given in table 7, the following settings turned out to be optimal for all of the object classes: taking the square root of image intensities before computing gradients; 20° orientation bins (9 in 180° or 18 in 360°); 2×2 blocks of 8×8 pixel cells; and an inter block stride of 8 pixels (so each cell belongs to 4 blocks). Two settings changed

**Table 7.** The key parameters for each trained detector

| Class | Window Size | Avg. Size | Orientation Bins | Normalization Method | Margin (see §6.6) |
|---|---|---|---|---|---|
| Person | 56×112 | Height 80 | 9 (0–180°) | L2-Hys | 12 |
| Car | 112×56 | Height 40 | 18 (0–360°) | L2-Hys | 8 |
| Motorbike | 144×80 | Width 112 | 18 (0–360°) | L1-Sqrt | 4 |

from class to class. *(i)* Including the signs of gradients (*i.e.* using orientation range 0–360° rather than 0–180°) is helpful for classes in which local contrasts typically have consistent signs (*e.g.* cars and motorcycles with their dark tyres on light rims), and harmful for less consistent classes (*e.g.* humans with their multicoloured clothing). *(ii)* Regarding normalization, L2-Hys (L2-norm followed by Lowe-style clipping and renormalization [32]) and L1-Sqrt (L1-norm followed by square root, *i.e.*, $\mathbf{v} \rightarrow \sqrt{\mathbf{v}/(\|\mathbf{v}\|_1 + \epsilon)}$ typically have comparable performance, but for the motorbike class L1-Sqrt significantly outperforms L2-Hys. We suspect that this happens because L1-Sqrt provides more robustness against the rapid fine-detail gradient changes that are common in motorcycle wheels.

**Multi-scale Detection Framework.** To use the above window-based classifier for object detection, it is scanned across the image at multiple scales, typically firing several times in the vicinity of each object. We need to combine these overlapping classifier hits to produce a detection rule that fires exactly once for each observed object instance. We treat this as a maximum finding problem in the 3D position-scale space. More precisely, we convert the classifier score to a weight at each 3D point, and use a variable bandwidth Mean Shift algorithm [9] to locate the local maxima of the resulting 3D "probability density". Mean Shift requires positive weights, and it turns out that clipped SVM scores max(score, 0) work well. The (variable) bandwidth for each point is given by $(\sigma_x s, \sigma_y s, \sigma_s)$ where $s$ is the detection scale and $\sigma_x, \sigma_y, \sigma_s$ are respectively the $x, y$ and scale bandwidths. We use $\sigma_s = 30\%$ and set $(\sigma_x, \sigma_y)$ to $(8, 16)$ for the Person class and $(16, 8)$ for the Motorbike and Car classes – *i.e.* proportional to the aspect ratio of the detection window, as in practice the multiple detections tend to be distributed in this way.

We perform one final step. The challenge rules consider detections to be false if they have less than 50% area overlap with the marked object box, and as our detection windows have been slightly enlarged to include some background context, we need to shrink them again. Different classes occupy different amounts of their bounding boxes on average, so we do this adaptively. For each class, we learn a final classifier on the combined *train+val* data set (with settings chosen by validation on *val* after training on *train*). Using this classifier on *train+val*, we calculate precision-recall curves for several different window shrinkage factors and choose the factor that gives the best overall performance. Table 7 lists the chosen shrinkage margins in pixels relative to the detection window size. Note that this tuning is based on training data. For each challenge we performed just one run on test set, whose results were submitted to the challenge.

**Additional Comments.** We did not have time to optimize the window size of our motorbike classifier before the challenge, but afterwards we found that larger windows are preferable – $144 \times 80$ here, versus $112 \times 56$ in our original challenge submission. The performance of the new classifier is comparable to the two best results in the challenge.

### 6.7 INRIA-Dorko

**Participants:** Gyuri Dorkó, Cordelia Schmid
**Affiliation:** INRIA Rhône-Alpes, Montbonnot, France
**E-mail:** {gyuri.dorko,cordelia.schmid}@inrialpes.fr

**Introduction.** We have participated in the localization competition for people and motorbikes. Our method combines class-discriminative local features with an existing object localization technique to improve both its speed and performance. Our system learns the spatial distribution of the object positions for automatically created discriminative object-parts, and then, uses the generalized Hough-transform to predict object locations on unseen test images.

**Feature Extraction.** Images are described by sparse local features extracted with a scale-invariant interest point operator. We use a modified version of the multi-scale Harris detector [21]. Interest regions are described by the Scale Invariant Feature Transform (SIFT) [32] computed on a 4x4 grid and for 8 orientation bins, resulting in a 128 dimensional descriptor.

**Training.** We first learn a vocabulary of size 1200 from the scale-invariant features of the training set. We use expectation-maximization (EM) to estimate a Gaussian Mixture Model with a diagonal covariance matrix. Then, we assign a rank to each cluster based on its discriminative power as in [15]. Our criterion is derived from the likelihood score, and prefers rare but very discriminative object-parts. The rank for cluster $C_i$ is defined as:

$$\tilde{P}^{+}(C_i) = \frac{\sum_{\mathbf{v_j} \in D^+} P(C_i|\mathbf{v_j})}{\sum_{\mathbf{v_j} \in D^+} P(C_i|\mathbf{v_j}) + \sum_{\mathbf{v_j} \in D^-} P(C_i|\mathbf{v_j})} \tag{3}$$

where $D^+$ and $D^-$ are the set of descriptors extracted from positive and negative images respectively and $P(C_i|\mathbf{v_j})$ is the probability of component $C_i$ given descriptor $\mathbf{v_j}$. We then learn the spatial distribution of the object positions and scales for each cluster. For each training image, we assign all descriptors inside the rectangle locating the object to its cluster (by MAP), and record the centre $(x,y)$ and the scale (width and height) of the rectangle with respect to the assigned cluster. This step is equivalent to [29] with the difference that we collect the width and height separately and that we do not use the figure-ground segmentation of the object. The output of our training is a list of clusters with the following properties:

- the mean and variance representing the appearance distribution of the cluster,
- a probabilistic score for its discriminative power,
- and a spatial distribution of the object positions and scales.

**Localization by Probabilistic Hough Voting.** The localization procedure on a test image is similar to the initial hypothesis generation of Leibe *et al.*

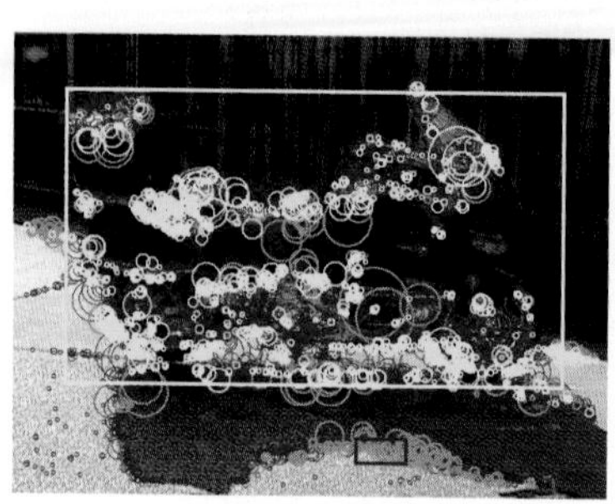

Motorbike

People

**Fig. 10.** *INRIA-Dorko:* Example detections on test images for motorbike (left) and people (right). Blue (dark) points are eliminated due to feature selection, and yellow (bright) points vote for the best solution (yellow rectangle). Non-yellow rectangles indicate false detections with lower confidence.

[29]. The difference is that we incorporate the discriminative capacity into the voting scheme: only the 100 most discriminative clusters participate in the voting, and the probabilistic score is integrated into the voting scheme. This allows better confidence estimations for the different hypotheses. Our algorithm is the following. The extracted scale-invariant features of the test image are assigned to the closest cluster by appearance (MAP). Then, the chosen clusters vote for possible object locations and scales (4D space). In practice we simplified the voting scheme from [29] by only allowing one cluster per descriptor to vote, and extended their formulation by weighting each vote with the discriminative score from (3). The predicted object locations and scales are found as maxima in the 4D voting space using the Mean-Shift[8] algorithm with a scale-adaptive balloon density estimator[9, 29]. The confidence level for each detection is determined by the sum of the votes around the object location in the voting space. Fig. 10 shows example detections on test images.

### 6.8 INRIA-Jurie

**Participants:** Frederic Jurie, Gyuri Dorkó, Diane Larlus, Bill Triggs
**Affiliation:** INRIA Rhône-Alpes, Montbonnot, France
**E-mail:** `frederic.jurie@inrialpes.fr`

We participated in the competition 1 for all four categories.

Our method is based on an SVM classifier trained on feature vectors built using local image descriptors. Our approach is purely appearance based, i.e. it does not explicitly use the local structures of object classes. The learning consists of four steps (see Fig. 11). First, we extract local image features using a dense multi-scale representation. Our novel clustering method is then applied

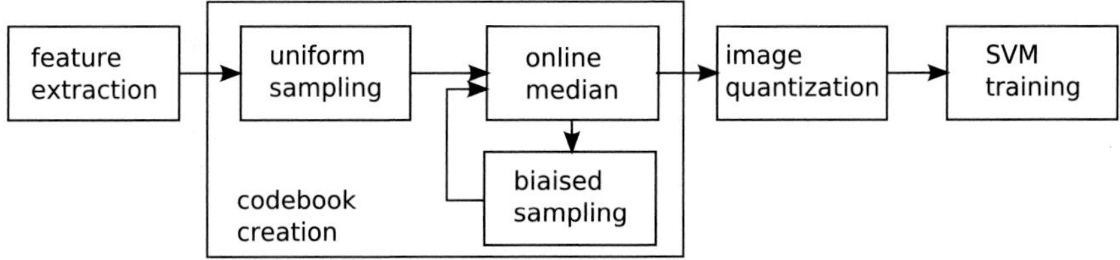


**Fig. 11.** *INRIA-Jurie:* Outline of the learning steps. See text for details.

to build a codebook of visual words. This codebook is used to compute "bag of features" representation for each image, similar to [10], then an SVM classifier is trained to separate between object images and the background (the other classes of the database). In the following we describe in detail each step of our method.

**Feature Extraction.** Overlapping local features are extracted on each scale according to a regular grid defined to be sufficiently dense to represent the entire image. Our parameters are set to extract approximately 20000 regions per image. Each region is then represented by a 128 dimensional SIFT descriptor [32], i.e. a concatenated 8-bin orientation histograms on a 4x4 grid.

**Codebook Creation.** The extracted set of dense features has two important properties. First, it is very highly populated; the large number of features per image leads to a total of several hundred thousand for the entire training set (`train+val`). Second, the dense feature set is extremely unbalanced as was shown in [24]. Therefore, to obtain a discrete set of labels on the descriptors we have designed a new clustering algorithm [27] taking into account these properties. The method has two main advantages. It can discover low populated regions of the descriptor space, and it can easily cope with a large number of descriptors.

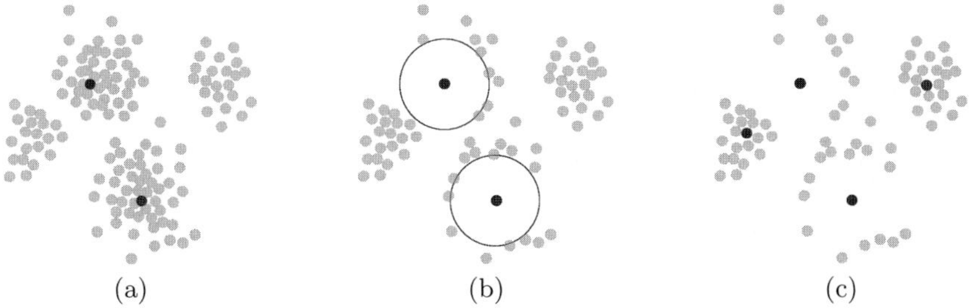


**Fig. 12.** *INRIA-Jurie:* Biased sampling. (a) assumes that we discovered 2 new centres in the previous step, which is marked by the two black points. (b) The influence radius determines an affectation ball around each centre. (c) All descriptors within these balls are removed and the remaining portion is then random sampled.

Our iterative approach discovers new clusters at each step by consecutively calling a sampling and a k-median algorithm (see Fig. 11) until the required total number of clusters are found. In order to decrease the importance of highly populated regions we use biased sampling: new regions are discovered far enough from previously found centres. This is realized by introducing an *influence radius* to affect points close to already found centres. All affected descriptors are then excluded from any further sampling. Fig. 12 illustrates our sampling step. The influence radius ($r = 0.6$) and the total number of clusters ($k = 2000$) are parameters of our method.

The biased sampling is followed by the *online median* algorithm proposed by Mettu and Plaxton [34]. Their method is based on the *facility location* problem and chooses the centres one by one. At each iteration of our algorithm we discover 20 new centres by this algorithm.

We keep all the parameters of our codebook creation algorithm fixed and set by our earlier experience, *i.e.* they are not tuned for the PASCAL Challenge database. For the creation of the codebook we originally cropped the training images based on the provided bounding boxes, but later we discovered that our result remain the same using the full images. (ROC curves are reported with the cropped images.)

**Image Quantization.** Both learning and testing images are represented by the *bag of features* approach [10], i.e by frequency histograms computed using the occurrence of each visual word of our codebook. We associate each descriptor to the closest codebook element within the predefined influence radius. Our association discards descriptors that fall out of all affectation balls; they are considered as outliers. To measure the distance between SIFT features we used the Euclidean distance as in [32].

**Classification.** We used the implementation of [6] to train linear SVM classifiers on the normalized image histograms. In the first set of experiments (indicated by `dcb_p1` on our reports) we trained the SVMs on binary histograms, each bin indicating the presence or absence of the codebook elements. In the second set of experiments (indicated by `dcb_p2`), a standard vector normalisation is used.

### 6.9 INRIA-Zhang

**Participants:** Jianguo Zhang, Cordelia Schmid
**Affiliation:** INRIA Rhône-Alpes, Montbonnot, France
**E-mail:** `{jianguo.zhang,cordelia.schmid}@inrialpes.fr`

**Abstract.** Our approach represents images as distributions of features extracted from a sparse set of keypoint locations and learns a Support Vector Machine classifier with a kernel based on an effective measure for comparing distributions. Results demonstrate that our approach is surprisingly effective for classification of object images under challenging real-world conditions, including significant intra-class variations and substantial background clutter.

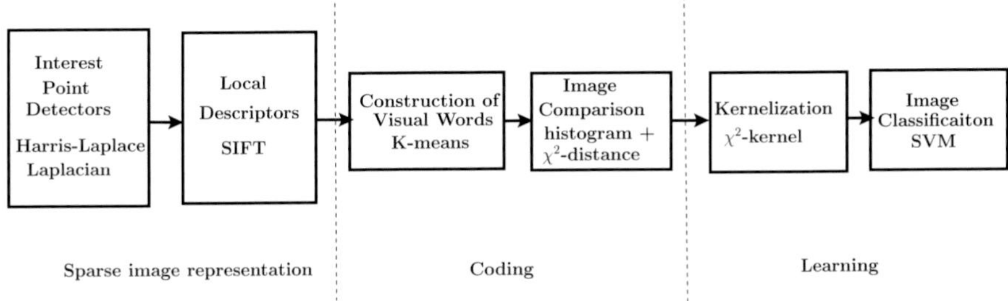


**Fig. 13.** *INRIA-Zhang:* Architecture of the approach

**Introduction.** Fig. 13 illustrates the different steps of our approach. We first compute a sparse image representation by extracting a set of keypoint locations and describing each keypoint with a local descriptor. We then compare image distributions based on frequency histograms of visual words. Finally, images are classified with a $\chi^2$-kernel and a Support Vector Machine (SVM).

A large-scale evaluation of our approach is presented in [44]. This evaluation shows that to achieve the best possible performance, it is necessary to use a combination of several detectors and descriptors together with a classifier that can make effective use of the complementary types of information contained in them. It also shows that using local features with the highest possible level of invariance usually does not yield the best performance. Thus, a practical recognition system should seek to incorporate multiple types of complementary features, as long as their local invariance properties do not exceed the level absolutely required for a given application. An investigation of the influence of background features on recognition performance shows the pitfalls of training on datasets with uncluttered or highly correlated backgrounds, since this yields disappointing results on test sets with more complex backgrounds.

**Sparse Image Representation.** We use two complementary scale-invariant detectors to extract salient image structures: *Harris-Laplace* [37] and *Laplacian* [31]. Harris-Laplace detects corner-like structures, whereas the Laplacian detects blob-like ones. Both detectors output circular regions at a characteristic scale.

SIFT features [32] are used to describe the scale normalized regions; it has been shown to outperform a set of existing descriptors [38]. SIFT computes the gradient orientation histogram for the support region. We use 8 orientation planes. For each orientation, the gradient image is sampled over a 4×4 grid of locations, resulting in a 128 feature vector.

For the training images and test set 1 of the PASCAL challenge (1373 images in total), the average number of points detected per image is 796 for Harris-Laplace and 2465 for the Laplacian. The minimum number of points detected for an image is 15 for Harris-Laplace and 71 for the Laplacian. This illustrates the sparsity of our image representation.

**Comparing Distributions of Local Features.** We first construct a visual vocabulary from the local features and then represent each image as a histogram of visual words. The vocabulary for the PASCAL challenge is obtained as follows: 1) We randomly select 50000 descriptors from the training images of one class. 2) We cluster these features with k-means ($k = 250$). 3) We concatenate the cluster centres of the 4 classes to build the global vocabulary of 1000 words.

A histogram measures the frequency of each word in an image. Each feature in the image is assigned to the closest word. We use the $\chi^2$ distance to compare histograms:

$$\chi^2 = \sum_i \frac{(h_1(i) - h_2(i))^2}{h_1(i) + h_2(i)}$$

where $h_1$ and $h_2$ are the histograms of two different images.

**Kernel-Based Classification.** We use an extended Gaussian kernel [7]:

$$K(S_i, S_j) = \exp(-1/A \cdot D(S_i, S_j))$$

where $D(S_i, S_j)$ is the $\chi^2$ distance and $S_i, S_j$ are vocabulary histograms. The resulting $\chi^2$ *kernel* is a Mercer kernel.

Each detector/descriptor pair can be considered as an independent channel. To combine different channels, we sum their distances, i.e., $D = \sum D_i, i = 1, ..., n$ where $D_i$ is the similarity measure of channel $i$. The kernel parameter $A$ is obtained by 5-fold cross validation on the training images.

For classification, we use *Support Vector Machines* [40]. For a two-class problem the decision function has the form $g(x) = \sum_i \alpha_i y_i K(x_i, x) - b$, where $K(x_i, x)$ is the value of a *kernel function* for the training sample $x_i$ and the test sample $x$. The $y_i \in \{-1, +1\}$ and $\alpha_i$ are the class label and the learned weight of the training sample $x_i$. $b$ is a learned threshold parameter. The training samples with $\alpha_i > 0$ are usually called *support vectors*.

We use the two-class setting for binary detection, i.e., classifying images as containing or not a given object class. If we have $m$ classes ($m = 4$ for the PASCAL challenge), we construct a set of binary SVM classifiers $g_1, g_2, ..., g_m$, each trained to separate one class from the others. The SVM score is used as a confidence measure for a class (normalized to $[0, 1]$).

**Conclusions.** Our bag-of-keypoints method achieves excellent results for object category classification. However, successful category-level object recognition and localization is likely to require more sophisticated models that capture the 3D shape of real-world object categories as well as their appearance. In the development of such models and in the collection of new datasets, bag-of-keypoints methods can serve as effective baselines and calibration tools.

### 6.10 METU

**Participants:** Ilkay Ulusoy[1], Christopher M. Bishop[2]
**Affiliation:** [1]Middle Eastern Technical University, Ankara, Turkey
[2]Microsoft Research, Cambridge, UK
**E-mail:** ilkay@metu.edu.tr, cmbishop@microsoft.com

We follow several recent approaches [32, 37] and use an interest point detector to focus attention on a small number of local patches in each image. This is followed by invariant feature extraction from a neighbourhood around each interest point. Specifically we use DoG interest point detectors, and at each interest point we extract a 128 dimensional SIFT feature vector [32]. Following [3] we concatenate the SIFT features with additional colour features comprising average and standard deviation of $(R, G, B)$, $(L, a, b)$ and $(r = R/(R+G+B)$, $g = G/(R+G+B))$, which gives an overall 144 dimensional feature vector.

We use $\mathbf{t_n}$ to denote the image label vector for image $n$ with independent components $t_{nk} \in \{0,1\}$ in which $k = 1, \ldots K$ labels the class. Each class can be present or absent independently in an image. $\mathbf{X_n}$ denotes the observation for image $n$ and this comprises a set of $J_n$ feature vectors $\{\mathbf{x_{nj}}\}$ where $j = 1, \ldots, J_n$. Note that the number $J_n$ of detected interest points will in general vary from image to image.

On a small-scale problem it is reasonable to segment and label the objects present in the training images. However, for large-scale object recognition involving thousands of categories this will not be feasible, and so instead it is necessary to employ training data which is at best 'weakly labelled'. Here we consider a training set in which each image is labelled only according to the presence or absence of each category of object.

Next we associate with each patch $j$ in each image $n$ a binary label $\tau_{njk} \in \{0,1\}$ denoting the class $k$ of the patch. These labels are mutually exclusive, so that $\sum_{k=1}^{K} \tau_{njk} = 1$. These components can be grouped together into vectors $\tau_{\mathbf{nj}}$. If the values of these labels were available during training (corresponding to strongly labelled images) then the development of recognition models would be greatly simplified. For weakly labelled data, however, the $\{\tau_{\mathbf{nj}}\}$ labels are hidden (latent) variables, which of course makes the training problem much harder.

Consider for a moment a particular image $n$ (and omit the index $n$ to keep the notation uncluttered). We build a parametric model $y_k(\mathbf{x_j}, \mathbf{w})$ for the probability that patch $\mathbf{x_j}$ belongs to class $k$. For example we might use a simple linear-softmax model with outputs

$$y_k(\mathbf{x_j}, \mathbf{w}) = \frac{\exp(\mathbf{w_k^T x_j})}{\sum_{\mathbf{l}} \exp(\mathbf{w_l^T x_j})}$$

which satisfy $0 \leqslant y_k \leqslant 1$ and $\sum_k y_k = 1$. The probability of a patch label $\tau_{\mathbf{j}}$ to be class $k$ is then given directly by the output $y_k$:

$$p(\tau_{\mathbf{j}}|\mathbf{x_j}) = \prod_{\mathbf{k=1}}^{\mathbf{K}} \mathbf{y_k}(\mathbf{x_j}, \mathbf{w})^{\tau_{\mathbf{jk}}}$$

Next we assume that if one, or more, of the patches carries the label for a particular class, then the whole image will. Thus the conditional distribution of the image label, given the patch labels, is given by

$$p(\mathbf{t}|\tau) = \prod_{\mathbf{k}=\mathbf{1}}^{\mathbf{K}} \left[ \mathbf{1} - \prod_{\mathbf{j}=\mathbf{1}}^{\mathbf{J}} [\mathbf{1} - \tau_{\mathbf{jk}}] \right]^{\mathbf{t_k}} \left[ \prod_{\mathbf{j}=\mathbf{1}}^{\mathbf{J}} [\mathbf{1} - \tau_{\mathbf{jk}}] \right]^{\mathbf{1}-\mathbf{t_k}}$$

In order to obtain the conditional distribution $p(\mathbf{t}|\mathbf{X})$ we have to marginalize over the latent patch labels. Although there are exponentially many terms in this sum, it can be performed analytically for our model to give

$$\begin{aligned} p(\mathbf{t}|\mathbf{X}) &= \sum_{\tau} \left\{ p(\mathbf{t}|\tau) \prod_{\mathbf{j}=\mathbf{1}}^{\mathbf{J}} \mathbf{p}(\tau_{\mathbf{j}}|\mathbf{x_j}) \right\} \\ &= \prod_{k=1}^{K} \left[ 1 - \prod_{j=1}^{J} [1 - y_k(\mathbf{x_j}, \mathbf{w})] \right]^{t_k} \left[ \prod_{j=1}^{J} [1 - y_k(\mathbf{x_j}, \mathbf{w})] \right]^{1-t_k} \end{aligned} \tag{4}$$

Given a training set of $N$ images, which are assumed to be independent, we can construct the likelihood function from the product of such distributions, one for each data point. Taking the negative logarithm then gives the following error function

$$E(\mathbf{w}) = -\sum_{n=1}^{N} \sum_{k=1}^{K} \{t_{nk} \ln [1 - Z_{nk}] + (1 - t_{nk}) \ln Z_{nk}\}$$

where we have defined

$$Z_{nk} = \prod_{j=1}^{J_n} [1 - y_k(\mathbf{x_{nj}}, \mathbf{w})]$$

The parameter vector $\mathbf{w}$ can be determined by minimizing this error (which corresponds to maximizing the likelihood function) using a standard optimization algorithm such as scaled conjugate gradients [4]. More generally the likelihood function could be used as the basis of a Bayesian treatment, although we do not consider this here.

Once the optimal value $\mathbf{w}_{\mathrm{ML}}$ is found, the corresponding functions $y_k(\mathbf{x}, \mathbf{w}_{\mathrm{ML}})$ for $k = 1, \ldots, K$ will give the posterior class probabilities for a new patch feature vector $\mathbf{x}$. Thus the model has learned to label the patches even though the training data contained only image labels. Note, however, that as a consequence of the noisy 'OR' assumption, the model only needs to label one foreground patch correctly in order to predict the image label. It will therefore learn to pick out a small number of highly discriminative foreground patches, and will classify the remaining foreground patches, as well as those falling on the background, as 'background' meaning non-discriminative for the foreground class.

An example of patch labelling and image classification for each class is given in Figure 14.

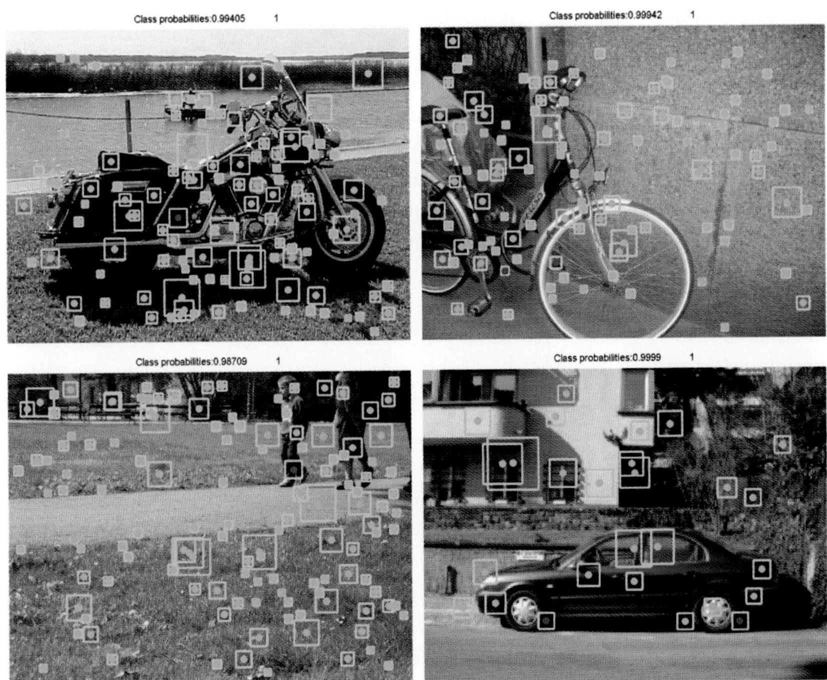


**Fig. 14.** *METU:* One patch labelling example for each class (motorbike, bike, people and car). Red and green dots denote foreground and background respectively. The patch labels are obtained by assigning each patch to the most probable class.

### 6.11 MPITuebingen

**Participants:** Jan Eichhorn, Olivier Chapelle
**Affiliation:** Max Planck Institute for Biological Cybernetics, Tübingen, Germany
**E-mail:** {jan.eichhorn,olivier.chapelle}@tuebingen.mpg.de

**Main Concepts.** For the absent/present object categorization task we used a Support Vector Classifier. Each image is converted to a collection of Local Image Descriptors (LIDs) and a kernel for sets is applied to this representation.

As LID we used the widely known SIFT-descriptors [32] but instead of the standard difference of Gaussians multiscale interest point detector we applied a basic Harris corner detector at one single scale. Each image was converted to a collection of LIDs where each LID contains coordinates, orientation and appearance of a particular salient region whose location was selected by the interest point detector (IPD). Note that, no data dependent post-processing of the LIDs was performed (as for example PCA or clustering in the appearance space of the training set).

For the successful use of Support Vector Classifiers it is necessary to define a kernel function appropriate for the underlying type of data representation. This function acts as a similarity measure (in our application for images) and should reflect basic assumptions about similarity in the categorization sense. For technical reasons it has to be a positive definite function.

To measure the similarity of two images, a possible strategy could be to find salient image regions of similar appearance (e.g. in SIFT-space) and thereby establishing a geometrical correspondence between the objects on the images (implicitly assuming that similar regions represent similar object parts).

In our method we avoid the complications of finding correspondences between images and neglect all geometry information at scales larger than the size of the extracted salient regions. In practice this means we ignore the coordinates of the LID and simply use its appearance part. Consequently the representation of a single image is reduced to a set of appearance vectors. On top of this representation we can now apply a kernel function for sets, the so called Bhattacharyya kernel [25]. Details of this kernel are described in the following Section. As a minor kernel we always used a standard Gaussian RBF-kernel $k_{\mathrm{RBF}}(x, x') = \exp(-\frac{\|x-x'\|}{2\sigma^2})$.

Maybe it is interesting to note that we observed a decreasing performance when using during training the segmentation mask of the objects that was provided with the datasets. This behaviour might indicate that the method can use information from the image background to infer the absence or presence of an object. In case of more realistic datasets and true multi-class categorization this effect should vanish.

**Bhattacharyya Kernel [25].** The name of this kernel function arises from the fact that it is based on the Bhattacharyya affinity, a similarity measure that is defined for probability distributions:

$$k_{\mathrm{bhatt}}(p, p') = \int \sqrt{p(x) \cdot p'(x)}\, \mathrm{d}x$$

To define a kernel function between two sets $\mathbf{L}$ and $\mathbf{L}'$, it was suggested in [25] to fit a Gaussian distribution to each of the sets: $\mathbf{L} \sim \mathcal{N}(\mu, \Sigma)$ and $\mathbf{L}' \sim \mathcal{N}(\mu', \Sigma')$. Then, the value of the *Bhattacharyya kernel* is the Bhattacharyya affinity of the corresponding Gaussians, which can be formulated as a closed expression

$$\begin{aligned} K_{\mathrm{bhatt}}(\mathbf{L}, \mathbf{L}') =& |\Sigma|^{-\frac{1}{4}}\, |\Sigma'|^{-\frac{1}{4}}\, |\Sigma^{\dagger}|^{\frac{1}{2}} \\ & \exp\left[-\frac{1}{4}\left(\mu^{\top}\Sigma^{-1}\mu + \mu'^{\top}\Sigma'^{-1}\mu'\right) + \frac{1}{2}\mu^{\dagger^{\top}}\Sigma^{\dagger}\mu^{\dagger}\right] \end{aligned}$$

where $\Sigma^{\dagger} = 2\left(\Sigma^{-1} + \Sigma'^{-1}\right)^{-1}$ and $\mu^{\dagger} = \frac{1}{2}\left(\Sigma^{-1}\mu + \Sigma'^{-1}\mu'\right)$.

Since the Gaussian approximation reflects only a limited part of the statistics of the empirical distribution, the authors further propose to map the set elements into a feature space induced by a minor kernel. The Bhattacharyya affinity can be computed in feature space by use of the kernel trick and doing so allows to capture more structure of the empirical distribution. However, in feature space the covariance matrices of each of the sets ($\Sigma$ and $\Sigma'$ respectively) are structurally rank-deficient and therefore it is necessary to involve a regularization step before computing the inverse:

$$\tilde{\Sigma}^{-1} = (\Sigma + \eta \cdot \mathrm{Tr}(\Sigma) \cdot I)^{-1}$$

Hereby a new parameter $\eta$ is introduced, which adjusts the amount of regularization. The larger $\eta$ is the more similar the two covariance matrices appear and the more the kernel depends only on the difference of the set means[5].

A more detailed analysis of other kernel functions for images represented by LIDs is under review for publication. A preliminary version can be found in a technical report [16].

### 6.12 Southampton

**Participants:** Jason D. R. Farquhar, Hongying Meng, Sandor Szedmak, John Shawe-Taylor
**Affiliation:** University of Southampton, Southampton, UK
**E-mail:** ss03v@ecs.soton.ac.uk

**Introduction.** Our method consists of two main phases, as shown in Figure 15, a machine vision phase which computes highly discriminative local image features, and a machine learning phase which learns the image categories based upon these features. We present two innovations: 1) the Bhattacharyya kernel is used to measure the similarity of the sets of local features found in each image, and, 2) an extension of the well-known SVM, called SVM_2K, is used to combine different features and improve overall performance. Each of the main components of our approach is described next.

**Image Feature Extraction.** On every image an interest point detector is applied to find the *interesting* local patches of the image (usually centred around corners). The types of the detectors used were, Multi-scale Harris-Affine, and Laplacian of Gaussians (LoG). To reduce the feature dimension and increase robustness to common image transformations (such as illumination or perspective) a local feature is generated for each patch using the *SIFT* descriptor. For more details see [32] or [36].

**Dimensionality Reduction.** As the dimension of the SIFTs is relatively high dimensionality reduction is used to improve the generalisation capability of the learning procedure and diminish the overall training time. The two types of dimensionality reduction tried are: Principal Component analysis (PCA), which finds directions of maximum variance in the input data, and Partial Least

[5] If the covariance matrices are identical ($\Sigma = \Sigma'$) the Bhattacharyya kernel reduces to: $K_{\mathrm{bhatt}}(\mathbf{L}, \mathbf{L}') = \exp\left(-\frac{1}{4}(\mu - \mu')^\top \Sigma^{-1}(\mu - \mu')\right)$.

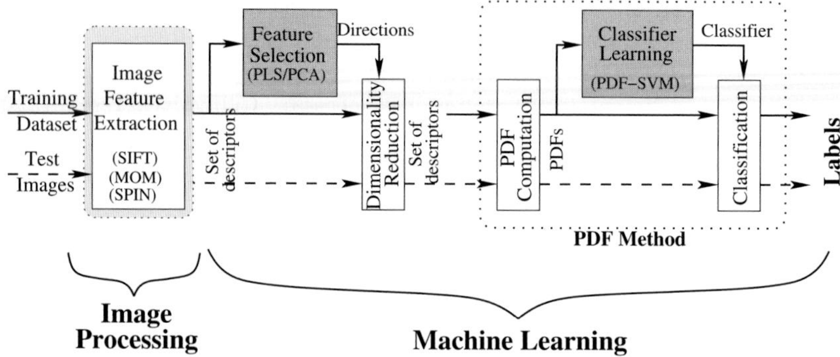


**Fig. 15.** *Southampton:* General classification schema

Squares Regression (PLS) [2], which finds directions of maximum covariance between input data and output labels.

**PDF Computation.** Image feature generation and dimensionality reduction output a set of local descriptors per image. As most machine learning algorithms cannot cope with variable length feature sets, previously histograms have been used to map these to a fixed length representation. An alternative approach is to model the set of features as a probability distribution (PDF) over feature space and then define a kernel between PDFs, which can be used in any kernelised learning algorithm, such as the SVM. We assumed that the set of image features follow Gaussian distribution and then the Bhattacharyya kernel [25], $K(\mathrm{Pr}_1(x), \mathrm{Pr}_2(x)) = \int \sqrt{\mathrm{Pr}_1(x)}\sqrt{\mathrm{Pr}_2(x)}dx$, was used to measure similarity of them.

**Classifier Learning.** To date only maximum margin based classifiers have been used, specifically either a conventional SVM [42] or our modified multi-feature SVM, called SVM_2K. As shown in Figure 16, SVM_2K combines two distinct feature sources (or kernels) to maximise the output classifier performance. The details can be found in [33].

**Experiments.** Three learning methodologies within the framework outlined above were submitted which differed only in the types of interest point detector used (LoG or multi-scale Harris affine) and the classifier used (SVM or SVM_2K),

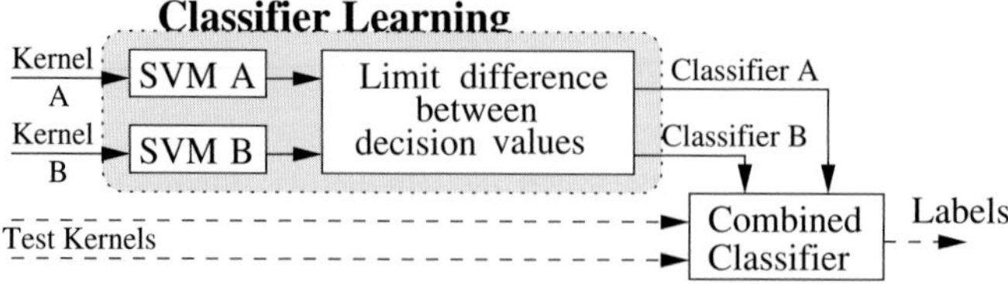


**Fig. 16.** *Southampton:* SVM_2K combines feature vectors arriving from distinct sources

with both LoG and Harris-Affine features used for SVM_2K. From initial experiments it was found that a 20 dimensional PLS reduction gave best performance so this was applied in all cases.

## 7 Results: Classification Task

### 7.1 Competition 1: `test1`

Table 8 lists the results of classification competition 1. In this competition, training was carried out using only the `train+val` image set, and testing performed on the `test1` image set. For each object class and submission, the EER and AUC measures are listed. Some participants submitted multiple results, and results for all submissions are shown. The ROC curves for the competition are shown in Figures 18–21, with each figure showing the results for a particular object class. In these figures, only the "best" result submitted by each participant is shown to aid clarity; the EER measure was used to choose the best result for each participant.

The INRIA-Jurie method performed consistently best in terms of both EER and AUC, achieving EER of 0.917–0.977 depending on the class. This method uses the "bag of words" representation with local descriptors extracted at points

**Table 8.** Results for competition 1: *classification*, train using the `train+val` image set and test on the `test1` image set. For each object class and submission, the EER and AUC measures are shown. Note that some participants submitted multiple results. Bold entries in each column denote the "best" methods for that object class according to EER or AUC.

| | **Motorbikes** | | **Bicycles** | | **People** | | **Cars** | |
|---|---|---|---|---|---|---|---|---|
| **Submission** | EER | AUC | EER | AUC | EER | AUC | EER | AUC |
| Aachen: ms-2048-histo | 0.926 | 0.979 | 0.842 | 0.931 | 0.861 | 0.928 | 0.925 | 0.978 |
| Aachen: n1st-1024 | 0.940 | 0.987 | 0.868 | 0.954 | 0.861 | 0.936 | 0.920 | 0.979 |
| Darmstadt: ISM | 0.829 | 0.919 | – | – | – | – | 0.548 | 0.578 |
| Darmstadt: ISMSVM | 0.856 | 0.882 | – | – | – | – | 0.644 | 0.717 |
| Edinburgh: bof | 0.722 | 0.765 | 0.689 | 0.724 | 0.571 | 0.597 | 0.793 | 0.798 |
| HUT: final1 | 0.921 | 0.974 | 0.795 | 0.891 | 0.850 | 0.927 | 0.869 | 0.956 |
| HUT: final2 | 0.917 | 0.970 | 0.816 | 0.895 | 0.833 | 0.931 | 0.908 | 0.968 |
| HUT: final3 | 0.912 | 0.952 | 0.781 | 0.864 | 0.845 | 0.919 | 0.847 | 0.934 |
| HUT: final4 | 0.898 | 0.960 | 0.767 | 0.880 | 0.857 | 0.921 | 0.909 | 0.971 |
| INRIA-Jurie: dcb_p1 | 0.968 | 0.997 | 0.918 | 0.974 | **0.917** | **0.979** | **0.961** | **0.992** |
| INRIA-Jurie: dcb_p2 | **0.977** | **0.998** | **0.930** | 0.981 | 0.901 | 0.965 | 0.938 | 0.987 |
| INRIA-Zhang | 0.964 | 0.996 | **0.930** | **0.982** | **0.917** | 0.972 | 0.937 | 0.983 |
| METU | 0.903 | 0.966 | 0.781 | 0.822 | 0.803 | 0.816 | 0.840 | 0.920 |
| MPITuebingen | 0.875 | 0.945 | 0.754 | 0.838 | 0.731 | 0.834 | 0.831 | 0.918 |
| Southampton: develtest | 0.972 | 0.994 | 0.895 | 0.961 | 0.881 | 0.943 | 0.913 | 0.972 |
| Southampton: LoG | 0.949 | 0.989 | 0.868 | 0.943 | 0.833 | 0.918 | 0.898 | 0.959 |
| Southampton: mhar.aff | 0.940 | 0.985 | 0.851 | 0.930 | 0.841 | 0.925 | 0.901 | 0.961 |

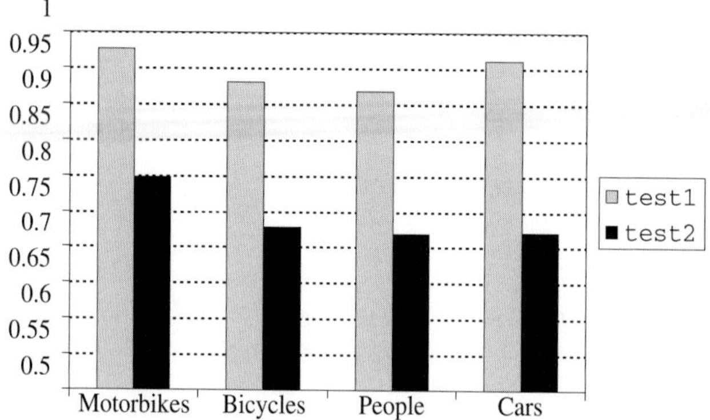


**Fig. 17.** Equal error rate (EER) results for *classification* competitions 1 and 2 by class and test set. The "best" (in terms of EER) result obtained for each class and each test set is shown. Note that results were much better for the `test1` set than for the `test2` set. There is perhaps surprisingly little difference in performance across classes.

on a dense grid. Performance of the INRIA-Zhang method was very similar; this method also uses the bag of words representation, but uses interest point detection to extract a sparser set of local features. For three of the classes, the ROC curves for the two methods intersect several times, making it impossible to determine which method performs best overall; only for the "cars" class was the performance of the INRIA-Jurie method consistently better over the whole range of the ROC curve (Figure 21).

Performance of two of the other methods using distributions of local features: Aachen and Southampton, was also similar but typically slightly worse than the INRIA methods, though the Southampton method performed particularly well on the "motorbikes" class. The Aachen method uses a log-linear model for classification, and the Southampton method the Bhattacharyya kernel instead of the bag of words representation.

The MPITuebingen method, which is similar to the Southampton method in the use of the Bhattacharyya kernel had consistently lower performance; reasons might include differences in the method for extraction of local features. The Edinburgh method, which is very similar to the INRIA-Zhang method gave consistently worse results; Section 6.3 discusses the likely reasons for this.

The HUT method, which is based on segmented image regions, performed comparably to the methods based on local features for all but the "bicycles" class; the poorer performance on this class might be anticipated because of the difficulty of segmenting a bicycle from the background. The METU method, based on individual local descriptors, performed worse than the methods using the global distribution of local features except on the "motorbikes" class.

The "recognition by detection" method submitted by Darmstadt did not perform well on this competition. Darmstadt chose to train only using side views, and this will have limited the performance. Another possible reason is that there was correlation between the object class presence and the appearance of the background, which this method is unable to exploit.

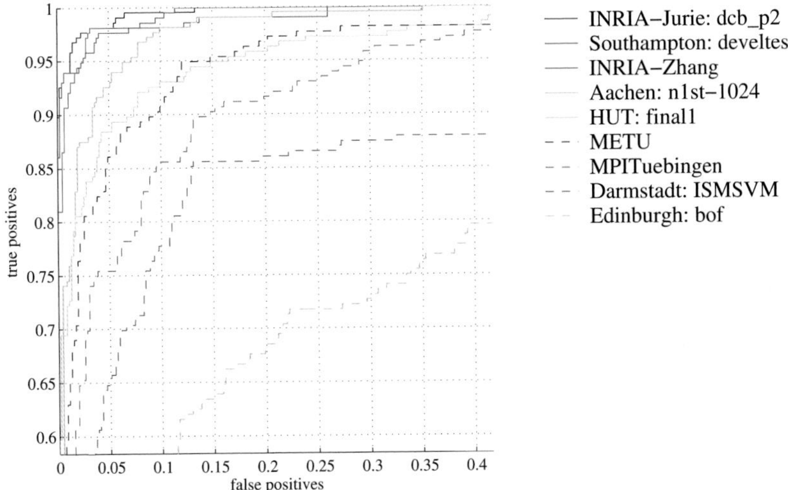


**Fig. 18.** ROC curves for *motorbikes* in competition 1: classification, train using the `train+val` image set and test on the `test1` image set. The best result in terms of EER from each participant is shown, with curves ranked by decreasing EER. The axes cover a range equal to two times the maximum EER of the submitted results.

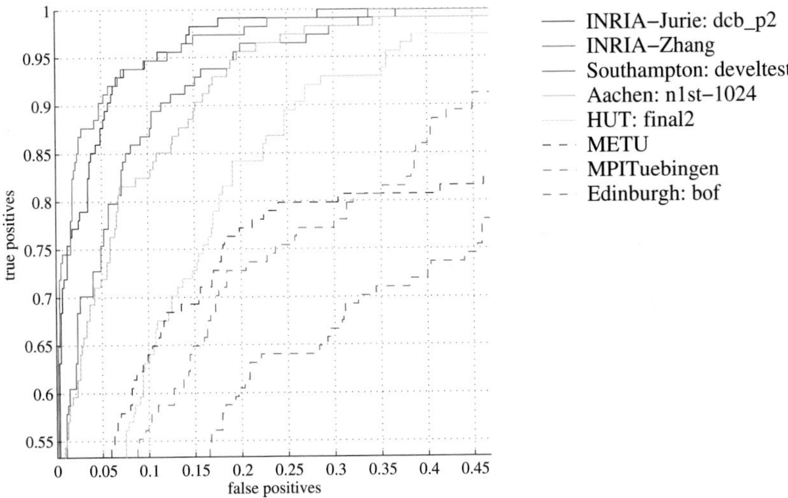


**Fig. 19.** ROC curves for *bicycles* in competition 1: classification, train using the `train+val` image set and test on the `test1` image set. The best result in terms of EER from each participant is shown, with curves ranked by decreasing EER. The axes cover a range equal to two times the maximum EER of the submitted results.

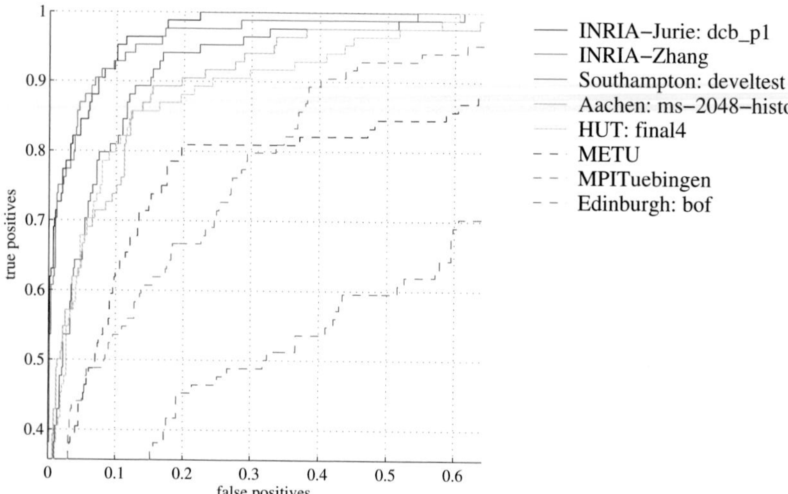


**Fig. 20.** ROC curves for *people* in competition 1: classification, train using the `train+val` image set and test on the `test1` image set. The best result in terms of EER from each participant is shown, with curves ranked by decreasing EER. The axes cover a range equal to two times the maximum EER of the submitted results.

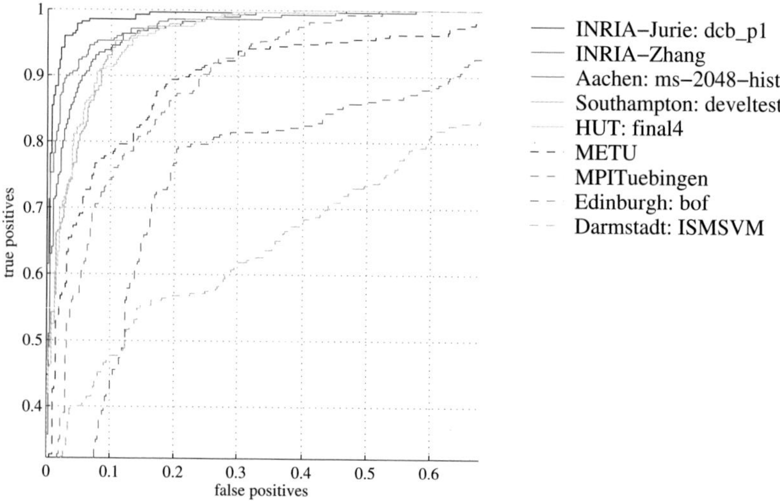


**Fig. 21.** ROC curves for *cars* in competition 1: classification, train using the `train+val` image set and test on the `test1` image set. The best result in terms of EER from each participant is shown, with curves ranked by decreasing EER. The axes cover a range equal to two times the maximum EER of the submitted results.

### 7.2 Competition 2: `test2`

Table 9 lists the results of classification competition 2. In this competition, training was carried out using only the `train+val` image set, and testing performed

**Table 9.** Results for competition 2: *classification*, train using the `train+val` image set and test on the `test2` image set. For each object class and submission, the EER and AUC measures are shown. Note that some participants submitted multiple results. Bold entries in each column denote the "best" methods for that object class according to EER or AUC.

| | Motorbikes | | Bicycles | | People | | Cars | |
|---|---|---|---|---|---|---|---|---|
| **Submission** | EER | AUC | EER | AUC | EER | AUC | EER | AUC |
| Aachen: ms-2048-histo | 0.767 | 0.825 | 0.667 | 0.724 | 0.663 | 0.721 | 0.703 | 0.767 |
| Aachen: n1st-1024 | 0.769 | 0.829 | 0.665 | 0.729 | 0.669 | 0.739 | 0.716 | 0.780 |
| Darmstadt: ISM | 0.663 | 0.706 | – | – | – | – | 0.551 | 0.572 |
| Darmstadt: ISMSVM | 0.683 | 0.716 | – | – | – | – | 0.658 | 0.683 |
| Edinburgh: bof | 0.698 | 0.710 | 0.575 | 0.606 | 0.519 | 0.552 | 0.633 | 0.655 |
| HUT: final1 | 0.614 | 0.666 | 0.527 | 0.567 | 0.601 | 0.650 | 0.655 | 0.709 |
| HUT: final2 | 0.624 | 0.693 | 0.604 | 0.647 | 0.614 | 0.661 | 0.676 | 0.740 |
| HUT: final3 | 0.594 | 0.637 | 0.524 | 0.546 | 0.574 | 0.618 | 0.644 | 0.694 |
| HUT: final4 | 0.635 | 0.675 | 0.616 | 0.645 | 0.587 | 0.630 | 0.692 | 0.744 |
| INRIA-Zhang | **0.798** | **0.865** | **0.728** | **0.813** | **0.719** | **0.798** | **0.720** | **0.802** |
| MPITuebingen | 0.698 | 0.765 | 0.616 | 0.654 | 0.591 | 0.655 | 0.677 | 0.717 |

on the `test2` image set. The ROC curves for the competition are shown in Figures 22–25, with each figure showing the results for a particular object class. Only the "best" result submitted by each participant is shown to aid clarity; the EER measure was used to choose the best result for each participant.

Fewer participants submitted results for competition 2 than competition 1. The best results were obtained by the INRIA-Zhang method both in terms of EER and AUC, and for all object classes; this method also performed close to best in competition 1.

The Aachen method performed similarly to the INRIA-Zhang method in competition 2, and better relative to the other methods than it did in competition 1; it may be that this method offers more generalization which is helpful on the more variable images in the `test2` image set, but not for `test1`.

Performances of the Edinburgh, HUT, and MPITuebingen methods were all similar but varied over the object classes. The poorer performance of the Edinburgh method on the `test1` images was not clear for the `test2` images.

In competition 2, the performance of the Darmstadt method was comparable to the others, whereas it performed poorly in competition 1. It may be that in the `test2` dataset there are fewer regularities in the image context of the object classes, so methods such as the Darmstadt one, which ignore the background, are more effective.

### 7.3 Comparison of Competitions 1 and 2

Figure 17 shows the best EER obtained for each object class in competition 1 (`test1`) and competition 2 (`test2`). The `test2` image set seems to be much more challenging; this was the intention in collecting this set of images. In terms of EER, performance on the `test2` images were worse than on the `test1` images,

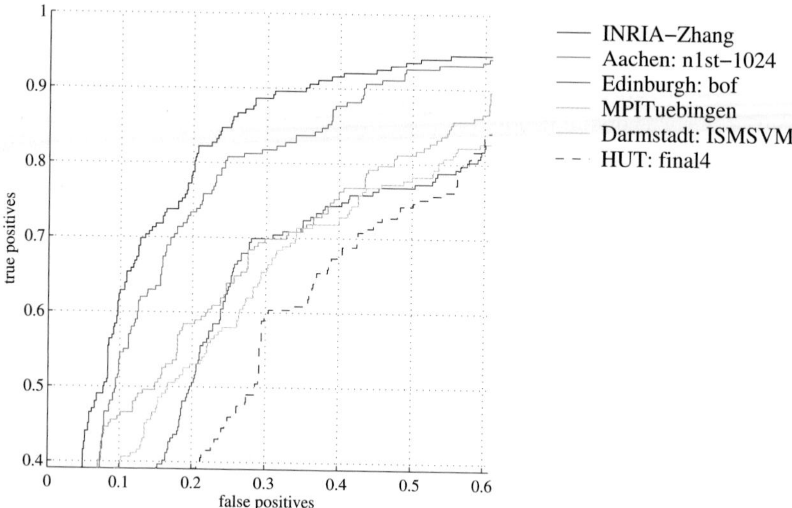


**Fig. 22.** ROC curves for *motorbikes* in competition 2: classification, train using the `train+val` image set and test on the `test2` image set. The best result in terms of EER from each participant is shown, with curves ranked by decreasing EER. The axes cover a range equal to two times the maximum EER of the submitted results.

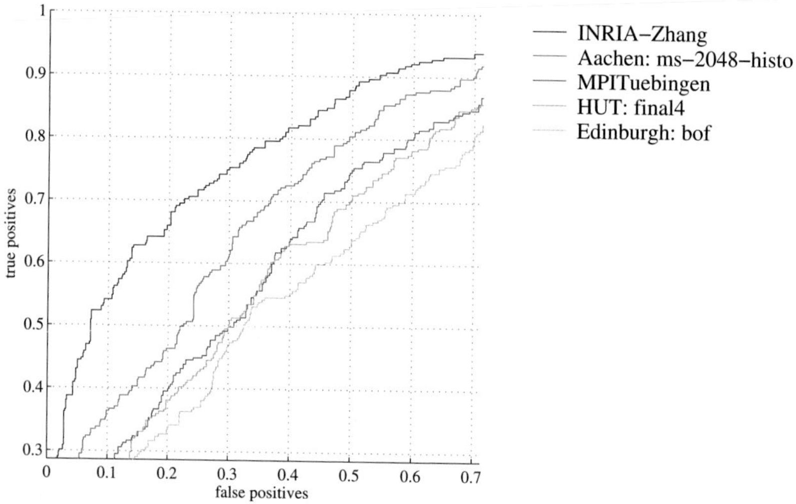


**Fig. 23.** ROC curves for *bicycles* in competition 2: classification, train using the `train+val` image set and test on the `test2` image set. The best result in terms of EER from each participant is shown, with curves ranked by decreasing EER. The axes cover a range equal to two times the maximum EER of the submitted results.

with EER in the range 0.720–0.798 for the best method, depending on the object class, compared to 0.917–0.977 for competition 1. Recall that this second test set was intended to provide a set of images with higher variability than those in the first image set; it seems that this intention has been met.

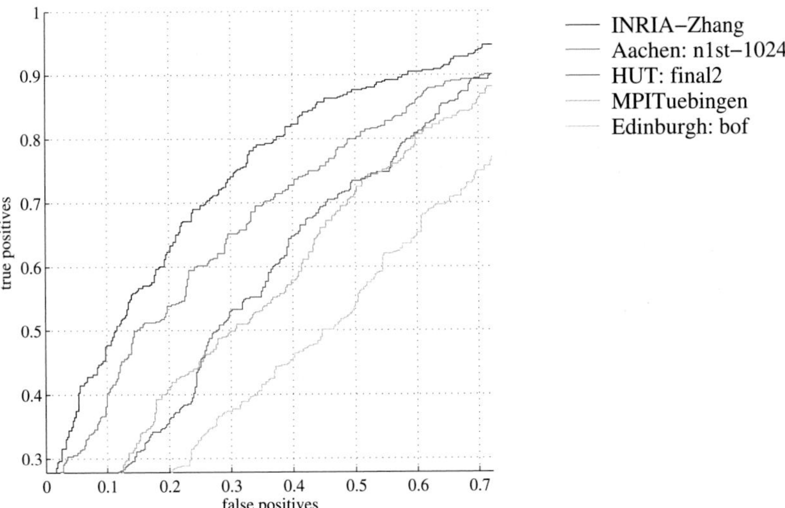


**Fig. 24.** ROC curves for *people* in competition 2: classification, train using the `train+val` image set and test on the `test2` image set. The best result in terms of EER from each participant is shown, with curves ranked by decreasing EER. The axes cover a range equal to two times the maximum EER of the submitted results.

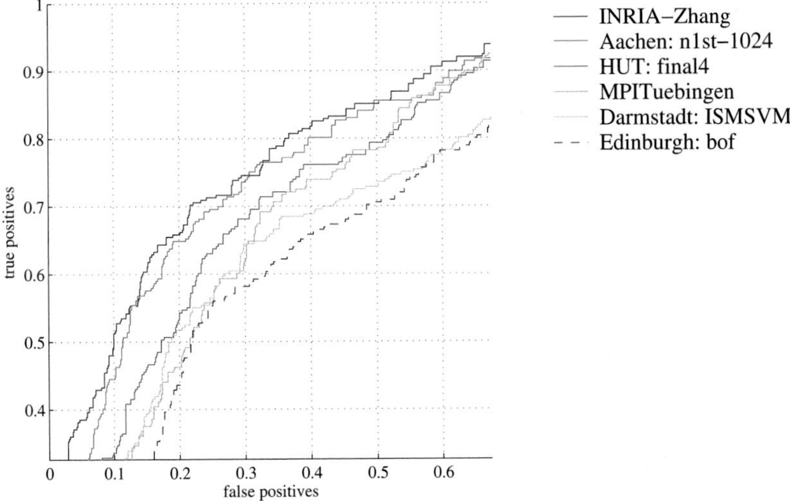


**Fig. 25.** ROC curves for *cars* in competition 2: classification, train using the `train+val` image set and test on the `test2` image set. The best result in terms of EER from each participant is shown, with curves ranked by decreasing EER. The axes cover a range equal to two times the maximum EER of the submitted results.

There is surprisingly little difference in performance of the best methods across object classes, using either the `test1` or `test2` image sets. While performance on the two object classes that the object recognition community might typically consider 'easier': motorbikes and cars, was indeed better than for the other two classes on the `test1` image set, the differences to the other classes are small. One might expect recognition of bicycles to be much harder because of their "wiry" structure which makes segmentation from the background difficult, or means that local features will a contain significant area of background; humans might be considered difficult to recognize because of the high variability of shape (e.g. different poses) and appearance (clothes, etc.). It is not possible to offer a conclusive explanation of the results here; one possibility is unintended regularity in the background giving a strong cue to the object class. Because none of the methods used here except the Darmstadt method delineate the object(s) in the image which result in a positive classification, it is hard to tell which parts of the image are being used by the classifier.

# 8 Results: Detection Task

## 8.1 Competition 5: `test1`

Table 10 lists the results of detection competition 5. In this competition, training was carried out using only the `train+val` image set, and testing performed on the `test1` image set. For each object class and submission, the AP measure is listed. Some participants submitted multiple results, and results for all submissions are shown. The precision/recall curves for the competition are shown in Figures 27–30, with each figure showing the results for a particular object class.

Performance of methods on the detection tasks varied much more greatly than for the classification task, and there were fewer submissions. For the "motorbikes" class, the Darmstadt method performed convincingly better than

**Table 10.** Results for competition 5: *detection*, train using the `train+val` image set and test on the `test1` image set. For each object class and submission, the AP measure is shown. Note that some participants submitted multiple results. Bold entries in each column denote the "best" methods for that object class according to AP.

| Submission | Motorbikes | Bicycles | People | Cars |
|---:|---:|---:|---:|---:|
| Darmstadt: ISM | 0.865 | – | – | 0.468 |
| Darmstadt: ISMSVM | **0.886** | – | – | 0.489 |
| Darmstadt: ISMSVM_2 | – | – | – | 0.439 |
| Edinburgh: meanbb | 0.216 | 0.007 | 0.000 | 0.000 |
| Edinburgh: puritymeanbb | 0.470 | 0.015 | 0.000 | 0.000 |
| Edinburgh: siftbb | 0.453 | 0.098 | 0.002 | 0.000 |
| Edinburgh: wholeimage | 0.118 | **0.119** | 0.000 | 0.000 |
| FranceTelecom | 0.729 | – | – | 0.353 |
| INRIA-Dalal | 0.490 | – | **0.013** | **0.613** |
| INRIA-Dorko | 0.598 | – | 0.000 | – |

other methods, with an average precision of 0.886. The variant using an SVM verification stage (ISMSVM) was slightly better than that without it (ISM). The FranceTelecom method also performed well on this class, giving good precision across all recall levels, but was consistently outperformed by the Darmstadt method. The INRIA-Dorko method, which is a variant of the Darmstadt method, performed only slightly worse than the Darmstadt method at low recall, but precision dropped off sharply at recall above 0.5. The Darmstadt submission used segmentation masks for training, while the INRIA-Dorko method used only the bounding boxes, and this may account for the difference in results.

The INRIA-Dalal method performed significantly worse for motorbikes than the other methods. Section 6.6 reports improved results by modifying the window size used by the detector. In the challenge, performance was close to the better of the baseline methods provided by Edinburgh. These baseline methods used the bag of words classifier to assign confidence to detections and predicted a single bounding box either simply as the mean bounding box taken from the training data, or as the bounding box of all Harris points in the image; the difference in performance between these two methods was small. The success of these simple methods can be attributed to the lack of variability in the `test1` data: many of the motorbikes appear in the centre of the image against a fairly uniform background.

For the “bicycles” class, the only results submitted were for Edinburgh’s baseline methods. The method predicting the bounding box as the bounding box of all Harris points did best, suggesting that uniform background may have been the reason.

For the “people” class, INRIA-Dalal, INRIA-Dorko and Edinburgh submitted results. The INRIA-Dalal method performed best but AP was very low at 0.013. The INRIA-Dorko method and baselines all gave almost zero average precision. The poor results on this task may be attributed to the small size of the training set relative to the large variability in appearance of people.

For the “cars” class, the INRIA-Dalal method achieved the highest AP of 0.304. For recall below 0.5, the Darmstadt method also performed well, with the ISMSVM_2 run giving greater precision than the INRIA-Dalal method; precision dropped off sharply at higher levels of recall. Darmstadt chose to train only on *side* views of cars and this explains the drop off in precision as the method fails to find cars from other views.

The FranceTelecom method did not perform as well as the INRIA-Dalal or Darmstadt methods, but was consistently much better than any of the Edinburgh baselines. The failure of the baselines suggests that the car images exhibited much less regularity than the motorbike images.

### 8.2 Competition 6: `test2`

Table 11 lists the results of detection competition 6. In this competition, training was carried out using only the `train+val` image set, and testing performed on the `test2` image set. The precision/recall curves for the competition are shown in Figures 31–34, with each figure showing the results for a particular object class.

**Table 11.** Results for competition 6: *detection*, train using the `train+val` image set and test on the `test2` image set. For each object class and submission, the AP measure is shown. Note that some participants submitted multiple results. Bold entries in each column denote the "best" methods for that object class according to AP.

| Submission | Motorbikes | Bicycles | People | Cars |
|---:|---:|---:|---:|---:|
| Darmstadt: ISM | 0.292 | – | – | 0.083 |
| Darmstadt: ISMSVM | 0.300 | – | – | 0.181 |
| Darmstadt: ISMSVM_2 | **0.341** | – | – | – |
| Edinburgh: meanbb | 0.055 | 0.000 | 0.000 | 0.000 |
| Edinburgh: puritymeanbb | 0.116 | 0.004 | 0.000 | 0.000 |
| Edinburgh: siftbb | 0.088 | **0.113** | 0.000 | 0.028 |
| Edinburgh: wholeimage | 0.020 | 0.006 | 0.000 | 0.005 |
| FranceTelecom | 0.289 | – | – | 0.106 |
| INRIA-Dalal | 0.124 | – | **0.021** | **0.304** |

Overall performance on the `test2` image set was much worse than on the `test1` images. The best results were obtained for motorbikes, and for this class AP dropped from 0.886 on `test1` to 0.341 on `test2`.

The relative performance of the methods was largely unchanged from that observed in competition 5. For motorbikes, the Darmstadt method performed best, and for cars the INRIA-Dalal method. For the "cars" class, the INRIA-Dalal method performed convincingly better than the Darmstadt method, which achieved high precision but lower recall in competition 5. The reason for this may be that the `test2` images contain an even lower proportion of side views of cars than in the `test1` data.

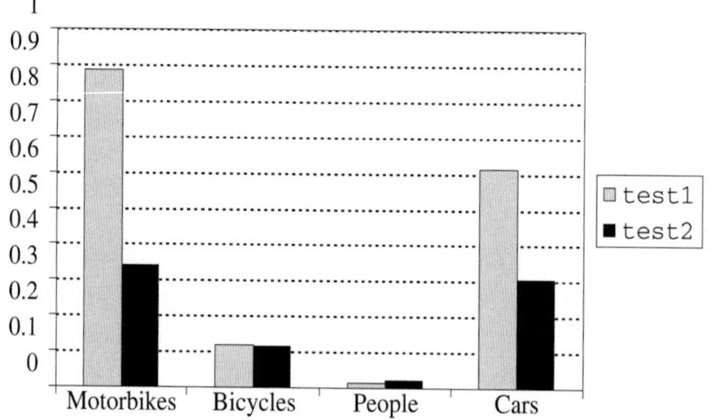


**Fig. 26.** Average precision (AP) results for *detection* competitions 5 and 6 by class and test set. The "best" (in terms of AP) result obtained for each class and each test set is shown. For the motorbike and car classes the results were much better for the `test1` set than for the `test2` set. There is a large difference in performance across classes; however note that few groups submitted results for bicycles and people.

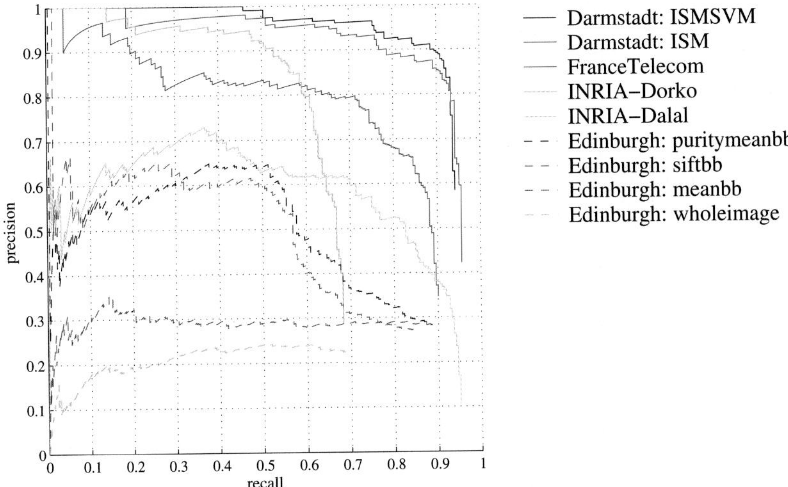


**Fig. 27.** PR curves for *motorbikes* in competition 5: detection, train using the `train+val` image set and test on the `test1` image set. All results submitted by each participant are shown, with curves ranked by decreasing AP.

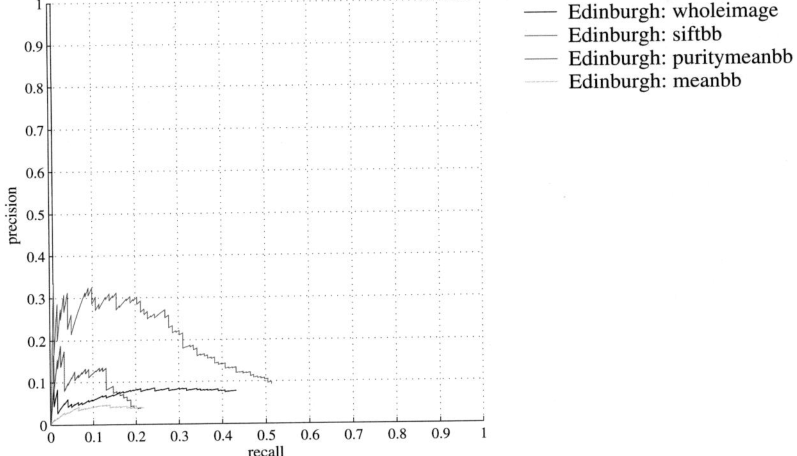


**Fig. 28.** PR curves for *bicycles* in competition 5: detection, train using the `train+val` image set and test on the `test1` image set. All results submitted by each participant are shown, with curves ranked by decreasing AP.

The FranceTelecom method also gave results well above the baselines for the "motorbikes" class, but results for the "cars" class were poor, with precision dropping off at very low recall.

For the "people" class, only INRIA-Dalal and Edinburgh submitted results. The precision/recall curve of the INRIA-Dalal method was consistently above

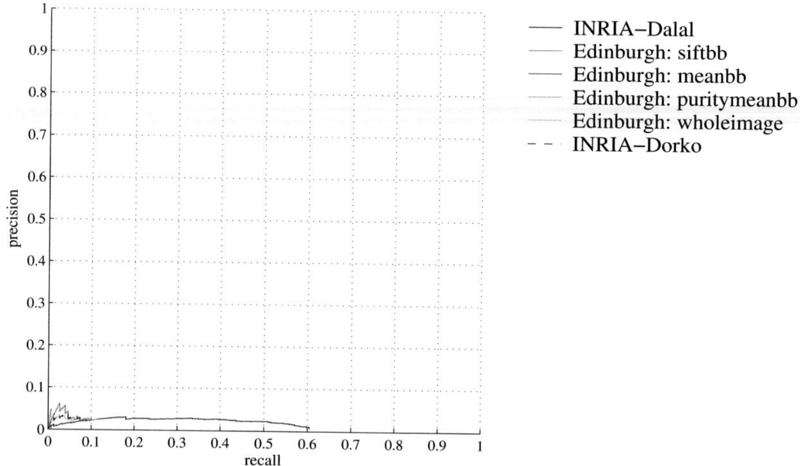


**Fig. 29.** PR curves for *people* in competition 5: detection, train using the `train+val` image set and test on the `test1` image set. All results submitted by each participant are shown, with curves ranked by decreasing AP.

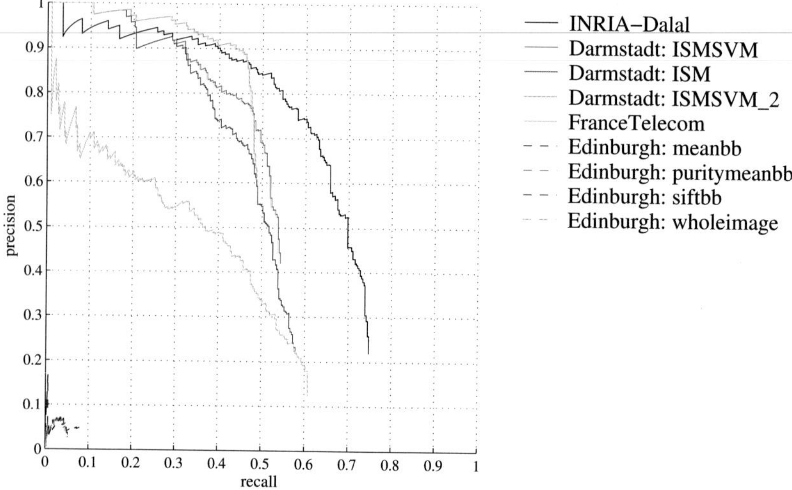


**Fig. 30.** PR curves for *cars* in competition 5: detection, train using the `train+val` image set and test on the `test1` image set. All results submitted by each participant are shown, with curves ranked by decreasing AP.

any of the baseline methods, but AP was very low at 0.021; this is probably due to the limited training data.

For all classes except people the Edinburgh baselines did surprisingly well, though consistently worse than the other methods. In particular, the method proposing the bounding box of all Harris points gave good results. This suggests that there may still be a significant bias toward objects appearing on a uniform background in the `test2` images.

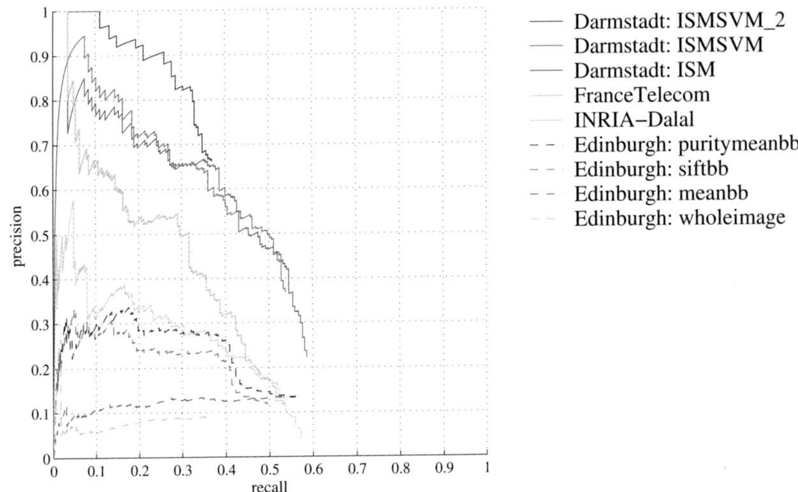


**Fig. 31.** PR curves for *motorbikes* in competition 6: detection, train using the `train+val` image set and test on the `test2` image set. All results submitted by each participant are shown, with curves ranked by decreasing AP.

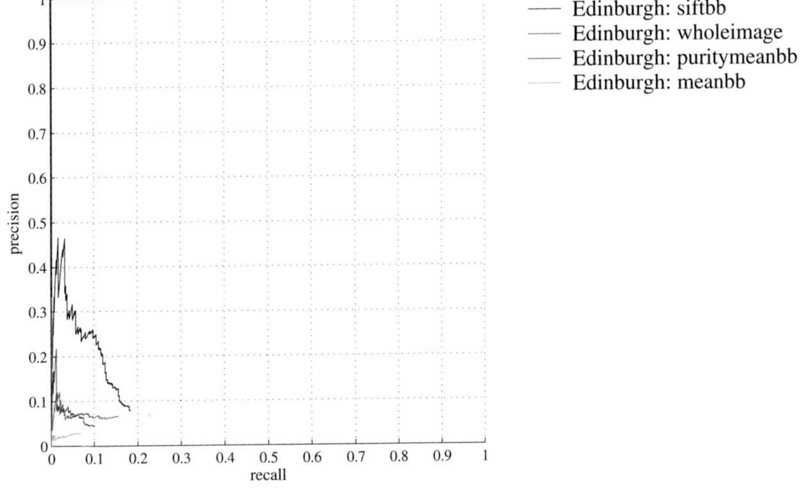


**Fig. 32.** PR curves for *bicycles* in competition 6: detection, train using the `train+val` image set and test on the `test2` image set. All results submitted by each participant are shown, with curves ranked by decreasing AP.

## 8.3 Comparison of Competitions 5 and 6

Figure 26 shows the best AP obtained for each object class in competition 5 (`test1`) and competition 6 (`test2`). For the "motorbikes" and "cars" classes, for which results significantly better than the baselines were achieved, results on

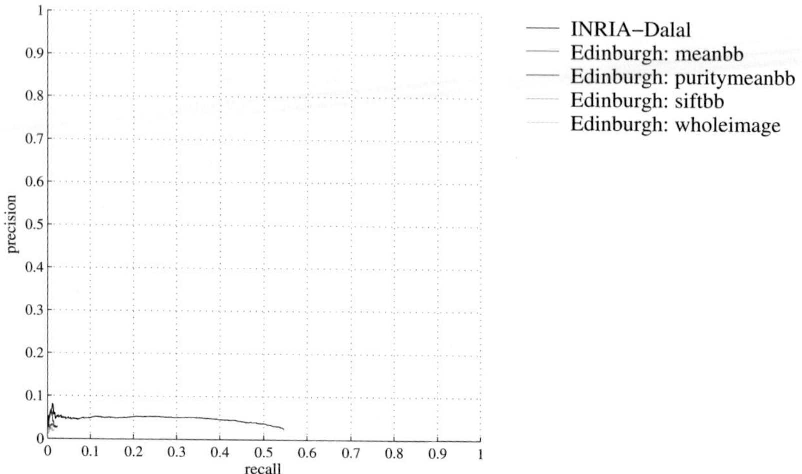


**Fig. 33.** PR curves for *people* in competition 6: detection, train using the `train+val` image set and test on the `test2` image set. All results submitted by each participant are shown, with curves ranked by decreasing AP.

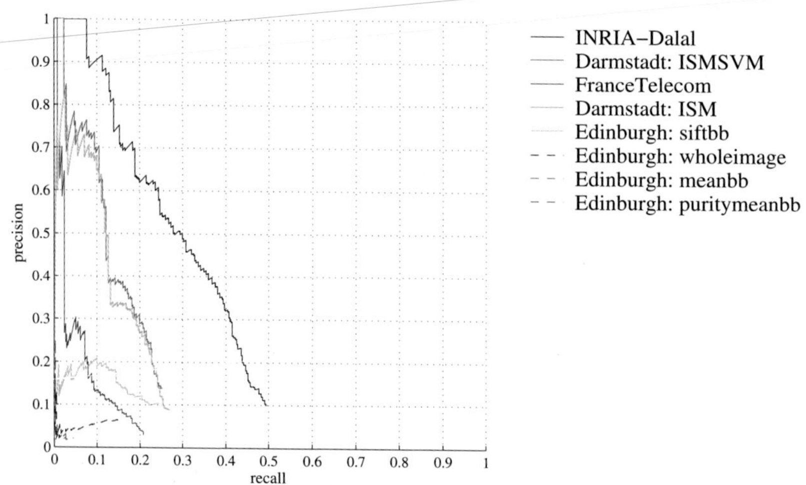


**Fig. 34.** PR curves for *cars* in competition 6: detection, train using the `train+val` image set and test on the `test2` image set. All results submitted by each participant are shown, with curves ranked by decreasing AP.

`test1` were much better than on `test2` suggesting that the second test set is indeed much more challenging, as was the intention.

Performance across the object classes varied greatly on both test sets. Note however that for bicycles only results for “baseline” methods were submitted, and for people results for only two methods were submitted for `test1`, and only one method for `test2`.

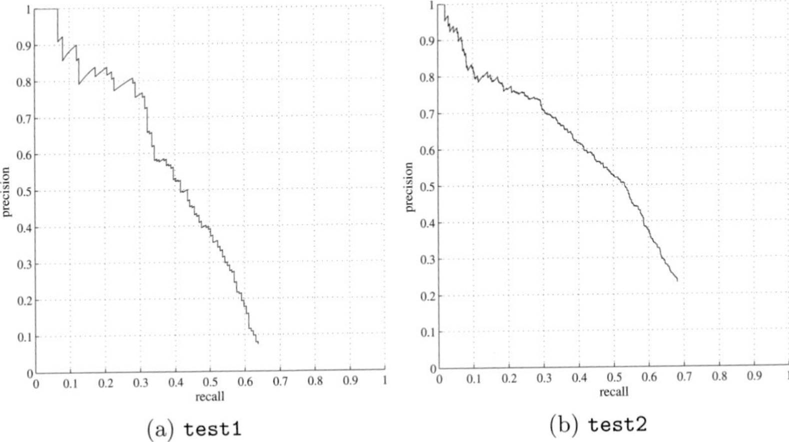


(a) `test1` (b) `test2`

**Fig. 35.** PR curves for *people* in competitions 7 and 8: detection, train using any data other than the provided test sets. Results shown are for the sole submission, from INRIA-Dalal.

For the `test1` images, performance for motorbikes was better than that for cars, which is interesting since one might expect cars to be easier to recognize because of their more convex structure. The reason may be due to less variation in the pose of motorbikes (mostly side views) relative to cars in the `test1` images. Results on the two classes for the `test2` images were about equal, suggesting that there is less bias in the second test set.

### 8.4 Competitions 7 and 8

Competitions 7 and 8 allowed participants to use any training data other than the test data provided for the challenge. Only one participant submitted results: INRIA-Dalal tackled the "people" class on both test sets. Figure 35 shows precision/recall curves for these results. Average precision was 0.410 for the `test1` images, and 0.438 for the `test2` images. These results are strikingly different than those obtained using the same method but only the provided training data: AP of 0.013 for `test1` and 0.021 for `test2`. This suggests that, certainly for this method, the size of the training set provided for the "people" class was inadequate.

## 9 Discussion

The challenge proved a worthwhile endeavour, with participation from twelve groups representing nine institutions. A range of methods for object classification and detection were evaluated providing a valuable snapshot of the state of the art in these tasks. The experience gained in the challenge, and discussion at the challenge workshop, resulted in a number of issues for consideration in future challenges.

**Errors in the Data.** Several participants commented on errors in the provided data. Undoubtedly there remained some errors in the first data set which arose from incomplete labelling of the original image databases from which the images were taken. Future challenges should improve the quality of this data. In terms of evaluation, all participants used the same data so any errors should not have caused bias toward a particular method. A key aspect of machine learning is the ability of a learning method to cope with some proportion of errors in the training data. It might be interesting for future challenges to consider data sets with known and varying proportion of errors to test methods' robustness to such errors.

A related issue is the difficulty of establishing ground truth, particularly for the detection task. For many images it is hard for a human observer to judge whether a particular object is really recognizable, or to segment individual objects, for example a number of bicycles in a bike rack. A unique aspect of the challenge was that the images were collected without reference to a particular method, whereas many databases will have been collected and annotated with a particular approach e.g. window-based or parts-based in mind. Future challenges might employ multiple annotations of the same images to allow some consensus to be reached, or increasing the size of the datasets might reduce the effect of such ambiguity on evaluation results. The results of existing methods might also be used to judge the "difficulty" of each image.

**Limited Training Data.** One participant commented that the training data provided for the person detection task was insufficient. However, there is a move in the object recognition community toward use of small training sets, as little as tens of images for some object classes, so there is some value in testing results with small training sets. Future challenges might consider providing larger training sets.

**Difficulty Level of the Data.** One participant commented that the `train+val` data was too "easy" with respect to the test data. Images were assigned randomly to the `train`, `val`, and `test1` image sets, so the training data should have been unbiased with respect to `test1`. It is quite possible that for current methods, the `train+val` data was not sufficient to learn a method successful on `test2` images. This is more a comment of current methods than the data itself, for example most current methods are "view-based" and require training on different views of an object; other methods might not have such requirements.

**Releasing Test Data.** In the challenge, the test data with associated ground truth was released to participants. Code to compute the ROC and PR curves was given to participants and the computed curves were returned to the organizers. This protocol was followed to minimize the burden on both participants and organizers, however, because the participants had access to the ground truth of the test sets, there was a risk that participants might optimize their methods on the test sets.

It was suggested that for future challenges the test data and/or ground truth not be released to participants. This gives two alternatives: (i) release images but not ground truth. One problem here is that participants may informally generate their own ground truth by "eye-balling" their results (this is much less of a problem in most machine learning contests, where it is hard for humans to generate predictions based on the input features); (ii) release no test data. This would require that participants submit binaries or source code to the organizers who would run it on the test data. This option was not taken for the challenge because of anticipated problems in running participants' code developed on different operating systems, with different shared libraries, etc. Submitting source code e.g. MATLAB code would also raise issues of confidentiality.

**Evaluation Methods.** Some participants were concerned that the evaluation measures (EER, AUC, AP) were not defined before results were submitted. In future challenges it might be productive to specify the evaluation measures, though this does run the risk of optimizing a method with respect to a particular measure. It might be useful to further divide the datasets to obtain a more informative picture of what each method is doing, for example detecting small vs. large objects, or particular views.

It was also suggested that evaluation of discrimination between classes carried out more directly (e.g. in the forced-choice scenario), rather than in a set of binary classification tasks would be informative. Because of the use of images containing objects from multiple classes, this requires defining new evaluation measures; one possibility is to measure classification accuracy as a function of a "refusal to predict" threshold.

**Increasing the Number of Classes.** Future challenges might increase the number of classes beyond the four used here. This would be useful to establish how well methods scale to a large number of classes. Other work has looked at discrimination of 101 classes [17] but only in the case that each image contains a single object (using the "forced choice" scenario). New data sets must be acquired to support evaluation in the more realistic case of multiple objects in an image. A number of researchers are collecting image databases which could contribute to this.

**Measuring State-of-the-Art Performance.** The challenge encouraged participants to submit results based on their own (unlimited) training data, but only one such submission was received. This was disappointing because it prevented judgement of just how well these classification and detection tasks can be achieved by current methods with no constraints on training data or other resources. Future challenges should provide more motivation for participants to submit results from methods built using unlimited resources.

## Acknowledgements

We are very grateful to those who provided images and their annotations; these include: Bastian Leibe & Bernt Schiele (TU-Darmstadt), Shivani Agarwal, Aatif Awan & Dan Roth (University of Illinois at Urbana-Champaign), Rob Fergus

& Pietro Perona (California Institute of Technology), Antonio Torralba, Kevin P. Murphy & William T. Freeman (Massachusetts Institute of Technology), Andreas Opelt & Axel Pinz (Graz University of Technology), Navneet Dalal & Bill Triggs (INRIA), Michalis Titsias (University of Edinburgh), and Hao Shao (ETH Zurich). The original PASCAL Object Recognition database collection and web pages `http://www.pascal-network.org/challenges/VOC/` were assembled by Manik Varma (University of Oxford). We are also grateful to Steve Gunn (University of Southampton) for enabling creation of the challenge web pages, Rebecca Hoath (University of Oxford) for help assembling the challenge database, and to Kevin Murphy for spotting several glitches in the original development kit.

Funding for this challenge was provided by the IST Programme of the European Community, under the PASCAL Network of Excellence, IST-2002-506778. This publication only reflects the authors' views.

## References

1. S. Agarwal, A. Awan, and D. Roth. Learning to detect objects in images via a sparse, part-based representation. *IEEE Transactions on Pattern Analysis and Machine Intelligence*, 20(11):1475–1490, 2004.
2. M. Barker and W. Rayens. Partial least squares for discrimination. *Journal of Chemometrics*, 17:166–173, 2003.
3. K. Barnard, P. Duygulu, D. Forsyth, N. Freitas, D. Blei, and M. I. Jordan. Matching words and pictures. *Journal of Machine Learning Research*, 3:1107–1135, 2003.
4. C. M. Bishop. *Neural Networks for Pattern Recognition.* Oxford University Press, 1995.
5. E. Borenstein and S. Ullman. Class-specific, top-down segmentation. In *Proceedings of the 7th European Conference on Computer Vision, Copenhagen, Denmark*, pages 109–124, 2002.
6. C.-C. Chang and C.-J. Lin. *LIBSVM: a library for support vector machines*, 2001. Software available at http://www.csie.ntu.edu.tw/~cjlin/libsvm.
7. O. Chapelle, P. Haffner, and V. Vapnik. Support vector machines for histogram-based image classification. *IEEE Transactions on Neural Networks*, 10(5):1055–1064, Oct. 1999.
8. D. Comaniciu and P. Meer. Distribution free decomposition of multivariate data. *Pattern Analysis and Applications*, 2:22–30, 1999.
9. D. Comaniciu, V. Ramesh, and P. Meer. The variable bandwidth mean shift and data-driven scale selection. In *Proceedings of the 8th IEEE International Conference on Computer Vision, Vancouver, Canada*, volume 1, pages 438–445, July 2001.
10. G. Csurka, C. Dance, L. Fan, J. Williamowski, and C. Bray. Visual categorization with bags of keypoints. In *ECCV2004 Workshop on Statistical Learning in Computer Vision*, pages 59–74, 2004.
11. N. Dalal and B. Triggs. Histograms of oriented gradients for human detection. In *Proceedings of the IEEE International Conference on Computer Vision and Pattern Recognition*, pages 886–893, San Diego, CA, USA, June 2005.

12. T. Deselaers, D. Keysers, and H. Ney. Discriminative training for object recognition using image patches. In *Proceedings of the IEEE International Conference on Computer Vision and Pattern Recognition*, volume 2, pages 157–162, San Diego, CA, USA, June 2005.
13. T. Deselaers, D. Keysers, and H. Ney. Improving a discriminative approach to object recognition using image patches. In *DAGM 2005*, volume 3663 of *LNCS*, pages 326–333, Vienna, Austria, August/September 2005.
14. G. Dorko and C. Schmid. Selection of scale-invariant parts for object class recognition. In *Proceedings of the 9th IEEE International Conference on Computer Vision, Nice, France*, pages 634–640, Oct. 2003.
15. G. Dorkó and C. Schmid. Object class recognition using discriminative local features. Technical report, INRIA, Feb. 2005.
16. J. Eichhorn and O. Chapelle. Object categorization with SVM: kernels for local features. Technical report, Max Planck Institute for Biological Cybernetics, July 2004.
17. L. Fei-Fei, R. Fergus, and P. Perona. Learning generative visual models from few training examples: an incremental bayesian approach tested on 101 object categories. In *Proceedings of the Workshop on Generative-Model Based Vision, Washington, DC, USA*, June 2004.
18. R. Fergus, P. Perona, and A. Zisserman. Object class recognition by unsupervised scale-invariant learning. In *Proceedings of the IEEE International Conference on Computer Vision and Pattern Recognition, Madison, Wisconsin, USA*, June 2003.
19. M. Fritz, B. Leibe, B. Caputo, and B. Schiele. Integrating representative and discriminant models for object category detection. In *Proceedings of the 10th IEEE International Conference on Computer Vision, Beijing, China*, Oct. 2005.
20. C. Garcia and M. Delakis. Convolutional face finder: A neural architecture for fast and robust face detection. *IEEE Transactions on Pattern Analysis and Machine Intelligence*, 26(11):1408–1423, Nov. 2004.
21. C. Harris and M. Stephens. A combined corner and edge detector. In *Proceedings of the 4th Alvey Vision Conference*, pages 147–151, 1988.
22. T. Joachims. Text categorization with support vector machines: Learning with many relevant features. In C. Nédellec and C. Rouveirol, editors, *Proceedings of the 10th European Conference on Machine Learning, Chemnitz, Germany*, pages 137–142. Springer Verlag, Heidelberg, Germany, 1998.
23. T. Joachims. Making large-scale SVM learning practical. In B. Schölkopf, C. Burges, and A. Smola, editors, *Advances in Kernel Methods - Support Vector Learning*. The MIT Press, Cambridge, MA, USA, 1999.
24. F. Jurie and W. Triggs. Creating efficient codebooks for visual recognition. In *Proceedings of the 10th IEEE International Conference on Computer Vision, Beijing, China*, 2005.
25. R. Kondor and T. Jebara. A kernel between sets of vectors. In *Proceedings of the 20th International Conference on Machine Learning, Washingon, DC, USA*, 2003.
26. J. Laaksonen, M. Koskela, and E. Oja. PicSOM—Self-organizing image retrieval with MPEG-7 content descriptions. *IEEE Transactions on Neural Networks, Special Issue on Intelligent Multimedia Processing*, 13(4):841–853, July 2002.
27. D. Larlus. Creation de vocabulaires visuels efficaces pour la categorisation d'images. Master's thesis, Image Vision Robotic, INPG and UJF, june 2005.
28. B. Leibe, A. Leonardis, and B. Schiele. Combined object categorization and segmentation with an implicit shape model. In *ECCV2004 Workshop on Statistical Learning in Computer Vision*, pages 17–32, Prague, Czech Republic, May 2004.

29. B. Leibe and B. Schiele. Scale invariant object categorization using a scale-adaptive mean-shift search. In *Proceedings of the 26th DAGM Annual Pattern Recognition Symposium*, Tuebingen, Germany, Aug. 2004.
30. B. Leibe, E. Seemann, and B. Schiele. Pedestrian detection in crowded scenes. In *Proceedings of the IEEE International Conference on Computer Vision and Pattern Recognition*, San Diego, CA, USA, June 2005.
31. T. Lindeberg. Feature detection with automatic scale selection. *International Journal of Computer Vision*, 30(2):79–116, 1998.
32. D. G. Lowe. Distinctive image features from scale-invariant keypoints. *International Journal of Computer Vision*, 60(2):91–110, 2004.
33. H. Meng, J. Shawe-Taylor, S. Szedmak, and J. R. D. Farquhar. Support vector machine to synthesise kernels. In *Proceedings of the Sheffield Machine Learning Workshop*, Sheffield, UK, 2004.
34. R. R. Mettu and C. G. Plaxton. The online median problem. In *Proceedings of the 41st Annual Symposium on Foundations of Computer Science*, page 339. IEEE Computer Society, 2000.
35. K. Mikolajczyk, B. Leibe, and B. Schiele. Local features for object class recognition. In *Proceedings of the 10th IEEE International Conference on Computer Vision, Beijing, China*, Oct. 2005.
36. K. Mikolajczyk and C. Schmid. A performance evaluation of local descriptors. In *Proceedings of the IEEE International Conference on Computer Vision and Pattern Recognition, Madison, Wisconsin, USA*, volume 2, pages 257–263, June 2003.
37. K. Mikolajczyk and C. Schmid. Scale and affine invariant interest point detectors. *International Journal of Computer Vision*, 60:63–86, 2004.
38. K. Mikolajczyk and C. Schmid. A performance evaluation of local descriptors. *IEEE Transactions on Pattern Analysis and Machine Intelligence*, 27(10):1615–1630, 2005.
39. A. Opelt, A. Fussenegger, A. Pinz, and P. Auer. Weak hypotheses and boosting for generic object detection and recognition. In *Proceedings of the 8th European Conference on Computer Vision, Prague, Czech Republic*, volume 2, pages 71–84, 2004.
40. B. Schölkopf and A. Smola. *Learning with Kernels: Support Vector Machines, Regularization, Optimization and Beyond.* The MIT Press, Cambridge, MA, USA, 2002.
41. E. Seemann, B. Leibe, K. Mikolajczyk, and B. Schiele. An evaluation of local shape-based features for pedestrian detection. In *Proceedings of the 16th British Machine Vision Conference*, Oxford, UK, 2005.
42. J. Shawe-Taylor and N. Cristianini. *Kernel Methods for Pattern Analysis.* Cambridge University Press, 2004.
43. M. Weber, M. Welling, and P. Perona. Unsupervised learning of models for recognition. In *Proceedings of the 6th European Conference on Computer Vision, Dublin, Ireland*, pages 18–32, 2000.
44. J. Zhang, M. Marszalek, S. Lazebnik, and C. Schmid. Local features and kernels for classification of texture and object categories: An in-depth study. Technical report, INRIA, 2005.

# The PASCAL Recognising Textual Entailment Challenge

Ido Dagan[1], Oren Glickman[1], and Bernardo Magnini[2]

[1] Bar Ilan University, Ramat Gan 52900, Israel
{dagan, glikmao}@cs.biu.ac.il
http://cs.biu.ac.il/~{dagan, glikmao}/
[2] ITC-irst, 38100 Trento, Italy
magnini@itc.it
http://tcc.itc.it/people/magnini.html

**Abstract.** This paper describes the PASCAL Network of Excellence first *Recognising Textual Entailment* (RTE-1) Challenge benchmark[1]. The RTE task is defined as recognizing, given two text fragments, whether the meaning of one text can be inferred (entailed) from the other. This application-independent task is suggested as capturing major inferences about the variability of semantic expression which are commonly needed across multiple applications. The Challenge has raised noticeable attention in the research community, attracting 17 submissions from diverse groups, suggesting the generic relevance of the task.

## 1 Introduction

### 1.1 Rational

A fundamental phenomenon of natural language is the variability of semantic expression, where the same meaning can be expressed by, or inferred from, different texts. This phenomenon may be considered as the dual problem of language ambiguity, together forming the many-to-many mapping between language expressions and meanings. Many natural language processing applications, such as Question Answering (QA), Information Extraction (IE), (multi-document) summarization, and machine translation (MT) evaluation, need a model for this variability phenomenon in order to recognize that a particular target meaning can be inferred from different text variants.

Even though different applications need similar models for semantic variability, the problem is often addressed in an application-oriented manner and methods are evaluated by their impact on final application performance. Consequently it becomes difficult to compare, under a generic evaluation framework, practical inference methods that were developed within different applications. Furthermore, researchers within one application area might not be aware of relevant methods that were developed in the context of another application. Overall,

[1] See http://www.pascal-network.org/Challenges/RTE/ for the first and second RTE challenges.

J. Quiñonero-Candela et al. (Eds.): MLCW 2005, LNAI 3944, pp. 177–190, 2006.

there seems to be a lack of a clear framework of generic task definitions and evaluations for such "applied" semantic inference, which also hampers the formation of a coherent community that addresses these problems. This situation might be confronted, for example, with the state of affairs in syntactic processing, where clear application-independent tasks, communities (and even standard conference session names) have matured.

The *Recognising Textual Entailment* (RTE) Challenge is an attempt to promote an abstract generic task that captures major semantic inference needs across applications. The task requires to recognize, given two text fragments, whether the meaning of one text can be inferred (entailed) from another text. More concretely, our applied notion of *textual entailment* is defined as a directional relationship between pairs of text expressions, denoted by $T$ - the entailing "Text", and $H$ - the entailed "Hypothesis". We say that $T$ *entails* $H$ if, typically, a human reading $T$ would infer that $H$ is most likely true. This somewhat informal definition is based on (and assumes) common human understanding of language as well as common background knowledge. It is similar in spirit to evaluation of applied tasks such as Question Answering and Information Extraction, in which humans need to judge whether the target answer or relation can indeed be inferred from a given candidate text. Table 1 includes a few examples from the dataset along with their gold standard annotation.

As in other evaluation tasks our definition of textual entailment is operational, and corresponds to the judgment criteria given to the annotators who decide whether this relationship holds between a given pair of texts or not. Recently there have been just a few suggestions in the literature to regard entailment recognition for texts as an applied, empirically evaluated, task (see [4], [6] and [12]).

It seems that major inferences, as needed by multiple applications, can indeed be cast in terms of textual entailment. For example, a QA system has to identify texts that entail a hypothesized answer. Given the question "*Who painted 'The Scream'?*", the text "*Norway's most famous painting, 'The Scream' by Edvard Munch,...*" entails the hypothesized answer form "Edvard Munch painted 'The Scream'." (see corresponding example 568 in Table 1). Similarly, for certain Information Retrieval queries the combination of semantic concepts and relations denoted by the query should be entailed from relevant retrieved documents. In IE entailment holds between different text variants that express the same target relation. In multi-document summarization a redundant sentence, to be omitted from the summary, should be entailed from other sentences in the summary. And in MT evaluation a correct translation should be semantically equivalent to the gold standard translation, and thus both translations should entail each other. Consequently, we hypothesize that textual entailment recognition is a suitable generic task for evaluating and comparing applied semantic inference models. Eventually, such efforts can promote the development of entailment recognition "engines" which may provide useful generic modules across applications.

Our applied notion of Textual entailment is also related, of course, to classical semantic entailment in the linguistics literature. A common definition of

**Table 1.** Examples of Text-Hypothesis pairs

| ID | TEXT | HYPOTHESIS | TASK | VALUE |
|---|---|---|---|---|
| 568 | *Norway's most famous painting, "The Scream" by Edvard Munch, was recovered Saturday, almost three months after it was stolen from an Oslo museum.* | *Edvard Munch painted "The Scream".* | QA | True |
| 1586 | *The Republic of Yemen is an Arab, Islamic and independent sovereign state whose integrity is inviolable, and no part of which may be ceded.* | *The national language of Yemen is Arabic.* | QA | True |
| 1076 | *Most Americans are familiar with the Food Guide Pyramid– but a lot of people don't understand how to use it and the government claims that the proof is that two out of three Americans are fat.* | *Two out of three Americans are fat.* | RC | True |
| 1667 | *Regan attended a ceremony in Washington to commemorate the landings in Normandy.* | *Washington is located in Normandy.* | IE | False |
| 13 | *iTunes software has seen strong sales in Europe.* | *Strong sales for iTunes in Europe.* | IR | True |
| 2016 | *Google files for its long awaited IPO.* | *Google goes public.* | IR | True |
| 2097 | *The economy created 228,000 new jobs after a disappointing 112,000 in June.* | *The economy created 228,000 jobs after dissapointing the 112,000 of June.* | MT | False |
| 893 | *The first settlements on the site of Jakarta were established at the mouth of the Ciliwung, perhaps as early as the 5th century AD.* | *The first settlements on the site of Jakarta were established as early as the 5th century AD.* | CD | True |
| 1960 | *Bush returned to the White House late Saturday while his running mate was off campaigning in the West.* | *Bush left the White House.* | PP | False |
| 586 | *The two suspects belong to the 30th Street gang, which became embroiled in one of the most notorious recent crimes in Mexico: a shootout at the Guadalajara airport in May, 1993, that killed Cardinal Juan Jesus Posadas Ocampo and six others.* | *Cardinal Juan Jesus Posadas Ocampo died in 1993.* | QA | True |
| 908 | *Time Warner is the world's largest media and Internet company.* | *Time Warner is the world's largest company.* | RC | False |
| 1911 | *The SPD got just 21.5% of the vote in the European Parliament elections, while the conservative opposition parties polled 44.5%.* | *The SPD is defeated by the opposition parties.* | IE | True |

entailment in formal semantics ([3]) specifies that a text $t$ entails another text $h$ (hypothesis, in our terminology) if $h$ is true in every circumstance (*possible world*) in which $t$ is true. For example, in example 13 from Table 1 we'd assume humans to agree that the hypothesis is necessarily true in any circumstance for which the text is true. In such intuitive cases, our proposed notion of textual entailment corresponds to the classical notions of semantic entailment.

However, our applied definition allows for cases in which the truth of the hypothesis is highly plausible, for most practical purposes, rather than certain. In Table 1, examples 1586, 1076, 893 and 586 were annotated as True even though the entailment in this cases is not certain. This seems to match the types of uncertain inferences that are typically expected from text based applications. [7] present a first attempt to define in probabilistic terms a coherent notion and generative setting of textual entailment. For a discussion on the relation between Textual Entailment and some classical linguistic notions such as presupposition and implicature see [16]. There is also considerable classical work on fuzzy or uncertain inference (e.g. [1], [8], [9]). Making significant reference to this rich body of literature and deeply understanding the relationships between our operational textual entailment definition and relevant linguistic notions is an ongoing research topic, and is beyond the scope of this paper. Finally, it may be noted that from an applied empirical perspective much of the effort is directed at recognizing meaning-entailing variability at rather shallow linguistic levels, rather than addressing relatively delicate logical issues as typical in classical literature.

### 1.2 The Challenge Scope

As a first step towards the above goal we created a dataset of Text-Hypothesis ($T$-$H$) pairs of small text snippets, corresponding to the general news domain (see Table 1). Examples were manually labeled for entailment - whether $T$ entails $H$ or not - by human annotators, and were divided into *development* and *test* datasets. Participating systems were asked to decide for each $T$-$H$ pair whether $T$ indeed entails $H$ (denoted as *True*) or not (*False*), and results were compared to the manual gold standard.

The dataset was collected with respect to different text processing applications, as detailed in the next section. Each portion of the dataset was intended to include typical $T$-$H$ examples that may correspond to success and failure cases of the actual applications. The collected examples represent a range of different levels of entailment reasoning, based on lexical, syntactic, logical and world knowledge, at different levels of difficulty.

The distribution of examples in this challenge has been somewhat biased to choosing nontrivial pairs, and also imposed a balance of True and False examples. For this reason, systems performances in applicative settings might be different than the figures for the challenge data, due to different distributions of examples in particular applications. Yet, the data does challenge systems to handle properly a broad range of entailment phenomena. Overall, we were aiming at an explorative rather than a competitive setting, hoping that meaningful baselines and analyses for the capabilities of current systems will be obtained.

Finally, the task definition and evaluation methodologies are clearly not mature yet. We expect them to change over time and hope that participants' contributions, observations and comments will help shaping this evolving research direction.

## 2 Dataset Preparation and Application Settings

The dataset of Text-Hypothesis pairs was collected by human annotators. It consists of seven subsets, which correspond to typical success and failure settings in different applications, as listed below. Within each application setting the annotators selected both positive entailment examples (*True*), where $T$ is judged to entail $H$, as well as negative examples (False), where entailment does not hold (a 50%-50% split). Typically, $T$ consists of one sentence (sometimes two) while $H$ was often made a shorter sentence (see Table 1). The full datasets are available for download at the Challenge website[2].

In some cases the examples were collected using external sources, such as available datasets or systems (see Acknowledgements), while in other cases examples were collected from the web, focusing on the general news domain. In all cases the decision as to which example pairs to include was made by the annotators. The annotators were guided to obtain a reasonable balance of different types of entailment phenomena and of levels of difficulty. Since many $T$-$H$ pairs tend to be quite difficult to recognize, the annotators were biased to limit the proportion of difficult cases, but on the other hand to try avoiding high correlation between entailment and simple word overlap. Thus, the examples do represent a useful broad range of naturally occurring entailment factors. Yet, we cannot say that they correspond to a particular representative distribution of these factors, or of True vs. False cases, whatever such distributions might be in different settings. Thus, results on this dataset may provide useful indications of system capabilities to address various aspects of entailment, but do not predict directly the performance figures within a particular application.

It is interesting to note in retrospect that the annotators' selection policy yielded more negative examples than positive ones in the cases where $T$ and $H$ have a very high degree of lexical overlap. This anomaly was noticed also by Bos and Markert, Bayer et al. and Glickman et al. (this Volume), and affected the design or performance of their systems

### 2.1 Application Settings

**Information Retrieval (IR).** Annotators generated hypotheses ($H$) that may correspond to meaningful IR queries that express some concrete semantic relations. These queries are typically longer and more specific than a standard keyword query, and may be considered as representing a semantic-oriented variant within IR. The queries were selected by examining prominent sentences in news stories, and were then submitted to a web search engine. Candidate texts ($T$) were selected from the search engine's retrieved documents, picking candidate texts that either do or do not entail the hypothesis.

**Comparable Documents (CD).** Annotators identified $T$-$H$ pairs by examining a cluster of comparable news articles that cover a common story. They

[2] http://www.pascal-network.org/Challenges/RTE/

examined "aligned" sentence pairs that overlap lexically, in which semantic entailment may or may not hold. Some pairs were identified on the web using Google news[3] and others taken from an available resource of aligned English sentences (see Acknowledgments). The motivation for this setting is the common use of lexical overlap as a hint for semantic overlap in comparable documents, e.g. for multi-document summarization.

**Reading Comprehension (RC).** This task corresponds to a typical reading comprehension exercise in human language teaching, where students are asked to judge whether a particular assertion can be inferred from a given text story. The challenge annotators were asked to create such hypotheses relative to texts taken from news stories, considering a reading comprehension test for high school students.

**Question Answering (QA).** Annotators used the TextMap Web Based Question Answering system available online (see Acknowledgments). The annotators used a resource of questions from CLEF-QA[4] (mostly) and TREC[5], but could also construct their own questions. For a given question, the annotators chose first a relevant text snippet ($T$) that was suggested by the QA system as including the correct answer. They then turned the question into an affirmative sentence with the hypothesized answer "plugged in" to form the hypothesis ($H$). For example, given the question, "Who is Ariel Sharon?" and taking a candidate answer text "Israel's Prime Minister, Ariel Sharon, visited Prague" ($T$), the hypothesis $H$ is formed by turning the question into the statement "Ariel Sharon is Israel's Prime Minister", producing a True entailment pair.

**Information Extraction (IE).** This task is inspired by the Information Extraction application, adapting the setting for pairs of texts rather than a text and a structured template. For this task the annotators used an available dataset annotated for the IE relations "kill" and "birth place" produced by UIUC (see acknowledgments), as well as general news stories in which they identified manually "typical" IE relations. Given an IE relation of interest (e.g. a purchasing event), annotators identified as the text ($T$) candidate news story sentences in which the relation is suspected to hold. As a hypothesis they created a straightforward natural language formulation of the IE relation, which expresses the target relation with the particular slot variable instantiations found in the text. For example, given the information extraction task of identifying killings of civilians, and a text "Guerrillas killed a peasant in the city of Flores.", a hypothesis "Guerrillas killed a civilian" is created, producing a True entailment pair.

**Machine Translation (MT).** Two translations of the same text, an automatic translation and a gold standard human translation (see Acknowledgements), were compared and modified in order to obtain $T$-$H$ pairs. The automatic translation

[3] http://news.google.com
[4] http://clef-qa.itc.it/
[5] http://trec.nist.gov/data/qa.html

was alternately taken as either $T$ or $H$, where a correct translation corresponds to True entailment. The automatic translations were sometimes grammatically adjusted, being otherwise grammatically unacceptable.

**Paraphrase Acquisition (PP).** Paraphrase acquisition systems attempt to acquire pairs (or sets) of lexical-syntactic expressions that convey largely equivalent or entailing meanings. Annotators selected a text $T$ from some news story which includes a certain relation, for which a paraphrase rule from a paraphrase acquisition system (see Acknowledgements) may apply. The result of applying the paraphrase rule on $T$ was chosen as the hypothesis $H$. Correct paraphrases suggested by the system, which were applied in an appropriate context, yielded True $T$-$H$ pairs; otherwise a False example was generated. For example, given the sentence "*The girl was found in Drummondville.*" and by applying the paraphrase rule $X\ was\,found\,in\ Y \Rightarrow Y\ contains\ X$, we obtain the hypothesis "*Drummondville contains the girl.*" Yielding a False example.

## 2.2 Additional Guidelines

Some additional annotation criteria and guidelines are listed below:

- Given that the text and hypothesis might originate from documents at different points in time, tense aspects are ignored.
- In principle, the hypothesis must be fully entailed by the text. Judgment would be False if the hypothesis includes parts that cannot be inferred from the text. However, cases in which inference is very probable (but not completely certain) are still judged at True. In example #586 in Table 1 one could claim that the shooting took place in 1993 and that (theoretically) the cardinal could have been just severely wounded in the shooting and has consequently died a few months later in 1994. However, this example is tagged as True since the context seems to imply that he actually died in 1993. To reduce the risk of unclear cases, annotators were guided to avoid vague examples for which inference has some positive probability that is not clearly very high.
- To keep the contexts in $T$ and $H$ self-contained annotators replaced anaphors with the appropriate reference from preceding sentences where applicable. They also often shortened the hypotheses, and sometimes the texts, to reduce complexity.
- Annotators were directed to assume common background knowledge of the news domain such as that a company has a CEO, a CEO is an employee of the company, an employee is a person, etc. However, it was considered unacceptable to presume highly specific knowledge, such as that Yahoo bought Overture for 1.63 billion dollars.

## 2.3 The Annotation Process

Each example $T$-$H$ pair was first judged as True/False by the annotator that created the example. The examples were then cross-evaluated by a second judge, who received only the text and hypothesis pair, without any additional information from the original context. The annotators agreed in their judgment for roughly 80% of the examples, which corresponded to a 0.6 Kappa level (moderate agreement). The 20% of the pairs for which there was disagreement among the judges were discarded from the dataset. Furthermore, one of the organizers performed a light review of the remaining examples and eliminated an additional 13% of the original examples, which might have seemed controversial. Altogether, about 33% of the originally created examples were filtered out in this process.

The remaining examples were considered as the gold standard for evaluation, split to 567 examples in the development set and 800 in the test set, and evenly split to True/False examples. Our conservative selection policy aimed to create a dataset with non-controversial judgments, which will be addressed consensually by different groups. It is interesting to note that few participants have independently judged portions of the dataset and reached high agreement levels with the gold standard judgments, of 95% on all the test set (Bos and Markert), 96% on a subset of roughly a third of the test set (Vanderwende et al.) and 91% on a sample of roughly 1/8 of the development set (Bayer et al.).

## 3 Submissions and Results

### 3.1 Submission Guidelines

Submitted systems were asked to tag each *T*-*H* pair as either True, predicting that entailment does hold for the pair, or as False otherwise. In addition, systems could optionally add a confidence score (between 0 and 1) where 0 means that the system has no confidence of the correctness of its judgment, and 1 corresponds to maximal confidence. Participating teams were allowed to submit results of up to 2 systems or runs.

The development data set was intended for any system tuning needed. It was acceptable to run automatic knowledge acquisition methods (such as synonym collection) specifically for the lexical and syntactic constructs present in the test set, as long as the methodology and procedures are general and not tuned specifically for the test data[6].

In order to encourage systems and methods which do not cover all entailment phenomena we allowed submission of partial coverage results, for only part of the test examples. Naturally, the decision as to on which examples the system abstains were to be done automatically by the system (with no manual involvement).

### 3.2 Evaluation Criteria

The judgments (classifications) produced by the systems were compared to the gold standard. The percentage of matching judgments provides the accuracy of the run, i.e. the fraction of correct responses.

[6] We presumed that participants complied with this constraint. It was not enforced in any way.

As a second measure, a Confidence-Weighted Score (cws, also known as Average Precision) was computed. Judgments of the test examples were sorted by their confidence (in decreasing order), calculating the following measure:

$$cws = \frac{1}{n}\sum_{i=1}^{n}\frac{\#correct - up - to - rank - i}{i}$$

where $n$ is the number of the pairs in the test set, and $i$ ranges over the sorted pairs. The Confidence-Weighted Score ranges between 0 (no correct judgments at all) and 1 (perfect classification), and rewards the systems' ability to assign a higher confidence score to the correct judgments than to the wrong ones. Note that in the calculation of the confidence weighted score correctness is with respect to classification - i.e. a negative example, in which entailment does not hold, can be correctly classified as false. This is slightly different from the common use of average precision measures in IR and QA, in which systems rank the results by confidence of positive classification and correspondingly only true positives are considered correct.

### 3.3 Submitted Systems and Results

Sixteen groups submitted the results of their systems for the challenge data, while one additional group submitted the results of a manual analysis of the dataset (Vanderwende et al., see below). As expected, the submitted systems incorporated a broad range of inferences that address various levels of textual entailment phenomena. Table 2 presents some common (crude) types of inference components which, according to our understanding, were included in the various systems (see [2] and [13] who propose related breakdowns of inference types).

The most basic type of inference measures the degree of word overlap between T and H, possibly including stemming, lemmatization, part of speech tagging, and applying a statistical word weighting such as idf. Interestingly, a non-participating system that operated solely at this level, using a simple decision tree trained on the development set, obtained an accuracy level of 58%, which might reflect a knowledge-poor baseline (see [5]). Higher levels of lexical inference considered relationships between words that may reflect entailment, based either on statistical methods or WordNet. Next, some systems measured the degree of match between the syntactic structures of $T$ and $H$, based on some distance criteria. Finally, few systems incorporated some form of "world knowledge", and a few more applied a logical prover for making the entailment inference, typically over semantically enriched representations. Different decision mechanisms were applied over the above types of knowledge, including probabilistic models, probabilistic Machine Translation models, supervised learning methods, logical inference and various specific scoring mechanisms.

Table 2 shows the results for the runs as submitted to the challenge (later post-submission results may appear in this Volume). Overall system accuracies were between 50 and 60 percent and system cws scores were between 0.50 and 0.70. Since the dataset was balanced in terms of true and false examples, a system

**Table 2.** Accuracy and cws results for the system submissions, ordered by first author. Partial coverage refers to the percentage of examples classified by the system out of the 800 test examples. (The results of the manual analysis by Vanderwende at al. (MSR) are summarized separately in the text.)

| First Author (Group) | accuracy | cws | partial coverage | System description | | | | | |
|---|---|---|---|---|---|---|---|---|---|
| | | | | Word overlap | Statistical lexical relations | WordNet | Syntactic matching | world knowledge | Logical inference |
| Akhmatova (Macquarie) | 0.519 | 0.507 | | X | | | | | X |
| Andreevskaia (Concordia) | 0.519 | 0.515 | | | | X | X | | |
| | 0.516 | 0.52 | | | | | | | |
| Bayer (MITRE) | 0.586 | 0.617 | | | X | | | | |
| | 0.516 | 0.503 | 73% | | | | | X | X |
| Bos (Edinburgh & Leeds) | 0.563 | 0.593 | | X | | X | | X | X |
| | 0.555 | 0.586 | | X | | | | | |
| Delmonte (Venice & irst) | 0.606 | 0.664 | 62% | | | X | X | | X |
| Fowler (LCC) | 0.551 | 0.56 | | | | X | | X | X |
| Glickman (Bar Ilan) | 0.586 | 0.572 | | | X | | | | |
| | 0.53 | 0.535 | | | | | | | |
| Herrera (UNED) | 0.566 | 0.575 | | X | X | | X | | |
| | 0.558 | 0.571 | | X | | | | | |
| Jijkoun (Amsterdam) | 0.552 | 0.559 | | X | X | | | | |
| | 0.536 | 0.553 | | X | | X | | | |
| Kouylekov (irst) | 0.559 | 0.607 | | X | X | | X | | |
| | 0.559 | 0.585 | | | | | | | |
| Newman (Dublin) | 0.563 | 0.592 | | X | X | | | | |
| | 0.565 | 0.6 | | | | | | | |
| Perez (Madrid) | 0.495 | 0.517 | | X | | | | | |
| | 0.7 | 0.782 | 19% | | | | | | |
| Punyakanok (UIUC) | 0.561 | 0.569 | | | | | X | | |
| Raina (Stanford) | 0.563 | 0.621 | | | X | X | X | | X |
| | 0.552 | 0.686 | | | | | | | |
| Wu (HKUST) | 0.512 | 0.55 | | | X | | X | | |
| | 0.505 | 0.536 | | | | | | | |
| Zanzotto (Rome-Milan) | 0.524 | 0.557 | | | | X | X | | |
| | 0.518 | 0.559 | | | | | | | |

that uniformly predicts True (or False) would achieve an accuracy of 50% which constitutes a natural baseline. Another baseline is obtained by considering the distribution of results in random runs that predict True or False at random. A run with $cws > 0.540$ or $accuracy > 0.535$ is better than chance at the 0.05 level and a run with $cws > 0.558$ or $accuracy > 0.546$ is better than chance at the 0.01 level.

Unlike other system submissions, Vanderwende et al. (this Volume) report an interesting manual analysis of the test examples. Each example was analyzed as whether it could be classified correctly (as either True or False) by taking into account only syntactic considerations, optionally augmented by a lexical thesaurus. An "ideal" decision mechanism that is based solely on these levels of inference was assumed. Their analysis shows that 37% of the examples could (in principle) be handled by considering syntax alone, and 49% if a thesaurus is also consulted.

The Comparable Documents (CD) task stands out when observing the performance of the various systems broken down by tasks. Generally the results on this task are significantly higher than results on the other tasks with results as high as 87% accuracy and cws of 0.95. This behavior might indicate that in comparable documents there is a high prior probability that seemingly matching sentences indeed convey the same meanings. We also note that for some systems it is the success on this task which pulled the figures up from the insignificance baselines.

Our evaluation measures do not favor specifically recognition of positive entailment. A system which does well in recognizing when entailment does not hold would do just as well in terms of accuracy and cws as a system tailored to recognize true examples. In retrospect, standard measures of precision, recall and $f$ in terms of the positive (entailing) examples would be appropriate as additional measures for this evaluation. In fact, some systems recognized only very few positive entailments (a recall between 10-30 percent). None of the systems performed significantly better than the $f$=0.67 baseline of a system which uniformly predicts true.

## 4 Discussion

As a new task and a first challenge, Textual Entailment Recognition is still making its first steps towards becoming a mature discipline within the Natural Language Processing community. We received a lot of feedback from the participants and other members of the research community, which partly contributed to the design of the second challenge (RTE-2) which is planned for 2006. Following are some issues that came up at the panels and discussions at the challenge workshop.

**Multi Valued Annotation.** In our setting we used a binary {True, False} annotation - a hypothesis is either entailed from the text or not. An annotation of False was used to denote both cases in which the truth value of the hypothesis is either (most likely) false or unknown given the text. Yet, one might want to distinguish between cases (such as example 1667 in Table 1) for which the hypothesis is False given the text and cases (such as example 2097) for which it is unknown whether the hypothesis is True or False. For this reason, a 3-valued annotation scheme ({True, False, Unknown}; see [10]) was proposed as a possible alternative. Furthermore, given the fuzzy nature of the task, it is not clear whether a 3-valued annotation would suffice and so n-valued annotation or even a Fuzzy logic scheme ([15]) may be considered as well. Allowing for a richer annotation scheme may enable to include the currently discarded examples on which there was no agreement amongst the annotators (see Section 2.3).

**Assumed Background Knowledge.** Textual inferences are based on information that is explicitly asserted in the text and often on additional assumed background knowledge not explicitly stated in the text. In our guidelines (see Section 2.2) we allowed annotators to assume common knowledge of the news domain. However, it is not clear how to separate out linguistic knowledge from world knowledge, and different annotators might not agree on what constitutes common background knowledge. For example, in example 1586 in Table 1 one needs to assume world knowledge regarding Arab states and the Arab language in order to infer the correctness of the hypothesis from the text. Furthermore, the criteria defining what constitutes acceptable background knowledge may be hypothesis dependant. For example, it is inappropriate to assume as background knowledge that The national language of Yemen is Arabic when judging example 1586, since this is exactly the hypothesis in question. On the other hand, such background knowledge might be assumed when examining the entailment "Grew up in Yemen" → "Speaks Arabic". Overall, there seemed to be a consensus that it is necessary to assume the availability of background knowledge for judging entailment, even though it becomes one of the sources for certain disagreements amongst human annotators.

**Common Preprocessing.** Textual Entailment systems typically rely on the output of several NLP components prior to performing their inference, such as tokenization, lemmatization, part-of-speech tagging, named entity recognition and syntactic parsing. Since different systems differ in their preprocessing modules it becomes more difficult to compare them. In the next Challenge we plan to supply some common pre-processing of the data in order to enable better system comparison and to let participants focus on the inference components.

**Entailment Subtasks.** Textual entailment recognition is a complex task and systems typically perform multiple sub-tasks. It would therefore be interesting to define and compare performance on specific relevant subtasks. For example, [2] and [7] define lexical and lexical-syntactic entailment subtasks and [11] define an entailment-alignment subtask. Datasets that are annotated for such subtasks may be created in the future.

**Inference Scope.** Textual Entailment systems need to deal with a wide range of inference types. So far we were interested in rather direct inferences that are based mostly on information in the text and background knowledge. Specialized types of inference, such as temporal reasoning, complex logical inference or arithmetic calculations (see example 1911 from Table 1) were typically avoided but may be considered more systematically in the future.

## 5 Conclusions

The PASCAL *Recognising Textual Entailment* (RTE) Challenge is an initial attempt to form a generic empirical task that captures major semantic inferences across applications. The high level of interest in the challenge, demonstrated by the submissions from 17 diverse groups and noticeable interest in the research community, suggest that textual entailment indeed captures highly relevant core tasks.

The results obtained by the participating systems may be viewed as typical for a new and relatively difficult task (cf. for example the history of MUC benchmarks). Overall performance figures for the better systems were significantly higher than some baselines. Yet, the absolute numbers are relatively low, with small, though significant, differences between systems. Interestingly, system complexity and sophistication of inference did not correlate fully with performance, where some of the best results were obtained by rather naïve lexically-based systems. The fact that quite sophisticated inference levels were applied by some groups, with 6 systems applying logical inference, provides an additional indication that applied NLP research is progressing towards deeper semantic reasoning. Additional refinements are needed though to obtain sufficient robustness for the Challenge types of data. Further detailed analysis of systems performance, relative to different types of examples and entailment phenomena, are likely to yield future improvements.

Being the first benchmark of its types there are several lessons for future similar efforts. Most notably, further efforts can be made to create "natural" distributions of Text-Hypothesis examples. For example, $T$-$H$ pairs may be collected directly from the data processed by actual systems, considering their inputs and candidate outputs. An additional possibility is to collect a set of multiple candidate texts that might entail a given single hypothesis, thus reflecting typical ranking scenarios. Data collection settings may also be focused on typical "core" semantic applications, such as QA, IE, IR and summarization. Some of these improvements are planned for the 2nd PASCAL Recognising Textual Entailment Challenge. Overall, we hope that future similar benchmarks will be carried out and will help shaping clearer frameworks, and corresponding research communities, for applied research on semantic inference.

## Acknowledgements

The following sources were used in the preparation of the data:

- Document Understanding Conferences (DUC) 2004 Machine Translation evaluation data, from the National In-stitute of Standards and Technology (NIST). http://duc.nist.gov/duc2004/
- TextMap Question Answering online demo, from the Information Sciences Institute (ISI). http://brahms.isi.edu:8080/textmap/
- Relation Recognition dataset, from University of Illinois at Urbana-Champaign. http://l2r.cs.uiuc.edu/~cogcomp/
- DIRT paraphrase database (online demo), from the University of southern California. http://www.isi.edu/~pantel/Content/Demos/demosDirt.htm
- The output of the TEASE system for extracting entailment relations and paraphrases ([14]).
- Corpus of Sentence Alignment in monolingual comparable corpora, Columbia University. http://www.cs.columbia.edu/~noemie/alignment/

We would like to thank the people and organizations that made these sources available for the challenge.

We would also like to acknowledge the people involved in creating and annotating the data: Danilo Giampiccolo, Tracy Kelly, Einat Barnoy, Allesandro

Valin, Ruthie Mandel, and Melanie Joseph. This work was supported in part by the IST Programme of the European Community, under the PASCAL Network of Excellence, IST-2002-506778. This publication only reflects the authors' views. We wish to thank the managers of the PASCAL Challenges program, Florence d'Alché-Buc and Michele Sebag, for their enthusiastic efforts and assistance, and Eileen Simon and John Shawe-Taylor from PASCAL for being so supportive all along.

## References

1. Bacchus, F.: Representing and Reasoning with Probabilistic Knowledge, M.I.T. Press (1990).
2. Bar-Haim, R., Szpektor, I., Glickman O.: Definition and Analysis of Intermediate Entailment Levels. ACL-05 Workshop on Empirical Modeling of Semantic Equivalence and Entailment. (2005)
3. Chierchia, G., McConnell-Ginet, S.: Meaning and grammar: An introduction to semantics, 2nd. edition. Cambridge, MA: MIT Press (2001).
4. Condoravdi, C., Crouch, D., de Paiva, V., Stolle, R., Bobrow, D.G.: Entailment, intensionality and text understanding. HLT-NAACL Workshop on Text Meaning (2003)
5. Corley,C., Mihalcea, R.: Measuring the Semantic Similarity of Texts. Proceedings of the ACL Workshop on Empirical Modeling of Semantic Equivalence and Entailment, pages 1318, Ann Arbor, June 2005.
6. Dagan, I., Glickman, O.: Probabilistic Textual Entailment: Generic Applied Modeling of Language Variability. PASCAL workshop on Learning Methods for Text Understanding and Mining, 26 - 29 January (2004), Grenoble, France.
7. Glickman, O., Dagan, I., Koppel, M.: A Lexical Alignment Model for Probabilistic Textual Entailment. This Volums.
8. Halpern, J.Y.: An analysis of first-order logics of probability. Artificial Intelligence 46:311-350 (1990).
9. Keefe, R., Smith P. (ed.): Vagueness: A Reader. The MIT Press. 1997.
10. Lukasiewicz, J.: Selected Works, L. Borkowski Ed., North Holland, London, 1970.
11. Marsi, E., Krahmer, E.: Classification of Semantic Relations by Humans and Machines. Proceedings of the ACL Workshop on Empirical Modeling of Semantic Equivalence and Entailment, 2005.
12. Monz, C., de Rijke, M.: Light-Weight Entailment Checking for Computational Semantics. the third workshop on inference in computational semantics (ICoS-3). (2001)
13. Lucy Vanderwende and William B. Dolan: What Syntax can Contribute in the Entailment Task. This Volume.
14. Szpektor, I., Tanev, H., Dagan, I.,Coppola, B.: Scaling Web-based Acquisition of Entailment Relations. Empirical Methods in Natural Language Processing (EMNLP). (2004).
15. Zadeh, L.: Fuzzy sets. Information and Control, 8 , 1965.
16. Zaenen, A., Karttunen, L., Crouch, R.: Local Textual Inference: Can it be Defined or Circumscribed?. Proceedings of the ACL Workshop on Empirical Modeling of Semantic Equivalence and Entailment, 2005.

# Using Bleu-like Algorithms for the Automatic Recognition of Entailment*

Diana Pérez and Enrique Alfonseca

Department of Computer Science,
Universidad Autónoma de Madrid,
Madrid, 28049, Spain
{diana.perez, enrique.alfonseca}@uam.es

**Abstract.** The BLEU algorithm has been used in many different fields. Another possible application is the automatic recognition of textual entailment. BLEU works at the lexical level, by comparing a candidate text with several reference texts in order to calculate how close the candidate text is to the references. In this case, the candidate is the text part of the entailment and the hypothesis is the unique reference. The algorithm achieves an accuracy of around 50%. Moreover, in this paper we explore the application of BLEU-like algorithms, finding that they can reach an accuracy of around 56%, which proves its possible use as a baseline for the task of recognizing entailment.

## 1 Introduction

In the framework of the Pascal Challenge, a fairly new and interesting task was tackled: the automatic recognition of textual entailment (RTE). It consists of deciding if a certain expression, a text called the entailment hypothesis (H), can be inferred by another expression, the text (T), and thus whether it can be said that T entails H or not.

This task deals with many different linguistic phenomena, such as language variability, since there are many different possible paraphrasings that can confuse an automatic system. For instance, if T and H are, respectively:

(1) a. Eyeing the huge market potential, currently led by Google, Yahoo took over search company Overture Services Inc last year.
    b. Yahoo bought Overture.

a human annotator would know that, in this context, *"to take over"* is another way to say *"to buy"*. Hence, he or she would ignore the rest of the information and would mark the entailment as true. However, this task is not so straightforward for a computer. In fact, if it is not provided with some kind of resource indicating the paraphrase between T and H, it would mark the entailment as false.

* This work has been sponsored by the Spanish Ministry of Science and Technology, project number TIN2004-03140.

J. Quiñonero-Candela et al. (Eds.): MLCW 2005, LNAI 3944, pp. 191–204, 2006.

Obviously, it is a complex task that needs both a preliminary study to find out the most suitable techniques that can be applied to solve it, and the development of new techniques specifically designed for it. This problem has attracted a great deal of attention from the research community. In particular, seventeen different systems have been presented in the Pascal Challenge using several Natural Language Processing (NLP) techniques. These systems can be grouped according to the highest linguistic level in which their NLP techniques work:

- **Lexical:** systems that rely on studying word overlapping and/or statistical lexical relationships. For instance, the MITRE system [1].
- **Syntactic/Semantic:** systems that are based on the use of parsers to analyze and to match the sentences according to their syntactic structure. An example is the UIUC system [2]. They can also be underpinned by the use of world knowledge and/or the application of some kind of logical prover. For example, the Stanford system [3].

It is interesting to observe that according to the metrics given by the challenge organizers [4], the best result was an accuracy of 0.586 achieved by the systems [1, 5] (both of them working only at the lexical level) and a 0.686 Confidence Weight Score (CWS) value achieved by the Stanford system [3] (using statistical lexical relations, WordNet, syntactic matching, world knowledge and logical inference).

These facts lead us to our main motivation, that is to discuss if this problem can be addressed with just shallow techniques. If that is not the case, it will be interesting to know what the advantages of deep analyses are, and how the results differ from just using shallow techniques.

In this paper, we use the BLEU algorithm [6, 7], that works at the lexical level, to compare the entailing text (T) with the hypothesis (H). Once the algorithm was applied, it turned out that, despite its simplicity, it was able to achieve a result as good as an accuracy of 54% for the development set, and of around a 50% for the test set (CWS=52%).

It is important to highlight that BLEU requires less than two hours programming time and it does not use any NLP resource. On the other hand, it is our hypothesis that, in order to improve the results, it is appropriate to apply some NLP techniques. In order to test it, we have also tried other BLEU-like algorithms, increasing the accuracy up to 56% (CWS=54%). These results confirmed the use of BLEU-like algorithms as a possible baseline for the automatic recognition of textual entailment. Furthermore, they show how a shallow technique can reach an accuracy of around 56%.

This article is organized as follows: Section 2 explains how BLEU and other similar algorithms work in general, and next Section 3 details the application of these algorithms for recognizing entailment and gives the results achieved. Section 4 explores how shallow and deeper NLP techniques can contribute to this task. Finally, Section 5 ends with the main conclusions of the paper and some possible lines of future work.

## 2 BLEU-like Algorithms

The BLEU (BiLingual Evaluation Understudy) algorithm was created by Papineni *et al.* [6] as a procedure to rank systems according to how well they translate texts from one language to another. Basically, the algorithm looks for n-gram coincidences between a candidate text (the automatically produced translation) and a set of reference texts (the human-made translations). This algorithm is as follows:

- For several values of N (typically from 1 to 4), calculate the percentage of n-grams from the candidate translation that appear in any of the human translations. The frequency of each n-gram is limited to the maximum frequency with which it appears in any reference.
- Combine the marks obtained for each value of N, as a weighted linear average.
- Apply a Brevity Penalty factor to penalize short candidate texts (which may have n-grams in common with the references, but may be incomplete). If the candidate is shorter than the references, this factor is calculated as the ratio between the length of the candidate text and the length of the reference which has the most similar length.

It can be seen that BLEU is not only a keyword matching method between pairs of text. It considers several other factors that make it more robust:

- It takes into account the length of the text in comparison with the lengths of reference texts. This is because the candidate text should be similar to the reference texts (if the translation has been well done). Therefore, the fact that the candidate text is shorter than the reference texts is indicative of a poor quality translation and thus, BLEU penalizes it with a Brevity Penalty factor that lowers the score.
- The measure of similarity can be considered as a precision value that calculates how many of the n-grams from the candidate appear in the reference texts. This value has been modified, as the number of occurrences of an n-gram in the candidate text is clipped at the maximum number of occurrences it has in the reference texts. Therefore, an n-gram that is repeated very often in the candidate text will not increment the score if it only appears a few times in the references.
- The final score is the result of the weighted sum of the logarithms of the different values of the precision, for n varying from 1 to 4. It is not advisable to use higher values of n since coincidences longer than four-grams are very unusual.

BLEU's output indicates how similar the candidate and reference texts are. In fact, the higher the value is, the more similar they are. Papineni *et al.* report a correlation above 96% when comparing BLEU's scores with the human-made scores [6].

This algorithm has also been applied to evaluate text summarization systems with the modification that, in this case, the stress is put on the recall rather than on the precision [8]. This has motivated us to try a similar change in the original BLEU algorithm.

In particular, BLEU measures the recall in a rough way by penalizing very short translations using the Brevity Penalty factor. We have focused on improving this factor, by calculating it as the percentage of the reference text that is covered by the candidate text.

The resulting algorithm is called BLEU+**recall** and it is as follows:

1. For each value of $N$ (typically from 1 to 4), calculate the Modified Unified Precision ($MUP_N$) as the percentage of $N$-grams from the candidate answer which appears in the reference text.
2. Calculate the weighted linear average of $MUP_N$ obtained for each value of $N$. Store it in $combMUP$.
3. Calculate the Modified Brevity Penalty ($MBP$) factor, which is intended to penalize answers with a very high precision, but which are too short, to measure the recall:
   (a) For $N$ from a maximum value (e.g. 10) down to 1, look whether each $N$-gram from the candidate text appears in the reference. In that case, mark the words from the found $N$-gram, both in the candidate and in the reference.
   (b) The $MBP$ factor is the percentage of the reference that has been found in the candidate text.
4. The final score is the result of multiplying the $MBP$ factor by $e^{combMUP}$.

BLEU+recall has been conveniently applied in the assessment of free-text answers combined with some shallow NLP techniques [9], using the `wraetlic` tools[1] [10]. These techniques are the following:

- **Stemming (ST):** To reduce each word to its stem or root form to facilitate the task of finding words with similar meanings but in different morphological forms. For instance, to match *books* and *book* as the former word is just the plural form of the latter.
- **Removal of closed-class words (CC):** To ignore functional words that have been tagged as closed-class words (e.g. prepositions, conjunctions, determiners, etc.) because they do not convey the main meaning of the sentence.
- **Word Sense Disambiguation (WSD):** To identify the sense in which polysemous words are used, using WordNet as the repository of word senses (see Section 3 for more details).

## 3 Application of BLEU-like Algorithms for Automatically Recognizing Textual Entailment

The corpus provided by the Pascal RTE Challenge organizers [4] consisted of 567 development entailment pairs and 800 test pairs. They have been gathered so that different linguistic levels were necessary to automatically judge entailment

[1] www.ii.uam.es/~ealfon/eng/research/wraetlic.html

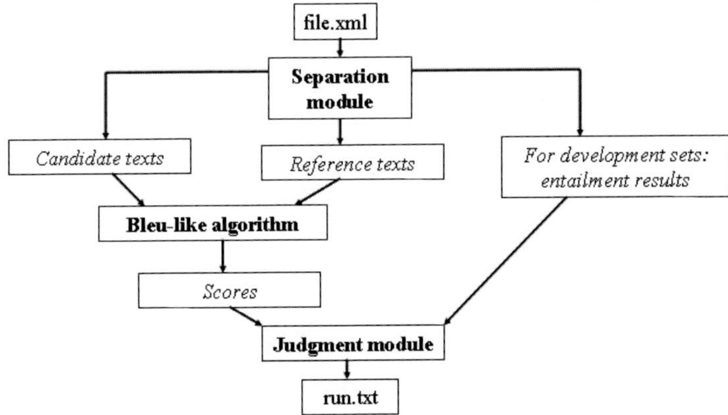


**Fig. 1.** Procedure to automatically recognize textual entailment using a BLEU-like algorithm

as TRUE or FALSE. They were also selected to produce a balanced corpus in which half of the entailment were TRUE according to human annotators. Whenever there was a disagreement between the human annotators about the nature of a pair, it was discarded.

Figure 1 shows the procedure for recognizing entailment using a BLEU-like algorithm. The first step is to use the *"Separation Module"* to split the initial corpus in two different sets[2], one with the T part of the entailment pairs and the other with the H part.

The second step is to decide whether the candidate text should be considered as the text part of the entailment (T) or as the hypothesis (and, as a consequence whether the reference text should be considered as the H or the T part). In order to make this choice, the length of the T and H parts and the dependency of the BLEU algorithm on the references should be taken into account. Initially, we considered the T part as the reference and the H as the candidate. This setting should have the advantage that the T part is usually longer than the H part and thus the reference would contain more information than the candidate. It could help BLEU's comparison process since the quality of the references is crucial and, in this case, the number of them has been dramatically reduced to only one (when in the rest of the applications of BLEU the number of references is always higher).

Then, the third step is to apply the algorithm as described in Section 2. The output is a score for each pair that enters the *"Judgement module"* to give a TRUE or FALSE value to each pair and also to be used as its confidence score. We performed an optimization procedure for the development set that chose the best threshold according to the percentage of success of correctly recognized entailment pairs. The value obtained was 0.157. Thus, if BLEU's output is higher than 0.157 the entailment is marked as TRUE, otherwise as FALSE.

[2] For the development sets, another output of this module is a file with the human annotators judgment for each pair.

**Table 1.** Results of using BLEU for recognizing the entailment in the development sets, considering from the first to seventh columns the T part of the entailment as the reference text (threshold = 0.157) and, from the eight to the final column the T part of the entailment as the candidate text (threshold = 0.1). The acronyms in the columns indicate: task id; number of entailment pairs (NTE); accuracy (A); number of pairs correctly judged as true (NTR); number of pairs correctly judged as false (NFR); number of pairs incorrectly judged as true (NTW); and, number of pairs incorrectly judged as false (NFW).

| Task | NTE | A | NTR | NFR | NTW | NFW | NTE | A | NTR | NFR | NTW | NFW |
|---|---|---|---|---|---|---|---|---|---|---|---|---|
| CD | 98 | 77% | 39 | 36 | 12 | 11 | 98 | 72% | 40 | 31 | 17 | 10 |
| IE | 70 | 44% | 16 | 15 | 20 | 19 | 70 | 50% | 23 | 12 | 23 | 12 |
| MT | 54 | 52% | 18 | 10 | 17 | 9 | 54 | 52% | 21 | 7 | 20 | 6 |
| QA | 90 | 41% | 9 | 28 | 17 | 36 | 90 | 50% | 22 | 23 | 22 | 23 |
| RC | 103 | 51% | 30 | 23 | 28 | 22 | 103 | 50% | 33 | 19 | 32 | 19 |
| PP | 82 | 57% | 22 | 25 | 18 | 17 | 82 | 60% | 25 | 24 | 19 | 14 |
| IR | 70 | 44% | 10 | 21 | 14 | 25 | 70 | 41% | 8 | 21 | 14 | 27 |
| Total | 567 | 53% | 144 | 158 | 126 | 139 | 567 | 54% | 172 | 137 | 147 | 111 |

**Table 2.** Results for the test set using BLEU (threshold = 0.1). Columns indicate: task id; confidence-weighted score or average precision (CWS); and, the accuracy.

| TASK | CWS | Accuracy |
|---|---|---|
| CD | 0.7823 | 0.7000 |
| IE | 0.5334 | 0.5000 |
| MT | 0.2851 | 0.3750 |
| QA | 0.3296 | 0.4231 |
| RC | 0.4444 | 0.4571 |
| PP | 0.6023 | 0.4600 |
| IR | 0.4804 | 0.4889 |
| TOTAL | 0.5168 | 0.4950 |

The results achieved are gathered in Table 1 (left). In order to confirm our insight that considering the T part of the entailment as the reference reaches better results, we repeated the experiment this time choosing the T part of the pair as the candidate and the H part as the reference. The results are shown in Table 1 (right). In this case, the best threshold has been 0.1. This is the value that has been fixed as threshold for the test set.

It can be seen how the results contradict our insight that the best setting would be to have the T part as the reference text. In fact, the results are not so much different for both configurations. A possible reason for this could be that all cases when BLEU failed to correctly judge the entailment are problematic in both settings. BLEU cannot deal with these cases neither taking the T part as the reference text nor taking it as the candidate text.

It is also important to highlight that the average accuracy achieved was of 54%. Moreover, it reached an accuracy of 72% for the Comparable Document

**Table 3.** Results for the test set using BLEU+**recall** (threshold = 0.9). Columns indicate: task id; confidence-weighted score or average precision (CWS); and, the accuracy considering the T part of the entailment pairs as the candidate text; and, next, then considering the H part of the pairs as the reference text.

| TASK | CWS | Accuracy | CWS | Accuracy |
|---|---|---|---|---|
| CD | 0.5847 | 0.6333 | 0.4629 | 0.4800 |
| IE | 0.5524 | 0.5333 | 0.4311 | 0.5000 |
| MT | 0.4771 | 0.4667 | 0.3632 | 0.4083 |
| QA | 0.5517 | 0.5846 | 0.5944 | 0.5000 |
| RC | 0.4976 | 0.5071 | 0.5872 | 0.5000 |
| PP | 0.4829 | 0.4600 | 0.4954 | 0.5200 |
| IR | 0.5091 | 0.5444 | 0.3814 | 0.5000 |
| TOTAL | 0.5194 | 0.5425 | 0.4730 | 0.4838 |

(CD) task. This result was expected since BLEU's strength relies on making comparisons between texts in which the lexical level is the most important.

The results for the test set (although a slightly lower than for the development test) confirm the same conclusions drawn before. In fact, for the first run in which BLEU was used for all the tasks, it achieved a confidence-weighted score of 52% and an accuracy of 50%. See Table 2 for details.

It can be seen that the results are better choosing the T part as the candidate text, and the H part as the reference, contrary to our initial insight. After analyzing the data set, we have seen that in many cases H is implied by T, but the reverse is not applicable, i.e. the entailment is unidirectional. This implies that it may be the case that most of H is covered by T, but a large portion of T is not covered by H. Therefore, the score returned by BLEU is lower if we consider T as the reference, because in these cases the hypothesis text is penalized by the Brevity Penalty Factor.

As can be seen, not only the overall performance continues being similar to accuracy obtained with the development test. Also, the best task for the test set keeps being the CD. To highlight this fact, we implemented a preliminary step of the algorithm in which there was a filter for the CD pairs, and only they were processed by BLEU. In this way, we created a second run with the CD set that achieved a CWS of 78% and an accuracy of 70%. This high result indicates that, although, in general, BLEU should only be considered as a baseline for recognizing textual entailment, in the case of CD, it can probably be used as a stand-alone system.

As indicated in Section 2, we have also tried several BLEU-like algorithms. For all them the threshold to decide whether the entailment should be judged as TRUE or FALSE was empirically determined as 0.9. They are the following:

- BLEU+**recall:** Following the procedure previously described but, using the algorithm described in Section 2 with the new Modified Brevity Penalty (MBP) factor, which takes into account not only the precision but also the recall. Table 3 shows the results both for considering the T part of the

**Table 4.** Results for the test set using BLEU+**recall+ST** (threshold = 0.9). Columns indicate: task id; confidence-weighted score or average precision (CWS); and, the accuracy considering the T part of the entailment pairs as the candidate text; and, next, considering the H part of the pairs as the reference text.

| TASK | CWS | Accuracy | CWS | Accuracy |
|---|---|---|---|---|
| CD | 0.5962 | 0.6200 | 0.4382 | 0.4667 |
| IE | 0.5475 | 0.5167 | 0.4375 | 0.5000 |
| MT | 0.4674 | 0.5083 | 0.3735 | 0.4167 |
| QA | 0.5799 | 0.6000 | 0.5857 | 0.5000 |
| RC | 0.4746 | 0.5143 | 0.5870 | 0.5000 |
| PP | 0.4902 | 0.4800 | 0.5257 | 0.5200 |
| IR | 0.5731 | 0.5556 | 0.4075 | 0.5000 |
| TOTAL | 0.5333 | 0.5500 | 0.4704 | 0.4825 |

**Table 5.** Results for the test set using BLEU+**recall+CC** (threshold = 0.9). Columns indicate: task id; confidence-weighted score or average precision (CWS); and, the accuracy considering the T part of the entailment pairs as the candidate text; and, next, considering the H part of the pairs as the reference text.

| TASK | CWS | Accuracy | CWS | Accuracy |
|---|---|---|---|---|
| CD | 0.5986 | 0.6067 | 0.5141 | 0.5000 |
| IE | 0.5522 | 0.5750 | 0.4437 | 0.5000 |
| MT | 0.4614 | 0.5000 | 0.5058 | 0.4667 |
| QA | 0.5310 | 0.5385 | 0.5896 | 0.5000 |
| RC | 0.4457 | 0.4500 | 0.5972 | 0.5000 |
| PP | 0.4703 | 0.5000 | 0.5124 | 0.5200 |
| IR | 0.5423 | 0.5111 | 0.4011 | 0.5000 |
| TOTAL | 0.5152 | 0.5300 | 0.5145 | 0.4963 |

entailment as the candidate or the reference and the H part as the reference or the candidate. It can be seen that while the CWS is kept of around 52%, the accuracy has been increased up to 54%. Using the T part as the candidate which continues to be the best configuration.

- BLEU+**recall+ST:** The improvement observed with the previous algorithm makes us think that, by further tuning the algorithm, more promising results could be achieved. Hence, we added an initial pre-processing step in which both the T and H part of the entailment pairs were stemmed. The results shown in Table 4 confirm our insight, as with this new step and using the T part as the candidate, an accuracy of 55% is reached and a CWS of 53%.
- BLEU+**recall+CC:** Although the removal of stop-words can produce worse results (e.g. [11]), we were intrigued about the effect of combining this step with BLEU+recall. However, it turned out that in our case it has also a negative effect decreasing the accuracy down to 53% and the CWS down to 52% (see Table 5). Perhaps, it could be solved by only removing certain stop-words and not all of them.

**Table 6.** Results for the test set using BLEU+**recall+WSD** (threshold = 0.9). Columns indicate: task id; confidence-weighted score or average precision (CWS); and, the accuracy considering the T part of the entailment pairs as the candidate text; and, next, considering the H part of the pairs as the reference text.

| TASK | CWS | Accuracy | CWS | Accuracy |
|---|---|---|---|---|
| CD | 0.6287 | 0.6200 | 0.4231 | 0.4667 |
| IE | 0.5804 | 0.5583 | 0.4333 | 0.5000 |
| MT | 0.4848 | 0.5250 | 0.3690 | 0.4167 |
| QA | 0.5554 | 0.5846 | 0.6028 | 0.5000 |
| RC | 0.4795 | 0.5143 | 0.5539 | 0.4929 |
| PP | 0.5351 | 0.4800 | 0.5173 | 0.5200 |
| IR | 0.5540 | 0.5444 | 0.4009 | 0.5000 |
| TOTAL | 0.5405 | 0.5550 | 0.4627 | 0.4813 |

**Table 7.** Results for the test set using BLEU+**recall+ST+CC+WSD** (threshold = 0.9). Columns indicate: task id; confidence-weighted score or average precision (CWS); and, the accuracy considering the T part of the entailment pairs as the candidate text; and, next, considering the H part of the pairs as the reference text.

| TASK | CWS | Accuracy | CWS | Accuracy |
|---|---|---|---|---|
| CD | 0.6035 | 0.5867 | 0.4413 | 0.4800 |
| IE | 0.5631 | 0.5583 | 0.4123 | 0.5000 |
| MT | 0.4729 | 0.4833 | 0.4613 | 0.4083 |
| QA | 0.5264 | 0.5615 | 0.5906 | 0.5000 |
| RC | 0.4739 | 0.4643 | 0.6113 | 0.5000 |
| PP | 0.5278 | 0.5000 | 0.5063 | 0.5200 |
| IR | 0.5375 | 0.5222 | 0.4973 | 0.5111 |
| TOTAL | 0.5267 | 0.5288 | 0.4979 | 0.4925 |

- BLEU+**recall+WSD:** This variant of the algorithm incorporates the use of WordNet 2.0 to identify the sense in which each word from the entailment pairs is used, using a WSD algorithm similar to [12], as described in [13] that measures the similarity between the context of the polysemous word in the entailment pair and the definition of the glosses in WordNet for its several senses. The gloss more similar to the context of the polysemous word is the one chosen and thus, the sense associated to that gloss is assigned to the word. The similarity metric is the cosine similarity based on the Vector Space Model (VSM). Given that one of the main problems to face when recognizing entailment is to deal with paraphrasings, we believe that this approach should give better results than the previous ones. This insight is proved by the results achieved: an accuracy of 56% and a CWS of 54% (see Table 6). It can be seen how both the accuracy and the CWS have reached with this configuration their highest value.
- BLEU+**recall+ST+CC+WSD:** The last algorithm that we have tried consists in combining BLEU+recall with all the NLP techniques contemplated.

**Table 8.** Results for several BLEU-like algorithms according to all the metrics used in the Pascal RTE Challenge[4]

| Algorithm | Accuracy | CWS | Precision | Recall | f-measure |
|---|---|---|---|---|---|
| BLEU+recall | 0.5425 | 0.5194 | 0.5282 | 0.7950 | 0.6347 |
| BLEU+recall+ST | 0.5500 | 0.5333 | 0.5312 | 0.8500 | 0.6538 |
| BLEU+recall+CC | 0.5300 | 0.5152 | 0.5349 | 0.4600 | 0.4946 |
| BLEU+recall+WSD | **0.5550** | **0.5405** | 0.5381 | 0.7775 | 0.6360 |
| BLEU+recall+ST+CC+WSD | 0.5267 | 0.5288 | 0.5406 | 0.3825 | 0.4480 |

Thus, the process would be as follows: first, the words of the entailment pairs are stemmed and the polysemous words are disambiguated, then the stop-words are removed and BLEU+recall is applied to give a score to each pair so that the "Judgment module" can decide according to the 0.9 threshold whether the entailment holds or not. Table 7 shows the results for this experiment. Again the configuration that uses T as the candidate gives the best results. It achieves an accuracy of 53% and a CWS of 53% that do not improve the only use of WSD (perhaps because of the negative effect of using the removal of closed-class words is still noticed when combined with other NLP techniques).

Finally, Table 8 summarizes the results for accuracy, CWS, precision, recall and f-measure for the five BLEU-like algorithms under test considering the T part of the entailment as the candidate text and with the 0.9 threshold.

## 4 Discussion

Automatically recognizing textual entailment is an interesting task that involves many complex linguistic phenomena. Seventeen different systems were presented at the Pascal RTE Challenge. They were based on very diverse techniques working at different linguistic levels. Nonetheless, all the results achieved were in the small range from 50% to 59% of accuracy. This section discusses how far shallow approaches can deal with this task and whether it is worthwhile to use deeper NLP techniques.

First of all, it is unclear whether this task can be completely solved just with automatic techniques. As indicated, the pairs used in the test set were those on which all the human annotators agreed. Even so, when several human researchers were asked to manually recognize entailment they only achieved an agreement of 91% [1]. Therefore, the complete task, including the discarded examples, can be considered difficult even for human judges. Perhaps, a possible solution for this can be to mark the entailment pairs not only as TRUE or FALSE, but also as DON'T KNOW, as proposed by Bos and Markert [14].

Our approach in the article has been to use BLEU-like algorithms. They only work at the lexical level and, thus, they cannot deal with examples in which the syntactic or semantic level are crucial to correctly solve the entailment. For example, those cases in which the T and H parts are the same except for just one word that reverses the whole meaning of the text, as in the pair number 148 in the development set, whose T and H parts are

(2) a. The Philippine Stock Exchange Composite Index rose 0.1 percent to 1573.65
b. The Philippine Stock Exchange Composite Index dropped.

This is a very difficult case for BLEU-like algorithms. It will be misleading since they would consider that both T and H are saying something very similar, while in fact, the only words that are different in both texts, *"rose"* and *"dropped"*, are antonyms, making the entailment FALSE.

Another example is the pair number 1612 of the development set, whose T and H part are

(3) a. With South Carolina being Jesse Jackson's home state, there was a very strong incentive in the black community.
b. Jesse Jackson was born in South Carolina.

Any human annotator would know that this pair is true since in the T part it is said that South Carolina is Jesse Jackson's home state which is another way to say that Jesse Jackson was born in South Carolina. However, no BLEU-like algorithm would be able to identify this relationship without having any knowledge about this paraphrasing.

Other authors have found similar results such as Jijkoun *et al.* [15] that claimed their need for exploring deeper text features, Akhmatova [16] that stated that a deep semantic and syntactical analysis is vital to solve this problem and Herrera *et al.* [17] that declared that matching-based approaches were not enough (except perhaps for CD tasks) since a higher lexical overlap does not imply a higher semantic entailment.

On the other hand, it can be observed that despite the simplicity of BLEU and that it only works at the lexical level, it could be considered as a baseline for recognizing textual entailment [7]. In fact, this was our motivation to test similar algorithms such as BLEU+recall and combinations of BLEU+recall with NLP techniques such as stemming, removal of closed-class words and WSD. The results confirm our insight. In fact, BLEU+recall+WSD has reached an accuracy of 56% and a CWS of 54%, that are better than chance at the 0.05 level.

Some examples that are easily solved by these BLEU-like algorithms are:

- The pair of the development test with identifier 583, with the following T and H snippets:
  (4) a. While civilians ran for cover or fled to the countryside, Russian forces were seen edging their artillery guns closer to Grozny, and Chechen fighters were offering little resistance.
  b. Grozny is the capital of Chechnya.
  
  Since only the word Grozny is present both texts it will correctly mark it as false.
- The pair number 950 of the development set, with the following T and H snippets:

(5) a. Movil Access, a Grupo Salinas company, announced today that Gustavo Guzman will appoint Jose Luis Riera as company CFO of Grupo Iusacell.
b. Movil Access appoints Jose Luis Riera as CFO.

As the T part is included in the H part, the entailment will be correctly judge as true.

Furthermore, Bos and Markert [14] have observed that, when a shallow system is extended with deep NLP methods, the difference between the results they achieve is small. In fact, the accuracy of the first system is 0.5550, and that of the second system is just slightly higher, 0.5625.

## 5 Conclusion and Future Work

The discovery of entailment relationships is important for many NLP tasks [18]. In the framework of the Pascal RTE Challenge, an overview of the state-of-the-art of the field and, a study of which are the most promising techniques that should be used to face this task, took place.

Our approach is based on the use of the BLEU algorithm. Some conclusions that can be drawn from the experiments described in Section 2 are:

- BLEU can be used as a baseline for the task of recognizing entailment pairs, considering the candidate text as T and the reference text as the H part of the entailment, since it has achieved an accuracy of around 50%.
- BLEU's results depend greatly on the task considered. For example, for the Comparable Documents (CD) task it reaches its maximum value (77%) and for Information Retrieval (IR) the lowest (41%).
- BLEU has a slight tendency to consider a hypothesis as TRUE. In 319 out of 567 pairs, BLEU said the entailment was true. Out of these, it was right in 172 cases, and it was wrong in 147 cases. On the other hand, there were only 111 false negatives.

It is also interesting to observe that, although the origin of BLEU is to evaluate MT systems, the results for the MT task are not specially higher. The reason for that could be that BLEU is not being used here to compare a human-made translation to a computer-made translation, but two different sentences which contain an entailment expression, but which are not alternative translations of the same text in a different language.

Regarding BLEU-like algorithms, it has been seen how the potential of BLEU for this task can be further exploited reaching up to an accuracy of 56% and a CWS of 54% when a modification of BLEU takes into account the recall and incorporates WSD relying on WordNet was used.

The main limit of BLEU is that it does not use any semantic information and, thus, sentences with many words in common but with a different meaning will not be correctly judged.

A main conclusion of this paper is that shallow NLP techniques cannot be disregarded in this task. They have proved how useful they are, not only to serve as baselines, but also as the basis for more complex systems and to obtain in a simple and fast way fairly good results compared to those reached by deeper techniques. All the same, in order to completely solve this task, we agree with the general opinion of the field that more resources are necessary. In particular, our best configuration used WordNet.

It would be interesting, as future work, to complement the use of BLEU+recall with some kind of syntactic processing and some treatment of synonyms and antonyms. For example, by combining it with a parser that translates all sentences from passive to active and allowed the comparison by syntactic categories such as subject, direct object, indirect object, etc.

As the Pascal Challenge organizers stated, it would be interesting to work towards the building of "semantic engines". This work would not only benefit the automatic recognition of entailment but several related NLP fields that suffer from similar problems such as the need of dealing with paraphrasings in the automatic assessment of free-text answers.

## References


1. Bayer, S., Burger, J., Ferro, L., Henderson, J., Yeh, A.: Mitre's submissions to the eu pascal rte challenge. In: Proceedings of the PASCAL Recognising Textual Entailment workshop, U.K. (2005)
2. Salvo-Braz, R., Girju, R., Punyakanok, V., Roth, D., Sammons, M.: An inference model for semantic entailment in natural language. In: Proceedings of the PASCAL Recognising Textual Entailment workshop, U.K. (2005)
3. Raina, R., Haghighi, A., Cox, C., Finkel, J., Michels, J., Toutanova, K., MacCartney, B., Marneffe, M., Manning, C., Ng, A.Y.: Robust textual inference using diverse knowledge sources. In: Proceedings of the PASCAL Recognising Textual Entailment workshop, U.K. (2005)
4. Dagan, I., Glickman, O., Magnini, B.: The pascal recognising textual entailment challenge. In: Proceedings of the PASCAL Recognising Textual Entailment workshop, U.K. (2005)
5. Glickman, O., Dagan, I., Koppel, M.: Web based probabilistic textual entailment. In: Proceedings of the PASCAL Recognising Textual Entailment workshop, U.K. (2005)
6. Papineni, K., Roukos, S., Ward, T., Zhu, W.: BLEU: a method for automatic evaluation of machine translation. Research report, IBM (2001)
7. Perez, D., Alfonseca, E.: Application of the bleu algorithm for recognising textual entailments. In: Proceedings of the PASCAL Recognising Textual Entailment workshop, U.K. (2005)
8. Lin, C., Hovy, E.: Automatic evaluation of summaries using n-gram co-occurrence statistics. In: Proceedings of the Human Technology Conference 2003 (HLT-NAACL-2003). (2003)
9. Alfonseca, E., Pérez, D.: Automatic assessment of short questions with a BLEU-inspired algorithm and shallow nlp. In: Advances in Natural Language Processing. Volume 3230 of Lecture Notes in Computer Science. Springer Verlag (2004) 25–35
10. Alfonseca, E.: Wraetlic user guide version 2.0 (2005)
11. Wu, D.: Textual entailment recognition based on inversion transduction grammars. In: Proceedings of the PASCAL Recognising Textual Entailment workshop, U.K. (2005)

12. Lesk, M.: Automatic sense disambiguation using machine readable dictionaries. In: Proceedings of the 5th International Conference on Systems Documentation. (1986) 24–26
13. Ruiz-Casado, M., Alfonseca, E., Castells, P.: Automatic assignment of wikipedia encyclopedic entries to wordnet synsets. In: Advances in Web Intelligence. Volume 3528 of Lecture Notes in Artificial Intelligence. Springer Verlag (2005) 380–386
14. Bos, J., Markert, K.: Combining shallow and deep nlp methods for recognizing textual entailment. In: Proceedings of the PASCAL Recognising Textual Entailment workshop, U.K. (2005)
15. Jijkoun, V., Rijke, M.: Recognizing textual entailment using lexical similarity. In: Proceedings of the PASCAL Recognising Textual Entailment workshop, U.K. (2005)
16. Akhmatova, E.: Textual entailment resolution via atomic propositions. In: Proceedings of the PASCAL Recognising Textual Entailment workshop, U.K. (2005)
17. Herrera, J., Penas, A., Verdejo, F.: Textual entailment recognition based on dependency analysis and wordnet. In: Proceedings of the PASCAL Recognising Textual Entailment workshop, U.K. (2005)
18. Szpektor, I., Tanev, H., Dagan, I., Coppola, B.: Scaling web-based acquisition of entailment relations. In Lin, D., Wu, D., eds.: Proceedings of the EMNLP, Association for Computational Linguistics. (2004) 41–48

# What Syntax Can Contribute in the Entailment Task

Lucy Vanderwende and William B. Dolan

Microsoft Research,
Redmond, WA 98052
{lucyv, billdol}@microsoft.com

**Abstract.** We describe our submission to the PASCAL Recognizing Textual Entailment Challenge, which attempts to isolate the set of Text-Hypothesis pairs whose categorization can be accurately predicted based solely on syntactic cues. Two human annotators examined each pair, showing that a surprisingly large proportion of the data - 34% of the test items - can be handled with syntax alone, while adding information from a general-purpose thesaurus increases this to 48%.

## 1 Introduction

The data set made available by the PASCAL Recognizing Textual Entailment Challenge provides a great opportunity to focus on a very difficult task, determining whether one sentence (the hypothesis, H) is entailed by another (the text, T).

Our goal was to isolate the class of T-H pairs whose categorization can be accurately predicted based solely on syntactic cues. This work is part of a larger ablation study aimed at measuring the impact of various NLP components on entailment and paraphrase.

We have chosen to provide a partial submission that addresses the following question: what proportion of the entailments in the PASCAL test set could be solved using a robust parser? We are encouraged that other entrants chose to focus on different baselines, specifically those involving lexical matching and edit distance. Collectively, these baselines should establish what the minimal system requirements might be for addressing the textual entailment task.

## 2 Details of Microsoft Research Submission

Various parsers providing constituent level analysis are now available to the research community, and state-of-the-art parsers have reported accuracy of between 89% and 90.1% F-measure (Collins and Duffy, 2002, Henderson 2004; see Ringger et al., 2004 for results with a non-treebank parser). There are also efforts to produce parsers that assign argument structure (Gildea and Jurafsky, 2002, and for example, Hacioglu et al., 2004). With these developments, we feel that

J. Quiñonero-Candela et al. (Eds.): MLCW 2005, LNAI 3944, pp. 205–216, 2006.

syntax can be defined broadly to include such phenomena as argument assignment, intra-sentential pronoun anaphora resolution, and a set of alternations to establish equivalence on structural grounds.

Our goal was to establish a baseline for the entailment task that reflects what an idealized parser could accomplish, abstracting away from the analysis errors that any specific parsing system would inevitably introduce. We decided therefore to rely on human annotators to decide whether syntactic information alone is sufficient to make a judgment. Two human annotators evaluated each T-H pair, indicating whether the entailment was:

- True by Syntax,
- False by Syntax,
- Not Syntax,
- Can't Decide

Additionally, we allowed the annotators to indicate whether recourse to information in a general purpose thesaurus entry would allow a pair to be judged True or False. Both annotators were skilled linguists, and could be expected to determine what an idealized syntactic parser could accomplish. We should note at this point that it could prove impossible to automate the judgment process described in this paper; the rules-of-thumb used by the annotators to make True or False judgments could turn out to be incompatible with an operational system.

We found that 34% of the test items can be handled by syntax, broadly defined; 48% of the test items can be handled by syntax plus a general purpose thesaurus. The results of this experiment are summarized in Table 1:

**Table 1.** Summary of Microsoft Research partial submission; Run1 is without thesaurus, Run2 is with thesaurus

| | Without thesaurus | Using thesaurus |
|---|---|---|
| True | 69 (9%) | 147 (18%) |
| False | 197 (25%) | 243 (30%) |
| Not syntax | 534 (67%) | 410 (51%) |

Overall, inter-annotator agreement was 72%. Where there were disagreements, the annotators jointly decided which judgment was most appropriate in order to annotate all test items. Of the disagreements, 60% were between False and Not-Syntax, and 25% between True and Not-Syntax; the remainder of the differences involved either annotation errors or cases where one or both annotators chose Can't Decide. This confirms our anecdotal experience that it is easier to decide when syntax can be expected to return True, and that the annotators were uncertain when to assign False. In some cases, there are good syntactic clues for assigning False, which is why we designed the evaluation to force a choice between True, False, and Not-Syntax. But in many cases, it is simply the absence of syntactic equivalence or parallelism that results in a judgment of False, and most of the disagreements centered on these cases.

## 3 Results of Partial Submission

Our test results are not comparable to those of other systems, since obviously, our runs were produced by human annotators. In this section, we only want to briefly call attention to those test items which showed a discrepancy between our adjudicated human annotation and those provided as gold standard. It is worth mentioning that we believe the task is well-defined, at least for the test items we evaluated. For the 295 test items returned in Run1 of our submission, 284 matched the judgment provided as gold standard, so that our inter-annotator agreement on this subset of the test set was 96%.

In Run1 (using an idealized parser, but no thesaurus), there were 11 discrepancies. Of the 3 cases where we judged the test item to be True but the gold standard for the item is False, one is clearly an annotation error (despite having two annotators!) and two are examples of strict inclusion, which we allowed as entailments but the data set does not (test items 1839 and 2077); see (1).

1. (pair id="2077", value="FALSE", task="QA")
   <T> They are made from the dust of four of Jupiters tiniest moons.
   <H> Jupiter has four moons.

More difficult to characterize as a group are the 8 cases where we judged the test item to be False but the gold standard for the item is True (although 5/8 are from the QA section) The test items in question are: 1335, 1472, 1487, 1553, 1584, 1586, 1634, and 1682. It does appear to us that more knowledge is needed to judge these items than simply what is provided in the Text and Hypothesis. We therefore believe that these items should be removed from the data set, since pairs for which there was disagreement among the judges were discarded. Item 1634 is a representative example.

2. (pair id="1634", value="TRUE", task="IE")
   <T> William Leonard Jennings sobbed loudly as was charged with killing his 3-year-old son, Stephen, who was last seen alive on Dec. 12, 1962.
   <H> William Leonard Jennings killed his 3-year-old son, Stephen.

## 4 Requirements for a Syntax-Based System

We analyzed our human judgments to establish which syntactic phenomena a robust parser would need to handle in order to complete the entailment task. We can distinguish two categories: the level of syntactic analysis, further described in 4.1, and a set of alternations, described in 4.2. Section 4.3 describes the special handling of syntactic analysis for the purpose of establishing a T-H pair to be False. Most of the examples will be from the subset of judgments that are True and based solely on syntactic cues, because these sentence pairs often isolate the specific phenomena under discussion. We have included a list of syntactic phenomena and alternations for each judgment type in the Appendix, from which the cooccurence of phenomena can also be ascertained.

Additionally, we enumerate in the Appendix those test items, representing only a small fraction (3.5%) of the test set, which can be judged using single word replacement alone. An example of single-word replacement is the following:

3. (pair id="1996", value="TRUE", task="PP")
<T> Iraqi militants abduct 2 Turks in Iraq.
<H> Iraqi militants kidnap 2 Turks in Iraq.

### 4.1 Syntactic Analysis

The best illustration of the role played by syntactic evidence involves cases where predicate-argument assignment gives clear evidence for the judgment. (4a) and (4b) are good examples:

4. <T> Latvia, for instance, is the lowest-ranked team in the field but defeated World Cup semifinalist Turkey in a playoff to qualify for the final 16 of Euro 2004.

4a. (pair id="1897", value="TRUE", task="IE")
<H> Turkey is defeated by Latvia.

4b. (pair id="1896", value="FALSE", task="IE")
<H> Latvia is defeated by Turkey.

A more straightforward case is for a parser (in most cases, a preprocessing component to the parser) to account for Named Entity Recognition, identifying various expressions of an entity as equivalent, as in (5), where the strings *Reverend Frank Chikane* and *Rev Frank Chikane* refer to the same person.

5. (pair id="847", value="TRUE", task="CD")
<T> On hand to meet him with Mbeki were (... ) and director general in the presidency, Reverend Frank Chikane.
<H>On hand to meet him with Mbeki were (....) and director general in the presidency, Rev Frank Chikane.

Other syntactic phenomena frequently observed in the data are T-H pairs that differ only in nominalization, as in (6), coordination, prepositional phrase attachment, and negation.

6. (pair id="1021", value="TRUE", task="RC")
<T> Sunday's election results demonstrated just how far the pendulum of public opinion has swung away from faith in Koizumi's promise to bolster the Japanese economy and make the political system more transparent and responsive to the peoples' needs.
<H> Koizumi promised to bolster the Japanese economy.

We also assume that a parser, broadly defined, will be capable of identifying the inferences invited by the apposition construction and by the predicate-complement constructions. In example (7), if the predicate holds for not only the subject, but also for the apposition to the subject, then this sentence pair can also be handled straightforwardly:

7. (pair id="1616", value="TRUE", task="IE ")

<T> In 1833, Benjamin Harrison, the 23rd president of the United States, was born in North Bend, Ohio.

<H> The 23rd President of the United States was born in Ohio.

The examples presented above attempt to illustrate each syntactic phenomena in isolation. However, at least half of the T-H pairs require the identification of multiple phenomena simultaneously. The example in (8) involves Named Entity Recognition (*Honecker* = *Erich Honeker*), including identification of spelling variants, two instances of pronominal anaphora (*he* = *Honecker/Homeker*), and vp-cataphora (*did* = *build the Berlin Wall*). Nevertheless, if a parser is able to provide this level of syntactic analysis, the system can return a True judgment with confidence.

8. (pair id="621", value="TRUE", task="QA")

<T> Although Honecker led the Communist East German state between 1971 and 1989, he will be remembered most for what he did long before – building the Berlin Wall.

<H>Erich Honeker built the Berlin Wall.

Finally, the identification of negation naturally plays a significant role in determining entailment, including the identification of morphological variants expressing negation. For Hypotheses that match an embedded clause in the Text, the subordinating conjunction and the semantic type of the main verb is also of importance; this phenomenon was relatively frequent in all but the subset of the test set we judged to be true using syntax alone. Consider examples (9) and (10):

9. (pair id="2025", value="FALSE", task="IR")

<T> There are a lot of farmers in Poland who worry about their future if Poland joins the European Union.

<H> Poland joins the European Union.

10. (pair id="2055", value="FALSE", task="QA")

<T> The fact that Einstein was invited to be the president of Israel is critical to an accurate understanding of one of the greatest individuals in modern history.

<H> Einstein is the president of Israel.

### 4.2 Syntactic Alternations

By far the most frequent alternation between Text and Hypothesis that a system needs to identify is an appositive construction promoted to main clause in the Hypothesis. This alternation alone accounted for approximately 24% of the subset of the data we judged could be handled with syntactic analysis[1].

[1] This distribution is likely to be a result of the instructions given for the creation of the IE subtask in the PASCAL RTE data set, in particular, which focused on several well-known relationship types from IE, such as "born in" and "organizational role".

11. (pair id="760", value="TRUE", task="CD")
<T> The Alameda Central, west of the Zocalo, was created in 1592.
<H> The Alameda Central is west of the Zocalo.

Another frequent alternation involves material in a relative clause being promoted to a main clause in the Hypothesis, as in example (12), which includes named entity recognition as well:

12. (pair id="1060", value="TRUE", task="RC")
<T> (...) when Silva was sent in by Rio de Janeiro state Gov. Rosinha Matheus, who also is an Evangelical Christian.
<H> Rosinha Matheus is an Evangelical Christian.

Examples of other frequent alternations that need to be identified are: predicate nominal / premodifier (13), *of*-prepositional phrase / premodifier (14), and *have* / possessive (15).

13. (pair id="1088", value="TRUE", task="RC")
<T> Eight of the 51 Philippine humanitarian troops in Iraq have already left the country, Philippine Foreign Affairs Secretary Delia Albert said early Wednesday.
<H> Delia Albert is the Philippine Foreign Affairs Secretary.

14. (pair id="1096", value="TRUE", task="RC")
<T> A longtime associate of al Qaeda leader Osama bin Laden surrendered to Saudi Arabian officials.
<H> Osama bin Laden is the leader of al Qaeda.

15. (pair id="1010", value="TRUE", task="RC")
<T> (...) photographs of a hazy orange Titan – the largest of Saturn's 31 moons, about the size of the planet Mercury.
<H> Saturn has 31 moons.

Lastly, there are additional alternations which largely derive from the Information Extraction subset of the test data, where the creators of the test set were requested to select a few targeted types of relations, such as "X was born in Y" and "X is located in Y", and construct T-H pairs. Such alternations can be found in the appendix.

### 4.3 Establishing False Entailment

We found two main categories of T-H pairs that we judged to be False: False, where there was a mismatch in the syntactic structure, and False, where there was no syntactic structure shared by the T-H pair. Although we can annotate this by hand, we are unsure whether it would be possible to create a system to automatically detect the absence of syntactic overlap. Though mismatched main verbs are the primary cue to the absence of overlap, all possible major and minor argument types were found unaligned, each potentially leading to a judgment of False entailment; see the Appendix for the details.

Examples of judging False by mismatch of syntactic structure are those in which the Subject and Verb align (with or without thesaurus), but the Object does not, as in (16):

16. (pair id="103", value="FALSE", task="IR")
<T> The White House ignores Zinni's opposition to the Iraq War.
<H> White House ignores the threat of attack.

The following examples illustrate the absence of shared syntactic structure in the major argument positions. In (17), the entailment is judged False since *baby girl* is not the subject of any verb of *buying*, nor is *ambulance* the object of any verb of *buying*; additionally, there is no mention of *buying* in T at all. In (18), the entailment is judged False because there is no mention of *Douglas Hacking* in the Text, nor any mention of *physician*. While a system using lexical matching might well rule the second example False, there are enough lexical matches in the former that a system using syntax is likely required.

17. (pair id="2179", value="FALSE", task="RC")
<T> An ambulance crew responding to an anonymous call found a 3-week-old baby girl in a rundown house Monday, two days after she was snatched from her mother at a Melbourne shopping mall.
<H> A baby girl bought an ambulance at a Melbourne shopping mall.

18. (pair id="2169", value="FALSE", task="CD")
<T> Scott and Lance Hacking talked with their younger brother at the hospital July 24.
<H>Douglas and Scott Hacking are physicians.

## 5 Interesting "Not Syntax" Examples

The number of examples that can be handled using syntax, broadly defined, is significant, but more than 50% were judged to be outside the realm of syntax, even allowing for the use of a thesaurus.

Some test items exhibited phrasal-level synonymy, which the annotators did not expect would be available in a general purpose thesaurus. Consider, *X bring together Y* and *Y participate in X* in (19):

19. (pair id="287", value="TRUE", task="IR")
<T> The G8 summit, held June 8-10, brought together leaders of the world's major industrial democracies, including Canada, France, Germany, Italy, Japan, Russia, United Kingdom, European Union and United States.
<H>Canada, France, Germany, Italy, Japan, Russia, United Kingdom and European Union participated in the G8 summit.

There are some examples with apparent alternation, but the alternation cannot easily be supported by syntax. Consider *three-day* and *last three days* in the following example:

20. (pair id="294", value="TRUE", task="IR")
<T> The three-day G8 summit will take place in Scotland.
<H> The G8 summit will last three days.

In other cases, the annotators considered that there were too many alternations and thesaurus replacements necessary to confidently say that syntax could be used. Consider the following example, where *more than half* has to align with *many*, *saying* aligns with *thinking*, and *not worth fighting* aligns with *necessary*.

21. (pair id="306", value="TRUE", task="IR")
<T> The poll, for the first time, has more than half of Americans, 52 percent, saying the war in Iraq was not worth fighting.
<H> Many Americans don't think the war in Iraq was necessary.

## 6 Discussion and Conclusion

Our goal was to contribute a baseline consisting of a system which uses an idealized parser, broadly defined, that can detect alternations, and optionally has access to a general purpose thesaurus. In order to explore what is possible in the limit, we used two human annotators and resolved their disagreements to produce a partial submission. It is interesting to note that the task is well-defined; of the 295 test items returned in our submission (Run1, without thesaurus), 284 matched the judgment provided as gold standard, so that our inter-annotator agreement on this subset is 96%.

An idealized syntax-based system can account for 34% of the test items, and, with the addition of information from a general purpose thesaurus, 48%. This finding is promising, though we expect the numbers to decrease subject to an implementation with a real-world parser and set of matching rules. An implemented system will also need to take the interaction of various alternations and syntactic phenomena as well. It may well be that there is a limit on the number of interactions an operational system can tolerate before its accuracy declines.

A syntax-based approach appears to be more powerful at deciding when T-H pairs exhibit False entailment: a syntax-only approach categorizes only 9% of the test items as True entailments successfully vs. 24% as False entailments. We have some concern that this imbalance is a consequence of the test creation process, as described in Dagan et al.. The test set authors were instructed for some subtasks to take a given sentence as the Text, and to produce a Hypothesis with either significant word overlap (but False) or no word overlap (but True); the first creation method would favor syntax-based methods. While the current RTE 1 test set is a rich collection of many of the possible types of mappings that can hold between Text and Hypothesis, a test collection that is a representative sampling of the mappings that occur for any subtask will be a valuable resource for system applications that include entailment.

Our baseline results need to be compared with those obtained by the systems using lexical matching and edit distance, as we expect that some of the items that can be handled by syntax alone could also be accounted for by these simpler methods.

We hope that the challenge workshop is well served by offering this study of the capabilities of an idealized parser. While approximately half of the RTE 1 test items are amenable to an approach using syntax augmented with a general purpose thesaurus, it is clear that the remainder of the test set represents an opportunity for work on fundamental entailment and paraphrase problems.

## Acknowledgements

The authors wish to thank the organizers of the RTE Challenge and PASCAL for creating this dataset and making it available. The authors also thank Deborah Coughlin for her linguistic judgments as one of the annotators, and for help with data analysis. We also thank the Butler Hill Group (www.butlerhill.com) for designing and maintaining the annotation environment.

## References

1. Michael Collins and Nigel Duffy. 2002. New Ranking Algorithms for Parsing and Tagging: Kernels over Discrete Structures, and the Voted Perceptron. *Proceedings of ACL 2002*, Philadelphia, PA.
2. Ido Dagan, Oren Glickman and Bernardo Magnini. 2005. "The PASCAL Recognising Textual Entailment Challenge." *In the Proceedings of the PASCAL Recognising Textual Entailment Challenge*, April 2005.
3. Daniel Gildea and Daniel Jurafsky. 2002. Automatic Labeling of Semantic Roles. *Computational Linguistics*, 28(3):245-288.
4. Kadri Hacioglu, Sameer Pradhan, Wayne Ward, James H. Martin, and Daniel Jurafsky, 2004. Semantic Role Labeling by Tagging Syntactic Chunks. *Proceedings of the Eighth Conference on Natural Language Learning (CONLL-2004)*, Boston, MA, May 6-7.
5. James Henderson. 2004. Discriminative training of a neural network statistical parser. *Proceedings of ACL 2004*, Barcelona, Spain.
6. Eric Ringger, Robert C. Moore, Eugene Charniak, Lucy Vanderwende, and Hisami Suzuki. 2004. Using the Penn Treebank to Evaluate Non-Treebank Parsers. *Proceedings of the 2004 Language Resources and Evaluation Conference (LREC)*. Lisbon, Portugal.

## Appendix

Files of the human judgments described in this paper are available on request from the authors.

- True by Syntax (with/without thesaurus)
- False by Syntax (with/without thesaurus)

Tables 2-5 contain categorization of human judgments regarding the syntactic phenomena and alternations required of a robust parser. Each category is followed by a list of the test items exhibiting the phenomena from the RTE 1 data set. For categories with ten or more examples, the distribution over the subtasks represented in RTE 1 is also given.

**Table 2.** Syntactic Phenomena Not Involving Alternation

| | |
|---|---|
| (Counter-)Factive | 174, 308, 472, 914, 962, 1076, 1121, 1284, 1300, 1358, 1359, 1421, 1634, 1876, 1907, 1981, 1982, 1983, 2024, 2025, 2041, 2055, 2062, 2121, 2122, 2135, 2167 |
| | CD: 3.7% IE: 14.8% IR: 29.6% MT: 7.4% PP: 22.2% QA: 7.4% RC: 14.8% |
| Anaphora | 298, 621, 936, 987, 1029, 1121, 1312, 1319, 1334, 1618, 1644, 1645, 1646, 1826, 1840, 1848, 1862, 1893, 1907, 2037, 2041 |
| | CD: 4.8% IE: 28.6% IR: 14.3% MT: 14.3% QA: 14.3% RC: 23.8% |
| Apposition | 741, 864, 901, 1144, 1203, 1263, 1387, 1556, 1584, 1616, 1617, 1618, 1648, 1822, 1907, 2036, 2090, 2190 |
| | CD: 22.2% IE: 33.3% MT: 11.1% QA: 16.7% RC: 16.7% |
| Attachment | 724, 893, 897, 1008, 1607, 1667 |
| Coordination | 300, 888, 898, 1004, 1042, 1082, 1342, 1370, 1536, 1634, 1640, 1831, 1861, 1895, 1896, 1964, 2014, 2020, 2113, 2129, 2169 |
| | CD: 28.6% IE: 23.8% IR: 14.3% MT: 4.8% PP: 4.8% QA: 4.8% RC: 19.0% |
| Ellipsis | 807, 2112 |
| Existential | 310, 840, 875, 1196, 2034 |
| Extraposition | 2041 |
| Named Entity Recognition | 39, 82, 103, 308, 315, 621, 692, 696, 821, 841, 847, 862, 864, 993, 1060, 1074, 1122, 1123, 1175, 1189, 1196, 1203, 1218, 1300, 1374, 1387, 1507, 1531, 1546, 1549, 1552, 1584, 1590, 1616, 2017, 2032, 2048, 2135, 2144, 2163 |
| | CD: 27.5% IE: 2.5% IR: 15.0% MT: 15.0% PP: 2.5% QA: 25.0% RC: 12.5% |
| Negation | 979, 1004, 1144, 1196, 1301, 1370, 1663, 1826, 1861, 1893, 1981, 1982, 1984 |
| | CD: 15.4% IE: 15.4% MT: 15.4% PP: 23.1% RC: 30.8% |
| Nominalization | 315, 962, 1021, 1092, 1358, 1422, 1625, 2073, 2135, 2176 |
| | CD: 10.0% IE: 10.0% IR: 40.0% PP: 10.0% QA: 10.0% RC: 20.0% |
| Passive-Active | 727, 1053, 1071, 1137, 1263, 1824, 1825, 1862, 1896, 1897, 1901, 1913, 1968, 1984, 1988, 2070 |
| | CD: 12.5% IE: 25.0% MT: 6.3% PP: 18.8% QA: 6.3% RC: 31.3% |
| Predeterminer | 1203, 1445, 2077, 2176 |
| Predicate Complement | 692, 938, 1092, 1325, 1468, 2006 |
| Relative/Infinitive Clause | 186, 472, 605, 727, 856, 887, 979, 1053, 1060, 1092, 1137, 1196, 1335, 1462, 1480, 1504, 1617, 1618, 1629, 1816, 1900, 1901, 1969 |
| | CD: 13.0% IE: 21.7% IR: 4.3% MT: 8.7% PP: 8.7% QA: 17.4% RC: 26.1% |
| Spelling variation/error | 743, 883, 888, 1556 |
| VP-Cataphora | 621 |

**Table 3.** Syntactic Phenomena Involving Alternation

| | |
|---|---|
| "be born" – Appositive "from" | 1584, 1621 |
| "be from" – "be born in" | 1672, 1687 |
| "be located" – in-PP | 1654 |
| "be located" – Appositive | 1074, 1123, 1549, 1655, 1944 |
| Adjective/Noun morphology | 878, 1203, 1203, 2176 |
| Auxiliary – no-aux | 1308 |
| Be – Equi | 48, 878, 1144 |
| Be – Appositive | 35, 139, 760, 843, 929, 996, 1009, 1011, 1073, 1091, 1093, 1142, 1555, 1613, 1836, 1903, 1905, 1998, 2039 |
| | CD: 10.5% IE: 21.1% PP: 5.3% QA: 10.5% RC: 52.6% |
| Be – Appositive (flipped) | 336, 901, 1032, 1062, 1065, 1134, 1826, 1940, 2037, 2092 |
| | CD: 10.0% IE: 20.0% QA: 10.0% RC: 60.0% |
| Genitive – Location | 35, 828, 1872 |
| Have – Possessive | 1010, 2077 |
| Location Alternation | 1361, 1820, 1871, 1872, 2082 |
| Non finite – Finite verb construction | 1263 |
| Of Prepositional Phrase – Premodifier | 864, 1096, 1203, 1325, 1358, 1451, 2037, 2096 |
| Postmodifier – hyphenated | 1122 |
| Postmodifier – Premodifier | 878, 1627, 2048 |
| PreDeterminer – Restrictive Relative Clause | 1662 |
| Predicate Nominative – Postmodifier | 1662 |
| Predicate Nominative – Premodifier | 166, 739, 739, 1031, 1088, 1096, 1451, 1620 |
| Premodifier – Noun Appositive | 39, 1028, 2039 |
| Relative Clause – Main Clause | 142, 825, 825, 962, 1007, 1041, 1122, 1609, 1687 |

**Table 4.** Single Word Replacement

| | |
|---|---|
| Single Word | 711, 834, 836, 846, 885, 1070, 1282, 1359, 1432, 1445, 1447, 1540, 1611, 1623, 1882, 1952, 1954, 1961, 1962, 1963, 1967, 1979, 1980, 1987, 1994, 1996, 2019, 2049, 2088 |
| | CD: 17.2% IE: 13.8% IR: 3.4% MT: 3.4% PP: 51.7% QA: 6.9% RC: 3.4% |

**Table 5.** Lack of Syntactic Parallelism

| | |
|---|---|
| Factoid | 828, 1820, 1824 |
| Location | 1334, 1530, 1531, 1547, 1620, 1624, 1628, 1667, 1672, 1821, 1874, 1999, 2027, 2134 |
| | IE: 50.0% IR: 7.1% MT: 7.1% QA: 21.4% RC: 14.3% |
| Main verb | 727, 887, 938, 965, 967, 993, 997, 1042, 1103, 1133, 1307, 1317, 1335, 1342, 1376, 1380, 1389, 1410, 1424, 1425, 1427, 1441, 1442, 1459, 1472, 1479, 1488, 1504, 1506, 1507, 1516, 1524, 1539, 1546, 1608, 1618, 1622, 1629, 1644, 1647, 1648, 1680, 1682, 1683, 1686, 1688, 1693, 1840, 1846, 1848, 1849, 1853, 1854, 1860, 1865, 1866, 1869, 1913, 1954, 1979, 1990, 1992, 1998, 2006, 2008, 2014, 2018, 2020, 2021, 2022, 2026, 2029, 2035, 2036, 2038, 2047, 2048, 2053, 2063, 2070, 2090, 2113, 2117, 2125, 2136, 2144, 2152, 2157, 2162, 2163, 2167, 2168, 2176, 2179, 2187, 2190 |
| | CD: 22.9% IE: 21.9% IR: 12.5% MT: 4.2% PP: 9.4% QA: 18.8% RC: 10.4% |
| Object | 103, 1012, 1013, 1071, 1308, 1319, 1321, 1389, 1642, 1816, 1825, 1896, 1901, 2102, 2123, 2124, 2127, 2129, 2145, 2146 |
| | CD: 15.0% IE: 15.0% IR: 25.0% MT: 20.0% RC: 25.0% |
| Of-Prepositional Phrase | 2028, 2092, 2133 |
| Postmodifier | 1530 |
| Predicate Adjective | 48 |
| Predicate Complement | 308, 1174, 1203, 1462, 1552, 1822, 1845 |
| Predicate Nominative | 35, 840, 1011, 1032, 1123, 1487, 1498, 1549, 1551, 1553, 1589, 1666, 1675, 2033, 2037, 2039, 2045, 2054, 2056, 2169 |
| | CD: 10.0% IE: 10.0% PP: 5.0% QA: 60.0% RC: 15.0% |
| Subject | 909, 910, 936, 981, 1008, 1016, 1028, 1040, 1055, 1056, 1218, 1301, 1317, 1319, 1325, 1334, 1363, 1367, 1374, 1501, 1536, 1554, 1586, 1590, 1607, 1645, 1646, 1831, 1837, 1848, 1849, 1862, 1863, 1896, 2042, 2043, 2090, 2123, 2127, 2134, 2190 |
| | CD: 12.2% IE: 12.2% IR: 12.2% MT: 14.6% QA: 17.1% RC: 31.7% |
| Subordinate Clause | 1051 |
| Time | 1829, 1890 |

# Combining Lexical Resources with Tree Edit Distance for Recognizing Textual Entailment

Milen Kouylekov[1,2] and Bernardo Magnini[1]

[1] ITC-irst, Centro per la Ricerca Scientifica e Tecnologica,
via Sommarive 14, 38050 Povo, Trento, Italy
[2] University of Trento,
via Sommarive 18, 38050 Povo, Trento, Italy
milen@kouylekov.net, magnini@itc.it

**Abstract.** This paper addresses Textual Entailment (i.e. recognizing that the meaning of a text entails the meaning of another text) using a Tree Edit Distance algorithm between the syntactic trees of the two texts. A key aspect of the approach is the estimation of the cost for the editing operations (i.e. Insertion, Deletion, Substitution) among words.

The aim of the paper is to compare the contribution of two different lexical resources for recognizing textual entailment: WordNet and a word-similarity database. In both cases we derive entailment rules that are used by the Tree Edit Distance Algorithm. We carried out a number of experiments over the PASCAL-RTE dataset in order to estimate the contribution of different combinations of the available resources.

## 1 Introduction

The problem of language variability (i.e. the fact that the same information can be expressed with different words and syntactic constructs) has attracted a lot of interest during the years and it has posed significant problems for systems that require some form of natural language understanding. The example below shows that recognizing the equivalence of the statements *came into power*, *was prime-minister* and *stepped in as prime-minister* is a challenging problem.

- Ivan Kostov came into power in 1997.
- Ivan Kostov was prime-minister of Bulgaria from 1997 to 2001.
- Ivan Kostov stepped in as prime-minister 6 months after the December 1996 riots in Bulgaria.

While the language variability problem is well known in Computational Linguistics, a general unifying framework has been proposed only recently in [3]. In this approach, language variability is addressed by defining *entailment* as a relation that holds between two language expressions (i.e. a text T and an hypothesis H) if the meaning of H as interpreted in the context of T, can be inferred from T. The entailment relation is directional as one expression can entail the other, while the opposite may not.

J. Quiñonero-Candela et al. (Eds.): MLCW 2005, LNAI 3944, pp. 217–230, 2006.

The Recognizing Textual Entailment (RTE) task takes as input a T/H pair and consists in automatically determining whether an entailment relation holds between T and H or not. The task covers almost all the phenomena in language variability: entailment can be due to lexical variations, as it is shown in example (1), to syntactic variation (example 2), to semantic inferences (example 3) or to complex combinations of all such levels. As a consequence of the complexity of the task, one of the crucial aspects for any RTE system is the amount of linguistic and world knowledge required for filling the gap between T and H. The following examples, taken from the RTE-PASCAL dataset, show the complexity of the problem:

1. *T* - Euro-Scandinavian media cheer Denmark v Sweden draw.
   *H* - Denmark and Sweden tie.
2. *T* - Jennifer Hawkins is the 21-year-old beauty queen from Australia.
   *H* - Jennifer Hawkins is Australia's 21-year-old beauty queen.
3. *T* - The nomadic Raiders moved to LA in 1982 and won their third Super Bowl a year later.
   *H* - The nomadic Raiders won the Super Bowl in 1983.

In example 1 the entailment relation is based on the synonymy between *draw* and *tie*; in example 2 we need to understand that the syntactic structures of the text and the hypothesis are equivalent; finally, in 3 we need to reason about temporal entities.

A crucial role in textual entailment is played by entailment rules which are defined [3] as language expressions with syntactic analysis and optional variables replacing sub-parts of the structure. They consist of entailing template (i.e. the left hand side of the rule) and an entailed template (i.e. the right hand side of the rule), which share the same variable scope. Prior or contextual (posterior) probability is assigned to the rule. As an example, a lexical and syntactic rules is show on Table 1.

**Table 1.** Lexical and Syntactic Rules

| Rule | Score |
|---|---|
| draw $\Rightarrow$ tie | 0.2 |
| Australia's X $\Rightarrow$ X from Australia | 0.8 |

This rules will allow to detect an entailment relation at the lexical level for the example 1 and on syntactic level for example 2 above.

However, for concrete applications, a huge amount of such entailment rules are necessary. We investigate the possibility to automatically derive entailment rules from already existing linguistic resources. The aim of the paper is to provide a clear and homogeneous framework for the evaluation of lexical resources for the RTE task. The framework is based on the intuition that the probability of an entailment relation between T and H is related to the ability to show that the whole content of H can be mapped into the content of T. The more straightforward the mapping can be established, the more probable is the entailment relation. Since a mapping can be described as the sequence of editing operations needed to transform T into H, where each edit operation has a cost associated with it, we assign an entailment relation if the overall cost of the transformation is below a certain threshold, empirically estimated on the training data.

Within the Tree Edit Distance (TED) framework, the evaluation of a linguistic resource for the RTE task is equivalent to the capability of the resource to provide entailment rules that are profitably used to allow edit operations with their corresponding costs. We have experimented the TED approach with three linguistic resources: (i) a non-annotated document collection, from which we have estimated the relevance of words; (ii) a database of similarity relations among words estimated over a corpus of dependency trees; (iii) WordNet, from which we have extracted entailment rules based on lexical relations.

Experiments, carried out on the PASCAL-RTE dataset, provide significant insight for future research on RTE.

The paper is organized as follows. In Section 2 we review some of the relevant approaches proposed by groups participating in the PASCAL-RTE challenge. Section 3 presents the Tree Edit Distance algorithm we have adopted and its application to dependency trees. Section 4 describes the architecture of the system. Section 5 describes the resources we have used for deriving entailment rules and how we have estimated cost functions over them. Section 6 presents the results we have obtained while Section 7 contains a general discussion and describes some directions for future work.

## 2 Relevant Approaches

The most basic inference technique used by participants at PASCAL-RTE is the degree of overlap between T and H. Such overlap is computed using a number of different approaches, ranging from statistic measures like *idf*, deep syntactic processing and semantic reasoning. The difficulty of the task explains the poor performance of all the systems, which achieved accuracy between 50-60%. In the rest of the Section we briefly mention some of the systems which are relevant to the approach we describe in this paper.

A similar approach to recognizing textual entailment is implemented in a system participating in PASCAL-RTE [7]. The authors use dependency parsing and extract lexical rules from WordNet.

In [1] the authors describe two systems for recognizing textual entailment. The first system is based on deep syntactic processing. Both T and H are parsed and converted into a logical form. An event-oriented statistical inference engine is used to separate the TRUE from FALSE pairs. The second system is based on statistical machine translation models.

A method for recognizing textual entailment based on graph matching is described in [17]. To handle language variability problems the system uses a maximum entropy coreference classifier and calculates term similarities using WordNet [5] by means of a similarity module based on techniques described in [15].

A system based on frequency-based term weighting in combination with different similarity measures is presented in [8]. The weight of the words in the hypothesis is calculated with normalized inverse frequency:

$$ICF(w) = \frac{\#occurrences\_of\_w}{\#occurrences\_of\_all\_words} \quad (1)$$

$$weight(w) = 1 - \frac{ICF(W) - ICF_{min}}{ICF_{max} - ICF_{min}} \quad (2)$$

where $ICF_{min}$ and $ICF_{max}$ are the minimum and maximum inverse frequencies. The second measure is the dependency based word similarity described in [10].

## 3 Tree Edit Distance on Dependency Trees

We adopted a tree edit distance algorithm applied to the syntactic representations (i.e. dependency trees) of both T and H. A similar use of tree edit distance has been presented by [16] for a Question Answering system, showing that the technique outperforms a simple bag-of-word approach. While the cost function presented in [16] is quite simple, for the RTE challenge we tried to elaborate more complex and task specific measures.

According to our approach, T entails H if there exists a sequence of transformations applied to T such that we can obtain H with an overall cost below a certain threshold. The underlying assumption is that pairs that exhibits an entailment relation have a low cost of transformation. The kind of transformations we can apply (i.e. deletion, insertion and substitution) are determined by a set of predefined entailment rules, which also determine a cost for each editing operation.

We have implemented the tree edit distance algorithm described in the paper from [20] and apply it to the dependency trees derived from T and H. Edit operations are defined at the level of single nodes of the dependency tree (i.e. transformations on subtrees are not allowed in the current implementation). Since the [20] algorithm does not consider labels on edges, while dependency trees provide them, each dependency relation R from a node A to a node B has been re-written as a complex label B-R concatenating the name of the destination node and the name of the relation. All nodes except the root of the tree are relabeled in this way. The algorithm is directional: we aim to find the better (i.e. less costly) sequence of edit operation that transform T (the source) into H (the target). According to the constraints described above, the following transformations are allowed:

- **Insertion:** Insert a node from the dependency tree of H into the dependency tree of T. When a node is inserted it is attached with the dependency relation of the source label.
- **Deletion:** Delete a node N from the dependency tree of T. When N is deleted all its children are attached to the parent of N. It is not required to explicitly delete the children of N as they are going to be either deleted or substituted on a following step.

- **Substitution:** Change the label of a node N1 in the source tree (the dependency tree of T) into a label of a node N2 of the target tree (the dependency tree of H). Substitution is allowed only if the two nodes share the same part-of-speech. In case of substitution the relation attached to the substituted node is changed with the relation of the new node.

## 4 System Architecture

The system is composed of the following modules, showed in Figure 1: (i) a text processing module, for the preprocessing of the input T/H pair; (ii) a matching module, which performs the mapping between T and H; (iii) a cost module, which computes the cost of the edit operations.

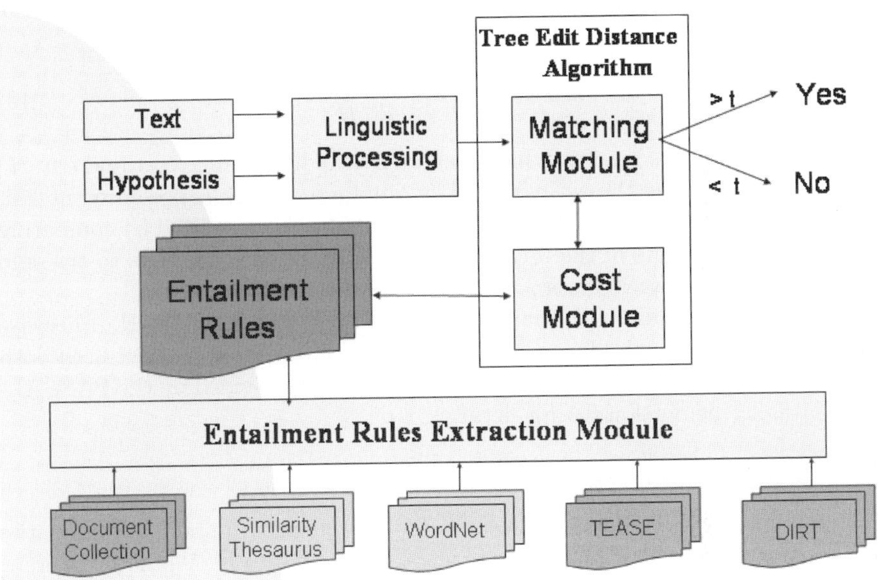


**Fig. 1.** System Architecture

### 4.1 Text Processing Module

The *text processing module* creates a syntactic representation of a T/H pair and relies on a sentence splitter and a syntactic parser. For sentence splitting we used *MXTerm* [18], a Maximum entropy sentence splitter. For parsing we used *Minipar*, a principle-based English parser [9] which has high processing speed and good precision.

A relevant problem we encountered, affecting about 30% of the pairs in the dataset we used, is that the parser represents in a different way occurrences of similar expressions, making it harder to apply edit transformations. For instance,

"Wal-Mart" and "Wal-Mart Stores inc." have different trees, where "Mart" the governing node in the first case and the governed node in the second. The problem could be addressed by changing the order of the nodes in T which is however complex because it introduces changes in the tree edit-distance algorithm. Another solution, which we intend to explore in the future, is the integration of specialized tools and resources for handling named entities and acronyms. In addition, for about 20% of the pairs, the parser did not produce the right analysis either for T or for H.

### 4.2 Matching Module

The *matching module* finds the best sequence (sequence with lower cost) of edit operations between the dependency trees obtained from T and H. It implements the edit distance algorithm described in Section 3.

The entailment score *score(T,H)* of a given pair is calculated in the following way:

$$score(T, H) = \frac{ed(T, H)}{ed(, H)} \tag{3}$$

where $ed(T, H)$ is the function that calculates the edit distance cost and $ed(, H)$ is the cost of inserting the entire tree H. A similar approach is presented in [14], where the entailment score of two document $d$ and $d'$ is calculated by comparing the sum of the weights of the terms that appear in both documents to the sum of the weights of all terms in $d'$.

We used a threshold $t$ such that if $score(T, H) < t$ then T entails H, otherwise no entailment relation holds for the pair. To set the threshold we have used both the positive and negative examples of the training set provided by the PASCAL-RTE dataset (see Section 6.1 for details).

### 4.3 Cost Module

The matching module makes requests to the *cost module* in order to receive the cost of single edit operations needed to transform T into H. We have different cost strategies for the three edit operations.

*Insertion.* The intuition underlying insertion is that its cost is proportional to the relevance of the word $w$ to be inserted (i.e. inserting an informative word has an higher cost than inserting a less informative word). More precisely:

$$Cost[Ins(w)] = Rel(w) \tag{4}$$

where $Rel(w)$, in the current version of the system, is computed on a document collection as the *inverse document frequency (idf)* of $w$, a measure commonly used in *Information Retrieval.* If $N$ is the number of documents in a text collection and $N_w$ is the number of documents of the collection that contain $w$ then the *idf* of $w$ is given by the formula:

$$idf(w) = \log \frac{N}{N_w} \tag{5}$$

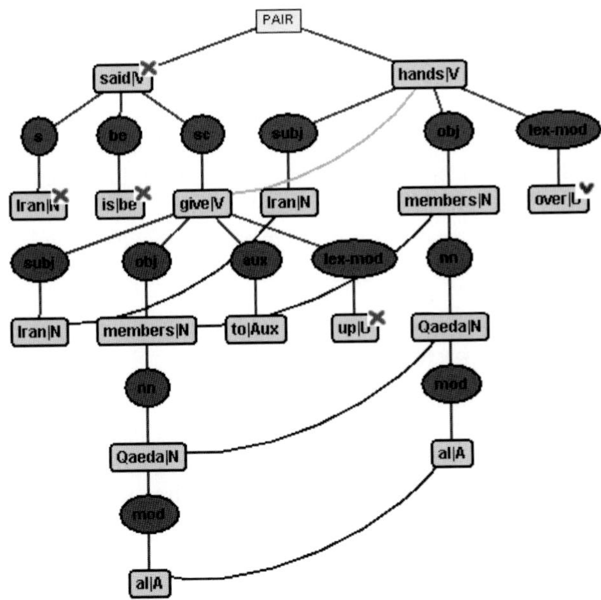


**Fig. 2.** An example of a T H pair mapping

The most frequent words (e.g. stop words) have a zero cost of insertion. In [14] the authors present similar approach to term weighting.

*Substitution.* The cost of substituting a word $w_1$ with a word $w_2$ can be estimated considering the semantic entailment between the words. The more the two words are entailed, the less the cost of substituting one word with the other.

We have used the following formula:

$$Cost[Subs(w_1, w_2)] = \\ Ins(w_2) * (1 - Ent(w_1, w_2)) \tag{6}$$

where $Ins(w_2)$ is calculated using (3) and $Ent(w_1, w_2)$ can be approximated with a variety of relatedness functions between $w_1$ and $w_2$.

There are two crucial issues for the definition of an effective function for lexical entailment: first, it is necessary to have a database of entailment relations with enough coverage; second, we have to estimate a quantitative measure for such relations. The availability of such resources is discussed in Section 5.

*Deletion.* In the PASCAL-RTE dataset H is typically shorter than T. As a consequence, we expect that much more deletions are necessary to transform T into H than insertions or substitutions. Given this bias toward deletion, in the current version of the system we set the cost of deletion to 0. This expectation has been empirically confirmed (see results of system 2 in Section 6.3).

An example of mapping between the dependency tree of T and H is depicted in Figure 2. The tree on the left is the dependency tree of the text: *Iran is said to give up al Qaeda members.* The tree on the right is the dependency tree corresponding to the hypothesis: *Iran hands over al Qaeda members.* The algorithm finds as the best mapping the subtree with root *give*. The verb *hands* is substituted by the verb *give* because it exists an entailment rule between them extracted from one of the resources. Lines connect the nodes that are exactly matched and nodes that are substitutions (give-hands) for which the similarity database represent is used. They represent the minimal cost match. Nodes in the text that do not participate in a mapping are removed. The lexical modifier *over* of the verb *hands* is inserted.

## 5 Resources for Lexical Entailment

This section presents the resources we experimented with in our approach to textual entailment to identifying semantic similarity during the substitution operation. Each resource is seen as a database of entailment rules, where each rule has associated a probability value determining the confidence of the relation. We have derived entailment rules from two available lexical resources, i.e. WordNet and a word-similarity database.

### 5.1 WordNet Similarity Rules

WordNet [5] is a lexical database which includes lexical and semantic relations among word senses. Originally developed for English, versions of WordNet are currently available also for other languages (e.g. Spanish, German and Italian).

We have defined a set of entailment rules (see Section 3) over the WordNet relations among synsets, with their respective probabilities. If A and B are synsets in WordNet (we used version 2.0), then we derived an entailment rule in the following cases:

- if A is hypernym of B then P(B A)
- if A is synonym of B then P(B A)
- if A entails B then P(B A)
- if A pertains to B then P(B A)

For all the relations between the synsets of two words, the probability of entailment is estimated with the following formula:

$$Ent_{wordnet}(w_1, w_2) = \frac{1}{S_{w_1}} * \frac{1}{S_{w_2}} \quad (7)$$

where $S_{w_i}$ is the number of senses of $w_i$; $\frac{1}{S_{w_1}}$ is the probability that $w_i$ is in the sense which participates in the relation; $Ent_{wordnet}(w_1, w_2)$ is the joined probability. The proposed formula is simplistic and does not take in to account the frequency of senses and the length of the relation chain between the synsets. We plan to improve it in our future work.

### 5.2 Word Similarity Database

As an alternative to the use of WordNet for determining the cost of substitutions, we experimented with the use of a dependency based thesaurus available at *http://www.cs.ualberta.ca/~lindek/downloads.htm.* For each word, the thesaurus lists up to 200 most similar words and their similarities. The similarities are calculated on a parsed corpus using frequency counts of the dependency triples. A complete review of the method including comparing with different approaches is presented in [10]. Dependency triples consists of a head, a dependency type and a modifier. They can be viewed as features for the head and the modifiers in the triples when calculating similarity.

The cost of a *substitution* is calculated by the following formula:

$$Ent_{sim}(w_1, w_2) = sim_{th}(w_1, w_2) \quad (8)$$

where $w_1$ is the word from T that is being replaced by the word $w_2$ from H and $sim_{th}(w_1, w_2)$ is the similarity between $w_1$ and $w_2$ in the thesaurus multiplied by the similarity between the corresponding relations.

## 6 Experiments and Results

We carried out a number of experiments in order to estimate the contribution of different combinations of the available resources. In this section we report on the dataset, the experiments and the results we have obtained.

### 6.1 Dataset

For the experiments we have used the PASCAL-RTE dataset [4]. The dataset [1] was collected by human annotators and is composed of 1367 text ($T$) - hypothesis ($H$) pairs split into positive and negative examples (a 50%-50% split).

Typically, $T$ consists of one sentence while $H$ was often made of a shorter sentence. The dataset has been split in a training (576 pairs) and a test (800 pairs) part.

### 6.2 Experiments

The following configurations of the system have been experimented with:

*System 1: Tree Edit Distance Baseline.* In this configuration, considered as a baseline for the Tree Edit Distance approach, the cost of the three edit operations are set as follows:
*Deletion*: always 0
*Insertion*: the *idf* of the word to be inserted
*Substitution*: 0 if $w_1 = w_2$, infinite in all the other cases.

[1] Available at http://www.pascal-network.org/Challenges/RTE/Datasets

In this configuration the system just needs a non-annotated corpus for estimating the *idf* of the word to be inserted. The corpus is composed of 4.5 million news documents from the CLEF-QA (Cross Language evaluation Forum) and TREC (Text Retrieval Conference) collections. Deletion is 0 because we expect much more deletions that insertions, due to the fact that $T$ is longer than $H$.

*System 2: Deletion as idf.* In this configuration we wanted to check the impact of assigning a cost to the deletion operation.
*Deletion*: the *idf* of the word to be deleted
*Insertion*: the *idf* of the word to be inserted
*Substitution*: same as System 1.

*System 3: Fixed Insert cost* In this configuration we wanted to fix the insert cost in order to check the impact of estimating the insert cost using local corpus. We chose a value of the *insertion* that was used in [16].
*Deletion*: 0
*Insertion*: 200
*Substitution*: same as System 1.

*System 4: Similarity Database.* This is the same than System 1, but we estimate the cost of substitutions using the similarity database described in Section 5.2. We expect a broad coverage with respect to the previous system.
*Deletion*: always 0
*Insertion*: the *idf* of the word to be inserted
*Substitution*: same as System 1, plus similarity rules.

*System 5: WordNet.* This is the same than System 1., but we estimate the cost of substitutions using the WordNet relations as described in Section 5.1. We expect a broader coverage with respect to System 1 and we want to compare it with System 4.
*Deletion*: always 0
*Insertion*: the *idf* of the word to be inserted
*Substitution*: same as system 1, plus WordNet rules.

*System 6: WordNet(constrained).* This is the same than System 5., but we have put constrain to the WordNet similarity score. Only entailment rules with score higher than 0.2 are used.
*Deletion*: always 0
*Insertion*: the *idf* of the word to be inserted
*Substitution*: same as system 1, plus WordNet rules(score $> 0.2$).

*System 7: Combination.* This is a combination of system 4 and system 6 aimed at checking the degree of overlap between rules of the two different resources.
*Deletion*: always 0
*Insertion*: the *idf* of the word to be inserted
*Substitution*: same as system 1, plus WordNet and similarity rules.

### 6.3 Results

For each system we have tested we report a table with the following data:

- #Attempted: the number of deletions, insertions and substitutions that the algorithm successfully attempted (i.e. which are included in the best sequence of editing transformations).
- %Success: the proportion of deletions, insertions and substitutions that the algorithm successfully attempted over the total of attempted edit transformations.
- Accuracy: the proportion of *T-H* pairs correctly classified by the system over the total number of pairs.
- CWS: Confidence Weighted Score (also known as Average Precision), is given by the formula:

$$cws = \frac{1}{n}\sum_{i=1}^{n}\frac{\#correct - upto - i}{i} \tag{9}$$

where $n$ is the number of the pairs in the test set, and $i$ ranges over the sorted pairs. The Confidence-Weighted Score ranges between 0 (no correct judgments at all) and 1 (perfect classification), and rewards the systems' ability to assign a higher confidence score to correct judgments than to incorrect ones.

**Table 2.** Results

| | System 1 | System 2 | System 3 | System 4 | System 5 | System 6 | System 7 |
|---|---|---|---|---|---|---|---|
| #deletions | 20325 | 19984 | 20220 | 20101 | 19971 | 20220 | 20101 |
| #insertions | 7927 | 7586 | 7822 | 7823 | 7573 | 7611 | 7823 |
| #substitutions | 2686 | 3027 | 2791 | 2910 | 3040 | 2790 | 2910 |
| %deletions | 0.88 | 0.87 | 0.88 | 0.83 | 0.86 | 0.88 | 0.83 |
| %insertions | 0.75 | 0.71 | 0.74 | 0.73 | 0.71 | 0.74 | 0.73 |
| %substitutions | 0.25 | 0.29 | 0.26 | 0.27 | 0.29 | 0.26 | 0.27 |
| accuracy | 0.560 | 0.481 | 0.550 | 0.566 | 0.548 | 0.572 | 0.566 |
| cws | 0.615 | 0.453 | 0.603 | 0.624 | 0.550 | 0.581 | 0.624 |

Table 2 shows the results obtained by the six systems we experimented with.

The hypothesis about the 0 cost of the deletion operation was confirmed by the results of System 2. Setting precise costs of the delete operation improve the performance of the system. For example, if we consider pair 908:

T - Time Warner is the world's largest media and Internet company.

H - Time Warner is the world's largest company.

the edit distance algorithm performs only three deletions of the nodes *'Internet'*, *'and'* and *'media'*. Still this operation modifies the semantics of T.

*System 3*, the system using fixed insertion cost, has lower performance than the baseline system. This shows that using a flexible insertion cost function increases the performance of the algorithm.

The similarity database used in system 4 increased the number of the successful substitutions made by the algorithm from 25% to 27%. It also increased the performance of the system for both *accuracy* and *cws*. The impact of the similarity database on the result is small because of the low similarity between the dependency trees of H and T.

The system based on Wordnet entailment rule, i.e. System 5, also increases the performance against the baseline system. The number of the substitutions is up to 26%. The accuracy is the highest achived using tree edit distance and it is 0.012 more than the baseline. In comparison with System 4 it makes less substitutions, because of the higher substitution cost (the word similarity score in the thesaurus is almost always higher than the WordNet similarity). This shows that increasing the number of substations does not mean an automatic increase of the performance. This is also fact for System 5. The best performing system makes less substitutions than systems 4 and 5. In fact, when the substitution cost is low the tree edit distance algorithm gives low distance score to trees that have similar structure. Reducing the cost of the substitution increases the importance of such trees against trees with more common nodes.

The combined run was completely dominated by the similarity database because of the lower cost of the substitution given by the word similarity thesaurus (higher similarity score).

## 7 Discussion and Future Work

We have presented an approach for recognizing textual entailment based on tree edit distance applied to the dependency trees of $T$ and $H$. We have also demonstrated that using lexical similarity resources can increase the performance of a system based on such algorithm.

The approach we have presented can be considered as a framework for testing the contribution of different kinds of linguistic resources for the textual entailment task. The intuition is that the performance of the system is correlated with the contribution, in terms of entailment rules, of the used resources. As an example, a wrong substitution with a low cost can significantly affect the optimal cost of the tree mapping (comparison between System 4, 5 and 6). A lesson we learned is that, in order to obtain good results, we should consider for substitution only pairs with high entailment score (in our experiment dependency or WordNet similarity). The experiments we have carried out show that a word similarity databases coupled with the edit distance algorithm can be used for successfully recognizing textual entailment. However, in order to test the specific contribution of a certain resource, a set of pairs from the RTE dataset which require specific lexical entailment rules must be selected.

The tree edit distance algorithm is designed to work with substitution on the level of tree nodes while our analysis of the PASCAL-RTE dataset show that sub-tree substitutions are more suitable for the task. In the future we plan to extend the usage of WordNet as an entailment resource. A method for calculating similarity between words in WordNet is presented in [2]. The potential of Extended WordNet [6] as an entailment resource is also discussed in [13] and [12] Other resources of entailment rules (e.g.paraphrases in [11], entailment patterns as acquired in [19]) could significantly widen the application of entailment rules and, consequently, improve performances. We estimated that for about 40% of the true positive pairs the system could have used entailment rules found in entailment and paraphrasing resources. As an example, the pair 565:

> T - Soprano's Square: Milan, Italy, home of the famed La Scala opera house, honored soprano Maria Callas on Wednesday when it renamed a new square after the diva.
>
> H - La Scala opera house is located in Milan, Italy.

could be successfully solved using a paraphrase pattern such as *Y home of X* <=> *X is located in Y*, which can be found in [11]. However, in order to use this kind of entailment rules, it would be necessary to extend the "single node" implementation of tree edit distance to address editing operations among subtrees. A system with an algorithm capable of calculating the cost of substitution on the level of subtrees can be used as a framework for testing paraphrase and entailment acquisition systems.

A drawback of the tree edit distance approach is that it is not able to observe the whole tree, but only the subtree of the processed node. For example, the cost of the insertion of a subtree in H could be smaller if the same subtree is deleted from T at a prior or later stage. A context sensitive extension of the insertion and deletion module will increase the performance of the system.

## References


1. Samuel Bayer, John Burger, Lisa Ferro, John Henderson and Alexander Yeh. MITRE's Submissions to the EU Pascal RTE Challenge *In Proceedings of PASCAL Workshop on Recognizing Textual Entailment* Southampton, UK, 2005
2. Alexander Budanitsky and Graeme Hirst Semantic distance in WordNet: An experimental, application-oriented evaluation of five measures. *In Workshop on WordNet and other Lexical Resources, Second meeting of the Nord American Chapter of the Association for Computational Linguistics.* Pittsburgh, 2001.
3. Ido Dagan and Oren Glickman. Generic applied modeling of language variability *In Proceedings of PASCAL Workshop on Learning Methods for Text Understanding and Mining* Grenoble, 2004
4. Ido Dagan, Oren Glickman and Bernardo Magnini. The PASCAL Recognizing Textual Entailment Challenge *In Proceedings of PASCAL Workshop on Recognizing Textual Entailment* Southampton, UK 2005
5. Christiane Fellbaum. WordNet, an electronic lexical database *MIT Press, 1998*
6. Sandra Harabagiu, George Miller and Dan Moldovan. WordNet 2 - A morphologically and Semantically Enhanced Resource. *In proceeding of ACL-SIGLEX99 Marylend 1999*

7. Jesus Herrera, Anselmo Peñas and Felisa Verdejo. Textual Entailment Recognition Based on Dependency Analysis and WordNet *In Proceedings of PASCAL Workshop on Recognizing Textual Entailment* Southampton, UK, 2005
8. Valentin Jijkoun and Maarten de Rijke. Recognizing Textual Entailment Using Lexical Similarity *In Proceedings of PASCAL Workshop on Recognizing Textual Entailment* Southampton, UK, 2005
9. Dekang Lin. Dependency-based evaluation of MINIPAR *In Proceedings of the Workshop on Evaluation of Parsing Systems at LREC-98.* Granada, Spain, 1998
10. Dekang Lin. An Information-Theoretic Definition of Similarity *Proceedings of International Conference on Machine Learning, Madison, Wisconsin*, July, 1998.
11. Dekang Lin and Patrick Pantel. Discovery of inference rules for Question Answering *Natural Language Engineering, 7(4)*, pages 343-360, 2001
12. Moldovan, D., Rus V. Logic Form Transformation and it's Applicability in Question Answering *In proceedings of ACL 2001.*
13. Moldovan, D., Harabagio, S., Girju, R., Morarescu, P., Lacatsu, F., Novischi, A LCC Tools for Question Answering. *NIST Special Publication: SP 500-251 The Eleventh Text Retrieval Conference (TREC 2002-2003).*
14. Christof Monz and Maarten de Rijke. Light-Weight Entailment Checking for Computational Semantics. *The third workshop on inference in computational semantics (ICoS-3, 2001)*
15. Tedd Pedersen , Siddharth Patwardhan and Jason Michelizzi. WordNet::Similarity - Measuring the relatedness of concepts *AAAI-2004*
16. Vasin Punyakanok, Dan Roth and Wen-tau Yih. Mapping Dependencies Trees: An Application to Question Answering *Proceedings of AI & Math*, 2004
17. Rajat Raina, Aria Haghighi, Christopher Cox, Jenny Finkel, Jeff Michels, Kristina Toutanova Bill MacCartney, Marie-Catherine de Marneffe, Christopher D. Manning and Andrew Y. Ng. Robust Textual Inference using Diverse Knowledge Sources *In Proceedings of PASCAL Workshop on Recognizing Textual Entailment* Southampton, UK, 2005
18. Adwait Ratnaparkhi. A Maximum Entropy Part-Of-Speech Tagger *In proceeding of the Empirical Methods in Natural Language Processing Conference, May 17-18*, 1996
19. Idan Szpektor, Hristo Tanev, Ido Dagan, and Bonaventura Coppola. Scaling Web-based Acquisition of Entailment Relations *In Proceedings of EMNLP-04 - Empirical Methods in Natural Language Processing*, Barcelona, July 2004
20. Kaizhong Zhang ,Dennis Shasha. Fast algorithm for the unit cost editing distance between trees *Journal of algorithms, vol. 11, p. 1245-1262*, December 1990

# Textual Entailment Recognition Based on Dependency Analysis and *WordNet*

Jesús Herrera, Anselmo Peñas, and Felisa Verdejo

Departamento de Lenguajes y Sistemas Informáticos,
Universidad Nacional de Educación a Distancia,
Madrid, Spain
{jesus.herrera, anselmo, felisa}@lsi.uned.es

**Abstract.** The Recognizing Textual Entailment System shown here is based on the use of a broad-coverage parser to extract dependency relationships; in addition, *WordNet* relations are used to recognize entailment at the lexical level. The work investigates whether the mapping of dependency trees from text and hypothesis give better evidence of entailment than the matching of plain text alone. While the use of *WordNet* seems to improve system's performance, the notion of mapping between trees here explored (inclusion) shows no improvement, suggesting that other notions of tree mappings should be explored such as tree edit distances or tree alignment distances.

## 1 Introduction

Textual Entailment Recognition (RTE) aims at deciding whether the truth of a text entails the truth of another text called hypothesis. This concept has been the basis for the PASCAL[1] RTE Challenge [3].

The system presented here is aimed at validating the hypothesis that (i) a certain amount of semantic information could be extracted from texts by means of the syntactic structure given by a dependency analysis, and that (ii) lexico-semantic information such as *WordNet* relations can improve RTE.

In short, the techniques involved in this system are the following:

- Dependency analysis of texts and hypothesises.
- Lexical entailment between dependency tree nodes using *WordNet*.
- Mapping between dependency trees based on the notion of *inclusion*.

For the experiments, the PASCAL RTE Challenge 2005 corpora have been used. Two corpora are available, one for training and a second used to test systems' performance after training. Each corpus is compound by a set of hypothesis and text pairs where the objective is to determine whether the text entails the hypothesis or not for each pair.

In section 2 the architecture of the proposed system is described. Section 3 shows how lexical entailment is accomplished. Section 4 presents the methodology followed to evaluate matching between dependency trees. Section 5 describes the experiments accomplished with the system. In section 6 the results obtained are shown. Finally, some conclusions are given.

---

[1] Pattern Analysis, Statistical Modeling and Computational Learning Network of Excellence. http://www.pascal-network.org/

J. Quiñonero-Candela et al. (Eds.): MLCW 2005, LNAI 3944, pp. 231–239, 2006.

## 2 System's Architecture

The proposed system is based on surface techniques of lexical and syntactic analysis. It works in a non-specific way, not giving any kind of special treatment for the different tasks considered in the Challenge (Comparable Documents, Question Answering, etcetera) [3].

System's components, whose graphic representation is shown in figure 1, are the following:

1. A dependency parser, based on Lin's *Minipar* [9], which normalizes data from the corpus of text and hypothesis pairs and accomplishes the dependency analysis, generating a dependency tree for every text and hypothesis.
2. A lexical entailment module, which takes the information given by the parser and returns the hypothesis' nodes that are entailed by the text. A node is a vertex of the dependency tree, associated with a lexical unit and containing all the information computed by the dependency parser (lexical unit, lemma, part-of-speech, etcetera). This module uses *WordNet* in order to find multiwords and synonymy, similarity, hyponymy, *WordNet*'s entailment and negation relations between pairs of lexical units, as shown in section 3.
3. A matching evaluation module, which searches for paths into hypothesis' dependency tree, conformed by lexically entailed nodes. It works as described in section 4.

The system accepts pairs of text snippets (text and hypothesis) at the input and gives a boolean value at the output: *TRUE* if the text entails the hypothesis and *FALSE* otherwise.

## 3 Lexical Entailment

A module of lexical entailment is applied over the nodes of both text and hypothesis, as shown in figure 1. This module gets its input from the output of the dependency parser (see figure 1); as described in section 2, the dependency parser provides a dependency tree for every text and hypothesis. The output of the module of lexical entailment is a

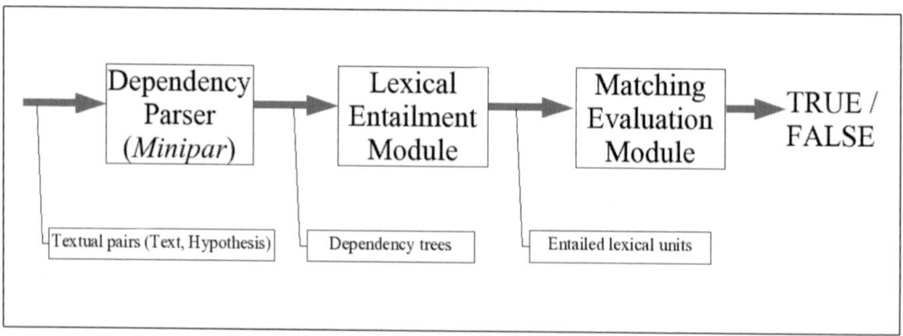


**Fig. 1.** System's architecture

list of pairs *(T,H)* where $T$ is a node in the text tree whose lexical unit entails the lexical unit of the node $H$ in the hypothesis tree. This entailment at the word level considers *WordNet* relations, detection of *WordNet* multiwords and negation, as follows:

### 3.1 Synonymy and Similarity

The lexical unit $T$ entails the lexical unit $H$ if they can be synonyms according to *WordNet* or if there is a relation of similarity between them. Some examples were found in the PASCAL Challenge training corpus such as, for example: *discover* and *reveal*, *obtain* and *receive*, *lift* and *rise*, *allow* and *grant*, etcetera.

The rule implemented in the lexical entailment module was the following:

- *entails(T, H)* IF *synonymy(T, H)* OR *WN_similarity(T, H)*

As an example, for the lexical units *allow* and *grant*, since *synonymy(allow, grant) is TRUE* then the module determines that *entails(allow, grant)*, i.e., *allow* and *grant* are lexically entailed by a synonymy relation. Another example is given for the lexical units *discover* and *reveal*: since *WN_similarity(discover, reveal) is TRUE*, then the module determines that *entails(discover, reveal) is TRUE*.

### 3.2 Hyponymy and *WordNet* Entailment

Hyponymy and entailment are relations between *WordNet* synsets having a transitive property. Some examples after processing the training corpus of PASCAL Challenge are: *glucose* entails *sugar*, *crude* entails *oil*, *kill* entails *death*.

The rules implemented were:

- *entails(T, H)* IF exists a synset $S_T$ including $T$ and a synset $S_H$ including $H$ such as *hyponymy*($S_T$,$S_H$)
- *entails(T, H)* IF exists a synset $S_T$ including $T$ and a synset $S_H$ including $H$ such as *WN_en-tailment*($S_T$,$S_H$)
- *entails(T, H)* IF exists a path from a synset $S_T$ including $T$ to a synset $S_H$ including $H$ conformed by hyponymy and/or *WordNet* entailment relations

Thus, $T$ entails $H$ if a synset $S_T$ including $T$ is a hyponym of a synset $S_H$ including $H$, considering transitivity. For example, *glucose* and *sugar* are lexically entailed because a path of an only hyponymy relation exists between a synset of *glucose* and a synset of *sugar*. Another example is given for the lexical units *kill* and *death*, where synsets containing them are related through a *WordNet* entailment relation.

### 3.3 Multiwords

There are many multiwords in *WordNet* showing useful semantic relations with other words and multiwords. The recognition of multiwords needs an extra processing in order to normalize their components. For example, the recognition of the multiword *came_down* requires the previous extraction of the lemma *come*, because the multiword present in *WordNet* is *come_down*.

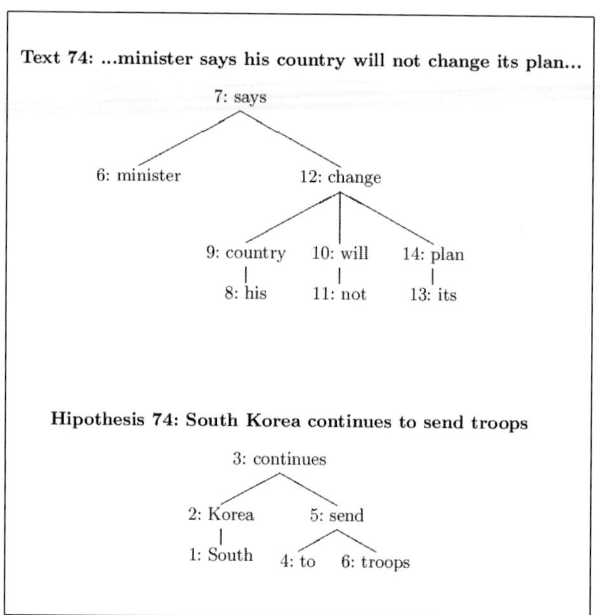


**Fig. 2.** Dependency trees for pair 74 from training corpus. Entailment is *TRUE*.

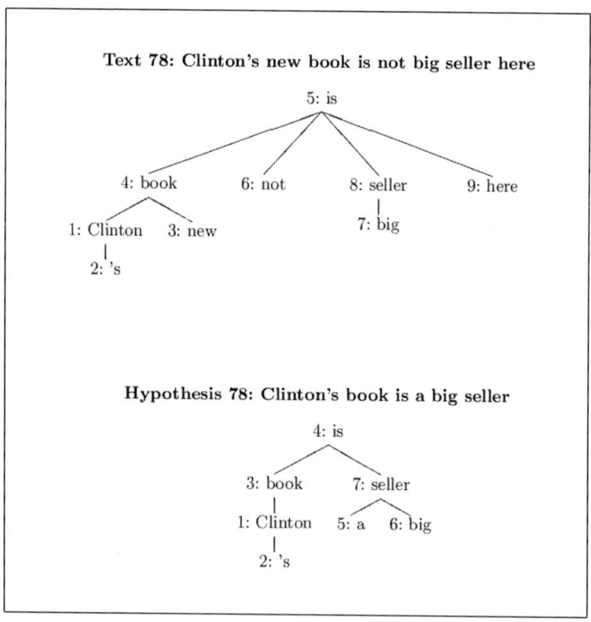


**Fig. 3.** Dependency trees for pair 78 from training corpus. Entailment is *FALSE*.

The variation of multiwords does not happen only because of lemmatization. Sometimes there are some characters that change as, for example, a dot in an acronym or a proper noun with different wordings. For this reason, a fuzzy matching between candidate and *WordNet* multiwords was implemented using the edit distance of Levenshtein [8]. If the two strings differ in less than 10%, then the matching is permitted. For example, the multiword *Japanise_capital* in hypothesis 345 of the training corpus was translated into the *WordNet* multiword *Japanese_capital*, allowing the entailment between *Tokyo* and it. These are some other examples of entailment after multiword recognition; because of synonymy *blood_glucose* and *blood_sugar*, *Hamas* and *Islamic_Resistance_Movement* or *Armed_Islamic_Group* and *GIA* can be found; because of hyponymy, some examples in the corpus are: *war_crime* entails *crime* and *melanoma* entails *skin_cancer.*

### 3.4 Negation and Antonymy

Negation is detected after finding leaves with a negation relationship with its father in the dependency tree. This negation relationship is then propagated to its ancestors until the head. For example, figures 2 and 3 show an excerpt of the dependency trees for the training examples 74 and 78 respectively. Negation at node 11 of text 74 is propagated to node 10 (*neg(will)*) and node 12 (*neg(change)*). Negation at node 6 of text 78 is propagated to node 5 (*neg(be)*). Therefore, entailment is not possible between a lexical unit and its negation. For example, before considering negation, node 5 in text 78 (*be*) entails node 4 in hypothesis 78 (*be*). Now, this entailment is not possible.

The entailment between nodes affected by negation is implemented considering the antonymy relation of *WordNet*, and applying the previous processing to them (sections 3.1, 3.2, 3.3). For example, since node 12 in text 74 is negated (*neg(change)*), the antonyms of *change* are considered in the entailment relations between text and hypothesis. Thus, *neg(change)* in text entails *continue* in the hypothesis because the antonym of *change*, *stay*, is a synonym of *continue*.

## 4 Mapping Between Dependency Trees

Dependency trees give a structured representation for every text and hypothesis. The notion of mapping [13] between dependency trees can give an idea about how semantically similar are two text snippets; this is because a certain semantic information is implicitly contained into dependency trees. The technique used here to evaluate a matching between dependency trees is inspired in Lin's proposal [10] and is based on the notion of tree inclusion [6].

An abstract hypothesis' dependency tree and its respective abstract text's dependency tree are shown in figure 4, as an example. Thick lines are used to represent both the hypothesis' matching branches and the text's branches containing nodes that show a lexical entailment with a node from the hypothesis. Note that not every node from a branch of the text's dependency tree must show a lexical entailment with another node from the hypothesis, while a branch from the hypothesis is considered a "matching branch" only if all its nodes are involved in a lexical entailment with a node from the respective branch from the text's dependency tree.

The subtree conformed by all the matching branches from a hypothesis' dependency tree is included in the respective text's dependency tree. The work hypothesis assumes that the larger is the included subtree of the hypothesis' dependency tree, the more semantically similar are the text and the hypothesis. Thus, the existence or absence of an entailment relation from a text to its respective hypothesis is determined by means of the portion of the hypothesis' tree that is included in the text's tree.

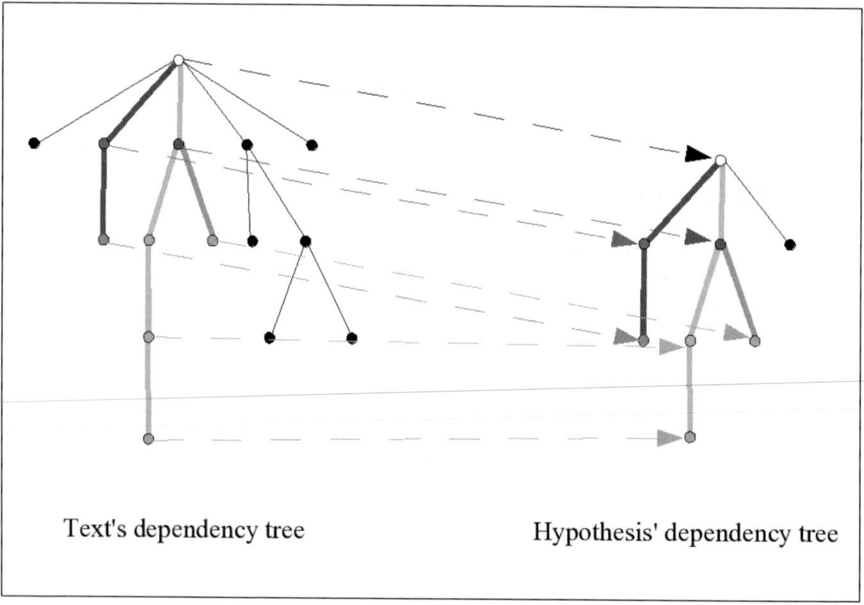


**Fig. 4.** Example for hypothesis' matching branches

Informally, this *tree overlap* measures how large is the hypothesis' dependency subtree *included* in the text's dependency tree with respect to the whole hypothesis' dependency tree. A higher degree of matching between dependency trees has been taken as indicative of a semantic relation. The threshold to determine whether there exists an entailment relation between a text and a hypothesis is obtained after training the system with the development corpus.

## 5 Experiments

Some experiments were accomplished in order to obtain feedback about successive improvements made to our system. For this purpose, several settings were trained over the development corpus and evaluated against the test corpus.

- System 1
  - Lexical level: No special processing for lexical entailment, but the coincidence between a word from the text and the hypothesis.

- Entailment decision: build a decision tree using C4.5 [11] over the training corpus and use this tree to classify the test samples. The set of attributes for building the decision tree were:
  - ∗ Number of nodes in the hypothesis' dependency tree.
  - ∗ Number of nodes in the hypothesis' dependency tree not entailed by any node in the text's dependency tree.
  - ∗ Percentage of entailed nodes from the hypothesis' dependency tree.

– System 2
  - Lexical level: lexical entailment as described in section 3.
  - Entailment decision: same as system 1.

– System 3
  - Lexical level: same as system 2.
  - Entailment decision: same as systems 1 and 2, but adding boolean attributes to the decision tree specifying whether nodes showing a subject or object relations with their fathers have failed or not (i.e., if they have not been entailed by any node from the text).

– System 4
  - Lexical level: same as systems 2 and 3.
  - Entailment decision: applying the algorithm from section 4 based on the notion of tree inclusion [6].

## 6 Results

Overall results are shown in table 1. The behavior of all the systems is quite similar except for system 4 that obtains the lower accuracy. The use of the lexical entailment module based on *WordNet* slightly increases accuracy (system 2 with respect to system 1); however, the inclusion of attributes in the decision tree related to the syntactic role (subject and object) does not improve the performance in our setting (system 3). Finally, the overlapping algorithm based on the notion of tree inclusion did not obtain the expected performance (system 4).

Some questions arise about the mapping between dependency trees approach. Though the notion of inclusion is not enough for RTE, some other notions such as tree alignment distance [2] [4] or tree edit distance [2] [4]] seem more promising as shown in [7]. Nevertheless, the results obtained by systems 2 and 3 are close to those obtained with the best approaches in PASCAL RTE Challenge [3].

**Table 1.** Accuracy values of the systems

| | Accuracy |
|---|---|
| System 1 | 55.87% |
| System 2 | 56.37% |
| System 3 | 56.25% |
| System 4 | 54.75% |

## 7 Conclusions and Future Work

The use of lexical resources such as *WordNet* aimed at recognizing entailment and equivalence relations at the lexical level for improving system's performance. In this direction, the next step is to recognize and evaluate entailment between numeric expressions, Named Entities and temporal expressions.

A mapping of dependency trees based on the notion of inclusion (as shown here) is not enough to tackle appropriately the problem, with the possible exception of Comparable Document [3] tasks. A higher lexical overlap does not mean a semantic entailment and a lower lexical overlap does not mean different semantics. Other mapping approaches based on the notions of tree edit distance or tree alignment distance seem more promising [7].

Both lexical and syntactic issues to be improved have been detected. At the lexical level, some kind of paraphrasing detection would be useful; for example, in pair 96 of the training corpus (see table 2) is necessary to detect the equivalence between *same-sex* and *gay* or *lesbian*; or, in pair 128 (see table 2), *come into conflict with* and *attacks* must be detected as equivalent. Previous work has been developed; for example, Szpektor et al. (2004) [12] propose a web-based method to acquire entailment relations; Barzilay and Lee (2003) [1] use multiple-sentence alignment to learn paraphrases in an unsupervised way; or Hermjakob et al. (2002) [5] show how *WordNet* can be extended as a reformulation resource.

**Table 2.** Pairs 96 and 128 from the training corpus

| |
|---|
| ***Text 96:*** The Massachusetts Supreme Judicial Court has cleared the way for lesbian and gay couples in the state to marry, ruling that government attorneys "failed to identify any constitutionally adequate reason" to deny them the right. |
| ***Hypothesis 96:*** U.S. Supreme Court in favor of same-sex marriage |
| ***Text 128:*** Hippos do come into conflict with people quite often. |
| ***Hypothesis 128:*** Hippopotamus attacks human. |

Sometimes, two related words are not considered because their lemmas (provided by the dependency parser) are different or a semantic relation between them can not be found; for example, in pair 128 of the training corpus the relations between *Hippos* and *Hippopotamus* and the relation between *people* and *human* are not detected.

Other problem is that, in certain cases, a high matching between hypothesis' nodes and text's nodes is given but, simultaneously, hypothesis' branches match with disperse text's branches; then, syntactic relations between substructures of the text and the hypothesis must be analyzed in order to determine the existence of an entailment.

Some other future lines of work include:

- A detailed analysis of the corpora, with the aim of determining what kinds of inference are necessary in order to tackle successfully the entailment detection. For example: temporal relations, spatial relations, numeric relations, relations between named entities, paraphrase detection, etcetera; and the development of the corresponding subsystems.

– The development of improved mapping algorithms between trees, such as the tree edit distance or an alignment distance [2] [4].

Hence, it is observed that for RTE is necessary to tackle a wide set of linguistic phenomena in a specific way, both at the lexical level and at the syntactic level.

## Acknowledgments

This work has been partially supported by the Spanish Ministry of Science and Technology within the following project: TIC-2003-07158-C04-02, R2D2-SyEMBRA.

## References

1. R. Barzilay and L. Lee. Learning to Paraphrase: An Unsupervised Approach Using Multiple-Sequence Alignment. In *NAACL-HLT*, 2003.
2. P. Bille. Tree Edit Distance, Alignment Distance and Inclusion. Technical Report TR-2003-23, IT Technical Report Series, March 2003.
3. I. Dagan, O. Glickman, and B. Magnini. The PASCAL Recognising Textual Entailment Challenge. In *Proceedings of the PASCAL Challenges Workshop on Recognising Textual Entailment, Southampton, UK*, pages 1–8, April 2005.
4. R. Gusfield. *Algoritms on Strings, Trees and Sequences*. Cambridge University Press, 1997.
5. U. Hermjakob, A. Echibabi, and D. Marcu. Natural Language Based Reformulation Resource and Web Exploitation for Question Answering. In *Proceedings of TREC*, 2002.
6. P. Kilpeläinen. Tree Matching Problems with Applications to Structured Text Databases. Technical Report A-1992-6, Department of Computer Science, University of Helsinki, Helsinki, Finland, November 1992.
7. M. Kouylekov and B. Magnini. Recognizing Textual Entailment with Tree Edit Distance Algorithms. In *Proceedings of the PASCAL Challenges Workshop on Recognising Textual Entailment, Southampton, UK*, pages 17–20, April 2005.
8. V. I. Levensthein. Binary Codes Capable of Correcting Deletions, Insertions and Reversals. In *Soviet Physics - Doklady*, volume 10, pages 707–710, 1966.
9. D. Lin. Dependency-based Evaluation of MINIPAR. In *Workshop on the Evaluation of Parsing Systems, Granada, Spain*, May 1998.
10. D. Lin and P. Pantel. DIRT - Discovery of Inference Rules from Text. In *Proceedings of ACM SIGKDD Conference on Knowledge Discovery and Data Mining*, pages 323–328, 2001.
11. J.R. Quinlan. *C4.5: Programs for Machine Learning*. Morgan Kaufman, 1993.
12. I. Szpektor, H. Tanev, I. Dagan, and B. Coppola. Scaling Web-Based Acquisition of Entailment Relations. In *Proceedings of Empirical Methods in Natural Language Processing (EMNLP-04)*, 2004.
13. G. Valiente. An Efficient Bottom-Up Distance Between Trees. In *Proceedings of the International Symposium on String Processing and Information REtrieval, SPIRE*, pages 212–219, 2001.

# Learning Textual Entailment on a Distance Feature Space

Maria Teresa Pazienza[1], Marco Pennacchiotti[1], and Fabio Massimo Zanzotto[2]

[1] University of Roma Tor Vergata, Via del Politecnico 1, Roma, Italy
{pazienza, pennacchiotti}@info.uniroma2.it
[2] DISCo, University of Milano Bicocca, Via B. Arcimboldi 8, Milano, Italy
zanzotto@disco.unimib.it

**Abstract.** Textual Entailment recognition is a very difficult task as it is one of the fundamental problems in any semantic theory of natural language. As in many other NLP tasks, Machine Learning may offer important tools to better understand the problem. In this paper, we will investigate the usefulness of Machine Learning algorithms to address an apparently simple and well defined classification problem: the recognition of Textual Entailment. Due to its specificity, we propose an original feature space, the *distance feature space*, where we model the distance between the elements of the candidate entailment pairs. The method has been tested on the data of the Recognizing Textual Entailment (RTE) Challenge.

## 1 Introduction

The task of recognizing if a textual expression, the text $T$, entails another expression, the hypothesis $H$, is a very difficult challenge. Indeed, as described in [1], Textual Entailment (TE) recognition (as referred in [2]) can be seen as the basic ability that any semantic theory for natural languages must have. Only those semantic theories able to detect textual entailment can be considered correct. Techniques for detecting textual entailment can be then seen as a first step in the building process of a semantic theory for natural language. We are thus facing a very complex problem.

Textual Entailment recognition can be tackled using two main strategies: *shallow and robust techniques* mostly based on shallow and probabilistic textual analysis, or more complex *syntactic-based models* involving a deeper syntactic analysis and the use of ad-hoc rules.

*Shallow and robust models* are based on the assumption of independence among words. They can be used to tackle Textual Entailment recognition, as it has already been done in several difficult open domain NLP tasks (e.g. Text Categorization and Information Retrieval). Even if these simple and effective models are still far from being perfect, they usually outperform more sophisticated techniques based on deep syntactic and semantic properties. For instance, in Text Categorization bag-of-word models seem to be more successful than any

J. Quiñonero-Candela et al. (Eds.): MLCW 2005, LNAI 3944, pp. 240–260, 2006.

other approach based on more complex "linguistic" features [3], even if in specific domain (e.g. the medical domain) performances are not so high [4].

As in Text Categorization, shallow models seem to be the most promising also for Textual Entailment recognition. Indeed, some top-performing approaches to TE strongly rely on the assumption that every word is independent from the other, as in the probabilistic textual entailment model presented in [5] and in the lexical model presented in [6]. The first approach [5] has been shown to have one of the highest performances in the 2005 Pascal Challenge on *Recognising Textual Entailment* (RTE) [7]. It assumes that the entailment $T \rightarrow H$ holds if the posterior probability $P(H|T)$ of $H$ being true given $T$ is higher than the prior probability $P(H)$. The actual probabilistic textual entailment indicator $P(H|T)$ is then evaluated at word level $P(w_H|w_T)$ and recombined using the word independence assumption. $P(w_H|w_T)$ is estimated over a large textual collection (i.e. the web) assuming that the joint event $(w_H, w_T)$ is verified when the two words, $w_H$ and $w_T$ are found in the same document, while $P(H)$ is set to a fix value for all pairs. The second approach [6] uses a very similar model (even if not probabilistic) where the distance between the two words, $w_H$ and $w_T$, is estimated over a semantic hierarchy (i.e. WordNet, [8]) with different semantic similarity measures (e.g. [9, 10]).

These approaches, even if top-performing, are still far from offering a satisfactory solution to the Textual Entailment task. In fact, on the RTE dataset [7] they reached an accuracy of less than 60%. The manual study in [11] suggests that there is room for improvement if more complex text representations are used than those based on independence assumption. According to this investigation, 49% cases of the RTE dataset can be correctly predicted using syntactic clues that consider the dependence between words in the sentence. Thus, the use of a *perfect* parser and syntactic constraint checking techniques would correctly predict (100% accuracy) all the 49% pairs identified in the study. Using a random guesser (50% accuracy) on the remaining 51% pairs, the overall accuracy would increase to 74%. Models based on structural syntactic information ("syntax-based models") should then guarantee a high margin of improvement.

*Syntax-based models*, generally rely on the notion of distance or similarity between the syntactic representations of the two text fragments T and H, as it usually happens for some lexical model. Moreover, sometimes these models include also semantic information (e.g. WordNet [8]). The approaches presented in [12] and in [13] define a distance between dependency syntactic graphs: these approaches, while being pretty similar, use different syntactic representations and parsers. Moreover, in [14] a variant of the edit distance, the *tree edit distance*, is applied to estimate differences between structures: this distance is defined on the dependency trees produced by the syntactic parser described in [15].

Syntax-based models are still far from the performance manually estimated in [11] (the "perfect" syntactic parser is still not available). Moreover, even using a "perfect" parser, it may happen that rules for detecting entailment, written in these syntactic models, are inadequate as not totally correct or not covering all entailment cases.

A solution to the inadequacy of manually built rules adopted in several NLP applications (e.g. Information Extraction [16]) is the application of supervised or semi-supervised machine learning algorithms able to extract weighted rules using set of training examples. Syntax-based models, that use Machine Learning to derive rules, appear promising, as they have the potential to improve and outperform shallow approaches in Textual Entailment recognition.

Following this approach, in this paper we investigate the possibility of using machine learning models to tackle the problem of Textual Entailment recognition. The aim is to understand whether or not machine learning represents a practical and promising way to improve the performance of a generic recognition model. It is evident that the application of classical machine learning algorithms to the Textual Entailment task is not straightforward, mainly because of the small number of training examples. As we believe that this number can never be large enough to learn significant regularities in a simple direct feature space (see Sec. 2), we propose an alternative feature space based on the distance between the elements of textual entailment pairs. We will discuss this distance feature space in Sec. 4. Finally, in Sec. 5, we will evaluate our model using SVM-light [17] on the RTE data [7].

## 2 Classifiers, Machine Learning, and Textual Entailment

Machine Learning algorithms learn how to classify instances into categories. Instances are seen in a feature space and the role of the algorithm is to learn regularities that help in the classification. The learnt final function $T$ maps elements in the feature space $F_1 \times \ldots \times F_n$ to one element in the final set of categories $C$, that is:

$$T : F_1 \times \ldots \times F_n \rightarrow C$$

where $F_1$, ..., $F_n$ are the features for observing instances.

One of the main issues in applying a learner to a particular classification task is to identify the most suitable feature space. However, as we will see later in this section, this is not the only problem when trying to exploit classifiers for the Textual Entailment task. For example, it is not clear which is the most suitable set of categories $C$ and, as a consequence, which equivalences should be learnt by the algorithms. In this section we analyse these problems, in order to explain the rationale behind our *distance feature space*.

At a first glance, the Textual Entailment task seems to be a clearly defined classification problem. Instances are represented as triples $(T, H, value)$ where $T$ is the text, $H$ is the hypothesis, and where $value$ is $true$ if $T \rightarrow H$ holds and $false$ otherwise. For example:

(1) **T**: *The carmine cat devoured the mouse in the garden*
**H**: *The cat killed the mouse*
**value**: *true*

This definition can lead to very simple feature spaces based on the bag-of-word abstraction. A good example is given by a bipartite bag-of-word feature space

$FS_T \times FS_H$, where $FS_T$ is related to the text $T$ while $FS_H$ is related to the hypothesis $H$. $FS_T$ and $FS_H$ are two complete bag-of-word feature spaces, where dimensions are words and values are 1 or 0 (i.e., a specific word is present or not in the text fragment $T$ or $H$). Finally, the classification is on the $\{true, false\}$ categories, that is, the pair is a positive or a negative instance of the entailment relation.

This *bipartite feature space* $FS_T \times FS_H$ is, in principle, inadequate for a small number of training examples and for the classification problem as it has been defined. Indeed, in this space, a learner is unlikely to infer useful properties. For instance (relating to previous example), the learner can infer that, if there is *cat* and *mouse* both in $FS_T$ and in $FS_H$, $T$ and $H$ can be positive instances of an entailment pair. This information is quite sparse and the solution cannot be obtained from adding the syntactic interpretation or some lexical semantic abstraction in the feature space.

In particular, tree kernels [18, 19] can be used to integrate syntactic information in the feature space; unfortunately, this is not a feasible solution, because of the sparseness of the space. For example, the possible syntactic interpretations of the sentences in the example (1) are:

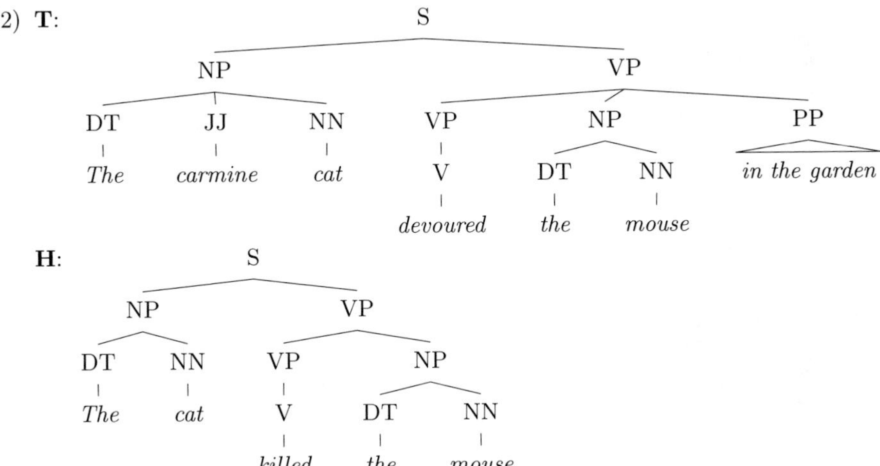


The regularities that can be learnt from this pair by a tree kernel are either too specific, e.g. both $T$ and $H$ should have the subtree (3), or too general, e.g. the subtree (4).

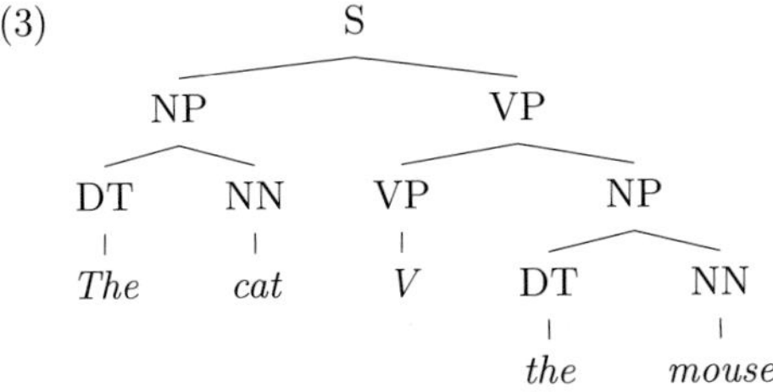

(4) 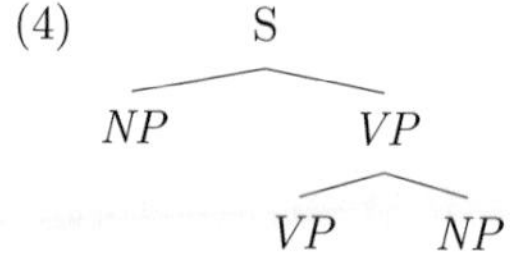


When working with a small number of examples, the equivalence between the elements in the two classes (entailed and not entailed pairs), may only be found at the level of general syntactic properties as the one in (4). This latter property may be read as: *both $T$ and $H$ should have a sentence that has a main verb and two direct arguments.* As such, this property is not a very significant clue to detect whether or not $T$ entails $H$, as it is too general. In the same way, too specific properties are not useful, as they lack generalization power and can thus be applied only to a small set of cases. For example the property in (3) states: *both $T$ and $H$ should have a sentence that has a main verb and two direct arguments, whose values must be "the cat" and "the mouse".*

In order to extract more useful properties for the TE classification task (neither too generic nor too specific) , the number of training examples should be bigger and bigger, and the classification problem should be differently formulated. In fact, the equivalence classes to be discovered should be more complex than the simple *true* and *false* entailment prediction. They should be centred on the hypothesis $H$: that is, in principle, each $H$ should correspond to an equivalence class. By consequence, the whole process of verifying if entailment holds for a (T;H) pair is divided in two steps. Firstly, the most suitable equivalence class is chosen for a fragment $T$, using ML classification. Then, entailment is said to hold if the predicted class corresponds to the H of the pair (T;H).

The step of categorising in equivalence classes representing possible $H$ is a neat shift with respect to the $true/false$ classification approach. As such, the classification subtask needs different types of features. Indeed, the feature set can not model the properties of the fragments $T$ and $H$ independently as for the bipartite feature space: in fact, the aim here is to find the equivalence class $H$ that is most similar to a given instance $T$. A sort of distance should then be evaluated between the instance $T$ (to be classified), and the elements of each possible class $H$. The feature space can then be the classical one as the text $T$ and the hypothesis $H$ should be modelled as different points.

Even if it seems an infeasible solution, due to the infinite number of possible $H$, this technique is adopted in learning a large number of equivalence classes often called *inference rules* [20]. We will use the *distributional hypothesis* [21] to cluster instances around an equivalence class that is the *inference rule* [20, 22]. Unluckily, these methods can not solve the problem in our case, as they need a large set of examples, that can be met only in very large corpora.

As a consequence, it emerges that the direct representation of $H$ and $T$ in a simple or a bipartite feature space is not an interesting solution. What is relevant should then be found elsewhere.

Let us consider again example (1). The interesting property of $H$ and $T$ is that they share two words, *cat* and *mouse*, not the specific words shared. The same consideration applies to the syntactic feature space (2). The relevant property is that $H$ and $T$ share the structure:

(5)

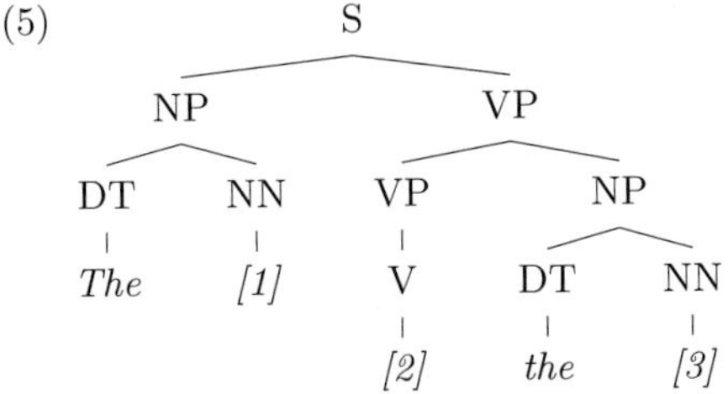


and that in position *[1]* and *[3]* they have the same words. The relevant property is then that $H$ and $T$ share a similar structure and that they share similar values in strategic positions of the structure itself. The actual values of *[1]* and *[3]* are not important, while it is important that they have similar meaning. A sort of syntactic-semantic "distance" between $T$ and $H$ could be then a more suitable approach to really grasp the notion of TE, as it is done in [12, 13, 14].

We propose to study the learnability on a feature space representing the distance between the two elements in the candidate entailment pair, instead of on the previously described bipartite feature space . This should make the entailment problem learnable with a small number of training examples as the problem is not studied on the actual values of the examples but on their distance. In the following section we describe both the formalisms and techniques to model the notion of distance between $T$ and $H$, while in Sec. 4 we will introduce our *distance feature space.*

## 3 Modelling Textual Entailment as Syntactic Graph Similarity

Here we introduce the model to investigate the similarity between syntactic graphs originally used to directly detect entailment. Furthermore, the model can also be used to build the distance feature space we are interested in, transforming textual entailment into a learnable classification problem. The distance feature space will be described in Sec. 4.

As textual entailment is mainly concerned with syntactic aspects (as outlined in [2] and observed in [11]), a model for its recognition should basically rely on lexical and syntactic techniques, enriched only with shallow semantic analysis.

We model the entailment pair $T-H$ as two *syntactic graphs* augmented with lexical and shallow semantic information. Each graph *node* represents a phrase of the sentence, together with its syntactic, morphological and semantic information. Each graph *edge* expresses a syntactic relation among phrases. We can thus consider the recognition process as the comparison between two graphs: the more similar the graphs are, the higher is the probability of entailment. A *similarity measure* among graphs can be meant as a measure of entailment, and *graph matching theory* can be used as a tool to verify if entailment relation holds.

In the following section we introduce the basic notions on graph theory needed to describe how we implemented the graph similarity measure. Then, in Sec.3.2 we introduce the Extended Dependency Graph (XDG), the syntactic graph formalism we rely on. Peculiar properties of textual entailment that require specific adaptations of graph matching theory are then outlined in Sec.3.3. Finally, the model for textual entailment recognition is described in Sec.3.4, together with the strategy we adopted to deal with syntactic transformations (Sec.3.5).

### 3.1 Graph Matching Theory

Graph matching theory aims to evaluate the similarity between two graphs. The power of graph matching theory resides in the generality of graphs, as they can be used to represent roughly any kind of objects. Graph matching is then used in many different settings, as vision applications (such as video indexing [23] and 3D object recognition [24]), case-based reasoning [25] and planning [26]. Graph nodes usually represent object parts, while edges represent relations among parts. Matching algorithms recognize how similar two objects are, looking at the structural similarity of their graph representation. It is thus possible, for instance, to turn a recognition problem of an unknown visual object, into a graph matching task over a given repository of known instances.

In the rest of this section we firstly outline basic definitions of graph matching theory, as presented in [27], and then briefly discuss how graph similarity is evaluated in practice.

**Definition 1.** *A* graph *is defined as 4-tuple $G = (N, E, \mu, \nu)$, where $N$ is the finite set of labelled nodes, $E$ the finite set of labelled edges connecting the nodes in $N$, $\mu : N \rightarrow L_N$ the function that assigns labels to nodes, and $\nu : E \rightarrow L_E$ the function that assigns labels to edges.*

**Definition 2.** *A* graph isomorphism *is a bijective function $f : N \rightarrow N'$, from a graph $G = (N, E, \mu, \nu)$ to a graph $G' = (N', E', \mu', \nu')$, such that:*

- *$\mu(n) = \mu'(f(n))$ for all $n \in N$*
- *for any edge $e \in E$ connecting two nodes $n_1$, $n_2$, it exists an edge $e'$ connecting $f(n_1), f(n_2)$, and vice versa.*

**Definition 3.** *A* subgraph isomorphism *is an injective function $f : N \rightarrow N'$, from $G = (N, E, \mu, \nu)$ to $G' = (N', E', \mu', \nu')$, if it exists a subgraph $S \subseteq G'$ such that $f$ is a graph isomorphism from $G$ to $S$.*

**Definition 4.** *A graph $G$ is called* common subgraph *between two graphs $G_1$ and $G_2$ if it exist a subgraph isomorphism from $G_1$ to $G$ and from $G_2$ to $G$.*

**Definition 5.** *The common subgraph $G$ of $G_1$ and $G_2$ with the highest number of nodes is called the* maximal common subgraph *($mcs(G_1, G_2)$).*

The concept of *maximal common subgraph* (*mcs*) is often central in the definition of a *similarity measure*. In fact, in real applications, errors and distortions in the input graphs are frequent. Consequently, as perfect matching between two objects becomes often impossible, graph matching algorithms must be error tolerant, returning as result a degree of similarity between graphs, rather than a deterministic matching value. As an example, in [28] a similarity measure between two graphs $G_1$ and $G_2$ is proposed as a *distance* between the number of nodes of the *mcs* and the number of nodes of the biggest graph:

$$d(G_1, G_2) = 1 - \frac{|mcs(G_1,G_2)|}{max(|G_1|,|G_2|)}$$

### 3.2 The XDG Formalism

In the context of textual entailment, graph matching theory can be applied to two graphs representing the syntactic structure of $T$ and $H$, together with relevant lexical information. As useful syntactic representation we decided to use the extended dependency graph (XDG) [29]. An XDG is a dependency graph whose nodes $C$ are *constituents* and whose edges $D$ are the *grammatical relations* among the constituents, i.e. $\mathcal{XDG} = (C, D)$.

The XDG formalism has two interesting properties: it hides unnecessary ambiguity in possibly underspecified constituents and it may represent alternative interpretations in a single graph.

Constituents (i.e. $c \in C$) are classical syntactic trees with explicit *syntactic heads*, $h(c)$, and *potential semantic governors*, $gov(c)$. Constituents can be represented as feature structures, having as relevant features:

- the *head* and the *gov*, having as domain $\mathcal{C}$ (the set of trees and subtrees derived from $C$), and representing respectively *syntactic heads* and *potential semantic governors*;
- the *type* representing the syntactic label of the constituent and having as domain $\Lambda$.

Moreover, a constituent can be either *complex* or *simple*. A *complex constituent* is a tree containing other constituents as sons (which are expressed by the feature *subConstituents*). A *simple constituent* represents a leaf node, i.e., a token span in the input sentence, that carries information about lexical items through the following features:

- $surface$, representing the actual form found in the token span,
- *lemma*, taking values in the lexicon $\mathcal{L}$ and representing the canonical form of the target surface,
- *morphology*, representing the morphological features of the inflected form.

On the other hand, dependencies in $(h, m, T) \in D$ represent typed (where $T$ is the type) and ambiguous relations among a constituent, the *head* $h$, and one of its $modifiers$ $m$. The ambiguity is represented using *plausibility*, a real value ranging between 0 and 1, where 1 stands for unambiguous. Then, $D$ is defined as a subset of $C \times C \times \Gamma \times (0, 1]$, where the sets represent respectively the domains of the features *head*, $modifier$, *type*, and *plausibility*.

The syntactic analysis of entailment couples has been carried out by Chaos [29], a robust modular parser based on the XDG formalism.

### 3.3 Adapting XDG and Graph Matching to Textual Entailment

In Sec.3.1 and Sec.3.2 a general methodology (graph matching) and a formalism (XDG) for recognizing textual entailment have been proposed. Entailment recognition can thus be described as a matching process between two XDG graphs representing the hypothesis and the text, where nodes are the set of constituents $C$ and edges are the set of dependencies $D$. In order to obtain a model of the process, it is necessary to verify if either the chosen formalism and methodology satisfy all the characteristics needed for entailment recognition or they need some adaptation.

Concerning the XDG formalism, it is necessary to define the specific kind of information that a graph for entailment recognition must hold. Then, it must be verified if XDG graphs are able to capture all this information. In order to be detected, entailment requires both syntactic and shallow lexical-semantic information:

- *syntactic information*: in general, graphs that have similar syntactic and lexical structure are likely to express the same fact. Moreover, syntactic addition to the $T$ graph with respect to $H$ can reveal a strict entailment relation, as capturing *syntactic subsumption entailment.* Finally, syntactic variations such as nominalization and active/passive transformations must be treated as invariant operations on graphs, since the meaning of the fact expressed is preserved. A graph is thus required to represent both syntactic dependencies and syntactic variations.
- *shallow lexical-semantic information*: syntactic similarity can be supported by lexical-semantic information needed to grasp *semantic subsumption entailment*, such as verb and noun generalization, antinomy and synonymy. Moreover, *direct implication* requires the recognition of verb entailments. As all these information must be modelled in the graph similarity measure, graphs must express all the morphological and lexical properties needed to carry out semantic operations, such as word stems and derivational properties.

The XDG formalism captures all needed information, as syntactic dependencies are explicitly represented, and lexical information about nodes is carefully treated.

Regarding the graph matching methodology, it seems suitable for the textual entailment task. In fact, a classical graph matching problem and textual entailment reveal some similarities:

- there are complex objects to be matched, composed by independent parts (represented as graph nodes) and relations among them (represented as edges).
- in order to tackle errors and distortion, it is better to adopt a similarity measure able to express the degree of similarity between two objects (e.g. using *mcs*), rather than a deterministic value.
- meta-operation can be performed over collection of objects, such as *graph clustering* and *graph querying.* For example, textual entailment clustering of $H$ and $T$ sentences can be viewed as a sort of semantic generalization of surface forms into semantic relation ([30]).

However, some peculiar properties of textual entailment require major adaptations of the standard graph matching methodology:

- *Node complexity.* In the graph theory, nodes are matched by simply looking at their *label level.* In textual entailment node similarity can not be reduced to a surface analysis, as both morphological and semantic variations must be taken into account (for example *ate*, *has eaten* and *devour* should have some degree of similarity). Moreover, textual entailment nodes are not atomic, since they represent complex constituents that can be further divided in sub-constituents for deeper lexical-semantic analysis. For these two reasons, matching between two nodes is a complex process, that can not produce a simple true value (as it usually happens at the label level). It is necessary to evaluate a graded level of linguistically motivated *node semantic similarity* $sm(c_h, c_t)$.
- *Edge complexity.* Edges are complex structures too: the matching over them must consider also the type of dependency they express. A graded *syntactic similarity* $ss(c_h, c_t)$ has then to be defined to capture this aspects.
- *Transformation invariance.* Textual entailment must account for graph invariant transformations: specific type of syntactic phenomena (nominalization, active/passive transformation, etc.) should be properly treated. Two graphs representing syntactic variations of the same fact, while structurally dissimilar, should be considered as equivalent.
- *Asymmetry.* Textual entailment, unlike the classical graph problems, is not symmetric, since it represents a direct relation of subsumption from $T$ to $H$. By consequence, the *graph isomorphism* definition must be further refined in a more specific notion of *XDG subsumption isomorphism.*

Considering these remarks, definition in Sec. 3.1 have been extended as follows.

**Definition 6.** *An* XDG subsumption isomorphism *is an oriented relation from a text* $\mathcal{XDG}_T = (C_T, D_T)$ *to an hypothesis* $\mathcal{XDG}_\mathcal{H} = (C_H, D_H)$ $(\mathcal{XDG}_H \preceq \mathcal{XDG}_T)$*, expressed by two bijective functions:*

- $f_C : C_T \rightarrow C_H$
- $f_D : D_T \rightarrow D_H$

*where* $f_C$ *and* $f_D$ *describe the oriented relation of subsumption between constituents (nodes) and dependencies (edges) of* $H$ *and* $T$*.*

$f_C$ and $f_D$ play the role of function $f$ in the definition of *graph isomorphism* in Sec. 3.1. Unluckily, due to the *node and edge complexity* factors, a definition of $f_C$ and $f_D$ can not be easily stated as for $f$. Sec. 3.4 will thus give an extensive description on how these two functions are modelled.

**Definition 7.** *A* subgraph subsumption isomorphism *between* $\mathcal{XDG}_H$ *and* $\mathcal{XDG}_T$*, written as* $\mathcal{XDG}_H \sqsubseteq \mathcal{XDG}_T$*, holds if it exists* $\mathcal{XDG}'_T \subseteq \mathcal{XDG}_T$ *so that* $\mathcal{XDG}_H \preceq \mathcal{XDG}'_T$*.*

As in the graph matching theory, an *mcs* must be defined in order to cope with distortions and errors in the input graphs. Specifically, in entailment recognition, errors are mainly introduced by syntactic parser erroneous interpretations, both at the morphological and syntactic level.

**Definition 8.** *The* maximal common subsumer subgraph *(*mcss*) between $\mathcal{XDG}_H$ and $\mathcal{XDG}_T$ is the graph with the highest number of nodes, among all the subgraph of $\mathcal{XDG}_H$ which are in isomorphic subgraph subsumption with $\mathcal{XDG}_T$.*

### 3.4 Graph Syntactic Similarity Measure for Textual Entailment

The similarity measure $\mathcal{E}(\mathcal{XDG}_T, \mathcal{XDG}_H)$, used to estimate the degree of confidence with which $\mathcal{XDG}_H$ and $\mathcal{XDG}_T$ are in entailment relation, must be modelled on the subsumption between nodes and edges in $T$ and $H$, grasping the notion of *mcss*. Four main steps are required:

1. *Model the bijective function* $f_C : C'_T \rightarrow C'_H$, that maps constituents in $C'_H \subseteq C_H$ to subsuming constituents in $C'_T \subseteq C_T$. A semantic similarity $sm(c_h, c_t)$ must be associated to each mapping. For example in the pair $H$:[the cat eats the mouse], $T$:[the cat devours the mouse], *eats* could be mapped in *devours*.
2. *Model the bijective function* $f_D : D'_T \rightarrow D'_H$, that maps dependencies in $D'_H \subseteq D_H$ to dependencies in $D'_T \subseteq D_T$. A syntactic similarity $ss(c_h, c_t)$ is then derived to better capture the implications of such mappings.
3. *Find the mcss*, that is, the common subgraph identified by $f_C$ and $f_D$. The *mcss* must be associate to an overall similarity, deriving from the *sm* and *ss* of its nodes and edges.
4. *Model* $\mathcal{E}(XDG_T, XDG_H)$ using *mcss* and the two input graphs $\mathcal{XDG}_H$ and $\mathcal{XDG}_T$. Textual entailment between a pair $T - H$ will be thus predicted verifying $\mathcal{E}(XDG_T, XDG_H)$ against a manually tuned threshold.

In the following paragraphs the different steps are described in detail. For an extensive example refer to Figure 1.

**Node Subsumption.** The node subsumption function $f_C$ must identify constituents in $C_H$ that can be mapped to constituents $C_T$. We will define the function with a set $A$ containing the *anchors* (the correspondences between the constituents of $C_H$ and $C_T$). The set $A$ will thus represent the nodes of the *mcss*.

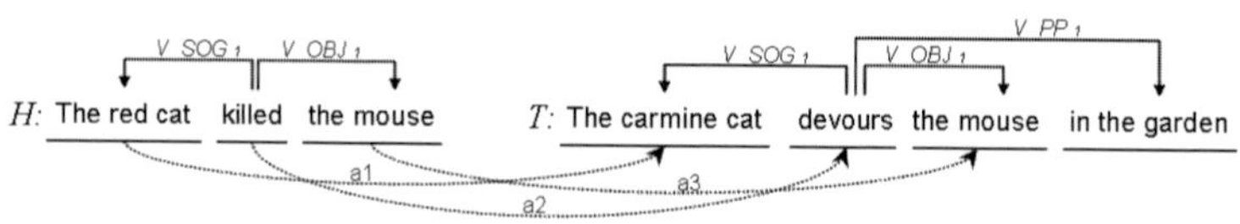


**Fig. 1.** A complete example of entailment pair, represented in the XDG formalism. Solid lines indicate grammatical relations $D$ (with *type* and *plausibility)*; dotted lines indicate anchors $a_i$ between $H$ and $T$ constituents.

In $A$, each constituent $c_h \in C_H$ is associated, where possible, to its most similar constituent $c_t \in C_T$ (that is, the $c_t$ that most likely subsumes $c_h$). The definition follows:

**Definition 9.** *Given the* anchors $a = (c_h, c_t)$ *as linking structures, connecting constituents* $c_h \in C_H$ *to constituents* $c_t \in C_T$ *and a function of* semantic similarity $sm(c_h, c_t) \in (0, 1]$ *expressing how much similar* $c_h$ *and* $c_t$ *are looking at their lexical and semantic properties, the set of anchors* $A$ *is:*

$$A = \{(c_h, c_t) | c_h \in C_H, c_t \in C_T, sm(c_h, c_t) = \max_{c \in C_T} sm(c_h, c) \neq 0\}$$

If a subsuming $c_t$ can not be found for a $c_h$ (i.e. $\max_{c \in C_T} sm(c_h, c) = 0$), then $c_h$ has no anchors. For example in the entailment pair of Fig. 1, $f_C$ produces the mapping pairs *[The red cat - The carmine cat]*, *[killed - devours]*, *[the mouse - the mouse]*.

The semantic similarity $sm(c_h, c_t)$ is derived on the basis of the syntactic type of $c_h$, that is, if it is a noun-prepositional phrase $sm(c_h, c_t) = sm_{np}(c_h, c_t)$ or a verb phrase $sm(c_h, c_t) = sm_{vp}(c_h, c_t)$. If $c_h$ is a noun-prepositional phrase, similarity $sm_{np}(c_h, c_t)$ is evaluated as:

$$sm_{np}(c_h, c_t) = \alpha * s(gov(c_h), gov(c_t)) + (1 - \alpha) * \frac{\sum_{sh \in S(c_h)} \max_{s_t \in S(c_t)} s(s_h, s_t)}{|S(c_h)|}$$

where $gov(c)$ is the governor of the constituent $c$, $S(c_h)$ and $S(c_t)$ are the set simple constituents excluding the governors respectively of $c_h$ and $c_t$, and $\alpha \in [0, 1]$ is an empirically evaluated parameter used to weigh the importance of the governor. Meanwhile, $s(s_h, s_t) \in [0, 1]$ expresses the similarity among two simple constituents: it is maximal if they have same surface or stem (e.g. *cat* and *cats*), otherwise a semantic similarity weight $\beta \in (0, 1)$ is assigned looking at possible WordNet relations (synonymy, entailment and generalization). For example, setting $\beta = 0.8$ for synonymy and $alpha = 0.5$, the constituents *ch:* [the red cat] and *ct:* [the carmine cat], have $sm = 0.95$, as the governors ($gov_{ch} = cat$ and $gov_{ct} = cat$) and the first simple constituents ($sh_1 = the$ and $st_1 = the$) have $s = 1$, and the second simple constituents are synonyms ($sh_2 = red$ and $st_1 = carmine$).

If $c_h$ is a verb phrase, different *levels* of similarity are taken into consideration, according to the semantic value of its modal. For example *must go-could go* should get a lower similarity than *must go-should go*. A verb phrase is thus composed by its governor *gov* and its modal constituents *mod*. The overall similarity is thus:

$$sm_{vp}(c_h, c_t) = \gamma * s(gov(c_h), gov(c_t)) + (1 - \gamma) * d(mod(c_h), mod(c_t))$$

where $d(mod(c_h), mod(c_t)) \in [0, 1]$ is empirically derived as the semantic distance between two modals (e.g., *must* is nearer to *should* than to *could*) (classified as generic auxiliaries, auxiliaries of possibility and auxiliaries of obligation).

**Edge Subsumption.** Once $f_C$ is defined, the existence of the bijective fuction $f_D$ can be easily verified by construction. The edge subsumption function $f_D$ maps $(c_h, c'_h, T_h) \in D_H$ to $f_D(c_h, c'_h, T_h) = (c_t, c'_t, T_t) \in D_T$ if $T_h = T_t$ and $(c_h, c_t), (c'_h, c'_t) \in A$. The set of mapped $D_H$ will thus represent the edges linking the nodes of the *mcss*.

The definition of $f_D$ allows to investigate the external *syntactic similarity* $ss(c_h, c_t)$ of a certain anchor $(c_h, c_t) \in A$. This should capture the similarity of the relations established by elements in the anchor. Our syntactic similarity $ss(c_h, c_t)$ depends on the semantic similarity of the constituents connected with the same dependency to $c_h$ and $c_t$ in their respective $\mathcal{XDG}$s, that is, the set $A(c_h, c_t)$ defined as:

$$A(c_h, c_t) = \{(c'_h, c'_t) \in A | f_D(c_h, c'_h, T) = (c_t, c'_t, T)\}$$

For example in Fig. 1, $A(killed, devours)$= $\{$([*the_red_cat*], [*the_carmine_cat*]), ([*the_mouse*], [*the_mouse*])$\}$. The syntactic similarity $ss(c_h, c_t)$ is then defined as:

$$ss(c_h, c_t) = \frac{\sum\limits_{(c'_h, c'_t) \in A(c_h, c_t)} sm(c'_h, c'_t)}{|D_H(c_h)|}$$

where $D_H(c_h)$ are the dependencies in $D_H$ originating in $c_h$.

**Similarity measure.** Once nodes and edges of the *mcss* have been identified through $f_C$ and $f_D$, an overall similarity $S(mcss)$ is evaluated for *mcss*. $S(mcss)$ must express how much similar the two subgraphs $\mathcal{XDG}'_T$ and $\mathcal{XDG}'_H$ in isomorphic subsumption are, both from a syntactic and a semantic point of view.

For each pair $(c_h, c_t) \in A$ a global similarity $S$ is thus derived as:

$$S(c_h, c_t) = \delta * sm(c_h, c_t) + (1 - \delta) * ss(c_h, c_t)$$

where $\delta$ is a manually tuned parameter. The similarity measure $\mathcal{E}(\mathcal{XDG}_T, \mathcal{XDG}_H)$ can be evaluated in analogy to the measure described in Sec. 3.1. In this specific case, numerator and denominator will not be expressed as the number of nodes, but as probabilities, since, as stated before, textual entailment must account for node and edges complexity. The numerator will thus be the overall *mcss* similarity . The denominator will express the best case, in which *mcss* corresponds to $\mathcal{XDG}_H$, and all nodes and edges match with probability 1 to elements of a hypothetic $T$.

$$\mathcal{E}(\mathcal{XDG}_T, \mathcal{XDG}_H) = \frac{S(mcss)}{|C_H|} = \frac{\sum\limits_{(c_h, c_t) \in A} S(c_h, c_t)}{|C_H|}$$

### 3.5 Graph Invariant Transformations

Entailment pairs are often expressed through syntactic variations. For example in the pair:

$H$:[The cat killed the mouse], $T$:[The killing of the mouse by the cat] entailment is syntactically express by a nominalization. We had thus to model some of the basic and most important variation phenomena in our system, in order to cope with pairs with different syntactic structures used and expressing the same fact. That is, a graph matching must be guaranteed for $H$ and $T$ when they have two different syntactic graphs which are one the syntactic variation of the other. Before the graph matching procedure can be activated, a set of graph transformation rules have been applied to $\mathcal{XDG}_H$ and $\mathcal{XDG}_T$, in order to normalize form sentences that have a syntactic variation. For example in the abovementioned example, the text is brought back to the normal form $T$:[the cat killed the mouse]. We modelled the following type of invariant transformation:

- *nominalization in $T$*. Different cases such as $T$:[The killing of the mouse by the cat] and $T$:[The cat is the killer of the mouse] are treated. Only nominalization of $T$ is taken into consideration, as usually in entailment relations nominalization happens only in $T$;
- *passivization in $H$ or $T$*. Passive sentences are brought to active forms, e.g. $H$:[the cat eats the mouse], $T$:[the mouse is eaten by the cat];
- *negation in $H$ or $T$*. If one sentence is the negative form of the other, the two sentences are recognized to be not in entailment (*negative subsumption*). Negation can be expressed in different ways. For example $H$:[the cat eats the mouse], could have two simple negative counterparts T:[the cat doesn't eat the mouse] or T:[the cat does not eat the mouse].

Due to the RTE deadlines, at the time of the experiments presented in this paper only the above mentioned syntactic normalization were integrated in the system. In order to improve performance and coverage of the entailment phenomenon, much more normalization rules should be taken into account. Argument movements, verb subcategorization frames and other syntactic inversion could in fact play a crucial role in the recognition process. In this line, two major issues should be addressed.

On the one hand, it could be useful to study extensively the relevance and the impact of syntactic normalizations on the Textual Entailment task, in order to understand if the integration of fine-grained normalizations is feasible and worthwhile. In [11] a first analysis of syntactic alternations in the RTE corpus was carried out. It resulted that the most frequent alternation (24% of all entailment pairs) was simple *apposition*, e.g. $H$:[the cat, killer of the mouse], $T$:[the cat is the killer of the mouse]. Our system properly treated such cases as a generic alternation.

On the other hand, it could be useful to investigate into the use of specific grammars, such as the Inversion Transuction Grammars [31], to better formalize and handle such normalization phenomena in a real operational framework.

## 4 A Distance Feature Space for Textual Entailment

The syntactic similarity measure we proposed in the previous section is a possible detector of entailment between $T$ and $H$ (once the acceptability threshold has been set) while it is also a good base to build the *distance feature space.*

A simple distance feature space may be defined with one only feature: the similarity between $H$ and $T$ with the value $\mathcal{E}(\mathcal{XDG}_T, \mathcal{XDG}_H)$. In this case, the target of the learning problem would be setting the threshold. However, as it emerges from the previous sections, this trivial distance feature space suffers the limits of the measure $\mathcal{E}(\mathcal{XDG}_T, \mathcal{XDG}_H)$. The measure depends on many parameters ($\alpha$, $\beta$, $\gamma$, and $\delta$) that should just be empirically evaluated. To better use the machine learning algorithms, some more complex distance feature spaces not depending on these parameters could be useful.

The limitation of the $\mathcal{E}(\mathcal{XDG}_T, \mathcal{XDG}_H)$ measure relates to several aspects. One major problem is that similarity rules used in the measure may be incomplete to detect the entailment between $T$ and $H$. We will tackle this problem by using the notion of distance feature space. The point is to study sentences in $H$ not as a whole but as a collection of pieces (i.e., constituents, such as [the cat], [devours], and [the mouse]) and the distance feature space should represent how these pieces are covered by fragments of the text $T$. We will not use a bag-of-word space as it would suffer the previously discussed limits (Sec. 2).

To set up a distance feature space we have to solve a major problem. As we cannot rely on the bag-of-word model, each feature should represent the distance of a specific portion of the sentence $H$ with respect to the most similar portion in $T$. Such kind of distance feature space can be defined only if the structure of the sentence $H$ is stable and known in advance. We then focus our attention to the sentence structure `Subject-Verb-Object`. This structure can represent a fact that is the typical target of the textual entailment recognition task (see [7]) even if the verb has some more arguments to better define the fact. If the target structure of $H$ is defined, the distance feature space can be easily settled: every feature can represent the distance of each relevant element of $H$ (i.e. the *Subject*, the *Verb*, and the *Object*) to the most similar element in $T$. We will refer to $S$ as the *Subject*, to $V$ as the main *Verb*, and to $O$ as the *Object*. We will call $\mathcal{G}$ the basic distance feature space. The mnemonic feature names and the way to compute their values are then described in Fig. 2 where the functions $ss(c_h, c_t)$, $s(c_h, c_t)$, and $sm(c_h, c_t)$ are those defined in Sec. 3. Moreover, $c_h^S$, $c_h^V$, and $c_h^O$ are respectively the subject, the verb, and the object constituents of the hypothesis $H$. $c_t^S$, $c_t^V$, and $c_t^O$ are the constituents of the text $T$ most similar to respectively $c_h^S$, $c_h^V$, and $c_h^O$. This similarity is evaluated using $ss(c_h, c_t)$.

We also enriched the distance feature space with further information:

- a set of features $\mathcal{A}$ related to the percent of commonly anchored dependencies both in $H$ and in $T$, i.e.:

$$\mathcal{A} = \{\frac{|\bigcup_{c_h \in C_H} D_H(c_h)|}{|D_H|}, \frac{|\bigcup_{c_t \in C_T} D_T(c_t)|}{|D_T|}\}$$

- a set of features $\mathcal{T}$ related to the textual entailment subtasks (CD, MT, etc.).

Lastly, as simple feature spaces can work better than complex ones, we also used a less complex feature set $\mathcal{L}$. This should represent the distance at the lexical level in a bag-of-word fashion without any syntactic or semantic information. We

| feature name | value |
|---|---|
| $S_{sm}$ | $sm_{np}(c_h^S, c_t^S)$ |
| $S_{simsub}$ | $\frac{\sum_{sh \in S(c_h^S)} \max_{s_t \in S(c_t^S)} s(s_h, s_t)}{\lvert S(c_h^S)\rvert}$ |
| $S_{ss}$ | $ss(c_h^S, c_t^S)$ |
| $V_{sm}$ | $sm_{vp}(c_h^V, c_t^V)$ |
| $V_{ss}$ | $ss(c_h^V, c_t^V)$ |
| $O_{sm}$ | $sm_{np}(c_h^O, c_t^O)$ |
| $O_{simsub}$ | $\frac{\sum_{sh \in S(c_h^O)} \max_{s_t \in S(c_t^O)} s(s_h, s_t)}{\lvert S(c_h^O)\rvert}$ |
| $O_{ss}$ | $ss(c_h^O, c_t^O)$ |

**Fig. 2.** The $\mathcal{G}$ distance feature space

then used two features: the percent of $H$ tokens and of $H$ lemmas that are in common with $T$. As we will see this is the baseline model.

The application of the machine learning algorithm to the distance feature space can be also seen as a method of empirically estimating the parameters $\alpha$, $\gamma$, and $\delta$ of the overall $\mathcal{E}(\mathcal{XDG}_T, \mathcal{XDG}_H)$ measure. However, what the algorithm should do is something more than using this distance feature space $\alpha$, $\gamma$, and $\delta$ are related to the specific bit of text, that is *Subject*, *Verb*, and *Object*.

## 5 Experimental Evaluation

The RTE challenge has been the first test to evaluate our approach and to verify its performances. The data set used for the competition was formed by three sets of entailment pairs: a *First development set*, composed by 287 annotated pairs, a *Second development set*, composed by 280 annotated pairs, and a *Test set*, composed by 800 non annotated pairs. Participating systems were evaluated over the test set: a prediction value ($True$ and $False$) and an associated degree of confidence on the prediction $c \in [0, 1]$ have been provided for each pair. Two measures were used for evaluation: *accuracy* (fraction of correct responses) and the *confidence-weighted score (cws)* as defined in [7].

We performed the experiments on our distance feature space using SVM-light [17]. The experiments have been organised as follows: firstly, we investigated the performances of the different feature spaces using examples in the two development sets and we choose the more promising feature space; secondly, we trained the classifier on the chosen feature space using all the examples in the two development sets and we evaluated it on the *Test set*. Due to the maximal number of examples available for training, 567, the use of a distance feature space is perfectly justifiable. This number is enormously far from the examples methods like the ones based on the *Distributional Hypothesis* can have (see Sec. 2).

**Table 1.** Preliminary accuracy analysis on the two development sets with SVM

| | D1 | D3 | D4 | D5 | D6 |
|---|---|---|---|---|---|
| $\mathcal{L}$ | 51.16(±3.98) | - | - | - | - |
| $\mathcal{L}$,$\mathcal{T}$,$\mathcal{G}$ $\beta = 0.5$ | - | 55.28(±2.44) | 56.14(±2.51) | 56.40(±2.71) | 56.72(±2.92) |
| $\mathcal{L}$,$\mathcal{T}$,$\mathcal{G}$ $\beta = 1$ | - | 56.37(±2.45) | 57.14(±2.94) | 57.37(±3.45) | 57.12(±3.56) |
| $\mathcal{L}$,$\mathcal{T}$,$\mathcal{G}$,$\mathcal{A}$ $\beta = 1$ | - | - | 57.20(±3.01) | 57.42(±3.36) | 57.12(±3.38) |

In order to better understand the effectiveness and the value of the SVM approach, we compare its performance with those obtained by a second *Rule-Based system* we presented at the RTE challenge. The Rule-Based approach simply applies the similarity measure $\mathcal{E}(\mathcal{XDG}_T, \mathcal{XDG}_H)$ on the entailment pairs. Parameters ($\alpha$, $\beta$, $\gamma$, and $\delta$) were manually tuned on the training set.

The preliminary experiments have been carried out using the two development sets as source for an n-fold cross validation. We performed a 3-fold cross-validation repeated 10 times. Each number we report for these experiments is then given by 30 different runs. In Tab. 1, we report the mean accuracy and its standard deviation of SVM in the different feature spaces. Each row shows a different pair feature space and a value for the parameter $\beta$ when necessary: the baseline lexical distance feature space $\mathcal{L}$, the distance feature space $\mathcal{L}$,$\mathcal{T}$,$\mathcal{G}$ with $\beta = 0.5$ and $\beta = 1$, and, finally, the distance feature space with some more structural features $\mathcal{L}$,$\mathcal{T}$,$\mathcal{G}$,$\mathcal{A}$. The columns represent the degrees of the polynomial kernels used in SVM.

The results of the preliminary investigations suggest that every distance feature space is statistically significantly better than the lexical distance feature space $\mathcal{L}$. However a clear understanding of which feature space is better among all the others is not completely clear as they do not statistically differ. The higher mean is reached by the space $\mathcal{L}$,$\mathcal{T}$,$\mathcal{G}$,$\mathcal{A}$ with degree of the polynomial kernel equal to 5. Even if this is not statistically different from the other means that are around 57% of accuracy (all these performances can have represent the same statistical population), we choose this feature space to run the experiment on the competition.

The results over the competition *Test Set* are presented in Tab. 2. Results are divided in two tables: an overall analysis of the results and an analysis according to the different tasks. For comparison purposes, in Tab. 3 results of the Rule-Based system are also reported.

Not surprisingly, the overall results are only slightly above the chance threshold, in line with those obtained by other systems presented at RTE challenge. As stated in the introduction, Textual Entailment recognition is a fairly new task that encompasses many different NLP areas and issues (lexical semantics, syntactic and semantic analysis, etc.). Therefore, as every new demanding challenge in NLP, Textual Entailment needs to be investigated and handled carefully: the RTE challenge 2005 has been a first step in the study and the understanding of the linguistic phenomenon in its whole and most general definition. Indeed, the early experimental evidences obtained by the systems presented at the challenge are all still far from being satisfactory. Many interesting and very different

**Table 2.** Competition results with SVM approach

| *Measure* | *Result* |
|---|---|
| cws | 0.5591 |
| accuracy | 0.5182 |
| precision | 0.5532 |
| recall | 0.1950 |
| f | 0.2884 |

| TASK | *cws* | *accuracy* |
|---|---|---|
| CD | 0.7174 | 0.6443 |
| IE | 0.4632 | 0.4917 |
| MT | 0.4961 | 0.4790 |
| QA | 0.4571 | 0.4574 |
| RC | 0.5898 | 0.5214 |
| PP | 0.5768 | 0.5000 |
| IR | 0.4882 | 0.4889 |

**Table 3.** Competition results with Rule-Based approach

| *Measure* | *Result* |
|---|---|
| cws | 0.5574 |
| accuracy | 0.5245 |
| precision | 0.5265 |
| recall | 0.4975 |
| f | 0.5116 |

| TASK | *cws* | *accuracy* |
|---|---|---|
| CD | 0.8381 | 0.7651 |
| IE | 0.4559 | 0.4667 |
| MT | 0.5914 | 0.5210 |
| QA | 0.4408 | 0.3953 |
| RC | 0.5167 | 0.4857 |
| PP | 0.5583 | 0.5400 |
| IR | 0.4405 | 0.4444 |

approaches were presented, ranging from statistical methods to Rule-Based systems, operating at different level of analysis (lexical, syntactic, semantic, pragmatic). The variety of the approaches reveals both the intrinsically complex nature of the task and the early stage of analysis reached so far.

With regard to the results of our SVM system, two aspects are interesting to notice. Firstly, overall results are roughly in line with those obtained by the Rule-Based System in Tab. 3: the only surprising difference is in the level of recall, that is much higher for the Rule-Based. The very low level of recall achieved by SVM has to be further carefully analysed, in order to find a better trade-off between recall and precision. Moreover, the higher recall achieved by the Rule-Based is probably due also to the manual tuning process, that allowed a better set-up of the system.

Secondly, examining the results on the specific tasks, both the SVM and the Rule-Based approaches showed roughly the same performance on all tasks, apart from CD. Indeed, on the *Comparable Document* (CD) task SVM achieved cws 0.7174, while Rule-Based 0.8381. These results are similar to those obtained by the other RTE systems. The CD task is thus in general easier than the others. In fact, most of the CD pairs in the corpus reveal the same linguistic behaviours: entailment is mainly characterized by simple lexical and syntactic variations that can be easily captured by syntactic rules and lexical-semantic analysis. Therefore, the use of simple word distance metrics between $T$ and $H$ together with a shallow syntactic and semantic analysis appears to be well suited for the CD task. Our system metrics were able to capture this kind of phenomenon adequately. In the easiest case CD pairs could be successfully recognized by simple lexical-semantic hints, as in:

*T*: [A Union Pacific freight train hit five people.]
*H*: [A Union Pacific freight train struck five people.]

or by syntactic normalization:

*T*: [Ghazi Yawar, a Sunni Muslim who lived for years in Saudi Arabia, has been picked as president of Iraq...]
*H*: [Yawer is a Sunni Muslim.]

Complex entailments, mixing syntactic and semantic variation were still captured by our system:

*T*: [Last July, a 12-year-old boy in Nagasaki - a city just north of Sasebo - was accused of kidnapping, molesting and killing a 4-year-old by shoving him off the roof of a car garage.]
*H*: [Last year a 12-year-old boy in Nagasaki was accused of murdering a four-year-old boy by pushing him off a roof.]

Notwithstanding, the CD dataset contains also cases of complex entailments that need at least logical reasoning to be correctly handled, as in:

*T*: [Each hour spent in a car was associated with a 6 percent increase in the likelihood of obesity and each half-mile walked per day reduced those odds by nearly 5 percent, the researchers found.]
*H*: [The more driving you do means you are going to weigh more – the more walking means you are going to weigh less.]

Such cases could not be grasped by our systems.

Besides CD, the partly disappointing performances on all other tasks are due to the more complex nature of the entailment, that often requires world knowledge and some kind of reasoning, such in:

*T*: [On Feb . 1 , 1945 , the Polish government made Warsaw its capital , and an office for urban reconstruction was set up ]
*H*: [Warsaw remained Poland's capital after the war .]

As a consequence of the little knowledge we still have of the linguistic phenomena underlying Textual Entailment, not only syntactic normalizations must be better studied, but also other NLP area should be investigated for hints and suggestions for solutions. Indeed, as underlined in the introduction, only 49% of entailment pairs can be captured by syntax. Other resources and reasoning tools should then be needed to cope with the problem: generic and verb lexical resources, world and domain knowledge, logical reasoning and many other issues should be better investigated.

## 6 Conclusions

Textual Entailment recognition is far from being a resolved problem and, as any other complex NLP problem, it may be possible to significantly improve results by applying machine learning techniques. In this paper we introduced the *distance feature space* that, in our opinion, could overcome the problem of a limited number of examples given for training. Results are far from being satisfactory but we believe that this is a promising way to use robust machine learning models in this very difficult problem.

## References


1. Chierchia, G., McConnell-Ginet, S.: Meaning and Grammar: An introduction to Semantics. MIT press, Cambridge, MA (2001)
2. Dagan, I., Glickman, O.: Probabilistic textual entailment: Generic applied modeling of language variability. In: Proceedings of the Workshop on Learning Methods for Text Understanding and Mining, Grenoble, France (2004)
3. Basili, R., Moschitti, A., Pazienza, M.T.: Empirical investigation of fast text categorization over linguistic features. In: Proceedings of the 15th European Conference on Artificial Intelligence (ECAI 2002), Lyon, France (2002)
4. Joachims, T.: Learning to Classify Text using Support Vector Machines: Methods, Theory, and Algorithms. Kluwer Academic Publishers (2002)
5. Glickman, O., Dagan, I.: A probabilistic setting and lexical coocurrence model for textual entailment. In: Proceedings of the ACL-Workshop on Empirical Modeling of Semantic Equivalence and Entailment, Ann Arbor, Michigan (2005)
6. Corley, C., Mihalcea, R.: Measuring the semantic similarity of texts. In: Proceedings of the ACL-Workshop on Empirical Modeling of Semantic Equivalence and Entailment, Ann Arbor, Michigan (2005)
7. Dagan, I., Glickman, O., Magnini, B.: The pascal recognising textual entailment challenge. In: PASCAL Challenges Workshop, Southampton, U.K (2005)
8. Miller, G.A.: WordNet: A lexical database for English. Communications of the ACM **38** (1995) 39–41
9. Resnik, P.: Using information content to evaluate semantic similarity. In: Proceedings of the 14th International Joint Conference on Artificial Intelligence, Montreal, Canada (1995)
10. Lin, D.: An information-theoretic definition of similarity. In: Proceedings of the 15th International Conference on Machine Learning, Madison, WI (1998)
11. Vanderwende, L., Coughlin, D., Dolan, B.: What syntax can contribute in entailment task. In: Proceedings of the 1st Pascal Challenge Workshop, Southampton, UK (2005)
12. Pazienza, M.T., Pennacchiotti, M., Zanzotto, F.M.: A linguistic inspection of textual entailment. In Bandini, S., Manzoni, S., eds.: AI*IA 2005: Advances in Artificial Intelligence. Volume LNAI 3673., Milan, Italy, Springer-Verlag (2005)
13. Raina, R., Haghighi, A., Cox, C., Finkel, J., Michels, J., Toutanova, K., MacCartney, B., de Marneffe, M.C., Manning, C.D., Ng, A.Y.: Robust textual inference using diverse knowledge sources. In: Proceedings of the 1st Pascal Challenge Workshop, Southampton, UK (2005)
14. Kouylekov, M., Magnini, B.: Tree edit distance for textual entailment. In: Proceedings of the International Conference Recent Advances of Natural Language Processing (RANLP-2005), Borovets, Bulgaria (2005)
15. Lin, D.: Dependency-based evaluation of minipar. In: Proceedings of the Workshop on Evaluation of Parsing Systems at LREC-98, Granada, Spain (1998)
16. Proceedings of the Seventh Message Understanding Conference (MUC-7), Virginia USA, Morgan Kaufmann (1998)
17. Joachims, T.: Making large-scale svm learning practical. In Schlkopf, B., Burges, C., Smola, A., eds.: Advances in Kernel Methods-Support Vector Learning, MIT Press (1999)
18. Collins, M., Duffy, N.: New ranking algorithms for parsing and tagging: Kernels over discrete structures, and the voted perceptron. In: Proceedings of the ACL-02, Philadelphia, PA (2002)

19. Moschitti, A.: A study on convolution kernels for shallow semantic parsing. In: Proceedings of the ACL-04, Barcellona, Spain (2004)
20. Lin, D., Pantel, P.: DIRT, discovery of inference rules from text. In: Knowledge Discovery and Data Mining. (2001) 323–328
21. Harris, Z.: Distributional structure. In Katz, J., ed.: The Philosophy of Linguistics, New York, Oxford University Press (1985)
22. Glickman, O., Dagan, I.: Identifying lexical paraphrases from a single corpus: A case study for verbs. In: Proceedings of the International Conference Recent Advances of Natural Language Processing (RANLP-2003), Borovets, Bulgaria (2003)
23. Shearer, K., Bunke, H., Venkatesh, S., Kieronska, D.: Efficient graph mathicng for video indexing. Technical Report 1997, Department of Computer Science, Curtin University (1997)
24. Cho, C., Kim, J.: Recognizing 3-d objects by forward checking constrained tree search. PRL **13** (1992) 587–597
25. Borner, K., Pippig, E., Tammer, E.C., Coulon, C.H.: Structural similarity and adaptation. In: EWCBR. (1996) 58–75
26. Sanders, K.E., Kettler, B.P., Hendler, J.: The case for graph-structured representations. In: Proceedings of the Second International Conference on Case-based Reasoning, Springer-Verlag (1997) 245–254
27. Bunke, H.: Graph matching: Theoretical foundations, algorithms, and applications. In: Vision Interface 2000, Montreal, Springer-Verlag (2000) 82–88
28. Bunke, H., Shearer, K.: A graph distance metric based on the maximal common subgraph. Pattern Recogn. Lett. **19** (1998) 255–259
29. Basili, R., Zanzotto, F.M.: Parsing engineering and empirical robustness. Natural Language Engineering **8/2-3** (2002)
30. Pazienza, M.T., Pennacchiotti, M., Zanzotto, F.M.: Identifying relational concept lexicalisations by using general linguistic knowledge. In: ECAI. (2004) 1071–1072
31. Wu, D.: Stochastic inversion transduction grammars, with application to segmentation, bracketing, and alignment of parallel corpora. In: Computational Linguistics. Volume 23. (1997) 207–223

# An Inference Model for Semantic Entailment in Natural Language

Rodrigo de Salvo Braz, Roxana Girju, Vasin Punyakanok, Dan Roth, and Mark Sammons

Department of Computer Science,
University of Illinois at Urbana-Champaign,
Urbana IL 61801, USA

**Abstract.** *Semantic entailment* is the problem of determining if the meaning of a given sentence entails that of another. We present a principled approach to semantic entailment that builds on inducing re-representations of text snippets into a hierarchical knowledge representation along with an optimization-based inferential mechanism that makes use of it to prove semantic entailment. This paper provides details and analysis of the knowledge representation and knowledge resources issues encountered. We analyze our system's behavior on the PASCAL text collection[1] and the PARC collection of question-answer pairs[2]. This is used to motivate and explain some of the design decisions in our hierarchical knowledge representation, that is centered around a predicate-argument type abstract representation of text.

## 1 Introduction

*Semantic entailment* is the task of determining, for example, that the sentence: "*WalMart defended itself in court today against claims that its female employees were kept out of jobs in management because they are women*" entails that "*WalMart was sued for sexual discrimination*".

Determining whether the meaning of a given text snippet *entails* that of another or whether they have the same meaning is a fundamental problem in natural language understanding that requires the ability to abstract over the inherent syntactic and semantic variability in natural language [1]. This challenge is at the heart of many high level natural language processing tasks including Question Answering, Information Retrieval and Extraction, Machine Translation, and others that attempt to reason about and capture the meaning of linguistic expressions.

Research in natural language processing in the last few years has concentrated on developing resources that provide multiple levels of syntactic and semantic analysis, resolve context sensitive ambiguities, and identify relational structures and abstractions (from syntactic categories like POS tags to semantic categories such as named entities).

[1] http://www.pascal-network.org/Challenges/RTE/

[2] The data is available at http://l2r.cs.uiuc.edu/~cogcomp/data.php

J. Quiñonero-Candela et al. (Eds.): MLCW 2005, LNAI 3944, pp. 261–286, 2006.

However, we believe that in order to move beyond this level and support fundamental tasks such as inferring semantic entailment between two text snippets, there needs to be a unified knowledge representation of the text that **(1)** provides a hierarchical encoding of the structural, relational and semantic properties of the given text, **(2)** is integrated with learning mechanisms that can be used to induce such information from raw text, and **(3)** is equipped with an inferential mechanism that can be used to support inferences over such representations.

Relying on general purpose knowledge representations — FOL, probabilistic or hybrids — along with their corresponding general purpose inference algorithms does not resolve the key issues of *what to represent* and *how to derive a sufficiently abstract representation* and, in addition, may lead to brittleness and complexity problems. On the other hand, relying only on somewhat immediate correspondences between question and candidate answers, such as shared words or shared named entities, has strong limitations. We avoid some of these problems by *inducing* an abstract representation of the text which does not attempt to represent the full meaning of text, but provides what could be seen as a *shallow semantic* representation; yet, it is significantly more expressive than extraction of straightforward phrase-level characteristics. We induce this into a description-logic based language that is more restricted than FOL yet is expressive enough to allow both easy incorporation of language and domain knowledge resources and strong inference mechanisms.

Unlike traditional approaches to inference in natural language [2, 3, 4] our approach (1) makes use of *machine learning* based resources in order to induce an abstract representation of the input data, as well as to support multiple inference stages and (2) models inference as an *optimization* process that provides robustness against inherent variability in natural language, inevitable noise in inducing the abstract representation, and missing information.

We present a principled computational approach to *semantic entailment* in natural language that addresses some of the key problems encountered in traditional approaches – knowledge acquisition and brittleness. The solution includes a hierarchical knowledge representation language into which we induce appropriate representations of the given text and required background knowledge. The other main element is a sound inferential mechanism that makes use of the induced representation to determine an extended notion of subsumption, using an optimization approach that supports abstracting over language variability and representation inaccuracies. Along with describing the key elements of our approach, we present a system that implements it, and an evaluation of this system on two corpora, PASCAL and PARC text collections.

### 1.1 General Description of Our Approach

Specifically, given two text snippets $S$ (source) and $T$ (target) where typically, but not necessarily, $S$ consists of a short paragraph and $T$ a sentence, textual semantic entailment is the problem of determining if $S \models T$, which we read as "*$S$ entails $T$*". This informally means that *most people would agree that the meaning of $S$ implies that of $T$*. More formally, we say that $S$ *entails* $T$ when some representation of $T$ can be "matched" (modulo some meaning-preserving transformations to be defined below) with some (or part of a) representation of $S$, at some level of granularity and abstraction. The approach consists of the following components:

A Description Logic based hierarchical knowledge representation, **EFDL** (Extended Feature Description Logic), [5], into which we re-represent the surface

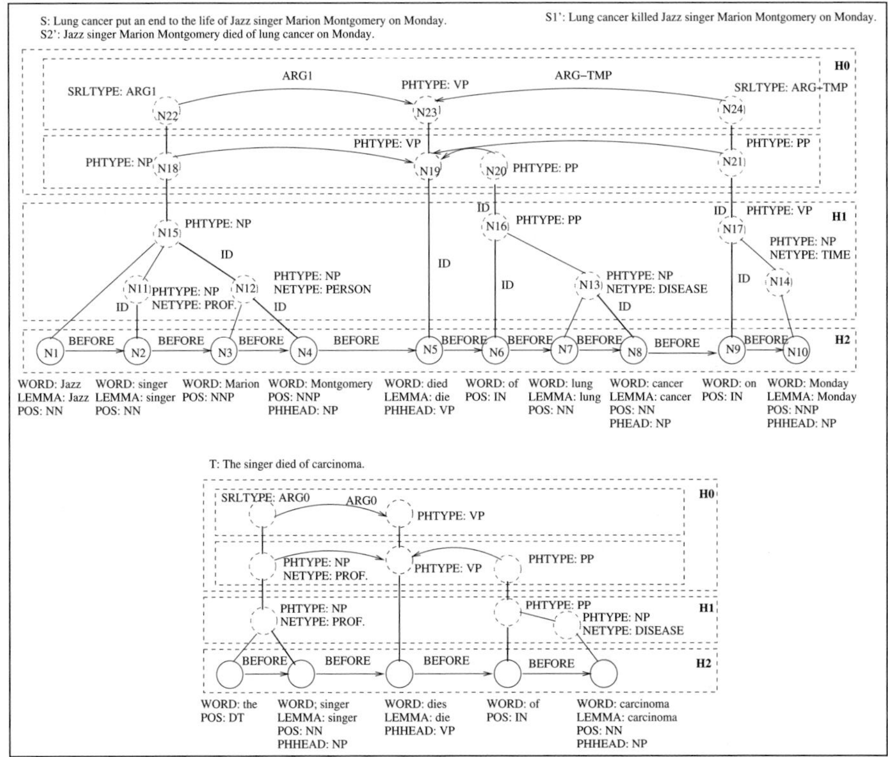


**Fig. 1.** Example of *Re-represented Source & Target* pairs as concept graphs. The original source sentence $S$ generated several alternatives including $S_1'$ and the sentence in the figure ($S_2'$). Our algorithm was not able to determine entailment of the first alternative (as it fails to match in the extended subsumption phase), but it succeeded for $S_2'$. The dotted nodes represent phrase level abstractions. $S_2'$ is generated in the first phase by applying the following chain of inference rules: #1 (genitives): "Z's W → W of Z"; #2: "X put end to Y's life → Y die of X". In the extended subsumption, the system makes use of WordNet hypernymy relation ("*lung cancer*" IS-A "*carcinoma*") and NP-subsumption rule ("*Jazz singer Marion Montgomery*" IS-A "*singer*"). The rectangles encode the hierarchical levels ($H_0, H_1, H_2$) at which we applied the extended subsumption. Also note that entailment follows even though the structure corresponding to "on Monday" is not present in the target sentence, since "event happened on Monday" entails "event happened".

level text, augmented with induced syntactic and semantic parses and word and phrase level abstractions.

**A knowledge base** consisting of syntactic and semantic rewrite rules, written in EFDL.

**An extended subsumption algorithm** which determines subsumption between EFDL expressions (representing text snippets or rewrite rules). "Extended" here means that the basic unification operator is extended to support several word level and phrase level abstractions.

First, a set of machine learning based resources are used to induce the representation for $S$ and $T$. The entailment algorithm then proceeds in two phases: (1) it incrementally generates re-representations of the original representation of the source text $S$ by augmenting it with heads of subsumed re-write rules, and (2) it makes use of an optimization based (extended) subsumption algorithm to check whether any of the alternative representations of the source entails the representation of the target $T$. The extended subsumption algorithm is used both in checking final entailment and in determining when and how to generate a re-representation in slightly different ways. Figure 1 provides a graphical example of the representation of two text snippets, along with a sketch of the extended subsumption approach to decide the entailment.

Along with the formal definition and justification developed here for our computational approach to semantic entailment, our knowledge representation and algorithmic method provide a novel solution that addresses some of the key issues the natural language research community needs to resolve in order to move forward towards higher level tasks of this sort. Namely, we provide ways to represent knowledge, either external or induced, at multiple levels of abstractions and granularity, and reason with it at the appropriate level. The evaluation of our approach is very encouraging and illustrates the significance of some of its key contributions, while also exhibiting the key areas where significant progress is needed – that of the rewrite rule knowledge base.

## 2 Algorithmic Semantic Entailment

Let $\mathcal{R}$ be a knowledge representation language with a well defined syntax and semantics over any domain $\mathcal{D}$. Specifically, we think of elements in $\mathcal{R}$ as expressions in the language or, equivalently, as the set of interpretations that satisfy it [6]. Let $r$ be a mapping from a set of text snippets $\mathcal{T}$ to a set of expressions in $\mathcal{R}$. Denote the representations of two text snippets $S, T$, under this mapping by $r_S, r_T$, respectively. Note that we will use the word *expression* and *representation* interchangeably. Given the set of interpretations over $\mathcal{D}$, let $M$ be a mapping from an expression in $\mathcal{R}$ to the corresponding set of interpretations it satisfies. For expressions $r_S, r_T$, the images of $S, T$ under $\mathcal{R}$, their model theoretic representations thus defined are denoted $M(r_s)$, $M(r_t)$.

Conceptually, as in the traditional view of semantic entailment, this leads to a well defined notion of entailment, formally defined via the model theoretic view; traditionally, the algorithmic details are left to a *theorem prover* that uses the syntax of the representation language, and may also incorporate additional knowledge in its inference. We follow this view, and use a notion of *subsumption* between elements in $\mathcal{R}$, denoted $u \sqsubseteq v$, for $u, v \in \mathcal{R}$, that is formally defined via the model theoretic view — when $M(u) \subseteq M(v)$. Subsumption between representations provides an implicit way to represent entailment, where additional knowledge is conjoined with the source to "prove" the target.

However, the proof theoretic approach corresponding to this traditional view is unrealistic for natural language. Subsumption is based on *unification* and requires, in order to prove entailment, that the representation of $T$ is entirely embedded in the representation of $S$. Natural languages allow for words to be replaced by synonyms, for modifier phrases to be dropped, etc., without affecting meaning. An extended notion of subsumption is therefore needed which captures sentence, phrase, and word-level abstractions.

Our algorithmic approach is thus designed to alleviate these difficulties in a proof theory that is too weak for natural language. Conceptually, a weak proof theory is overcome by entertaining multiple representations that are equivalent in meaning. We provide theoretical justification below, followed by the algorithmic implications.

We say that a representation $r \in \mathcal{R}$ is *faithful* to $S$ if $r$ and $r_S$ have the same model theoretic representation, i.e., $M(r) = M(r_s)$. Informally, this means that $r$ is the image under $\mathcal{R}$ of a text snippet with the same meaning as $S$.

**Definition 1.** *Let $S, T$ be two text snippets with representations $r_S, r_T$ in $\mathcal{R}$. We say that $S {\models} T$ (read: $S$* semantically entails *$T$) if there is a representation $r \in R$ that is faithful to $S$ and that is subsumed by $r_T$.*

Clearly, there is no practical way to exhaust the set of all those representations that are faithful to $S$. Instead, our approach searches a space of faithful representations, generated via a set of rewrite rules in our KB.

A *rewrite rule* is a pair $(lhs, rhs)$ of expressions in $\mathcal{R}$, such that $lhs \sqsubseteq rhs$. Given a representation $r_S$ of $S$ and a rule $(lhs, rhs)$ such that $r_S \sqsubseteq lhs$, the augmentation of $r_S$ via $(lhs, rhs)$ is the representation $r'_S = r_S \wedge rhs$.

**Claim:** The representation $r'_S$ generated above is faithful to $S$.

To see this, note that as expressions in $\mathcal{R}$, $r'_S = r_S \wedge rhs$, therefore $M(r'_S) = M(r_S) \cap M(rhs)$. However, since $r_S \sqsubseteq lhs$, and $lhs \sqsubseteq rhs$, then $r_S \sqsubseteq rhs$ which implies that $M(r_S) \subseteq M(rhs)$. Consequently, $M(r'_S) = M(r_S)$ and the new representation is faithful to $S$.

The claim gives rise to an algorithm, which suggests incrementally *augmenting* the original representation of $S$ via the rewrite rules, and computing subsumption using the "weak" proof theory between the augmented representation and $r_T$. Informally, this claim means that while, in general, augmenting the representation of $S$ with an expression $rhs$ may restrict the number of interpretations the resulting expression has, in this case, since we only augment the representation when the left hand side $lhs$ subsumes $r_S$, we end up with a new representation that is in fact equivalent to $r_S$. Therefore, given a collection of rules $\{(lhs \sqsubseteq rhs)\}$ we can chain their applications, and incrementally generate faithful representations of $S$. Consequently, this algorithm is a sound algorithm[3] for semantic entailment according to Def. 1, but it is not complete. Its success depends on the size and quality of the rule set[4] applied in the search.

Two important notes are in order. First, since rewrite rules typically "modify" a small part of a sentence representation (see Fig. 1), the augmented representation provides also a compact way to encode a large number of possible representations. Second, note that while the rule augmentation mechanism provides a justification for an algorithmic process, in practice, applying rewrite rules is somewhat more complicated. The key reason is that many rules have a large fan-out; that is, a large number of heads are possible for a given rule body. Examples include synonym rules, equivalent ways to represent names of people (e.g., John F. Kennedy and JFK), etc. We therefore implement the mechanism in two ways; one process which supports chaining well, in which we explicitly augment the representation with low fan-out rules (e.g., Passive-Active rules); and a second, appropriate to the large fan-out rules. In the latter, we abstain from augmenting the representation with the many possible heads but take those rules into account when comparing the augmented source with the target. For example, if a representation includes the expression "JFK/PER", we do not augment it with all the many expressions equivalent to "JFK" but, when comparing it to a candidate in the target, such as "President Kennedy", these equivalencies are taken into account. Semantically, this is equivalent to augmenting the representation. Instead of an explicit list of rules, the large fan-out rules are represented as a functional black box that can, in principle, contain any procedure for deciding comparisons. For this reason, this mechanism is called *functional subsumption*. The resulting algorithmic approach is therefore:

**(1)** After inducing a representation for $S$ and $T$, the algorithm incrementally searches the rewrite rules in KB to find a rule with a body that subsumes the representation of $S$. In this case, the head of the rule is used to *augment* the representation of $S$ and generate a new (equivalent) representation $S_i'$ of $S$. KB consists of syntactic and semantic rewrite rules expressed at the word, syntactic and semantic categories, and phrase levels; the resulting new representations capture alternative ways of expressing the surface level text.

**(2)** Representation $S_i'$s are processed via the extended subsumption algorithm against the representation of $T$. The notion of extended subsumption captures, just like the rewrite rules, several sentence, phrase, and word-level abstractions. The extended subsumption process is also used when determining whether a rewrite rule applies.

Rewrite rules and extended subsumption decisions take into account relational and structural information encoded in the hierarchical representation, which is

[3] Soundness depends on a "correct" induction of the representation of the text; we do not address this theoretically here.

[4] The power of this search procedure is in the rules. $lhs$ and $rhs$ might be very different at the surface level, yet, by satisfying model theoretic subsumption they provide expressivity to the re-representation in a way that facilitates the overall subsumption.

discussed below. In both cases, decisions are quantified as input to an optimization algorithm that attempts to generate a "proof" that $S$ entails $T$, and is discussed later in the paper.

## 3 High-Level System Description

The full entailment system implements the algorithm described in Sec. 2. This section provides a description of this system as well as some implementation-driven deviations from the abstract algorithm.

First, sentence pairs are annotated with various machine learning tools and parsed into the hierarchical representation described in Sec. 4 (denoted by PARSE on the diagram in Fig. 2).

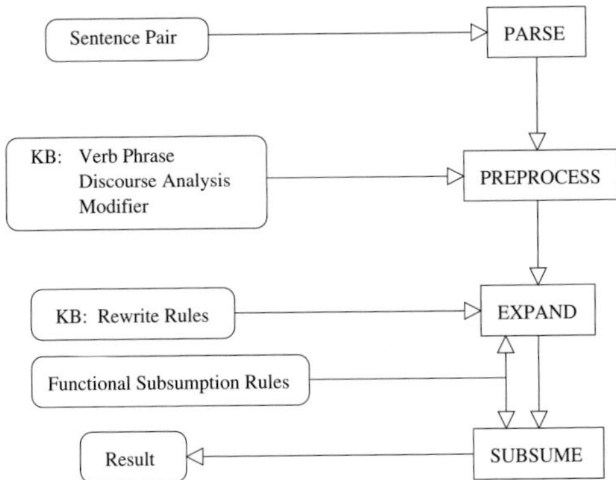


**Fig. 2.** System block diagram

The expansion described in Sec. 2 is subdivided into two stages: the first stage, labeled PREPROCESS on the accompanying diagram, applies a set of *semantic analysis* modules comprising rewrite rules that need only be applied once. Once these have been applied, the second sub-stage expands the source sentence only with rules from the Rewrite Rule knowledge base module. (The distinction between the rules in the semantic analysis modules and the rules in the Rewrite Rule knowledge base module is explained in Sec. 3.1.) The preprocessing module also uses heuristics to simplify complex predicate arguments.

The second expansion stage (EXPAND in the diagram) applies rewrite rules to the source sentence, and may chain these rules over successive iterations. (Expansion terminates either when no new rules can be applied without duplicating a previous application or after a fixed number of iterations).

After expansion, the system checks for subsumption (SUBSUME in the diagram) by comparing elements of the source and target sentences, generating a cost solution for the comparison as described in Sec. 5, and comparing the minimum cost to a threshold. In both the expansion and subsumption stages, the extended subsumption knowledge base is used as necessary.

Changes to the system can be realized by adding or removing semantic analysis modules, by changing the subsumption algorithm, or by changing the weights on those variables in the optimization formulation corresponding to the relevant attribute/edge types in the representation and on the variables describing applications of different categories of rewrite rules.

### 3.1 Semantic Analysis Modules

The semantic analysis modules are essentially groupings of rewrite rules, separated from the more general rewrite rules because they deal with structural principles such as tense and auxiliary verb constructions rather than more specific paraphrasing. They behave in most respects like the general rewrite rules described in Sec. 5, except for the following distinctions:

1. They are applied to both S and T.
2. The Verb Processing module allows its rules to modify T by *rewriting* the verb construction in T instead of simply *expanding* the original T, as described in the Verb Processing Module section below.
3. These rules may not be chained indefinitely; either they add an attribute to a node which is then preserved through all subsequent rule applications, or they permanently simplify a multi-node structure to a simpler structure.

The system presently supports three semantic analysis modules: verb phrase compression, discourse analysis, and modifier analysis. Note that we use Discourse Analysis to denote semantic analysis of interaction between predicates (a refinement of the traditional denotation of relationships between sentences, as such interactions could occur between predicates in different, as well as within, sentences). The different semantic analysis modules depend on different levels of structure and the corresponding rules are therefore phrased at different levels of representation: verb phrase compression requires word order and part of speech; discourse analysis requires full parse information and part of speech, and modifier analysis requires full and shallow parse information and part of speech.

#### 3.1.1 The Verb Phrase Module

The Verb Processing (VP) module rewrites certain verb phrases as a single verb with additional attributes. It uses word order and part of speech information to identify candidate patterns and, when the verbs in the construction in the sentence match a pattern in the VP module, the verb phrase is replaced by a single predicate node with additional attributes representing modality (MODALITY) and tense (TENSE). Simple past and future tenses are detected and represented, as are some conditional tenses.

The rules in the VP module are applied differently from those in other modules, allowing the sentence representation to be changed by substituting the verb construction specified by the rule head for that specified by the rule body (rather than simply expanding the sentence representation by adding the head structure). This is permissible because the rules in this module have extremely high precision, so few or no errors are introduced by these alterations.

The VP module presently recognizes modal constructions, tense constructions, and simple verb compounds of the form "VERB to VERB" (such as "*manage to enter*"). In each case, in the functional subsumption step of rule application, the first verb is compared to a list that maps verb lemmas to tenses and modifiers; for example, in the verb phrase "*has entered*", "*has*" is recognized as a tense auxiliary and results in the attribute "TENSE: past" being added to the second verb's node. The "*has*" node is then eliminated and the graph structure corrected.

#### 3.1.2 Discourse Analysis Module

The Discourse Analysis (DA) module detects the effects of an embedding predicate on the embedded predicate. It uses the full parse tree to identify likely candidate structures, then compares the embedding verb to a list mapping verbs to MODALITY. Presently the main distinction is between "FACTUAL" and a set of values that distinguish various types of uncertainty. This allows different assumptions to be supported; for example, if we assume that when something is said, it is taken as truth, we can treat the MODALITY value, "REPORTED", as entailing "FACTUAL". The module attaches the appropriate MODALITY value to the embedded verb node; if this attribute is not matched during subsumption, subsumption fails.

#### 3.1.3 Modifier Module

The Modifier module allows comparison of noun modifiers such as "all", "some", "any", "no", etc. This module is important when two similar sentences differ in the generality of one or more arguments of otherwise identical predicates. For full effectiveness, this requires that the system determine whether the predicate in question is upward or downward monotonic, i.e. whether the source target entails more general or more specific cases. This problem is non-trivial and has not yet been resolved for this system.

Instead, we assume that predicates are upward monotonic. For example, a source sentence predicate with an argument modified by an adjective subsumes an identical target predicate with the same argument without the modifying adjective. This is non-reflexive, i.e. a target predicate with an argument having an adjectival modifier will not be subsumed by an identical source predicate with no adjectival modifier (or a modifier different in meaning).

### 3.2 Rewrite Rule Module

The Rewrite Rule module contains rules encoding paraphrase and logical rewrite information. Paraphrase rules encode valid substitutions for one verb (-phrase) with another (e.g. "*hawked*" may be replaced with "*sold*" given similar argument structure); logical rules encode predicates that may be inferred from existing predicates (e.g. if A sold B to C, then C bought B from A).

The Rewrite Rule module is implemented independently of the semantic analysis modules, and behaves as described in Sec. 2. Most rewrite rules require Semantic Role Labeling (SRL) information (Sec. 4), though some use only word order and the words. The Rewrite Rule knowledge base can be used independently of the other modules, but may benefit from them—e.g. VP module may compress a tense construction, allowing a rewrite rule to fire. To avoid the obvious problem of potentially generating grammatically incorrect sentences, the following restriction is imposed on rewrite rules that modify the node/edge structure of the sentence representation: A rewrite rule encoding predicate-level information must add a new node for the substituted predicate, connected to the relevant arguments of the existing predicate matching the rule body.

A sentence is not read as a sequence of words; rather, it is read as a collection of predicates. As such, it can be thought of as a set of trees whose roots (predicates) do not overlap, but whose leaves (arguments) may be shared by more than one predicate.

### 3.3 Variations of the Entailment System

By changing the weighting scheme of the cost function in the module that checks for subsumption, it is possible to restrict the kinds of information available to the system. For example, if only variables corresponding to words and SRL information are given non-zero weights, only rewrite rules using a subset of this information and the information itself will be represented in the final cost equation. Any distinct information source may be given its own weight, thus allowing different information sources to be given preference. At present, these weights are found by brute force search; our current efforts are directed at learning these weights more efficiently.

For the experimental evaluation of the system, we also tried a hybrid system that used high-level semantic information and general rewrite rules, but which used a relatively basic word level approach (LLM; see Sec. 7) to compare the arguments of predicates.

## 4 Hierarchical Knowledge Representation

Our semantic entailment approach relies heavily on a hierarchical representation of natural language sentences, defined formally over a domain $\mathcal{D} = \langle \mathcal{V}, \mathcal{A}, \mathcal{E} \rangle$ which consists of a set $\mathcal{V}$ of typed elements, a set $\mathcal{A}$ of attributes of elements, and a set $\mathcal{E}$ of relations among elements. We use a Description-Logic inspired language, *Extended Feature Description Logic (EFDL)*, an extension of FDL [5] . As described there, expressions in the language have an equivalent representation as *concept graphs*, and we refer to the latter representation here for comprehensibility.

*Nodes* in the concept graph represent elements — words, (multiple levels of) phrases (including arguments to predicates), and predicates. *Attributes* of nodes represent properties of elements. Examples of attributes (they are explained in more detail later) include {LEMMA, WORD, POS, PREDICATE_VALUE, PHTYPE, PHHEAD, NETYPE, ARGTYPE, NEGATION, MODALITY, TENSE}. The first three are word level, the next three are phrase level, NETYPE is the named entity of a phrase, ARGTYPE is the set of semantic arguments as defined in PropBank [7],

NEGATION is a negation attribute, MODALITY encodes a proposition's modality (by tagging its main verb), and TENSE applies only to verbs. Only attributes with non-null values need to be specified.

*Relations* (roles) between two elements are represented by labeled edges between the corresponding nodes. Examples of roles (again, explained in more detail later) include: {BEFORE, ARG0, ... ARG5}; BEFORE indicates the order between two individuals, and ARG0, ... ARG5 represent the relations between a predicate (verb) and its argument.

Figure 1 shows a visual representation of a pair of sentences re-represented as concept graphs. Concept graphs are used both to describe instances (sentence representations) and rewrite rules. The expressivity of these differ — the body and head of rules are simple chain graphs, for inference complexity reasons. (Restricted expressivity is an important concept in Description Logics [8], from which we borrow several ideas and nomenclature.)

Concept graph representations are induced via state of the art machine learning based resources such as a part-of-speech tagger [9], a syntactic parser [10], a semantic parser [11, 12], a named entity recognizer [5], and a name coreference system [13] with the additional tokenizer and lemmatizer derived from WordNet [14]. Rewrite rules were filtered from a large collection of paraphrase rules developed in [15]. These are inference rules that capture lexico-syntactic paraphrases, such as "*X wrote Y*" synonymous with "*X is the author of Y*".

The rules are compiled into our language. Moreover, a number of non-lexical rewrite rules were generated manually. Currently, our knowledge base consists of approximately 300 inference rules.

### 4.1 Rule Representation

A rule is a pair (*lhs*, *rhs*) of concept graphs (*lhs* is the rule's *body*, while *rhs* is its *head*). These concept graphs are restricted in that they must be *paths*. This restricts the complexity of the inference algorithm while keeping them useful enough for our purposes.

*lhs* describes a structure to match in the sentence concept graph, while *rhs* describes a new predicate (and related attributes and edges) to be added to the sentence concept graph in case there is a match. *rhs* can also describe attributes to add to one or more existing nodes without adding a new predicate, provided no new edges are introduced. These restrictions ensure that the data representation always remains, from the subsumption algorithm's perspective, a set of overlapping trees.

Variables can be used in *lhs* so that we can specify which entities have edges/attributes added by *rhs*. Rules thus allow modification of the original sentence; e.g. we encode DIRT [15] rules as predicate-argument structures and use them to allow (parts of) the original sentence to be re-represented via paraphrase, by linking existing arguments with new predicates.

[5] Named entity recognizer from Cognitive Computation Group, available at http://l2r.cs.uiuc.edu/~cogcomp

# 5 Inference Model and Algorithm

This section describes how the extended subsumption process exploits the hierarchical knowledge representation and how inference is modeled as optimization.

## 5.1 Modeling Hierarchy and Unification Functions

An exact subsumption approach that requires the representation of $T$ be entirely embedded in the representation of $S_i'$ is unrealistic. Natural languages allow words to be replaced by synonyms, modifier phrases to be dropped, etc., without affecting meaning.

We define below our notion of extended subsumption, computed given two representations, which is designed to exploit the hierarchical representation and capture multiple levels of abstractions and granularity of properties represented at the sentence, phrase, and word-level.

Nodes in a concept graph are grouped into different hierarchical sets denoted by $H = \{H_0, \ldots, H_j\}$ where a lower value of $j$ indicates higher hierarchical level (more important nodes). This hierarchical representation is derived from the underlying concept graph and plays an important role in the definitions below.

We say that $S_i'$ entails $T$ if $T$ can be *unified into* $S_i'$. The significance of definitions below is that we define unification so that it takes into account both the hierarchical representation and multiple abstractions.

Let $V(T)$, $E(T)$, $V(S_i')$, and $E(S_i')$ be the sets of nodes and edges in $T$ and $S_i'$, respectively. Given a hierarchical set $H$, a *unification* is a 1-to-1 mapping $U = (U_V, U_E)$ where $U_V : V(T) \mapsto V(S_i')$, and $U_E : E(T) \mapsto E(S_i')$ satisfying:

1. $\forall (x, y) \in U$ : $x$ and $y$ are in the same hierarchical level.
2. $\forall (e, f) \in U_E$ : their sinks and sources must be unified accordingly. That is, for $n_1$, $n_2$, $m_1$, and $m_2$ which are the sinks and the sources of $e$ and $f$ respectively, $(n_1, m_1) \in U_V$ and $(n_2, m_2) \in U_V$.

Let $\mathcal{U}(T, S_i')$ denote the space of all unifications from $T$ to $S_i'$. In our inference, we assume the existence of a unification function $G$ that determines the cost of unifying pairs of nodes or edges. $G$ may depend on language and domain knowledge, e.g. synonyms, name matching, and semantic relations. When two nodes or edges cannot be unified, $G$ returns infinity. This leads to the definition of *unifiability*.

**Definition 2.** *Given a hierarchical set $H$, a unification function $G$, and two concept graphs $S_i'$ and $T$, we say that $T$ is* unifiable *to $S_i'$ if there exists a unification $U$ from $T$ to $S_i'$ such that the cost of unification defined by*

$$D(T, S_i') = \min_{U \in \mathcal{U}(T, S_i')} \sum_{H_j} \sum_{(x,y) \in U | x,y \in H_j} \lambda_j G(x, y)$$

*is finite, where $\lambda_j$ are some constants s.t. the cost of unifying nodes at higher levels dominates those of the lower levels.*

Because top levels of the hierarchy dominate lower ones, nodes in both graphs are checked for subsumption in a top down manner. The levels and corresponding processes are:

`Hierarchy set` $H_0$ corresponds to sentence-level nodes, represented by the verbs in the text. The inherent set of attributes is {PHTYPE, PREDICATE_VALUE, LEMMA}. In order to capture the argument structure at sentence-level, each verb in $S'_i$ and $T$ has a set of edge attributes {$\text{ARG}_i$, $\text{PHTYPE}_i$}, where $\text{ARG}_i$ and $\text{PHTYPE}_i$ are the semantic role label and phrase type of each argument $i$ of the verb considered [7].

For each verb in $S'_i$ and $T$, check if they have the same attribute set and argument structure at two abstraction levels:

1. The semantic role level (SRL attributes). eg: ARG0 verb ARG1 : *[Contractors]*/ARG0 *build [houses]*/ARG1 *for $100,000.*
2. The syntactic parse level (parse tree labels). Some arguments of the verb might not be captured by the semantic role labeler (SRL); we check their match at the syntactic parse level. eg: NP verb NP PP : *[Contractors]*/NP *build [houses]*/NP *[for $100,000]*/ PP.

At this level, if all nodes are matched (modulo functional subsumption), the cost is 0, otherwise it is infinity.

`Hierarchy set` $H_1$ corresponds to phrase-level nodes and represents the semantic and syntactic arguments of the $H_0$ nodes (verbs). If the phase-level nodes are recursive structures, all their constituent phrases are $H_1$ nodes. For example, a complex noun phrase consists of various base-NPs. Base-NPs have edges to the words they contain.

The inference procedure recursively matches the corresponding $H_1$ nodes in $T$ and $S'_i$ until it finds a pair whose constituents do not match. In this situation, a *Phrase-level Subsumption* algorithm is applied. The algorithm is based on subsumption rules that are applied in a strict order (as a decision list) and each rule is assigned a confidence factor. The algorithm makes sure two $H_1$ nodes have the same PHTYPE, but allows other attributes such as NETYPE to be optional. Each unmatched attribute results in a uniform cost.

`Hierarchy set` $H_2$ corresponds to word-level nodes. The attributes used here are: {WORD, LEMMA, POS}. Unmatched attributes result in a uniform cost.

Figure 1 exemplifies the matching order between $S'_i$ and $T$ based on constraints imposed by the hierarchy.

### 5.2 Inference as Optimization

We solve the subsumption problem by formulating an equivalent Integer Linear Programming (ILP) problem[6]. An ILP problem involves a set of integer variables

[6] Despite the fact that this optimization problem is NP hard, commercial packages such as Xpress-MP (by Dash Optimization, http://www.dashoptimization.com) have very good performance on sparse problems. See [16, 17] for details on modeling problems as ILP problems.

$\{v_i\}$ and a set of linear equality or inequality constraints among them. Each variable $v_i$ is associated with a cost $c_i$, and the problem is to find an assignment to the variables that satisfies the constraints and minimizes $\sum_i c_i v_i$.

To prove $S \sqsubseteq T$, we first start with the graph $S$ (the initial graph). Then we extend $S$ by adding the right hand sides of applicable rules. This is repeated up to a fixed number of rounds and results in an expanded graph $S'_d$. The formulation allows us to solve for the optimal unification from $T$ to $S'_d$ that minimizes the overall cost.

To formulate the problem this way, we need a set of variables that can represent different unifications from $T$ to $S'_d$, and constraints to ensure the validity of the solution, i.e. that the unification does not violate any nonnegotiable property. We explain this below. For readability, we sometimes express constraints in a logic form that can be easily transformed to linear constraints.

#### 5.2.1 Representing Unification

We introduce Boolean variables $u(n,m)$ for each pair of nodes $n \in V(T)$ and $m \in V(S'_d)$ in the same hierarchical level, and $u(e,f)$ for each pair of edges $e \in E(T)$ and $f \in E(S'_d)$ in the same level.

To ensure that the assignment to the matching variables represents a valid unification from $T$ and $S'_d$, we need two types of constraints. First, we ensure the unification preserves the node and edge structure. For each pair of edges $e \in E(T)$ and $f \in E(S'_d)$, let $n_i$, $n_j$, $m_k$, and $m_l$ be the sources and the sinks of $e$ and $f$ respectively. Then $u(e,f) \Rightarrow u(n_i,m_k) \bigwedge u(n_j,m_l)$. Finally, to ensure that the unification is a 1-to-1 mapping from $T$ to $S'_d$, $\forall n_i \in V(T) \sum_{m_j \in S'_d} u(n_i,m_j) = 1$, and $\forall m_j \in V(S'_d) \sum_{n_i \in T} u(n_i,m_j) \leq 1$.

#### 5.2.2 Finding a Minimal Cost Solution

We seek the unification with a minimum (and, of course, finite) cost: $\sum_{H_j} \sum_{u(x,y)|x,y \in H_j} \lambda_j G(x,y) u(x,y)$, where $\lambda_j$ is the constant and $G$ the cost of unification as we explained in the previous sections. The minimal subgraph $S'_i$ of $S'_d$ that $T$ is unified to is also the minimal representation of $S$ that incurs minimal unification cost.

## 6 Previous Work

Knowledge representation and reasoning techniques have been studied in NLP for a long time [2, 3, 4]. Most approaches relied on mapping to a canonical First Order Logic representations with a general prover and without using acquired rich knowledge sources.

Significant development in NLP, specifically the ability to acquire knowledge and induce some level of abstract representation could, in principle, support more sophisticated and robust approaches. Nevertheless, most modern approaches developed so far are based on shallow representations of the text that capture lexico-syntactic relations based on dependency structures and are mostly built from grammatical functions in an extension to keyword-base matching [18]. Some systems make use of some semantic information, such as WordNet lexical chains

[19], to slightly enrich the representation. Other have tried to learn various logicical representations [20]. However, none of these approaches makes global use of a large number of resources as we do, or attempts to develop a flexible, hierarchical representation and an inference algorithm for it, as we present here.

Recently, as part of the PASCAL effort, more thought has been given to representation and inference with them. While most of the approaches presented there are still relatively shallow, some are more involved, including Glickman et. al [21] and Raina et. al [22]. The former provides an attempt to formalize the semantic entailment problem probabilistically, but the corresponding implementation focuses mostly on lexical level processing techniques. The latter is more similar to ours. Specifically, it is more related to one of our earlier attempt to model sentence equivalence via tree mapping [23]. Similar to our approach they use a large number of resources (such as a dependency parser, WordNet semantic information, and a PropBank semantic parser) to enrich a graph-based representation of source and target sentences. This information is then used to perform a number of lexico-syntactic and semantic transformations that would potentially lead to the source-target match. However, in contrast to our system, they do not attempt to formalize their approach.

## 7 Experimental Evaluation

We tested our approach on two corpora: a set of question-answer pairs provided by the PARC AQUAINT team[7], and the PASCAL challenge data set[8].

We first describe the performance of the system on the PARC data set, organizing the rewrite rules into separate components and examining the contribution of each. We then examine the system's performance on the PASCAL data set, and the need for different weights in the optimization function for this corpus. In the tables in this section, all numerical results represent the accuracy of the system when predictions are made for all examples in the corpus under consideration, i.e. for a recall of 100%.

### 7.1 Experiments Using the PARC Data Set

In this set of experiments, we tested our approach on a collection of question-answer pairs developed by Xerox PARC for a pilot evaluation of Knowledge-Oriented Approaches to Question Answering under the ARDA-AQUAINT program. The PARC corpus consists of 76 Question-Answer pairs annotated as "true", "false" or "unknown" (and an indication of the type of reasoning required to deduce the label). The question/answer pairs provided by PARC are designed to test different cases of linguistic entailment, concentrating on examples of strict and plausible linguistic (lexical and constructional) inferences, and indicating whether each involves some degree of background world knowledge. The focus is on inferences that can be made purely on the basis of the meaning

[7] The data is available at http://l2r.cs.uiuc.edu/~cogcomp/data.php

[8] http://www.pascal-network.org/Challenges/RTE/

of words and phrases. The questions are straightforward and therefore easily rewritten (by hand) into statement form.

For evaluation reasons, we used only two labels in our experiments , "true" and "false", corresponding to "S entails T" and "S does not entail T". The "unknown" instances were classified as "false". Of these 76 sentence pairs, 64 were perfectly tagged by our Semantic Role Labeler (SRL), and were used as a second noise-free test set to evaluate our system under "ideal" conditions.

This section illustrates the contributions of high-level (semantic) analysis modules to system performance and compares the full entailment system with the baseline LLM — lexical-level matching based on a bag-of-words representation with lemmatization and normalization. For each semantic analysis component we give one or more examples of sentence pairs affected by the new version/component. Finally, we present a summary of the performance of each system on the noise-free (perfect) and noisy (full) data sets.

The full system uses Semantic Role Labeling, full parse and shallow parse structure, which allows use of all semantic analysis modules. This version of the system, labeled "SRL+deep", also uses Named Entity annotation from our Named Entity Recognizer (NER).

### 7.1.1 LLM

The LLM system ignores a large set of stopwords — including some common verbs, such as "go" — which for certain positive sentence pairs allows entailment when the more sophisticated system requires a rewrite rule to map from the predicate in S to the predicate in T. For example: since the list of stopwords includes forms of "*be*", the following sentence pair will be classified "true" by LLM, while the more sophisticated system requires a KB rule to link "*visit*" to "*be (in)*":

S: *[The diplomat]*/ARG1 *visited [Iraq]*/ARG1 *[in September]*/AM_TMP

T: *[The diplomat]*/ARG1 *was in [Iraq]*/ARG2

Of course, LLM is insensitive to small changes in wording. For the following sentence pair, LLM returns "true", which is clearly incorrect:

S: *Legally, John could drive.*

T: *John drove.*

### 7.1.2 SRL + Deep Structure

The entailment system without the high-level semantic modules correctly labels the following example, which is incorrectly labeled by the LLM system:

S: *No US congressman visited Iraq until the war.*

T: *Some US congressmen visited Iraq before the war.*

The entailment system includes the determiners "*no*" and "*some*" as modifiers of their respective entities; subsumption fails at the argument level because these modifiers don't match. (Note: this does not require the MODIFIER module, as in this instance, the lexical tokens themselves are different.)

However, the new system also makes new mistakes:

S: *The room was full of women.*

T: *The room was full of intelligent women.*

The LLM system finds no match for "intelligent" in S, and so returns the correct answer, "false". However, the SRL+deep structure system allows unbalanced T adjective modifiers, assuming that S must be more general than T, and allows subsumption.

*7.1.2.1 Verb Phrase (VP) Module.* The Verb Phrase module is beneficial when two similar sentences are distinguished by a modal construction.

In the example below, the VP recognizes the modal construction and adds the modifying attribute "MODALITY: potential" to the main verb node, "*drive*":

S: *Legally, John could drive.*

T: *John drove.*

Subsumption in the entailment system then fails at the verb level, making entailment less likely.

This module also acts as an enabler for other resources (such as the Knowledge Base). This may result in a decrease in performance when those modules are not present, as it corrects T sentences that may have failed subsumption in the more restricted system because the auxiliary verb was not present in the corresponding S sentence:

S: *Bush said that Khan sold centrifuges to North Korea.*

T: *Centrifuges were sold to North Korea.*

The system without the VP module returns the correct answer, "false", for this example, but for the wrong reason: SRL generates a separate predicate frame for "*were*" and for "*sold*" in T, and there is no matching verb for "were" in S.

When the VP module is added, the auxiliary construction in T is rewritten as a single verb with tense and modality attributes attached; the absence of the auxiliary verb means that SRL generates only a single predicate frame for "*sold*". This matches its counterpart in S, and subsumption succeeds, as the qualifying effect of the verb "said" in S cannot be recognized without the deeper parse structure and the Discourse Analysis module.

On the PARC corpus, the net result of applying the VP module when the KB is not enabled is either no improvement or a decrease in performance, due to the specific mix of sentences. However, the importance of such a module to correctly identify positive examples becomes evident when the knowledge base is enabled, as the performance jumps significantly over that of the same system without VP enabled.

*7.1.2.2 Discourse Analysis (DA) Module.* The following example highlights the importance of the way an embedded predicate is affected by the embedding predicate. In this example, the predicate "*Hanssen sold secrets to the Russians*" is embedded in the predicate "*The New York Times reported...*".

S: *The New York Times reported that Hanssen sold FBI secrets to the Russians and could face the death penalty.*

T: *Hanssen sold FBI secrets to the Russians.*

Our system identifies the following verb frames in S and T:

S-A: *[The New York Times]*/ARG0 *reported [that Hanssen sold FBI secrets to the Russians... ]*/ARG1

S-B: *[Hanssen]*/ARG0 *sold [FBI secrets]*/ARG1 *to [the Russians]*/ARG3
T-A: *[Hanssen]*/ARG0 *sold [FBI secrets]*/ARG1 *to [the Russians]*/ARG3

During preprocessing, our system detects the pattern "[VERB] that [VERB]", and classifies the first verb as affecting the confidence of its embedded verb. The system marks the verb (predicate) "*sold*" in S with attribute and value "MODALITY: REPORTED". Thus the subsumption check determines that entailment fails at the verb level, because by default, verbs are given the attribute and value "MODALITY: FACTUAL", and the MODALITY values of the "*sold*" nodes in S and T do not match. This is in contrast to the baseline LLM system, which returns the answer "true".

The next example demonstrates that the implementation of this embedding detection is robust enough to handle a subtly different sentence pair: in this case, the sentence structure "*Hanssen, who sold...*" indicates that the reader should understand that it is already proven (elsewhere) that Hanssen has sold secrets:
S: *The New York Times reported that Hanssen, who sold FBI secrets to the Russians, could face the death penalty.*
T: *Hanssen sold FBI secrets to the Russians.*

Our system identifies the following verb frames in S and T (using the full parse data to connect "who" to "Hanssen"):
S-A: *[The New York Times]*/ARG0 *reported [that Hanssen, who sold FBI secrets to the Russians... ]*/ARG1
S-B: *[Hanssen]*/ARG0 *sold [FBI secrets]*/ARG1 *to [the Russians]*/ARG3
T-A: *[Hanssen]*/ARG0 *sold [FBI secrets]*/ARG1 *to [the Russians]*/ARG3

During preprocessing, the system does not detect an embedding of "*sold*" in "*reported*", and so does not attach the attribute and value "MODALITY: REPORTED" to the verb "*sold*" in S. During the subsumption check, the "*sold*" verbs now match, as both are considered factual.

*7.1.2.3 Modifier (Mod) Module.* In the experimental results summarized below, adding the Modifier module does not improve performance, because in all the PARC examples involving modifiers, a different modifier in S and T corresponds to a negative label.

However, the modifier module will correctly analyze the following sentence pair, which is a reordered pair from the PARC corpus:
S: *All soldiers were killed in the ambush.*
T: *Many soldiers were killed in the ambush.*

The default rule — non-identical argument modifiers cause subsumption to fail — is incorrect here, as S entails T. The Modifier module correctly identifies the entailment of "many" by "all", and subsumption will succeed.

**Table 1.** System's performance on the PARC corpus with different optimization weighting schemes

| Corpus Version | Baseline (LLM) | Weighting Scheme | |
|---|---|---|---|
| | | PARC scheme | PASCAL scheme |
| Perfect | 59.38 | 88.21 | 57.81 |
| Full | 61.84 | 77.63 | 56.58 |

**Table 2.** System's performance obtained for the PARC question-answer pairs with perfect SRL. This corresponds to 64 question-answering pairs. N/A indicates that the module could not be used with the corresponding system configuration.

| Module | without KB | | with KB | |
|---|---|---|---|---|
| | LLM | SRL + Deep | LLM | SRL + Deep |
| Base | 59.38 | 62.50 | 62.50 | 68.75 |
| + VP | N/A | 62.50 | N/A | 75.00 |
| + DA | N/A | 71.88 | N/A | 82.81 |
| + Mod | N/A | 71.88 | N/A | 82.81 |

**Table 3.** System's performance obtained for the PARC question-answer pairs on the full data set. N/A indicates that no knowledge information could be used.

| Module | without KB | | with KB | |
|---|---|---|---|---|
| | LLM | SRL+Deep | LLM | SRL+Deep |
| Base | 61.84 | 61.84 | 64.47 | 67.11 |
| + VP | N/A | 60.52 | N/A | 69.74 |
| + DA | N/A | 68.42 | N/A | 77.63 |
| + Mod | N/A | 68.42 | N/A | 77.63 |

### 7.1.3 Experimental Results: PARC

We present the results of the experiments on the PARC data set with two differently weighted inference formulations, which show that for the PARC data set, a formulation where weights on higher levels in the hierarchy described in Sec. 5 dominate performed better than a formulation favoring lower-level hierarchy elements.

Table 1 shows the overall performance of the system on the PARC data set for two sets of weights on the final inference formulation, one suited to the PARC data set and one suited to the PASCAL data set. In both cases the weights were determined empirically and the KB of rewrite rules was enabled.

The breakdown of the contributions of different modules are presented in Table 2 and 3. We compare the baseline and the full entailment system (SRL+ Deep). Table 2 presents the evaluation of the system with and without the KB inference rules, comparing the baseline and the full entailment system (SRL+Deep) when SRL is perfect, i.e. considering only examples on which our SRL tool gives correct annotation. Table 3 presents the evaluation when the entire dataset is used, including those examples on which the SRL tool makes mistakes.

The results obtained with perfect semantic argument structure (perfect SRL) are provided here to illustrate the advantages of the hierarchical approach, as noise introduced by SRL errors can obscure the effects of the different levels of the hierarchical representation/subsumption. The system behaves consistently, showing improvement as additional hierarchical structure and additional semantic analysis resources are added. These results validate the benefit of the hierarchical approach.

## 7.2 Experiments Using the PASCAL Data Set

In this experiment we tested our approach on a set of sentence pairs developed for the PASCAL challenge. As the system was designed to test for semantic entailment, the PASCAL test data set is well suited, being composed of 800 source — target sentence pairs, with a truth value indicating whether the source logically entails the target. The set is split into various tasks: CD (Comparable Documents), IE (Information Extraction), IR (Information Retrieval), MT (Machine Translation), PP (Prepositional Paraphrases), QA (Question Answering), and RC (Reading Comprehension). The typical sentence size varies from 11 (IR task) to 25 (MT task) words.

#### 7.2.1 Experimental Results: PASCAL

Table 4 shows the system's performance. We first used the optimization function weighting scheme that was most successful for the PARC dataset (labeled "PARC scheme"); the resulting performance was poor. Error analysis revealed many mistakes at the predicate-argument level, probably due to the greater complexity of the PASCAL corpus. This led us to try other weighting schemes that emphasized lower-level information such as lexical tokens and word order; the most successful of these yielded the results labeled "PASCAL scheme".

**Table 4.** System's performance obtained for each experiment on the PASCAL corpus and its subtasks

| System | Overall | Task | | | | | | |
|---|---|---|---|---|---|---|---|---|
| | | CD | IE | IR | MT | PP | QA | RC |
| PARC Scheme | 51.38 | 54.67 | 50.00 | 51.11 | 50.83 | 54.00 | 50.00 | 50.00 |
| PASCAL Scheme | 58.63 | 82.67 | 54.17 | 53.33 | 51.67 | 50.00 | 53.85 | 53.57 |
| LLM | 55.00 | 84.00 | 45.83 | 44.44 | 50.00 | 42.00 | 53.85 | 48.57 |

The system using the PASCAL weighting scheme does significantly better than the baseline LLM system, which shows evidence in some categories of negative correlation between matched keywords in the source and target sentences and entailment of T by S. Both do significantly better than the system using the PARC weighting scheme. Clearly, for the PASCAL corpus, higher level information (such as predicate-argument structure) is unhelpful to the system (reasons for this are suggested in the Error Analysis and Discussion sections below). However, the optimization formulation is robust enough to allow reasonably good performance even on this corpus.

#### 7.2.2 Error Analysis

Error analysis of the system's output for the PASCAL test corpus revealed that the high-level semantic resources had a high error rate. These errors lead to missing or misleading information that is then included in the final subsumption step. This section gives some examples of these errors.

*7.2.2.1 Rewrite Rules.* One major problem is the very incomplete coverage of our Knowledge Base of rewrite rules relating verb phrases. There are many entailment pairs in which very different verbs or verb phrases must be identified as having the same meaning to correctly determine subsumption, such as:

S: *Vanunu converted to Christianity while in prison, and has been [living]/*MAINVERB *in an anglican cathedral in Jerusalem since his release on April 21.*

T: *A convert to Christianity, Vanunu has [sequestered himself]/*MAINVERB *at a Jerusalem church since he was freed on April 21.*

Our system relies on our Knowledge Base of rewrite rules to allow modification of the source sentence and therefore allow it to match the corresponding part of the target sentence, and this incompleteness is a significant problem.

We are confident that the new VerbNet resources soon to be available will provide a good resource for more complete rewrite rules.

*7.2.2.2 Semantic Role Labeling.* The high-level resources depend heavily on the Semantic Role Labeler correctly identifying predicates (verbs) and arguments. While the SRL's performance on each element of a given verb frame is good — e.g. approaching 90% f-value for identifying ARG0 and ARG1 (similar to Subjects and Direct Objects) — it often makes mistakes on one or more elements in a given sentence. Moreover, when arguments are complex noun phrases (containing more than one base Noun Phrase), the system's higher-level analysis modules use heuristics to find the main entity of the argument; these heuristics introduce additional errors.

Study of a 10% sample of the test corpus suggests that SRL or the supporting argument analysis module makes a "significant" error (i.e., one that will interfere with subsumption) on about 58% of all cases. The following examples indicate the types of errors SRL and its supporting module makes.

*Incorrect Verb:*

In the next example, the SRL tags 'articulate' in T as a verb, and generates a redundant verb frame.

S: *Clinton [is]/*MAINVERB *a very charismatic person.*

T: *Clinton [is]/*MAINVERB *[articulate]/*MAINVERB.

This adds incorrect predicate-argument information to the Target graph and interferes with subsumption.

*Missing Argument:*

In the following example, SRL correctly identifies all constituents of the verb frames for 'said' and 'wearing' in both $S$ and $T$. However, SRL finds the subject of "carry" in T but not in S:

S: *Witnesses said the gunman was wearing gray pants and a tan jacket and was [carrying]/*MAINVERB *[a gray bag]/*ARG1.

T: *Witnesses said [the gunman]/*ARG0 *was wearing gray pants and a tan jacket COMMA and [carrying]/*MAINVERB *[a gray bag]/*ARG1.

This leads to high-level information being absent from S that is present in T, and interferes with subsumption.

*Incorrect Argument Type:*

In the next example, SRL mislabels a key argument of the main verb in T:

S: *[Satomi Mitarai]/*ARG1 *[died]/*MAINVERB *of blood loss.*

T: *[Satomi Mitarai]/*AM_EXT *[bled]/*MAINVERB *to death.*

This leads to mismatched high-level information in S and T, interfering with subsumption.

*Incorrect Argument Simplification:*

In the next example, the preprocessing module that simplifies complex arguments oversimplifies a key argument for the verb frame '[threatens to] dismiss':

S: *[Israeli Prime Minister Ariel Sharon]*/ARG0 *threatened to [dismiss]*/MAINVERB *[cabinet ministers]*/ARG1 *who don 't support his plan to withdraw from the Gaza Strip.*

T: *[Israeli Prime Minister Ariel Sharon]*/ARG0 *threatened to [fire]*/MAINVERB *[cabinet opponents]*/ARG1 *of his Gaza withdrawal plan .*

This oversimplification results in mismatched arguments in S and T, and impedes subsumption.

*7.2.2.3 Verb Phrase Compression.* The verb phrase compression module requires a good mapping from compressible verb phrase structures — such as auxiliary and modal verb structures, and structures where one verb modifies another (like "manages to enter") — to their compressed counterparts.

As with the PARC corpus, this module does not have a marked effect in isolation; rather, it potentially enables better subsumption between verb phrases that differ mainly in structure. In the last example, for instance, the VP module replaces the structure "threaten to dismiss" with the verb "dismiss" plus an associated MODALITY attribute "POTENTIAL".

*7.2.2.4 Discourse Analysis.* The Discourse Analysis module detects embedding structures, and is useful when the embedding structure affects the truth value of the embedded predicate. However, there are few such cases in the PASCAL corpus: for example, all "reported" structures are considered true (whereas PARC considers them "unknown", which our system treats as "false"). For example:

S: *A spokeswoman said there were no more details available.*

T: *No further details were available.*

In the PARC corpus, this sentence pair would get the label "UNKNOWN"; in PASCAL, it is considered "TRUE". As such, there is no advantage in activating the DA module over simply assuming "TRUE", as the "reported" embedding is the predominant case, with few other embedding constructions.

*7.2.2.5 Modifier Analysis.* The Modifier Analysis module works at the argument level, and is mainly of use when the two sentences being compared are similar. There are very few cases in the PASCAL corpus where such distinctions are important (i.e., when an argument subtype differs in otherwise identical predicate-argument pattern in S and T). Hence, this module has little effect.

The following examples show how the PASCAL weighted optimization model compares to the baseline LLM system.

*Example 1:*

S: "*A militant group in Iraq is holding seven foreign truck drivers.*"

T: "*The militant group said it had released the Iraqi driver.*"

In this example, LLM matches the majority of (non-stop-) words in T with words in S, and gives it the incorrect label "TRUE". However, the weighted optimization function takes into account other low level information such as word order, and correctly identifies this example as a case where S does not entail T.

The weighting scheme for the PASCAL data set does not give special weight to elements such as numbers; this can result in false positives:

*Example 2:*
S: "*Jennifer Hawkins is the 21-year-old beauty queen from Australia.*"
T: "*Jennifer Hawkins is Australia's 20-year-old beauty queen.*"

Our system matches almost all the key words in T with those in S; as numbers do not carry more weight than other word elements, our system allows subsumption, resulting in a false positive. LLM makes the same error.

### 7.3 Discussion

The results obtained for the different corpora, and the need for different weighting schemes for the optimization function used to resolve subsumption, indicate that the system can adapt to different corpora if the correct weights are learned. At present, these weights are not learned, but set by trial and error; devising appropriate learning mechanisms must be the next focus of research.

This section describes the way the optimization function is set up and how the weighting schemes differ for the two corpora.

#### 7.3.1 The Optimization Function

The hierarchical optimization function described in Sec. 5 is realized as three levels in these experiments:

1. Full predicate-argument information;
2. An intermediate level of information, using phrase level nodes in the concept graph representation;
3. A basic level of information using word-level information.

The function optimized in the inference step of the algorithm represents with weighted variables both the attributes and edges that encode this hierarchical information and the rules applied by the various knowledge modules.

The optimization problems formulated by the system for the two data sets are of the same form as they represent all three levels in each. However, we found empirically that different weights for some of the variables gave the best performance for the two data sets (meaning the weights on the variables associated with rule application and levels of representation).

While these weights can be learned, we got the best results from setting them by hand. For the PARC data set, weights were balanced between all three levels, while for the PASCAL data set, the weights for the third level dominated.

#### 7.3.2 The Need for Different Weighting Schemes

The need for the different weighting schemes is due to the greater complexity of the sentences in the PASCAL corpus, which have a number of relevant characteristics:

1. Many sentences are more complex in structure, with arguments of predicates widely separated from their predicates; this reduces SRL performance.
2. Many sentences have multiple predicates; particularly when T has multiple predicates, this increases the chance that an SRL error is made and therefore impedes entailment.
3. Many sentence pairs require verb phrase recognition and paraphrasing. Rules for making the appropriate substitution are hard to generate and apply, and SRL performance on recognizing verb phrase predicates is poorer than on single- verb predicates.
4. Many sentence pairs require complex "world knowledge", i.e. reasoning resources that extend beyond paraphrasing and even simple predicate-level inference (A left B $\Rightarrow$ A was in/at B).

The error analysis detailed above indicates that the elements of our system that yield high-level information about predicates and arguments are not yet mature enough to handle many of the complexities of the PASCAL data set. It makes sense, then, that in the optimization formulation for the PASCAL data set, variables relating to the rules/resources from level 1 are not very significant, and those representing more general (low-level) features are more useful; in the formulation for the PARC data set, however, the variables relating to stricter, higher-level features/rule applications are more relevant (given that the sentences are typically very similar, and the amount of information to be gained from lower-level features is small).

### 7.4 Summary

The entailment system is flexible enough to handle two very different corpora by using different weighting schemes for the optimization function that resolves subsumption. In effect, the system emphasizes lower-level information (such as lexical tokens and word order) for the harder PASCAL corpus, as the accuracy and coverage of higher-level information (such as the predicate-argument structure) is poor. For the simpler PARC corpus, higher level resources perform well and provide useful information; the weighting scheme for the optimization function for this corpus reflects this increased relevance.

Future work will involve improving the knowledge base using resources such as VerbNet, learning weights for the optimization functions via machine learning techniques, and improving the accuracy of key system resources. These should improve the value of the higher-level information and allow efficient optimization of the coefficients in the hierarchical optimization function, improving performance on harder corpora such as PASCAL.

## 8 Conclusions and Future Work

This paper presents a principled, integrated approach to *semantic entailment.* We developed an expressive knowledge representation that provides a hierarchical encoding of structural, relational and semantic properties of the text and populated it using a variety of machine learning based tools. An inferential mechanism over a knowledge representation that supports both abstractions and several levels of representations allows us to begin to address important issues in abstracting over the variability in natural language. Our preliminary evaluation is very encouraging, yet leaves a lot to hope for. Improving our resources and developing ways to augment the KB are some of the important steps we need to take. Beyond that, we intend to tune the inference algorithm by incorporating a better mechanism for choosing the appropriate level at which to require subsumption. Given the fact that we optimize a linear function, it is straight forward to learn the cost function. Moreover, this can be done in such a way that the decision list structure is maintained.

**Acknowledgments.** We thank Dash Optimization for a free academic license to the Xpress-MP software. This work was supported by the Advanced Research and Development Activity (ARDA)s Advanced Question Answering for Intelligence (AQUAINT) program, NSF grant ITR-IIS-0085980 and ONRs TRECC and NCASSR programs.

## References

1. Dagan, I., Glickman, O.: Probabilistic textual entailment: Generic applied modeling of language variability. In: Learning Methods for Text Understanding and Mining, Grenoble, France (2004)
2. Schubert, L.K.: From english to logic: Contex-free computation of 'conventional' logical translations. In Grosz, B.J., Sparck Jones, K., Webber, B.L., eds.: Natural Language Processing. Kaufmann, Los Altos, CA (1986)
3. Moore, R.C.: Problems in logical form. In Grosz, B.J., Sparck Jones, K., Webber, B.L., eds.: Natural Language Processing. Kaufmann, Los Altos, CA (1986)
4. Hobbs, J.R., Stickel, M., Martin, P., Edwards, D.: Interpretation as abduction. In: Proc. of the 26th Annual Meeting of the Association for Computational Linguistics (ACL). (1988) 95–103
5. Cumby, C.M., Roth, D.: Learning with feature description logics. In Matwin, S., Sammut, C., eds.: The 12th International Conference on Inductive Logic Programming (ILP-02), Springer (2003) 32–47 LNAI 2583.
6. Lloyd, J.W.: Foundations of Logic Progamming. Springer (1987)
7. Kingsbury, P., Palmer, M., Marcus, M.: Adding semantic annotation to the Penn treebank. In: Proc. of the 2002 Human Language Technology conference (HLT)., San Diego, CA (2002)
8. Baader, F., Calvanese, D., McGuinness, D., Nardi, D., Patel-Schneider, P.: Description Logic Handbook. Cambridge (2003)
9. Even-Zohar, Y., Roth, D.: A sequential model for multi class classification. In: Proc. of the 2001 Conference on Empirical Methods for Natural Language Processing (EMNLP). (2001) 10–19
10. Collins, M.: Head-driven Statistical Models for Natural Language Parsing. PhD thesis, Computer Science Department, University of Pennsylvenia, Philadelphia (1999)
11. Punyakanok, V., Roth, D., Yih, W., Zimak, D.: Semantic role labeling via integer linear programming inference. In: Proc. of the 20th International Conference on Computational Linguistics (COLING), Geneva, Switzerland (2004)

12. Punyakanok, V., Roth, D., Yih, W.: The necessity of syntactic parsing for semantic role labeling. In: Proc. of the 19th International Joint Conference on Artificial Intelligence (IJCAI). (2005)
13. Li, X., Morie, P., Roth, D.: Identification and tracing of ambiguous names: Discriminative and generative approaches. In: Proc. of the 19th National Conference on Artificial Intelligence (AAAI). (2004)
14. Fellbaum, C.: WordNet: An Electronic Lexical Database. MIT Press (1998)
15. Lin, D., Pantel, P.: DIRT: discovery of inference rules from text. In: Proc. of ACM SIGKDD Conference on Knowledge Discovery and Data Mining 2001. (2001) 323–328
16. Roth, D., Yih, W.: A linear programming formulation for global inference in natural language tasks. In: Proceedings of CoNLL-2004. (2004) 1–8
17. Roth, D., Yih, W.: Integer linear programming inference for conditional random fields. In: Proceedings of the International Conference on Machine Learning (ICML). (2005)
18. Durme, B.V., Huang, Y., Kupsc, A., Nyberg, E.: Towards light semantic processing for question answering, HLT Workshop on Text Meaning (2003)
19. Moldovan, D., Clark, C., Harabagiu, S., Maiorano, S.: Cogex: A logic prover for question answering. In: Proc. of HLT-NAACL 2003. (2003)
20. Thompson, C., Mooney, R., Tang, L.: Learning to parse NL database queries into logical form. In: Workshop on Automata Induction, Grammatical Inference and Language Acquisition. (1997)
21. Glickman, O., Dagan, I., Koppel, M.: A probabilistic classification approach for lexical textual entailment. In: Proc. of AAAI 2005. (2005)
22. Raina, R., Ng, A., Manning, C.: Robust textual inference via learning and abductive reasoning. In: Proc. of AAAI 2005. (2005)
23. Punyakanok, V., Roth, D., Yih, W.: Natural language inference via dependency tree mapping: An application to question answering. Technical Report No. UIUCDCS-R-2004-2443), UIUC Computer Science Department (2004)

# A Lexical Alignment Model for Probabilistic Textual Entailment

Oren Glickman, Ido Dagan, and Moshe Koppel

Bar Ilan University, Ramat Gan 52900, Israel
{glikmao, dagan, koppel}@cs.biu.ac.il
http://cs.biu.ac.il/~{glikmao, dagan, koppel}/

**Abstract.** This paper describes the Bar-Ilan system participating in the Recognising Textual Entailment Challenge. The paper proposes first a general probabilistic setting that formalizes the notion of textual entailment. We then describe a concrete alignment-based model for lexical entailment, which utilizes web co-occurrence statistics in a bag of words representation. Finally, we report the results of the model on the *Recognising Textual Entailment* challenge dataset along with some analysis.

## 1 Introduction

Many Natural Language Processing (NLP) applications need to recognize when the meaning of one text can be expressed by, or inferred from, another text. Information Retrieval (IR), Question Answering (QA), Information Extraction (IE), text summarization and Machine Translation (MT) evaluation are examples of applications that need to assess this semantic relationship between text segments. The Recognising Textual Entailment (RTE) task ([8]) has recently been proposed as an application independent framework for modeling such inferences. Within the applied textual entailment framework, a text $t$ is said to entail a textual hypothesis $h$ if the truth of $h$ can be most likely inferred from $t$.

Textual entailment indeed captures generically a broad range of inferences that are relevant for multiple applications. For example, a QA system has to identify texts that entail a hypothesized answer. Given the question "*Does John Speak French?*", a text that includes the sentence "*John is a fluent French speaker*" entails the suggested answer "*John speaks French.*" In many cases, though, entailment inference is uncertain and has a probabilistic nature. For example, a text that includes the sentence "*John was born in France.*" does not strictly entail the above answer. Yet, it is clear that it does increase substantially the likelihood that the hypothesized answer is true.

The uncertain nature of textual entailment calls for its explicit modeling in probabilistic terms. We therefore propose a general generative probabilistic setting for textual entailment, which allows a clear formulation of probability spaces and concrete probabilistic models for this task. We suggest that the proposed setting may provide a unifying framework for modeling uncertain semantic inferences from texts.

J. Quiñonero-Candela et al. (Eds.): MLCW 2005, LNAI 3944, pp. 287–298, 2006.

An important sub task of textual entailment, which we term *lexical entailment*, is recognizing if the lexical concepts in a hypothesis $h$ are entailed from a given text $t$, even if the relations which hold between these concepts in $h$ may not be entailed from $t$. This is typically a necessary, but not sufficient, condition for textual entailment. For example, in order to infer from a text the hypothesis "*Chrysler stock rose*," it is a necessary that the concepts of *Chrysler*, *stock* and *rise* must be inferred from the text. However, for proper entailment it is further needed that the right relations would hold between these concepts. In this paper we demonstrate the relevance of the general probabilistic setting for modeling lexical entailment, by devising a preliminary alignment-based model that utilizes document co-occurrence probabilities in a bag of words representation.

Although our proposed lexical system is relatively simple, as it doesn't rely on syntactic or other deeper analysis, it nevertheless achieved an overall accuracy of 59% and an average precision of 0.57. The system did particularly well on the Comparable Documents (CD) task achieving an accuracy of 83%. These results may suggest that the proposed probabilistic framework is a promising basis for improved implementations that incorporate richer information.

## 2 A Probabilistic Setting for Textual Entailment

### 2.1 Motivation

A common definition of entailment in formal semantics ([5]) specifies that a text $t$ entails another text $h$ (hypothesis, in our terminology) if $h$ is true in every circumstance (*possible world*) in which $t$ is true. For example, in examples 1 and 3 from Table 1 we'd assume humans to agree that the hypothesis is necessarily true in any circumstance for which the text is true. In such intuitive cases, textual entailment may be perceived as being certain, or, taking a probabilistic perspective, as having a probability of 1. In quite many other cases, though, entailment inference is uncertain and has a probabilistic nature. In example 2, the text doesn't contain enough information to infer the hypothesis' truth. And in example 4, the meaning of the word hometown is ambiguous and therefore one cannot infer for certain that the hypothesis is true. In both of these cases there are conceivable circumstances for which the text is true and the hypothesis is false. Yet, it is clear that in both examples, the text does increase substantially the likelihood of the correctness of the hypothesis, which naturally extends the classical notion of certain entailment. Given the text, we expect the probability that the hypothesis is indeed true to be

**Table 1.** Example sentence pairs

| example | text | hypothesis |
|---|---|---|
| 1 | *John is a French Speaker* | *John speaks French* |
| 2 | *John was born in France* | *John speaks French* |
| 3 | *Harry's birthplace is Iowa* | *Harry was born in Iowa* |
| 4 | *Harry is returning to his Iowa hometown* | *Harry was born in Iowa* |

relatively high, and significantly higher than its probability of being true without reading the text. Aiming to model application needs, we suggest that the probability of the hypothesis being true given the text reflects an appropriate confidence score for the correctness of a particular textual inference. In the next subsections we propose a concrete generative probabilistic setting that formalizes the notion of truth probabilities in such cases.

## 2.2 A Probabilistic Setting and Generative Model

Let $T$ denote a space of possible texts, and $t \in T$ a specific text. Let $H$ denote the set of all possible hypotheses. A hypothesis $h \in H$ is a propositional statement which can be assigned a truth value. It is assumed here that $h$ is represented as a textual statement, but in principle it could also be expressed as a text annotated with additional linguistic information or even as a formula in some propositional language.

A semantic state of affairs is captured by a mapping from $H$ to {0=false, 1=true}, denoted by $w : H \rightarrow \{0, 1\}$, called here *possible world* (following common terminology). A possible world $w$ represents a concrete set of truth value assignments for all possible propositions. Accordingly, $W$ denotes the set of all possible worlds.

We assume a probabilistic generative model for texts and possible worlds. In particular, we assume that texts are generated along with a concrete state of affairs, represented by a possible world. Thus, whenever the source generates a text $t$, it generates also corresponding hidden truth assignments that constitute a possible world $w$. The probability distribution of the source, over all possible texts and truth assignments $T \times W$, is assumed to reflect inferences that are based on the generated texts. That is, we assume that the distribution of truth assignments is not bound to reflect the state of affairs in a particular "real" world, but only the inferences about propositions' truth which are related to the text. The probability for generating a true hypothesis $h$ that is not related at all to the corresponding text is determined by some prior probability $P(h)$. For example, $h$="*Paris is the capital of France*" might have a prior smaller than 1 and might well be false when the generated text is not related at all to Paris or France. In fact, we may as well assume that the notion of textual entailment is relevant only for hypotheses for which $P(h) < 1$, as otherwise (i.e. for tautologies) there is no need to consider texts that would support h's truth. On the other hand, we assume that the probability of $h$ being true (generated within $w$) would be higher than the prior when the corresponding $t$ does contribute information that supports $h$'s truth.

## 2.3 Probabilistic Textual Entailment Definition

We define two types of events over the probability space for $T \times W$:

I) For a hypothesis $h$, we denote as $Tr_h$ the random variable whose value is the truth value assigned to $h$ in a given world. Correspondingly, $Tr_h = 1$ is the event of h being assigned a truth value of 1 (true).

II) For a text $t$, we use $t$ itself to denote also the event that the generated text is $t$ (as usual, it is clear from the context whether $t$ denotes the text or the corresponding event).

We say that a text $t$ *probabilistically entails* a hypothesis $h$ (denoted as $t \Rightarrow h$) if $t$ increases the likelihood of $h$ being true, that is, if $P(Tr_h = 1|t) > P(Tr_h = 1)$, or equivalently if the pointwise mutual information, $I(Tr_h = 1, t)$, is greater then 0. Once knowing that $t \Rightarrow h$, $P(Tr_h = 1|t)$ serves as a probabilistic confidence value for $h$ being true given $t$.

Application settings would typically require that $P(Tr_h = 1|t)$ obtains a high value; otherwise, the text would not be considered sufficiently relevant to support $h$'s truth (e.g. a supporting text in QA or IE should entail the extracted information with high confidence). Finally, we ignore here the case in which $t$ contributes negative information about $h$, leaving this relevant case for further investigation.

### 2.4 Model Properties

It is interesting to notice the following properties and implications of our probabilistic setting:

**A)** Textual entailment is defined as a relationship between texts and propositions whose representation is typically based on text as well, unlike logical entailment which is a relationship between propositions only. Accordingly, textual entailment confidence is conditioned on the actual generation of a text, rather than its truth. For illustration, we would expect that the text "*His father was born in Italy*" would logically entail the hypothesis "*He was born in Italy*" with high probability - since most people who's father was born in Italy were also born there. However we expect that the text would actually not probabilistically textually entail the hypothesis since most people for whom it is specifically reported that their father was born in Italy were not born in Italy [1].

**B)** We assign probabilities to propositions (hypotheses) in a similar manner to certain probabilistic reasoning approaches (e.g. [1], [13]). However, we also assume a generative model of text, similar to probabilistic language models and statistical machine translation, which supplies the needed conditional probability distribution. Furthermore, since our conditioning is on texts rather than propositions we do not assume any specific logic representation language for text meaning, and only assume that textual hypotheses can be assigned truth values.

**C)** Our framework does not distinguish between textual entailment inferences that are based on knowledge of language semantics (such as *murdering* $\Rightarrow$ *killing*) and inferences based on domain or world knowledge (such as *live in Paris* $\Rightarrow$ *live in France*). Both are needed in applications and it is not clear where and how to put such a borderline.

---

[1] This seems to be the case when analyzing the results of entering the above text in a web search engine.

**D)** An important feature of the proposed framework is that for a given text many hypotheses are likely to be true. Consequently, for a given text $t$, $\sum_h P(Tr_h = 1|t)$ does not sum to 1. This differs from typical generative settings for IR and MT (e.g. [4], [19]), where all conditioned events are disjoint by construction. In the proposed model, it is rather the case that $P(Tr_h = 1|t) + P(Tr_h = 0|t) = 1$, as we are interested in the probability that a single particular hypothesis is true (or false).

**E)** An implemented model that corresponds to our probabilistic setting is expected to produce an estimate for $P(Tr_h = 1|t)$. This estimate is expected to reflect all probabilistic aspects involved in the modeling, including inherent uncertainty of the entailment inference itself (as in example 2 of Table 1), possible uncertainty regarding the correct disambiguation of the text (example 4), as well as uncertain probabilistic estimates that stem from the particular model structure and implementation.

## 3 A Lexical Entailment Model

We suggest that the proposed setting above provides the necessary grounding for probabilistic modeling of textual entailment. Since modeling the full extent of the textual entailment problem is clearly a long term research goal, in this paper we rather focus on the above mentioned subtask of *lexical entailment* - identifying when the lexical elements of a textual hypothesis are inferred from a given text.

To model lexical entailment we first assume that the meaning of each individual content word $u$ in a hypothesis can be assigned a truth value. One possible interpretation for such truth values is that lexical concepts are assigned existential meanings. For example, for a given text $t$, $Tr_{book} = 1$ if it can be inferred in $t$'s state of affairs that a book exists. Our model does not depend on any such particular interpretation, though, as we only assume that truth values *can* be assigned for lexical items but do not explicitly annotate or evaluate this subtask.

Given this lexically-projected setting, a hypothesis is assumed to be true if and only if all its lexical components are true as well. This captures our target perspective of lexical entailment, while not modeling here other entailment aspects. When estimating the entailment probability we assume that the truth probability of a term $u$ in a hypothesis $h$ is independent of the truth of the other terms in $h$, obtaining:

$$\begin{aligned} P(Tr_h = 1|t) &= \prod_{u \in h} P(Tr_u = 1|t) \\ P(Tr_h = 1) &= \prod_{u \in h} P(Tr_u = 1) \end{aligned} \tag{1}$$

In order to estimate $P(Tr_u = 1|t)$ for a given word $u$ and text $t = \{v_1, \ldots, v_n\}$, we further assume that the majority of the probability mass comes from a specific entailing word in $t$, allowing the following approximation:

$$P(Tr_u = 1|t) = \max_{v \in t} P(Tr_u = 1|T_v) \tag{2}$$

where $T_v$ denotes the event that a generated text contains the word $v$. This corresponds to expecting that each word in $h$ will be entailed from a specific word in $t$ (rather than from the accumulative context of $t$ as a whole). One can view Equation 2 as inducing an alignment between terms in the hypothesis and terms in the text, somewhat similar to alignment models in statistical MT (e.g. [4]).

Thus we obtain an estimate for the entailment probability based on lexical entailment probabilities from (1) and (2) as follows:

$$P(Tr_h = 1|t) = \prod_{u \in h} \max_{v \in t} P(Tr_u = 1|T_v) \tag{3}$$

### 3.1 Web-Based Estimation of Lexical Entailment Probabilities

We perform unsupervised empirical estimation of the lexical entailment probabilities, $P(Tr_u = 1|T_v)$, based on word co-occurrence frequencies from the web. Following our proposed probabilistic model (cf. Section 2.2), we assume that the web is a sample generated by a language source. Each document represents a generated text and a (hidden) possible world. Given that the possible world of the text is not observed we do not know the truth assignments of hypotheses for the observed texts. We therefore further make the simplest assumption that all hypotheses stated verbatim in a document are true and all others are false and hence $P(Tr_u = 1|T_v) \approx P(T_u|T_v)$, the probability that $u$ occurs in a text given that $v$ occurs in that text. The lexical entailment probability estimate is thus derived from (3) as follows:

$$P(Tr_h = 1|t) \approx \prod_{u \in h} \max_{v \in t} P(T_u|T_v) \tag{4}$$

The co-occurrence probabilities are easily estimated based on maximum likelihood counts:

$$P(T_u|T_v) = \frac{n_{u,v}}{n_v} \tag{5}$$

where $n_v$ is the number of documents containing word $v$ and $n_{u,v}$ is the number of documents containing both $u$ and $v$. In the experiments we obtained the corresponding counts by performing queries to a web search engine, since the majority of RTE examples were based on web snippets.

## 4 Experimental Setting

The text and hypothesis of all pairs in the RTE development and test sets were tokenized by the following simple heuristic - split at white space and remove any preceding or trailing of the following punctuation characters: ([{)]}"'`.,;:-!?. A standard stop word list was applied to remove frequent tokens. Counts were obtained using the AltaVista search engine[2], which supplies an estimate for the number of results (web-pages) for a given one or two token query.

[2] http://www.av.com/

We empirically tuned a threshold, $\lambda$, on the the estimated entailment probability to decide if entailment holds on not. For a $t-h$ pair, we tagged an example as true (i.e. entailment holds) if $p = P(Tr_h = 1|t) > \lambda$, and as false otherwise. We assigned a confidence of $p$ to the positive examples ($p > \lambda$) and a confidence of $1 - p$ to the negative ones.

The threshold was tuned on the 567 annotated text-hypothesis example pairs in the development set for optimal *confidence weighted score* (*cws*). The optimal threshold of $\lambda = 0.005$ resulted in a *cws* of 0.57 and *accuracy* of 56% on the development set. This threshold was used to tag and assign confidence scores to the 800 pairs of the test set.

## 5 Analysis and Results

The resulting accuracy on the test set was of 59% and the resulting confidence weighted score was of 0.57. Both are statistically significantly better then chance at the 0.01 level.

Table 2 lists the accuracy and cws when computed separately for each task. As can be seen by the table the system does well on the CD and MT tasks, and quite poorly (not significantly better than chance) on the RC, PP, IR and QA tasks. It seems as if the success of the system is attributed almost solely to

**Table 2.** Accuracy and cws by task

| task | accuracy | cws |
|---|---|---|
| Comparable Documents (CD) | 0.8333 | 0.8727 |
| Machine Translation (MT) | 0.5667 | 0.6052 |
| Information Extraction (IE) | 0.5583 | 0.5143 |
| Reading Comprehension (RC) | 0.5286 | 0.5142 |
| Paraphrase (PP) | 0.5200 | 0.4885 |
| Information Retrieval (IR) | 0.5000 | 0.4492 |
| Question Answering (QA) | 0.4923 | 0.3736 |

its success on the CD and MT tasks. Indeed it seems as if there is something common to these two tasks, which differentiates them from the others - in both tasks high overlap of content words (or their meanings) tends to correlate with entailment.

### 5.1 Success and Failure Cases

The system misclassified 331 out of the 800 test examples. The vast majority of these mistakes (75%) were false positives - pairs the system classified as true but were annotated as false. It is also interesting to note that the false negative errors were more common among the MT and QA tasks while the false positive errors were more typical to the other tasks. An additional observation from the recall-precision curve (Figure 3) is that high system confidence actually

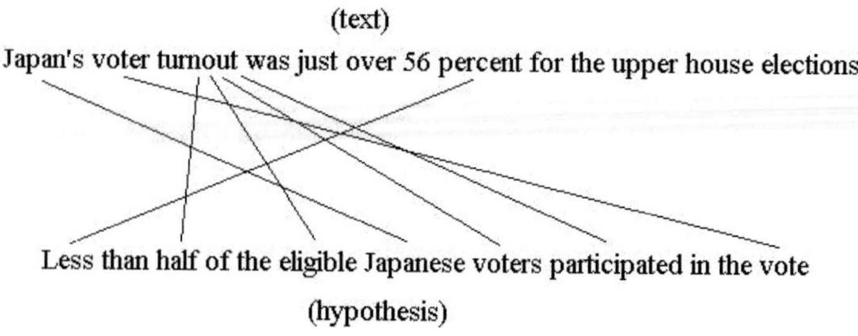


**Fig. 1.** System's underlying alignment for example 1026 (RC). gold standard - false, system - false.

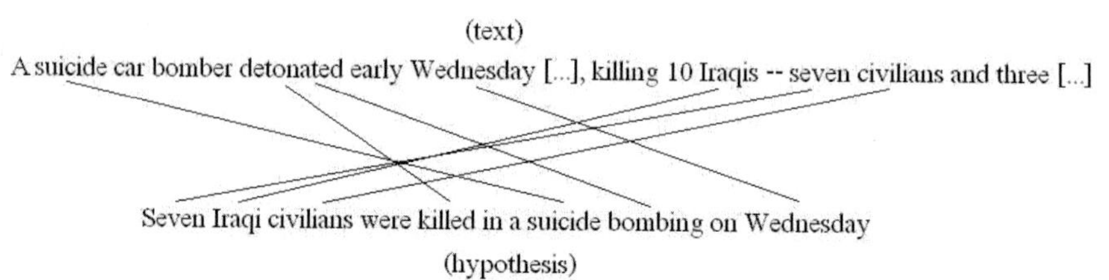

(text)
A suicide car bomber detonated early Wednesday [...], killing 10 Iraqis -- seven civilians and three [...]
Seven Iraqi civilians were killed in a suicide bombing on Wednesday
(hypothesis)


**Fig. 2.** System's underlying alignment for example 1095 (RC). gold standard - true, system - true.

corresponds to false entailment. This is attributed to an artifact of this dataset by which examples with high word overlap between the text and hypothesis tend to be biased to negative examples (see [8]).

In an attempt to 'look under the hood' we examined the underlying alignment obtained by our system on a sample of examples. Figure 1 illustrates a typical alignment. Though some of the entailing words correspond to what we believe to be the correct alignment (e.g. voter → vote, Japan's → Japanese), the system also finds many dubious lexical pairs (e.g. turnout → half, percent → less).

Furthermore, the induced alignments do not always correspond to the "expected" alignment. For example, in Figure 2 - based on the web co-occurrence statistics, *detonated* is a better trigger word for both *killed* and *bombing* even though one would expect to align them with the words *killing* and *bomber* respectively. Obviously, co-occurrence within documents is only one factor in estimating the entailment between words. This information should be combined with other statistical criteria that capture complementary notions of entailment, such as lexical distributional evidence as addressed in ([9], [10], [11]), or with lexical resources such as WordNet ([17]).

### 5.2 Comparison to Baseline

As a baseline model for comparison we use a heuristic score proposed within the context of text summarization and Question Answering ([18], [20]). In this score semantic overlap between two texts is modeled via a word overlap measure,

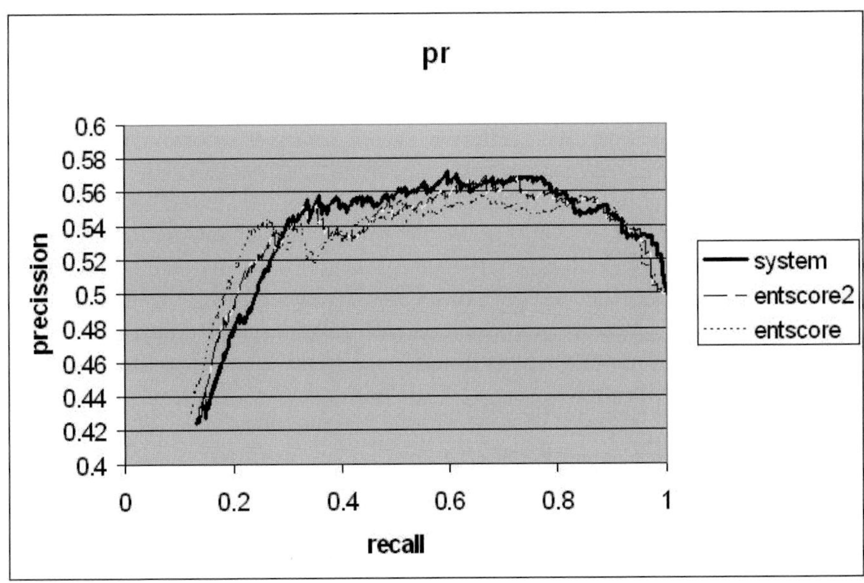


**Fig. 3.** Comparison to baselines (*system* refers to our probabilistic model)

considering only words that appear in both texts weighted by *inverse document frequency* (*idf*). More concretely, this directional entailment score between two texts, denoted here by $entscore(t,h)$, is defined as follows:

$$entscore(t,h) = \frac{\sum_{w \in t \wedge h} idf(w)}{\sum_{w \in h} idf(w)} \tag{6}$$

where $idf(w) = log(N/n_w)$, $N$ is the total number of documents in the corpus and $n_w$ the number of documents containing word $w$. We have tested the performance of this measure in predicting entailment on the RTE dataset. Tuning the classification threshold on the development set (as done for our system), *entscore* obtained a somewhat lower accuracy of 56%.

To further investigate the contribution of the co-occurrence probabilities we extended the *entscore* measure by incorporating lexical co-occurrence probabilities in a somewhat analogous way to their utilization in our model. In this extended measure, termed $entscore_2$, we compute a weighted average of the lexical probabilities, rather than their product in our model (Equation 3), where the weights are the *idf* values, following the rational of the *entscore* measure. More concretely, $entscore_2$ is defined as follows:

$$entscore_2(t,h) = \frac{\sum_{u \in h} idf(u) * max_{v \in t} P(Tr_u = 1|v)}{\sum_{u \in h} idf(u)} \tag{7}$$

$P(Tr_u = 1|v)$ is approximated by $P(T_u|T_v)$ and estimated via co-occurrence counts, as in our model (equations 4 and 5). Note that when using this approximation, $P(Tr_u = 1|v) = 1$ when $u = v$ and thus the max value in (7) is obtained as 1 for hypothesis words that appear also in the text, naturally extending the rational of *entscore*.

Figure 3 compares the recall-precision curves for our system and the two baseline entailment scores. The different recall points are obtained by varying a threshold over the entailment score (or probability), considering all examples with a score higher than the threshold as positive classifications. The figures show that on this dataset our system has higher precision over most recall ranges. [3] In addition, $entscore_2$, which incorporates lexical co-occurrence probabilities, performs somewhat better than the baseline *entscore* which considers only literal lexical overlap. These results demonstrate the marginal contribution of (i) utilizing lexical co-occurrence probabilities and (ii) embedding them within a principled probabilistic model.

### 5.3 Working at the Lexical Level

The proposed lexical model is quite simple and makes many obviously wrong assumptions. Some of these issues were addressed in another work by the authors ([12]), which was tested in a different setting. That model views lexical entailment as a text classification task. Entailment is derived from the entire context in the sentence (rather than word-to-word alignment) and Naïve Bayes classification is applied in an unsupervised setting to estimate the hidden lexical truth assignments. It would be interesting for future work to thoroughly compare and possibly combine the two models and thus capture entailment from a specific text term as well as the impact of the entire context within the given text.

Clearly, there is an upper bound of performance one would expect from a system working at the lexical level (see the analysis in [2]). Incorporating additional linguistic levels into the probabilistic entailment model, such as syntactic matching, co-reference resolution and word sense disambiguation, becomes a challenging target for future research.

## 6 Related Work

Modeling semantic overlap between texts is a common problem in NLP applications. Many techniques and heuristics were applied within various applications to model such relations between text segments. Within the context of Multi Document Summarization, [18] propose modeling the directional entailment between two texts $t$, $h$ via the entailment score of Equation 6 to identify redundant information appearing in different texts. A practically equivalent measure was independently proposed in the context of QA in [20]. This baseline measure captures word overlap, considering only words that appear in both texts and weighs them based on their inverse document frequency.

[3] Note the anomaly that high lexical overlap, which yields high system confidence, actually correlates with false entailment (as noted in [8]). This anomaly explains the poor precision of all systems at the lower recall ranges, while the generally more accurate models are effected more strongly by this anomaly.

Different techniques and heuristics were applied on the RTE-1 dataset to specifically model textual entailment. Interestingly, a number of works (e.g. [3], [6], [14]) applied or utilized a lexical based word overlap measure similar to Equation 7. The measures vary in the word-to-word similarity used and the weighting scheme. Distributional similarity (such as [16]) and WordNet based similarity measures (such as [15]) were applied. In addition, the different works vary in the preprocessing done (tokenization, lemmatization, etc.) and in the corpora used to collect statistics. For this reason it is difficult to compare the performance of the different measure variants of different systems. Nevertheless the reported results were all comparable, which may suggest that these lexical techniques are somewhat close to exhausting the potential of lexical based systems.

## 7 Conclusions

This paper described the Bar-Ilan system participating in the First Recognising Textual Entailment Challenge. We proposed a general probabilistic setting that formalizes the notion of textual entailment. In addition we described an alignment-based model in a bag of words representation for lexical entailment, which was applied using web co-occurrence statistics. Although our proposed lexical system is relatively simple, as it does not rely on syntactic or other deeper analysis, it nevertheless achieved competitive results. These results may suggest that the proposed probabilistic framework is a promising basis for improved implementations that would incorporate deeper types of information.

## Acknowledgments

This work was supported in part by the IST Programme of the European Community, under the *PASCAL Network of Excellence*, IST-2002-506778. This publication only reflects the authors' views.

## References

1. Bacchus, F.: Representing and Reasoning with Probabilistic Knowledge, M.I.T. Press (1990).
2. Bar-Haim, R., Szpektor, I., Glickman O.: Definition and Analysis of Intermediate Entailment Levels. ACL-05 Workshop on Empirical Modeling of Semantic Equivalence and Entailment. (2005)
3. Bos, J., Markert, K.: Recognising Textual Entailment with Robust Logical Inference. This Volume.
4. Brown, P.F., Della Pietra, V.J., Della Pietra, S.A., Mercer, R.L.: The Mathematics of Statistical Machine Translation: Parameter Estimation. Computational Linguistics, 19(2):263-311 (1993).
5. Chierchia, G., McConnell-Ginet, S.: Meaning and grammar: An introduction to semantics, 2nd. edition. Cambridge, MA: MIT Press (2001).
6. Corley, C., Mihalcea, R.: Measuring the Semantic Similarity of Texts. ACL 2005 Workshop on Empirical Modeling of Semantic Equivalence and Entailment.

7. Dagan, I., Glickman, O.: Probabilistic Textual Entailment: Generic Applied Modeling of Language Variability. PASCAL workshop on Learning Methods for Text Understanding and Mining (2004).
8. Dagan, I., Glickman, O., Magnini, B.: The PASCAL Recognising Textual Entailment Challenge. This Volume.
9. Geffet, M., Dagan, I.: Feature Vector Quality and Distributional Similarity. Coling 2004.
10. Geffet, M., Dagan, I.: The Distributional Inclusion Hypotheses and Lexical Entailment. ACL 2005.
11. Glickman, O., Dagan, I.: Identifying Lexical Paraphrases From a Single Corpus: A Case Study for Verbs. Recent Advantages in Natural Language Processing (RANLP). 2003.
12. Glickman, O., Dagan, I., Koppel, M.: A Probabilistic Classification Approach for Lexical Textual Entailment, Twentieth National Conference on Artificial Intelligence (AAAI) 2005.
13. Halpern, J.Y.: An analysis of first-order logics of probability. Artificial Intelligence 46:311-350 (1990).
14. Jijkoun, V., de Rijke, M.: Recognizing Textual Entailment: Is Lexical Similarity Enough?. This Volume.
15. Leacock, C., Chodorow, M., and Miller, G.: Using corpus statistics and wordnet relations for sense disambiguation. Computational Linguistics 24, 1 1998, 147–165.
16. Lin, D.: Automatic Retrieval and Clustering of Similar Words. COLING-ACL, 1998.
17. Miller, G., A.: WordNet: A Lexical Databases for English. CACM, 38(11):39–41, 1995.
18. Monz, C., de Rijke, M.: Light-Weight Entailment Checking for Computational Semantics. In Proc. of the third workshop on inference in computational semantics (ICoS-3) (2001).
19. Ponte, J.M., Croft W.B.: A Language Modeling Approach to Information Retrieval. SIGIR conference on Research and Development in Information Retrieval (1998).
20. Saggion, H., Gaizauskas, R., Hepple, M., Roberts, I., Greenwood, M.: Exploring the Performance of Boolean Retrieval Strategies for Open Domain Question Answering. Proceedings of the Workshop on Information Retrieval for Question Answering. SIGIR 2004.

# Textual Entailment Recognition Using Inversion Transduction Grammars

Dekai Wu

Human Language Technology Center, HKUST,
Department of Computer Science, University of Science and Technology,
Clear Water Bay, Hong Kong
dekai@cs.ust.hk

**Abstract.** The PASCAL Challenge's textual entailment recognition task, or RTE, presents intriguing opportunities to test various implications of the strong language universal constraint posited by Wu's (1995, 1997) Inversion Transduction Grammar (ITG) hypothesis. The ITG Hypothesis provides a strong inductive bias, and has been repeatedly shown empirically to yield both efficiency and accuracy gains for numerous language acquisition tasks. Since the RTE challenge abstracts over many tasks, it invites meaningful analysis of the ITG Hypothesis across tasks including information retrieval, comparable documents, reading comprehension, question answering, information extraction, machine translation, and paraphrase acquisition. We investigate two new models for the RTE problem that employ simple generic Bracketing ITGs. Experimental results show that, even in the absence of any thesaurus to accommodate lexical variation between the Text and the Hypothesis strings, surprisingly strong results for a number of the task subsets are obtainable from the Bracketing ITG's structure matching bias alone.

## 1 Introduction

The *Inversion Transduction Grammar* or *ITG* formalism, which historically was developed in the context of translation and alignment, hypothesizes strong expressiveness restrictions that constrain paraphrases to vary word order only in certain allowable nested permutations of arguments—even across different languages (Wu 1997). The textual entailment recognition (RTE) challenge (Dagan *et al.*2005) provides opportunities for meaningful analysis of the ITG Hypothesis across a broad range of application domains, since alignment techniques in general (Wu 2000) appear to be highly applicable to the RTE task.

The strong inductive bias imposed by the ITG Hypothesis has been repeatedly shown empirically to yield both efficiency and accuracy gains for numerous language acquisition tasks, across a variety of language pairs and tasks. Zens and Ney (2003) show that ITG constraints yield significantly better alignment coverage than the constraints used in IBM statistical machine translation models on both German-English (Verbmobil corpus) and French-English (Canadian Hansards corpus). Zhang and Gildea (2004) find that unsupervised alignment

J. Quiñonero-Candela et al. (Eds.): MLCW 2005, LNAI 3944, pp. 299–308, 2006.

using Bracketing ITGs produces significantly lower Chinese-English alignment error rates than a syntactically supervised tree-to-string model (Yamada and Knight 2001). With regard to translation rather than alignment accuracy, Zens *et al.* (2004) show that decoding under ITG constraints yields significantly lower word error rates and BLEU scores than the IBM constraints. Zhang and Gildea (2005) obtain improved alignment by lexicalizing the ITG. Chiang (2005) and Vilar and Vidal (2005) also obtain improved alignment and translation performance by imposing ITG constraints on their models.

The present studies on the RTE challenge are motivated by the following observation: the empirically demonstrated suitability of ITG paraphrasing constraints across languages should hold, if anything, even more strongly in the monolingual case.

The simplest class of ITGs, *Bracketing ITGs*, are particularly interesting in applications like the RTE challenge, because they impose ITG constraints in language-independent fashion, and in the simplest case do not require any language-specific linguistic grammar or training. In Bracketing ITGs, the grammar uses only a single, undifferentiated non-terminal (Wu 1995a). The key modeling property of Bracketing ITGs that is most relevant to the RTE challenge is that they assign strong preference to candidate Text-Hypothesis pairs in which nested constituent subtrees can be recursively aligned with a minimum of constituent boundary violations. Unlike language-specific linguistic approaches, however, the shape of the trees are driven in unsupervised fashion by the data. One way to view this is that the trees are hidden explanatory variables. This not only provides significantly higher robustness than more highly constrained manually constructed grammars, but also makes the model widely applicable across languages in economical fashion without a large investment in manually constructed resources.

Formally, ITGs can be defined as the restricted subset of syntax-directed transduction grammars or SDTGs (Lewis and Stearns 1968) where all of the rules are either of *straight* or *inverted* orientation. Ordinary SDTGs allow any permutation of the symbols on the right-hand side to be specified when translating from the input language to the output language. In contrast, ITGs only allow two out of the possible permutations. If a rule is straight, the order of its right-hand symbols must be the same for both language. On the other hand, if a rule is inverted, then the order is left-to-right for the input language and right-to-left for the output language. Since inversion is permitted at any level of rule expansion, a derivation may intermix productions of either orientation within the parse tree. The ability to compose multiple levels of straight and inverted constituents gives ITGs much greater expressiveness than might seem at first blush.

Moreover, for reasons discussed by Wu (1997), ITGs possess an interesting intrinsic combinatorial property of permitting roughly up to four arguments of any frame to be transposed freely, but not more. This matches suprisingly closely the preponderance of linguistic verb frame theories from diverse linguistic traditions that all allow up to four arguments per frame. Again, this property emerges naturally from ITGs in language-independent fashion, without any hardcoded language-specific knowledge. This further suggests that ITGs should do well at picking out Text-Hypothesis pairs where the order of up to four arguments per frame may vary freely between the two strings. Conversely, ITGs should do well at rejecting pairs where (1) too many words in one sentence find no correspondence in the other, (2) frames do not nest in similar ways in the candidate sentence pair, or (3) too many arguments must be transposed to achieve an alignment—all of which would suggest that the sentences probably express different ideas.

As an illustrative example, in common similarity models, the following pair of sentences (found in actual data arising in our experiments below) would receive an inappropriately high score, because of the high lexical similarity between the two sentences:

Chinese president Jiang Zemin arrived in Japan today for a landmark state visit .

江泽民 将 是 到 日本 做 国事访问 的 首位 中国 国家 主席 .
*(Jiang Zemin will be the first Chinese national president to pay a state vist to Japan.)*

However, the ITG based model is sensitive enough to the differences in the constituent structure (reflecting underlying differences in the predicate argument structure) so that it assigns a low score, according to our experiments. On the other hand, the experiments also show that it successfully assigns a high score to other candidate bi-sentences representing a true Chinese translation of the same English sentence, as well as a true English translation of the same Chinese sentence.

We investigate two new models for the RTE problem that employ simple generic Bracketing ITGs, both with and without a stoplist. The experimental results show that, even in the absence of any thesaurus to accommodate lexical variation between the Text and the Hypothesis strings, surprisingly strong results for a number of the task subsets are obtainable from the Bracketing ITG's structure matching bias alone.

## 2 Scoring Method

Each Text-Hypothesis pair of the test set was scored via the ITG biparsing algorithm described in Wu and Fung (2005) which is essentially similar to the dynamic programming approach of Wu (1997), as follows.

Note that all words of the vocabulary are included among the lexical transductions, allowing exact word matches between the two strings of any candidate paraphrase pair. No other lexical similarity model was used in these experiments, which allows us to study the effects of the ITG bias independently of lexical similarity models.

Let the input English sentence be $\mathbf{e}_1, \ldots, \mathbf{e}_T$ and the corresponding input Chinese sentence be $\mathbf{c}_1, \ldots, \mathbf{c}_V$. As an abbreviation we write $\mathbf{e}_{s..t}$ for the sequence of words $\mathbf{e}_{s+1}, \mathbf{e}_{s+2}, \ldots, \mathbf{e}_t$, and similarly for $\mathbf{c}_{u..v}$; also, $\mathbf{e}_{s..s} = \epsilon$ is the empty string. It is convenient to use a 4-tuple of the form $q = (s, t, u, v)$ to identify each node of the parse tree, where the substrings $\mathbf{e}_{s..t}$ and $\mathbf{c}_{u..v}$ both derive from the node $q$. Denote the nonterminal label on $q$ by $\ell(q)$. Then for any node $q = (s, t, u, v)$, define

$$\delta_q(i) = \delta_{stuv}(i) = \max_{\text{subtrees of} q} P[\text{subtree of } q, \ell(q) = i, i \stackrel{*}{\Rightarrow} \mathbf{e}_{s..t}/\mathbf{c}_{u..v}]$$

as the maximum probability of any derivation from $i$ that successfully parses both $\mathbf{e}_{s..t}$ and $\mathbf{c}_{u..v}$. Then the best parse of the sentence pair has probability $\delta_{0,T,0,V}(\mathrm{S})$.

The algorithm computes $\delta_{0,T,0,V}(\mathrm{S})$ using the following recurrences. Note that we generalize argmax to the case where maximization ranges over multiple indices, by making it vector-valued. Also note that $[]$ and $\langle\rangle$ are simply constants, written mnemonically; they represent *straight* and *inverted*, the two permutations allowed by ITGs. The condition $(S - s)(t - S) + (U - u)(v - U) \neq 0$ is a way to specify that the substring in one but not both languages may be split into an empty string $\epsilon$ and the substring itself; this ensures that the recursion terminates, but permits words that have no match in the other language to map to an $\epsilon$ instead.

1. *Initialization*

$$\delta_{t-1,t,v-1,v}(i) = b_i(\mathbf{e}_t/\mathbf{c}_v), \qquad \begin{matrix} 1 \le t \le T \\ 1 \le v \le V \end{matrix}$$

$$\delta_{t-1,t,v,v}(i) = b_i(\mathbf{e}_t/\epsilon), \qquad \begin{matrix} 1 \le t \le T \\ 0 \le v \le V \end{matrix}$$

$$\delta_{t,t,v-1,v}(i) = b_i(\epsilon/\mathbf{c}_v), \qquad \begin{matrix} 0 \le t \le T \\ 1 \le v \le V \end{matrix}$$

2. *Recursion.* For all $i, s, t, u, v$ such that $\left\{ \begin{smallmatrix} 1 \le i \le N \\ 0 \le s < t \le T \\ 0 \le u < v \le V \\ t-s+v-u > 2 \end{smallmatrix} \right.$

$$\delta_{stuv}(i) = \max[\delta^{[]}_{stuv}(i), \delta^{\langle\rangle}_{stuv}(i)]$$

$$\theta_{stuv}(i) = \begin{cases} [] \text{ if } \delta^{[]}_{stuv}(i) \ge \delta^{\langle\rangle}_{stuv}(i) \\ \langle\rangle \text{ otherwise} \end{cases}$$

where

$$\delta^{[]}_{stuv}(i) = \max_{\substack{1 \le j \le N \\ 1 \le k \le N \\ s \le S \le t \\ u \le U \le v \\ (S-s)(t-S)+(U-u)(v-U) \ne 0}} a_{i \to [jk]}\, \delta_{sSuU}(j)\, \delta_{StUv}(k)$$

$$\begin{bmatrix} \iota^{[]}_{stuv}(i) \\ \kappa^{[]}_{stuv}(i) \\ \sigma^{[]}_{stuv}(i) \\ \upsilon^{[]}_{stuv}(i) \end{bmatrix} = \operatorname*{argmax}_{\substack{1\le j\le N \\ 1\le k\le N \\ s\le S\le t \\ u\le U\le v \\ (S-s)(t-S)+(U-u)(v-U)\neq 0}} a_{i\to[jk]}\, \delta_{sSuU}(j)\, \delta_{StUv}(k)$$

$$\delta^{\langle\rangle}_{stuv}(i) = \max_{\substack{1\le j\le N \\ 1\le k\le N \\ s\le S\le t \\ u\le U\le v \\ (S-s)(t-S)+(U-u)(v-U)\neq 0}} a_{i\to\langle jk\rangle}\, \delta_{sSUv}(j)\, \delta_{StuU}(k)$$

$$\begin{bmatrix} \iota^{\langle\rangle}_{stuv}(i) \\ \kappa^{\langle\rangle}_{stuv}(i) \\ \sigma^{\langle\rangle}_{stuv}(i) \\ \upsilon^{\langle\rangle}_{stuv}(i) \end{bmatrix} = \operatorname*{argmax}_{\substack{1\le j\le N \\ 1\le k\le N \\ s\le S\le t \\ u\le U\le v \\ (S-s)(t-S)+(U-u)(v-U)\neq 0}} a_{i\to\langle jk\rangle}\, \delta_{sSUv}(j)\, \delta_{StuU}(k)$$

3. *Reconstruction.* Initialize by setting the root of the parse tree to $q_1=(0,T,0,V)$ and its nonterminal label to $\ell(q_1) = \mathrm{S}$. The remaining descendants in the optimal parse tree are then given recursively for any $q = (s,t,u,v)$ by:

$$\textsc{Left}(q) = \begin{cases} \text{NIL} & \text{if } t-s+v-u\le 2 \\ (s, \sigma^{[]}_q(\ell(q)), u, \upsilon^{[]}_q(\ell(q))) & \text{if } \theta_q(\ell(q)) = [] \\ (s, \sigma^{\langle\rangle}_q(\ell(q)), \upsilon^{\langle\rangle}_q(\ell(q))) & \text{if } \theta_q(\ell(q)) = \langle\rangle \end{cases}$$

$$\textsc{Right}(q) = \begin{cases} \text{NIL} & \text{if } t-s+v-u\le 2 \\ (\sigma^{[]}_q(\ell(q)), t, \upsilon^{[]}_q(\ell(q)), v) & \text{if } \theta_q(\ell(q)) = [] \\ (\sigma^{\langle\rangle}_q(\ell(q)), t, u, \upsilon^{\langle\rangle}_q(\ell(q))) & \text{if } \theta_q(\ell(q)) = \langle\rangle \end{cases}$$

$$\ell(\textsc{Left}(q)) = \iota_q^{\theta_q(\ell(q))}(\ell(q))$$

$$\ell(\textsc{Right}(q)) = \kappa_q^{\theta_q(\ell(q))}(\ell(q))$$

As mentioned earlier, biparsing for ITGs can be accomplished efficiently in polynomial time, rather than the exponential time required for classical SDTGs. The result in Wu (1997) implies that for the special case of Bracketing ITGs, the time complexity of the algorithm is $\Theta\left(T^3V^3\right)$ where $T$ and $V$ are the lengths of the two sentences. This is a factor of $V^3$ more than monolingual chart parsing, but has turned out to remain quite practical for corpus analysis, where parsing need not be real-time.

The ITG scoring model can also be seen as a variant of the approach described by Leusch *et al.* (2003), which allows us to forego training to estimate true probabilities; instead, rules are simply given unit weights (with caveats discussed in the Results section). The ITG scores can be interpreted as a generalization of classical Levenshtein string edit distance, where inverted block transpositions are also allowed. Even without probability estimation, Leusch *et al.* found excellent correlation with human judgment of similarity between translated paraphrases.

## 3 Experimental Method

We evaluated two different versions of the Bracketing ITG based RTE models.

In the basic version, all words of the vocabulary are included among the lexical transductions, allowing exact word matches between the Text and the Hypothesis.

The second version excludes a list of 172 words from a stoplist from the lexical transductions. The motivation for this model was to discount the effect of words such as "the" or "of" since, more often than not, they could be irrelevant to the RTE task. Negation words such as "not" were excluded from the stoplist, since they often critically determine whether entailment is true or false.

No significant training was performed with the available development sets. Rather, the aim was to establish foundational baseline results, to see in this first round of RTE experiments what results could be obtained with the simplest versions of the ITG models.

The RTE test set consists of 800 Text-Hypothesis string pairs, selected from various sources by human collectors. Each string pair is labeled according to the task category that the data was drawn from. These labels divide the data into seven task subsets, which we analyze individually below. While the collectors were attempting to build a representative dataset, it is difficult to make claims about distributional neutrality, due to the arbitrary nature of the example selection process.

## 4 Results

Across all subsets overall, the basic model produced a confidence-weighted score of 54.97% (better than chance at the 0.05 level). All examples were labeled, so precision, recall, and f-score are equivalent; the accuracy was 51.25%.

Surprisingly, the stoplisted model produced worse results. The overall confidence-weighted score was 53.61%, and the accuracy was 50.50%. We discuss the reasons below in the context of specific subsets.

As one might expect, the Bracketing ITG models performed better on the subsets more closely approximating the tasks for which Bracketing ITGs were designed: comparable documents (CD), paraphrasing (PP), and information extraction (IE). We will discuss some important caveats on the machine translation (MT) and reading comprehension (RC) subsets. The subsets least close to the Bracketing ITG models are information retrieval (IR) and question answering (QA).

### 4.1 Comparable Documents (CD)

The CD task definition can essentially be characterized as recognition of noisy word-aligned sentence pairs. Among all subsets, CD is perhaps closest to the noisy word alignment task for which Bracketing ITGs were originally developed, and indeed produced the best results for both of the Bracketing ITG models. The basic model produced a confidence-weighted score of 79.88% (accuracy 71.33%), while the stoplisted model produced an essentially unchanged confidence-weighted score of 79.83% (accuracy 70.00%).

The results on the RTE Challenge datasets closely reflect the larger-scale findings of Wu and Fung (2005), who demonstrate that an ITG based model yields far more accurate extraction of parallel sentences from quasi-comparable non-parallel corpora than previous state-of-the-art methods. Wu and Fung's results also use the evaluation metric of uninterpolated average precision (i.e., confidence-weighted score).

Note also that we believe the results here are artificially lowered by the absence of any thesaurus, and that significantly further improvements would be seen with the addition of a suitable thesaurus, for reasons discussed below under the MT subsection.

### 4.2 Paraphrase Acquisition (PP)

The PP task is also close to the task for which Bracketing ITGs were originally developed. For the PP task, the basic model produced a confidence-weighted score of 57.26% (accuracy 56.00%), while the stoplisted model produced a lower confidence-weighted score of 51.65% (accuracy 52.00%). Unlike the CD task, the greater importance of function words in determining equivalent meaning between paraphrases appears to cause the degradation in the stoplisted model.

The effect of the absence of a thesaurus is much stronger for the PP task as opposed to the CD task. Inspection of the datasets reveals much more lexical variation between paraphrases, and shows that cases where lexis does not vary are generally handled accurately by the Bracketing ITG models. The MT subsection below discusses why a thesaurus should produce significant improvement.

### 4.3 Information Extraction (IE)

The IE task presents a slight issue of misfit for the Bracketing ITG models, but yielded good results anyhow. The basic Bracketing ITG model attempts to align all words/collocations between the two strings. However, for the IE task in general, only a substring of the Text should be aligned to the Hypothesis, and the rest should be disregarded as "noise". We approximated this by allowing words to be discarded from the Text at little cost, by using parameters that impose only a small penalty on null-aligned words from the Text. (As a reasonable first approximation, this characterization of the IE task ignores the possibility of modals, negation, quotation, and the like in the Text.)

Despite the slight modeling misfit, the Bracketing ITG models produced good results for the IE subset. The basic model produced a confidence-weighted score of 59.92% (accuracy 55.00%), while the stoplisted model produced a lower confidence-weighted score of 53.63% (accuracy 51.67%). Again, the lower score of the stoplisted model appears to arise from the greater importance of function words in ensuring correct information extraction, as compared with the CD task.

### 4.4 Machine Translation (MT)

One exception to expectations is the machine translation subset, a task for which Bracketing ITGs were developed. The basic model produced a confidence-weighted score of 34.30% (accuracy 40.00%), while the stoplisted model produced a comparable confidence-weighted score of 35.96% (accuracy 39.17%).

However, the performance here on the machine translation subset cannot be directly interpreted, for two reasons.

First, the task as defined in the RTE Challenge datasets is not actually crosslingual machine translation, but rather evaluation of monolingual comparability between an automatic translation and a gold standard human translation. This is in fact closer to the problem of defining a good MT evaluation metric, rather than MT itself. Leusch *et al.* (2003 and personal communication) found that Bracketing ITGs as an MT evaluation metric show excellent correlation with human judgments.

Second, no translation lexicon or equivalent was used in our model. Normally in translation models, including ITG models, the translation lexicon accommodates lexical ambiguity, by providing multiple possible lexical choices for each word or collocation being translated. Here, there is no second language, so some substitute mechanism to accommodate lexical ambiguity would be needed.

The most obvious substitute for a translation lexicon would be a monolingual thesaurus. This would allow matching synonomous words or collocations between the Text and the Hypothesis. Our original thought was to incorporate such a thesaurus in collaboration with teams focusing on creating suitable thesauri, but time limitations prevented completion of these experiments. Based on our own prior experiments and also on Leusch *et al.*'s experiences, we believe this would bring performance on the MT subset to excellent levels as well.

### 4.5 Reading Comprehension (RC)

The reading comprehension task is similar to the information extraction task. As such, the Bracketing ITG model could be expected to perform well for the RC subset. However, the basic model produced a confidence-weighted score of just 49.37% (accuracy 47.14%), and the stoplisted model produced a comparable confidence-weighted score of 47.11% (accuracy 45.00%).

The primary reason for the performance gap between the RC and IE domains appears to be that RC is less news-oriented, so there is less emphasis on exact lexical choices such as named entities. This puts more weight on the importance of a good thesaurus to recognize lexical variation. For this reason, we believe the addition of a thesaurus would bring performance improvements similar to the case of MT.

### 4.6 Information Retrieval (IR)

The IR task diverges significantly from the tasks for which Bracketing ITGs were developed. The basic model produced a confidence-weighted score of 43.14% (accuracy 46.67%), while the stoplisted model produced a comparable confidence-weighted score of 44.81% (accuracy 47.78%).

Bracketing ITGs seek structurally parallelizable substrings, where there is reason to expect some degree of generalization between the frames (heads and arguments) of the two substrings from a lexical semantics standpoint. In contrast, the IR task relies on unordered keywords, so the effect of argument-head binding cannot be expected to be strong.

### 4.7 Question Answering (QA)

The QA task is extremely free in the sense that questions can differ significantly from the answers in both syntactic structure and lexis, and can also require a significant degree of indirect complex inference using real-world knowledge. The basic model produced a confidence-weighted score of 33.20% (accuracy 40.77%), while the stoplisted model produced a significantly better confidence-weighted score of 38.26% (accuracy 44.62%).

Aside from adding a thesaurus, to properly model the QA task, at the very least the Bracketing ITG models would need to be augmented with somewhat more linguistic rules that include a proper model for *wh-* words in the Hypothesis, which otherwise cannot be aligned to the Text. In the Bracketing ITG models, the stoplist appears to help by normalizing out the effect of the *wh-* words.

## 5 Conclusion

We have reported results and analysis on our preliminary round of experiments using two simple Bracketing ITG models on the RTE datasets.

What we find highly interesting is the perhaps surprisingly large effect obtainable from this structure matching bias alone, which already produces good results on a number of the subsets—especially on the IE subtask, which appeared from the results to be the hardest of the seven subtasks—even without yet incorporating any lexical similarity or thesaurus model into the ITG.

Clearly the most serious omission in our experiments with Bracketing ITG models was the absence of any lexical similarity model, allowing zero lexical variation between the Text and Hypothesis. This forced the models to rely entirely on the Bracketing ITG's inherent tendency to optimize structural match between hypothesized nested argument-head substructures. We plan to remedy the absence of a thesaurus as the obvious next step. This could be expected to raise performance significantly on all subsets.

Wu and Fung (2005) also discuss how to obtain any desired tradeoff between precision and recall. This would be another interesting direction to pursue in the context of recognizing textual entailment.

Finally, using the development sets to train the parameters of the Bracketing ITG model via expectation-maximization would improve performance Wu (1995b). It would only be feasible to tune a few basic parameters, however, given the small size of the development sets.

**Acknowledgment.** The author would like to thank the Hong Kong Research Grants Council (RGC) for supporting this research in part through grants

RGC6083/99E, RGC6256/00E, and DAG03/04.EG09, and Marine Carpuat and Yihai Shen for invaluable assistance in preparing the datasets and stoplist.

## References

David Chiang: A hierarchical phrase-based model for statistical machine translation. In: 43rd Annual Meeting of the Association for Computational Linguistics (ACL-2005), Ann Arbor (2005) 263–270

Ido Dagan, Oren Glickman, and Bernardo Magnini: The PASCAL Recognising Textual Entailment Challenge. In: PASCAL Challenges Workshop on Recognising Textual Entailment, Southampton, UK (2005)

Gregor Leusch, Nicola Ueffing, and Hermann Ney: A novel string-to-string distance measure with applications to machine translation evaluation. In: Machine Translation Summit, New Orleans (2003)

P. M. Lewis and R. E. Stearns: Syntax-directed transduction. Journal of the Association for Computing Machinery **15** (1968) 465–488

Juan Miguel Vilar and Enrique Vidal: A recursive statistical translation model. In: ACL-2005 Workshop on Building and Using Parallel Texts, Ann Arbor (2005) 199–207

Dekai Wu: An algorithm for simultaneously bracketing parallel texts by aligning words. In: 33rd Annual Meeting of the Association for Computational Linguistics Conference (ACL-95), Cambridge, MA, Association for Computational Linguistics (1995)

Dekai Wu: Trainable coarse bilingual grammars for parallel text bracketing. In: 3rd Annual Workshop on Very Large Corpora (WVLC-3), Cambridge, MA (1995) 69–81 Also in Susan Armstrong, Kenneth W. Church, Pierre Isabelle, Sandra Manzi, Evelyne Tzoukermann, and David Yarowsky (editors), Natural Language Processing Using Very Large Corpora. Dordrecht: Kluwer. ISBN 0-7923-6055-9. Nov 1999.

Dekai Wu: Stochastic inversion transduction grammars and bilingual parsing of parallel corpora. Computational Linguistics **23** (1997)

Dekai Wu: Alignment. In Dale, R., Moisl, H., Somers, H., eds.: Handbook of Natural Language Processing. Marcel Dekker, New York (2000) 415–458

Dekai Wu and Pascale Fung: Inversion transduction grammar constraints for mining parallel sentences from quasi-comparable corpora. In: Second International Joint Conference on Natural Language Processing (IJCNLP-2005), Jeju, Korea (2005)

Kenji Yamada and Kevin Knight: A syntax-based statistical translation model. In: 39th Annual Meeting of the Association for Computational Linguistics Conference (ACL-01), Toulouse, France, Association for Computational Linguistics (2001)

Richard Zens and Hermann Ney: A comparative study on reordering constraints in statistical machine translation, Hong Kong (2003) 192–202

Richard Zens, Hermann Ney, Taro Watanabe, and Eiichiro Sumita: Reordering constraints for phrase-based statistical machine translation. In: Proceedings of COLING, Geneva (2004)

Hao Zhang and Daniel Gildea: Syntax-based alignment: Supervised or unsupervised? In: Proceedings of COLING, Geneva (2004)

Hao Zhang and Daniel Gildea: Stochastic lexicalized inversion transduction grammar for alignment. In: 43rd Annual Meeting of the Association for Computational Linguistics (ACL-2005), Ann Arbor (2005) 475–482

# Evaluating Semantic Evaluations: How RTE Measures Up

Sam Bayer, John Burger, Lisa Ferro, John Henderson, Lynette Hirschman, and Alex Yeh

The MITRE Corporation, 202 Burlington Road, Bedford, MA 02144, USA
{sam, john, lferro, jhndrsn, lynette, asy}@mitre.org

**Abstract.** In this paper, we discuss paradigms for evaluating open-domain semantic interpretation as they apply to the PASCAL Recognizing Textual Entailment (RTE) evaluation (Dagan et al. 2005). We focus on three aspects critical to a successful evaluation: creation of large quantities of reasonably good training data, analysis of inter-annotator agreement, and joint analysis of test item difficulty and test-taker proficiency (Rasch analysis). We found that although RTE does not correspond to a "real" or naturally occurring language processing task, it nonetheless provides clear and simple metrics, a tolerable cost of corpus development, good annotator reliability (with the potential to exploit the remaining variability), and the possibility of finding noisy but plentiful training material.

## 1 Introduction

Our research group at MITRE has a long-term interest in development and implementation of evaluation paradigms for language processing applications, e.g., in the areas of text understanding (Hirschman 1998a; Hirschman et al. 2005), text translation (Papineni et al. 2002), speech-to-speech translation (Aberdeen et al. 2005), and spoken dialogue (Aberdeen et al. 2000; Walker et al. 2001). For the last several years, we have been exploring ways of evaluating *open-domain* semantic interpretation, focusing primarily on the paradigm of reading comprehension (Hirschman et al. 1999; Wellner et al. 2005). This exploration has led us to the Recognizing Textual Entailment (RTE) evaluation (Dagan et al. 2005) sponsored by the European Union PASCAL Network (Pattern Analysis, Statistical modeling and ComputAtional Learning). In this paper, we discuss a number of dimensions of our involvement with RTE, concentrating on its suitability and potential as an evaluation of open-domain semantic interpretation.

## 2 The Path to RTE

### 2.1 What Is RTE?

In the RTE evaluation, a system is presented with two short passages (usually, one sentence each): a premise, called the *text*, and a possible conclusion,

J. Quiñonero-Candela et al. (Eds.): MLCW 2005, LNAI 3944, pp. 309–331, 2006.

called the *hypothesis*. The system makes a binary judgment: does the text entail the hypothesis? By "entailment", RTE does not mean a strict logical proof; a certain degree of world knowledge, either factual or situational, is permitted. Nevertheless, following RTE, we use "entailment" to refer to this relation.

RTE has already generated an enormous amount of interest. Seventeen groups from three continents participated in the initial RTE 2004 evaluation, and the paradigm has already yielded a workshop at NAACL 2005 and a follow-on RTE evaluation for 2006. We believe this level of interest is well-justified, and that it demands a closer inspection of the strengths and weaknesses of the RTE evaluation.

## 2.2 What Makes a Good Evaluation?

One of the great advances in computational language processing has been the creation of carefully developed, metrics-based evaluations of language processing capabilities. RTE clearly qualifies as such an evaluation. But evaluations vary broadly in applicability, reliability, usefulness, and cost. Where does RTE stand on these criteria, and how does it compare with other open-domain evaluations which have been proposed?

Over the years, we have participated in, and helped design, many language processing evaluations. In the course of this work, we have developed a range of criteria for good evaluations. We discuss these criteria here in detail, as background for our exploration of RTE.

**Criterion 1: Realism or Applicability.** A successful language evaluation ought to have at least plausible applicability to some task of general interest to some significant set of users. A plausibly applicable task enhances the understandability of, and justification for, the evaluation for interested nontechnical observers; it raises the likelihood that the evaluation will drive applicable research; and it helps to guide the development of corpora for the evaluation. The evaluation can be applicable or "real" in a number of ways.

An end-to-end evaluation, for instance, evaluates system behavior which mimics or resembles a real application. One such evaluation is the TREC question answering (QA) evaluation, which corresponds fairly directly to a service that nontechnical users are interested in. Evaluations of system components, on the other hand, rely for their motivation on the plausible exploitation of such a component in a real application. An example of this latter type of evaluation is the evaluation of named entity identification (Sundheim 1995; Grishman and Sundheim 1995), which has been an important component of information extraction tasks.

If the application scenario is clear, the form of the corpus will be clear as well. For instance, the distribution of document types ought to mirror the distribution of document types in the actual task corpus; similarly for the density of relevant material, the difficulty of the test items, and a range of other features. On the other hand, if the application scenario is a mystery, the appropriate form of the corpus will be obscure. And while a clear application scenario certainly carries the risk of driving overly specific research, an evaluation which isn't clearly applicable carries the risk that the work it drives will not be relevant or applicable.

**Criterion 2: Clear Metrics.** The evaluation should employ easy-to-interpret (and easy-to-reproduce) evaluation metrics. The evaluation also ought to provide stable results; that is, it should be possible to compare results over time.

**Criterion 3: Cost.** A primary aspect of evaluations is their cost. These costs arise both in preparing the evaluation and in running it, and there are tradeoffs between these two costs.

In preparing the evaluation, one of the largest expenses is the cost of creating resources. For instance, the test set must be large enough to distinguish reliably among the different participating systems. It's less clear that size is important for the training and development sets; however, the ability to build corpora easily is definitely an asset for an evaluation, both for those approaches which use statistical training techniques and for those who want to apply the evaluation to a different domain. It's not always necessary for these training sets to be hand-annotated; in some cases, it might be useful to develop noisy but useful training corpora through various efficient means (see, for example, Morgan et al. (2004)). No matter what, the more expensive it is to prepare the required training and test corpora, the less data there will be. These costs may appear in several forms, e.g.: the cost of creating material *de novo*; the cost of acquiring "found" material; the cost of cleaning "found" material; and the cost of annotating material.

In running the evaluation, costs can arise in assessing the system answers. The TREC QA evaluation faces this issue (see below for a more extensive discussion). But a cost-effective evaluation might require a cost-intensive corpus, and it's important to find the appropriate balance. It's also possible that a cost-effective evaluation might not yield as much information about the systems as a more cost-intensive one. This issue of the "information gained per dollar spent" in evaluations is broad and complex, and deserves considerable further study.

**Criterion 4: Annotation Reliability.** People must be able to perform the annotation task reliably, because if people cannot agree, then there is no hope of providing consistent training data or a high-quality gold standard for evaluation. Controlled measures of inter-annotator agreement provide a good measure of task tractability and accuracy of gold-standard corpora for testing. The annotation task should also be efficient, because inefficient data preparation raises the cost (and, thus, lowers the quantity) of the data. These dimensions of reliability and efficiency are clearly related, but still distinct; a task which people can do consistently but slowly is problematic, as is a task which people can do quickly but can't agree on.

Other criteria are that the evaluation should be appropriately difficult (not too easy, not too hard) and appealing to the community (so researchers will participate and contribute shared resources); while important, these are not the focus of our paper.

Before we move our attention to RTE, it will be informative to see how these criteria are assessed for a paradigmatic example of a successful evaluation strategy: evaluating speech recognition (SR) by comparing system transcriptions to a gold standard using the metric of word error rate (WER).

- **Realism/applicability:** The SR transcription evaluation clearly applies to end-to-end tasks like dictation. It is also informative (although less so) as a component evaluation of complex systems which include SR.
- **Clear metrics:** The WER metric is easy for non-experts to understand and correlates well with comprehensibility of a transcript of spoken input, something potential end users care about.
- **Cost:** The cost of creating transcriptions is not negligible, but it can be done quite efficiently compared to other sorts of corpus creation. The real cost turns out to hinge on whether the speech corpora themselves already exist (e.g., collections of news broadcasts) or whether they must be specially collected (e.g., spontaneous human-machine interaction dialogues). In some cases, existing speech corpora have transcriptions ("found" data), but these transcriptions require significant cleaning to be useful: they may not be word-for-word, they may not spell out numbers or abbreviations, and they may have "cleaned up" disfluencies like false starts and corrections. The evaluation cost is minimal, since the WER metric can be automatically computed.
- **Annotation reliability:** Although detailed transcription requires an agreement on how to handle various disfluencies (pauses, repetitions, corrections, non-linguistic noise such as throat-clearing, etc.), it is relatively straightforward for annotators to learn, and the task is familiar to any native speaker. See Deshmukh et al. (1996) for a thorough discussion.
- **Appropriate difficulty:** Transcription evaluations have been very successful in pushing technology development forward. As WER decreased, the speech research community chose new tasks of greater difficulty in one or more dimensions: increased vocabulary, spontaneous speech vs. read speech or environments with increasing noise.
- **Community appeal:** Transcription evaluations using WER are the standard in the SR community, and have been for a number of years. An enormous number of community-created corpora are available, for a variety of scenarios (news broadcasts, spoken dialogues), and a range of languages.

With this example in mind, we turn to how we can use these criteria to assess the range of currently available open-domain semantic evaluations.

### 2.3 A Brief History of Open-Domain Semantic Evaluations

In this section, we assess three strategies for open-domain semantic evaluation: semantic interpretation matching, question answering (QA), and reading comprehension (RC). Afterward, we identify the significant questions for RTE raised by this discussion.

**Semantic Interpretation Matching.** Semantic interpretation matching refers to an evaluation strategy in which the evaluation target is some abstract representation of the meaning of the input text. This strategy has been reasonably successful in fixed domain evaluations such as event template extraction (Sundheim 1995; Grishman and Sundheim 1995) or spoken language understanding (Hirschman et al. 1993). But attempts to apply this strategy to open-domain evaluations have foundered; Grishman and Sundheim (1995) document the problems with the SemEval semantic evaluation effort, and we encountered similar difficulties in the LogicForms evaluation in Senseval-3 (Bayer et al. 2004).

The problem is the form of the evaluation target. For instance, for SR transcription evaluations, the target is the transcribed text; this target is concrete, relatively intuitive, and enjoys broad agreement among the speakers of most written languages. Open-domain semantic representations share none of these properties. First, the evaluation target is conceptually far removed from the evaluation input (i.e., speech or text). Second, while fixed domains constrain and focus the form and content of the evaluation target, an open domain does not. As a result, the range of potential variation in representation is huge, and engenders enormous (sometimes religious) debate. For the same reasons, practical questions become intractable. What are the semantic atoms? How much context do we represent? What is the syntax of the representation? Even if we were to resolve all these questions, the human annotation process for any such target would be exceptionally complex, and this complexity affects both annotation reliability and the likelihood of developing a large corpus for testing.

It appears, then, that whatever evaluation strategy we choose, it can't require this sort of abstract representation.

**Question Answering.** The question answering (QA) task addresses the representation issue. Its input is a question and a corpus of documents, and its target is in the form of language (i.e., the answer to the question). One such evaluation is the TREC QA evaluation. The answers in TREC QA are text sequences drawn from the documents in the TREC information retrieval corpus. The QA task is clearly realistic, since users search for answers in document collections all the time. The metric it uses is relatively easy to understand and reproduce. The answer assessment process for TREC QA can be expensive, because each novel system answer has to be assessed by hand; however, the assessors can reuse these assessments when another system presents the same answer, and the document collection is closed. And while there's a corresponding potential expense to providing answers to questions for a training corpus, one can easily imagine "found" sources for the questions themselves, e.g., the logs of a Web site such as AskJeeves, or of calls to a library reference desk.

In summary, while the cost of corpus creation and answer assessment is important to keep in mind, QA has a number of appealing properties as an evaluation of open-domain understanding.

**Reading Comprehension.** Our work in reading comprehension (RC), begun in 1998, was motivated by a desire to create an open-domain language understanding evaluation which addressed the issue of data cost. We hypothesized that an approach using "found" data might alleviate this problem, and so we worked to exploit existing human reading comprehension tests (Hirschman et al. 1999; Wellner et al. 2005). This sort of evaluation is now generating considerable interest in the NLP community (Brachman 2005). These tests differ from the question answering scenario in that the test taker is given the document in which to look for the answers, and the answers are guaranteed to be found in that document.

Although one motivation for using "found" RC test was to reduce corpus development costs, this benefit was complicated by two factors. First, real reading comprehension tests have significant educational and commercial value. They are closely held, sometimes so that they may be reused for subsequent generations of students, and sometimes so that the tests may be sold as practice materials to future students. Second, while we did develop and make available several reading comprehension corpora (Light et al. 2001), these required significant expense and expertise to prepare and were consequently small in scale.

The cost of running the evaluation was also a factor, since our version of the RC task required the system to produce an answer, and thus incurred some of the expense of hand assessment of the results. However, it's also possible to use multiple-choice RC tests for an evaluation like this. A multiple-choice RC test adds a significant but one-time cost of creating distractor answers, but reduces the assessment cost to zero. These tests can include "none of the above" as an option, which increases the difficulty of the test by requiring the test taker to decide not simply which answer is best, but also whether any answer is good enough.

Finally, RC doesn't really correspond to a compelling task. It's hard to imagine a circumstance when it would be relevant to quiz a computer on how well it comprehended a document or set of documents (as opposed to a task like QA, where the computer is required to "apply" its ability to comprehend). We feel this shortcoming is significant.

### 2.4 Asking Questions About RTE

Our final two criteria are not at issue here. First, the community appeal of RTE is already apparent. Second, the evaluation is difficult, but not impossible. The RTE training and test corpora were split 50/50 between true and false entailment pairs; while the highest accuracy score in the official evaluation was 59%, at least two participants reported accuracy scores above 60% in work done between the submission deadline and the workshop itself. We will not discuss these criteria further.

The remaining criteria, on the other hand, require some significant attention.

- **Realism/applicability:** Does the RTE evaluation model a "real" task or applicable component?
- **Clear metrics:** While assessing RTE results requires no human intervention, how consistently can the scores be applied?

- **Cost:** Does the binary nature of the RTE judgment lead to efficient corpus creation? Is there "found" data we can use? What is the cost of entailment pair creation?
- **Annotation reliability:** Is inter-judge agreement sufficiently high?

In the sections which follow, we address these questions. We begin with a description of our own RTE system. We chose a simple, large-corpus technique, not because we believed it would be successful, but because it provided a good basis for us to explore a range of issues related to RTE itself, specifically the cost and difficulty of creating a gold-standard corpus; the complexity of the judgment guidelines; and the potential for building noisy training corpora automatically.

We then describe development of additional training materials, based on pairs of headlines and lead paragraphs extracted from news stories. We next report our experiments on inter-annotator agreement, for both our headline corpus and the RTE corpus as a whole. We then review our analysis of task difficulty, using a Rasch analysis based on the joint assessment of test item difficulty and system performance. We conclude by returning to these four criteria as they apply to the RTE evaluation, and discuss how it compares to the other evaluations we've described.

## 3 Text Alignment and Similarity as Entailment

MITRE's primary submission to the RTE evaluation took its inspiration from statistical machine translation (SMT). We thought that it might be informative to view the RTE entailment pairs as an aligned corpus of "translations", in which entailment serves as the noisy channel instead of a mapping between languages. To be sure, we do not believe that this approach can identify legitimate entailment pairs with anything approaching reliability; in fact, as we discuss below, we were compelled to expand our range of text comparison metrics beyond alignment in order to achieve any significant results. Rather, this strategy provides a framework in which to consider the implications of large-corpus approaches to the RTE task.

SMT explicitly models the probability that a sentence in a source language will translate to a sentence in the target language. Following Brown et al. (1993), most SMT models decompose this probability into probabilities relating individual word pairs in the two sentences. There are also mechanisms in the models for explaining spurious words in the source and target, by aligning them with the null string. SMT is a large-corpus approach to machine translation, and the 567 training pairs provided by the RTE evaluation are inadequate by orders of magnitude. We addressed this issue by automatically deriving a large, noisy training corpus of 100,000 entailment pairs from newswire articles, using initial article paragraphs as RTE texts and headlines as RTE hypotheses (see the following section for a detailed discussion). For testing purposes, we hand-annotated a separate set of 1000 pairs drawn from the same corpus.

We used the GIZA++ toolkit (Och and Ney 2003) to induce alignment models from these 100,000 training pairs. Figure 1 shows one such induced alignment. Most of the source words either align with their identical counterparts or fail to align, although there are some alignments which reflect synonymy or other dimensions of relatedness: *surrounded* with *engulf*, *Bushehr* with *Iran*. Some notable word correspondences found by the model are shown in Figure 2; as the *differing/equal* pair shows, both similarity of context and similarity of meaning drive the alignment.

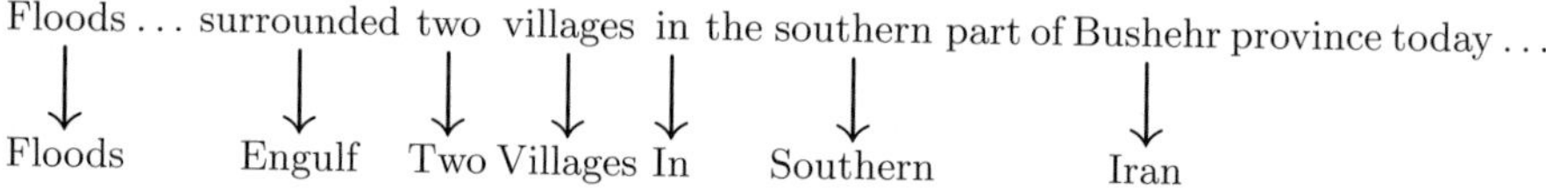


**Fig. 1.** GIZA++ alignment for an entailment training pair

| | |
|---|---|
| differing | equal |
| heroism | gallantry |
| spaceflight | spacecraft |
| railmen | railworkers |
| procrastination | timing |
| hirsute | hair |
| engulf | surround |
| outplay | defeats |
| mountaineer | climber |

**Fig. 2.** A subset of the top word alignments acquired by GIZA++

We explored three methods of applying this alignment model to the RTE task.

In the first method, we exploited the fact that the proportion of true vs. false entailment pairs in the RTE test corpus was known (namely, 50/50). We first determined the proportion of true and false pairs in our hand-annotated test set of 1000 pairs, which was 60%; this was also the base rate for the experiment, since this proportion of pairs meant that 60% accuracy should be achievable by chance. Next, we applied the alignment model to each of these 1000 pairs, ranked them by their alignment score, and used the 60% threshold as the boundary between true and false pairs in the ranking. This process assigned the correct truth value to these pairs with 80% accuracy.

Unfortunately, when we applied this model to the RTE development set, we were able to predict entailment correctly only slightly above chance. One possible reason for this discrepancy is that the non-entailing examples in our training corpus had very little word overlap, while a number of the examples in the RTE corpus were specifically designed to probe for phenomena like negation.

**Text:** Clinton's new book is not a big seller here.
**Hypothesis:** Clinton's book is a big seller.

**Text:** After trial, Family Court found defendant guilty of willfully violating the order of protection and sentenced him to six months incarceration.
**Hypothesis:** Family Court cannot punish the guilty

**Fig. 3.** Non-entailing RTE examples with high word overlap

These RTE pairs, illustrated in Figure 3, exhibit high rates of words in common, but are false.

For our subsequent approaches, we turned to `libparis` (Henderson and Morgan 2005), a library of string similarity metrics assembled by MITRE, to add more dimensions of sensitivity to the determination of entailment. Some of these metrics are inspired by MT evaluation, and some are based on standard string-matching algorithms (Gusfield 1997). We tried two ways of combining features extracted from the GIZA++ alignment models with these `libparis` metrics. We first used the SVM-light support vector machine package (Joachims 2002) to build a classifier on the RTE development data using these features, but cross-validation experiments showed this to be unpromising. For our final approach, we combined all the features using a simple k-nearest-neighbor classifier that chose, for each test pair, the dominant truth value among the five nearest neighbors in the development set (Bayer et al. 2005). Results are shown in Figure 4; as an indication of the poor performance of current systems on "real" comprehension tasks like RTE, our system was one of the highest-scoring submissions to the evaluation.

| | | |
|---|---|---|
| Pairs | | 800 |
| Correctly | T | 231/400 |
| labeled | F | 238/400 |
| Accuracy | | 0.59 |
| Precision | | 0.59 |
| Recall | | 0.58 |
| F-measure | | 0.58 |

**Fig. 4.** Alignment system results

## 4 Developing a Large Corpus of RTE Pairs

For development, the RTE organizers provided 567 exemplar sentence pairs. This quantity of exemplars is clearly inadequate for a large-corpus technique like SMT; successful SMT models are trained from a corpus which is typically larger by orders of magnitude than the RTE development set. In this section, we describe our attempt to develop a large corpus of entailment pairs.

**Text:** John murdered Bill yesterday.
**Hypothesis** (entailment): Bill is dead.
**Hypothesis** (paraphrase): Bill was killed by John.

**Fig. 5.** Contrast between entailment and paraphrase

Although RTE stands for "Recognizing Textual Entailment", the RTE development corpus exemplified a relationship between pairs which is both weaker and stronger than entailment. On the one hand, a large subset of RTE pairs exhibit plausible inference, rather than strict logical entailment; on the other hand, the overwhelming majority of the pairs illustrate a bidirectional plausible inference relation (i.e., paraphrase) between the hypothesis and a portion of the text, as illustrated in Figure 5. We found that 94% (131/140) of the true pairs in the second half of the RTE development corpus were these sorts of paraphrases.

Our challenge, then, was to find a naturally-occurring corpus which exhibits these properties, and furthermore might lend itself to automatic truth/falsity judgment at a high enough level of accuracy and purity to be useful in training a SMT model. This investigation led us fairly quickly to the relationship between news articles and their headlines. In particular, we observed that the headline of a news article is often a partial paraphrase of the lead paragraph, or is sometimes a genuine entailment, in approximately the same way the RTE data is. We thus posited that headlines and their corresponding lead paragraphs might provide a readily available source of training data. In the remainder of this section, we describe our exploration of this hypothesis.

### 4.1 Entailment Pairs in News Corpora

Because our goal was to automatically generate an extremely large corpus of exemplars, we focused on large data sources. Our first candidate was the news corpus collected by the MiTAP system (Damianos et al. 2003), which collects over one million articles per month from approximately 75 different sources. While our hand judgment of a sample of the MiTAP corpus did not yield good overall results (cf. Burger and Ferro (2005)), it was apparent that some news sources tended to be more fruitful than others. We were thus motivated to continue looking for high-quality sources.

The judgment task we defined differed slightly from the RTE task. For each article, we had a human judge determine whether the lead paragraph entailed the headline, but instead of a two-way judgment, the judge rendered a judgment of *yes*, *no*, or *maybe*, where *maybe* meant that the headline was very close to being an entailment or paraphrase. For the purposes of the RTE task, *maybe* and *no* are equivalent; however, we expected that these "near miss" pairs would be useful for our statistical training algorithms, since they represent some of the most difficult decisions. We developed a simple Web-based tool which provided transparent support for this judgment task (see Burger and Ferro (2005) for details).

After MiTAP, we turned to the Gigaword newswire corpus (Graff 2003). Gigaword contains over 4 million documents from four different news sources:

- Associated Press Worldstream English Service (APW)
- Agence France Press English Service (AFE)
- The New York Times Newswire Service (NYT)
- The Xinhua News Agency English Service (XIE)

For each source, Gigaword articles are classified into one of three types: news articles, digests of news briefs, and "other" (sports scores, stock prices, etc.). We restricted our investigations to news articles. We hand-judged 103 articles drawn from this corpus. We found that the overall distribution of judgments was very similar to those for the MiTAP corpus, but also that the Xinhua documents yielded 85% positive pairs (see Figure 6). Consequently, we chose to focus on this portion of the corpus.

| Source | Yes | No | Maybe | Total |
|---|---|---|---|---|
| APW | 8 (31%) | 12 (46%) | 6 (23%) | 26 |
| AFE | 14 (56%) | 4 (16%) | 7 (28%) | 25 |
| NYT | 8 (31%) | 17 (65%) | 1 (4%) | 26 |
| XIE | 22 (85%) | 4 (15%) | 0 (0%) | 26 |
| Total | 52 (50%) | 37 (36%) | 14 (14%) | 103 |

**Fig. 6.** Gigaword corpus results

A team of three judges tagged approximately 900 randomly selected Gigaword documents, including 520 from Xinhua. This larger tagging effort showed that an estimated 70% of the XIE headlines in Gigaword are entailed by the corresponding lead paragraph. (This is noticeably lower than our original estimate of 85%, which was based on a much smaller sample.) We hoped for a higher rate of purity, so we looked for more discriminators.

As in the MiTAP corpus, we found different rates of purity in different categories of articles. For example, articles about sports or entertainment often had whimsical (non-entailed) headlines, while articles about politics or business more frequently had the lead-entails-headline property we sought. These differences led us to use text classification techniques to try to find the mix of genres or topics that would most likely possess the lead-entails-headline property.

Once again, we employed an SVM strategy, but in this case, we used it as a document classifier rather than a pair classifier, with a goal of building a corpus of entailment pairs, rather than performing the RTE discrimination task. So in this case, we made use of the entire article and its metadata, not just the headline and lead paragraph. We experimented with a variety of feature representations and SVM parameters, but found the best performance with a Boolean bag-of-words representation, and a simple linear kernel. Leave-one-out cross-validation estimates indicate that SVM-light could identify whether documents exhibit the lead-entails-headline property with 77% accuracy. We attempted further refinements using active learning (Tong and Koller 2000), but we were not able to improve on this initial result.

To try to refine the corpus further, we ran the trained SVM on all 679,000 of the unjudged XIE documents, and selected the 100,000 instances which most strongly evinced the lead-entails-headline property, according to the SVM. This 100,000 document subset is the one we used to train our MT-alignment-based system for the RTE evaluation. We attempted to show that this subset was more "pure" than the entire XIE document set, but the sample we hand-annotated for this purpose was too small to demonstrate statistical significance. Nevertheless, it did show a suggestive improvement over the base rate. See Burger and Ferro (2005) for details.

Ultimately, we achieved our goal of developing a large, albeit noisy, training corpus for the RTE task. Our initial exploration of the MiTAP corpus suggested that it might be possible to find a source of sufficient purity, and we found such a source in the Xinhua subset of the Gigaword corpus. Although the hand-judged base rate for Xinhua was lower than our initial inspection (70% vs. 85%), and subsequent attempts to improve the purity of the corpus did not clearly succeed, the result was a corpus which exhibited the lead-entails-headline property to a significant extent.

### 4.2 Inter-judge Reliability

To determine the upper bound on system accuracy, and to evaluate the complexity and feasibility of the judgment task, we measured inter-judge reliability on both our own Gigaword corpus and the RTE development corpus.

Dagan et al. (2005) report that in preparing the RTE corpus (development and test), their two annotators achieved approximately 80% agreement. The 20% on which the annotators disagreed were discarded from the corpus, along with an additional 13% which a further review suggested might be controversial. These results align quite closely with the results from our annotation effort, although some problems remain.

For Gigaword, we added a second judge for 300 of the hand-judged XIE articles. We performed this double-judgment in two rounds, in order to assess the intuitive understandability of the task and the amount of judge training required. For the first round, an experienced judge gave a brief verbal overview of the task to a second, novice judge, and the two judges both hand-judged 100 documents. At that point, the more experienced judge reviewed the differences in judging and drafted a set of guidelines which provided a synopsis of the official RTE guidelines, plus a few rules unique to headlines (e.g., what to do when partial entailment only held if the lead were combined with location or date information from the dateline). The two judges then judged a second set of 200 articles.

As described previously, our judges rendered a judgment of *yes*, *no*, or *maybe*, where *maybe* meant that the pair did not exhibit the entailment relation, but was

| Condition | Round 1 (100 docs) | | Round 2 (200 docs) | |
|---|---|---|---|---|
| yes/yes | 54 | (54%) | 112 | (56%) |
| no/no | 20 | (20%) | 31 | (15.5%) |
| maybe/maybe | 1 | (1%) | 14 | (7%) |
| no/maybe | 9 | (9%) | 5 | (2.5%) |
| RTE agreement (maybe=no) | 84 | (84%) | 162 | (81%) |
| no/yes | 12 | (12%) | 12 | (6%) |
| yes/maybe | 4 | (4%) | 26 | (13%) |

**Fig. 7.** Inter-judge agreement for two XIE data sets

very close. Our *maybe* judgment, then, appears to align with the final RTE filter for controversial items. Figure 7 shows the various rates of inter-judge agreement and disagreement.

We see from this table that our inter-judge agreement rate is quite similar to the RTE organizers, especially after closer coordination on guidelines (81% on round 2 vs. 80% RTE). It is also close to the 83% agreement rate reported by Dolan et al. (2005) for their judgments on a similar task involving "more or less semantically equivalent" pairs. Our rate of controversial examples also appears to be comparable to the RTE organizers. On our round 2, for instance, the two uncontroversial conditions (*yes/yes* and *no/no*) comprised 71.5% of the examples (143 pairs), compared to 67% (80% - 13%) for the RTE organizers. It's interesting that our inter-judge agreement rate declined slightly from round 1 to round 2; Figure 7 shows that the reason is that the number of *no/maybe* conflicts (which don't affect the agreement rate) declined, while the number of *yes/maybe* conflicts (which do affect the agreement rate) increased.

For the RTE development corpus, we compared our judgments to the final judgments of the RTE development team. An experienced annotator judged 70 pairs drawn from the second half of the RTE training set (10 pairs from each of the seven application scenarios). Our judge achieved an agreement rate of 91% (64/70) with the truth/falsity judgments provided in this (already filtered) training set. Similar studies by RTE participants achieved higher agreement rates; e.g., Bos and Markert (2005) report an agreement rate of 95% with the entire 800-item test set.

We reviewed the sources of disagreement, and found three problem areas.

The first reason is specific to the Gigaword corpus. Because this corpus was automatically collected and zoned, the headlines in particular contained a number of irregularities that made it difficult to judge their appropriateness. Such irregularities included truncations (*Chinese President Vows to Open New Chapters With*), absence of propositions (subject headings like *Mandela's Speech*), prepended alerts like *URGENT:*, and bylines and date lines miszoned into the headline.

Second, our judges found they had irreconcilable differences about synonymy, both in the RTE training set and the Gigaword corpus. For example, in the lead/headline pair shown in Figure 8, the judges disagreed about whether *safe operation* in the lead paragraph and *operates smoothly* in the headline induced the appropriate entailment relation. Similarly, for pair 823 in the RTE training set, our two judges disagreed on whether *in bloody clothes* and *covered in blood* were related in the required way.

**Lead:** As of Saturday, Shanghai's Hongqiao Airport has performed safe operation for some 2,600 consecutive days, setting a record in the country
**Headline:** Shanghai's Hongqiao Airport Operates Smoothly

**Text:** The body of Satomi Mitarai was found by a teacher after her attacker returned to class in bloody clothes.
**Hypothesis:** Mitarai's body was found by a teacher after her killer returned to their classroom covered in blood.

**Fig. 8.** Synonym disagreements

Third, even though our extended guidelines provided some explicit direction on world knowledge, our judges disagreed on the amount of knowledge that was permissible. For instance, in the RTE training pair in Figure 9, a positive judgment is more convincing if one understands the implications of the references to *al Qaeda* and *September 11, 2001* in the text. Similarly, the lead/headline pair only leads to a positive judgment if the reader knows that *Sudan* and *the Khartoum government* are codescriptive.

**Lead:** Eritrea has accused the Khartoum government of taking more hostile moves against its nationals living in Sudan
**Headline:** Eritrea Accuses Sudan Of Taking Hostile Move

**Text:** The White House failed to act on the domestic threat from al Qaeda prior to September 11, 2001.
**Hypothesis:** White House ignored the threat of attack

**Fig. 9.** World knowledge disagreements

After each round of annotation, the judges attempted to reconcile their disagreements. We found that the judges could not reconcile a number of the judgments on which they disagreed. For the first round, 15 out of 100 pairs (15%) were left unreconciled, and for the second round, 42 out of 200 (21%) were left unreconciled. Eleven of the irreconcilable pairs in the second round were due to confusion stemming from the telegraphic nature of many well-formed headlines (e.g., *Crackdown on Auto-Mafia in Bulgaria*), which led to misunderstandings about how to judge truncated headlines and headlines lacking propositions. Despite the high number of irreconcilable pairs, the judges' detailed comments revealed that on pairs where they disagreed on how to label the pair, they often agreed on what the problem was.

Our study of inter-judge agreement suggests that this sort of annotation task consistently yields agreement rates in the 80% range, across a variety of groups and task definitions. While a good deal of the disagreement appears to be simply irreconcilable, simply eliminating these disagreements appears to be a good (albeit more expensive) strategy, as shown by the higher agreement rates between the judgments in the purified RTE corpus and independent judgments by RTE participants.

## 5 Evaluation Suitability: Rasch Analysis

There are many ways to think about the suitability of an evaluation: the cost and efficiency of setting it up and running it, its correlation with actual user tasks, etc. In this section, we consider another dimension of suitability: the comparability of system scores and the calibration of test elements.

### 5.1 An Overview of Rasch Analysis

What does it mean when one system outscores another by three items? It's very difficult to tell, because it depends on how consistently the individual test elements predict the performance of each system, and the difficulty of the test items that each system got right (and, consequently, the difficulty of the ones they got wrong, as well). An approach known as *Rasch analysis* (Bond and Fox 2001) can provide mathematically well-motivated insight into this issue. In previous joint work, MITRE participated in a Rasch analysis on the results of the TREC QA 2002 evaluation (Lange et al. 2004). We found these results provided useful insights, and so in this section, we apply this technique to the results of the RTE evaluation.

Rasch analysis uses the performance of test-takers on individual test items to generate a model of interconnected estimates of test-taking ability (in our case, system performance) and item difficulty. Under the Rasch model, the probability that a particular test-taker got a particular test item correct is a function of the difference between the test-taker's ability score and the item's difficulty score. Rasch analysis is used by a number of communities; in the educational testing world, it is used to assign test-independent levels of ability to test-takers, to calibrate tests, and to assign population-independent difficulty scores to test items. Rasch analysis also has the advantage that partial test results can be evaluated.

Rasch analysis is founded on the idea that most of the test-takers should agree on which items are easy and which are hard. So Rasch analysis is unusual in that one of its goals is to improve the goodness of fit of its models by changing the tests which generate the models; that is, the idea of Rasch analysis is not simply to assess the reliability of a given test, but to provide guidance for improving the reliability by replacing poorer test items with better ones.

For each subject S and test item Q, Rasch predicts the probability of S getting Q correct. *Outfit* is a measure of how far the actual results deviate from these predictions. Subject outfit is determined by examining how that subject did on all the test items; test item outfit is determined by examining how all the subjects did on that item. Outfit is often expressed as a "mean square" measure whose expected value is 1.0 (the minimum is 0, the maximum is unlimited).

Although outfit works in both directions, Rasch practitioners seem most interested in excessively large outfit: the degree to which a subject, for instance, "did better" overall on the "harder" test items than the Rasch model predicts. The better (more predictive) the test, the fewer the number of items which exceed the chosen outfit threshold. However, the appropriate threshold for outfit is, surprisingly, a matter of great contention in the Rasch community. To choose this threshold, Rasch practitioners use rules of thumb. One such rule of thumb is to flag something as exhibiting excessive outfit when it exceeds a threshold of 1.3 for a sample less than 500, 1.2 for sample sizes between 500 and 1000, and 1.1 for sample sizes larger than 1000 (Bond and Fox 2001, p. 208). For the novice, the motivation for choosing one rule of thumb over another is extremely obscure, and the difference among thresholds will not affect the discussion to follow.

## 5.2 Rasch Analysis of RTE

Figure 10 shows the Rasch analysis plots for systems and items from the RTE 2004 evaluation. We considered full submissions only (of which there were 23), against 779 test items (i.e., entailment pairs). One pair that every system got wrong and 20 pairs that every system got right were removed from the 800 pairs in the evaluation because they weren't discriminative; 19 of these 20 correct pairs came from the CD (comparable documents) application setting, which was the easiest of the seven application settings in the corpus.

The fine dotted lines show the large outfit threshold according to the rule of thumb given above (1.3 for a sample size of 23 systems to measure test item outfit; 1.2 for a sample size of 779 items to measure system outfit). The staggered dotted lines show an alternative large outfit threshold, applied by Lange et al. (2004) to the 2002 TREC QA evaluation. This evaluation featured 67 systems and 490 questions, which is comparable to the RTE evaluation.

The scales of these two graphs differ considerably. The Y axis of the item difficulty graph ranges from -4 to 4, while the Y axis of the system ability graph ranges from -1 to 1. In other words, the spread of system ability is very small. We didn't need Rasch analysis to observe this, but it's relevant to the discussion of outfit. According to either outfit bound, the test items are well-behaved; but this shouldn't surprise us, because the spread of system abilities is so narrow. That is, the item outfit is within bounds, because the differences among systems isn't enough to make it excessive.

The system outfit graph shows a few outliers (5 at the 1.2 threshold, 2 at the 1.6 threshold). If we want to reduce the number of outfitting items, and thus

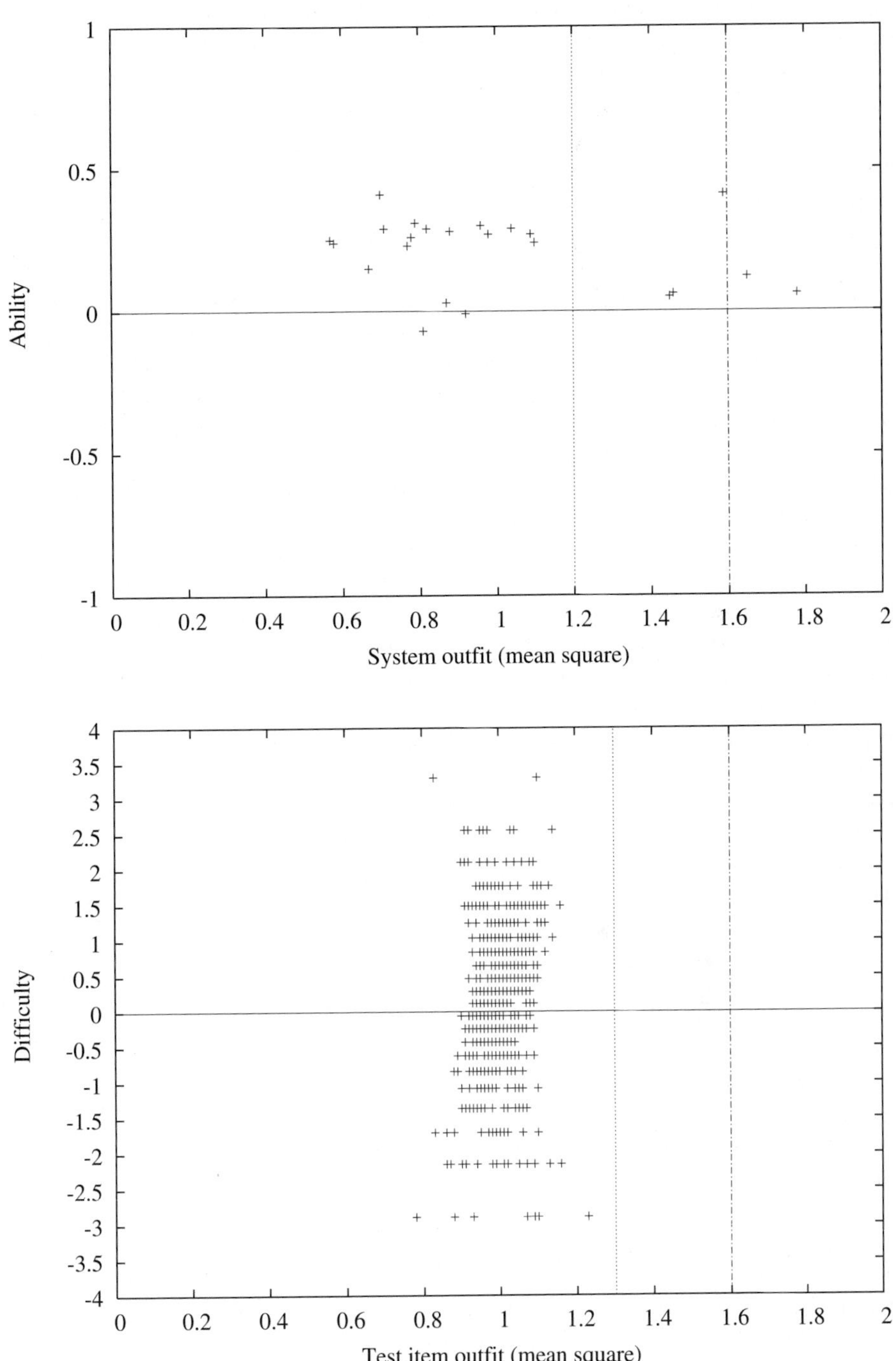


**Fig. 10.** Rasch system and item outfit for RTE 2005 evaluation

improve the test, how might we go about this? Rasch models are unidimensional models; that is, they are intended for tests that measure one thing in the target population of test takers. For instance, a test might be intended to measure mathematical ability among third graders. Outfitting items suggest that the test is measuring more than one thing; so our math test might also be unintentionally testing reading ability (say, by presenting mathematical word problems), possibly resulting in outfit among good math students who are poor readers.

For RTE, there are a number of possible dimensions at play besides reasoning ability. For instance, the RTE corpus was constructed from a number of data sources, representing tasks like information retrieval, information extraction, QA, etc. It may be that these sources are introducing an additional dimension. Alternatively, it might be differences in strictness of entailment, amount of world knowledge, or the presence of negation. We can start to look for these extra dimensions by isolating the outlying systems and studying the pairs the Rasch model predicted they shouldn't have responded to correctly. Once we identify these dimensions, we can refine the test accordingly, either by eliminating all but the dimension of interest, or by dividing the test into parallel sub-evaluations, each of which is unidimensional.

While the data from this population of test takers (i.e., RTE systems) does not suggest this evaluation is multidimensional, it shouldn't surprise us if it did. These systems vary widely in their approaches to the RTE task, and the novelty of the task hasn't allowed for the convergence of approaches found in more established evaluations. As time goes by, it may be that these various approaches will converge, and in this sense the RTE evaluation might affect the evolution of system capabilities in a way that human tests cannot, simply by asserting that the particular mix of phenomena found in the RTE corpus *ought* to be a unitary system capability. (This convergence is not necessarily a good thing, since it also may have the effect of reducing the diversity of research.) Alternatively, the outfit analysis might motivate the RTE evaluation to narrow the types of test items to focus the evaluation. Either way, Rasch analysis gives us a valuable tool to track and analyze both the test and the population of test takers.

## 6 Assessing RTE

With these results in hand, we finally focus on our criteria for evaluations as they bear on RTE.

### 6.1 Criterion 1: Realism or Applicability

The appeal of RTE seems to lie in the perception that it exemplifies a technology which is broadly required, and that any system which can perform the RTE task well would almost certainly have to have enough "smarts" to lead to considerably enhanced approaches to MT, information extraction, question answering, and the like. But the RTE task does not correspond to a "real" application; nor does it clearly correspond to a component of such an application. In other words, the criterion of realism presents a vexing issue.

While the simplicity of RTE is one of its strengths, it's also the reason for this problem. RTE is a decision task, rather than a generation task, and the vast majority of language processing tasks are generation tasks. The RTE corpus is "inspired" by a range of language processing scenarios, most of which can't exploit the RTE capability directly. For example:

- **Information retrieval:** The metric of comparison between query and document in IR is relevance, not entailment, and queries are keywords, not structured information or propositions.
- **Reading comprehension:** While one might be able to interpret an RC question as a premise which entails the answer, and it might be feasible to compare the question to each sentence in the text, three problems remain: the truth/falsity judgment in the RTE task selects only appropriate entailments, and can't choose between them; the answer might be distributed among multiple regions of the text (due to, e.g., pronominal reference); and finding the appropriate sentence which contains the answer isn't the same as finding the answer.
- **Question answering:** The problems for QA are similar to those for RC, and QA additionally presents the overhead of selecting the appropriate document from a large corpus.
- **Information extraction:** IE doesn't really have a candidate text to match against the "hypotheses" in the document; the goal, rather, is to find information of a particular category, likely spread throughout the document.
- **Machine translation:** Every good translation is entailed by its source, but this fact does not help much in generating that translation.
- **Paraphrase acquisition:** It might be possible to use an MT alignment approach to bootstrap paraphrase acquisition (as Figure 2 might suggest), but it's much more likely that a well-understood corpus of paraphrases would support an RTE task, rather than the other way around.

To be sure, there are applications for which an RTE module might be useful. For instance, identifying comparable documents is also one of the motivating RTE scenarios, and one could imagine a sentence-level pairwise entailment judgment as a component of a system which performs this task. Similarly, certain approaches to summarization or identifying novel documents might also be able to exploit such a capability.

The "realness" of an evaluation is a crucial dimension of its motivation, and a crucial guide for corpus creation. If the RTE evaluation were to focus on one or more of these plausible scenarios, it might fulfill this criterion; however, its scope is clearly intended to be broader, and as a result, we are denied this crucial guidance for creating a representative RTE corpus.

In a fixed application, the evaluation corpus can be crafted to reflect the target application in the ratio of relevant to irrelevant documents, the linguistic register and style, etc. On the one hand, such a corpus allows developers to tune the application, by ignoring or paying little attention to linguistic phenomena which appear infrequently; on the other hand, if the corpus is representative of the task, and the goal is to build a system which performs well on the task, this strategy is wise and appropriate. But we don't know what we're going to do with an RTE system, and so we're left with a host of questions. What proportion of entailment pairs should require world knowledge? What proportion should be easy or hard? What should the balance be between positive and negative examples? Without the answers to these questions, we run the very real risk of optimizing for a task which is unrepresentative of any of the applications it will be applied to.

Against this criterion, RTE clearly suffers in comparison with QA, which has clear utility, and is no better than RC, which also lacks a compelling task.

### 6.2 Criterion 2: Clear Metrics

Like QA and RC, the evaluation metric for RTE is intuitive. Rasch analysis suggests that the RTE evaluation probably fits a well-accepted statistical model of well-behaved tests, and appears to be comparable to the 2002 TREC QA evaluation in that regard (cf. Lange et al. (2004)). As a result, it's possible for RTE developers to use a subset of the evaluation items to calibrate results across years.

### 6.3 Criterion 3: Cost

As we show, RTE differs from QA and RC in presenting the possibility of using noisy corpora as training material. For some systems, this feature may be a considerable advantage. However, the preparation of gold-standard test (or training) data is surprisingly costly, due to the various manipulations which even our lead/headline pairs must undergo: tenses ought to be modified, pronouns must be replaced by proper names, etc. The cost of developing gold-standard RC material is also considerable, as we learned in the course of our RC research. On the other hand, the cost of answer assessment in RTE is zero, which compares favorably to QA and free-answer RC. At this point, it's too early to say whether any of these evaluations provide any advantages over the others along this dimension.

One notable shortcoming of RTE is that, unlike QA and free-answer RC, each RTE item provides one bit of information. In other words, the simplicity of the evaluation also compromises the informativeness of each item. This issue must be factored into the cost of developing an RTE corpus. One possible avenue of exploration is to develop a version of RTE which asks for a truth/falsity judgment for multiple candidate hypotheses for each premise, rather than only one, in the hope that the marginal cost of developing additional candidates is lower than that of developing another entailment pair. However, in this scenario, the resulting pairs will not be independent of each other, which has implications for statistical models like Rasch.

### 6.4 Criterion 4: Annotation Reliability

We found that the entailment judgment task is tolerably efficient; an informal review of our hand-judgment of the Gigaword corpus suggested a judgment speed as high as 100 pairs per hour for a trained judge. And our work on inter-judge agreement showed that the RTE judgment task is reasonably robust. Furthermore, we suspect that, unlike other annotation tasks, we can actually exploit the variability we found here.

Variability of interpretation is the natural state of affairs in human language. It should not surprise us at all that human judges differ about synonymy and acceptable levels of required world knowledge. Furthermore, this variability is *informative*. The developers of the initial RTE training corpus discarded pairs about which the judges disagreed. We suggest that this is the wrong thing to do, and that the RTE task ought to *capture* the variability of interpretation, especially since no set of judgment guidelines will ever be extensive enough to resolve the potential issues. Two possible strategies for capturing variability suggest themselves.

The first strategy is to make the truth/falsity judgment a scale rather than a binary choice. This might be as simple as adding "don't know" as an option, or may involve something like a five-point scale, ranging from clearly true to clearly false. Adding a third value might be the optimal choice, if judges end up spending a disproportionate amount of time on the difficult-to-decide cases. The second strategy is to preserve the binary choice, but have three judges judge all pairs, yielding a four-way classification ranging from 3T (true for all judges) to 0T (false for all judges).

We feel that there are at least two advantages to capturing this variability. First, system developers will have a wider range of judgments to choose from when training their systems; they'll know which judgments are strong and which are weak. Second, we now have the possibility of assessing the correlation between system confidence and human confidence, which will yield a more realistic task.

## 7 Summary

The PASCAL RTE evaluation has generated an enormous amount of interest. In this paper, we have tried to evaluate the evaluation. We used a general set of criteria for assessing the goodness of language evaluations to scrutinize RTE's cost, relevance, and suitability, and compared it to existing evaluations of open-domain understanding according to these criteria. We found that although RTE does not correspond to a "real" or naturally occurring language processing task, it nonetheless provides clear and simple metrics, a tolerable cost of corpus development, good annotator reliability (with the potential to exploit the remaining variability), and the possibility of finding noisy but plentiful training material.

## Acknowledgements

This paper reports on work supported by the MITRE Sponsored Research Program. We would like to thank MITRE's Laurie Damianos, who provided us with statistics on MiTAP's resources and served as one of the evaluators in our inter-judge reliability study, and Warren Greiff, for his insights about Rasch analysis.

In addition, we are grateful to Rense Lange, of Integrated Knowledge Systems, for his advice and expertise on Rasch analysis. Finally, we would like to thank the organizers of the RTE and ACL workshops, especially Ido Dagan, Oren Glickman, and Bill Dolan, for their comments and encouragement.

## References

Aberdeen, J., Condon, S., Doran, C., Harper, L., Oshika, B., Phillips, J.: Evaluation of speech-to-speech translation systems. Unpublished manuscript (2005)

Aberdeen, J., Hirschman, L., Walker, M.: Evaluation for DARPA Communicator spoken dialogue systems. In: Proceedings of the 2nd Conference on Language Resources and Evaluation (2000)

Bayer, S., Burger, J., Ferro, L., Henderson, J., Yeh, A.: MITRE's submissions to the EU Pascal RTE challenge. In: PASCAL Proceedings of the First Challenge Workshop, Recognizing Textual Entailment, Southampton, U.K. (2005)

Bayer, S., Burger, J., Greiff, W., Wellner, B.: The MITRE logical form generation system. In: Proceedings of Senseval-3: The Third International Workshop on the Evaluation of Systems for the Semantic Analysis of Text (2004) 69–72

Bond, T.G., Fox, C.M.: Applying the Rasch Model: Fundamental Measurement in the Human Sciences. University of Toledo Press (2001)

Bos, J., Markert, K.: Combining shallow and deep NLP methods for recognizing textual entailment. In: PASCAL Proceedings of the First Challenge Workshop, Recognizing Textual Entailment, Southampton, U.K. (2005)

Brachman, R.: (AA)AI: More than the sum of its parts. AAAI Presidential Address, presented at AAAI-2005 (2005)

Brown, P.F., Della Pietra, S.A., Della Pietra, V.J., Mercer, R.L.: The mathematics of statistical machine translation. Computational Linguistics **19** (1993)

Burger, J., Ferro, L.: Generating an entailment corpus from news headlines. In: ACL Workshop on Empirical Modeling of Semantic Equivalence and Entailment, Ann Arbor, MI (2005)

Dagan, I., Glickman, O., Magnini, B.: The PASCAL recognizing textual entailment challenge. In: PASCAL Proceedings of the First Challenge Workshop, Recognizing Textual Entailment, Southampton, U.K. (2005)

Damianos, L., Wohlever, S., Kozierok, R., Ponte, J.: MiTAP for real users, real data, real problems. In: Proceedings of the Conference on Human Factors of Computing Systems, Fort Lauderdale, FL (2003)

Deshmukh, N., Duncan, R., Ganapathiraju, A., Picone, J.: Benchmarking human performance for continuous speech recognition. In: Proceedings of the Fourth International Conference on Spoken Language Processing, Philadelphia, Pennsylvania, USA (1996) 2486–2489

Dolan, B., Brockett, C., Quirk, C.: Microsoft Research paraphrase corpus. `http://research.microsoft.com/research/nlp/msr_paraphrase.htm` (2005)

Graff, D.: English Gigaword. `http://www.ldc.upenn.edu/Catalog/CatalogEntry.jsp?catalogId=LDC2003T05` (2003)

Grishman, R., Sundheim, B.: Design of the MUC-6 evaluation. In: Proceedings of the Sixth Message Understanding Conference (MUC-6), Columbia, MD NIST, Morgan Kaufmann (1995)

Gusfield, D.: Algorithms on Strings, Trees and Sequences. Cambridge University Press (1997)

Henderson, J., Morgan, W.: Paris: an automated MT evaluation metric toolkit; and a survey of metric performance on the segment ranking task. Technical report, MITRE (2005) to appear.

Hirschman, L.: The evolution of evaluation: Lessons from the message understanding conferences. Computer Speech and Language **12** (1998) 281–305

Hirschman, L.: Language understanding evaluations: Lessons learned from MUC and ATIS. In: Proceedings of LREC-1998, Granada (1998)

Hirschman, L., Bates, M., Dahl, D., Fisher, W.M., Garafolo, J., Pallet, D.S., Hunicke-Smith, K., Price, P., Rudnicky, A., Tzoukermann, E.: Multisite data collection and evaluation in spoken language understanding. In: Proceedings of the DARPA Workshop on Human Language Technology, Princeton, NJ (1993) 19–24

Hirschman, L., Light, M., Breck, E., Burger, J.D.: Deep Read: A reading comprehension system. In: Proceedings of the 37th Annual Meeting of the Association for Computational Linguistics (1999)

Hirschman, L., Yeh, A., Blaschke, C., Valencia, A.: Overview of BioCreAtIvE: Critical assessment of information extraction for biology. BMC Bioinformatics **6** (2005) Suppl 1.

Joachims, T.: Learning to Classify Text Using Support Vector Machines. Kluwer (2002)

Lange, R., Moran, J., Greiff, W., Ferro, L.: A probabilistic Rasch analysis of question answering evaluations. In: Proceedings of HLT-NAACL 2004 (2004) 65–72

Light, M., Mann, G.S., Riloff, E., Breck, E.: Analyses for elucidating current question answering technology. Natural Language Engineering **7** (2001) 325–342

Morgan, A., Hirschman, L., Colosimo, M., Yeh, A., Colombe, J.: Gene name identification and normalization using a model organism database. Journal of Biomedical Informatics **37** (2004) 396–410

Och, F.J., Ney, H.: A systematic comparison of various statistical alignment models. Computational Linguistics **29** (2003)

Papineni, K., Roukos, S., Ward, T., Henderson, J., Reeder, F.: Corpus-based comprehensive and diagnostic MT evaluation: Initial Arabic, Chinese, French, and Spanish results. In: Proceedings of the 2002 Conference on Human Language Technology, San Diego, CA (2002) 124–127

Sundheim, B.: Overview of results of the MUC-6 evaluation. In: Proceedings of the Sixth Message Understanding Conference (MUC-6), Columbia, MD. NIST, Morgan Kaufmann (1995)

Tong, S., Koller, D.: Support vector machine active learning with applications to text classification. In: Proceedings of ICML-00, 17th International Conference on Machine Learning (2000)

Walker, M., Aberdeen, J., Boland, J., Bratt, E., Garofolo, J., Hirschman, L., Le, A., Lee, S., Narayanan, S., Papineni, K., Pellom, B., Polifroni, J., Potamianos, A., Prabhu, P., Rudnicky, A., Sanders, G., Seneff, S., Stallard, D., Whittaker, S.: DARPA Communicator dialog travel planning systems: The June 2000 data collection. In: Proceedings of Eurospeech 2001, Aalborg, Denmark (2001)

Wellner, B., Ferro, L., Greiff, W., Hirschman, L.: Reading comprehension tests for computer-based understanding evaluation. Natural Language Engineering (2005), to appear

# Partial Predicate Argument Structure Matching for Entailment Determination

Alina Andreevskaia, Zhuoyan Li, and Sabine Bergler

Concordia University,
1455 De Maisonneuve Blvd. West,
Montreal, Quebec, H3G 1M8 Canada
{andreev, zhuoy_li, bergler}@cse.concordia.ca

**Abstract.** The Computational Linguistics at Concordia laboratory system for textual entailment determination is based on shallow, partial predicate-argument structure matching combined with a WordNet-based lexical similarity measure. In this paper we describe experiments with different system settings conducted to assess the potential and limitations of partial predicate-argument structures in textual entailment determination.

## 1 Introduction

Establishing entailment relationships between two statements is important for many NLP tasks [1] and the problem is gaining interest in the research community. Most current work relies on the analysis of corpora - single or parallel- using machine learning and statistical methods (see [2, 3, 4, 5, 6]) to induce entailment-specific knowledge. Approaches to the determination of textual entailment between pairs of text snippets include techniques ranging from the BLEU algorithm [7] to complex methods making use of logic formalisms [8, 9, 10], theorem proving [11, 12], and a variety of statistical approaches [9, 13, 14, 15, 16]. In contrast, we approach the textual entailment problem using general mechanisms and strategies based uniquely on partial predicate argument structure (PPAS) and WordNet-based [17] lexical similarity measures.

A system that can determine entailment relations has many possible applications, including a test whether a sentence condensed for purposes of summarization is still a correct statement, given the original sentence was true. Entailment is a semantic notion originally defined over propositions, but extended here to sentences, as shown in Example 1.

(1) **Pair #1597 RTE:** ***True***
**T:** Nelson Mandela's Long Walk to Freedom began as scraps of paper, buried under the floor of his prison cell.
**H:** Nelson Mandela's autobiography is called "The Long Walk to Freedom".

As this example illustrates, entailment is not a clear cut notion: while in the context of the article from which the first sentence is taken (and indeed from world knowledge) the entailment may be clearly true, in isolation we feel it is

J. Quiñonero-Candela et al. (Eds.): MLCW 2005, LNAI 3944, pp. 332–343, 2006.

not necessarily so and thus, a system that is limited to just the two sentences cannot be expected to make this inference (after all, *The Long Walk to Freedom* might be a novel or a campaign slogan).

Evaluating entailment relations, as this example shows, is open to inter-annotator disagreements, as is the case with evaluating summaries [18]. But entailments between sentences are more constrained (context has to be ignored), and, therefore, less open to interpretation and presumably easier to evaluate. Yet they have a more stringent definition (subsumption of truth) and should thus be harder to approximate with means that do not include semantics.

The Recognising Textual Entailment (RTE) Challenge [19] provides a data set to test our ideas for a shallow semantics. Based on our summarization systems ERSS 2004 and Multi-ERSS [20, 21], we wanted to see how far a small extension of our tools would go towards capturing shallow semantics. Under the premise that the most basic aspect of semantics is the predicate argument structure of the sentence combined with a lexical resource, such as WordNet [17], our system produces a partial predicate argument structure from the sentence, which contains only the stipulated subject, the predicate, and the stipulated object.[1] The system matches PPASs in the pair, using WordNet and a conservative strategy (if in doubt, say no.) Our goal was to see how far very shallow predicate argument structures can be useful to determine entailment. This paper attempts to outline some of the insights gained in the process.

## 2 System Overview

The Computational Linguistic at Concordia (CLaC) Lab's system for the RTE Challenge is based on systems our laboratory developed for text summarization. The environment is implemented in the GATE architecture [24] and provides tagging, NP chunking, and knowledge-poor fuzzy NP coreference resolution [20, 21, 25]. The flexible GATE architecture allows for the creation of modular components that can be used in different combinations depending on the task. For the purposes of the textual entailment resolution we used two full parsers [22, 23] to construct the partial predicate structures (PPAS), then matched the structures in the data pairs using noun phrase coreference [25] within the same PPAS constituent (i.e. matching subjects with subjects, objects with objects, predicates with predicates), extended with a few specialized heuristics for particular problems that were encountered in the PASCAL RTE challenge development set, as discussed below.

### 2.1 Main Strategy

The system uses partial predicate-argument structures (PPASs) and a WordNet-based measure of lexical similarity to determine the entailment between the two components of a pair.

[1] We use two full fledged parsers, LINK [22] and RASP [23], to arrive at this truncated notion of PPAS; in hindsight we should have used the complete set of grammatical relations provided by the parsers directly.

Partial predicate-argument structures cover only the verb, its subject and object (if there is one) as in Example 2. PPASs are produced based on the dependency tree output of two parsers, the Link parser [22] and the RASP parser [26]. One of these two parsers can be set as default, the second to be used only when the default parser doesn't produce a parse. When both parsers are given equal priority, the system chooses for each sentence the parser that generates more PPASs. This last strategy produced marginally better results in the test runs and it is the default setting for the system.

(2) Two-thirds of the Scottish police force will be deployed at the happening.
s:[Two-thirds of the Scottish police force] v:[will be deployed] a:[p:[at] a:[the happening]]

Lexical similarity between structurally related items in the pairs is measured as the length of the path obtained while traversing the WordNet [17] tree-like hierarchy from one word to another via "is_a" relation. A shorter distance indicates a closer relationship, 0 corresponds to members of the same synset. The distance has to be within a pre-established threshold. We tested different thresholds varying from 0 to 4 and found that a more permissive approach resulted in slightly better recall at the expense of a comparable decrease in precision, while accuracy and CWS remained practically the same. The threshold of 0 was kept as the default setting for the system.

A matching heuristic establishes whether $H$ (hypothesis) is entailed by $T$ (text) based on PPASs and WordNet distance. Subjects are compared to subjects, verbs to verbs and objects to objects. Passive constructions are transformed into active ones before the comparison. The comparison stops when a match is found, thus ignoring any possible matches between other PPASs in the pair. This matching algorithm limits the number of potential cases that are considered for entailment to those that have very similar syntactic structures.

**Algorithm** *Entailment Detection*
(∗ **true**: entailment detected, **false** otherwise )

```
1.  Use the coreference resolution system to produce coreference chains both
    for T and H separately and for the pair as a unit
2.  for each pair
3.     for each sentence
4.        Extract Noun Phrases and Verb Groups
5.        Select a parse among parses from two parsers with weighted scheme
6.        Determine PPAS
7.  Apply cardinality filter
8.     for each numeric value from h
9.        if there is no corresponding cardinality value in t
10.       then return false
11. Apply Predicate Argument Structure comparison
12.    Transform passive constructions into active ones
13.    for each PPAS pair
14.       Compute WN distance for verbs in T and H
```

```
        if WN distance <= threshold
            if both PPASs have comparable structures²
                if there is coreference between corresponding parts³
                then return true
Apply Be-Heuristic
    if H contains the pattern "X is Y" and X∈H and X'∈T and {X, X'}
    belong to the same inter-sentence coreference chain and Y∈H and Y'∈T
    and {Y, Y'} belong to the same inter-sentence coreference chain and X'
    corefers with Y'
    then return true
return false
```

The algorithm favors precision over recall, therefore all entailment values are set to *False* unless the system finds compelling evidence to the contrary.

This approach is very shallow: it does not use the full dependency information in the parses, ignoring, for instance, adjuncts. In a few cases this didn't matter, as in Example 3. More often, however, the crucial information for entailment determination is thus ignored, resulting in incorrect assessments, as in Example 4, where the identical PPAS is constructed for both $T$ and $H$.

(3) **Pair #825, RTE: *True*, our system: *True***
**T:** A car bomb that exploded outside a U.S. military base near Beiji, killed 11 Iraqis.
**H:** A car bomb exploded outside a U.S. base in the northern town of Beiji, killing 11 Iraqis.

(4) **Pair #2040. RTE: *False*, our system: *True***
**T:** Stjepan Mesic was the first Croatian president to deliver a public address at Harvard.
**H:** Stjepan Mesic was the first Croatian president.
**PPAS:** s:[Stjepan Mesic] v:[was] a:[Croatian president]

This phenomenon was stronger in the test set than the development set and thus wasn't corrected for the Challenge. The development set suggested, however, some other, additional strategies; for instance a *be-heuristic* for Hypotheses of the form "X is Y", that uses coreference chains within $T$ and between $T$ and $H$ to decide whether the Hypothesis is *True* given the data in $T$. The development data contains many examples of this type in the QA task, but the phenomenon was less frequent in the test data.

(5) **Pair #336. RTE: *True***
**T:**The centre-right European People's Party (EPP), the largest group in the European Parliament, has warned that it will reject the Taoiseach, Berni Ahern, if he is nominated as the next president of the European Commission.
**H:** Berni Ahern is the Taoiseach.

[2] *Comparable structure* means they both have subject(s) and/or argument(s).

[3] e.g. subjects and/or arguments of the two PPASs being compared.

Another heuristic was introduced to reduce some negative impact of the shallow character of our partial predicate-argument structures. In Example 6, the non-entailment relation is determined by constituents which are ignored in our PPAS matching approach. A special *"cardinality"* heuristic ensures that such cases do not produce false positives when the ignored information concerns numbers.

(6) **Pair #768. RTE:** ***False***
**T:** A small bronze bust of Spencer Tracy sold for £174,000.
**H:** A small bronze bust of Spencer Tracy made £180,447.

## 3 Data

The RTE dataset envisions different tasks that require entailment determination and is thus divided into different types of pairs. These have been collected using different methods [19]: in the CD (comparable documents) task sub-set, pairs were manually selected from sets of lexically overlapping pairs of sentences (Example 7). This part of the PASCAL RTE challenge data showed the highest degree of both syntactical and lexical similarity between $T$ and $H$. In the Information Retrieval (IR), Reading Comprehension (RC), and Information Extraction (IR) tasks, annotators manually created the hypotheses that corresponded to the $T$ part of the pair. Such pairs had much greater variability in structure and word choice (Example 8). A similar approach was taken for the Paraphrase Acquisition (PP) task where the hypotheses were generated by annotators using automatically acquired pairs of lexical-syntactic expressions (Example 9). The Machine Translation (MT) task pairs were made of gold standard human translations and machine translations of the same sentence. This part of the data is characterized by occasional lack of proper grammatical structure and presents many non-standard expressions as in Example 10. Finally, for the Question Answering (QA) task, hypotheses were manually chosen from the output of an automatic QA system and were in most cases very different in syntactic structure from the $T$ part (Example 11).

(7) **Pair #898. RTE:** ***True***
**T:** After the war the city was briefly occupied by the Allies and then was returned to the Dutch.
**H:** After the war, the city was returned to the Dutch.

(8) **Pair #1030. RTE:** ***True***
**T:** De la Cruz's family said he had gone to Saudi Arabia a year ago to work as a driver after a long period of unemployment.
**H:** De la Cruz was unemployed.

(9) **Pair #39. RTE:** ***True***
**T:** Mr. Clinton received a hefty advance for the book, reportedly $10m, but he joked that by the time he finished the 937-page tome "I was just about down to minimum wage".
**H:** Bill Clinton received a reported $10 million advance.

(10) **Pair #1252. RTE: *True***
**T:** Well-known businessman, Representative Badi Flaha, whose term is expiring, thought that reforms are essential to develop the economy "but in Syria we prefer" to implement them slowly but assuredly.
**H:** Flaha explained that slow but sure progress was the "Syrian way. "

(11) **Pair #605. RTE: *True***
**T:** According to the Encyclopedia Britannica, Indonesia is the largest archipelagic nation in the world, consisting of 13,670 islands.
**H:** 13,670 islands make up Indonesia.

Thus, the data provided by the challenge organizers is diverse, covering a wide range of problems that constitute the task of textual entailment determination. While such diversity means that the data poses significant challenges and may not lend itself well to processing by a single method, it also provides excellent material for testing different strategies for a variety of NLP tasks. The complexity of the pairs ranges from relatively simple cases that can be handled by knowledge-poor methods (Example 12) to complex entailments that require world knowledge and are hard to analyze even for humans (Example 13).

(12) **Pair #836. RTE: *True***
**T:** A Union Pacific freight train hit five people.
**H:** A Union Pacific freight train struck five people.

(13) **Pair #836. RTE: *True***
**T:** Google files for its long awaited IPO.
**H:** Google goes public.

**Pair #1266. RTE: *True***
**T:** Mohammad Galal Abd Al-Kawi, author of the 15-episode series "The Priest and the Sheikh", says in a conversation with Agence France Presse today, Sunday, that he wrote these episodes "to respond to the biased campaigns in some Western media outlets, which are being directed by Jews, for the purpose of inciting subversion between Moslems and Copts."
**H:** Mohammad Galal Abd Al-Kawi wrote the series, "The Priest and the Sheikh" in retaliation to what he sees as Jewish propaganda of some Western media.

The analysis of the PASCAL RTE challenge data set showed that it has a relatively high inter-annotator agreement. Vanderwende et al. [27] report an agreement of 96% on approximately one-third of the test data, Bos et al. [12] report 95% for the complete test set, while our own agreement rate is 97%. For instance, in Example 1 nothing in $T$ implies that "Long Walk to Freedom" is an autobiography, in Example 14 nothing in $T$ suggests that the name of the ex-cop is Rios (also from a legal point of view, we cannot equal being accused of a murder with being a murderer).

(14) **Pair #966. RTE: *True*, our assessment: *False***
**T:** A former police officer was charged with murder Thursday in the slaying

of a college student who allegedly had threatened to expose their sexual relationship, authorities said.
**H:** Ex-cop Rios killed student.

## 4 Results

Table 1 presents the results of our best run submitted to the PASCAL RTE challenge. These results do not significantly exceed the chance level. There is a considerable difference among the results for different tasks. Our system (as most other systems in the competition) performed best on CD data that has the highest percentage of syntactically similar pairs. MT and QA tasks turned out to be the most difficult for our approach, mostly due to the difference in the predicate-argument structures and complexity of lexical paraphrases employed there.

**Table 1.** System results over different categories

| Task | Precision | Recall | Accuracy | CWS |
|---|---|---|---|---|
| All | 0.57 | 0.15 | 0.52 | 0.51 |
| CD | 0.89 | 0.32 | 0.64 | 0.64 |
| IE | 0.56 | 0.08 | 0.51 | 0.55 |
| MT | 0.40 | 0.10 | 0.47 | 0.43 |
| QA | 0.23 | 0.04 | 0.45 | 0.47 |
| RC | 0.52 | 0.17 | 0.51 | 0.48 |
| PP | 0.50 | 0.28 | 0.50 | 0.54 |
| IR | 0.62 | 0.11 | 0.52 | 0.49 |

The poor results with the original settings, where partial predicate-argument structures and the WordNet-based semantic similarity measure were combined, led us to explore the potential of using these two components separately to investigate the role each of them played in the system's decisions. Table 2 shows the results of these post-competition runs as compared to the results of the original run (row 2). In the first of these experiments (presented in Table 2 in row 1 as "PPAS, no WordNet"), system's decisions were made based only on PPAS similarity and string overlap between corresponding constituents. The results are slightly worse but overall very similar to those produced by the run where PPAS matching was coupled with WordNet-based similarity measure. In order to assess why adding WordNet does not increase the system performance, we produced the runs where PPAS matching was turned off.

In the experiments where PPASs were not employed by the system, we used the percentage of lexically similar tokens found in $T$ and $H$ to determine entailment: if the number of tokens in $H$ that had a matching a counterpart in $T$ was greater than a pre-set threshold value (established as percentage of matched tokens out of total tokens in the shorter sentence), $T$ was deemed to entail $H$. Three thresholds were tested: an overlap of at least 75%, of 50% and the lenient threshold of 30%. The 50% threshold produced the best results. When all parse

**Table 2.** Influence of syntactic and semantic components

| Setting | Precision | Recall | Accuracy | CWS |
|---|---|---|---|---|
| PPAS, no WordNet | 0.57 | 0.14 | 0.51 | 0.50 |
| PPAS + WN | 0.57 | 0.15 | 0.52 | 0.51 |
| No PPAS; threshold = 50% | 0.53 | 0.83 | 0.54 | 0.55 |

information was ignored, the precision went down but recall considerably increased, while both accuracy and CWS were better than chance at the 0.05 level.

The comparison of the three runs suggests that simplified PPAS matching results in a considerable drop in recall. This is due to the limitation that our matching procedure imposes on sentence components that are allowed to be tested for similarity. Our syntactic matching accepts as comparable only PPASs that have the same type and the same number of constituents, thereby ruling out a large number of pairs where syntactic structures of $T$ and $H$ are not exactly the same (as in the Example 11). Moreover, the experiments with WordNet-based similarity measure used without PPAS matching demonstrated that such over-restrictive matching prevents other system components from realizing their full potential.

The next section will consider the main types of our system's errors and how they are related to the shallow character of our PPAS matching.

## 5 Discussion

The PASCAL RTE challenge gave us an opportunity to explore the potential and the limitations of the shallow PPAS matching approach. The analysis of the system's errors that was conducted following the competition allowed the identification of major types of errors made by the system and revealed opportunities for further development of the system that will lead to more sophisticated methods for entailment determination.

The qualitative analysis of the observed errors permits to conclude that there are three major factors that contribute to system errors: the limitations of partial predicate-argument structures matching, the system's inability to deal with semantic similarity of units larger than words, and the lack of world knowledge. These factors often work in combination, but can also be a single source of the system's errors. In order to assess the role of shallow PPAS structures construction and matching in the system's performance we computed the percentage of errors attributable to (1) PPAS construction and matching alone; (2) the limitations of our PPAS construction and matching combined with other factors; (3) all errors related to PPAS, and (4) errors not related to PPAS, that were attributable to other factors (Table 3). The data in the table shows that errors and constraints related to PPAS construction and matching contribute to the majority of errors (82%), either alone (43%) or in combination with other factors (39%).

**Table 3.** Role of PPAS in system's errors (% of total number of errors per task)

| Task | Source of Errors | | | |
|---|---|---|---|---|
| | Errors related to PPAS only | PPAS in comb. with other factors | Total errors related to PPAS | Errors not related to PPAS |
| All | 43% | 39% | 82% | 18% |
| CD | 52% | 22% | 74% | 26% |
| IE | 42% | 51% | 93% | 7% |
| MT | 39% | 35% | 74% | 26% |
| QA | 21% | 70% | 91% | 9% |
| RC | 67% | 20% | 87% | 13% |
| PP | 59% | 5% | 64% | 36% |
| IR | 30% | 42% | 72% | 28% |

The information left out by our partial predicate-argument structures did not have significant impact on the system's performance: it accounted for only 2.5% of errors. The errors in the process of PPAS construction (bad parses lead to 14% of errors) and a very restrictive character of PPAS matching algorithm used are the main factors that contributed to the low performance of our system. For instance, if our syntactic component could handle nominalizations, such as the finite verb transformations in Example 15, precision would improve by about 2%. Nominalizations can be handled using a specialized heuristic and resources such as CatVar [28] [4] that contains part-of-speech variants of English lexemes. Overall, lack of provisions for common syntactic alternations contributed to more than 25% of system's errors.

(15) **Pair #1421. RTE:** ***True*****, our system:** ***False***
**T:** The Gaza unrest prompted Ahmed Qurei, prime minister, to threaten to quit.
**H:** The Gaza unrest triggered Ahmed Qurei's threat to quit.

The limitations of real-world parsers and our PPAS matching algorithm are also responsible for the difference between our results and manual assessments. A comparison of results for the system run that used only shallow PPAS matching in combination with string overlap, and the manual assessment reported by Vanderwende et al. [27] shows an interesting difference. Vanderwende et al. [27] states that annotators considered that 78 pairs can be correctly labeled as *True* based on syntax alone (it corresponds to recall of 19.5%) while our system correctly labeled 56 true entailments (14%).

The limitations of shallow PPAS matching described above compound with the limitations of WordNet-based similarity measures, lead to a number of errors (5% of all system errors), as in Example 16 where an inverted syntactic structure is accompanied by a lexical paraphrase with conversives. WordNet does not contain any information about most conversives, however, some inference patterns in [29] reflect this relationship.

[4] http://clipdemos.umiacs.umd.edu/catvar/

(16) **Pair #1512. RTE: *True*, our system: *False***
**T:** Lisa Marie was aware of the pressures of being Elvis Presley's daughter, so she didn't exactly pursue songwriting that seriously.
**H:** Lisa Marie Presley's father was Elvis Presley.

Phrasal-level paraphrases (Example 17), where a single lexeme can be replaced by a phrase (e.g., *battlefield — site of fighting*) or one collocation by another (*scored its worst performance — didn't do well*), cannot be handled by our system which considers only semantic similarity at the word level.

(17) **Pair #337. RTE: *True*, our system: *False***
**T:** It asserted that "within this framework, we draw your attention (People's Congress members) to Legislation 24 dealing with foreign currency circulation, which is no longer applicable and it has become one of the most significant obstacles to economic and investment activities.
**H:** Article 24 is obsolete, and is hindering the economy.

The inability of our system to handle phrasal level paraphrases as illustrated in Example 17, was the main reason of 3% of all errors and one of the factors in 8% of wrong guesses. The problem of automatic acquisition of paraphrases has attracted considerable interest in question-answering ([29]), information extraction ([30, 5]) and paraphrasing ([31, 6, 32]). Different methods of extraction of single and multi-word patterns from corpora have been proposed (see, for example, [6, 33, 2, 5, 1]), and recent work by Weeds et al. [34] extends the distributional similarity measures to sub-parses. The incorporation of phrasal level paraphrases into our system has been identified as one of the directions for future research.

## 6 Conclusions

The PASCAL RTE Challenge provided a good opportunity for exploration of the potential and limitations of the shallow PPAS matching approach employed in our system. The comparison of the results of system runs, as well as the analysis of system's errors demonstrated that PPASs are a good starting point for entailment determination. Our analysis showed that in order to take a full advantage of the information they contain, PPASs should be used as an input into a more sophisticated matching algorithm that can handle differences in syntactic structures of the sentences and phrasal-level paraphrases.

## References

1. Szpektor, I., Tanev, H., Dagan, I., Coppola, B.: Scaling web-based acquisition of entailment relations. In Lin, D., Wu, D., eds.: Proceedings of EMNLP 2004, Barcelona, Spain, Association for Computational Linguistics (2004) 41–48
2. Lin, D., Pantel, P.: DIRT-discovery of inference rules from text. In: Proceedings of ACM SIGKDD Conference on Knowledge Discovery and Data Mining. (2001) 323–328

3. Chklovski, T., Pantel, P.: VerbOcean: Mining the web for fine-grained semantic verb relations. In Lin, D., Wu, D., eds.: Proceedings of EMNLP 2004, Barcelona, Spain, Association for Computational Linguistics (2004) 33–40
4. Dagan, I., Glickman, O.: Probabilistic textual entailment: Generic applied modeling of language variability. In: Learning Methods for Text Understanding and Mining Workshop. (2004)
5. Shinyama, Y., Sekine, S.: Paraphrase acquisition for information extraction. In: Proceedings of the Second International Workshop on Paraphrasing: Paraphrase Acquisition and Applications (IWP2003) at ACL 2003, Sapporo, Japan (2004)
6. Barzilay, R., Lee, L.: Learning to paraphrase: An unsupervised approach using multiple-sequence alignment. In: Proceedings of HLT-NAACL 2003. (2003) 16–23
7. Perez, D., Alfonesca, E.: Application of the Bleu algorithm for recognizing textual entailments. In: Proceedings of the PASCAL Challenges Workshop on Recognising Textual Entailment, http://www.cs.biu.ac.il/ glikmao/rte05/index.html (2005) 9–12
8. Braz, R.d.S., Girju, R., Punjakanok, V., Roth, D., Sammons, M.: An inference model for semantic entailment in natural language. In: Proceedings of the PASCAL Challenges Workshop on Recognising Textual Entailment, http://www.cs.biu.ac.il/ glikmao/rte05/index.html (2005) 29–32
9. Bayer, S., Burger, J., Ferro, L., Henderson, J., Yeh, A.: MITRE's submissions to the EU pascal RTE challenge. In: Proceedings of the PASCAL Challenges Workshop on Recognising Textual Entailment, http://www.cs.biu.ac.il/glikmao/rte05/index.html (2005) 41–45
10. Fowler, A., Hauser, B., Hodges, D., Nikes, I., Novischi, A., Stephan, J.: Applying COGEX to recognize textual entailment. In: Proceedings of the PASCAL Challenges Workshop on Recognising Textual Entailment, http://www.cs.biu.ac.il/glikmao/rte05/index.html (2005) 69–72
11. Raina, R., Haghighi, A., Cox, C., Finkel, J., Michels, J., Toutanova, K., MacCartney, B., de Marneffe, M.C., Manning, C., Ng, A.Y.: Robust textual inference using diverse knowledge sources. In: Proceedings of the PASCAL Challenges Workshop on Recognising Textual Entailment, http://www.cs.biu.ac.il/glikmao/rte05/index.html (2005) 53–56
12. Bos, J., Markeret, K.: Combining shallow and deep NLP methods for recognizing textual entailment. In: Proceedings of the PASCAL Challenges Workshop on Recognising Textual Entailment, http://www.cs.biu.ac.il/glikmao/rte05/index.html, PASCAL (2005) 65–69
13. Glickman, O., Dagan, I., Koppel, M.: Web based probabilistic textual entailment. In: Proceedings of the PASCAL Challenges Workshop on Recognising Textual Entailment, http://www.cs.biu.ac.il/ glikmao/rte05/index.html (2005) 33–37
14. Jijkoun, V., de Rijke, M.: Recognizing textual entailment using lexical similarity. In: Proceedings of the PASCAL Challenges Workshop on Recognising Textual Entailment, http://www.cs.biu.ac.il/ glikmao/rte05/index.html (2005) 73–76
15. Kouyelekov, M., Magnini, B.: Recognizing textual entailment with tree edit distance algorithms. In: Proceedings of the PASCAL Challenges Workshop on Recognising Textual Entailment, http://www.cs.biu.ac.il/ glikmao/rte05/index.html (2005) 17–20
16. Newman, E., Stokes, N., Dunnion, J., Carthy, J.: UCD IIRG approach to the textual entailment challenge. In: Proceedings of the PASCAL Challenges Workshop on Recognising Textual Entailment, http://www.cs.biu.ac.il/glikmao/rte05/index.html (2005) 53–56
17. Fellbaum, C., ed.: WordNet: An Electronic Lexical Database. MIT Press (1998)

18. Over, P., Yen, J.: An introduction to duc 2004 intrinsic evaluation of generic new text summarization systems. In: Proceedings of the HLT-NAACL Workshop on Automatic Summarization, DUC 2004, Boston, MA (2004)
19. Dagan, I., Glickman, O., Magini, B.: The PASCAL recognizing textual entailment challenge. In: Proceedings of the PASCAL Challenges Workshop on Recognising Textual Entailment, http://www.cs.biu.ac.il/ glikmao/rte05/index.html (2005) 1–9
20. Bergler, S., Witte, R., Khalife, M., Li, Z., Rudzicz, F.: Using knowledge-poor coreference resolution for text summarization. In: Proceedings of the HLT Workshop on Automatic Summarization, DUC 2003, Edmonton, Canada (2003)
21. Bergler, S., Witte, R., Khalife, M., Li, Z., Chen, Y., Doandes, M., Andreevskaia, A.: Multi-ERSS and ERSS 2004. In: Proceedings of the HLT-NAACL Workshop on Automatic Summarization, DUC 2004, Boston, MA (2004)
22. Sleator, D.D., Temperley, D.: Parsing English with a link grammar. In: Third International Workshop on Parsing Technologies. (1993)
23. Carroll, J., Briscoe, T., Sanfilippo, A.: Parser evaluation: a survey and a new proposal. In: Proceedings, First International Conference on Language Resources and Evaluation, Granada, Spain, European Language Resources Association (1998) 447–454
24. Cunningham, H., Maynard, D., Bontcheva, K., Tablan, V.: GATE: A framework and graphical development environment for robust NLP tools and applications. In: Proceedings of the 40th Anniversary Meeting of the Association for Computational Linguistics. (2002)
25. Witte, R., Bergler, S.: Fuzzy coreference resolution for summarization. In: Proceedings of 2003 International Symposium on Reference Resolution and Its Applications to Question Answering and Summarization (ARQAS), Venice, Italy, Università Ca' Foscari (2003) 43–50
26. Briscoe, E., Carroll, J.: Robust accurate statistical annotation of general text. In: Proceedings of the Third International Conference on Language Resources and Evaluation (LREC 2002), Las Palmas, Canary Islands (2002) 1499–1504
27. Vanderwende, L., Coughlin, D., Dolan, B.: What syntax can contribute in entailment task. In: Proceedings of the PASCAL Challenges Workshop on Recognising Textual Entailment, http://www.cs.biu.ac.il/ glikmao/rte05/index.html (2005) 13–17
28. Habash, N., Dorr, B.: Recognizing system demonstration CatVar: A database of categorial variations for English. In: Proceedings of the MIT Summit, New Orleans, LA (2003) 471–474
29. Lin, D., Pantel, P.: Discovery of inference rules for question-answering. Natural Language Engineering **7** (2001) 343–360
30. Harabagiu, S.M., Maiorano, S.J.: Acquisition of linguistic patterns for knowledge-based information retreival. In: LREC-2000, Athenes, Greece (2000)
31. Glickman, O., Dagan, I.: Acquiring lexical paraphrases from a single corpus. In: Recent Advances in Natural Language Processing, Amsterdam, John Benjamins Publishing Co. (2004)
32. Dolan, W.B., Quirk, C., Brockett, C.: Unsupervised construction of large paraphrase corpora: Exploiting massively parallel news sources. In: Proceedings of COLING 2004. (2004)
33. Barzilay, R., Elhadad, N.: Sentence alignment for monolingual comparable corpora. In: Proceedings of the EMNLP. (2003)
34. Weeds, J., Weir, D., Keller, B.: The distributional similarity of sub-parses. In: Proceedings of the ACL Workshop on Empirical Modeling of Semantic Equivalence and Entailment, ACL (2005) 7–13

# VENSES – A Linguistically-Based System for Semantic Evaluation

Rodolfo Delmonte, Sara Tonelli,
Marco Aldo Piccolino Boniforti, and Antonella Bristot

Department of Language Sciences, Laboratory of Computational Linguistics,
University Ca' Foscari, 30124 Venice, Italy
delmont@unive.it

**Abstract.** The system for semantic evaluation VENSES (Venice Semantic Evaluation System) is organized as a pipeline of two subsystems: the first is a reduced version of GETARUN, our system for Text Understanding. The output of the system is a flat list of augmented head-dependent structures with Grammatical Relations and Semantic Roles labels. The evaluation system is made up of two main modules: the first is a sequence of linguistic rules; the second is a quantitatively based measurement of input structures and predicates. VENSES measures semantic similarity which may range from identical linguistic items, to synonymous, lexically similar, or just morphologically derivable. Both modules go through General Consistency checks which are targeted to high level semantic attributes like presence of modality, negation, and opacity operators, temporal and spatial location checks. Results in cws, recall and precision are homogeneous for both training and test corpus and fare higher than 60%.

## 1 Introduction

The RTE Challenge has taken a special stance with respect to semantic inference evaluation which we quote from [2:1]:

> Textual entailment recognition is the task of deciding, given two text fragments, whether the meaning of one text is entailed (can be inferred) from another text. This task captures generically a broad range of inferences that are relevant for multiple applications.

As the authors comment in their introductory paper to the Workshop, semantic inference evaluation is viewed from an applied empirical perspective, with an effort at "recognizing meaning-entailing variability at the lexical and syntactic level" [2:2], rather than addressing logical representational issues. As a matter of fact, we believe that any applied semantic task would have to cope also with semantic and logical issues and not just in an empirical way, seen that the algorithm that each participant had to implement, was intended to work on a very large range of linguistic phenomena. In fact, in order to capture the "many-to-many mapping between language expression and meanings" – as the same authors comment [2:1] – the system for RTE evaluation has to address

J. Quiñonero-Candela et al. (Eds.): MLCW 2005, LNAI 3944, pp. 344–371, 2006.

lexical, syntactic, semantic, logical, and sometimes pragmatic aspects (whenever the intended meaning is not linguistically expressed).

As also mentioned in [13], when analysed in more detail, the problem of semantic inference evaluation is more complex: for instance, the "intersectivity" issue, as we call it, or what the authors define as the more specific/less specific semantic relation needs to be encoded appropriately if monotonicity has to be detected from syntactic analysis. In addition, in many if not in most cases, the relevant data are not clear-cut relatable to one or the other aspect of linguistic analysis. Lexical issues are mixed up with semantic, syntactic and logical issues in such a way that the implementation of semantic evaluation needs to address them all at the same time.

Even though we might be building some Logical Form to use for semantic inference and eventually logical proof, as [1,9,12] also do, we abandoned this idea. This decision has been supported by empirical data and also on theoretical grounds. In fact, our system can produce a Discourse Model [3] in Situation Semantics terms, which could be used to do reasoning and inferencing: we worked on such a hypothesis for the first three months of the RTE Challenge, on the development set, just to discover that the amount of information made available in the model was insufficient and in many cases it suffered too much from parser brittleness, to guarantee an inferential engine or a theorem prover to work properly. So we turned to a less theoretically demanding system setup and decided to use linear semantically Augmented Head Dependent representations which allowed us to work at a propositional level without sacrificing, however, any of the inferential and logical operations we intended to produce on the T/H pairs. There are also elements of uncertainly in FOL representation usually hard to deal with, which on the contrary play an important role in semantic inference: they may be summarized by the following points, which will be discussed below: Modality, Future Tense, Progressive Mood; Lexicalized Negation; Opaque Second Order Operators (Conditionality); Governing Verbs of Doubt, Verbs of Process, Non-Factives; Temporal Inference; Formulaic Expressions; Non-/Anti-intersective Modifiers.

## 2 System Description

The system for semantic evaluation VENSES (Venice Semantic Evaluation System) is organized as a pipeline of two subsystems: the first is a reduced version of GETARUNS, our system for Text Understanding [6]; the second is the semantic evaluator which was previously created for Summary and Question evaluation[4] and has now been thoroughly revised for the new more comprehensive RTE task.

The reduced GETARUNS is composed of the usual sequence of sub-modules common in Information Extraction systems, i.e. a tokenizer, a multiword and NE recognition module, a PoS tagger based on finite state automata; then a multilayered cascaded RTN-based parser which is equipped with an interpretation module that uses subcategorization information and semantic roles

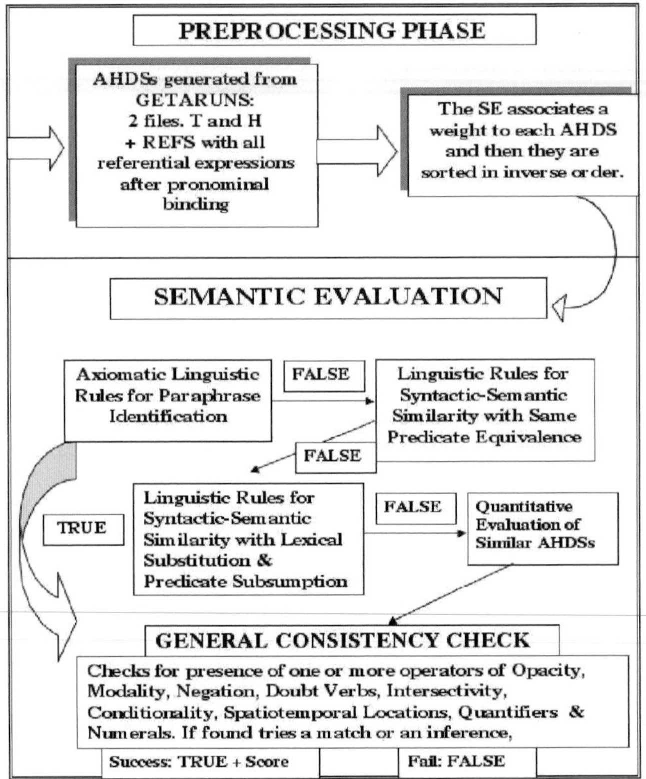


**Fig. 1.** Main Modules of VENSES

processing. The system has a pronominal binding module[7] that works at text/ hypothesis level separately for lexical personal, possessive and reflexive pronouns, which are substituted by the heads of their antecedents - if available. The output of the system is a flat list of head-dependent structures (HDS) with Grammatical Relations (GRs) and Semantic Roles (SRs) labels (for similar approaches see [9,10,11]). Notable additions to the usual formalism is the presence of a distinguished Negation relation; we also mark modals and progressive mood.

The evaluation system uses a cost model with rewards/penalties for T/H pairs where text entailment is interpreted in terms of semantic similarity: the closer the T/H pairs are in semantic terms the more probable is their entailment. Rewards in terms of scores are assigned for each "similar" semantic element; penalties on the contrary can be expressed in terms of scores or they can determine a local failure and a consequent FALSE decision – more on scoring below. In Fig.1 below is a presentation of the system:

The evaluation system accesses the output of GETARUN, i.e. the linguistic representation of the input texts, written on files. It is made up of four main

Modules: the first three are a sequence of linguistic rule-based sub-modules; the fourth is a quantitatively based measurement of input structures. The latter is basically a count of heads, dependents, GRs and SRs, scoring only similar elements in the T/H pair. Similarity may range from identical linguistic items, to synonymous or just morphologically derivable. As to GRs and SRs, they are scored higher according to whether they belong to the subset of core relations and roles, i.e. obligatory arguments, or not, that is adjuncts. All modules go through General Consistency checks which are targeted at high level semantic attributes like presence of modality, negation, and opacity operators, the latter ones as expressed either by the presence of discourse markers of conditionality or by a secondary level relation intervening between the main predicate and a governing higher predicate belonging to the class of non factual verbs. Two other general consistency checks regard temporal and spatial location modifiers which must be identical or entailed in one another, if present.

Linguistic rule-based sub-modules are organized into a sequence of rules going from those containing axiomatic-like paraphrase HDSs which are ranked higher, to rules stating conditions for similarity according to the scale of argumentality which are ranked lower. All rules address HDSs, GRs and Srs together with predicates in the form of lemmata or multiwords. All modules strive for True assessments: however, the Quantitative sub-module can output True or False according to general consistency and scoring. Modifying the scoring function may thus vary the final result dramatically: it may contribute more True decisions if relaxed, so it needs fine tuning. More experimentation has been carried out on a much bigger data set – the training data of the MSR made available by Microsoft on their website http://research.microsoft.com/research/nlp/msr_paraphrase.htm, (see also [8]) - to achieve a more general definition of this function, and will be discussed below.

The remainder of this paper is organized as follows: in section 2 we present our parser and its performance results. In section 3 we discuss the task of Semantic Inference evaluation, we give a linguistically-based definition of the task and present a set of semantic items heuristically related to T/H pairs taken from the RTE dataset. Also, in the same section we briefly comment on previous work. In section 4 we present the implementation of the Semantic Evaluator(SE). In section 5 we present results and a discussion of most common mistakes made by the SE.

### 2.1 An A-As Hybrid Parser

Our parser has been presented in detail lately in a number of papers [3,5] and has achieved 90% recall on the Greval Corpus and 89% recall on the XEROX-700 corpus, this latter test limited only to SUBJ/OBJ GRs. As in most robust parsers, we use a sequence or cascade of transducers: however, in our approach, since we intend to recover sentence level structure, the process goes from partial parses to full sentence parses. Sentence and then clause level parsing are crucial to the right assignment of Arguments and Adjuncts (hence A-As) to a governing predicate head. This is paramount in our scheme which aims at recovering predicate-argument structures, besides performing a compositional semantic translation of each semantically headed constituent.

The parser is organized into eleven layers as described below:

- Tokenizer produces input sentence which is a list of tokens obtained from the input text by sentence splitting;
- Tagger associates lexical categories to words from dictionary lookup or from morphological analysis;
- Tag disambiguation with finite-state automata and the aid of lexical information;
- Head-based Chunk building phase;
- Recursive argument/adjunct (A/A) constituent building procedure as a list of syntactic-semantic structures with tentative GFs labels, interspersed with punctuation marks;
- Clause builder that takes as input the A/A vector and tries to split it into separate clauses;
- Recursive clause-level interpretation procedure, that filters displaced or discontinuous constituents;
- Complex sentence organizer which outputs DAG structures;
- Logical Form with syntactic indices and Semantic Roles;
- Transducer from DAGs to AHDSs by recursive calls;
- Pronominal Binding at clause level.

We would like to define our parser "mildly bottom-up" because the structure building process cycles on a subroutine that collects constituents until it decides that what it has parsed might be analysed as Argument or Adjunct. This proceeds until a finite verb is reached and the parse is continued with the additional help of Verb Guidance by subcategorization information. Punctuation marks are also collected during the process and are used to organize the list of arguments and adjuncts into tentative clauses.

The clause builder looks for two elements in the input list: the presence of the verb-complex and punctuation marks, starting from the idea that clauses must contain a finite verb complex: dangling constituents will be adjoined to their left adjacent clause, by the clause interpreter after failure while trying to interpret each clause separately. The clause-level interpretation procedure interprets clauses on the basis of lexical properties of the governing verb: verbless clauses or fragments are dealt with by adding a default BE dummy predicate.

The final processor takes as input fully interpreted clauses which may be coordinate, subordinate, or main clauses. These are adjoined together according to their respective position. Care is taken to account for Reported Speech complex sentences which require the Parenthetical Clause to become Main governing clause. Specialized procedures are used to deal with non-declarative non-canonical structures like Questions, Imperatives, sentences with Reported Direct speech, Clausal Subject sentences and extraposed That-clause fronted sentences [see 4,7]. Fragments are computed at the end as a default strategy.

### 2.2 Parsing and Robust Techniques

As far as parsing is concerned, we purport the view that the implementation of a sound parsing algorithm must go hand in hand with sound grammar construction. Extra grammaticalities can be better coped with within a solid linguistic framework rather than without it. Our parser is a rule-based deterministic parser in the sense that it uses lookahead to reduce backtracking. It also implements Finite State Automata in the task of tag disambiguation, and produces multiwords whenever lexical information allows it. In our parser we use a number of parsing strategies and graceful recovery procedures which follow a strictly parameterized approach to their definition and implementation. Recovery procedures are also used to cope with elliptical structures and uncommon orthographic and punctuation patterns.

The grammar is equipped with a lexicon containing a list of fully specified inflected word forms where each entry is followed by its lemma and a list of morphological features, organized in the form of attribute-value pairs. However, morphological analysis for English has also been implemented and used for OutOfVocabulary words. The system uses a core fully specified lexicon, which contains approximately 10,000 most frequent entries of English, where every predicate – be it verb, noun, or adjective – is annotated for Syntactic Category, Aspectual Category, Semantic Category [6]; then the list of subcategorized arguments follows (if any exist), each argument being specified by Syntactic Constituency, Grammatical Function, Semantic Role and a list of Semantic Features from a set of 75, the same that we used to relabel WordNet . In addition to that, there are all lexical forms provided by a fully revised version of COMLEX. In order to take into account phrasal and adverbial verbal compound forms, we also use lexical entries made available by UPenn and TAG encoding. Their grammatical verbal syntactic codes have then been adapted to our formalism and is used to generate an approximate subcategorization scheme with an approximate aspectual and semantic class associated to it. Semantic inherent features for OOV words, be they nouns, verbs, adjectives or adverbs, are provided by a fully revised version of WordNet – 270,000 lexical entries - in which we used 75 semantic classes similar to those provided by CoreLex. These are all consulted at runtime. We use these features to induce semantic similarity for two entities whenever at least 2 identical features are matched in their feature list.

Another important element of analysis is constituted by Semantic Roles: we have reformatted all publicly available inventories, such as FrameNet, VerbNet and PropBank, and use them in that order, seen that FrameNet has more specific labels than the other two lexica. However, we also produced our own fully specified lexicon which is accessed before VerbNet.

Our training corpus for the complete system is made up 200,000 words and is organized by a number of texts taken from different genres, portions of the UPenn WSJ corpus, test-suits for grammatical relations, narrative texts, and sentences taken from COMLEX manual.

We don't have space here to describe the Pronominal Binding module which accesses Referential Heads at clause level and establishes possible antecedent-pronoun candidate lists which are then weighted and the best one chosen (but see [7]). As fpr the 1367 T/H pairs of the RTE Challenge, the parser has spotted 85 pronominal expressions which have received an antecedent: we checked the bindings and the result is 82% accuracy.

As an example of an ADHS consider Snippets 78[1] reported here below:

T. Clinton's new book is not big seller here.
H. Clinton's book is a big seller.

Whose structure is computed respectively as follows:

T.
**be(adj-locative, here).**
**seller(ncmod, big).**
**book(ncmod-specif, 'Clinton-s_').**
**be(xcomp-prop, seller).**
**be(subj-theme_bound, book).**
**be(neg, not).**

H.
**seller(ncmod, big).**
**book(ncmod-specif, 'Clinton-s_').**
**be(xcomp-prop, seller).**
**be(subj-theme_bound, book).**

The presence of the negation operator in the T portion of the snippet will prevent the evaluator from assessing to TRUE even though the relevant HD structures are identical.

## 3 The Task of Semantic Inference Evaluation

Even though at the bottom of any computation, semantic evaluation - in any case of non equality of the linguistic descriptions involved - needs lexical chains of some kind to be produced or attempted, we consider it less relevant than an appropriate setup for semantic inference. Here below we assess the contribution of a number of different linguistic scenarios – which will be further commented below – that we tried to set apart as can be derived from our SE. In Table 1. we can see their productivity in terms of number of T/H pairs inferred as TRUE, disregarding for the moment the fact that some of these might be false positives.

All rule types will be commented in detail below. What we wanted to highlight at this point, is the minimal impact of the Rule set used for Paraphrase evaluation, where we actually use the lemmas to be matched together in axiomatic-like structures: in other words, it is only in these cases that the actual linguistic

[1] All examples are from the corpus released for the RTE Challenge available at: http://www.pascal-network.org/Challenges/RTE, and have the same identifier.

**Table 1.** Ratio of TRUE classified snippets by Rule type accessed by the SE

| Rule Type/Datasets | Test set | Training Set | Test + Train |
|---|---|---|---|
| Quantitative evaluation | 66 20.5% | 52 21.7% | 118 21% |
| Paraphrase evaluation | 31 9.62% | 23 9.58% | 54 9.61% |
| Syntactic + Semantic eval. | 128 39.7% | 99 41.2% | 227 40.39% |
| Lexical chains evaluation | 75 23.3% | 51 21.2% | 126 22.42% |
| Hybrid for short snippets | 22 6.8% | 15 6.2% | 37 6.58% |
| Total no. snippets | 322 100% | 240 100% | 562 100% |

expressions play a determining role in the task to derive a semantic inference. The number of axioms we built on the basis of Development and Test sets is 47: considering the number of T/H pairs evaluated to True, the mapping is almost one rule to each pair. On the contrary, the great majority of rules applied by the SE come from the combination of Syntactic and Semantic Inference, where Lexical Inference also plays a role.

We also want to point out that our system produced antecedents for pronominal expressions at snippet level, however we haven't been able to find many examples in which such information would have been useful to the RTE task – they are all discussed below. We are not here referring to all those cases defined as Control in LFG theory, where basically the unexpressed subject of an untensed proposition (infinitival, participial, gerundive) either lexically, syntactically or structurally controlled is bound to some argument of the governing predicate.

We have also been working on the MSR training dataset, made available by Microsoft, which has 4076 T/H pairs. We noticed however that it has a major flaw: the annotators judged True pairs in which anaphoric binding applied between T and H. Under the entailment perspective, we think this impossible and a bad mistake, considering the fact that snippets are just small portions of text taken randomly and not in the appropriate context – same text, sequentially with the antecedent preceding the pronoun – to allow such an inference. However, under the "Paraphrase" perspective, i.e. under the additional constraints that the two snippets are taken from a cluster with the same content, it is certainly correct: there are some 250 such cases. Results obtained by our system – which we will not report in this paper - are close to the ones obtained under RTE (accuracy is 59.46%), with the proviso however that the proportion of FALSE to TRUE pairs was 1/3, and accuracy for TRUE is 63%.

### 3.1 Defining the Task of the Semantic Evaluator (SE)

As the examples discussed here below will make clear, the task of the SE is in no way definable on a purely theoretical semantic basis (but see [13]). One such particularly revealing case is the one constituted by the socalled (Non/Anti)-Intersective modifiers dealt with in current semantic and linguistic literature. It is a fact that presence of an intersective attribute in the Text and its omission in the Hypothesis hampers the entailment in theoretical terms, but not always in the application-oriented scenario of RTE. A typical case is shown in the following examples,

i. John bought a red car.
ii. John bought a car.

where example i. is more informative than example ii. due to the presence of the adjective "red". In addition, "car" and "red" can be interpreted compositionally so that ii. is entailed by i. Consider the next pairs:

iii. John was presented to an alleged great Italian scientist.
iv. John was presented to a great Italian scientist.
v. John was presented to a great scientist.
vi. John was presented to a scientist.

In iii. we inserted a "non-intersective" adjective "alleged", which causes the referential expression headed by "scientist" to become non extensional - the same applies to "anti-intersective" modifiers like "fake". In this case the two sentences cannot be interpreted compositionally and are not entailed; also sentence v. is not entailed in iv. in our context, by virtue of the presence of a geographical/intersective modifier in iv.; on the contrary vi. is entailed in v. "great" being a subjective modifier, but theoretically it belongs to "relative intersective" class which is not compositional.

To cope with similar problems, all modifiers that imply non-entailment have been listed separately and constitute a checklist against which modifier heads are checked when attempting to assess the entailment of two snippets.

**RTE LINGUISTIC RULE – Definition 1.** A linguistically based approximation to a sound definition of the task at hand may be represented by the Rule below:

**Two text fragments approximate the same meaning - are semantically equivalent - whenever they are**

- **a. linguistically coherent**
- **b. semantically consistent**
- **c. propositionally compatible**

In order to make the definition above more concrete, we created a set of Syntactic-Semantic Classes, both theoretically and empirically derived from the RTE examples dataset. They are divided up into two subsets because the actions carried out by our Semantic Evaluator address conditions necessary for True T/H pairs separately from those for False T/H pairs. We would like to comment extensively each semantic item with an example from RTE dataset: however this would make the paper too lengthy. So we decided to limit our analysis to an abbreviated comment of relevant linguistic elements (see also [13]). All snippets are individuated by their original number and the texts are included in an Appendix at the end of the paper. All these cases are positively dealt with by our SE.

### Syntactic-Semantic Classes for Linguistic Coherence

*i. Conditions for TRUE*
Same Main Heads; Same Main Dependents; Identity of GRs; Identity of SRs; Morphologically derived Heads
*i. Examples*
*Snippets 238* TRUE (Same SUBJect, Assassination/Assassinate, Same Temporal Adjunct)
*Snippets 693* TRUE (Invasion/Invade, Swedish/Swedes, Entailed Temporal Adjunct)
*Snippets 947 TRUE* (murder/kill,police commander/police officer)

*ii. Conditions for FALSE*
Opposite GRs/SRs; Non-identical GRs/SRs; Argument/Adjunct Swap; Missing Argument; Missing Main Predicate; Modifier/Attribute Swap
*ii. Examples*
*Snippets 152* FALSE (Same SUBJect swapped, same verb predicate)
*Snippets 602* FALSE (Same verb predicate, same Patient SUBJect/OBJect, missing omitted Agent/SUBJect)

### Syntactic-Semantic Classes for Semantic Consistency

*i. Conditions for TRUE*
Synonyms with adequate GRs / SRs; Entailment of Main Predicates with adequate GRs/SRs; Definitional Paraphrase; Formulaic Expressions; Pronominal Binding
*i. Examples*
*Snippets 466* TRUE (Same SUBJect, presence of formulaic expression "would like to acknowledge and thank"/recognize, same OBJect)
*Snippets 496* TRUE (Same SUBJect, Same main predicate BE, paraphrase indirectly derivable from definitions in WordNet)
*Snippets 648* TRUE (Same SUBJect, appositive nominal head "widow" in text entails "wife" in hypothesis)
*Snippets 783* TRUE (Same SUBJect, "fire" predicate/"send letter dismissal" complex predicate, same OBJect/ToOBJect)
*Snippets 876* TRUE (Same SUBJect, Kill and Die are treated as antonyms but they also share a part of same meaning – Die is implied in the action of Kill, the SUBJects have different SRs, same temporal location)
*Snippets 912* TRUE (Same/entailed SUBJect, "hurl obscenity"complex predicate/"curse" predicate, same IndirectOBJect)
*Snippet 933* TRUE (Same SUBJect, Synonym Main Predicate: same GRs with same SRs)
*Snippets 1121* TRUE (Pronominal SUBJect "it" bound as controller for Relevant Verb Predicate BUY/ACQUIRE, same OBJect) *see also Snippets 74; Snippets 201 below.*

*Snippets 1639* TRUE (Synonym Main Predicate more/less specific, same SUBJect-OBJect arguments with different GRs vs same SRs)

*ii. Conditions for FALSE*
Antonymity; Non-coincidence of Referential Attributes; Propositional/Full Paraphrase; Opposite Entailment (Non)-Intersective Modifiers; Inexistent Relevant Semantic Relations
*ii. Examples*
*Snippets 12* FALSE (Same SUBJect, opposite meaning of governed verb keep_from/release, lexical inference for OBJect form/document)
*Snippets 46* FALSE (PP adjunct nominal head morphologically derived/main verb Hypothesis – loss/lose, reverted GRs-SRs)
*Snippets 67* FALSE (Same SUBJect, opposite meaning of main verb come_down/rise)
*Snippets 148* FALSE (Same SUBJect, opposite meaning of main verb rise/drop)
*Snippets 220* FALSE (Same main phrasal verb predicate – begin legal action, reverted GRs/SRs)
*Snippets 2049* FALSE (Same SUBJect, same verb complement, non synonym, non entailed main verb predicate – order/demand – non identical SRs)
*Snippets 2064* FALSE (Same clause, Intersective modifier in Text – Western, geographical adjective/omitted non entailed modifier due to superlative relation)
*Snippets 2084* FALSE (Same clause, Different non entailed nominal predicate – "Israel" predicate nominal postmodifier)
*Snippets 2120* FALSE (SUBJect non entailed – less specific, different cardinality, spatial location specified for main verb FREE in Text not it Hypothesis)
*Snippets 2141* FALSE (SUBJect negated in Text, main verb negated in Text)
Inexistent Relevant Semantic Relations: *Snippets 620* FALSE; *Snippets 619* FALSE; *Snippets 700* FALSE; *Snippets 712* FALSE; *Snippets 677* FALSE

**Syntactic-Semantic Classes for Propositional Compatibility**

*i. Conditions for TRUE*
Modality, Future Tense, Progressive Mood; Negation, Lexicalized Negation; Light Verbs (Copulative, SpatioTemporal locating, etc.); Governing Verbs of Doubt; Governing Verbs of Process; Opaque Second Order Operators; Factuality and Counterfactuality; Temporal Inference & Operators
*i. Examples*
*Snippets 74* TRUE (Same SUBJect – by virtue of pronominal binding, his/ foreign ministry; and lexical inference country/South Korea -, continue/Negated Modal Verb won't + change governing main verbal head SEND)
*Snippets 172* TRUE (Same SUBJect, verbal head Suspect governing light verb BE/Modal May governing Cause, Same OBJects – More/Less Specific)
*Snippets 294* TRUE (Same SUBJect,Take_place/Last, three-day/three day)
*Snippets 1014* TRUE (Same SUBJect, More/less specific Heads, Lexicalized Negation Paraphrase Verb+It+Predicate Adjective /Modal Verb + negation)

*Snippets 1164* TRUE (Same SUBJect,Tell/Lexically inferred verbal head Announce, Negated morphologically derived Noun OBJect Cooperation/Negated main verbal head)
*Snippets 1168* TRUE (Same SUBJect, lexically inferrable main predicate tell/say, Negated Modal verb cannot + Operator unless, Same governing verb LIFT, Synonymous OBJect noun heads blockade/embargo)
*Snippets 1197* TRUE (Similar Adjunct with synonymous main verb Focus/Concentrate, main IndirectOBJect noun head matched to Adverbial Modifier + main verb, Future Tense / Modal Verb)
*Snippets 1214* TRUE (Same SUBJect, Same main verb Head, Temporal Inference and Modal Verbs (will + by the end of year 2001/should + before 2002)
*Snippets 1261* TRUE (Operators but-until + negation on main verb/if, Light verb HOLD/propose, Nominal head AGREEMENT morphologically derived from verbal head AGREE)
*Snippets 1265* TRUE (Same SUBJect, main verbal head Prepare is synonymous with Make in hypothesis, Progressive Mood / Future Tense)
*Snippets 1284* TRUE (Lexical Transformation noun Reduction/verb Reduce in Hypothesis; verb Reduce negated in Text but governed by Expect)

*ii. Conditions for FALSE*
Negation; Modality; Conditionality; Opacity; Doubt Verbs
*ii. Examples*
*Snippets 60* FALSE (Operator IF with conditional clause, non entailed main verb predicate try/continue)
*Snippets 73* FALSE (opaque nominal predicate governor – discussion, same inferrable clause – allow/grant, same governed TO_OBJect/main OBJect)
*Snippets 77* FALSE (opaque governing predicate talk_about, same clause – Dow_Jones be_down)
*Snippets 98* FALSE (SUBJect non inferrable by Knowledge of the world – Arafat/prime minister, same governed verb predicate, same IndirectOBJect)
*Snippets 171* FALSE (Same/entailed SUBJect, verbal head Suspect governing Same verb/nominal predicate of BE, Same/entailed OBJects – More/Less Specific)
*Snippets 227* FALSE (Same SUBJect, lexically inferrable main verb predicate say/decide, negated/quantified governed clause SUBJect, deontic/can modality on governed clause verb predicate, same OBJect)
*Snippets 516* FALSE (Modal + governing verb/Same verb predicate, same OBJect)

## 4 Implementing the Semantic Evaluator (SE)

As said above, the SE is organized into two main group of modules: a quantitatively based module, and a sequence of linguistic rules where quantitive scoring is also taken into account when needed, to increase confidence in the decision process. The two modules must then undergo General Consistency Checks which ascertain the presence of possible mismatches at semantic level. In particular, these checks take care of the following semantic items:

- presence of spatiotemporal locations relative to the same governing predicate, or a similar one as has been computed from previous modules;
- presence of opacity operators like discourse markers for conditionality having scope over the governing predicate under analysis;
- presence of quantifiers and other referentiality related determiners attached to the same nominal head in the T/H pair under analysis and chosen as relevant one by previous computation;
- presence of antonyms in the T/H pair at the level of governing predicates;
- presence of predicates belonging to the class of "doubt" expressing verbs, governing the relevant predicate shared by the T/H pair.

In some cases the General Consistency Checks have to be suspended: in particular whenever both T/H pairs contain opacity operators and negation, as for instance in Snippets no. 1014 reported in the Appendix, and other similar examples.

### 4.1 The Linguistic Rule-Based Modules

These Modules are organized as a sequence of sub-modules which start from exceptional cases down to default cases.

Exceptional cases of Semantic Inference are those constituted by Paraphrase and Reformulation rules where axiomatic structures are addressed; then Lexical Inference follows in snippets where the linguistic elements checked should be identical, synonymous, morphologically derivable or sharing a congruent number of semantic features; Syntactic and Semantic inference rules follow in which different structures are transformed and checked on the basis of GRs and SRs first, then lexical chains are attempted; finally Hybrid (partially heuristic) rules are tried in which both structures and lexical items are matched.

Each rule operates at propositional level within each clause to find matches: however, head-dependent representations are just an unordered and set of terms where the hierarchical organization of syntactic structures needs to be reconstructed. Since predicate-argument structures have to be addressed separately from predicate-adjuncts ones, before entering the semantic evaluator, we assign scores to GRs and SRs and then sort AHDSs accordingly. In this way, the core arguments are always in the front of the list contaning all current structures, as for instance in Snippet 46 reported here below,

T - The Yankees split Hollywood with something to feel OK about after last night's 5-4 loss to the Dodgers.
H - Dodgers lose first game ever at Fenway.

**1000-loss(ncmod-specif, '5/4').**
**1000-loss(ncmod-specif, 'night-s_').**
**1000-loss(ncmod-specif, to, dodger).**

**400-feel(ncmod-temporal, after, loss).**
**200-feel(obj-theme, ok).**
**250-split(xcomp-prop, feel).**
**100-feel(subj-agent, 'Hollywood').**
**20-split(iobj-comitative, with, something).**
**10-split(obj-source, hollywood).**
**0-split(subj-theme, 'Yankee').**
**1500-lose(adj-mod, ever).**
**1000-lose(ncmod-location, at, 'Fenway').**
**50-lose(xcomp-agent, game).**
**0-lose(subj-theme_aff, dodger).**

We also address main clause first always by means of scoring, seen that SUBJects and OBJects of secondary clauses are weighted differently.

The level of main clause is then switched to that of dependent clause when needed. Dependent clauses may be very important to determine the outcome of an inference: they may be tensed (head label CCOMP) or untensed (head label XCOMP). The governing head predicate is responsible for the factitivity of the dependent. To this aim, important elements checked at propositional level are opacity, modality, and negation. Opacity is determined by type of governing predicates, basically those belonging to the class of nonfactive predicates. Modality is revealed by the presence of modal verbs at this level of computation. Modality could also be instantiated at sentence level by adverbials, and be verified by General Consistency Checks. Finally, negation may be expressed locally as an adjunct of the verb, but also as a negative conjuction and negative adverbial – see examples above. It may also be present in the determiner of the nominal head and checked separately when comparing referring expressions considered in the inference. Negation may also be incorporated lexically in the verb in the class of the so-called "doubt" verbs.

**The Paraphrase Rule Sub-module.** This sub-module addresses definition-like H sentences, or simple paraphrases of the meaning expressed by the main predicate of the T text. Generally speaking, every time one such rule is fired, the T/H pair contains a conceptually complex lexical predicate and its paraphrase in conceptually simple components.

Examples of such cases are constituted by pairs like the following:

a. interview --> conduct an interview
b. pressurise --> apply pressure
c. treat --> receive treatment (provide)
d. fire --> send letter of dismissal

where both a. and b. were actually present in WordNet while c. did not figure with the same predicates but rather with the one in brackets; d. was totally absent.

Definitions and paraphrases are looked up at first in the glosses made available by WordNet. In case of failure a list of some 50 manually made up axiomatic rules are accessed – built on the basis of the training dataset. Each such rule addresses main predicates in the T/H pair, together with the presence of semantically relevant dependent if needed, and whenever the concept expressed by the lexically complex predicate requires it. Together with the predicates, the rules select relevant GRs and SRs when needed. In addition, more restrictions are introduced on additional arguments or adjuncts. As is the case with all the rules, penalties are explored in terms of semantic operators of the main predicate like negation, modality and opacity inducing verbs which must either be absent or be identical in the T/H pair. Below we report one of the axiomatic-like rules[2],

```
    complex\_induct(Text,apply,\_,pressure,obj-\_),
    complex\_induct(Text,pressure,\_,Ent,ncmod-\_),
    nonvar(Ent),
    (complex\_induct(Hypo,pressurize,Ent,\_,obj-\_);
    complex\_induct(Hypo,pressurise,Ent,\_,obj-\_)),

assess\_penalty([apply,pressurise],Hypo,Text,Scores),
    Scores=[],
    !.
```

where Text contains all AHDSs for Text snippet, Hypo contains all AHDSs for Hypothesis snippet; "complex_induct" is a recursive call that looks into the list of AHDSs and tries to instantiate the appropriate structure with the constants indicated above: i.e., APPLY as head predicate, with PRESSURE as dependant, with the GR "obj". In the second call, the head predicate must be PRESSURE and the GR ncmod. "Ent" should not be empty and will have to be instantiated in the same linguistic expression in the following calls, applied this time to the Hypothesis list of AHDSs, where the main head predicate should be PRESSURIZE and its spelling variant PRESSURISE. The two main predicates are checked for propositional level penalties, if any: Scores should be empty otherwise a fail will ensue.

**The Syntactic-Semantic Rule Sub-module.** The syntactic-semantic rule sub-module is organized into a sequence of subcalls where the T/H pairs are checked for semantic similarity starting from sameness of main predicates to semantic approximate match.

The first subcall requires the presence of same HDs as main predicates with core arguments, i.e. the ones which have been computed as subject, object, indirect object, arg_mod (passive "by" agent adjunct), xcomp. Nonconflicting SRs are checked in all subcalls: i.e. subject-agent are allowed to match with arg_mod-agent and subject-theme_affected with object-theme_affected but not viceversa. These matches take care of what are usually referred to as lexical alternations for verb sucategorization frames, and lexical rules in LFG terms which encompass such syntactic phenomena as passive, intransitivization, ergativization, dative shift, etc. Here below we report one example of such rules,

[2] The SE is written in SWI Prolog and runs under Unix or any other compatible system.

```
    same\_pred(Hypo,Text,Pred,Score1),
    best\_role1(Hypo,Text,Role),
    evaluate\_opaques(Pred, Hypo,Text),
    assess\_penalty(Pred, Hypo,Text,Score), Score=[],
    check\_veridicity(Pred, Hypo,Text,Head),
    same\_mainhead(Hypo,Text,Score2),
    same\_role(Role,First,Score3),
    same\_head(Rte,First,Score4),

evaluate\_scoring(Score1,Score2,Score3,Score4,Weight),
    !.
```

where "same_pred" looks for identical governing head predicate which is then further checked for best role, again by cycling in the lists of AHDSs for Text and Hypothesis. From this point onward, the SE checks at propositional level for the presence of possible penalty issuing main governing predicates with the two calls "evaluate_opaques" and "access_penalty". The following calls on the contrary check predicate-argument structures for the soundness of Semantic Roles and Grammatical Relations. Scores are then produced which are summed up and computed as Weight. This is then finally evaluated at higher level together with high level General Consistency Checks.

The second subcall requires the presence of semantically similar HDs as a combination of main head and main dependent and at least another identical HD structure within the core argument subset. Other subcalls included in this group check nominalization derivational relations intervening between main predicate of T and H, which in one case is checked with edit distance measures. A certain number of additional rules checks for semantic similarity, which can range from synonymous, down to morphologically derived.

The third subcall takes as input a list of "light-verbs" in semantic terms, i.e. verbs including "be", "have", "appear", and other similar copulative and locational verbs – like "live", "hold", "take_place", "participate", etc. - which are used to either make a definition, assert a property of the subject, individuate a location of the subject etc. These verbs are matched against main predicates and core arguments of the T portion, which must be identical to H. Quantitative measures are added to confirm the choice. Notable exceptions are sentences containing "be_born" predication which require specific constructions on the other member of the T/H pair.

The fourth subcall takes as input at least one identical main predicate HD non argument structure and one additional core argument or adjunct structure. Quantitative measures are added to confirm the choice.

The fifth subcall looks for different main predicates with core arguments which however must be non antonyms, non negative polarity and be synonyms. In addition, there must be at least another important identical non argument HD structure shared. Quantitative measures are added to confirm the choice. One such case is represented by Snippets 1639 reported in the Appendix.

These cases must be treated appropriately to distinguish them from what happens in real opposite meaning snippets where the SE considers SRs which must also be opposite, as in snippets 933; or cases in which the snippet is rescued due to the presence of same SRs, see Snippets 876, where DIE and KILL have entailed meaning; but when KILL is used in the passive, the SRs attached to their SUBJects will be identical.

### 4.2 The Quantitative Module

In this module all Heads, Dependents, GRs and SRs are collected for each member of the T/H pair and then they are passed to a scoring function that takes care of identical or similar members by assigning a certain score to every hit. Penalties correspond to high scores, while rewards correspond to low scores. A threshold is then set at a certain value which should encode the presence of a comparatively high number of identical/similar linguistic items. As said above, higher scores are assigned to core GRs and there is a scale also for SRs where Agent has higher score.

As with previous subcalls, at the end of the computation semantic consistency and integrity is checked by collecting and comparing semantic operators, as well as performing a search of possible governing "doubt" verbs.

Generally speaking, we also treat short utterances differently from long ones. A stricter check is performed whenever an utterance has 3 or less HD structures, the reason being that in these structures some of the above mentioned subcalls would fail due to insufficient information available. (This could be related to Application Domain, in particular QA having always shorter Hypotheses than others).

## 5 Results and Discussion

The RTE task is a hard task: this may be partly due to the way in which it has been formulated – half of the snippets are TRUE, the other half are FALSE. It is usually the case that 10-15% of mistakes are ascribable to the parser or any other analysis tool – at least this is what we expect from our parser, or other off-the-shelf parsers freely available from the web; another 5-10% mistakes will certainly come from insufficient semantic information – and this is what we measured on our results. Whenever a system makes 20% errors this is doubled to 40% due to corpus setup, and the final result will become 60% overall Recall.

As far as the Test set is concerned, our system correctly classified 285/400 False annotated snippets, and 194/400 True annotated snippets. As a result, the system misclassified 321 pairs out of 800 examples. The majority of mistakes – 193, i.e. 60.1% - were false negatives, which are T/H pairs which the system classified as false but were annotated as true. The number of false positives is 128, i.e. 39.9%, which the system wrongly classified as true. If we compute the internal consistency of classification of the algorithm, we come up with the following data: 128 false positives over an overall number of 322 pairs classified as true by the system corresponds to 60.3% overall accuracy for true snippets; 193 false negatives over a total number of 478 pairs classified as false by the system corresponds to 59.5% overall accuracy for false snippets.

As can be seen from Tab. 2, the system has produced different result in each Application domain, so we will now look with more details at accuracy data for each of the seven application fields:

- IR cws:0.7163 accuracy:0.6556
- CD cws:0.7139 accuracy:0.6667
- PP cws:0.8563 accuracy:0.8200

These three fields are by far those obtaining the best scoring by our system. In particular the Paraphrase Acquisition dataset fares higher simply because we acquired a good number of paraphrases from a number of sources including WordNet Definitions and turned them into appropriate "axiom-like" rules as described above. As to Comparable Documents and Information Retrieval, both syntax and semantics play a role in selecting the required synonyms and antonyms, within the appropriate predicate-argument structure as defined by GRs and SRs. The second set of data fares somewhat worse:

- IE cws:0.6534 accuracy:0.5833
- QA cws:0.5295 accuracy:0.5692
- RC cws:0.5796 accuracy:0.5357

In all these cases, results are better than chance overall but they are not up to the expected results partly because of semantic inadequacies in the thesaurus, as RC may suggest. But also partly because of the lack of suitable syntactic transformation rules for syntactic alternations, in particular all those cases involving

**Table 2.** Ratio of TRUE classified snippets by Rule type accessed by the SE

| **Test-set Results** | **Training-set Results** |
|---|---|
| cws: 0.6306 | cws: 0.6459 |
| accuracy: 0.5950 | accuracy: 0.6032 |
| precision: 0.6180 | precision: 0.6250 |
| recall: 0.4975 | recall: 0.5124 |
| f: 0.5512 | f: 0.5631 |
| QA cws:0.5295 acc:0.5692 | QA cws:0.6360 acc:0.5556 |
| PP cws:0.8563 acc:0.8200 | PP cws:0.6249 acc:0.6585 |
| IE cws:0.6534 acc:0.5833 | IE cws:0.6119 acc:0.6000 |
| CD cws:0.7139 acc:0.6667 | CD cws:0.7416 acc:0.6633 |
| IR cws:0.7163 acc:0.6556 | IR cws:0.6795 acc:0.6286 |
| RC cws:0.5796 acc:0.5357 | RC cws:0.5529 acc:0.5243 |
| MT cws:0.4693 acc:0.4750 | MT cws:0.6359 acc:0.6111 |

modifiers treated as arguments in one of the T/H pair. Finally the worst result obtained by the system,

- MT cws:0.4693 accuracy:0.4750

is represented by the MT data subset. The strange thing is that the Development set diverges only in this case from the Test set, by reaching a much higher result

- MT cws:0.6359 accuracy:0.6111

The other divergent case is represented by the PP results which fare lower than the ones obtained for the Test set,

- PP cws:0.6249 accuracy:0.6585

On a closer look, reasons for these differences are not due to system performance but to differences in distribution of the two application settings in Test and Development datasets, which are almost reversed: in the Test set MT pairs are almost the double of the PP pairs; the opposite applies to the Development set. In fact, if looked at from this perspective the results become absolutely comparable. These are the total figures in the two datasets:

- TEST SET
  - MT – 120 T/H pairs = 15%
  - PP – 50 T/H pairs = 6.25%
- DEVELOPMENT SET
  - MT – 54 T/H pairs = 9.5%
  - PP – 82 T/H pairs = 14.5%

In other words, the system performs slightly over chance in the MT application field - summing up the accuracy data and dividing by 2 we get 50.4%. In the PP field the results fare around 74% accuracy, still higher than other fields but no so much as 82% of the test set.

We looked into our mistakes to evaluate the impact of the parser on final Recall and we found out that: 10 snippets out of 100 TRUE ones have a wrong parse which can be regarded the main cause of the mistake. In other words only 10% of wrong results can be ascribed to bad parses. The remaing 10% is due to insufficient semantic information. In turn, this may be classified as follows:

- 80% is due to lack of paraphrases and definitions;
- 10% is due to wrong SemanticRole assignment;
- 10% is due to lack of synonym/antonym relations.

When we started working on the training corpus, verb predicates synsets made available by WordNet have been augmented by the information contained in Grady Ward's MOBY Thesaurus (http://www.dcs.shef.ac.uk/research/ilash/

Moby/). Additional information has been derived from a manually reorganized version of Roget's Thesaurus, again limited though to verb predicates. In particular, antonymity is lacking in WordNet where the choice has been that of listing only contradictory items (male/female). However antonymity has two more types to be taken into account: scalar antonyms where the two items don't need to be one or the other and can be between the two extremes of a particular scale (hot/cold); then relational opposites which are pairs that don't represent extremes of some scale (stop/go).

We also felt we needed information related to negative polarity verb predicates which we derived from Harvard Dictionary derived from Harvard IV-4 e Laswell's dictionary on the Dynamics of Culture (http://www.wjh.harvard.edu/). The paraphrase and definition list for verb predicates taken from WordNet and transformed into HD structures was also updated in order to cover some missing cases. For instance, we had to implement a new paraphrase for the verb FIRE which is paraphrased as "send dismissal letter to" in Snippets 783. The list of HDSs will be accessed by the Evaluator in the appropriate Module.

## 6 Related Work

Our approach to textual entailment can be compared to other similar approaches based on deep parsing, in particular see [1,12], which however, eventually derive a logical form to undertake semantic processing by means of a theorem prover. As a matter of fact, we also produce a logical form of each snippet, where syntactic indices generated by the parser are accompanied by semantic role labels, and levels of dependency or modification are encoded in embedding. However, since unification could only be applied whenever lexical substitutions or lexical paraphrases for semantically similar predicates have been accomplished, we assume our system to be a better tool for achieving the same goal. In this sense, we follow closely what [11,16] also do in their system, apart again from the theorem prover. Also [10] can be regarded another example of a system using dependency trees to do semantic similarity measures. We believe our structures to be a much better approximation of what other systems can produce: in particular in [11,16], only syntactic constituency is being produced and no further semantic processing is carried out, apart from semantic role assignment directly at word level. The same applies more or less to [1,12], seen that these approaches rely on the output of a constituency only syntactic parser. Only superficially relevant relations will be encoded by these system: all lexically unexpressed relations will be omitted. So not only SUBJects of untensed clauses, but also long distance dependency syntactically controlled arguments will not appear. On the contrary this is fully expressed in our representation which can thus be regarded syntactic-semantic in the intended sense. As to the use of a theorem prover, we rather prefer a more flexible rule-based semantic approach, as discussed above; in addition, Equality and Subsumption can be expressed very effectively by the paradigm of variable and constraints instantiation in Prolog, once the appropriate information is available. So in a nutshell, the real problem is getting the appropriate representation: we think that dependency structure are to be regarded equivalent to any other flat or hierarchical logical structure.

Another different case is constituted by [10] which computes syntactic constituency on the basis of a chomskian approach and then a mapping into Grammatical Relations is produced by the system. When we look at results reported by [1], we see that the best accuracy scores are obtained by the Hybrid Task and the domains with better score are CD and IR; the same applies to [12] where best scores are obtained by CD, PP, and IR. This is very much in line with our results and reflects some bias involved in the deep parsing approach.

If we consider probabilistic Bag Of Words (BOWs) approaches - see for instance [11,14,15] – the picture changes dramatically. In this cases, semantic similarity is derived from term cooccurence frequency measures, usually taken from a big corpus or the web itself. The main criticism we can raise to these approaches is that semantic elements contained in a sentence very often coincide with stopwords such as negation, auxiliaries, modals, prepositions. All these are function words which shouldn't be erased, because they are used to express relations (grammatical, semantic, discourse), which these systems attempt to capture by the usual cooccurence paradigm contained in such measures as Inverse Document Frequency (idf) or the Mutual Information. Even though we think that such approaches are needed in a real life application setting, they are nonetheless in themselves insufficient to determine with enough confidence whether what is being measured is actually semantic similarity at propositional level – i.e. the two snippets are saying the same thing – or just an instance with good approximation of parallel texts. If we look at results reported in [14], we see a remarkably high accuracy in two domains, CD and MT. The same appears to be the case in [11] where MT, QA and CD receive a very high accuracy score – over 80%; [15] doesn't report separate evaluations for each domain, so we are left with a single overall score. Best systems seem to be [14] and [15]: both fare around 59% accuracy. In all the three papers, error analysis is omitted: we take this to be a fundamental step in assessing the validity of their approach and look forward to see it in future papers. However, this seems to be a weakness of BOWs approaches.

## 7 Conclusions

We have presented an approach based on linguistic rules where representations are intended to convey all possible syntactic and semantic knowledge in a linear dependency-based compact but consistent format. Limitations of this approach are basically due to parsing errors and insufficient semantic/world knowledge, so we don't expect to go over 62/64% accuracy in future experiments with a similar dataset as the one provided by RTE. While deep parsing accuracy cannot reasonably be expected to improve easily beyond the 85% threshold, we hope to achieve better results with augmented thesauri and other semantic similarity repositories available on the web. Another possibility would be that of assuming a probabilistically based BOWs approach on the same issue, in order to recover missing information for term cooccurence, especially in such thorny cases as paraphrase and definition related semantic similarities. Approaches attested in the literature seem to be quite successful and could thus be integrated with the linguistically-based stance of our system. We are currently experimenting with a version of LinkGrammar (LG) ported under SWI Prolog, where we have implemented our semantically and discourse oriented labelling modules which provide information as to semantic roles, pronominal binding and other relevant logical operators and discourse markers. We intend to produce an evaluation based on the augmented LG output in order to ascertain whether it compares positively with our system.

## References

1. Bos, J., Clark, S., Steedman, M., Curran, J., Hockenmaier, J.: Wide-coverage semantic representations from a ccg parser. In: Proc. of the 20th International Conference on Computational Linguistics. Geneva, Switzerland (2004)
2. Dagan, I., Glickman, O., Magnini, B.: The pascal recognising textual entailment challenge. In: Proceedings of the Recognising Textual Entailment Challenge, Southampton (UK), (2005) 1-8
3. Delmonte, R.: Evaluating GETARUNS Parser with GREVAL Test Suite, Proc. ROMAND - 20th International Conference on Computational Linguistics - COLING, University of Geneva. (2004) 32-41
4. Delmonte, R.: Text Understanding with GETARUNS for Q/A and Summarization, Proc. ACL 2004 - 2nd Workshop on Text Meaning & Interpretation, Barcelona, Columbia University (2004) 97-104
5. Delmonte R.: GETARUN PARSER - A parser equipped with Quantifier Raising and Anaphoric Binding based on LFG, Proc. LFG2002 Conference, Athens, at http://cslipublications.stanford.edu/hand/miscpubsonline.html (2002) 130-153
6. Delmonte R.: Semantic Parsing with an LFG-based Lexicon and Conceptual Representations. Computers & the Humanities, 5-6 (1990) 461-488
7. Delmonte, R., Bianchi D.: Binding Pronominals with an LFG Parser. In: Proceeding of the Second International Workshop on Parsing Technologies, Cancun (Mexico), ACL. (1991) 59-72
8. Dolan, W.B., Quirk, C., Brockett, C.: Unsupervised construction of large paraphrase corpora: Exploiting massively parallel news sources. In: *Proceedings of the 20th International Conference on Computational Linguistics*, Geneva, Switzerland. (2004)
9. Harabagiu, S., Pasca, M., Maiorano S.: Open-Domain Question Answering Techniques. Natural Language Engineering 1 (1), CUP. (2003) 1-38
10. Lin, D., Pantel, P.: DIRTdiscovery of inference rules from text. In: Knowledge Discovery and Data Mining, (2001) 323–328
11. Punyakanok, V., Roth, D., Yih. W.: Natural language inference via dependency tree mapping: An application to question answering. Computational Linguistics (2004)
12. Raina, R., Haghighi, A., Cox, C., Finkel, J., Michels, J., Toutanova, K., MacCartney, B., Marneffe, M.C., Manning, C.D., Ng, A. Y.: Robust Textual Inference using Diverse Knowledge Sources. In: Proc. of the 1st. PASCAL Recognision Textual Entailment Challenge Workshop, Southampton, U.K., (2005) 57-60

13. Zaenen, A., Karttunen, L., Crouch, R.: Local Textual Inference: Can it be Defined or Circumscribed?. In: Proc. Workshop Empirical Modeling of Semantic Equivalence and Entailment, ACL05, University of Michigan, Ann Arbor Michigan, (2005) 31-36
14. Glickman, O., Dagan, I., Koppel, M.: A Probabilistic Classification Approach for Lexical Textual Entailment, Twentieth National Conference on Artificial Intelligence (AAAI-05), (2005)
15. Corley, C., Mihalcea, R.: Measuring the Semantic Similarity of Texts , in Proceedings of the ACL 2005 Workshop on "Empirical Modeling of Semantic Equivalence and Entailment", Ann Arbor, MI. (2005) 13-18
16. Braz, R., Girju, R., Punyakanok, V., Roth, D., Sammons, M.: An Inference Model for Semantic Entailment in Natural Language. In: Proc. of the 1st. PASCAL Recognision Textual Entailment Challenge Workshop, Southampton, U.K., (2005) 29-32

## Appendix

Examples of T/H pairs used in the text are all reported here below.

T/H pair 12
Oracle had fought to keep the forms from being released.
Oracle released a confidential document.
T/H pair 46
The Yankees split Hollywood with something to feel OK about after last night's 5-4 loss to the Dodgers.
Dodgers lose first game ever at Fenway.
T/H pair 60
If a Mexican approaches the border, he's assumed to be trying to illegally cross.
Mexicans continue to illegally cross border.
T/H pair 67
Total coal stocks with the thermal power stations came down to 9.6 million tonnes on March 3, 2003 from 11 million tonnes on October 1, 2002.
Coal stocks rise.
T/H pair 73
There are discussions in California and Arizona to allow illegal aliens to have driver's licenses.
California driver's licenses granted to illegal immigrants.
T/H pair 74
South Korea's deputy foreign minister says his country won't change its plan to send three-thousand soldiers to Iraq, despite the kidnapping of a South Korean man there.
South Korea continues to send troops.
T/H pair 77
The media always talk about the Dow being up or down a certain number of points.
Dow Jones is down.

T/H pair 98
Sharon warns Arafat could be targeted for assassination.
prime minister targeted for assassination.
T/H pair 148
The Philippine Stock Exchange Composite Index rose 0.1 percent to 1573.65.
The Philippine Stock Exchange Composite Index dropped.
T/H pair 152
Twenty-five of the dead were members of the law enforcement agencies and the rest of the 67 were civilians.
25 of the dead were civilians.
T/H pair 170
Bombs exploded in two Turkish cities Thursday only days before Turkey plays host to a NATO summit.
Turkey plays host to suicide bombers.
T/H pair 171
The terrorist is suspected of being behind several deadly kidnappings and dozens of suicide attacks in Iraq.
Terrorist kidnaps dozens of Iraqis.
T/H pair 172
The terrorist is suspected of being behind several deadly kidnappings and dozens of suicide attacks in Iraq.
The terrorist may have caused suicide attacks and kidnappings.
T/H pair 205
In any case, the fact that this week Michael Melvill, a 63-year-old civilian pilot, guided a tiny rocket-ship more than 100 kilometres above the Earth and then glided it safely back to Earth, is a cause for celebration.
Michael Melvill guided more than 100 rocket-ships above the Earth.
T/H pair 220
Canadian wireless technology licensing company Wi-LAN has begun legal action against Cisco, alleging the networking giant's Linksys and Aironet products are making use of its intellectual property without permission.
Linksys and Aironet begin legal action against a Canadian company.
T/H pair 227
A closely divided U.S. Supreme Court said on Thursday its 2002 ruling that juries and not judges must impose a death sentence applies only to future cases, a decision that may affect more than 100 death row inmates.
The Supreme Court decided that only judges can impose the death sentence.
T/H pair 238
Following the assassination attempt in 1981, Reagan said he felt God had spared him for a purpose, and he intended to devote the rest of his life in dedication to his God and to that purpose.
Regan was almost assassinated in 1981.
T/H pair 294
The three-day G8 summit will take place in Scotland. The G8 summit will last three days.

T/H pair 466
The Yellowstone Park Foundation recognizes the following organizations for their generous support in helping to protect the wonders and wildlife of Yellowstone National Park.
The Yellowstone Park Foundation would like to acknowledge and thank the following organizations for their generous support.
T/H pair 496
Like Jews and Christians, Muslims believe there is only one God.
Muslims are monotheistic.
T/H pair 516
If this challenge interests you, you might enjoy reading "Punished by Rewards" by Alfie Kohn.
I read "Punished by Rewards" by Alfie Kohn.
T/H pair 526
Successful plaintiffs recovered punitive damages in Texas discrimination cases 53% of the time.
Legal costs to recover punitive damages are a deductible business expense.
T/H pair 602
Historians estimate that 800,000 Chechens were stuffed into rail cars and deported to Kazakhstan and Siberia, and 240,000 of them died en route.
Stalin deported 800,000 Chechens.
T/H pair 619
Fiat's Gianni Agnelli, owner of Juventus, was quoted by Italian newspapers as saying that when Baggio came off the field after the Mexico game, "He looked like a wet rabbit".
Giovanni Agnelli is the president of Fiat.
T/H pair 620
PERSPECTIVE ON BOSNIA; A BALKANS PEACE THAT CANNOT LAST.
Bosnia is located in the former Yugoslavia.
T/H pair 648
Yoko Ono, widow of murdered Beatles star John Lennon, has plastered the small German town of Langenhagen with backsides.
Yoko Ono was John Lennon's wife.
T/H pair 677
The Dutch, who ruled Indonesia until 1949, called the city of Jakarta Batavia.
Formerly (until 1949) Batavia, Jakarta is largest city and capital of Indonesia.
T/H pair 693
This growth proved short-lived, for a Swedish invasion (1655-56) devastated the flourishing city of Warsaw.
Warsaw was invaded by the Swedes in 1655, and the city was devastated.
T/H pair 700
There are many Baroque churches of the Counter-Reformation period, including the Jesuit Church next to the cathedral and the Church of the Holy Cross, which contains Chopin's heart.
Sigismund made Warsaw the capital of Poland in 1611.

T/H pair 712
To the south of Castle Hill rises the higher Gellert Hill (771 feet), a steep limestone escarpment overlooking the Danube, which provides a panoramic view of the whole city.
To the south is Gellert Hill, which features the 19th-century Citadel.
T/H pair 783
Sharon sent dismissal letters to Benny Elon and Avigdor Lieberman, who oppose his withdrawal plan, on Friday.
On Friday,Sharon fired Benny Elon and Avigdor Lieberman.
T/H pair 811
Monica Meadows, a 22-year-old model from Atlanta, was shot in the shoulder on a subway car in New York City.
Monica Meadows, 23, was shot in shoulder while riding a subway car in New York City.
T/H pair 876
Officials said Michael Hamilton was killed when gunmen opened fire and exchanged shots with Saudi security forces yesterday
Michael Hamilton died yesterday.
T/H pair 933
Crude Oil Prices Slump.
Oil prices drop.
T/H pair 942
The U.S. handed power on June 30 to Iraq's interim government chosen by the United Nations and Paul Bremer, former governor of Iraq.
The United Nations officialy transferred power to Iraq.
T/H pair 947
The extraditables today claimed responsibility for the murder of Antioquia police commander colonel Waldemar Franklin Quintero, which occurred this morning in Medellin.
police officer killed.
T/H pair 1014
The thick atmosphere of Titan makes it difficult for even the largest telescopes on Earth to see anything clearly.
Telescopes on Earth cannot see Titan clearly.
T/H pair 1121
Continuing its buying spree, IBM said Wednesday that it plans to acquire Alphablox, a Mountain View, Calif.-based analytics software company.
IBM plans to buy Alphablox.
T/H pair 1149
The American State Department announced that Russia recalled her ambassador to the United States "for consultation" due to the bombing operations on Iraq.
The American Ministry of Foreign Affairs announced that Russia called the United States about the bombings on Iraq.

T/H pair 1164
Ramadan told reporters at the opening ceremony of the Baghdad International Exposition, "No cooperation and no inspection or monitoring by the American Zionist espionage commission (the Special Commission for disarming Iraq's banned weapons - UNSCOM) before Iraq's demands are met.".
Ramadan announced that Iraq will not cooperate with the inspectors.
T/H pair 1168
Ramadan told reporters in Baghdad that "Iraq cannot deal positively with whoever represents the Security Council, unless there was a clear stance on the issue of lifting the blockade.
Ramadan said that Iraq would cooperate when the UN considers lifting the embargo.
T/H pair 1197
Contact with the press will be restricted to "perodic meetings", as promised by all three parties, in order to "focus their energies" on the most important issues.
The delegations may only speak periodically to the press, in order to concentrate on the issues.
T/H pair 1214
It is planned that by the end of the year 2001, France will have minted 7.6 billion Euro coins weighing 30 thousand tons or approximately four times the equivalent weight of the Eiffel Tower.
According to plans, France should have minted 7.6 billion Euro coins before 2002.
T/H pair 1215
A statement issued by Royal Moroccan Airlines, a copy of which was received by Agence France Presse today, said that the company decided to start two flights a week between Casablanca and Gaza as soon as the Palestinian airport is opened there.
With the opening of the Palestinian airport, Royal Moroccan Airlines will fly between Casablanca and Gaza.
T/H pair 1261
Zeroual proposed February 25 as elections date, but this date will not become final until after the agreement between all of the political partners, according to what was reported by the First Secretary of the Socialist Forces Front, Ahmed Djeddai.
The election will be held on the 25th of February if all of the political partners agree.
T/H pair 1265
Egyptian television is preparing to film a series that highlights the unity and cohesion of Moslems and Copts as the single fabric of the Egyptian society, exemplifying in particular the story of former United Nations Secretary-General Boutros Ghali.
Egyptian television will make a series about Moslems, Copts and Boutros Boutros Ghali.

T/H pair 1284
Economic experts were surprised by this coordinated reduction of interest rates; they were expecting, before the meetings of officials in the German Central Bank and French Central Bank today, that the two main central banks in the Euro countries would not reduce interest rates this week.
Two main banks reduced their interest rates.
T/H pair 1639
Lennon was murdered by Mark David Chapman outside the Dakota on Dec. 8, 1980.
Mark David Chapman killed Lennon.
T/H pair 2049
Five other soldiers have been ordered to face courts-martial.
Five other soldiers have been demanded to face courts-martial.
T/H pair 2064
The Osaka World Trade Center is the tallest building in Western Japan.
The Osaka World Trade Center is the tallest building in Japan.
T/H pair 2084
Microsoft Israel was founded in 1989 and became one of the first Microsoft branches outside the USA.
Microsoft was established in 1989.
T/H pair 2120
Six hostages in Iraq were freed.
The four Jordanian hostages, kidnapped about a week ago, were freed.
T/H pair 2141
No Weapons of Mass Destruction Found in Iraq Yet.
Weapons of Mass Destruction Found in Iraq.

# Textual Entailment Recognition Using a Linguistically–Motivated Decision Tree Classifier

Eamonn Newman[1], Nicola Stokes[2], John Dunnion[1], and Joe Carthy[1]

[1] School of Computer Science and Informatics, University College Dublin, Ireland
{eamonn.newman, john.dunnion, joe.carthy}@ucd.ie
[2] NICTA Victoria Laboratory, Department of Computer Science and Software Engineering, University of Melbourne, Australia
nicola.stokes@nicta.com.au

**Abstract.** In this paper we present a classifier for Recognising Textual Entailment (RTE) and Semantic Equivalence. We evaluate the performance of this classifier using an evaluation framework provided by the PASCAL RTE Challenge Workshop. Sentence–pairs are represented as a set of features, which are used by our decision tree classifier to determine if an entailment relationship exisits between each sentence–pair in the RTE test corpus.

## 1 Introduction

In this paper, we present work undertaken by the Text Summarisation group at University College Dublin on the development of a classification system for recognising Textual Entailment (TE), where a text $T$ entails a hypothesis $H$ if the meaning of $H$ can be inferred from the meaning of $T$ [1].

Automatic text summarisation has a number of distinct stages. Radev [2] describes them thus: "content identification", when the topics of the original text(s) are identified; "conceptual organization", when the concepts to be covered by the summary are selected and ordered; and "realization", the actual generation of the summary. Multi–Document Summarisation (MDS) is the generation of a single summary from multiple documents. An MDS system must consider issues such as managing conflicting contradictory sources, identifying redundant sources and information overlap, adapting to user needs, and being mindful of authors' intentions, etc. One of the most critical issues in this list is the identification of redundant information, since the fundamental objective of the summarisation process is to avoid including repetitive information in the summary at all costs.

Redundancy removal is generally only a problem which arises in MDS, because information is being collated across multiple sources related through overlapping information (especially in certain domains, such as news stories, where a topic will often be introduced in every article described in the cluster). Obviously, this is less of a problem in single–document summarisation because an author is unlikely to continually repeat themselves in a text.

J. Quiñonero-Candela et al. (Eds.): MLCW 2005, LNAI 3944, pp. 372–384, 2006.

Most MDS redundancy removal techniques are based on some type of word overlap comparison. While this is a somewhat effective approach, we believe that the development of a deeper semantic analysis method would improve summary quality, since shallow methods are prone to missing certain cases (e.g., negation) which would be captured by deeper methods. This was the main motivation behind our participation in the PASCAL RTE Challenge. However, we found that the evaluation framework of the workshop was insufficient for our purposes, since only certain types of information redundancy (or semantic equivalence) were represented in RTE corpora.

The rest of this paper is presented as follows: in Section 2 we review related work in both summarisation research and textual entailment in general; Section 3 provides an overview of our system, the features it uses, and how they are used to detect entailment pairs; Section 4 describes in detail results of our experiments presented at the RTE workshop; and finally, in Section 5, we discuss some future directions for our research.

## 2 Related Work

In this section, we will first describe some of the research recently published as a result of the RTE challenge, followed by an overview of some related research from the text summarisation community on redundancy removal, i.e. the removal of repetitive information from machine–generated summaries.

### 2.1 Recognising Textual Entailment and Semantic Equivalence

There are a variety of approaches that can be used to address the problem of Recognising Textual Entailment and Semantic Equivalence (RTESE), as is evident by the breadth of the applications presented at the PASCAL RTE workshop [1] and the ACL workshop on Empirical Modeling of Semantic Equivalence and Entailment [3].

Most of these systems use some sort of lexical matching, be it simple word overlap or some more complex statistical co-occurrence relation (e.g. Latent Semantic Indexing). While these systems perform better than those without lexical matching, it was widely agreed that matching at a word-level alone was not sufficient for the PASCAL corpus. Corley [4] presents an overview of similarity metrics based on WordNet concepts. They showed that a combination of WordNet similarity measures [5] with a lexical matching metric (based on the number of shared words in a sentence–pair) acheived scores on the PASCAL corpus of up to 58.9%, which is comparable with other high–ranking systems at the workshop.

A number of the systems (de Salvo Braz et al. [6]; Akhmatova [7]; Bos and Markert [8]) used logical inference in which a representation of the text and hypothesis is constructed, and then a proof of the hypothesis is derived for the text (some of these systems appealed to world knowledge (hand–coded [9]; geographical [8]), or to formal lexical resources such as WordNet).

A number of systems represented the texts as parse trees (e.g. syntactic, dependency, semantic)(Pazienza [10]; Herrera [11]). This action reduces the problem of textual entailment recognition to one of (sub–)graph matching.

Interestingly, Vanderwende [12] showed that using no more than syntactic matching, one could match up to 37% of classifications correctly. Appealing to a thesaurus yields up to 49%. This is supported by empirical evidence from Herrera et al. [11] and Marsi and Krahmer [13]. Hence, it seems that relatively simple metrics used in combination perform better than more complex, "deeper" metrics such as logical inference or the incorporation of world knowledge into the classification computation. We suggest that this is the case because deep linguistic and inferential analysis is more prone to errors due to problems arising from word sense disambiguation.

One of the top systems in the PASCAL evaluation (Raina et al. [14, 15]) used all of the methods outlined above to some degree or another. Parsed sentences are represented as logical formulae. A theorem prover is then used to find the minimum cost of "proving" that the hypothesis is entailed by the text. These costs are learned from syntactic and semantic features and resources such as WordNet.

### 2.2 MDS Redundancy Removal

In this section, we describe some of the similarity detection and redundancy removal techniques which have been used in various multi-document summarisation systems. Many of the techniques used have evolved from similarity measures used in areas such as Information Retrieval [16, 17].

Possibly the most well-known and successful approach to similarity detection in automatic summarisation is the SimFinder [18] system. SimFinder is a multi–document summariser which uses clustering to reduce redundancies in its summaries. The similarity of texts (paragraphs or sentences) are judged using 43 separate features, from common words to synonyms and hypernym/hyponym matching. Texts are then clustered using a learning algorithm. This algorithm selected 11 of the 43 available features for its final set of classification rules, validating the authors' claims that "more than word matching is needed for effective paragraph matching". The clusters generated by SimFinder have been used by Barzilay in her system (described below) and by Centrifuser, where summaries are generated by selecting one sentence from each cluster.

Maximal Marginal Relevance [19] is a technique, based around the cosine similarity metric, that was was originally developed to detect diversity in a list of retrieved documents relevant to a specific query. It measures the relevance and the novelty of a document independently, and linearly combines the two measures to calculate the "marginal relevance". This technique has also been applied to multi–document summarisation research by Goldstein [20] in which MMR was used to select passages from multiple documents. More specifically, given a selection of relevant documents, MMR can be parameterised to rank passages according to certain criteria, such as whether the summary should be very specific to a particular topic, or whether it should cover a wide range of related issues.

More recently, Allan et al. [21] describe a method that generates temporal summaries from online news streams by adding novel information to a summary as news stories describing a particular event arrive. Although this work focusses on novelty detection, this task is obviously analogous to redunancy detection and so is relevant to our current discussion. Allan et al. define two concepts of *novelty* and *usefulness* using probabilistic language models. Novelty applies to a relevant sentence which is new to the presentation, e.g. the first sentence about an event is obviously novel. Usefulness refers to all relevant sentences which have the potential to contribute to the summary. The models are based on all of the previously–seen documents. These models are then used to determine if an incoming sentence is either novel or useful. If so, then they are added to the summary. In other words, the model is trying to capture novelty based on the "probability that the later sentence could have been generated from the same language model as the earlier sentence". A second novelty model was also investigated which compares the incoming sentence to clusters of related setences in order to overcome the data sparsity problem associated with generating language models for single sentences. This model proved to be the better–performing approach of the two.

In contrast Barzilay [22, 23, 24] adopted a more linguistically–motivated approach to the measurement of semantic equivalence. Her research focussed on the generation of abstractive summaries. In particular, her technique analysed dependency graph [25] representations of sentences to identify common paraphrase units between two potentially redundant sentences in a summary. Once these paraphrases (or redundancies) have been detected this information facilitates "information fusion", and the generation of a single sentence representing the information in both sentences. This text generation technique is used by the Columbia NewsBlaster MDS system [26].

From this discussion, it can be seen that advances in the area of Recognising Textual Entailment and Semantic Equivalence would be of great benefit to the Text Summarisation community.

## 3 System Description

In this section, we present an overview of our Textual Entailment Recognition system, which was originally presented at the PASCAL RTE workshop. Our system uses a decision tree classifier to detect an entailment relationship between pairs of sentences which are represented using a number of difference features such as lexical, semantic and grammatical attributes of nouns, verbs and adjectives. We generated our classifier from the RTE training data using the C5.0 machine learning algorithm [27]. We chose to use C5.0 as it can be used to build a decision–tree classifier which can branch on a numeric range, as opposed to many other such algorithms, which can only work on discrete values.

The features used are calculated using the WordNet taxonomy [28], the VerbOcean semantic network [29] (developed at ISI) and a Latent Semantic Indexing [30, 31] technique. Other features are based on the ROUGE (Recall–Oriented Understudy for Gisting Evaluation) [32] n-gram overlap metrics and cosine similarity between the text and hypothesis.

Our most sophisticated linguistic feature finds the longest common subsequence in the sentence–pair, and then detects contradictions in the pair by examining verb semantics for the presence of synonymy, near-synonymy, negation or antonymy in the subsequence.

In addition to these measures, there is also a **task** feature which identifies the application domain from which the sentence pair was derived. This allows the system to build separate classifiers for each task in order to capture the different aspects of entailment specific to each task.

We investigated the usefulness of a number of distinct features during the development of our decision tree approach to textual entailment. These features were developed using the training part of the corpus made available for the PASCAL Recognising Textual Entailment Workshop [1][1]. Not all of these features were contributing factors in our final classification systems, but we list all of them here for the sake of completeness because some features are combinations of other atomic features. Table 1 gives a list of the features we used, and their C5.0 data types.

**Table 1.** Features used by decision–tree classifier. <*name*>indicates a tuple of related features.

| Feature | data type |
|---|---|
| `entails` | boolean, unknown |
| `<rouge>` | continuous |
| `<wordnet>` | continuous |
| `LSI` | continuous |
| `cosine` | continuous |
| `<verbOcean>` | continuous |
| `negation_t` | continuous |
| `negation_h` | continuous |
| `negdiff` | continuous |
| `<lcs>` | boolean |
| `lcs+not` | boolean |

## 3.1 Sentence–Pair Features

The first of our equivalence features are derived using the **ROUGE metrics**, which were used as a means of evaluating summary quality against a set of human–generated summaries in the 2004 Document Understanding Conference workshop [35]. The metrics provide a measure of word overlap (i.e. unigram,

[1] The corpus may be downloaded from:
`http://www.pascal-network.org/Challenges/RTE/Datasets`

bigram, trigram and 4-gram), and a weighted and unweighted longest common subsequence measure.

In the **WordNet–based measure**, we define the similarity between two sentences as the sum of the maxmimal similarity scores between component words in WordNet, using the Hirst–St-Onge measure [28, 5]. To implement this we used Perl language Wordnet modules [33, 34] and WordNet version 2.0.

WordNet was used to identify entailment between sentence pairs where corresponding synonyms are used. Words from the same synset (set of one or more synonyms, as defined by WordNet) were considered to indicate a greater likelihood of entailment. We believe that the accuracy of this feature could be greatly improved by disambiguating the sentence pair before calculating synset overlap. More specifically, in some instances multiple senses of a single term could be matched with terms in the corresponding entailment pair, resulting in sentences appearing more semantically similar than they actually are.

A simple method for measuring sentence similarities is to use a vector–based method such as **cosine similarity** [16]. We use a vector-space model [17] as the primary data structure in the Cosine Similarity and Latent Semantic Indexing measures. Sentences are stopped and stemmed using the Porter stemming algorithm [36], and a count of all the words used in the sentences of the corpus is calculated. This count provides us with the information to construct the *termspace*, an $n$-dimensional vector space, where $n$ is the number of unique terms found in the corpus. With a vector representation of all of the sentences in the corpus, we can take a simple measure of the similarity of any pair of sentences by looking at the size of the angle between their vectors: the smaller the angle, the greater the similarity.

**Latent Semantic Indexing** [30, 31] takes as input a term–document matrix constructed in exactly the same way as for Cosine Similarity. Before applying a similarity measure between the vectors, an *information spreading* technique known as Singular Value Decomposition is applied to the matrix.

This technique scrutinises the term–document matrix for significant levels of word co–occurence and modifies magnitudes along appropriate dimensions (i.e. scores for particular words) accordingly. Thus, a sentence such as "The Iraqi leader was deposed" may have its vector representation modified with increased magnitude along dimensions corresponding to the terms "Saddam Hussein", "Baghdad" and "George W. Bush", for example.

Using a Latent Semantic Indexing matrix constructed from the DUC 2004 corpus, we attempted to identify words in entailment pairs which have high cooccurrence statistics. We took a term–document matrix of 10028 terms and converted this to a LSI matrix of 50 dimensions, using the GNU Scientfic Library for C [37].

**VerbOcean** is a lexical resource that provides fine–grained semantic relationships between verbs. These related verb–pairs and their relationship strengths were gleaned from the web using lexico–syntactic patterns that captured 5 distinct verb relationships:

- similar–to (e.g., *escape*, *flee*)
- strength (e.g., *kill* is stronger than *wound*)
- antonymy (e.g., *win*, *lose*)
- enablement (e.g., *fight*, *win*)
- happens–before (*marry* happens before *divorce*)

The VerbOcean online demo searches for paths between nodes in a semantic network generated from the VerbOcean data [38]. Given that the VerbOcean semantic network is not currently available for download but the verb pairs, their relationship types, and strengths are, we used this data to build our own verb–verb association matrix. We then extracted additional semantic relationships between verbs in the VerbOcean data by calculating the similarity between each verb vector pair using the cosine metric. In our experiments we only examined VerbOcean antonym and similar–to relationships when analysing verb semantics in the entailment pair; however, all VerbOcean relationships were used to generate the association matrix.

We also identify **adverbial negation** in the sentences. Adverbial negation occurs where the presence of a word (e.g., "nor", "not") modifies the meaning of the verb in the sentence. We generate three features from this information:

- **negation_t** counts the number of occurences of adverbial negation in the text
- **negation_h** counts the number of occurences of adverbial negation in the hypothesis.
- **negdiff** is the difference between negation_t and negation_h.

Examination of the development set suggested that for a significant proportion of sentence pairs, the **longest common subsequence**[2] is largely similar to the hypothesis element, i.e. most of the hypothesis is contained in the text element. For this feature, we only examined verb semantics in the longest common subsequence of the two sentences rather than in the full sentences. An example is shown in Figure 1. There are three variations of this feature: lcs, lcs_pos and lcs_neg.

- The **lcs** feature holds one of three values $\{-1, 0, 1\}$, which correspond to the presence of an antonym, no relationship, or a synonym relationship between the longest common subsequence of the text and the hypothesis sentence, respectively.
- **lcs_pos** and **lcs_neg** are simpler features which indicate the presence of a synonym relationship or antonym relationship, respectively.

**lcs+not** is another feature based on the longest common subsequence. It combines the above lcs features and also looks for the presence of words like "not", which reverse the meaning of the sentence. Thus, for example, if an antonym and "not" occur in a sentence then this is considered to be a positive indication of entailment. Even though lcs+not is a combination of our lcs

[2] The Longest Common Subsequence of a sentence pair is the longest (not necessarily contiguous) sequence of words which is common to both text and hypothesis.

id=1954; task=PP; judgement=FALSE
Text: *France on Saturday* flew *a planeload of United Nations aid into eastern Chad* where French soldiers prepared to deploy from their base in Abeche towards the border with Sudan's Darfur region.
Hypothesis: *France on Saturday* crashed *a planeload of United Nations aid into eastern Chad*

**Fig. 1.** Longest Common Subsequence. Italics denote the longest common subsequence.

features we still retain the simpler features as it has been shown that they improve entailment accuracy.

## 4 Experiments

We submitted two systems to the PASCAL workshop. The systems are described below, evaluated according to the workshop criteria and this evaluation is analysed in the following section.

### 4.1 System Performance

Our two submitted systems differ only in the parameters they use: System 1 uses all the syntactic equivalence features, the atomic lcs features and the task feature; System 2 uses the syntactic equivalence features, the composite lcs+not feature, and does not use the task feature.

This gave rise to System 1 performing much better for some tasks, but System 2 performed (marginally) better on average. This is shown in Tables 2 and 3. Our choice of features for each system was based on their performance on the second development set, having been trained on the first development set.

As already stated, when the task feature is enabled, the C5.0 algorithm uses it to make specific classifiers for each task. This seems to lead to over–fitting in

**Table 2.** Accuracy results for the classifiers. Scores marked with ** are statistically significant to 99% confidence.

| | Sys 1 | Sys 2 | Sys 3 | Sys 4 |
|---|---|---|---|---|
| Average | 0.5625** | 0.5650** | 0.5675** | 0.5663** |
| CD | 0.7467 | 0.7400 | 0.7467 | 0.8467 |
| IE | 0.5583 | 0.4917 | 0.5167 | 0.5417 |
| IR | 0.4456 | 0.5444 | 0.4333 | 0.5556 |
| PP | 0.5200 | 0.5600 | 0.5600 | 0.5000 |
| MT | 0.4750 | 0.5083 | 0.5667 | 0.4083 |
| QA | 0.5154 | 0.5385 | 0.5000 | 0.4846 |
| RC | 0.5714 | 0.5286 | 0.5714 | 0.5286 |

**Table 3.** Confidence–weighted scores (CWS) for the classifiers. Scores marked with ** are statistically significant to 99% confidence.

| | Sys 1 | Sys 2 | Sys 3 | Sys 4 |
|---|---|---|---|---|
| Average | 0.5917** | 0.6000** | 0.5818** | 0.5794** |
| CD | 0.8602 | 0.7764 | 0.7873 | 0.7526 |
| IE | 0.5083 | 0.5260 | 0.4958 | 0.5715 |
| IR | 0.3789 | 0.6130 | 0.4585 | 0.5201 |
| PP | 0.3968 | 0.5006 | 0.5320 | 0.4651 |
| MT | 0.5536 | 0.5130 | 0.5498 | 0.4108 |
| QA | 0.6003 | 0.5006 | 0.4684 | 0.4846 |
| RC | 0.6003 | 0.5685 | 0.5961 | 0.5866 |

some cases, e.g., especially on the IR and PP tasks, but it can help in certain cases such as the RC and IE tasks.

To examine the effects of using all the available features, we ran two new systems: System 3 uses all available features, and System 4 uses all features except the task feature.

The training sets indicated the extra features did not contribute anything to the classifiers and since we could only submit two systems to the workshop we ran our system submissions without these features.

Subsequently, we ran further experiments to fully investigate the effect of the features on classification accuracy. We found that accuracy scores for particular tasks (most notably, CD and PP) showed a significant increase. However, the average accuracy score across all tasks does not vary significantly.

Examination of the classifications made by each system (see Table 4) show that Systems 1 and 3, the systems using the task feature, tended to be quite balanced in their classifications, i.e. they had approximately the same number of positive and negative classifications. On the other hand, Systems 2 and 4 showed a bias towards marking instances as cases of true entailment (between 75% and 85% of cases were classified as "true"). This shows that the task indicator is highly informative to the classifiers, allowing them to specialise for particular tasks and thus improve their performance.

**Table 4.** Precision, Recall and F1 scores on Positive and Negative Entailments

| | Sys 1 | Sys 2 | Sys 3 | Sys 4 |
|---|---|---|---|---|
| | **Positive Entailment** | | | |
| Precision | 0.5459 | 0.5458 | 0.5692 | 0.5458 |
| Recall | 0.5500 | 0.8200 | 0.5555 | 0.8050 |
| F1 | 0.5479 | 0.6563 | 0.5620 | 0.6490 |
| | **Negative Entailment** | | | |
| Precision | 0.5466 | 0.6382 | 0.5659 | 0.6268 |
| Recall | 0.5425 | 0.3175 | 0.5800 | 0.3275 |
| F1 | 0.5445 | 0.4240 | 0.5729 | 0.4302 |

### 4.2 Analysis

In this section, we discuss with examples some common system errors made by our decision tree classifier. It is clear from our system description in Section 3 that the majority of our features deal with the identification of word–level, atomic paraphrase units (e.g., child = kid; eat = devour). Consequently, there are a number of examples where phrasal and compositional paraphrasing has resulted in misclassifications by our system. Some examples of this are shown in Figure 2.

id=1560; task=QA; judgement=TRUE
Text: The technological triumph known as GPS - the Global Positioning System of satellite-based navigation - was incubated in the mind of Ivan Getting.
Hypothesis: Ivan Getting invented the GPS.

id=858; task=CD; judgement=TRUE
Text: Each hour spent in a car was associated with a 6 percent increase in the likelihood of obesity and each half-mile walked per day reduced those odds by nearly 5 percent, the researchers found.
Hypothesis: The more driving you do means you're going to weigh more – the more walking means you're going to weigh less.

**Fig. 2.** Compositional Paraphrases (misclassified by our system)

Another important type of paraphrase, not addressed explicitly by our system, is the syntactic paraphrase (e.g., "I ate the cake" or "the cake was eaten by me"). However, although we didn't include a parse tree analysis in our approach, it appears that the ROUGE metrics (and to some extent the cosine metric) were an adequate means of detecting syntactic paraphrases. The position of the ROUGE features in high-level nodes in the decision tree confirms that n-gram overlap is an important aspect of textual entailment, but obviously not the full story. However, we also observed that in some cases syntactic paraphrases prevented the detection of longest common subsequences, and reduced the effectiveness of features that relied on this syntactic analysis. Consequently, parse tree analysis and subsequent normalisation of sentence structure could be an effective solution to this problem.

Overall, our LCS–based features were critical to the classification decision; however, we did find instances where sentence pairs were misclassified by over–simplification of the textual entailment task. For example, pair 2028 in Figure 3 shows how the true meaning of the text sentence can extend beyond the longest common subsequence. In addition, pair 1964 shows how coverage limitations in the VerbOcean resource resulted in this example being misclassified as negative, because an antonym relationship between "agree" and "oppose" was not listed.

Finally, during our manual examination of the results we also noticed another crucial analysis component missing from our system: numerical string evaluation. An example is shown in Figure 4. Future development will focus on a normalisation method for evaluating numeric values in the entailment pair.

id=2028; task=QA; judgement=FALSE
Text: *Besancon is the capital of France*'s watch and clock-making industry and of high precision engineering.
Hypothesis: *Besancon is the capital of France.*

id=1964; task=PP; judgement=FALSE
Text: Under the avalanche of Italian outrage *London Underground* has apologised and agreed *to withdraw the poster.*
Hypothesis: *London Underground* opposed *to withdraw the poster.*

**Fig. 3.** Longest Common Subsequence Faults

id=868; task=CD; judgement=FALSE
Text: Several other people, including a woman and two children, suffered injuries in the incident.
Hypothesis: Several people were slightly wounded, including a woman and three children.

**Fig. 4.** Numerical example (misclassified by our system)

## 5 Future Work

There are a number of planned improvements for our system. In particular, we will consider new sentence features in the detection process such as a measure of numerical equivalence between sentence pairs as illustrated in example 4, and a syntactic analysis component. Currently, our system does not have the capacity to recognise the different syntactic forms that a sentence may take.

In addition, we also intend to replicate Pantel's VerbOcean semantic network to allow us to search along paths in the network and thus increase the system's ability to detect semantically related verbs.

An empirical evaluation of other machine learning algorithms is also planned, to investigate if any other techniques would yield a better classifier than the C5.0 algorithm.

We also intend to further evaluate our RTE system by judging its performance as a module in a Multi–Document Summarisation system. We will aim to show that the identification of semantically–equivalent sentences using our RTE system improves the overall performance of the multi-document summariser.

## References

1. Dagan, I., Glickman, O., Magnini, B.(eds): Proceedings of the PASCAL Recognising Textual Entailment Challenge Workshop. April 11th-13th 2005, Southampton, UK.
2. Radev, D.: *Summarisation Tutorial.* SIGIR 2004. At `http://www.summarization.com/sigirtutorial2004.ppt`

3. Dolan, B., and Dagan, I. (eds): Proceedings of the ACL Workshop on Empirical Modeling of Semantic Equivalence and Entailment. June 30th 2005, Ann Arbor, Michigan, USA.
4. Corley, C., and Mihalcea, R.: *Measuring the Semantic Similarity of Texts.* In Proceedings of ACL Workshop on Empirical Modelling of Semantic Equivalence and Entailment, ACL, June 2005.
5. Budanitsky A. and Hirst G.: *Semantic distance in WordNet: An experimental, application-oriented evaluation of five measures.* In Proceedings of Workshop on WordNet and Other Lexical Resources, Second meeting of the North American Chapter of the Association for Computational Linguistics. 2001.
6. de Salvo Braz, R., Girju, R., Punyakanok, V., Roth, D. and Sammons, M: *An Inference Model for Semantic Entailment in Natural Language.* In Proc. PASCAL Workshop on Recognising Textual Entailment, 2005.
7. Akhmatova, E.: *Textual Entailment Resolution via Atomic Propositions.* In Proc. PASCAL Workshop on Recognising Textual Entailment, 2005.
8. Bos, J. and Markert, K.: *Combining Shallow and Deep NLP methods for Recognizing Textual Entailment.* In Proc. PASCAL Workshop on Recognising Textual Entailment, 2005.
9. Fowler, A., Hauser, B., Hodges, D., Niles, I., Novischi, A., and Stephan J.: *Applying* COGEX *to Recognize Textual Entailment.* In Proc. PASCAL Workshop on Recognising Textual Entailment, 2005.
10. Pazienza, M. T., Pennacchiotti, M., Zanzotto, F. M.: *Textual Entailment as Syntactic Graph Distance.* In Proc. PASCAL Workshop on Recognising Textual Entailment, 2005.
11. Herrera, J., Peñas, A., Verdejo, F.: *Textual Entailment Recognition based on dependency analysis and WordNet.* In Proc. PASCAL Workshop on Recognising Textual Entailment, 2005.
12. Vanderwende, L., Coughlin, D., Dolan, W.: *What Syntax can Contribute in Entailment Task.* In Proc. PASCAL Workshop on Recognising Textual Entailment, 2005.
13. Marsi, E. and Krahmer, E.: *Classification of semantic relations by humans and machines.* In Proc. ACL Workshop on Empirical Modeling of Semantic Equivalence and Entailment, Ann Arbor, June 2005.
14. Raina, R., et al.: *Robust Textual Inference using Diverse Knowledge Sources.* In Proc. PASCAL Workshop on Recognising Textual Entailment, 2005.
15. Raina, R., Ng, A. Y., Manning, C. D.: *Robust Textual Inference via Learning and Abductive Reasoning.* AAAI, 2005.
16. van Rijsbergen, C. J.: *Information Retrieval,* `http://www.dcs.gla.ac.uk/Keith/Preface.html`
17. Baeza-Yates, R. and Ribeiro-Neto, B.: *Modern Information Retrieval,* ACM Press, 1999.
18. Hatzivassiloglou, V., et al.: SIMFINDER*: A Flexible Clustering Tool for Summarization.* In Workshop on Automatic Summarization, NAACL, Pittsburg, USA, 2001.
19. Carbonell, J., and Goldstein, J.: *The use of MMR, Diversity–Based Reranking for Reordering Documents and Producing Summaries.* SIGIR, 1998, Melbourne, Australia.
20. Goldstein, J., Mittal, V., Carbonell, J., and Kantrowitz, M.: *Multi–Document Summarization by Sentence Extraction.* Automatic Summarization, Proceedings of the ANLP/NAACL Workshop, April 2000, Seattle, WA

21. Allan, J., Gupta, R., and Khandewal, V.: *Temporal Summaries of News Topics.* In Proceedings of SIGIR 2001.
22. Barzilay, R and McKeown, K. R.: *Sentence Fusion for Multidocument News Summarization.* Computational Linguistics, 2005.
23. Barzilay, R. and Elhadad, N.: *Sentence Alignment for Monolingual Comparable Corpora.* Proceedings of Empirical Methods in Natural Language Processing (EMNLP), Sapporo, Japan, 2003.
24. Barzilay, R.: *Multidocument Summarizer*, PhD Thesis, 2002, Columbia University.
25. Melcuk, I.: *Dependency Syntax: Theory and Practice*, Albany, State of New York University Press.
26. NewsBlaster: Columbia University, 2005. `http://newsblaster.cs.columbia.edu/`
27. Quinlan, J.R.: *C5.0 Machine Learning Algorithm.* At `http://www.rulequest.com`
28. Miller, G. A., et al.: *WordNet: Lexical Database for the English language*, Cognitive Science Laboratory, Princeton University. At `http://www.cogsci.princeton.edu/~wn`
29. Chklovski, T., Pantel, P.: *VerbOcean: Mining the Web for Fine–Grained Semantic Verb Relations.* Proc. Conf. Empirical Methods in Natural Language Processing (EMNLP-04), 2004.
30. Deerwester, S., Dumais, S. T., Furna, G. W., Landauer, T. K., and Harshman, R.: *Indexing by Latent Semantic Analysis.* Journal of the American Society for Information Science, 1990.
31. Landauer, T.K., Foltz, P.W., Latham, D: *Introduction to Latent Semantic Analysis.* Discourse Processes, 1998.
32. Lin, C.-Y., Hovy, E.: *Automatic Evaluation of Summaries using n-gram co–occurence statistics.* Proc. Document Understanding Conference (DUC), National Institute of Standards and Technology, 2004.
33. Patwardhan, S., Michelizzi, J., Banerjee, S., and Pedersen, T.: *WordNet::Similarity Perl Module* At `http://search.cpan.org/dist/WordNet-Similarity/lib/WordNet/Similarity.pm`
34. Rennie, J: *WordNet::QueryData Perl Module* At `http://search.cpan.org/~jrennie/WordNet-QueryData-1.39/QueryData.pm`
35. Document Understanding Conference (DUC), National Institute of Standards and Technology, USA. At `http://duc.nist.gov`.
36. Porter, M.: *An Algorithm for Suffix Stripping*, in Progam, vol. 14, no. 3, July 1980. At `http://www.tartarus.org/~martin/PorterStemmer/def.txt`.
37. Galassi, M., et al,: *GNU Scientific Library Reference Manual (2nd Ed.)* At `http://www.gnu.org/software/gsl/`
38. Chklovski, T., Pantel, P.: *Global Path-based Refinement of Noisy Graphs Applied to Verb Semantics.* In Proceedings of The Second International Joint Conference on Natural Language Processing (IJCNLP-05), Jeju Island, South Korea, October 11-13, 2005.

# Recognizing Textual Entailment Via Atomic Propositions

Elena Akhmatova and Diego Mollá

Centre for Language Technology, Division of Information and Communication Sciences, Macquarie University, North Ryde, NSW–2109, Australia
{elena, diego}@ics.mq.edu.au

**Abstract.** This paper describes Macquarie University's Centre for Language Technology contribution to the PASCAL 2005 Recognizing Textual Entailment challenge. Our main aim was to test the practicability of a purely logical approach. For this, atomic propositions were extracted from both the text and the entailment hypothesis and they were expressed in a custom logical notation. The text entails the hypothesis if every proposition of the hypothesis is entailed by some proposition in the text. To extract the propositions and encode them into a logical notation the system uses the output of Link Parser. To detect the independent entailment relations the system relies on the use of Otter and WordNet.

## 1 Introduction

Despite its study for over two millennia, Natural language is still a complex and somewhat mysterious system which does not stop to surprise us with its variety of phenomena, and which provides scholars with new and interesting tasks to solve. The advent of computers and the recent availability of increasingly large volumes of digitally-stored textual data have provided new opportunities and challenges for current researchers.

The first PASCAL Recognizing Textual Entailment Challenge (Dagan et al. 2005) highlights the relevance of recognizing textual entailment (henceforth RTE) as a core task within the area of Language Technology. The PASCAL challenge consisted of the recognition of textual entailment between coherent sentences T (*text*) and H (*hypothesis*) where T entails H if the meaning of H, as interpreted in the context of T, can be inferred from the meaning of T. In the following examples, the texts of the pairs labelled as A entail their respective hypotheses, whereas the texts of the pairs labelled as B do not entail their hypotheses:

1. **A text.** *Iraqi militants said Sunday they would behead Kim Sun-Il, a 33-year-old translator, within 24 hours unless plans to dispatch thousands of South Korean troops to Iraq were abandoned.*
   **hypothesis.** *Translator was kidnapped in Iraq.*
   **B text.** *Two Turkish engineers and an Afghan translator kidnapped in December were freed Friday.*
   **hypothesis.** *Translator was kidnapped in Iraq.*

J. Quiñonero-Candela et al. (Eds.): MLCW 2005, LNAI 3944, pp. 385–403, 2006.

2. **A text.** *A The privately owned spacecraft only got about 400 feet into space, according to radar measurements, but it was enough to confirm that it no longer takes a well-heeled government project to organize space travel.*
   **hypothesis.** *Private spaceship launches.*

   **B text.** *The Federal Aviation Administration's Associate Administrator for Commercial Space Transportation (FAA/AST) has given license approval to Scaled Composites of Mojave, California, permitting the firm to expand flight testing of SpaceShipOne – a privately-financed rocket plane to carry passengers to suborbital altitude.*
   **hypothesis.** *Private spaceship launches.*

RTE has been recognized as a principal task in various Language Technology areas, including Question Answering (QA), Information Retrieval (IR), Information Extraction (IE) and (multi-) document summarisation. Even the task of recognizing paraphrases can be reduced to a RTE task, since if X entails Y and Y entails X then X and Y paraphrase each other. Within the area of QA, to give an example of the relevance of textual entailment, given the question *Who killed Kennedy?*, the text *the assassination of Kennedy by Oswald* entails the expected answer *Oswald killed Kennedy*, even though it does not match the wording of the question fully. It would be advisable, therefore, to solve the general problem of text entailment and to apply the acquired solution to any applications that might need it.

A difficulty in the recognition of textual entailment is the fact that information can be expressed in a great variety of forms. Just to give an example, *X wrote Y* and *X is an author of Y* are paraphrases of each other. But the most important difficulty of textual entailment is the frequent use of word knowledge and common sense axioms to draw inferences. For example, *X's new novel Y appeared in the bookstores* expresses the idea that *X is an author of Y* and consequently *X wrote Y*. The task of textual entailment can only be truly solved via a process of fully understanding the text and the hypothesis. Still, we believe that it is possible to recognize textual entailment to a level of success that improves the related language technologies listed above.

The structure of this paper is as follows. Section 2 focuses on the various sources of entailment in natural language. Section 3 proposes a classification of entailments based on the types of tools required for the entailment task. The tools and resources that could be used in an automatic algorithm for entailment recognition are discussed in Section 4. Section 5 describes the architecture of our system and presents the results of the system performance on the PASCAL RTE test data. Section 6 contains a brief comparison of the system with respect to other participants in the RTE challenge. Finally, Section 7 concludes the paper.

## 2 Sources of Entailment

In this section we introduce a simple entailment classification according to the possible sources of entailment. There are three main sources of entailment, *syntactic information*, *semantic information*, and *logical information*.

### 2.1 Syntax

Some forms of entailment are derived from specific syntactic transformations. Natural language allows us to convey information compactly, to hide a part of the information, or alternatively, to give more details about the same fact and even emphasize some particular parts of the message. For example, let us suppose that we want to describe the fact that a new house was built. The following sentences could be used, depending on the main intention of our message:

1. *The builders have built the house.*
2. *The new house has been built by builders.*
3. *A new house has been built.*
4. *It is a new house that has been built.*
5. *It is the builders who have built a new house.*
6. *The building of a new house has just been finished.*
7. *The building of a new house by the builders has just been finished.*
8. *The builders managed to build the new house in time.*
9. *The builders finished building the new house in time.*
10. *The builders had to hurry a lot while building a new house.*
11. *The builders had to hurry. They had to build the house fast.*
12. *A house that has been recently built by the builders is very beautiful.*
13. *A house recently built by the builders is very beautiful.*
14. *The desired construction, namely a new house, has been built.*

As illustrated in these examples, the usual way to communicate who made an action is to use an active form. This is shown, for example, in Sentence 1. If it is not important or even not known who has done the action, a passive form such as Sentence 3 can be used. On the contrary, to stress who built the house (say, if one wonders whether this new house has been built by an owner himself, or by the builders), then a cleft sentence like Sentence 5 can be used. Sometimes information is provided in a more compact form, as in Sentence 6. In this case there are two facts in one sentence. It is supposed here that the reader knew beforehand about the construction of a new house in the district and wanted to get some information about an action as a whole.

As one could see, even if two sentences may express the same information they may give a slightly different connotation. Also, it depends on the kind of information that is already known by the reader, what is the most important to him. We may also distinguish between the text genres under consideration. An article in a newspaper or a book summary will compact information to a higher degree than in an essay or the book content itself. All of this will result in differences between the grammatical constructions used.

Some of the above sentences transmit more information, some less, but all of them entail that a new house was built. A general rule of entailment is that if a sentence expresses two nuggets of information, A and B, then the sentence entails both A and B. Thus, sentences containing more information entail the less informative sentences. As we will see below, we will exploit this central idea in our approach to the PASCAL RTE challenge.

For RTE the awareness of such syntactical diversity of the language will help to recognize that, for example, *The building of a new house has just been finished* entails *A new house has been built.*

### 2.2 Semantics

Another source of textual entailment is the actual meanings of the words. Not all kinds of past studies in lexical semantics are useful for our purposes. For example, take the traditional classification of nouns between proper and common nouns, or the classification between count and uncount nouns (Quirk et al. 1985, Page 245). They all help to characterize the meaning of a noun. Similarly the traditional classification between dynamic verbs and stative verbs (Quirk et al. 1985, Page 201) help us give a semantic description of a verb. But these are largely syntactically driven categorizations. There are syntactic constructions in the language that take into account this kind of knowledge. The division between proper and common nouns gives us the rules for the usage of articles (in the languages where there are articles), for example. Usually proper nouns are used without an article, though the usage of an article gives us some additional information sometimes. Thus, A Dr. Smith = Some Dr. Smith. *The* Robinsons is a family of Robinsons. *The* Netherlands is a country name, containing the plural. Similarly, dynamic verbs allow the use of progressive forms *He is running*, but stative verbs become unacceptable (or generate marked readings) when used in the progressive *He is knowing the truth.*

More useful for us are the semantic relations existing between words. This type of semantic information shows us the place of the word within a hierarchy of words linked by relations such as hyponymy/hypernymy, synonymy, antonymy, and plain entailment. For example, one can state that the meanings of two words are equal to each other if the words belong to the same synonym group, or that the meaning of one word entails the meaning of all of its hypernyms. For example, *The man saw a poodle* entails *The man saw a dog*, as dog is a hypernym of *poodle.*

### 2.3 Logic and Knowledge

We have left the logic source of textual entailment to the end of our list though this is the most intuitive one. One sentence entails another sentence if the logical concept of the first implies the logical concept of the second. For example, from the sentence *Russian president Vladimir Putin visited US* one can entail that *Vladimir Putin is a president of Russia* and *Vladimir Putin visited US.* As people have common sense and can use world knowledge we would easily deduce also that Vladimir Putin exists, he is human, he is a resident of Russia, and provided that one knows that it is a constitutional rule that only a person over 35 can become a president in Russia, one can also deduce that Putin is older than 35 years old. Also, if the sentence was found in a news article, we would deduce that it is most probably told about an official visit of president Putin to US, and probably many other things. Consequently, linguistic expressions of all these concepts are entailed from the same sentence.

The source of these entailments would not come through syntactic or lexical analysis this time, though these two types of linguistic information might play an auxiliary role in the process. Instead, the source of these entailments is knowledge representation and reasoning. An example of knowledge representation is a knowledge base that holds lexical axioms such as:

president(X) :– human(X), resident(X), over_age_limits(X).

This knowledge base would be complemented with a tool for reasoning that could work with this type of information.

In the work presented in this paper we use limited world knowledge. In particular we use only information that can be extracted from a lexical resource, plus a few general axioms. But a central idea in our work is the general entailment principle that a sentence entails every piece of information that it conveys or a conjunction of them.

In practice, textual entailment is the combination of syntax, semantics, and logic. This can be seen with the example *Peter tracked down and killed the man.* This sentence is a conjunction of two pieces of information, and therefore it entails *Peter killed the man.* A simple syntactic transformation allows the sentence to entail *The man was killed.* Furthermore, there is a cause-effect relation between *kill* and *die*, and therefore the sentence entails *The man was dead.* Finally, common sense tells us that, modulo very exceptional circumstances, someone who is dead becomes dead forever. Therefore, the sentence entails *The man is dead.*

## 3 Classification of Entailment

With respect to the tools to be used to find an entailment relation one can distinguish between three types of entailment:

- **Lexico-syntactic entailments:** Entailments that could be detected with the help of syntactic and lexical knowledge only. In other words, the hypothesis is just a lexico-syntactic variant of the text sentence.
- **Descriptive entailments:** Entailments of this group are characterized by the substitution of entire descriptions or definitions with a shorter expression.
- **Knowledge-based entailments:** Entailments that would need some extra knowledge, possibly from some entailment database. Lexical resources and syntax play an auxiliary role only.

### 3.1 Lexico-Syntactic Entailment

Lexico-syntactic entailment is a type of entailment where the hypothesis is a lexico-syntactic variant of the text. That means that the only tools required to prove the entailment relation are those concerned with the extraction of syntactic structures of the text and hypothesis, plus a lexical database. Examples of this type of entailment are:

**text.** *A Union Pacific freight train hit five people.*
**hypothesis.** *A Union Pacific freight train struck five people.*

**text.** *Satomi Mitarai died of blood loss.*
**hypothesis.** *Satomi Mitarai bled to death.*

The lexical correspondence might be fairly complicated. In the first example the correspondence is word to word, but this is not always the case. For example, a transitive predicate with its object could correspond to an intransitive predicate, *to bleed* = *to lose blood*, *to dine* = *to have dinner*, etc. A noun phrase could be expanded or bunched up in a hypothesis. *a dead man* = *a man who was killed*, *a writing pen* = *a pen for writing*, *a dinner cake* = *a cake prepared for dinner*. These complex correspondences between words add a lot of complications to the RTE task.

There might be a verb ellipsis, as in the following example, where only common sense helps one to assume that a rock group performs during a concert rather than attend it:

**text.** *Phish disbands after a final concert in Vermont on August 15.*
**hypothesis.** *Rock band Phish holds final concert in Vermont.*

In contrast to paraphrases we do not have to know this transformation in advance but we need a tool to estimate how probable the change is: we need to find an *entailment score.*

Vanderwende et al. (2005) have shown that up to 49% of all the entailment pairs in the RTE development set belong to this group of entailments. These figures were obtained using an *ideal* parser and an *ideal* lexical database. In particular, 37% of the test items of their evaluation can be handled by syntax, and 49% of the test items can be handled by syntax plus a general purpose thesaurus.

### 3.2 Descriptive Entailment

Entailments of this group are characterized by the fact that a definition or description is substituted with a term which is equivalent in meaning or more generic. See the description of the notions of *opponents* and *discrimination* in the examples of this section. Besides that, some compression techniques could be used to make it possible to convey as much information as possible in brief sentences. This is done not only via syntactic transformations (e.g. nominalizations) but also via the substitution of words. Consequently, knowledge about the syntactic structure of the sentence alone would not be sufficient to recognize all instances of this type of entailment.

For example:

**text.** *Israeli Prime Minister Ariel Sharon threatened to dismiss Cabinet ministers who don't support his plan to withdraw from the Gaza Strip.*
**hypothesis.** *Israeli Prime Minister Ariel Sharon threatened to fire cabinet opponents of his Gaza withdrawal plan.*

The following syntactic compression has been made in the above entailment example:

- Generalization: *Gaza Strip→Gaza*
- Nominalization: *plan to withdraw→withdrawal plan*
- Lexical substitution: *to dismiss→to fire*
- Definition substitution: *ministers who do not support X's plan→opponents.*

The above definition substitution is difficult to detect automatically given that it would most likely not appear in standard lexical knowledge bases.

Another example:

> **text.** *The country's largest private employer, Wal-Mart Stores Inc., is being sued by a number of its female employees who claim they were kept out of jobs in management because they are women.*
> **hypothesis.** *Wal-Mart is sued for sexual discrimination.*

The following transformations have been made:

- Lexical substitution: *Wal-Mart Stores Inc.→Wal-Mart.*
- Definition substitution: *to be sued by a number of its female employees who claim they were kept out of jobs in management because they are women→to be sued for sexual discrimination.*

Again, the definition substitution would be difficult to detect automatically.

### 3.3 Knowledge-Based Entailment

Finally, there are entailment pairs where common sense background knowledge is needed for their detection. We call them knowledge-based entailments.

> **text.** *Researchers at the Harvard School of Public Health say that people who drink coffee may be doing a lot more than keeping themselves awake — this kind of consumption apparently also can help reduce the risk of diseases.*
> **hypothesis.** *Coffee drinking has health benefits.*

> **text.** *Eating lots of foods that are a good source of fibre may keep your blood glucose from rising too fast after you eat.*
> **hypothesis.** *Fibre improves blood sugar control.*

> **text.** *Mexico City has a very bad pollution problem because the mountains around the city act as walls and block in dust and smog.*
> **hypothesis.** *Poor air circulation out of the mountain-walled Mexico City aggravates pollution.*

This type of entailment is much harder than the other two for the simple reason that currently there are no knowledge bases containing all the common-sense knowledge required, and even if there were any it is not obvious how to find the required information among a sea of unrelated information — see, for example, Mahesh et al.'s (1996) study of the applicability of a well-known attempt to provide a common-sense knowledge base.

One of the important questions that needs to be addressed is what kind of entailment will prove to be useful in real applications. From the point of view of QA the lexico-syntactic and the descriptive entailments most probably will bring an improvement to the performance of a QA system. They are also more accessible to computational methods than the third, more complex type of entailment. Therefore, in our approach we have focused on the first two and left the third type (knowledge-based entailment) for future work.

## 4 Tools

This section we introduce the tools used in the current system for textual entailment recognition.

### 4.1 Parser

Given that syntax plays a role in text entailment, we decided not to experiment with bag-of-words approaches and used syntactic information instead. The output of the parser provides us with this syntactic information. For our system we used the Link Grammar Parser (Sleator and Temperley 1991) because it is a robust parser that outputs a ranked list of parse variants (not just the favourite parse). The grammar provided with this parser covers a wide range of sentence structures, and various independent evaluations (e.g. Sutcliffe et al. 1996, Molla and Hutchinson 2003) show that its accuracy is comparable to that of other wide-coverage parsers. Also the code is freely available, and has been implemented in the C programming language with a C API.

The issue about the availability of multiple parse variants is important because, implicitly or explicitly, parsers try to guess the right parse among a (possibly large) list of possible parses for syntactically ambiguous sentences. Syntactic disambiguation is one of the most important and difficult tasks for a parser, since a sentence may contain hundreds of alternative parses, and context external to the scope of the sentence is often required. Our plan is to allow all the possible inferences resulting from the combined parses of a sentence. Thus, the sentence *The man saw a girl with a telescope* would entail the hypotheses that *A girl has a telescope* as well as *The man has a telescope*, according to the two possible readings of the sentence.

Although our current implementation only uses the first parse returned by Link Parser, a parser that returns all possible parses allows further extensions of our method.

Probably, eventually a formal notion of *text coherence* (or *grammaticality*) should be introduced for textual entailment such that all the coherent interpretations of the text should be used for the task rather than one final parse given by a specific parser.

An additional and important use of the syntactic structures returned by a parser is the construction of the logical form of the sentence. The logical form is required if we want to use logical entailment as a means to find textual entailment, as we do in our system.

### 4.2 Lexical Database

As mentioned in Section 2.2, hierarchical information about words and word concepts is valuable for the task of entailment recognition. The most popular lexical resource for English is WordNet (Miller 1995). It contains hierarchical information about the concepts expressed by nouns, verbs, adjective and adverbs.

For the concept *table#n#2* (i.e. the second word sense of the noun table) with gloss *a piece of furniture having a smooth flat top that is usually supported by one or more vertical legs; "it was a sturdy table"*, for example, WordNet provides the following information:

> If *X is a table*, then *X is a piece of furniture*, *X is furnishings*, *X is an artefact*, *X is a physical object* and *X is an entity.*
> If *X is a booth*, *X is a breakfast table* or *X is a desk*, then *X is a table.*

Also, WordNet provides information about meronymy (has-part) relationships, derivational information, and synonymy information. For verbs, WordNet presents also relations of causation and entailment. All of this information is useful for the task of RTE. Hyponymy and synonymy are especially indicated to detect entailment. To be more precise, proposition P1 entails proposition $P_2$ if $P_2$ is more general than $P_1$. One can say that $P_2$ is more general than $P_1$ if all of the concepts in $P_2$ are either synonyms or they are more general (hypernyms) in $P_1$. To compare concepts one can use therefore the hypernym and synset information from WordNet.

The meaning comparison at the word level is a well-defined task that has been approached by many researchers. WordNet relatedness and similarity measures (see, for example, the review provided by Budanitsky and Hirst 2001) might be helpful tools to perform such a meaning comparison. The currently available measures have been developed for applications quite different from the entailment recognition. Still, some redevelopment or adjustment might be used successfully for the RTE task. Inspired in these measures, we have defined a custom-made measure that approximates the degree of entailment between two arbitrary words.

### 4.3 Logic Prover

Given that entailment is a logical relationship, it is only natural to try and find the logical form of the text and the hypothesis and use a logical prover to test if the text entails the hypothesis. The classical theory of computational semantics suggests first-order Predicate Logic or extensions thereof as a tool for the representation of the sentence meaning (see, for example, Jurafsky and Martin 2000, Chapter 14). Various formalisms have been devised, some of which include methods for the construction of the logical forms (what is called the *semantic interpretation* or *semantic analysis* of the sentence). Given that the comparison of logical forms would eventually be done through automated deduction systems (logic provers), it is important to use a logical form notation that can be converted into the format of the chosen automatic prover.

In addition to the logical forms of the text and hypothesis, the logic prover needs to have access to world knowledge encoded in form of axioms. To avoid flooding the prover with a large set of axioms that would not help detect the entailment, our system uses information extracted from WordNet based on the actual words of the sentences.

The process of finding the logical forms and appropriate world-knowledge axioms is potentially difficult, and the computing complexity of the logical proof could be time-consuming. For these reasons most of the systems participating in PASCAL tried methods that avoided the use of logical forms. We decided to try this natural method to assess its feasibility for the RTE task. In particular, our current system uses the theorem prover Otter (Kalman 2001), which is available on the WWW. We will show the usage of Otter using a very simple example.

**text.** *A boy bought a desk.*
**hypothesis.** *A boy bought a table.*

Axiom extracted from WordNet:

*X is a desk*→*X is a table*

Input for Otter:

exists $x$ exists $y$ exists $e$ ($boy(x)$ & $bought(e, x, y)$ & $desk(y)$).
all $x$ ($desk(x) \rightarrow table(x)$).
-(exists $x$, $y$, $e$ ($boy(x)$ & $bought(e, x, y)$ & $table(y)$)).

Having been given the above input, Otter is capable to prove that the hypothesis is entailed from the text.

## 5 The Proposed System

The central idea of our approach to RTE is to exploit the basic principle of logical entailment: *A and entails A*. In our approach, the entailment between the text and the hypothesis sentences is detected by comparing the *atomic propositions* found in both sentences. By an atomic proposition we mean a minimal declarative statement (or a small idea) that has truth-conditions (is either true T or false F) and whose truth or falsity does not depend on the truth or falsity of any other proposition. For example, given the sentence *Coffee boosts energy and provides health benefits*, the propositions are *Coffee boosts energy* and *Coffee provides health benefits*. Thus, the meaning of a sentence is represented as the set of atomic propositions contained in it. One has to compare the propositions in order to compare the sentences.

To implement the idea we have used Link Parser (Sleator and Temperley 1991) version 4.1a to obtain a syntactic structure of the sentence. The output of the parser was used to extract the atomic propositions of the sentence. These in turn were converted into logical formulae that served as an input for a logical prover, Otter (Kalman 2001) version 3.3 in our case.

The architecture of the system is presented in Figure 1. The system performs the same analysis for the text and for the hypothesis. In both cases there is a process of parsing and a process of proposition extraction. After the propositions

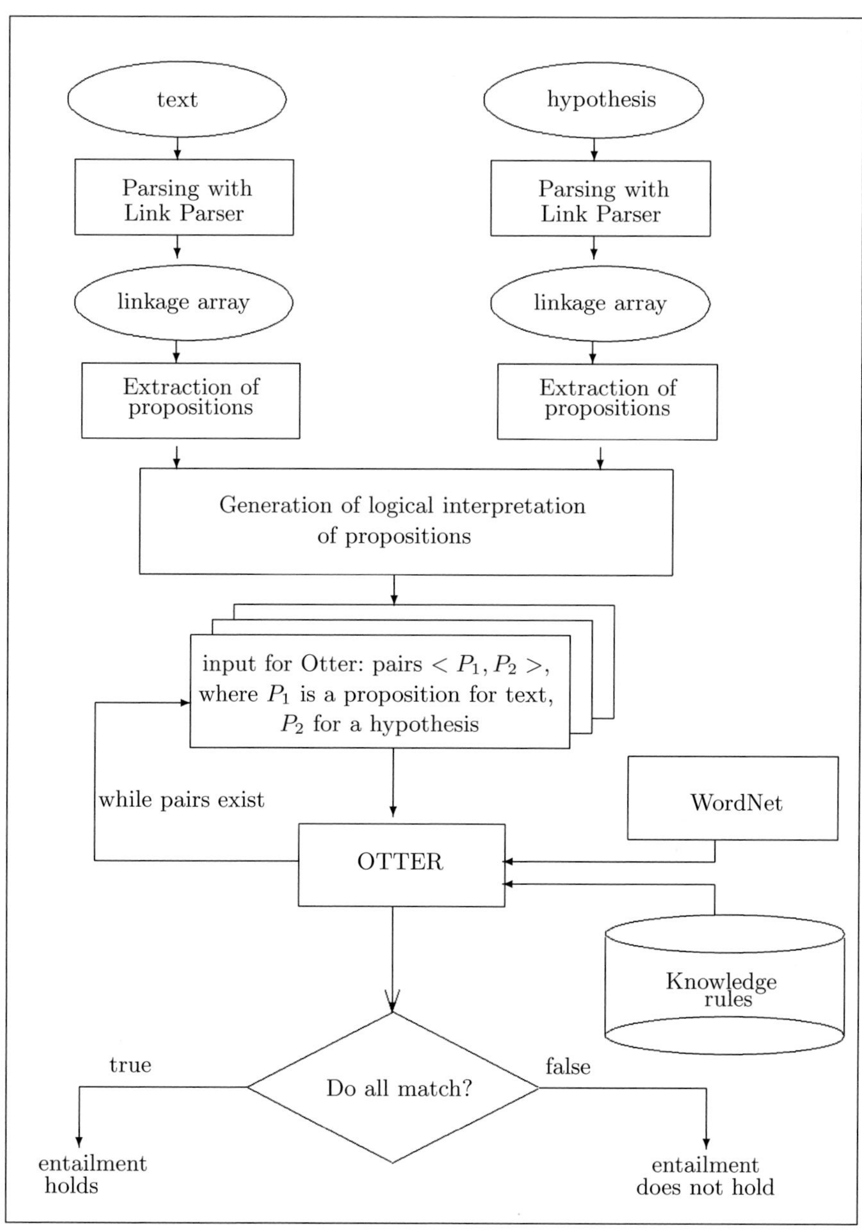


**Fig. 1.** Architecture of the system

have been extracted the system generates a logical form for every proposition. The logical forms of the propositions are given as an input to the theorem prover Otter. Data returned by Otter allows the system to make a decision about the relation of entailment between the text and the hypothesis.

Figure 2 shows an example the process of making a decision about the entailment relation between the text and the hypothesis. Every proposition of the hypothesis – *coffee gives health benefits* – is compared to all the propositions of the text sentence. In the example, since there is one proposition – *coffee provides health benefits* – that entails the only proposition of the hypothesis, the entailment holds.

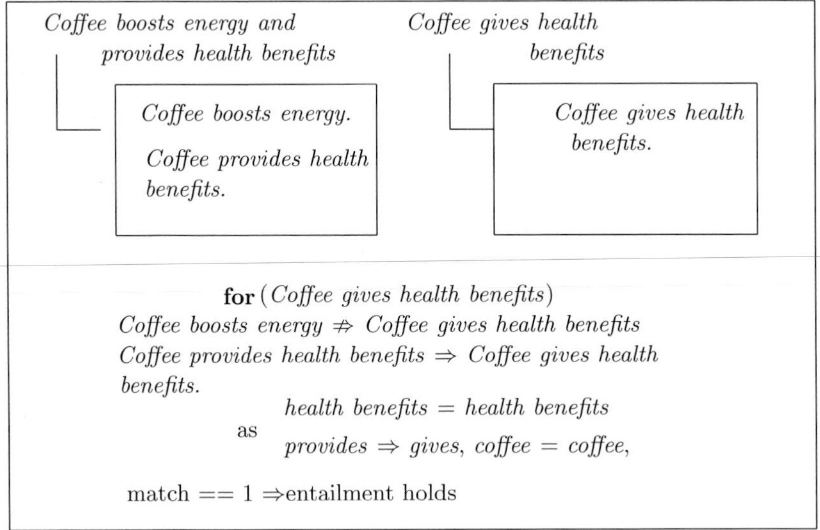


**Fig. 2.** Comparison of Propositions

### 5.1 Link Parser and Proposition Extraction

The current version of the system needs a full parse of the text and hypothesis sentences. Both sentences are parsed with the Link Parser. The output of the parser is an array of links (or *linkages*) between words.

In the example,

the subject of the sentence *coffee* is connected to the predicate *boosts* by means of the *Ss* link, that is defined as a relation between a subject in a singular number and its predicate. Capital *S* means subject, small *s* means singular. In a similar way *boosts* and *energy* are connected through the object-predicate linkage *Os*.

The full output of the Link Parser for the text sentence from our example may be represented graphically in the following two linkages:[1]

Xp
Wd Ss Os
L-WALL coffee.n boosts.v energy.n and provides.v health.n benefits.n .

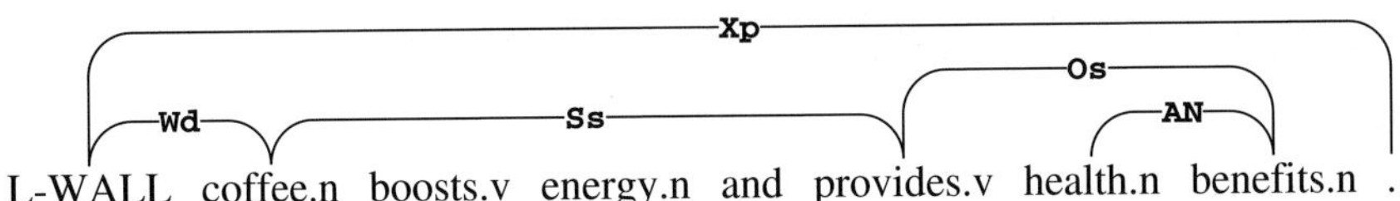


This output of the parser can be easily used to extract the atomic propositions from the sentences. One only needs to define which sets of links constitute a proposition and to check if there are coherent chains of such links in a sentence parse. *Ss* and *Os* links will give us a proposition, links between a noun, participle and its object, like in *boy playing chess*, will also constitute a proposition, and so on. Table 1 shows the basic combinations of links that constitute a proposition.

For our example text sentence two atomic propositions are extracted:

*coffee boosts energy* and *coffee provides health benefits.*

The hypothesis sentence contains only one proposition, namely

*coffee gives health benefits.*

## 5.2 Logical Forms and Automated Deduction

After the propositions are extracted they are converted into logical forms. These logical forms will constitute an input to the theorem prover. For this reason they are formatted according to the syntactic requirements of the particular theorem prover, Otter in our case.

The current logical representation is flat and syntax-dependent, and could be considered a simplified version of other logical representations proposed in the literature (e.g. Hobbs 1985, Copestake et al. Draft).

There are three types of objects: $Subj(x)$, $Obj(x)$, $Pred(x)$, and a meaning attaching element $iq(x, <meaning\ of\ x>)$. With this notation, the proposition *coffee boosts energy* has the following logical representation:

exists $x$ exists $y$ exists $z$ ($Subj(x)$ & $iq(x$, 'coffee') & $Pred(y)$ & $iq(y$, 'boosts') & $Obj(z)$ & $iq(z$, 'energy')).

Also, there are two variants of relationships $attr(x, y)$ and $prep(x, y)$; the following lines show an example of their usage:

Somali capital – $Subj(x)$ & $iq(x$, 'capital') & $attr(x, y)$ & $Subj(y)$ & $iq(y$, 'somali').
a zoo in Berlin – $Obj(x)$ & $iq(x$, 'zoo') & $prep(x, y)$ & $Obj(y)$ & $iq(y$, 'Berlin').

[1] Each picture shows one of the branches of the coordination as returned by Link Parser.

**Table 1.** The list of linkages used to extract propositions (only relevant links shown). For the reference to the meaning of the linkages visit the Link Grammar Documentation web-site http://bobo.link.cs.cmu.edu/link/dict/index.html.

| Linkages | Example | Proposition |
|---|---|---|
| *Ss/Sp Os/Op* | Links: Ss, Os<br>The boy.n plays.v chess.n | *boy plays chess* |
| *Mg Os/Op* | Links: Mg, Os<br>The boy.n playing.v chess.n is here | *boy plays chess* |
| *MX (with Xd, Xc)* | Links: MXs, Xd, Xc<br>The boy.n , a chess.n player.n , is here | *boy is a chess player* |
| *Bs/Bp (with R, RS)* | Links: Bs, R, RS, Os<br>The boy.n who plays.v chess.n is here | *boy plays chess* |
| *Bs/Bp (with R#, S#)* | Links: Bs, Rn, Ds, Ss<br>The boy.n the girl.n likes.v is here | *the girl likes the boy* |
| *Mv; Mv (with MVp, Js/Jp and by)* | Links: Js, Mv, MVp, Ds<br>The book.n read.v by the boy.n is good | *the boy read the book* |
| *Ss/Sp Pv MVp Js/Jp with by* | Links: Js, Ss, Pv, MVp, Ds<br>The book.n was.v read.v by the boy.n | *the boy read the book* |

As soon as a proposition is converted to its logical representation it is ready to be used as an input for Otter. However, Otter will not be able to prove anything without some background knowledge. The background knowledge provided to Otter comes from three different sources:

1. Knowledge about the relation between concepts, such as *give* and *provide*, or *table* and *furniture*. This is extracted from WordNet.
2. Knowledge about the relationships, like $attr(x, y)$, which could be substituted by $prep(x, y)$ under some circumstances.
3. Knowledge about the different representations of the same concept. A number, for example, could be represented as a word (*one*) or as a numeric expression (*1*).

The word relations provided by WordNet were used to compute a measure of entailment between pairs of words. Concept $c_i$ is in the entailment relation to a concept $c_j$, if $c_i$ is less generic than $c_j$ (by concept we mean here a particular sense of a word, or synset, using WordNet terminology). In a slightly more formal wording, $c_i$ entails $c_j$ if $c_i$ is equal to $c_j$ or $c_i$ is lower than $c_j$ in the WordNet hyponymy hierarchy. We generalize this idea to allow a degree of entailment between two arbitrary words. This degree of entailment depends on the length of the path between the two words, and the number of senses of each word. The final formula is:

$$rel(c_i, c_j) = p(c_i) \times p(c_j) \times score(c_i, c_j) \tag{1}$$

$$score(c_i, c_j) = C^{length(c_i, c_j) - 1} \tag{2}$$

where $p(c_i)$ is the probability that a word in a sentence is presented by the concept $c_i$, and $length(c_i, c_j)$ is the length of the path connecting the concepts. The constant $C$ $(0 < C \leq 1)$ has to be chosen empirically.

As it could be easily seen from the formula the final score is between zero and one. The idea behind the formula is the following. First, we assume that a word sense disambiguation system gives as an output the probability distribution over all the senses of a word. Secondly, we assert that the relation between concepts becomes weaker as the length of the path connecting the words increases. The constant $C$ helps to adjust the impact of the length between concepts in the final relatedness score.

Thus, for our example we can obtain the rule:

all $x$ ($iq(x$, 'provide') $\rightarrow iq(x$, 'give')).

Figure 3 shows the result obtained for the comparison of two lexical concepts, *provide* and *give*.

To account for the sources of information 1. and 2. the system used the following rules:

**provide - give** **relatedness score** $= 0.0042 > 0$
$\Rightarrow \forall x$ ($iq(x$, 'provide') $\rightarrow iq(x$, 'give')).
(verb chain); maximum path length - 3

1.**provide#1**(7)[2259805] –hyperonym– **give#3**(44)[2136207]
...
7.**provide#6**(7)[2155855]–hyperonym–**support#2**(11)[2155507] –hyperonym– **give#3**(44)[2136207]

**Fig. 3.** WordNet relatedness between the concepts *provide* and *give*; data and results. The figure shows the paths connecting the lexical concepts and the final relatedness score.

a) **Negation**: all $x$ all $x77$ ($niq(x, x77) \rightarrow -iq(x, x77)$).
b) **Attribute-preposition relation**: all $x$ all $y$ ($attr(x, y) \rightarrow prep(x, y)$).
c) **Numbers**: all $x$ ($iq(x, \text{'one'}) \rightarrow iq(x, \text{'1'})$).

Rule b) has been introduced to allow paraphrases of multi-word expressions, such as the ones below, where an attribute of a noun is converted into a prepositional phrase:

*night flight* ↔ *flight* ***in*** *(the) night*
*pet spray* ↔ *spray* ***for*** *pets*
*peanut butter* ↔ *butter* ***from*** *peanut*
*abortion problem* ↔ *problem* ***about*** *abortion*

### 5.3 Proposition Comparison

The text entails the hypothesis if for every proposition in the hypothesis there is one proposition in the text sentence that could entail it, as shown in Figure 2. The decision that proposition $p_1$ entails proposition $p_2$ can be easily made after sending Otter both propositions and all the background rules, including those obtained from the WordNet lexical database.

### 5.4 Results and Performance

The entailments addressed in the program belong to the class of lexico-syntactical entailments discussed in Section 3. As mentioned above, only around 49% of all entailment pairs in the RTE dataset are entailments of this kind. One might expect the system would not jump over the 50% barrier then. It is not true though. The results are different because the system also gets points for recognizing that there is no entailment relation between the text and hypothesis. It almost always states the absence of the entailment relation correctly.

Also the mistakes introduced on the stage of the parsing or during the process of proposition extraction brought some noise into the results, as some of the decisions that were made happened to be correct or incorrect because of the mistakes.

The actual results are shown in Table 2 and summarised here:

cws: 0.5067; accuracy: 0.5188; precision: 0.6119;
recall: 0.1025; f: 0.175.

The system successfully predicts the following types of entailments:

- **WordNet generalization** T: *The decision is made.* – H: *The determination is made.*
- **Logical generalization** T: *The good decision is made.* – H: *The decision is made.*
- **Syntactic variations** T: *The zoo built recently by the government is open for visitors now.* – H: *The zoo was built.*
- **NN syntactic structure** T: *The Brazilian president visited France.* – H: *The president of Brazil visited France.*

**Table 2.** Performance of the system according to the *PASCAL Recognizing Textual Entailment Challenge* evaluation method

| Task | Cws | Accuracy |
|---|---|---|
| CD | 0.6121 | 0.5867 |
| IE | 0.5519 | 0.5083 |
| MT | 0.4341 | 0.4917 |
| QA | 0.4649 | 0.4769 |
| RC | 0.4702 | 0.5214 |
| IR | 0.5452 | 0.5200 |
| PP | 0.4797 | 0.5111 |

Some of the mistakes of the system were caused by the overgeneralization of the logical forms for specific language structures. The two following examples illustrate this:

**text.** *The gastronomic capital of France is Lyon.*
**hypothesis.** *The capital of France is Lyon.*

**text.** *The man came to the park by car.*
**hypothesis.** *The man came to a car park.*

The first example is a typical intersective reading of adjectives. In general, the *gastronomic capital* of a country is not necessarily the *capital* of the country. However, all the predicates of the logical form of *capital of France* appear in the logical form of *gastronomic capital of France.* Therefore, an entailment is wrongly detected.

In the second example, our approach represents the dependency relation between *car* and *park* differently but the attribute-proposition relation rule makes the logic prover ignore the difference. Again, an entailment is wrongly detected.

## 6 Comparison with Other Systems

The majority of the systems presented at the PASCAL RTE Challenge tried to approximate entailment by computing lexical relations at the word level. The roughest approximation was found by applying the BLEU metric for the machine translation evaluation (Pérez and Alfonseca 2002) and lexical similarity scores (Jijkoun and de Rijke 2005).

Our system was one of the few approaches that used a logical representation of the input data. An example of another system relying on logic was the one by Bos and Markert (2005). It is interesting to note that ours was the only system where the sentence was divided into minimal semantic elements ("propositions") so that the subsequent data analysis was applied directly to propositions and not to the original sentences. This division simplifies significantly the process of creation of a logical representation of the sentence and emphasizes the logical nature of the entailment relation.

We have not proposed here any methods to extract information about entailments in order to construct an entailment knowledge database that may help to the recognition of entailment. One work on the topic deserving attention is the one by MITRE (Burger and Ferro 2005).

## 7 Summary and Future Work

The present work implements the basic logical property *A and B entails A*. For this, the system builds the logical form of each independent atomic proposition from the text and hypothesis sentences, and sends the logical forms to the Otter automatic prover. The information sent to Otter is extended with general axioms and background information about the words used by the text and hypothesis. WordNet is used as a lexical resource to detect the degree of entailment between individual words. Overall, the system is simple, based on fundamental concepts, and can be seen as a baseline on which to try to recognize more complex types of textual entailment.

This paper also presented a discussion of the nature of textual entailment with respect to the various sources of entailment and the types of entailments depending on the tools required for their recognition.

The next step is to work on a more accurate implementation of the algorithm, namely to include the analysis of more complex verb and noun groups, in particular with respect to the handling of prepositional attachments. We also plan to work on the background information that needs to be sent to the theorem prover. Finally, we are investigating alternative ways of assessing semantic similarity on the word level and its relation to entailment and other logical concepts.

We believe that our work shows the feasibility of the combined use of logical forms with lexical resources to detect the entailment between two sentences.

## References


Bos, J., Markert, K.: Combining Shallow and Deep NLP Methods for Recognizing Textual Entailment. Proceedings of the PASCAL Recognising Textual Entailment Challenge (2005) 65–68

Budanitsky, A., Hirst, G.: Semantic Distance in WordNet: An Experimental, application-oriented evaluation of five measures. Proceedings of the NAACL–2001 Workshop on WordNet and Other Lexical Resources. Pittsburg PA. (2001)

Burger, J., Ferro, L.: Generating an Entailment Corpus from News Headlines. Proceedings of the Empirical Modelling of Semantic Equivalence and Entailment, ACL-2005 (2005) 49–54

Copestake, A., Flickinger, D. Sag, I.A. Minimal Recursion Semantics: an Introduction (on-line draft). http://lingo.stanford.edu/sag/publications.html

Dagan, I., Glickman, O., Magnini, B.: The PASCAL Recognising Textual Entailment Challenge. Proceedings of the PASCAL Recognising Textual Entailment Challenge (2005)

Hobbs, J.R.: Ontological Promiscuity. Proceedings of the Association for Computational Linguistics (1985) 61–69

Jijkoun, V., de Rijke, M.: Recognizing Textual Entailment Using Lexical Similarity. In the Proceedings of the PASCAL Recognising Textual Entailment Challenge (2005) 73–76

Jurafsky, D., Martin, J.H. Speech and Language Processing: An Introduction to Natural Language Processing, Computational Linguistics and Speech Recognition. Prentice-Hall. Chapters 14–15 (2000)

Kalman, J.A.: Automated Reasoning with OTTER. Rinton Press. Paramus, NJ (2001)

Mahesh, K., Nirenburg, S., Cowie, J., Farwell, D. An Assessment of Cyc for Natural Language Processing. CRL technical report MCCS-96-302, New Mexico State University (1996)

Miller, G.: WordNet: A lexical database for English. Communications of the ACM, 38(11) (1995) 39–41

Mollá, D., Hutchinson, B. Intrinsic versus Extrinsic Evaluations of Parsing Systems. Proceedings of the 10th Conference of the European Chapter of the Association for Computational Linguistics (EACL), workshop on Evaluation Initiatives in Natural Language Processing (2003) 43–50.

Pérez, D., Alfonseca, E.: 2005. Application of BLEU algorithm for Recognizing Textual Entailments. In the Proceedings of the PASCAL Recognising Textual Entailment Challenge (2002) 9–12

Quirk, R., Greenbaum, S., Leech, G., Svartvik, J. A Comprehensive Grammar of the English Language. Longman, London (1985)

Sleator, D., Temperley, D.: Parsing English with a Link Grammar. Carnegie Mellon University Computer Science technical report CMU-CS-91-196 (1991)

Sutcliffe, R.F.E., Koch, H., McElligott, A., editors. Industrial Parsing of Software Manuals. Rodopi, Amsterdam (1996).

Vanderwende, L., Coughlin, D., Dolan, B.: What Syntax can Contribute in Entailment Task. In the Proceedings of the PASCAL Recognising Textual Entailment Challenge, (2005) 13–16

# Recognising Textual Entailment with Robust Logical Inference

Johan Bos[1] and Katja Markert[2]

[1] School of Informatics, University of Edinburgh, UK
jbos@inf.ed.ac.uk
[2] School of Computing, University of Leeds, UK
markert@comp.leeds.ac.uk

**Abstract.** We use logical inference techniques for recognising textual entailment, with theorem proving operating on deep semantic interpretations as the backbone of our system. However, the performance of theorem proving on its own turns out to be highly dependent on a wide range of background knowledge, which is not necessarily included in publically available knowledge sources. Therefore, we achieve robustness via two extensions. Firstly, we incorporate model building, a technique borrowed from automated reasoning, and show that it is a useful robust method to approximate entailment. Secondly, we use machine learning to combine these deep semantic analysis techniques with simple shallow word overlap. The resulting hybrid model achieves high accuracy on the RTE testset, given the state of the art. Our results also show that the various techniques that we employ perform very differently on some of the subsets of the RTE corpus and as a result, it is useful to use the nature of the dataset as a feature.

## 1 Introduction

Recognising textual entailment (RTE) is the task to find out whether some text T entails a hypothesis text H. This task has recently been the focus of the *RTE challenge*, an evaluation exercise organised by the PASCAL network in 2004/05 [DGM05]. Two examples from the dataset issued as part of this challenge are shown below.[1] In Example 1550 H follows from T (hence it is marked TRUE) whereas this is not the case in Example 731 (which is therefore annotated as FALSE).

Example: 1550 (TRUE)

**T**: In 1998, the General Assembly of the Nippon Sei Ko Kai (Anglican Church in Japan) voted to accept female priests.

**H**: The Anglican church in Japan approved the ordination of women.

[1] All examples in this article are from the corpus released as part of the RTE challenge, keeping the original example identifiers. This corpus is available via http://www.pascal-network.org/Challenges/RTE/.

J. Quiñonero-Candela et al. (Eds.): MLCW 2005, LNAI 3944, pp. 404–426, 2006.

Example: 731 (FALSE)

**T**: The city Tenochtitlan grew rapidly and was the center of the Aztec's great empire.

**H**: Tenochtitlan quickly spread over the island, marshes, and swamps.

The recognition of textual entailment needs access to a wide range of syntactic and lexical knowledge and is without doubt one of the ultimate challenges for any natural language processing (NLP) system: if it is able to recognise entailment with reasonable accuracy, it is clearly an indication that it has some thorough understanding of how language works. Moreover, recognising entailment bears similarities to Alan Turing's famous test to assess whether machines can think, as access to different sources of knowledge and the ability to draw inferences seem to be among the primary ingredients for an intelligent system. In addition, many NLP tasks have strong links to entailment: in summarisation, a summary should be entailed by the text; in machine translation, the source and target text should mutually entail each other; in question answering, a valid answer entails the question; and in information extraction, the extracted information should also be entailed by the text.

In this article we discuss two methods for recognising textual entailment. Firstly, we present a shallow method that relies mainly on weighted word overlap between text and hypothesis. Secondly, we use a method based on deep semantic analysis, borrowing techniques from the field of automated deduction, namely theorem proving and model building, to perform logical inference. As theory for natural language semantics we use Discourse Representation Theory, DRT [KR93]. Semantic representations are built in a compositional way for the text and hypothesis with the help of Combinatory Categorial Grammar, CCG [Ste01], using a wide-coverage statistical parser [CC04].

To increase transferrability to other datasets and tasks, both the shallow and deep method are domain-independent, and neither has been tailored to any particular test suite. In this article we test their accuracy and robustness on the RTE datasets as one of the few currently available datasets for textual inference. We also combine the two methods in a hybrid approach using an off-the-shelf machine learning tool.

In particular, we are interested in the following questions:

- Can either of the methods presented improve significantly over the baseline and what are the performance differences between them?
- How far does deep semantic analysis suffer from a lack of lexical and world knowledge and how can we perform robust logical inference in the face of potentially large knowledge gaps?
- Does the hybrid system using both shallow and deep semantic analysis improve over the individual use of these methods?
- How does the design of the test suite affect performance? Are there subsets of the test suite that are more suited to any particular textual entailment recognition method?

This article is organised as follows. First, we will describe the shallow semantic approach (Section 2). This is followed by a detailed description of the deep semantic approach in Section 3, where we will also explain how to integrate theorem proving and model building, and how this combination achieves a level of robustness in using logical inference. Both Sections 2 and 3 list the features derived from these methods that are then used in several machine learning experiments. Section 4 describes these experiments, including a hybrid deep/shallow system for entailment recognition. In Section 5 we perform an error analysis, and Section 6 discusses the RTE challenge in general. Finally, related work is presented in Section 7.

## 2 Shallow Semantic Analysis

We use several shallow surface features to model the text, hypothesis and their relation to each other. A basic shallow feature we believe might play a role in textual entailment is word overlap.

### 2.1 Word Overlap Measures

For many textual entailment example pairs there is a dependency between surface string similarity of text and hypothesis and the existence of entailment. In particular, the inclusion of all or almost all words of the hypothesis in the text makes entailment likely. A case in point is Example 125 below, where all words in the hypothesis are contained in the text and entailment holds.

Example: 125 (TRUE)

**T**: On November 25, 2001, a baby Asian elephant was born at the National Zoo in Washington, DC.

**H**: baby elephant born

In contrast, the occurrence of words in the hypothesis that are unrelated to any word in the text makes entailment unlikely. This is the case in Example 731 in the Introduction where the words *swamps*, *islands* and *marshes* in the hypothesis introduce new information that is not in the text.

Our general model for measuring word overlap is a simple bag-of-words model, i.e. word order and syntactic structure are ignored. The exact procedure is as follows:

1. Both text and hypothesis are tokenised and lemmatised.
2. The overlap measure between text and hypothesis is initialised as zero.
3. Should a lemma in the hypothesis be *related to* a lemma in the text, its *weight* is added to the overlap measure, otherwise it is ignored.
4. In the end the overlap is normalised by dividing it by the sum of the weights of all lemmas in the hypothesis. This ensures that the overlap is always a real number between 0 and 1 and also ensures independence of the length of the hypothesis.

Variations of this simple measure depend on the definition of word relatedness as well as on which formula for weighting lemmas is used. Thus, it is possible to define relatedness simply as equality of lemmas. This can handle examples like 125 above well, where all lemmas in the hypothesis are exactly matched in the text. However, it falls short of recognising, for example, simple synonym variation in word choice as the replacement of *found* by *discovered* in Example 1987 below.

Example: 1987 (TRUE)

**T**: The girl was found in Drummondville earlier this month.

**H**: The girl was discovered in Drummondville.

Therefore the word overlap we use takes into account equality, synonymy and morphological derivations. WordNet [Fel98] is used as the knowledge source for synonymy and derivations. We therefore say that a lemma $l_1$ in the hypothesis is said to be *related* to a lemma $l_2$ in the text iff $l_1$ and $l_2$ are equal, belong to the same WordNet synset (e.g., "murder" and "slay"), are related via WordNet derivations (e.g. "murder" and "murderer") or are related via a combination of synonymy and derivations (e.g. "murder" via "murderer" to "liquidator"). No word sense disambiguation is performed and *all* synsets for a particular lemma are considered.

Regarding weight assignment, each lemma in the hypothesis is assigned its inverse document frequency, accessing the Web as corpus via the GoogleAPI, as its weight. We prefer this procedure over equal weighting of all lemmas as it allows us to assign more importance to less frequent words.

### 2.2 Shallow Semantic Features

Apart from the overlap measure `wnoverlap` we take into account length (as measured by number of lemmas) of text and hypothesis, because in most true entailments the hypothesis is shorter than the text as it contains less information. This is covered by three numerical features measuring the length of the text, of the hypothesis and the relative length of hypothesis with regard to the text.

## 3 Deep Semantic Analysis

### 3.1 Overview

In a nutshell, the deep semantic analysis aims to produce fine-grained semantic representations for both the text and hypothesis of an entailment pair. It then uses techniques from automated deduction, in particular first-order theorem proving and finite model building, to predict whether the text entails the hypothesis or not.

To achieve this, both the text and hypothesis are tokenised using NLProcesser[2] and fed into a robust wide-coverage parser, which uses a statistical

[2] A product from Infogistics, see `http://www.infogistics.com/textanalysis.html`

model based on CCG [CC04]. The parser produces CCG-derivations. Consider for instance the derivations for Example 78 below:

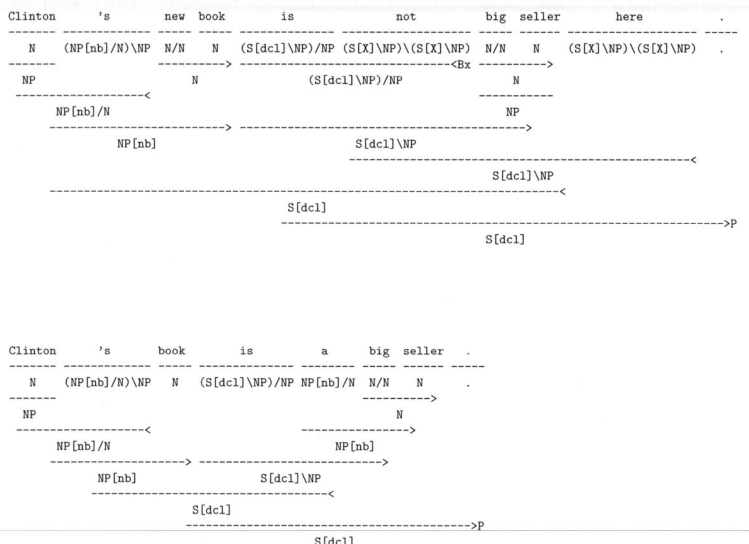


The CCG-derivations produced by the parser are the basis to construct discourse representation structures (DRSs, the semantic representations from DRT). This is done in a compositional way using the lambda-calculus as a "glue" to connect CCG with DRT [BCS+04, Bos05]. The semantic representations are then translated into first-order logic expressions. This allows us to perform inferences using a general-purpose theorem prover and model builder.

### 3.2 Semantic Interpretation

The semantic representation language is a first-order fragment of the DRS-language used in Discourse Representation Theory [KR93], conveying argument structure with a neo-Davidsonian analysis and including the recursive DRS structure to cover negation, disjunction, and implication. A basic DRS is an ordered pair of a set of discourse referents and a set of conditions imposed on these discourse referents. For convenience, we use the boxed notation to visualise DRSs, with the discourse referents at the top and the conditions at the lower part of the box. Consider for example the following entailment pair and the DRSs constructed for it:

Example: 78 (FALSE)

**T**: Clinton's new book is not big seller here.

**H**: Clinton's book is a big seller.

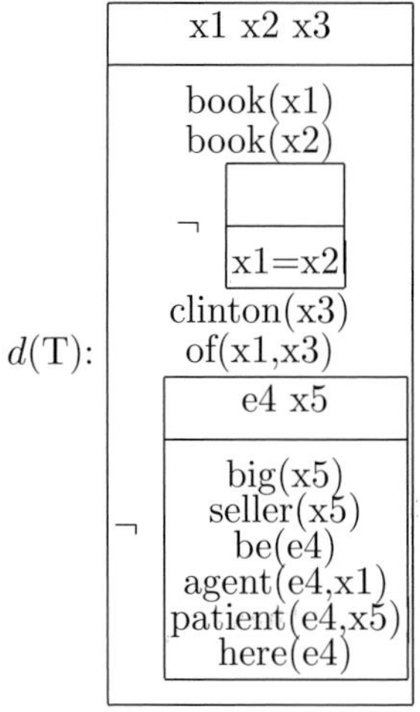


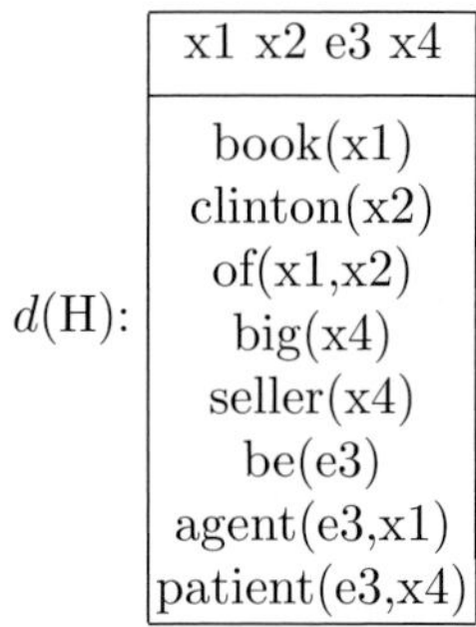


Proper names and definite descriptions are treated as anaphoric, and bound to previously introduced discourse referents if possible, otherwise accommodated [VdS92, Bos03]. Some lexical items are specified as presupposition triggers. An example is the adjective *new* which has a presuppositional reading, as shown by the existence of two different "book" entities in $d(\mathrm{T})$. Scope is fully specified.

The DRS language, with its quantifier free and rather flat representations, is useful for resolving ambiguities, such as pronoun resolution and presupposition projection. However, no efficient reasoning engines that work directly on DRSs exist. Therefore we use a translation from DRSs to first-order formula syntax, which opens the doors for using first-order theorem proving technology [BBKdN01]. The literature on DRT offers several translation functions that map DRS onto first-order logic — here we apply the so-called standard translation from DRS to first-order logic (see e.g. [KR93, BBKdN01]). This function, $f$, is defined by the following clauses:

$$f\left(\begin{array}{|c|}\hline \mathrm{x}_1 \ldots \mathrm{x}_n \\ \hline \mathrm{C}_1 \\ \vdots \\ \mathrm{C}_n \\ \hline \end{array}\right) = \exists \mathrm{x}_1 \ldots \exists \mathrm{x}_n \, (f(\mathrm{C}_1) \wedge \ldots \wedge f(\mathrm{C}_n))$$

$$f\left(\begin{array}{|c|}\hline \mathrm{x}_1 \ldots \mathrm{x}_n \\ \hline \mathrm{C}_1 \\ \vdots \\ \mathrm{C}_n \\ \hline \end{array} \Rightarrow \mathrm{B}\right) = \forall \mathrm{x}_1 \ldots \forall \mathrm{x}_n \, ((f(\mathrm{C}_1) \wedge \ldots \wedge f(\mathrm{C}_n)) \rightarrow f(\mathrm{B}))$$

$f(\mathrm{B}_1 \vee \mathrm{B}_2) = f(\mathrm{B}_1) \vee f(\mathrm{B}_2)$
$f(\neg\, \mathrm{B}) = \neg\, f(\mathrm{B})$
$f(\mathrm{x}{=}\mathrm{y}) = \mathrm{x}{=}\mathrm{y}$

$f$(P(x)) = P(x)
$f$(R(x,y)) = R(x,y)

Here B, $B_1$ and $B_2$ are variables ranging over DRSs, $C_i$ is a DRS-condition, P is a one-place predicate symbol and R a two-place predicate symbol. To illustrate the translation function, consider the result of translating $d$(T) and $d$(H) from Example 78 above:

$f(d$(T)): ∃x1 ∃x2 ∃x3 (book(x1) ∧ book(x2) ∧ ¬ (x1=x2) ∧ clinton(x3) ∧ of(x1,x3) ∧ ¬ ∃e4 ∃ x5( big(x5) ∧ seller(x5) ∧ be(e4) ∧ agent(e4,x1) ∧ patient(e4,x5) ∧ here(e4)))

$f(d$(H)): ∃x1 ∃x2 ∃e3 ∃x4 (book(x1) ∧ clinton(x2) ∧ of(x1,x2) ∧ big(x4) ∧ seller(x4) ∧ be(e3) ∧ agent(e3,x1) ∧ patient(e3,x4))

### 3.3 Theorem Proving

There are two kinds of first-order inference engines we use to perform reasoning: a theorem prover, and a model builder. First we will discuss the use of the theorem prover. We have integrated the prover Vampire [RV02] into our system, which is a general-purpose off-the-shelf theorem prover.

Given a textual entailment pair T/H, a theorem prover can be used to find an answer to conjecture (A):

$$f(d(\mathrm{T})) \rightarrow f(d(\mathrm{H})) \tag{A}$$

If the theorem prover manages to find a proof for this conjecture, then we predict that T entails H. (Note that we use the term "predict" here. There are cases in which the theorem prover finds a proof, although we are not actually dealing with a true entailment. This is due to inaccurate semantic analysis. See Section 5 for further discussion on this topic.)

In addition, we can also use a theorem prover to detect inconsistencies in a T/H pair by letting it handle the input (B):

$$\neg(f(d(\mathrm{T})) \wedge f(d(\mathrm{H}))) \tag{B}$$

If the theorem prover returns a proof for (B), we know that combining T and H yields an inconsistent state, thereby predicting that T does not entail H. An example is a pair T: *John is a doctor* and H: *John is not a doctor.* (Note that although it is the case that if T and H (combined) are inconsistent, then T does not entail H, the reverse does not hold. Therefore consistency checking is only a partial method to check for non-entailment.)

The RTE dataset contains only few inconsistent T/H pairs. Even although Example 78 might look like a case in point, it is not inconsistent. It would be if the T in the example were *Clinton's new book is not a big seller*. The addition of the adverb *here* makes T+H consistent.

Let's consider some examples that our system deals with successfully. Example 1005 is a case with apposition, and Example 898 one involving VP coordination.

Example: 1005 (TRUE)

**T**: Jessica Litman, a law professor at Michigan's Wayne State University, has specialized in copyright law and Internet law for more than 20 years.
**H**: Jessica Litman is a law professor.

Example: 898 (TRUE)

**T**: After the war the city was briefly occupied by the Allies and then was returned to the Dutch.
**H**: After the war, the city was returned to the Dutch.

Examples like these are rather trivial from the inference point of view, because they rely almost exclusively on correct syntactic analyses (here: apposition and coordination) and no additional knowledge is required to support the theorem prover. However, the majority of the entailment pairs require background knowledge to predict an entailment. In the next section we show what kind of background knowledge we use and how we integrate it.

### 3.4 Background Knowledge

To perform any interesting reasoning, the theorem prover needs background knowledge to support its proofs. For the RTE challenge we distinguished between three kinds of background knowledge: generic knowledge, lexical knowledge and geographical knowledge.

Knowledge is represented as axioms in first-order logic. Assume that BK is a conjunction of first-order axioms representing the relevant background knowledge for a T/H pair. The input to the theorem prover is then:

$$\text{BK} \wedge (f(d(\text{T})) \rightarrow f(d(\text{H}))) \qquad (\text{A}')$$

**Generic Knowledge.** Axioms for generic knowledge cover the semantics of possessives, active-passive alternation, and spatial knowledge. There are a dozen different axioms in the current system and these are the only manually generated axioms. Some examples include:

$\forall x \forall y \forall z(in(x,y) \wedge in(y,z) \rightarrow in(x,z))$
$\forall e \forall x \forall y(event(e) \wedge agent(e,x) \wedge in(e,y) \rightarrow in(x,y))$
$\forall e \forall x \forall y(event(e) \wedge patient(e,x) \wedge in(e,y) \rightarrow in(x,y))$
$\forall e \forall x \forall y(event(e) \wedge theme(e,x) \wedge in(e,y) \rightarrow in(x,y))$
$\forall x \forall y(in(x,y) \rightarrow \exists e(locate(e) \wedge patient(e,x) \wedge in(e,y)))$
$\forall x \forall y(of(x,y) \rightarrow \exists e(have(e) \wedge agent(e,y) \wedge patient(e,x)))$
$\forall e \forall x(event(e) \wedge agent(e,x) \rightarrow by(e,x))$

The last axiom in this list, for instance, helps Vampire to find a proof for Example 1977, which is a case of active-passive alternation.

Example: 1977 (TRUE)

**T**: His family has steadfastly denied the charges.

**H**: The charges were denied by his family.

**Lexical Knowledge.** Lexical knowledge is created automatically from WordNet. A hyponymy relation between two synsets A and B is converted into ∀x(A(x)→B(x)). Two synset sisters A and B are translated into ∀x(A(x)→ ¬B(x)). Here the predicate symbols from the DRS are mapped to WordNet synsets using a variant of Lesk's WSD algorithm [MS99]. The aforementioned Example 78 would be supported by the following lexical axioms:

∀x(clinton(x)→person(x))
∀x(book(x)→artifact(x))
∀x(artifact(x)→ ¬person(x))

Consider for instance Example 1952 below. The axiom ∀x(soar(x)→rise(x)) suffices for finding a proof for this entailment pair:

Example: 1952 (TRUE)

**T**: Crude oil prices soared to record levels.

**H**: Crude oil prices rise.

*d*(T):

e1 x2 x5 x6
crude(x5)
oil(x6)
nn(x6,x5)
price(x5)
soar(e1)
agent(e1,x5)
patient(e1,x2)
record(x2)
level(x2)

*d*(H):

e1 x2 x3
crude(x2)
oil(x3)
nn(x3,x2)
price(x2)
rise(e1)
agent(e1,x2)

**Geographical Knowledge.** Because a high number of examples in the development set required knowledge about geography, we automatically compiled a set of axioms from the CIA factbook (`http://www.cia.gov/cia/publications/factbook/` , covering knowledge about capitals, countries and US states. Some examples are:

∀x∀y(paris(x)∧france(y)→in(x,y))
∀x∀y(pago_pago(x)∧american_samoa(y)→in(x,y))

However, we could not find any examples where the theorem prover found a proof due to geographical knowledge in the test set.

### 3.5 Model Building

While theorem provers are designed to prove that a formula *is* a theorem (i.e., that the formula is true in any model), they are generally not good at deciding that a formula is *not* a theorem. Model builders are designed to show that a formula is true in at least one model. Hence, in addition to the Vampire theorem prover we also use the model builder Paradox [CS03].

To exploit the complementary approaches to inference, we use both a theorem prover and a model builder for any inference problem: the theorem prover attempts to prove the input whereas the model builder simultaneously tries to find a model for the negation of the input. If the model builder finds a model for

$$\neg(f(d(\mathrm{T}))\rightarrow f(d(\mathrm{H}))) \qquad (= \neg\mathrm{A})$$

we know that there cannot be a proof for its negation (hence no entailment). And if the model builder is able to generate a model for

$$f(d(\mathrm{T}))\wedge f(d(\mathrm{H})) \qquad (= \neg\mathrm{B})$$

we know that T and H are consistent (maybe entailment). (In practice, this is also a good way to terminate the search for proofs or models: if the theorem prover finds a proof for $\neg\phi$, we can halt the model builder to try and find a model for $\phi$ (because there won't be one), and vice versa.)

Another interesting property of a model builder is that it outputs a model for its input formula, if the input is satisfiable. A model is here the logical notion of a model, describing a situation in which the input formula is true. Formally, a model is a pair $\langle D, F\rangle$ where $D$ is the set of entities in the domain, and $F$ a function mapping predicate symbols to sets of domain members. For instance, the model returned for $f(d(\mathrm{T}))$ in Example 78 is one where the domain consists of three entities (domain size = 3):

```
D = {d1,d2,d3}       F(loc) = {}
F(book) = {d1,d2}    F(seller) = {}
F(clinton) = {d3}    F(be) = {}
F(of) = {(d1,d3)}    F(agent) = {}
F(big) = {}          F(patient) = {}
```

Model builders like Paradox generate such finite models by iteration. They attempt to create a model for domain size 1. If they fail, they increase the domain size and try again, until either they find a model or their resources run out. Thus, although there are possibly infinitely many models, model builders generally build a model with a minimal domain size. (For more information on model building consult [BB05]).

In the next section we show how to explore these finite models by using the domain and model size in predicting entailment.

### 3.6 Approximating Entailment

In an ideal world we calculate all the required background knowledge and by either finding a proof or a countermodel, decide how T and H relate with respect to entailment. However, it is extremely hard to acquire all the required background knowledge. This is partly due to the limitations of word sense disambiguation, the lack of resources like WordNet, and the lack of general knowledge in a form suitable for automated inference tasks.

To introduce an element of robustness into our approach, we use the models as produced by the model builder to measure the "distance" from an entailment. The intuition behind it is as follows. If H is entailed by T, the model for T+H is not informative compared to the one for T, and hence does not introduce new entities. Put differently, the domain size for T+H would equal the domain size of T. In contrast, if T does not entail H, H normally contains some new information (except when it contains negated information), and this will be reflected in the domain size of T+H, which then is larger than the domain size of T. It turns out that this difference between the domain sizes is a useful way of measuring the likelihood of entailment: large differences are mostly not entailments, small differences mostly are.

Consider the following example:

Example: 1049 (TRUE)

**T**: Four Venezuelan firefighters who were traveling to a training course in Texas were killed when their sport utility vehicle drifted onto the shoulder of a highway and struck a parked truck.

**H**: Four firefighters were killed in a car accident.

Although this example is judged as a true entailment, Vampire (the theorem prover that we use) does not find a proof because it lacks the background knowledge that one way of causing a car accident is to "drift onto the shoulder of the highway and strike something". On the other hand, Paradox, the model builder that we use, generates a model with domain size 11 for $f(d(\mathrm{T}))$, and a model with domain size 12 for $f(d(\mathrm{T})) \wedge f(d(\mathrm{H}))$. The absolute difference in domain sizes is small, and therefore likely to indicate an entailment. Apart from the absolute difference we also compute the difference relative to the domain size. For the example above the relative domain size yields $1/12 = 0.083$.

The domain size only tells us something about the number of entities used in a model—not about the number of established relations between the model's entities. Therefore, we also introduce the notion of model size. The model size is defined here by counting the number of all instances of two-place relations (and three-place relations, if there are any) in the model, and multiplying this with the domain size. For instance, the following (arbitrary) model

```
D = {d1,d2,d3}
F(cat) = {d1,d2}
F(john) = {d3}
F(of) = {(d1,d3)}
F(like) = {(d3,d1),(d3,d2)}
```

has a domain consisting of three entities and three instantiated two-place relations, yielding a model size of $3 * 3 = 9$.

Obviously, it is harder for model builders to generate a minimal model than just any model. In practice, a model builder like Paradox generally constructs models with a minimal domain size, but not necessarily one with a minimal model size. It is unclear how much this influenced our results but we plan to experiment with other model builders in future work, or taking aboard algorithms that transfer a model into a minimal model.

### 3.7 Deep Semantic Features

Given our approach to deep semantic analysis, we identified eight features relevant for recognising textual entailment. The theorem prover provides us with two features: `entailed` determining whether T implies H, and `inconsistent` determining whether T together with H is inconsistent. The model builder gives us six features: `domainsize` and `modelsize` for T+H as well as the absolute and relative difference between the sizes of T and T+H, both for the size of the domains (`domainsizeabsdif`, `domainsizereldif`) and the size of the models (`modelsizeabsdif`, `modelsizereldif`).

## 4 Experiments

There are not many test suites available for textual inference. We use throughout this section the dataset made available as part of the RTE challenge. We used the *t*-test for the difference between two proportions to measure whether the difference in accuracy between two algorithms or an algorithm and the baseline is statistically significant at the 5% level.

### 4.1 Dataset Design and Evaluation Measures

The organisers released a development set of 567 sentence pairs and a test set of 800 sentence pairs. In both sets, 50% of the sentence pairs were annotated as TRUE and 50% as FALSE, leading to a 50% most frequent class baseline for automatic systems.

The examples are further distinguished according to the way they were designed via a so-called *Task* variable. Examples marked CD (Comparable Documents) comprise sentences with high lexical overlap in comparable news articles, whereas the hypotheses of examples marked QA (Question Answering) were formed by translating questions from e.g., TREC into statements. The other subsets are IE (Information extraction), MT (Machine Translation) RC (Reading Comprehension), PP (Paraphrase Acquisition) and IR (Information Retrieval).

The different examples and subsets cover a wide variety of different aspects of entailment, from incorporation of background knowledge to lexical to syntactic entailment and combinations of all these. For a more exhaustive description of dataset design we refer the reader to [DGM05].

### 4.2 Experiment 1: Human Upper Bound

To establish a human upper bound as well as investigate the validity of the datasets issued, one of the authors annotated all 800 examples of the test set for entailment, following the short RTE annotation guidelines available at `http://www.pascal-network.org/Challenges/RTE/Instructions`. The annotation was performed before the release of the gold standard annotation for the test set and was therefore independent of the organisers' annotation. The organisers' and the author's annotation yielded a high percentage agreement of 95.25%. However, 33% of the originally created examples were already filtered out of the corpus before release by the organisers because of agreement-related problems. Therefore we expect that human agreement on textual entailment in general is rather lower. A further discussion of the gold standard dataset can be found in Section 6.

### 4.3 Decision Trees for Entailment Recognition

We expressed each example pair as a feature vector, using different subsets of the features described in Section 2 and Section 3 for each experiment. We then trained a decision tree for classification into TRUE and FALSE entailment on the development set, using the Weka machine learning tool [WF00], and tested on the test set.

Apart from a classification, Weka also computes a confidence value between 0.5 and 1 for each decision, dependent on the leaf in the tree that the classified example falls into: if the leaf covers $x$ examples in the training set, of which $y$ examples are classified wrongly, then the error rate is $y/x$ and the confidence value is $1 - y/x$.

Following the RTE challenge, the evaluation measures are accuracy (*acc*) as the percentage of correct judgements as well as confidence-weighted average score (*cws*), which rewards the system's ability to assign a higher confidence score to correct judgements than wrong ones [DGM05]: after the $n$ judgements are sorted in decreasing order by their confidence value, the following measure is computed:

$$cws = \frac{1}{n}\sum_{i=1}^{n}\frac{\#\text{correct-up-rank-}i}{i}$$

All evaluation measures are computed over the whole test set as well as on the 7 different subsets (CD, IE, etc.). The results are summarised in Table 1. We also computed precision, recall and F-measure for both classes TRUE and FALSE and will discuss the results in the text whenever of interest.

**Experiment 2: Shallow Features.** In this experiment only the shallow features (see Section 2) were used. The overall accuracy of 56.9% is significantly higher than the baseline.

Column 2 in Table 1 shows that this decent performance is entirely due to excellent performance on the CD subset. (Recall that the CD set was designed explicitly with examples with high lexical overlap in mind.)

In addition, the method overestimates the number of true entailments, achieving a Recall of 0.926 for the class TRUE, but a precision of only 0.547 on the same class. In contrast, it has good precision (0.761) but low recall (0.236) for the FALSE class. Thus, there is a correspondence between low word overlap and FALSE examples (see also the discussion of Example 731 in Section 2); high overlap, however, is normally necessary but not sufficient for TRUE entailment (see also Example 78 in Section 3).

**Table 1.** Summary of Results for Experiments 1 to 6

| Exp | 1: Human | | 2: Shallow | | 3: Strict | | 4: Deep | | 5: Hybrid | | 6: Hybr/Task | |
|---|---|---|---|---|---|---|---|---|---|---|---|---|
| Task | acc | cws | acc | cws | acc | cws | acc | cws | acc | cws | acc | cws |
| CD | 0.967 | n/a | **0.827** | **0.881** | 0.547 | 0.617 | 0.713 | 0.787 | 0.700 | 0.790 | **0.827** | 0.827 |
| IE | 0.975 | n/a | 0.508 | 0.503 | **0.542** | 0.622 | 0.533 | 0.616 | **0.542** | 0.639 | **0.542** | **0.627** |
| MT | 0.900 | n/a | 0.500 | 0.515 | 0.500 | 0.436 | **0.592** | **0.596** | 0.525 | 0.512 | 0.533 | 0.581 |
| QA | 0.961 | n/a | 0.531 | 0.557 | 0.461 | 0.422 | 0.515 | 0.419 | 0.569 | 0.520 | **0.577** | **0.531** |
| RC | 0.979 | n/a | 0.507 | 0.502 | **0.557** | 0.638 | 0.457 | 0.537 | 0.507 | 0.587 | **0.557** | **0.644** |
| PP | 0.920 | n/a | 0.480 | 0.467 | 0.540 | 0.581 | 0.520 | 0.616 | 0.560 | **0.667** | **0.580** | 0.619 |
| IR | 0.922 | n/a | 0.511 | 0.561 | 0.489 | 0.421 | 0.567 | 0.503 | **0.622** | **0.569** | 0.611 | 0.561 |
| all | 0.951 | n/a | 0.569 | 0.624 | 0.520 | 0.548 | 0.562 | 0.608 | 0.577 | 0.632 | **0.612** | **0.646** |

**Experiment 3: Strict Entailment.** To test the potential of entailment as discovered by theorem proving alone, we now use only the `entailment` and `inconsistent` features. As expected, the decision tree shows that, if a proof for T implies H has been found, the example should be classified as TRUE, otherwise as FALSE. The `inconsistent` feature was not used by the decision tree, which was not surprising as very few examples were covered by that feature.

The deep semantic analysis was able to create semantic representations and then search for proofs for 774 of all 800 T/H-pairs in the test data, achieving a coverage of 96.8%. The precision (0.767) for the class TRUE is reasonably high:

if a proof is found, then an entailment is indeed very likely. The exceptions where we found a proof but entailment did not hold are discussed further in Section 5. However, recall is very low (0.058) as only 30 proofs were found on the test set (for some examples see Section 3). This yields an F-measure of only 0.10 for the TRUE class. Due to the low recall, the overall accuracy of the system (0.52, see Table 1) is not significantly higher than the baseline.

Thus, this feature behaves in the opposite way to shallow lexical overlap and overgenerates the FALSE class. Missing lexical and background knowledge is the major cause for missing proofs.

**Experiment 4: Approximating Entailment.** As discussed in Section 3.6 we now try to compensate for missing knowledge and improve recall for TRUE entailments by approximating entailment with the features that are furnished by the model builder. Thus, Experiment 4 uses all eight deep semantic analysis features, including the features capturing differences in domain- and modelsizes. The recall for the TRUE class indeed jumps to 0.735. Although, unavoidably, the FALSE class suffers, the resulting overall accuracy (0.562, see Column 4 in Table 1) is significantly higher than when using the features provided by the theorem prover alone (as in Experiment 3). The confidence weighted score also rises substantially from 0.548 to 0.608. The approximation achieved can be seen in the different treatment of Example 1049 (see Section 3.6) in Experiments 3 and 4. In Experiment 3, this example is wrongly classified as FALSE as no proof can be found; in Experiment 4, it is correctly classified as TRUE due to the small difference between domain- and modelsizes for T and T+H.

There is hardly any overall difference in accuracy between the shallow and the deep classifier. However, it seems that the shallow classifier in its current form has very little potential outside of the CD subset whereas the deep classifier shows a more promising performance for several subsets.

**Experiment 5: Hybrid Classification.** As shallow and deep classifiers seem to perform differently on differently designed datasets, we hypothesized that a combination of these classifiers should bring further improvement. Experiment 5 therefore used all shallow and deep features together. However, the overall performance of this classifier (see Column 5 in Table 1) is not significantly better than either of the separate classifiers. Closer inspection of the results reveals that, in comparison to the shallow classifier, the hybrid classifier performs better or equally on all subsets but CD. In comparison to the deep classifier in Column 4, the hybrid classifier performs equally well or better on all subsets apart from MT. Overall, this means more robust performance of the hybrid classifier over differently designed datasets and therefore more independence from dataset design.

**Experiment 6: Dependency on Dataset Design.** As Experiment 5 shows, simple combination of methods, while maybe more robust, will not necessarily raise overall performance if the system does not know when to apply which method. To test this hypothesis further we integrated the subset indicator as a feature with the values CD, IE, MT, RC, IR, PP, QA into our hybrid system.

Indeed, the resulting overall accuracy (0.612) is significantly better than either shallow or deep system alone. In addition, the performance over all subsets is now more even and robust.

Note that using both a combination of methodologies *and* the subset indicator is necessary to improve on individual shallow and deep classifiers for this corpus. We integrated the subset indicator also into the shallow and deep classifier by themselves, yielding classifiers Shallow+Task and Deep+Task, with no or only very small changes in accuracy (these figures are not included in Table 1).

## 5 Error Analysis

A full error analysis of the hybrid system is beyond the scope of this paper as it incorporates a multitude of factors, including errors of shallow and deep methods as well as errors induced by the learning model and the combination of methods. We will, however, discuss error types of the shallow word overlap and the main theorem proving component of our system in the following two subsections.

### 5.1 Shallow Methods

As discussed in Experiment 2 above, the word overlap method tends to overgenerate the TRUE class. Typical examples that lead to such false positives can be summarized as follows:

- Negation that is not present in the hypothesis but is present in the text (see Example 78 in Section 3).
- Structural conversions, as we use a bag-of-words model only (for example, active-passive conversions).
- Conditional information in text or hypothesis, for example in "if"-clauses; ordinals; idioms. This includes Examples 1617, 2040, 2025, 2055, 2030, 2082 and 2079, which were also a problem for the theorem proving component and are in detail discussed in Section 5.2 below.
- Underestimation of crucial non-matching words in the hypothesis (see Example 828 below, where the mismatch of *20-year-old* is underestimated due to considerable overlap of other words like *Jennifer Hawkins*, *Australia*, *beauty queen* etc.).

  Example: 828 (FALSE)

  **T**: Jennifer Hawkins is the 21-year-old beauty queen from Australia.

  **H**: Jennifer Hawkins is Australia's 20-year-old beauty queen.

- Word sense ambiguity. As the shallow method does not perform any WSD, this can lead to incorrectly relating lemmata in hypothesis and text like *hit* and *shot* in Example 1959 below.

  Example: 1959 (FALSE)

  **T**: Kerry hit Bush hard on his conduct on the war in Iraq.

  **H**: Kerry shot Bush.

### 5.2 Strict Entailment

Experiment 3 showed that strict entailment creates many false negatives due to missing background knowledge. In contrast, when the theorem prover found a proof it was usually correct. Only 30 proofs were found by the system, of which 23 were annotated as entailments in the gold standard. These include adequately analysed phenomena such as apposition (5 times: 760, 929, 995, 1903, 1905), relative clauses (3 times: 142, 1060, 1900), coordination and attachment(3 times: 898, 807, 893), active-passive alternation (twice: 1007, 1897), possessives (once: 1010), the use of background knowledge (6 times: 236, 836, 1944, 1952, 1987, 1994) and more or less straightforward cases (3 times: 833, 1076, 741). Two of such examples (1005 from the training set and 898 from the test set) are given in Section 3.

Incorrect proofs were found for seven cases. It is interesting to find out why our system discovered a proof in these cases. It turns out that they are due to incorrect lexical semantics, the lack of dealing with metaphors, the restricted expressivity of first-order logic, and the inability to deal with idiomatic expressions. We will discuss these cases in detail.

Ordinals were not dealt with correctly in Examples 1617 and 2040. In both cases the relative clause (1617) and the infinitive construction (2040) were not part of the restriction of the ordinal, giving an incorrect semantic representation:

Example: 1617 (FALSE)

**T**: In 1782 Martin Van Buren, the first US president who was a native citizen of the United States, was born in Kinderhook, N.Y.
**H**: The first US president was born in Kinderhook, N.Y.

Example: 2040 (FALSE)

**T**: Stjepan Mesic was the first Croatian president to deliver a public address at Harvard.
**H**: Stjepan Mesic was the first Croatian president.

Example 2025 shows a text with a conditional. The current system does not adequately deal with all discourse adverbials yet, causing it to assert that Poland joins the EU rather than placing it in the antecedent of a conditional.

Example: 2025 (FALSE)

**T**: There are a lot of farmers in Poland who worry about their future if Poland joins the European Union.
**H**: Poland joins the European Union.

A rather similar case is Example 2055, where the system correctly associated Einstein to be the subject of being the president of Israel, but it incorrectly assumed that being invited to X is being X. A restriction on this class of modal verbs will fix this problem. (In the development data, however, there were similar cases that were annotated as entailments.)

Example: 2055 (FALSE)

**T**: The fact that Einstein was invited to be the president of Israel is critical to an accurate understanding of one of the greatest individuals in modern history.

**H**: Einstein is the president of Israel.

An interesting example is 2030. Here it seems that *capital* in 2030-T is used metaphorically, in the sense that it is the most important location with respect to gastronomy. As our system did not spot this, it incorrectly found a proof instead.

Example: 2030 (FALSE)

**T**: Lyon is actually the gastronomic capital of France.

**H**: Lyon is the capital of France.

A neo-Davidsonian analysis based on first-order logic is problematic for cases such as Example 2082. Although we analyse the modifiers of a verb all intersectively, it seems that *established in Italy* should be analysed restrictively.

Example: 2082 (FALSE)

**T**: Microsoft was established in Italy in 1985.

**H**: Microsoft was established in 1985.

Example 2079, finally, shows that some entailment pairs require a sophisticated analysis of idiomatic expressions:

Example: 2079 (FALSE)

**T**: US presence puts Qatar in a delicate spot.

**H**: Qatar is located in a delicate spot.

These examples of false positives show once more how hard recognising textual entailment is. Overall, however, the backbone of our deep semantic analysis is reasonably accurate. Its recall for TRUE entailments can be increased by finding methods for selecting appropriate background knowledge, and revising some of the lexical semantics will improve its precision.

## 6 Discussion of the Entailment Task

We will now discuss some observations we made on the task definition and the annotated data sets.

### 6.1 Task Definition

The current RTE dataset classified entailment as binary TRUE and FALSE. Following FRACAS, the semantic test suite in [CCVE+96], a classification that respects three values (yes, don't know, inconsistent), is probably more in its place. For instance, not only are examples 1301 and 1310 below not entailments, the hypotheses are inconsistent with the corresponding texts as well:

Example: 1301 (FALSE) (sic)

**T**: The former wife of the South African president did not ask for amnesty, and her activities were not listed in the political reports submitted by the African National Congress to the Truth and Reconciliation Commission in 1996 and 1997.

**H**: Winny Mandela, the President's ex-wife, is requesting amnesty.

Example: 1310 (FALSE) (sic)

**T**: Although the hospital insists that King Hussein is not fully free of the cancer, they are hopeful that he will recover.

**H**: The statement added that King Hussein has been cured completely.

### 6.2 Annotated Datasets

When establishing the upper bound in Experiment 1, we made several observations that could have an effect on the design of future test suites. The disagreements in annotation fell roughly into three categories. Firstly, the amount of background knowledge assumed by our annotation sometimes differed from the one taken into account by the gold standard annotation. Thus, the annotating author judged Example 825 below as FALSE, as she was not aware that Beiji was in the *north* of Iraq. The question of how much background knowledge can be assumed and how many examples should draw on extensive background knowledge in future datasets was extensively discussed at the RTE workshop.

Example: 825 (TRUE) (own annotation FALSE)

**T**: A car bomb that exploded outside a U.S. military base near Beiji, killed 11 Iraqis.

**H**: A car bomb exploded outside a U.S. base in the northern town of Beiji, killing 11 Iraqis.

Secondly, in a few cases, sentences that were isolated from their original context in the examples made it hard to annotate them correctly. Thus, our own annotation for Example 961 was FALSE as the first name of *Seiler* as *Audrey* is not inferrable from the text without a wider context.

Example: 961 TRUE (own annotation FALSE)

**T**: Seiler was reported missing March 27 and was found four days later in a marsh near her campus apartment.

**H**: Abducted Audrey Seiler found four days after missing.

Thirdly, several entailments were incorrectly annotated the gold standard in our opinion. Example 236 (see below), for instance, was judged as entailment. But taking tense into account (which, incidentally, our system is currently not able to do), it is strictly speaking not a textual entailment.

Example: 236 (TRUE) (sic)

**T**: Yasir Arafat has agreed to appoint a longtime loyalist as interior minister to take charge of the country's security.

**H**: Yasir Arafat nominated a loyalist as interior minister.

Another example is 893: the adverb *perhaps* in the text clearly expresses doubt on the date of establishment of settlements on Jakarta, and the hypothesis establishes it as a fact. This clearly is not entailment.

Example: 893 (TRUE) (sic)

**T**: The first settlements on the site of Jakarta were established at the mouth of the Ciliwung, perhaps as early as the 5th century AD.

**H**: The first settlements on the site of Jakarta were established as early as the 5th century AD.

## 7 Related Work

Our shallow analysis is similar to several shallow models presented as part of the RTE challenge, in particular the word overlap methods by [JdR05] and the shallow baselines by [HPV05]. The results achieved by us and them give a current upper bound of 55–57% accuracy for shallow overlap methods. This is also confirmed by [DGM05], who cite a non-participating system by Rada Mihalcea based on shallow features only with an accuracy of 56.8%. [PA05] adapted the BLEU algorithm that relies mainly on n-gram overlap. They report that the resulting system did not beat the 50% baseline. This difference in results might be due to the fact that the BLEU algorithm is not directional, i.e. it penalises difference in information and length between text and hypothesis also if the hypothesis is completely included and entailed by the text but, for example, contains much *less* information. All these approaches confirm the fact that shallow methods do best on the CD subtask and have the tendency to overestimate TRUE entailments. IDF models for entailment and question answering, but not within the RTE framework, have also been proposed by [MdR03, SGH+04].

The main idea of our deep analysis, using a detailed semantic analysis and first-order inference, goes back to [BB05]. Other approaches to textual entailment that are comparable to our "strict" entailment as carried out in Experiment 3 include the OTTER theorem prover [Akh05, FHH+05] and EPILOG in [BBF+05]. Both these systems (like our "strict" system) do not beat the baseline, with [BBF+05] explicitly mentioning lack of background knowledge and inference rules as the reason, confirming our experience. We incorporate model building as a central part of the inference mechanism as a partial solution to this problem, an approach not adopted by any other system as far as we know. We have shown that using model generation is a promising way to approximate entailment and can improve the low recall of theorem proving. It is interesting to compare our approach to [RNM05]. Although they do not use model builders, a similar basic idea of relaxing the constraints of strict theorem proving and weighing the differences between hypothesis and text underlies their weighted abduction approach.

As far as we are aware, our combination of a shallow with a deep approach into a single hybrid system is unique and adds to the robustness of our approach. We also show that differences in dataset design can be exploited by such a hybrid approach, resulting in a significant overall improvement. The task variable was also explored by [NSDC05] and [RNM05] with neither of them reporting statistically significant differences between their systems with and without the task variable. We believe the reason for this discrepancy compared to our results might lie in the fact that their systems do not incorporate two fundamentally different inference strategies. As discussed in Section 4, using the task variable with the deep or shallow approach alone does not improve results, whereas the combination of two different strategies plus the task variable yields improvements.

Results of other approaches to determining textual entailment indicate that it is an extremely hard task. The RTE workshop revealed that participating systems reached accuracy figures ranging between 0.50 and 0.59 and cws scores between 0.50 and 0.69 [DGM05]. Comparing this with our own results (accuracy 0.61 and cws 0.65) shows how well our systems performs on the same data set.

## 8 Conclusions

Relying on theorem proving as a technique for determining textual entailment yielded high precision but low recall due to a general lack of appropriate background knowledge. We used model building as an innovative technique to surmount this problem to a certain extent. Still, it will be unavoidable to incorporate automatic methods for knowledge acquisition to increase the performance of our approach. Future work will be directed to the acquisition of targeted paraphrases (as for example in [BL03]) that can be converted into background knowledge in the form of axioms.

Our hybrid approach combines shallow analysis with both theorem proving and model building and achieves high accuracy scores on the RTE dataset compared to other systems that we are aware of. The results for this approach also indicate that (a) the choice of entailment recognition methods might have to vary according to the dataset design and/or application and (b) that a method that wants to achieve robust performance across different datasets might need the integration of several different entailment recognition methods as well as an indicator of design methodology or application.

## Acknowledgements

We would like to thank Mirella Lapata and Malvina Nissim for their comments on earlier versions of this paper. We are also grateful to Valentin Jijkoun and Bonnie Webber for discussion on textual entailment and Steve Clark and James Curran for help on using the CCG-parser. Thanks to James for producing the fancy CCG-derivations in Section 3.

## References


[Akh05] E. Akhmatova. Textual entailment resolution via atomic propositions. In *Proceedings of the PASCAL Challenges Workshop on Recognising Textual Entailment*, pages 61–68, 2005.

[BB05] Patrick Blackburn and Johan Bos. *Representation and Inference for Natural Language. A First Course in Computational Semantics.* CSLI, 2005.

[BBF+05] S. Bayer, J. Burger, L. Ferro, J. Henderson, and A. Yeh. Mitre's submission to the eu pascal rte challenge. In *Proceedings of the PASCAL Challenges Workshop on Recognising Textual Entailment*, pages 41–44, 2005.

[BBKdN01] Patrick Blackburn, Johan Bos, Michael Kohlhase, and Hans de Nivelle. Inference and Computational Semantics. In Harry Bunt, Reinhard Muskens, and Elias Thijsse, editors, *Computing Meaning Vol.2*, pages 11–28. Kluwer, 2001.

[BCS+04] J. Bos, S. Clark, M. Steedman, J. Curran, and J. Hockenmaier. Wide-coverage semantic representations from a ccg parser. In *Proc of the* $20^{th}$ *International Conference on Computational Linguistics; Geneva, Switzerland; 2004*, 2004.

[BL03] Regina Barzilay and Lillian Lee. Learning to paraphrase: An unsupervised approach using multiple sequence alignment. In *NAACL-HLT 2003*, 2003.

[Bos03] J. Bos. Implementing the Binding and Accommodation Theory for Anaphora Resolution and Presupposition Projection. *Computational Linguistics*, 2003.

[Bos05] Johan Bos. Towards wide-coverage semantic interpretation. In *Proceedings of Sixth International Workshop on Computational Semantics IWCS-6*, pages 42–53, 2005.

[CC04] S. Clark and J.R. Curran. Parsing the WSJ using CCG and Log-Linear Models. In *Proceedings of the 42nd Annual Meeting of the Association for Computational Linguistics (ACL '04)*, Barcelona, Spain, 2004.

[CCVE+96] R. Cooper, R. Crouch, J. Van Eijck, C. Fox, J. Van Genabith, J. Jaspars, H. Kamp, M. Pinkal, D. Milward, M. Poesio, and S. Pulman. Using the framework. fracas: A framework for computationla semantics. Technical report, Fracas Deliverable D16., 1996.

[CS03] K. Claessen and N. Sörensson. New techniques that improve mace-style model finding. In *Model Computationa - Principles, Algorithms, Applications (Cade-19 Workshop)*, Miami, Florida., 2003.

[DGM05] Ido Dagan, Oren Glickman, and Bernardo Magnini. The pascal recognising textual entailment challenge. In *Proceedings of the PASCAL Challenges Workshop on Recognising Textual Entailment*, pages 1–8, 2005.

[Fel98] Christiane Fellbaum, editor. *WordNet: An Electronic Lexical Database.* MIT Press, Cambridge, Mass., 1998.

[FHH+05] A. Fowler, B. Hauser, D. Hodges, I. Niles, A. Novischi, and J. Stephan. Applying cogex to recognize textual entailment. In *Proceedings of the PASCAL Challenges Workshop on Recognising Textual Entailment*, pages 69–72, 2005.

[HPV05] Jesus Herrera, Anslemo Penas, and Felisa Verdejo. Textual entailment recognition based on dependency analysis and wordnet. In *Proceedings of the PASCAL Challenges Workshop on Recognising Textual Entailment*, 2005.

[JdR05] Valentin Jijkoun and Maarten de Rijke. Recognising textual entailment using lexical similarity. In *Proceedings of the PASCAL Challenges Workshop on Recognising Textual Entailment*, 2005.

[KR93] Hans Kamp and Uwe Reyle. *From Discourse to Logic. Introduction to Modeltheoretic Semantics of Natural Language, Formal Logic and Discourse Representation Theory.* Kluwer, Dordrecht, Netherlands, 1993.

[MdR03] C. Monz and M. de Rijke. Light-weight entailment checking for computational semantics. In *Proc. of the 3$^{rd}$ Workshop on Inference in Computational Semantics; 2003*, 2003.

[MS99] Christopher Manning and Hinrich Schuetze. *Foundations of Statistical Natural Language Processing.* MIT Press, 1999.

[NSDC05] Eamonn Newman, Nicola Stokes, John Dunnion, and Joe Carthy. Ucd iirg approach to the textual entailment challenge. In *Proceedings of the PASCAL Challenges Workshop on Recognising Textual Entailment*, 2005.

[PA05] Diana Perez and Enrique Alfonseca. Application of the bleu algorithm for recognising textual entailments. In *Proceedings of the PASCAL Challenges Workshop on Recognising Textual Entailment*, 2005.

[RNM05] R. Raina, A.Y. Ng, and C. Manning. Robust textual inference via learning and abductive reasoning. In *Proc. of AAAI 2005*, 2005.

[RV02] A. Riazanov and A. Voronkov. The design and implementation of Vampire. *AI Communications*, 15(2-3), 2002.

[SGH$^+$04] H. Saggion, R. Gaizauskas, M. Hepple, I. Roberts, and M Greenwood. Exploring the performance of boolean retrieval strategies for open domain question answering. In *Proc. of the Information Retrieval for Question Answering (IR4QA) Workshop at SIGIR 2004*, 2004.

[Ste01] M. Steedman. *The Syntactic Process.* The MIT Press, 2001.

[VdS92] R.A. Van der Sandt. Presupposition Projection as Anaphora Resolution. *Journal of Semantics*, 9:333–377, 1992.

[WF00] Ian H. Witten and Eibe Frank. *Data Mining: Practical Machine Learning Tools and Techniques with Java Implementations.* Morgan Kaufmann, San Diego, CA, 2000.

# Applying COGEX to Recognize Textual Entailment

Daniel Hodges, Christine Clark, Abraham Fowler, and Dan Moldovan

Language Computer Corporation, Richardson TX 75080, USA
{daniel, christine, abraham, moldovan}@languagecomputer.com

**Abstract.** This paper describes the system that LCC has devised to perform textual entailment recognition for the PASCAL RTE Challenge. Our system transforms each text-hypothesis pair into a two-layered logic form representation that expresses the lexical, syntactic, and semantic attributes of the text and hypothesis. A large set of natural language axioms are constructed for each text-hypothesis pair that help connect concepts in the hypothesis with concepts in the text. Our natural language logic prover is then used to prove entailment through abductive reasoning. The system's performance in the challenge resulted in an accuracy of 55%.

## 1 Introduction

The formal definition of logical entailment states that the a sentence $\beta$ is entailed by a sentence $\alpha$ if and only if in every world in which $\alpha$ is true, $\beta$ is also true [Russell and Norvig 2003]. In the natural language domain it becomes much more difficult to clearly define entailment due to the abundant number of ambiguities that are inherent in natural language. Many natural language sentences can be interpreted in a multitude of ways, and each interpretation can entail a different sets of sentences. As humans we can often use our common-sense reasoning ability to disambiguate the likely meaning of a sentence and determine if another sentence follows from it. Providing this level of reasoning ability to an automated system is a much more difficult task than strict logical entailment.

The PASCAL Recognizing Textual Entailment (RTE) Challenge attempts to evaluate an automated system's ability to recognize whether or not the meaning of one text fragment can be inferred from or entailed by another text fragment [Dagan et al. 2005]. The challenge evaluates a system's entailment recognition ability in seven application settings: Information Retrieval (IR), Comparable Documents (CD), Reading Comprehension (RC), Question Answering (QA), Information Extraction (IE), Machine Translation (MT), and Paraphrase Acquisition (PP). Though the objectives of these application settings are varied, the challenge serves to show how the ability to recognize entailment can be beneficial to any natural language processing system.

In this paper we describe LCC's approach to recognizing textual entailment through the use of an automated reasoning system. We have implemented a

J. Quiñonero-Candela et al. (Eds.): MLCW 2005, LNAI 3944, pp. 427–448, 2006.

natural language logic prover, called COGEX, that uniformly codifies text fragments, as well as world knowledge resources, in order to use its inference engine to verify any lexical and semantic relationships between two text fragments [Moldovan et al. 2003]. Details of COGEX's implementation are provided in Sections 3-5, the technique we use to determine whether entailment between two text fragments exists is explained in Section 6, and an analysis of our system's performance in the challenge is provided in Section 7.

## 2 Approach

A logic prover is an excellent tool for the entailment recognition task because the objective of a prover is to determine if there is a set of inference rules that can be applied to some given proposition to validate a hypothetical proposition. However, there are numerous complexities inherent to natural language that make the use of a logic prover to recognize textual entailment a non-trivial task. We have developed a natural language knowledge representation, axiom set, and reasoning methodology to account for the complexities of natural language.

COGEX generates a multi-layered first order logic representation for the text and hypothesis that encodes syntactic and semantic information expressed in text. The first layer represents the syntactic relations derived from the results of a statistical parser, similar to [Collins 2003], and also includes semantic entity class identifications detected by a named entity recognizer. The second layer provides semantic relations detected by our semantic parser, POLARIS, that express relations between words and phrases that are not expressed in the syntax layer and helps remove some of the syntax layer's ambiguity. The third layer of the representation, which expresses contextual knowledge as described in [Clark et al. 2005], is still under development and was not included for the entailment recognition task. Other research groups, such as PARC [Bobrow et al. 2005] and ASU [Tari and Baral 2005], have also implemented knowledge representations that attempt to capture syntactic, semantic, and contextual knowledge.

For each text-hypothesis pair COGEX uses three sources to produce axioms that will infer knowledge about the text during reasoning. WordNet, a publicly available database, is used to generate lexical chains between words in the text and hypothesis so COGEX can connect words that are semantically related. Linguistic equivalence rules are generated to accommodate common syntactic phenomenon. Additionally, some common-sense world knowledge axioms are provided to enable the prover to infer implicit knowledge from the text.

COGEX searches for entailment by performing "proof-by-contradiction" in which the prover negates the hypothesis and searches for a contradiction to the negated hypothesis. If a contradiction is found then there is evidence that the hypothesis is entailed by the text. A special backoff strategy is employed to allow COGEX to perform abductive reasoning. Upon completion of a proof, COGEX measures the soundness of the inferences applied in the proof to determine whether or not entailment holds.

Several other teams participating in the RTE Challenge also approached the entailment recognition task through logical inference. [Akhmatova 2005] also uses a logic prover but splits the text and hypothesis into multiple propositions and attempts to validate each proposition in the hypothesis. The Stanford [Raina et al. 2005] and UIUC [Braz et al. 2005] systems both use graphs for knowledge representation and employ graph matching algorithms to perform logical inference. The commonality between all of these systems is the attempt to push systems to a level of reasoning that is beyond that of lexical analysis.

## 3 Logic Form Representation

The knowledge representation used by COGEX for this entailment recognition task consists of two layers that express the syntactic and semantic propositions made by the text and hypothesis. The syntax-based representation and the semantic relation representation are detailed in the following subsections.

### 3.1 Syntax-Based Representation

The first layer of the logical representation is derived from a full syntactic parse and acknowledges syntax-based relationships such as: (1) syntactic subjects, (2) syntactic objects, (3) prepositional attachments, (4) complex nominals, and (5) adjectival/adverbial adjuncts. These syntax relations provide signals to the detection of semantic relations in the second layer. We also have a facility for detecting word sense but have chosen to disable it due to degraded performance caused by incorrect disambiguation.

As reported in [Moldovan and Rus 2002], there is a one-to-one mapping of the words of the text into the predicates in the logical form. A predicate is generated for every noun (NN), verb (VB), adjective (JJ), adverb (RB), preposition (IN), or conjunction (CC) encountered in the text and hypothesis. The name of the predicate is a concatenation of the lexeme's base form and the part of speech of the word. Nouns have predicates with a single argument. Adjectives and adverbs have a single argument that identifies what is being modified. Verb predicates have three arguments where the first represents the eventuality of the action, the second represents the syntactic subject of the action, and the third represents the direct object of the action.

Compound noun phrases (NNC), or complex nominals, are represented by a grouping predicate that has the participant nouns of the phrase as its arguments. Preposition (IN) predicates consist of two arguments where the first indicates the predicate of the phrase head to which the prepositional phrase is attached and the second argument indicates the prepositional object. Conjunctions (CC) are converted into grouping predicates as well and behave much like complex nominals. Additionally, named entities (NE) are detected by a named entity recognizer and are included in the logical representation. These predicates are named by the concatenation of the semantic class of the entity and a NE suffix and have a single argument for the entity being classified. The following example shows the first layer representation for the given text:

**Text:** *U.S. troops seized a relative and senior lieutenant to Sadr, who was also wanted for murder.*
**Logic Form:** `u_s_NN(x1) & _country_NE(x1) & troops_NN(x2) & nn_NNC(x3,x1,x2) & seize_VB(e1,x3,x6) & relative_NN(x4) & and_CC(x6,x4,x5) & senior_JJ(x5) & lieutenant_NN(x5) & _human_NE(x6) & to_TO(x6,x7) & Sadr_NN(x7) & _human_NE(x7) & also_RB(e2) & want_VB(e2,x8,x6) & for_IN(e2,x9) & murder_NN(x9)`

A notable feature of the logical form representation used in COGEX is the fixed-slot allocation mechanism of the verb predicates following the Davidsonian notation introduced in [Hobbs et al. 1993]. This enables the logic prover to distinguish the roles of the subjects and objects in a sentence. In the above example, if *"relative and senior lieutenant to Sadr"* is mistakenly taken to be the subject of the action and *"U.S. troops"* is mistakenly taken to be the direct object of the action, then the hypothesis, *"Sadr's senior lieutenant was apprehended."*, would no longer be entailed by the sentence.

### 3.2 Semantic Relation Representation

The second layer of the logical representation of the text is obtained by using a semantic parser, namely POLARIS. The semantic relations discovered by POLARIS are the underlying relations between concepts that exist within a word, between words, between phrases, and between sentences [Moldovan et al. 2004]. Polaris uses numerous classifiers, trained through machine learning techniques, and hand-coded rules to detect semantic relations. Table 1 lists the relations that Polaris extracts from text.

**Table 1.** List of semantic relations recognized by POLARIS

| Semantic Relations | | | |
|---|---|---|---|
| Possession | Source-From | Possibility | Kinship |
| Topic | Certainty | Property-Attribute Holder | Manner |
| Agent | Means | Result | Theme-Patient |
| Temporal | Accompaniment-Companion | Stimulus | Depiction |
| Part-Whole | Experiencer | Extent | Recipient |
| Hyponymy | Frequency | Belief | Predicate |
| Entail | Influence | Goal | Cause |
| Associated-with/Other | Meaning | Make-Produce | Measure |
| Instrument | Synonymy-Name | Explanation | Justification |
| Location-Space | Antonymy | Purpose | Plausibility-of |

Semantic relations provide the semantic background for text, which allows for a denser connectivity between the words and concepts expressed in the text, and express relations among the words of the text that are not explicitly stated. Semantic relations are also mapped to predicates where the name of the predicate consists of the relation that it represents and an SR suffix to indicate that it is a semantic relation. The arguments of these predicates are the events and entities that participate in the relation. In the following example the word *"seven"* is completely disconnected from *"truck drivers"* and the connection is only made through the `MEASURE` semantic relation. Further, the preposition *"in"* in this sentence is the only indicator of where this action is taking place and is disambiguated for the prover to its spatial sense by the `LOCATION` semantic relation.

**Text:** *A militant group in Iraq is holding seven foreign truck drivers.*
**Logic Form:** `militant_JJ(x1) & group_NN(x1) & in_IN(x1,x2) & iraq_NN(x2) & _country_NE(x2) & hold_VB(e1,x1,x6) & seven_NN(x3) & _number_NE(x3) & foreign_JJ(x6) & truck_NN(x4) & driver_NN(x5) & nn_NNC(x6,x4,x5)`
**Semantic Relations:**

- `HYPONYMY(militant group, group)`
- `PROPERTY_ATTRIBUTE_HOLDER(militant, group)`
- `LOCATION(Iraq, militant group)`
- `AGENT(militant group, holding)`
- `THEME(truck drivers, holding)`
- `MEASURE(seven, truck drivers)`
- `PROPERTY_ATTRIBUTE_HOLDER(foreign, truck drivers)`
- `HYPONYMY(truck driver, driver)`
- `THEME(driver, truck)`

## 4 Natural Language Axioms

The task of recognizing textual entailment in a logic prover requires the prover to be able to determine if the information in the hypothesis follows from the information in the text. COGEX depends on a suite of natural language axioms to derive new inferences from the text of a given pair while deciding if the hypothesis is in fact true. Specifically, COGEX uses (1) WordNet Lexical Chains to increase semantic connectivity, (2) Linguistic Rewriting Rules to drive the generation of paraphrasing axioms, (3) Semantic Relation Calculus to facilitate inference over the detected semantic relations in order to derive unstated semantic relations, and (4) World-Knowledge axioms to express knowledge that cannot otherwise be automatically derived. Each axiom class is detailed along with examples in the following subsections. Unless otherwise specified, all variables should be considered existentially quantified.

### 4.1 WordNet Lexical Chains

An important requirement of the entailment recognition task is the ability to recognize if a pair of different words are semantically related. For many of the text-hypothesis pairs in the data set, there are only one or two words that the text and hypothesis do not have in common, making the condition of entailment dependent on deriving valid connections between those dissimilar words.

WordNet lexical chains is the facility we have implemented to detect pairs of different words in the text and hypothesis that are semantically related, and generate axioms that express this relation.

WordNet [Miller 1990] consists of numerous sets of words called synonym sets or synsets, where each set of words share the same lexical concept. These synsets are linked together by WordNet relations that express how the different concepts are interrelated. Lexical chains are sequences of synsets related through WordNet relations that create a path between two words. A complete description of our lexical chains implementation is available in [Moldovan and Novischi 2002]. For example, there are *HYPERNYM* and *DERIVATION* relations between the first sense of the noun region and the third sense of the verb locate which produces the following lexical chain:

```
region:n#1 → HYPERNYM → location:n#1 →
DERIVATION → locate:vb#3
```

From each unmatched word in the hypothesis, we attempt to create a lexical chain to each word in the text. Initially, we only created lexical chains for the disambiguated senses of the words in the text and hypothesis, but due to inadequate disambiguation performance we were forced to generate lexical chains for all senses of the words in the pair. We attempt to ensure the relevancy of the lexical chains by limiting the path length to two relations. For every lexical chain found between the text and hypothesis, an axiom is created with the text word as the antecedent and the hypothesis word as the consequent. The corresponding axiom to the above lexical chain is provided below:

```
all x1 (region_NN(x1) → locate_VB(e1,x2,x1))
```

### 4.2 Linguistic Rewriting Rules

There are many examples in the challenge data set where the semantic content of the hypothesis and text is identical, but there are small syntactic and/or morphologic variations. COGEX uses linguistic rewriting rules to account for these variations and to provide some coreference ability as well. These axioms are instantiated based on patterns found in the parse trees for the text and hypothesis and are only made available to the text-hypothesis pair that generated them. Below we present examples of some of the more important axioms for the textual entailment recognition task.

**Complex Nominals and Coordinated Conjunctions.** Several forms of coreference need to be resolved between concepts used in text-hypothesis pairs. A special kind of coreference is the case of name alias, in which an entity is referred to by its full proper name, whereas the same entity may be referred to in another place by an acronym, a partial name, or by an alias. Consider the following example where the poll is referred to as an *"opinion poll"* in the text and just as a *"poll"* in the hypothesis:

**Text:** *The opinion poll was conducted on ...*
```
opinion_NN(x1) & poll_NN(x2) & nn_NNC(x3,x1,x2) &
conduct_VB(e1,x4,x3) & on_IN(e1,x5) & ...
```
**Hypothesis:** *The poll was carried out on ...*
```
poll_NN(x1) & carry_VB(e1,x2,x1) & out_RB(e1) &
on_IN(e1,x3) & ...
```

Above, the **nn_NNC** is the direct object of the verb in the text and **poll_NN** is the direct object of the verb in the hypothesis. The following axioms are generated by COGEX to facilitate coreference between *"opinion poll"* and *"poll"*:

1. `all x1 x2 x3 (opinion_NN(x1) & poll_NN(x2)& nn_NNC(x3,x1,x2) → opinion_NN(x3) & poll_NN(x3))`

2. `all x1 (opinion_NN(x1) | poll_NN(x1) → opinion_NN(x1) & poll_NN(x1) & nn_NNC(x1,x1,x1))`

The first axiom is utilized to coreference *"poll"* with *"opinion poll"*, but an unavoidable side effect of this axiom is that it also incorrectly coreferences *"opinion"* with *"opinion poll"*. It is insufficient to simply coreference the head word due to cases like *"Microsoft Corp."* where the head word, *"Corp"*, would be incorrectly coreferenced. Additionally, no evidence is offered by the hypothesis that the poll that is being referenced is in fact an opinion poll and not some other type of poll, but since these axioms will only be generated for this pair, the probability that they are the same poll is very high. Thus, even though this axiom is necessary to correctly recognize entailment in the above pair, it is unsound and has the ability to generate invalid proofs. For this reason, COGEX penalizes the score of proofs that utilize these axioms as discussed in Section 6.1. Similar axioms are used to handle coreferencing for coordinated conjunctions.

**Apposition Axioms.** Many of the text-hypothesis pairs have been designed strictly to test an entailment recognition system's ability to handle appositions. The following example requires a system to recognize that the substantive, *"a Sunni Muslim..."*, is referring to Ghazi Yawar:

**Text:** *Ghazi Yawar, a Sunni Muslim who lived for years in ...*
**Hypothesis:** *Yawar is a Sunni Muslim.*

COGEX handles appositions by creating an axiom that links the head of the noun phrase in the substantive to the head of the noun phrase it describes. For this pair, the following axiom is generated:

```
all x1 x2 x3 (ghazi_NN(x1) & yawar_NN(x2) & nn_NNC(x3,x1,x2) →
sunni_NN(x4) & muslim_NN(x5) & nn_NNC(x3,x4,x5))
```

### 4.3 Semantic Relation Calculus

One goal of the challenge preparers was to develop text-hypothesis pairs that tested if systems could recognize whether or not semantic entailment held when there is significant syntactic overlap between the text and hypothesis. With our semantic relations enabled, we can verify the semantic connectivity between the text and hypothesis by using a set of rule pairing axioms for the semantic relations. These enable inference of unstated semantics from those detected in the text. The first of the following examples of rule pairings can be interpreted as *"if x1 is the purpose of x2 and x3 is part of x2, then x1 is the purpose of x3."*

```
all x1 x2 x3 (purpose_sr(x1,x2) & partwhole_sr(x3,x2) → purpose_sr(x1,x3))
all x1 x2 x3 (synonymy_sr(x1,x2) & agent_sr(x1,x3) → agent_sr(x2,x3))
all x1 x2 (synonymy_sr(x1,x2) → synonymy_sr(x2,x1))
all x1 e1 e2 (agent_sr(x1,e1) & purpose_sr(e2,e1) → purpose_(e2,x1))
all x1 x2 x3 (cause_sr(x1,x2) & cause_sr(x2,x3) → cause_sr(x1,x3))
all x1 x2 x3 (purpose_sr(x1,x2) & topic_sr(x3,x1) → purpose_sr(x3,x2))
```

### 4.4 World Knowledge

We have incorporated a relatively small common-sense knowledge base of 310 hand-coded world knowledge axioms, where 80 have been tuned for the development set data and 230 have been tuned for the TREC 2002 and 2003 data. The axioms help to express common-sense knowledge that could not otherwise be automatically derived. We restricted ourselves from analyzing the test set in the process of creating these axioms, and consequently, the contribution of these axioms to COGEX's performance is more significant in the development set than in the test set. However, as discussed in Section 7.5, these axioms have a negative effect on the system's performance. In the following example, the detection of entailment is a trivial task if the world knowledge axiom, *"a hometown is where a person is born"*, is made available to the prover:

**Text:** *In Waco, near Nelson's hometown of Abbott, ...*
**Hypothesis:** *Nelson was born in Abbott.*
**World Knowledge Axiom:** `all x1 x2 x3 (_POS(x2,x1) & hometown_NN(x2) & of_IN(x2,x3) → bear_VB(e1,x4,x1) & in_IN(e1,x3))`

## 5 Reasoning Methodology

The proof method employed by COGEX is "reductio ad absurdum" or "proof by contradiction" in which a hypothetical proposition is proved by showing that it is impossible for the hypothetical proposition to be false. This is performed in the textual entailment domain by showing that there are statements made in the text that prevent the hypothesis from being false. Specifically, the logic form representation of the hypothesis is negated and inferences are drawn from the logic form representation of the text to determine if there is a contradiction between propositions in the negated hypothesis and propositions inferred from the text. The presence of a contradiction serves as evidence that the hypothesis is entailed by the text.

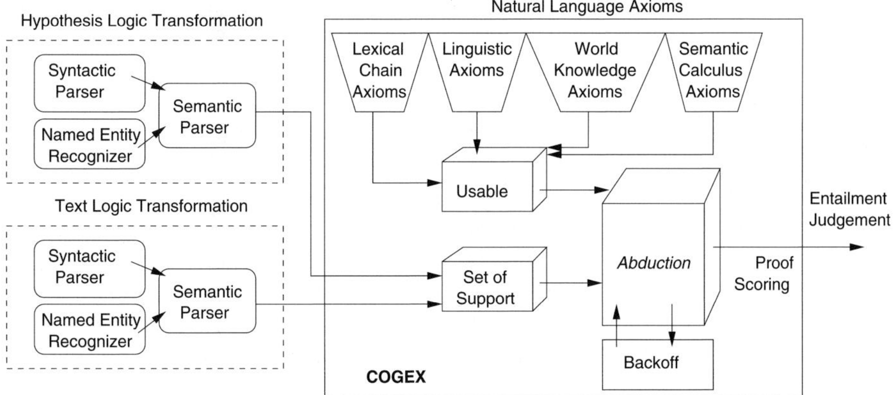


**Fig. 1.** COGEX Architecture

Figure 1 illustrates the high level components of COGEX and how they interact when detecting entailment for a text-hypothesis pair. A detailed explanation of these components is provided in the following subsections.

### 5.1 Axiom Partitioning

COGEX utilizes the Set of Support Strategy [Wos 1988] to divide the knowledge base into two sets of axioms called the Usable List and Set of Support (SOS). The SOS list consists of axioms that are supported by the problem under study, and the Usable list consists of auxiliary axioms that can be used to infer new information from the axioms in the SOS. Axioms in the SOS are weighted based on their lexical ordering and the weight indicates the order in which they should be chosen to participate in the search. At each step of the search COGEX removes the lightest-weight axiom from the SOS, places it in the Usable list, and performs hyperresolution and paramodulation to infer new axioms. Any newly resolved axioms are appropriately weighted based on their lexical ordering and placed in the Set of Support. The search continues in this fashion until a contradiction is found in the knowledge base or the Set of Support is empty.

For the textual entailment recognition task, the text and negated hypothesis logic form representations are placed in the Set of Support to guide the search. The natural language axioms described in Section 4 are placed in the Usable list so that they may be used to infer new information from the pair's text. The negated hypothesis is assigned the largest possible weight to ensure that it will be the last axiom to participate in the search, a requirement of COGEX's backoff strategy described in Section 5.2.

### 5.2 Backoff Strategy

COGEX's inability to find a proof once the Set of Support is empty indicates that there is some set of constraints posed by the negated hypothesis that cannot be resolved. The backoff strategy attempts to resolve these constraints by unbinding arguments in the predicates of the hypothesis logic form, and/or removing predicates that are not critical to the meaning of the hypothesis. The backoff strategy is necessary to account for defects that may occur in the logic form representation and the incompleteness of our knowledge base as described in Section 6.

The backoff strategy requires that the hypothesis be the last axiom to be evaluated by the prover so that it may guarantee that all possible knowledge that can be inferred from the text is already in the knowledge base. If no proof is found upon the insertion of the negated hypothesis, COGEX analyzes the hypothesis to determine what predicates in it are preventing a contradiction from occurring. Arguments of the predicate that prevented the contradiction from occurring are incrementally unbound until a contradiction is found or the predicate becomes disconnected from the rest of the logic form. If a predicate becomes disconnected and continues to prevent a contradiction from occurring, it is dropped from the hypothesis. COGEX continues in this manner, unbinding arguments and dropping predicates, until a proof is found. For each argument that is unbound and predicate that is dropped, COGEX penalizes the score of the final proof.

In cases where multiple predicates are preventing COGEX from finding a proof, the system attempts to drop the predicate of least importance first. This is performed by initially ordering the predicates of the hypothesis such that predicates of least syntactic importance, based on their part of speech class and connectedness nature, will be dropped first. Semantic relation and named entity predicates are first, complex nominals and coordinate conjunctions are second, nouns and verbs are third, adjectives and adverbs are fourth, and prepositions, possessives, and personal pronouns are last in the logical form ordering.

### 5.3 Example Proof

In this section we present a complete proof executed by COGEX for the following text-hypothesis pair:

**Text:** *Cedras, Biamby, and Francois also led the 1991 takeover.*
**Hypothesis:** *Cedras took part in the 1991 coup.*

Below are the logic form representations produced by COGEX for the text and hypothesis sentences. For clarity, only the first layer of the representation is presented since it is all that is required for the proof.

**Text LF:** `Cedras_NN(x1) & _human_NE(x1) & Biamby_NN(x2) & _human_NE(x2) & and_CC(x4,x1,x2,x3) & Francois_NN(x3) & _human_NE(x3) & also_RB(e1) & lead_VB(e1,x4,x6) & 1991_NN(x5) & _date_NE(x5) & takeover_NN(x6)`

**Hypothesis LF:** `Cedras_NN(x1) & _human_NE(x1) & take_part_VB(e1,x1,x2) & in_IN(e1,x4) & 1991_NN(x3) & _date_NE(x3) & coup_NN(x4)`

The axioms utilized by COGEX perform this proof are presented below as well as their classification. A lexical chain is created between *takeover* and *coup* because these words reside in the same synset. One of the linguistic rewriting rules that was not discussed in Section 4.2 is used to express that when a year is directly followed by a noun, that noun occurs in that year. Additionally, a world knowledge axiom is required to express that if someone or something leads something, they take part in it.

**WordNet Lexical Chains**
```
all x1 (takeover_nn(x1) → coup_nn(x1))
```

**Linguistic Rewriting Rules**
```
all x4 x5 (1991_nn(x4) & takeover_nn(x5) → in_in(x5,x4))
```

**World Knowledge**
```
all e1 x1 x2 (lead_vb(e1,x1,x2) → take_part_vb(e1,x1,x3) &
in_in(e1,x2))
```

The following is the resulting proof executed by COGEX:

```
1 [] -_human_ne(x1)| -_date_ne(x3)| -cedras_nn(x1)| -1991_nn(x3)|
-coup_nn(x4)| -take_part_vb(e1,x1,x2)| -in_in(e1,x4).
2 [] cedras_nn(x1).
3 [] _human_ne(x1).
4 [] lead_vb(e1,x7,x5).
5 [] 1991_nn(x4).
6 [] _date_ne(x4).
7 [] takeover_nn(x5).
8 [] -1991_nn(x4)| -takeover_nn(x5)|in_in(x5,x4).
9 [] -lead_vb(e1,x1,x2)|take_part_vb(e1,x1,$c1).
10 [] -lead_vb(e1,x1,x2)|in_in(e1,x2).
11 [] -takeover_nn(x1)| coup_nn(x1).
12 [hyper,7,11] coup_nn(x5).
13 [hyper,4,9] take_part_vb(e1,x7,c1).
14 [hyper,4,10] in_in(e1,x5).
15 [hyper,1,2,3,5,6,12,13,14] $F.
```

## 6 Entailment Recognition

Typically, a logic prover performs entailment recognition by attempting to find a finite set of axioms that can be applied to some pre-defined knowledge base to arrive at the given hypothesis. If the prover is unable to find a set of axioms that proves the hypothesis, then it can be concluded that entailment does not exist. A requirement of this methodology is that the knowledge base have access to an axiom set that is sound and complete for the domain of the proof. The difficulty in applying this strategy in the NLP domain for recognizing textual entailment is that the axiom set that we build for each entailment pair is neither sound nor complete and the logic form representation does not accurately represent all of the complexities of natural language. By creating lexical chains for all senses, a significant number of unsound axioms are created. As illustrated by examples in Section 4.2, it is difficult to create linguistic rewriting rules that guarantee sound behavior as well. Even world knowledge axioms are subject to unsound behavior when constructed too coarsely. Furthermore, the large set of axioms that are employed by COGEX is incomplete because they represent only a small portion of knowledge that is necessary to fully comprehend natural language. Additionally, the correctness of our logic form is contingent on the output of the statistical parser which is not always accurate.

We account for the incompleteness of our axiom set with the backoff strategy described in Section 5.2 which allows the prover to relax constraints in the hypothesis that are preventing it from finding a proof. With a complete axiom set, the prover can use deduction to determine if the constraints of the hypothesis are met by the text, but without completeness we must rely on abductive proofs [Hobbs et al. 1993] to determine whether or not entailment exists.

An unsound axiom set enables the prover to generate propositions that are not supported by the knowledge base, which in turn allows the prover to detect entailment where it does not exist. Thus, even without backoff strategies, COGEX cannot rely on the detection of a proof to indicate entailment in a text-hypothesis pair. Another hazard that can be encountered in an unsound knowledge base is the generation of conflicting propositions. When performing proof-by-refutation the goal is to find a set of propositions that will conflict with the negated hypothetical propositions, but this method cannot execute properly if a conflict is found between propositions inferred strictly from the knowledge base. However, this is currently not a concern with our system because negation is not represented in the text's logic form and there are no axioms that produce negated propositions; without any negated predicates, no contradiction can occur.

### 6.1 Proof Scoring

An evaluation of the validity of proofs returned by COGEX is made by initially assigning each proof with a perfect score and then assessing penalties for any possibly unsound actions taken. Unsound actions consists of the use of axioms that may be unsound and the relaxation of hypothesis constraints by unbinding arguments and dropping predicates. After an initial proof has been found, the prover continues searching for different proofs that can be found without relaxing any additional hypothesis constraints and upon completion returns the proof with the highest score.

For each set of axioms described in Section 4, a weight has been applied that indicates to the prover how much to penalize the resulting proof when one of the axioms in the set is used. The amount of weight applied to each set of axioms has been determined through empirical analysis over TREC 2002-2003 questions and signifies how likely it is that the axiom is unsound. Complex nominal decomposition axioms have been given the highest weight due to their ability to break down syntactic constraints and create incorrect syntactic relations between predicates. Lexical chain axioms must also be weighted heavily because without word sense disambiguation, a lexical chain only signifies that there is some concept in which the word pair is linked and there is no assurance that the concept in which they are linked is the same as the one being expressed in the text-hypothesis pair. A lexical chain axiom's weight is based on the type relations in the chain and the length of the chain. The other linguistic rewriting rules are not weighted heavily because they merely express syntactically equivalent forms of the text. Additionally, no weight is applied to our relatively small set of hand-crafted world knowledge axioms because we suspect the human element in the development process will help to ensure the soundness of these axioms.

As described in Section 5.2, the prover relaxes hypothesis constraints by unbinding predicate arguments and dropping terms from the hypothesis as necessary. Penalties are assessed to the proof for each argument that is unbound and each predicate that is dropped. Just as with the axioms, through experimentation we have discovered which classes of predicates have the most significant effect on the determination of the existence of entailment for a text-hypothesis pair. Uninformative part of speech elements, such as prepositions and conjunctions, receive a very small weight, while more informative elements such as verbs, nouns, and modifiers receive larger weights. Named entities and semantic relations are assigned the highest weight because they express some of the higher level concepts in the hypothesis that must be inferable from the text for entailment to exist.

After all of the appropriate penalties have been assessed, a normalized version of the score that takes into account the weight and number of predicates in the hypothesis logic form is calculated. If this normalization is not performed, hypotheses with fewer words would receive higher proof scores than those with more words, making it difficult to compare them and determine an effective threshold. The proof score is normalized by first determining the maximum penalty that could have been assessed by dropping all of the predicates of the hypothesis logic form. The actual penalty is divided by the maximum drop penalty to determine what percentage of the maximum penalty has been assessed and this value is subtracted from one to produce the normalized score as shown in Equation 1.

$$norm\_score = 1 - \left( \frac{max\_score - proof\_score}{max\_penalty} \right) \tag{1}$$

## 6.2 Judgment and Confidence Determination

True and false entailment are judged by determining if the normalized score of a text-hypothesis pair is above or below a given threshold. We utilized the development set to empirically determine the threshold at which the highest accuracy for the set is achieved. This threshold was then applied in the test set evaluation. Further experimentation with the development set revealed that the nature of the scores for each application setting were very different and for that reason different thresholds should be applied to each setting.

Confidence for each text-hypothesis pair is measured as the distance between the normalized score and the threshold. This enables scores that are further from the threshold to have a higher confidence score than scores that are closer to the threshold. The difference between the normalized score and the threshold is normalized such that the resulting confidence score is a value between zero and one.

## 7 Performance Analysis

### 7.1 Test Set

Results for COGEX's performance in the challenge are summarized in Table 2. Precision is defined as the number of pairs where entailment was correctly recognized divided by the number of pairs where entailment was recognized. Recall is defined as the number of pairs where entailment was correctly recognized divided by the number of pairs where entailment exists. The Confidence Weighted Score (CWS) is calculated by the algorithm presented in [Dagan et al. 2005]. Two additional metrics, mean true score and mean false score, were important to our own analysis of the system's performance during the development process. These metrics report the mean scores received by *true* and *false* entailment pairs in the data set. For our threshold technique, described in Section 6.2, to operate successfully, there needs to be a significant separation between the mean true and mean false scores.

**Table 2.** Results for the test set

| Task | Accuracy | CWS | Precision | Recall | F-measure | $\overline{true}$ | $\overline{false}$ |
|---|---|---|---|---|---|---|---|
| IR | .478 | .386 | .477 | .467 | .472 | .521 | .613 |
| CD | .780 | .822 | .920 | .613 | .736 | .641 | .248 |
| RC | .514 | .534 | .512 | .614 | .558 | .660 | .627 |
| QA | .485 | .434 | .484 | .477 | .481 | .568 | .594 |
| IE | .483 | .580 | .490 | .783 | .603 | .767 | .736 |
| MT | .542 | .440 | .564 | .367 | .444 | .498 | .525 |
| PP | .460 | .450 | .475 | .760 | .585 | .740 | .774 |
| all | .551 | .560 | .549 | .573 | .561 | .623 | .559 |

The data set construction methodology employed for each application setting had a significant effect on system performance as evidenced by the varied accuracies of COGEX. There is also a large variance in the mean true and mean false scores, which makes it extremely difficult to choose a single threshold that is appropriate for entailment detection in all application settings. We were originally reluctant to select different thresholds for each task because we felt that the presence or absence of entailment in a text-hypothesis pair should be independent of the source of the pair. However, as discussed in Section 6, without a sound and complete axiom set, it is impossible to implement a reasoning system that can uniformly recognize entailment for all possible text-hypothesis pairs. Thus, since we are reliant upon a threshold to determine whether entailment exists, it is appropriate to select different thresholds for each task. This also reflects real-word usage, since for each type of application the system would be tuned for best performance in that setting. Post-challenge experimentation with multiple threshold selection yielded an accuracy of 56.2% on the test set.

COGEX, and most other systems participating in the challenge, performed significantly better on the comparable documents application setting than the other tasks. Due to the way text-hypothesis pairs are chosen in this task, there is often little to no information in the text of false pairs that could help us logically infer the hypothesis, making it very difficult to find a case where the hypothesis cannot be false. Being unable to find contradictions with the hypothesis, the backoff strategy is forced to drop a large number of predicates from the hypothesis and return extremely low scores for the false entailment pairs. The large difference between the true and false entailment scores allows us to easily separate the pairs and establish an appropriate threshold which results in an extremely high precision. In the following example very few words overlap and there are no axioms that can be used to derive knowledge that supports the hypothesis, making it easy for COGEX to falsely derive entailment.

**Text:** *Hyperhidrosis is more common than you think. This condition affects 1 out of 25 people.*
**Hypothesis:** *Asians have an even higher rate of incidence—1 of every 5 suffers from hyperhidrosis.*

COGEX's worst accuracy was received in the paraphrase acquisition application setting. Additionally, the system's best recall is received in this application setting. This phenomenon is also due to the method in which this set of entailment pairs was constructed. The hypothesis and text sentences of these pairs tend to have a larger percentage of overlapping words which means that in cases where entailment exists, little inferencing work is required to prove it. However, when entailment does not exist, the backoff strategy is only required to relax a minimal number of constraints posed by hypothesis to arrive at a proof. Thus, high scores are returned for proofs whether or not entailment exists as shown by the mean true and mean false scores. The same can be said for the pairs in the information extraction application setting. The following is an example of a pair COGEX incorrectly labels as *True* due to the high word overlap.

**Text:** *Design problems would delay the release of mobile computer chipset dubbed Alviso until next year.*
**Hypothesis:** *Design problems would allow the release of mobile computer chipset dubbed Alviso until next year.*

The main hindrances to COGEX's performance were defects in the knowledge representation, unsound axioms, and an incomplete axiom set. The logic form representation utilized by COGEX is generated from a statistical parse which is not always accurate and without a correct parse it is impossible to generate a

**Table 3.** Accuracy of knowledge representations

| Layer | Component | Accuracy |
|---|---|---|
| 1 | Syntactic Parser and Logic Form Transformations | 86% |
| 2 | POLARIS Semantic Relations | 40% |

correct logic form. The semantic layer of the logic form representation is generated by our semantic parser which currently is only able to detect a subset of the semantic relations in open text. Table 3 summarizes the accuracy of each layer of the knowledge representation. We experimented by spending some time hand correcting a small set of the logic forms in the test set and immediately received a higher accuracy. Additionally, our current logic form representation does not support negation which is a necessary ability to handle a number of the pairs in the test set. An analysis of how unsoundness and incompleteness in the axiom set affected COGEX is provided in Section 7.5.

An additional hindrance to COGEX's performance is the scoring algorithm. The results in Table 2 show that in a number of the tasks the mean true score is less than the mean false score. This suggests that the current scoring algorithm, which was originally designed for our question answering system, may not be appropriate for all of these different entailment recognition tasks. This failure is exemplified by the paraphrase acquisition example presented above.

### 7.2 Development Set

Performance results for the development sets are presented in Table 4. There is a quite a large difference in the performance of the system between the two data sets and the test set, which indicates that there is not a sufficient number of text-hypothesis pairs in either set to provide a solid representation of the reasoning requirements of this entailment recognition task. Having only the development sets as training data for our system, we were forced to use them to determine appropriate thresholds for the system's operation on the test set.

**Table 4.** Results for the development set

| Data Set | Accuracy | CWS | Precision | Recall | F-measure |
|---|---|---|---|---|---|
| dev1 | .648 | .663 | .646 | .650 | .648 |
| dev2 | .609 | .510 | .589 | .736 | .654 |

### 7.3 Annotator Agreement

During the development process we attempted to produce our own set of annotations for the test set to get an idea of how the system was performing. During this annotation process there were numerous disagreements among ourselves and upon receiving the key we found even more disagreements with the "Gold Standard" annotations. Ultimately, we found 77 pairs in the test set for which we disagreed upon the appropriate annotation, yielding a Kappa statistic of 0.8075. The source of the disagreement among ourselves and the key set is due to the different accepted definitions of entailment. Implicature is used throughout natural language to express information that should be entailed by text without concretely stating it, making it difficult for any reasoning system to detect the presence of entailment. Another pitfall is in the underspecification of context information. A single natural language sentence can take on many meanings in different contexts, and understanding which context is being used is necessary to determine if entailment exists. Until a universally agreed-upon first order logic form representation of text can be developed, it will be impossible to develop an entailment data set with 100% agreement. Consequently, the annotator percentage of agreement should be established as an upper bound for the entailment recognition task.

### 7.4 Proof Difficulty

Before evaluating the text-hypothesis pairs in the test set with our system, we manually determined how difficult it is to prove entailment in each of the true entailment text-hypothesis pairs. We established five different difficulty levels: *easy*, *moderate*, *difficult*, *intractable*, and *invalid*. Proofs are considered easy in cases where the entailment is simply a matter of eliminating information from the first sentence, recognizing an apposition, or replacing one or two words with synonyms. Proofs are considered moderately difficult when one or more axioms are required to derive the second sentence of the entailment pair from the first one. The expectation is that all entailment pairs that have been deemed easy or moderate can be handled by our current system implementation provided sufficient axioms are created by the system. Difficult proofs are those that cannot be handled by COGEX without adding substantial new functionality, such as negation, coreference resolution, and predicate variables in axioms, or without using ad hoc axioms, those not applicable beyond the case which motivates them. We have labeled text-hypothesis pairs as intractable if we believe that entailment could not be correctly detected by an automated system. Invalid is used to indicate that, in our opinion, an entailment pair which was labeled TRUE should have been labeled FALSE.

Table 5 illustrates the distribution of text-hypothesis pairs for each difficulty level and the system's ability to detect entailment at the different difficulty levels. It is clear that COGEX's performance on the text-hypothesis pairs classified as easy or moderate is significantly better than its performance on other pairs. Many of the text-hypothesis pairs with the moderate classification require some external world knowledge or additional linguistic rewriting rules to enable COGEX to find better proofs. As expected, the system's unsound and incomplete axiom set is one of the biggest hindrance to its performance, but what is interesting is that completeness seems to be more important than soundness. We suspect that providing the system with additional resources for dynamic axiom

**Table 5.** Results for the true entailment pairs of the test set categorized by proof difficulty

| Difficulty | Pairs | Accuracy | CWS |
|---|---|---|---|
| easy | 81 | .852 | .892 |
| moderate | 122 | .582 | .610 |
| difficult | 126 | .444 | .413 |
| intractable | 1 | 1.000 | 1.000 |
| invalid | 70 | .457 | .501 |

generation should enable it to successfully prove many of these pairs classified as moderate. However, caution should be used in the generation of unsound axioms due to their ability to generate false positives. Since our system is designed to accurately detect entailment in only the easy and moderate cases, we expect that with a perfect axiom set the system can accurately detect entailment in 50.75% of the pairs in the test set.

### 7.5 Axiom Effectiveness

Having determined that the performance of the system is highly dependent upon the axiom set that is made available to it, we performed an analysis of the effectiveness of each axiom class employed by COGEX. For this analysis, we used the test set and different empirically chosen thresholds for each system run. It was necessary to choose different thresholds for each system run because the different axiom classes have a significant effect on proof scoring and accordingly, threshold selection. We ran these experiments with semantic relations enabled and disabled to determine the contribution they make to COGEX'S performance. The results of this analysis are provided in Tables 6 & 7. *None* corresponds to the system's baseline performance without any axioms, *LRR* corresponds to the linguistic rewriting rules described in Section 4.2, *LEX* corresponds to the lexical chain axioms described in Section 4.1, *WK* corresponds to the world knowledge axioms described in Section 4.4, and *all* corresponds to the system with all of the above axioms in place.

It is initially somewhat startling to see how well the system performs without any axioms enabled, but there is good reason for this. Without any axioms COGEX operates very much like a word overlap detector and word overlap is a property that is often exhibited by true entailment pairs. Additionally, an axiom-less COGEX is still able to verify syntax constraints posed by the hypothesis, allowing it to demote pairs in which these constraints are not met.

The addition of the linguistic rewriting rules to the axiom set only provides a small boost to the system's performance, which indicates that in many cases the barrier to entailment detection is not the syntax constraints that are resolved by these axioms. Also, many of the problems that these axioms are designed to resolve can be handled by unbinding predicate arguments, an action of the

**Table 6.** System performance per axiom set configuration without semantic relations

| Axiom Class | Accuracy | CWS | Precision | Recall | F-measure |
|---|---|---|---|---|---|
| none | .574 | .580 | .561 | .687 | .618 |
| LRR | .578 | .583 | .564 | .692 | .622 |
| LEX | .584 | .562 | .562 | .777 | .652 |
| WK | .572 | .577 | .556 | .722 | .628 |
| LRR+LEX | .585 | .563 | .563 | .769 | .650 |
| LRR+WK | .574 | .579 | .559 | .709 | .625 |
| LEX+WK | .582 | .558 | .557 | .805 | .658 |
| all | .584 | .560 | .561 | .784 | .654 |

**Table 7.** System performance per axiom set configuration with semantic relations

| Axiom Class | Accuracy | CWS | Precision | Recall | F-measure |
|---|---|---|---|---|---|
| none | .579 | .579 | .569 | .662 | .612 |
| LRR | .580 | .578 | .567 | .687 | .621 |
| LEX | .585 | .561 | .566 | .742 | .642 |
| WK | .578 | .573 | .565 | .689 | .621 |
| LRR+LEX | .585 | .561 | .563 | .764 | .648 |
| LRR+WK | .579 | .574 | .562 | .724 | .633 |
| LEX+WK | .587 | .553 | .563 | .779 | .654 |
| all | .588 | .555 | .566 | .764 | .650 |

backoff strategy that is not heavily penalized by COGEX. However, an important result of the addition of these axioms is that both precision and recall receive a proportionally significant boost which verifies that these axioms for the most part are sound and contribute to the completeness of the axiom set.

Lexical chain axioms provide a much more significant boost to COGEX's performance. The ability to recognize synonyms in the text and hypothesis is an important skill for this entailment recognition task. The most significant performance boost occurs for the recall metric which indicates that these axioms are of extreme importance to the completeness of the axiom set. The system's precision receives a proportionally small boost which leads us to believe that some of the lexical chain axioms being produced are unsound. The f-measure and accuracy show that this is clearly a case where sacrificing soundness for completeness is a good idea. The combination of linguistic rewriting rules and lexical chains produces the system's highest accuracy of 58.5%. In this case COGEX's recall is primariliy driven by the lexical chain axioms and the system receives a slight boost in precision with the addition of the linguistic rewriting rules. This configuration is optimal because both of these sets of axioms are able to contribute to the completeness of the axiom set without adding a significant amount of unsound behavior.

An interesting result occurs when the system has only the relatively small set of hand-coded world knowledge axioms available. The accuracy and precision both drop significantly, but the recall goes way up. Just as with the lexical chain axioms, the recall boost is a sign of the contribution to the axiom set's completeness and the precision drop is a sign of unsound axioms. This is a surprising result since this set of axioms was hand-coded, which we felt would ensure soundness and not necessarily completeness. However, the task of producing sound axioms is a much more difficult than it appears to be on the surface, and naturally we attempt to generate axioms that are as general as possible to encourage completeness which, in turn leads to unsoundness. Word sense disambiguation is a necessary element for these common-sense axioms because in most cases they apply for only one sense of the word, and since we were forced to do without it, it is not surprising to see the axioms being used in an unsound manner. Furthermore, all of these axioms were created without examining the test set, which prevented us from creating world knowledge axioms that were necessary for pairs in the test set. Just as with the lexical chains, the addition of linguistic rewriting rules to the world knowledge axioms improves COGEX's ability to recognize entailment in a few cases where linguistic knowledge is required. The addition of world knowledge axioms to the lexical chain axiom set results in the highest recall indicating that these two axiom sets do contribute significantly to COGEX's completeness but also lower accuracy and precision scores due to the unsoundness of the world knowledge base.

As expected from previous results, running the system with all axiom sets enabled produces slightly worse performance than running the system with just linguistic rewriting rules and lexical chain axioms. Here, the system's accuracy is being supported by the large number of sound axioms being generated by linguistic rewriting rules and the lexical chain axioms and only receives a small hit in performance due to the world knowledge axioms. Thus, we can conclude that there is a trade-off between soundness and completeness and the key to good performance is to utilize axiom sets that do not sacrifice too much of one for the other.

Overall, the addition of semantic relations to the logic form boosts accuracy and precision while hurting recall. Semantic relations force COGEX to reconcile the hypothesis's semantic constraints as well as the lexical and syntactic constraints posed by the first layer of the logic form. The additional constraints as well as the representation's incomplete semantic layer, due to semantic parser's accuracy, make it more difficult for COGEX to find proofs for each text-hypothesis pair, and as a result, recall drops. However, the new requirement that the semantics of the hypothesis be entailed by the semantics of the text significantly increases precision and accuracy.

With semantic relations enabled, it is no longer the case that the *LRR+LEX* axiom set combination produces the best performance. We suspect the reason for this is the significant weight that is given to semantic relation predicates. Due to the method in which normalized scores are calculated, as show in Equation 1, the addition of this weight to each semantic relation effectively diminishes the importance of all the other predicates in the logic form. Thus, the syntactic constraints of the hypothesis become less important and the addition of linguistic rewriting rules does little to improve performance. Our semantic relations parser is currently only returning a proportionally small number of relations and we suspect that as we are able to detect more semantic relations, COGEX's performance will increase for the entailment recognition task.

## 8 Conclusion

The ability to accurately recognize textual entailment adds significant value to any natural language processing system. Entailment recognition systems based purely on word overlap, lexical similarity, or statistical analysis cannot offer the level of reasoning that is required by the majority of the entailment pairs presented in this task and more importantly the level of reasoning required in real world applications. The logic prover is an essential tool in advancing the reasoning capabilities of natural language systems closer to the human level.

Our system, COGEX, shows great potential for performing high level reasoning in natural language. This paper has detailed the major components involved in our natural language prover and what barriers there are to it's performance. Our syntactically and semantically rich knowledge representation allows us to capture both explicit and implicit knowledge expressed in open text. The large collection of static and dynamically generated axioms produced by COGEX help to boost the accuracy and recall of our entailment recognition system. The novel backoff strategy employed by COGEX allows the system to handle the shortcomings of the knowledge representation and the axiom set.

The performance of COGEX in this entailment recognition task was on par with the rest of the systems in the challenge and we believe that through the development of a better syntactic parser and a knowledge representation that includes more high level concepts implicitly stated in text, we will be able to provide COGEX with a much more accurate representation of text. Additionally, the implementation of new resources for axiom generation will vastly improve the performance of COGEX.

## References

[Akhmatova 2005] Elena Akhmatova. Textual Entailment Resolution via Atomic Propositions. In *Proceedings of the PASCAL Challenges Workshop on Recognising Textual Entailment*, April 2005.

[Bobrow et al. 2005] D. Bobrow, C. Condoravdi, R. Crouch, R. Kaplan, L. Karttunen, T. King, V. dePaiva, and A. Zaenen 2005. A Basic Logic for Textual Inference. In *Papers from the AAAI 2005 Workshop on Inference for Textual Question Answering*, pages 47–51, AAAI Press.

[Braz et al. 2005] Rodrigo de Salvo Braz, Roxana Girju, Vasin Punyakanok, Dan Roth, and Mark Sammons. An Inference Model for Semantic Entailment in Natural Language. In *Proceedings of the PASCAL Challenges Workshop on Recognising Textual Entailment*, April 2005.

[Clark et al. 2005] C. Clark, D. Hodges, J. Stephan, and D. Moldovan. 2005. Moving QA Towards Reading Comprehension Using Context and Default Reasoning. In *Papers from the AAAI 2005 Workshop on Inference for Textual Question Answering*, pages 6–12, AAAI Press.

[Collins 2003] M. Collins. Head-Driven Statistical Models for Natural Language Parsing. *Computational Linguistics*, Volume 29, Number 4, pages 589–637, 2003.

[Dagan et al. 2005] Ido Dagan, Oren Glickman and Bernardo Magnini. The PASCAL Recognising Textual Entailment Challenge. In *Proceedings of the PASCAL Challenges Workshop on Recognising Textual Entailment*, April 2005.

[Hobbs et al. 1993] J. Hobbs, M. Stickel, and P. Martin. 1993. Interpretation as abduction. In *Artificial Intelligence, Vol 63*, pages 69–142.

[Miller 1990] G. Miller 1990. Wordnet: an online lexical database. In *International Journal of Lexicography, 3(4).*

[Moldovan et al. 2004] D. Moldovan, A. Badulescu, M. Tatu, D. Antohe, and R.C. Giru. 2004. Models for the semantic classification of noun phrases. In *Proceedings of HLT/NAACL, Computational Lexical Semantics workshop,* Boston, Massachusetts.

[Moldovan et al. 2003] D. Moldovan,C. Clark, S. Harabagiu, and S. Maiorano. 2003. Cogex: A Logic Prover for Question Answering. In *Proceedings of the Human Language Technology and North American Chapter of the Association for Computational Linguistics Conference (HLT-2003)*, Edmonton, Alberta, Canada,pages 87–93.

[Moldovan and Novischi 2002] D. Moldovan and A. Novischi. 2002. Lexical Chains for Question Answering. In *Proceedings of 19th International Conference on Computational Linguistics (COLING-2002)*, Taipei, Taiwan, pages 674–680.

[Moldovan and Rus 2002] D. Moldovan and V. Rus 2001. Logic Form Transformation of WordNet and its Applicability to QuestionAnswering. In *Proceedings of the 39th Annual Meeting of the Association for Computational Linguistics (ACL-2001)*, Toulouse, France, pages 394–401.

[Raina et al. 2005] R. Raina, A. Haghighi, C. Cox, J. Finkel, J. Michels, K. Toutanova, B. MacCartney, B Marneffe, C. D. Manning, and A. Y. Ng Robust Textual Inference using Diverse Knowledge Sources. In *Proceedings of the PASCAL Challenges Workshop on Recognising Textual Entailment*, April 2005.

[Russell and Norvig 2003] S. Russell and P. Norvig. 2003. *Artificial Inteligence - A Modern Approach.* Prentice Hall, 2003..

[Tari and Baral 2005] L. Tari and C. Baral 2005. Using AnsProlog with Link Grammar and WordNet for QA with deep reasoning. In *Papers from the AAAI 2005 Workshop on Inference for Textual Question Answering*, pages 13–21, AAAI Press.

[Wos 1988] L. Wos. 1998. *Automated Reasoning, 33 Basic Research Problems.* Prentice Hall, 1988.

# Recognizing Textual Entailment: Is Word Similarity Enough?

Valentin Jijkoun and Maarten de Rijke

Informatics Institute, University of Amsterdam,
Kruislaan 403, 1098 SJ Amsterdam, The Netherlands
{jijkoun, mdr}@science.uva.nl

**Abstract.** We describe the system we used at the PASCAL-2005 Recognizing Textual Entailment Challenge. Our method for recognizing entailment is based on calculating "directed" sentence similarity: checking the directed "semantic" word overlap between the text and the hypothesis. We use frequency-based term weighting in combination with two different word similarity measures.

Although one version of the system shows significant improvement over randomly guessing decisions (with an accuracy score of 57.3), we show that this is only due to a subset of the data that can be equally well handled by simple word overlap. Furthermore, we give an in-depth analysis of the system and the data of the challenge.

## 1 Introduction

The Recognizing Textual Entailment (RTE) challenge, which is organized within the PASCAL network (Pascal), is a task where systems are required to detect semantic entailment between pairs of natural language sentences. For example, the sentence

- *The memorandum noted the United Nations estimated that 2.5 million to 3.5 million people died of AIDS last year*

is considered to logically entail the sentence

- *Over 2 million people died of AIDS last year.*

While the recognition of textual entailment is not an end-to-end task in itself, it is generally felt that robust entailment checkers have the potential of improving the performance of systems for a variety of end-to-end tasks, including reading comprehension, question answering, information extraction, machine translation, and paraphrase acquisition.

In principle, the RTE challenge offers opportunities for a broad spectrum of techniques, ranging from shallow baseline approaches based on lexical overlap and word similarity measures well-known from the field of information retrieval to methods based on deep natural language processing that require significant amounts of elaborate knowledge engineering. At the PASCAL-2005 RTE challenge the whole spectrum was

J. Quiñonero-Candela et al. (Eds.): MLCW 2005, LNAI 3944, pp. 449–460, 2006.

represented; see (Dagan et al., 2005a). Our focus is on methods situated at the light-weight end of the scale. The main research aim for our participation in the PASCAL-2005 RTE challenge was to understand the potential and limitations of simple entailment checking methods based on word similarity. More specifically, in this paper we address the following issues:

- How well does a baseline entailment checker based on word similarity work? How much do similarity measures contribute to the performance?
- When determining whether a pair of sentences is a positive entailment instance, the similarity score between the two sentences needs to be above some threshold. How reliably can this threshold be estimated from development data?
- How well does our light-weight similarity measure separate positive and negative entailment examples?
- What are easy cases where word similarity methods are likely to succeed, and what are hard cases where they are likely to break down and where more elaborate methods are called for?

The remainder of the paper is organized as follows. In Section 2 we describe our system and provide details on the setting used for our experiments. Then, in Section 3 we compare several versions of the system and explore the contributions of its various components. In Sections 4–8 we describe more general and methodological issues, including thresholding, the distribution of positive and negative examples, and easy vs. hard cases for our system. We wrap up in Section 9.

## 2 System Description and Experimental Setting

At the Pascal-2005 RTE challenge, systems had to address the following task: given a pair of sentences $T$, $H$ (text, hypothesis), determine whether $T$ logically entails $H$ and provide an estimate of the system's confidence. The example entailment pairs come from a number of natural language processing (NLP) areas: comparable documents (CD), reading comprehension (RC), question answering (QA), information extraction (IE), machine translation (MT), and paraphrase acquisition (PP). See (Dagan et al., 2005a) for further details.

To address the RTE challenge, we proceed as follows. For every text, hypothesis pair $(T,H)$, we view each sentence as a bag of words and calculate a *directed sentence similarity score* between them. To check for entailment, we compare the score against a threshold. This method is implemented as shown in the pseudo-code in Figure 1. Essentially, for every word in the hypothesis $H$ we find the most similar word in the text $T$ according to the measure $\text{wordsim}(w_1,w_2)$. If such a similar word exists (i.e., *maxSim* is non-zero), we add the weighted similarity value to the total similarity score. Otherwise, we subtract the weight of the word, penalizing words in the hypothesis without matching words in the text.

The threshold for the final entailment checking is selected using the development corpus of text, hypothesis pairs (see Subsection 2.3). The confidence of a decision made by the system is determined by looking at the distance between the similarity value and the threshold. For example, for positive decisions (*sim* $\geq$ *threshold*):

**let** $T = (T_1, T_2, \ldots, T_n)$
**let** $H = (H_1, H_2, \ldots, H_m)$
$totalSim = 0$
$totalWeight = 0$
**for** $j = 1 \ldots m$ **do**
  $maxSim = \max_i \mathrm{wordsim}(T_i, H_j)$
  **if** $maxSim = 0$ **then** $maxSim = -1$
  $totalSim$ += $maxSim * \mathrm{weight}(H_j)$
  $totalWeight$ += $\mathrm{weight}(H_j)$
**end for**
$sim = totalSim / totalWeight$
**if** $sim \geq threshold$ **then return** TRUE
**return** FALSE

**Fig. 1.** Pseudo-code for our textual similarity method: determining whether the text $T$ entails the hypothesis $H$

$$confidence = \frac{sim - threshold}{1 - threshold}$$

The algorithm is parametrized with two functions:

- $\mathrm{weight}(w)$: the importance of the word $w$ for the similarity identification;
- $\mathrm{wordsim}(w_1, w_2)$: the similarity between the two words $w_1$ and $w_2$ , with range $[0, 1]$.

Next, we describe the choices we considered for these two functions.

### 2.1 Weighting Words

The weighting of words with respect to importance is based on core intuitions from research in Information Retrieval, where Inverse Document Frequency (IDF) is often used as a measure of term importance; see e.g., (Baeza-Yates and Ribeiro-Neto, 1999). Recently, Monz and de Rijke (2001) used IDF for light-weight entailment checking in the setting of information fusion: merge information (i.e., text snippets) on a single topic but try to avoid redundancy, i.e., if a snippet entails another segment, only the entailing segment should be included in the fused information; in that paper, evaluation was done using a purpose-built corpus.

For our experiments in the present paper we use the normalized *inverse collection frequency* of words, calculated on a large collection of newspaper texts. That is, for a word $w$ we compute

$$\mathrm{ICF}(w) = \log \frac{\#\text{ occurences of all words}}{\#\text{ occurences of } w},$$

and the actual weight of a word is calculated as normalized ICF, so that, for instance, the weight for the most frequent word ("*the*") is 0.

### 2.2 Word Similarity Measures

We experimented with two similarity measures: Dekang Lin's dependency-based word similarity (Lin, 1998) and the measure based on lexical chains in WordNet due to Hirst and St-Onge (1998). For both measures, words were first converted to lemmas. Our choice of the measures was motivated by their relative "promiscuity", i.e., the fact that they identify as similar more word pairs than other measures, as indicated by the analysis of five WordNet-related measures in (Budanitsky and Hirst, 2001) and our own experiments with Lin's dependency-based similarity. In future work we plan to study whether promiscuity is indeed helpful in the context of textual entailment.

We used both similiary measures for our official submission, as described in (Jijkoun and de Rijke, 2005). The dependency-based similarity measure performed somewhat better (accuracy 55.3 vs. 53.6). For this reason, we only focus on Lin's dependency-based word similarity in the remainder of this paper.

### 2.3 Experimental Setting

For the experiments described below, we used the material provided by the organizers of the Pascal-2005 RTE challenge: a development and test corpus, with 567 and 800 sentence pairs, respectively, manually annotated for logical entailment.

The evaluation measures used are accuracy (A), confidence-weighted score (CWS), as well as precision (P) and recall (R) for the entailment identification; see (Dagan et al., 2005a) for details.

## 3 Versions of the System

In this section we present and discuss several versions of our entailment checker. Our aim is to understand how well the word similarity-based system works and what the contribution of different components is, thus addressing the first of the research questions raised in the introduction.

The design of our system involves a number of important choices, whose effects are not obvious: (i) weighting words by importance, and (ii) using a word similarity measure. We want to determine whether the use of these techniques is justified.

In addition to these choices, we considered an option motivated by examples from the development corpus, like

T: Clinton's new book is not big seller here.
H: Clinton's book is a big seller.

Clearly, the text $T$ does not entail the hypothesis $H$ because of the presense of "*not*." We added a simple ad-hoc rule to the system, that checks for *not* or *n't* in both sentences of a pair, and rejects entailment if a particle is present in exacly one of the two sentences.

In our experiments we evaluated the following versions of the system:

- *M*: the main version, with word importance weighting, Lin's word similarity and the rule for handling *not*,
- *M-not*: the same but without the *not*-rule,

**Table 1.** Accuracy, precision, and recall scores for (different flavors of) our baseline system

| | *M* | *M-not* | *M-not-sim* | *M-not-sim-imp* |
|---|---|---|---|---|
| optimal threshold | 0.4 | 0.4 | 0.2 | 0.3 |
| accuracy on development corpus | 58.2 | 56.6 | 57.1 | 57.0 |
| accuracy on test corpus | 57.3 | 57.1 | 54.4 | 54.3 |
| precision on test corpus | 55.1 | 54.7 | 53.0 | 53.3 |
| recall on test corpus | 78.8 | 83.5 | 76.3 | 69.3 |

- *M-not-sim*: also without word similarity, and
- *M-not-sim-imp*: also without word weighting.

Note that the simplest version of the system, *M-not-sim-imp*, assigns entailment scores based solely on word overlap.

The results are presented in Table 1. There, we list the various flavors of our baseline system; the threshold values used as listed in row 2. Optimal thresholds were chosen so as to maximise accuracy on the development corpus.[1]

Interestingly, in Table 1 we see that the more "elaborate" system *M* outperformseach of its subsystems, both on the development corpus and on the test corpus with automatically selected threshold. Looking at the accuracy scores on the test corpus, we see that each component of the main system *M* adds to the overall score, weighting helps (54.4 vs. 54.3), word similarity helps (57.1 vs. 54.4) and the *not*-rule helps (57.3 vs. 57.1). Another thing worth noting is that the simplest system, *M-not-sim-imp*, does not perform significantly better than random (which was the intention of the organizers Dagan et al. (2005a)), while *M* does.

With respect to the 25 full runs submitted to the PASCAL-2005 RTE Challenge (Dagan et al., 2005a), both *M* and *M-not* (with accuracy scores of 57.3 and 57.1, respectively) perform above the median (55.2) and are only outperformed by the Web-based probabilistic system of Glickman et al. (2005) and the MT-based system of Bayer et al. (2005) (both with accuracy scores of 58.6). While this might be interpreted as a "success" for our simple methods, we interpret this outcome as an indication that deep language technology still faces very non-trivial challenges in recognizing textual entailment.

There are some further observations worth making. While differences in accuracy scores on the test corpus between the systems *M* and *M-not* are insignificant, their performance on the development corpus differs more substantially. However, in our further experiments with random splittings of the Pascal-2005 RTE collection into development and test data (see below), behavior of all versions of the system was similar on both corpora.

Summarizing our findings in this section, we claim that whereas simple word-overlap methods do not work well for the RTE task, they can be easily extended with

[1] As an aside, the system used to generate the official runs that were submitted for our participation in the Pascal-2005 RTE challenge (*M-not*) actually showed an accuracy score of 55.3; due to a bug, the threshold of 0.5 used there was selected based only on half of the development corpus. Had we used the entire development corpus for our official runs, the accuracy score would have been 57.1, as in Table 1, row 4.

simple weighting and word similarity measures, resulting in a system with a competitive performance.

## 4 Choosing a Threshold

Next, we turn to the second of our research questions from the introduction: How robust is the choice of thresholds? We approached this question from a number of angles.

To check how sensitive the different versions of the system are to varying corpora, we performed several experiments, splitting the entire collection randomly into development and test data, keeping the proportion of positive/negative examples and examples for the six subtasks as they were in the original split (i.e., in total 567 pairs for development and 800 pairs for testing). For each split and each version of the system, the optimal threshold was selected on the development data and then applied to the test data. The results, for the systems *M* and *M-not-sim-imp*, are presented in Table 2. While there is some variation in the resulting accuracy scores for *M*, all are significantly better than random at the 0.01 level (Dagan et al., 2005a). These experiments indicate that the system's behavior is consistent and that fine-tuning entailment thresholds on development data does generally produce good performance on test examples.

Our next observation concerns the performance on the development corpus vs. the performance on the test corpus: the former is not necessarily a good predictor of the latter. In particular, while simple subsystems (*M-not-sim* and *M-not-sim-imp*) perform reasonably well on the development corpus, their performance on the test corpus is substantially lower. In our experiments with random splittings, we observed a similar phenomena: whereas generally better performance on the development corpus led to better performance on the test data (with thresholds tuned on the development corpus), we were unable to establish strong statistical correlation (we used Spearman's rank correlation coefficient).

In an attempt to see how the choice of threshold depends on the choice of corpus, we looked at the performance of the versions of our system with different thresholds. Figure 2 shows the accuracy on the development and test data depending on a threshold, for the full system *M* (top) and the simplest subsystem *M-not-sim-imp* (bottom).

While for the simplest system, *M-not-sim-imp*, thresholds optimal for the development corpus are clearly suboptimal for the test corpus (the peaks in accuracy are located at different values of the threshold), for the full system, *M*, the correlation is very high. This does indeed indicate that for simple overlap (*M-not-sim-imp*) the optimal threshold is highly corpus-dependent, but that the choice is quite consistent in the more complex system (*M*). That is, *M*'s reasonable performance is not an accident.

**Table 2.** Accuracy scores based on alternative optimal thresholds: as estimated on the official development corpus (Official), and on 10 random splittings of the development and test corpus (Min, Max, Median)

| System | Official | Min | Max | Median |
|---|---|---|---|---|
| *M* | 57.3 | 54.9 | 57.8 | 57.0 |
| *M-not-sim-imp* | 54.3 | 52.5 | 56.5 | 55.1 |

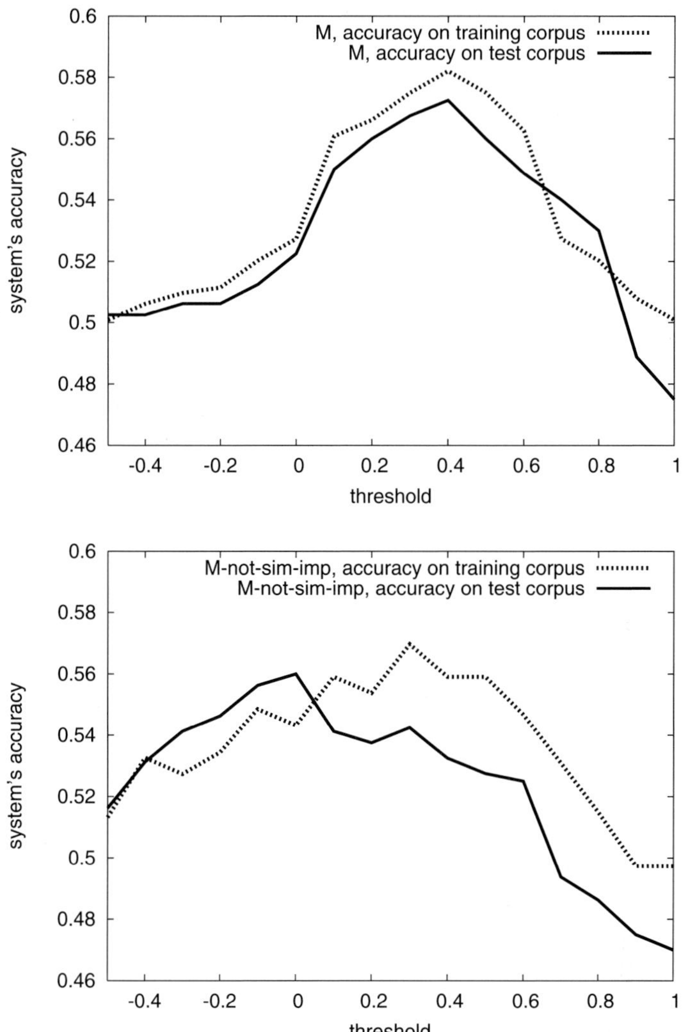


**Fig. 2.** (Top): thresholds on the main system *M*. (Bottom): thresholds on the simplest system *M-not-sim-imp*. The horizontal axis shows possible thresholds, and the vertical axis—accuracy of a system.

We have not systematically investigated how the size of the development corpus affects the quality of threshold, but anecdotal evidence (the bug in our official submission, see footnote 1) suggests that the size of the development corpus is an important issue, and that at least several hundreds of pairs are necessary for training.

Finally, we hypothesize that the optimal thresholds depend on the source of the examples, i.e., they may be different for the seven subtasks (CD, IE, MT, QA, RC, PP, IR). However, since currently only 50–100 entailment pairs are available for development per subtask, it is difficult to support this claim experimentally at this time.

## 5 The Distribution of Positive and Negative Examples

Every system that makes an entailment decision based on a threshold of some similarity score between the text and the hypothesis (e.g., most systems in the PASCAL-2005 RTE Challenge) is based on the assumption that the similarity scores somehow separate negative and positive examples. Ideally, for a good variant of a similarity scoring method,

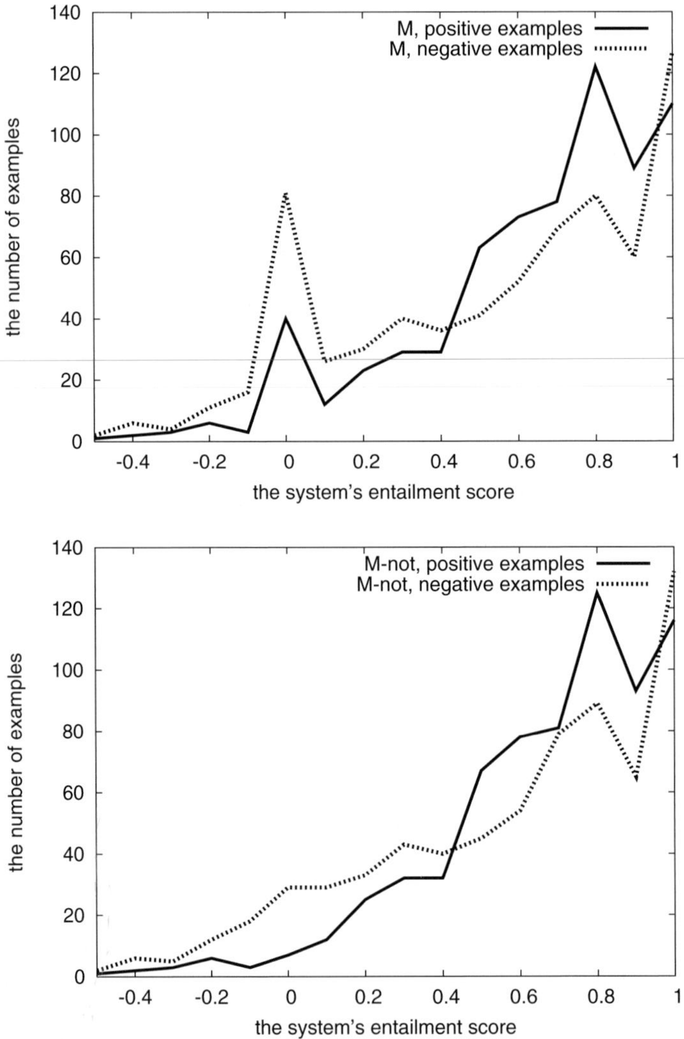


**Fig. 3.** Distribution of true positive and negative examples. (Top): for the full system *M*. (Bottom): for the system without the *not*-rule (*M-not*). The horizontal axis gives the possible values of the system's entailment score, and the vertical axis shows the number of pairs (positive vs. negative) with this entailment score.

negative examples would mostly have low scores and positive examples—mostly high scores.

To see whether this is indeed the case for our entailment checkers, we plotted the number of true positive and true negative entailment pairs that were assigned different scores by the system. Figure 3 shows the results for the systems *M* and *M-not* on the full corpus of 1367 entailment pairs.

Quite surprisingly, for the word-similarity based system *M-not* (Figure 3(Bottom)) the distributions of positive and negative examples with respect to the score of the system are very similar and the graphs have peaks near the same values. Most negative examples are "concentrated" around the same entailment score as positive examples. Moreover, there are actually more negative than positive examples with entailment score 1. This means that the system does not really manage to separate positive and negative examples, but simply uses the fact that the distribution of negatives is somewhat "flatter": the peak around score 0.8 is lower and some mass is moved left, to lower values. It seems that the "only" reason the system shows a performance that is better than random is that the distribution of the negative examples with respect to weighted word overlap is flatter than the distribution of the positive examples (except for the high peak in both distributions around score 1.0).

Note that the situation is somewhat different when we include our simple *not*-rule (Figure 3(Top)). Now, negative examples have a second clear peak around 0 (this is exactly the entailment score assigned by the *not*-rule). Apart from improving accuracy, it seems that the *not*-rule actually does something reasonable, providing for a somewhat clearer separation between positive and negative examples.

As an aside, for the other, simpler subsystems (*M-not-sim* and *M-not-sim-imp*), the slopes of the graphs are even flatter and the two curves are even closer together, making it even more difficult to separate positive and negative examples.

In sum, we conclude that in general, the similarity-based system *M* fails to actually separate positive and negative examples of the entailment pairs: their distributions with respect to the system's score are very similar. A more substantial separation is only achieved using the ad-hoc *not*-rule.

## 6 Easy vs. Hard Cases

Ideally, we would want to use our word similarity-based system to identify entailment pairs that are "hard" for a purely word-based systems, i.e., where more sophisticated analysis (syntactic relations, reasoning with world knowledge) is required. Can we use a variant of our entailment checking methods to find such "hard" cases?

Unfortunately, the answer seems to be "no." As the curves in Figure 3 indicate, there is no single region among possible entailment scores with a substantial number of TE examples and high confidence of the system (i.e., mostly positive or mostly negative examples). As mentioned previously, the distributions of positive and negative examples are fairly similar. The best observation we were able to make is that among TE pairs with scores less than 0.1 (216 pairs of 1367, or 16%), as much as 69% of the pairs were negative entailment examples. Still, we believe that the accuracy 0.69 is not high enough to consider these examples as "easy."

For now it seems that we need a different way of identifying "easy" vs. "hard" cases—a reliable category of "easy" examples is identified in the next section.

## 7 Performance on Different Subtasks

We also compared the performance of our entailment checking system on different subtasks, reflecting the different sources from which the entailment pairs were selected by the task organizers. The table below shows the accuracy, precision and recall of the system *M* for all subtasks:

| Subtask | Accuracy | Precision | Recall |
|---|---|---|---|
| CD | 84.0 | 84.9 | 82.7 |
| IE | 59.2 | 55.2 | 96.7 |
| MT | 45.8 | 46.8 | 60.0 |
| QA | 46.2 | 47.0 | 60.0 |
| RC | 52.1 | 51.2 | 92.9 |
| PP | 56.0 | 53.5 | 92.0 |
| IR | 50.0 | 50.0 | 71.1 |
| Overall | 57.3 | 55.0 | 78.8 |

From the table it is clear that the overall accuracy of the system is relatively high only due to the reasonable performance on the CD (comparable documents) subtask. This particular subtask appears to be quite easy for our system, whereas on other tasks the performance is not better than randomly guessing. Manual examination of the entailment candidate pairs from the CD subtask shows that the pairs usually have many words in common. Here are two examples:

(T) Voting for a new European Parliament was clouded by concerns over apathy.
(H) Voting for a new European Parliament has been clouded by apathy.
Entailment: TRUE, System's score: 0.88

(T) A small bronze bust of Spencer Tracy sold for $174,000.
(H) A small bronze bust of Spencer Tracy made $180,447.
Entailment: FALSE, System's score: 0.44

In the second example the similarity is substantially lower since the numbers (which occur relatively rarely in our newspaper collection, and thus get higher weight) are different.

In our subsequent analysis, we found that even the subsystem *M-not-sim-imp* (simple word overlap) performed well on the CD subtask, with an accuracy score of 86.0. This suggests that examples from the CD task can indeed be considered "easy" and that they probably need not be included in future editions of the RTE task.

When CD examples were removed from the development and testing corpora, the system did not perform better than random (accuracy 51.2). We interpret this as a good sign: examples from other subtasks, apparently, require other, deeper methods of entailment recognition.

## 8 Precision and Recall

For all subtasks, except CD, our precision scores are substantially worse than our recall scores. The system $M$ judged 72% of the test pairs as positive, compared to 50% true positives in the test set. This comes as no surprise: since most examples have entailment scores larger than the selected threshold (see Figure 3), most errors are also in this "positive" area, thus most errors are false positives.

In many classification problems thresholds can be used to fine-tune the precision-recall balance, which is obviously a very useful option for any real-world application. However, we found that for our system precision on the test data cannot be improved by changing the threshold. This is due to the great uncertainty for large values of the entailment score (Figure 3) and unseparability of positive and negative examples mentioned above.

## 9 Conclusions

We described a system for recognizing textual entailment based on lexical similarity. Although the system performs significantly better than randomly guessing, the reasonable performance is only based on one subtask (CD, comparable documents). For this subtask even much simpler systems (viz. plain word overlap) give similar performance. For all other subtasks none of the variants of our system performed better than random. Moreover, we found that the system cannot be further tuned without overfitting, which indicates that other, deeper textual features need to be explored.

## Acknowledgments

Both authors were supported by the Netherlands Organization for Scientific Research (NWO) under project number 220-80-001. In addition, Maarten de Rijke was supported by grants from NWO, under project numbers 017.001.190, 264-70-050, 365-20-005, 612.000.106, 612.000.207, 612.066.302, 612.069.006, and 640.001.501

## References

Ricardo Baeza-Yates and Berthier Ribeiro-Neto. *Modern Information Retrieval.* ACM Press, 1999.

Samuel Bayer, John Burger, Lisa Ferro, John Henderson, and Alexander Yeh. MITRE's submission to the EU Pascal RTE challenge. In Dagan et al. (2005b).

Alexander Budanitsky and Graeme Hirst. Semantic distance in wordnet: An experimental, application-oriented evaluation of five measures. In *Workshop on WordNet and Other Lexical Resources, Second meeting of the North American Chapter of the Association for Computational Linguistics*, 2001.

Ido Dagan, Oren Glickman, and Bernardo Magnini. The PASCAL Recognizing Textual Entailment Challenge. Dagan et al. (2005b).

Ido Dagan, Oren Glickman, and Bernardo Magnini, editors. *PASCAL. Proceedings of the first challenge workshop Recognizing Textual Entailment.* 2005b.

Oren Glickman, Ido Dagan, and Moshe Koppel. Web based probabilistic textual entailment. In Dagan et al. (2005b).

Graeme Hirst and David St-Onge. Lexical chains as representation of context for the detection and correction of malapropisms. In Fellbaum Christiane, editor, *WordNet: An electronic lexical database*. The MIT Press, 1998.

Valentin Jijkoun and Maarten de Rijke. Recognizing textual entailment using lexical similarity. In Dagan et al. (2005b).

Dekang Lin. An information-theoretic definition of similarity. In *Proceedings of International Conference on Machine Learning*, 1998.

Christof Monz and Maarten de Rijke. Light-weight entailment checking for computational semantics. In *Proceedings of the Workshop on Inference in Computational Semantics (ICoS-3)*, 2001.

Pascal. Pascal Recognising Textual Entailment Challenge, 2005. URL: `http://www.pascal-network.org/Challenges/RTE/`.

# Author Index


Akhmatova, Elena 385
Alfonseca, Enrique 191
Allan, Moray 117
Andreevskaia, Alina 332

Bayer, Sam 309
Bergler, Sabine 332
Bishop, Christopher M. 117
Boniforti, Marco Aldo Piccolino 344
Bos, Johan 404
Bousquet, Olivier 1
Bristot, Antonella 344
Burger, John 309

Carthy, Joe 372
Cawley, Gavin C. 56
Chapelle, Olivier 56, 117
Chawla, Nitesh V. 41
Clark, Christine 427

Dagan, Ido 177, 287
Dalal, Navneet 117
de Rijke, Maarten 449
de Salvo Braz, Rodrigo 261
Delmonte, Rodolfo 344
Deselaers, Thomas 117
Dolan, William B. 205
Dorkó, Gyuri 117
Duffner, Stefan 117
Dunnion, John 372

Eichhorn, Jan 117
Everingham, Mark 117

Farquhar, Jason D.R. 117
Ferro, Lisa 309
Fowler, Abraham 427
Fritz, Mario 117

Garcia, Christophe 117
Girju, Roxana 261
Glickman, Oren 177, 287
Griffiths, Tom 117

Henderson, John 309
Herrera, Jesús 231
Hirschman, Lynette 309
Hodges, Daniel 427

Jijkoun, Valentin 449
Jurie, Frederic 117

Keysers, Daniel 117
Kohonen, Jukka 95
Koppel, Moshe 287
Koskela, Markus 117
Kouylekov, Milen 217
Kurogi, Shuichi 78

Laaksonen, Jorma 117
Larlus, Diane 117
Leibe, Bastian 117
Li, Zhuoyan 332

Magnini, Bernardo 177, 217
Markert, Katja 404
Meng, Hongying 117
Moldovan, Dan 427
Mollá, Diego 385
Murray, Iain 33

Neal, Radford M. 28
Newman, Eamonn 372
Ney, Hermann 117

Pazienza, Maria Teresa 240
Peñas, Anselmo 231
Pennacchiotti, Marco 240
Pérez, Diana 191
Punyakanok, Vasin 261

Quiñonero-Candela, Joaquin 1

Rasmussen, Carl Edward 1
Roth, Dan 261

Sammons, Mark 261
Sawa, Miho 78
Schiele, Bernt 117

Schmid, Cordelia 117
Schölkopf, Bernhard 1
Seemann, Edgar 117
Shawe-Taylor, John 117
Sinz, Fabian 1
Snelson, Edward 33
Stokes, Nicola 372
Storkey, Amos 117
Suomela, Jukka 95
Szedmak, Sandor 117

Talbot, Nicola L.C. 56
Tanaka, Shinya 78
Tonelli, Sara 344
Triggs, Bill 117

Ulusoy, Ilkay 117

Van Gool, Luc 117
Vanderwende, Lucy 205
Verdejo, Felisa 231
Viitaniemi, Ville 117

Williams, Christopher K.I. 117
Wu, Dekai 299

Yeh, Alex 309

Zanzotto, Fabio Massimo 240
Zhang, Jianguo 117
Zisserman, Andrew 117

# Lecture Notes in Artificial Intelligence (LNAI)

Vol. 3946: T.R. Roth-Berghofer, S. Schulz, D.B. Leake (Eds.), Modeling and Retrieval of Context. XI, 149 pages. 2006.

Vol. 3944: J. Quiñonero-Candela, I. Dagan, B. Magnini, F. d'Alché-Buc (Eds.), Machine Learning Challenges. XIII, 462 pages. 2006.

Vol. 3930: D.S. Yeung, Z.-Q. Liu, X.-Z. Wang, H. Yan (Eds.), Advances in Machine Learning and Cybernetics. XXI, 1110 pages. 2006.

Vol. 3918: W.K. Ng, M. Kitsuregawa, J. Li, K. Chang (Eds.), Advances in Knowledge Discovery and Data Mining. XXIV, 879 pages. 2006.

Vol. 3910: S.A. Brueckner, G.D.M. Serugendo, D. Hales, F. Zambonelli (Eds.), Engineering Self-Organising Systems. XII, 245 pages. 2006.

Vol. 3904: M. Baldoni, U. Endriss, A. Omicini, P. Torroni (Eds.), Declarative Agent Languages and Technologies III. XII, 245 pages. 2006.

Vol. 3900: F. Toni, P. Torroni (Eds.), Computational Logic in Multi-Agent Systems. XVII, 427 pages. 2006.

Vol. 3899: S. Frintrop, VOCUS: A Visual Attention System for Object Detection and Goal-Directed Search. XIV, 216 pages. 2006.

Vol. 3898: K. Tuyls, P.J. 't Hoen, K. Verbeeck, S. Sen (Eds.), Learning and Adaption in Multi-Agent Systems. X, 217 pages. 2006.

Vol. 3891: J.S. Sichman, L. Antunes (Eds.), Multi-Agent-Based Simulation VI. X, 191 pages. 2006.

Vol. 3890: S.G. Thompson, R. Ghanea-Hercock (Eds.), Defence Applications of Multi-Agent Systems. XII, 141 pages. 2006.

Vol. 3885: V. Torra, Y. Narukawa, A. Valls, J. Domingo-Ferrer (Eds.), Modeling Decisions for Artificial Intelligence. XII, 374 pages. 2006.

Vol. 3881: S. Gibet, N. Courty, J.-F. Kamp (Eds.), Gesture in Human-Computer Interaction and Simulation. XIII, 344 pages. 2006.

Vol. 3874: R. Missaoui, J. Schmidt (Eds.), Formal Concept Analysis. X, 309 pages. 2006.

Vol. 3873: L. Maicher, J. Park (Eds.), Charting the Topic Maps Research and Applications Landscape. VIII, 281 pages. 2006.

Vol. 3863: M. Kohlhase (Ed.), Mathematical Knowledge Management. XI, 405 pages. 2006.

Vol. 3862: R.H. Bordini, M. Dastani, J. Dix, A.E.F. Seghrouchni (Eds.), Programming Multi-Agent Systems. XIV, 267 pages. 2006.

Vol. 3849: I. Bloch, A. Petrosino, A.G.B. Tettamanzi (Eds.), Fuzzy Logic and Applications. XIV, 438 pages. 2006.

Vol. 3848: J.-F. Boulicaut, L. De Raedt, H. Mannila (Eds.), Constraint-Based Mining and Inductive Databases. X, 401 pages. 2006.

Vol. 3847: K.P. Jantke, A. Lunzer, N. Spyratos, Y. Tanaka (Eds.), Federation over the Web. X, 215 pages. 2006.

Vol. 3835: G. Sutcliffe, A. Voronkov (Eds.), Logic for Programming, Artificial Intelligence, and Reasoning. XIV, 744 pages. 2005.

Vol. 3830: D. Weyns, H. V.D. Parunak, F. Michel (Eds.), Environments for Multi-Agent Systems II. VIII, 291 pages. 2006.

Vol. 3817: M. Faundez-Zanuy, L. Janer, A. Esposito, A. Satue-Villar, J. Roure, V. Espinosa-Duro (Eds.), Nonlinear Analyses and Algorithms for Speech Processing. XII, 380 pages. 2006.

Vol. 3814: M. Maybury, O. Stock, W. Wahlster (Eds.), Intelligent Technologies for Interactive Entertainment. XV, 342 pages. 2005.

Vol. 3809: S. Zhang, R. Jarvis (Eds.), AI 2005: Advances in Artificial Intelligence. XXVII, 1344 pages. 2005.

Vol. 3808: C. Bento, A. Cardoso, G. Dias (Eds.), Progress in Artificial Intelligence. XVIII, 704 pages. 2005.

Vol. 3802: Y. Hao, J. Liu, Y.-P. Wang, Y.-m. Cheung, H. Yin, L. Jiao, J. Ma, Y.-C. Jiao (Eds.), Computational Intelligence and Security, Part II. XLII, 1166 pages. 2005.

Vol. 3801: Y. Hao, J. Liu, Y.-P. Wang, Y.-m. Cheung, H. Yin, L. Jiao, J. Ma, Y.-C. Jiao (Eds.), Computational Intelligence and Security, Part I. XLI, 1122 pages. 2005.

Vol. 3789: A. Gelbukh, Á. de Albornoz, H. Terashima-Marín (Eds.), MICAI 2005: Advances in Artificial Intelligence. XXVI, 1198 pages. 2005.

Vol. 3782: K.-D. Althoff, A. Dengel, R. Bergmann, M. Nick, T.R. Roth-Berghofer (Eds.), Professional Knowledge Management. XXIII, 739 pages. 2005.

Vol. 3763: H. Hong, D. Wang (Eds.), Automated Deduction in Geometry. X, 213 pages. 2006.

Vol. 3755: G.J. Williams, S.J. Simoff (Eds.), Data Mining. XI, 331 pages. 2006.

Vol. 3735: A. Hoffmann, H. Motoda, T. Scheffer (Eds.), Discovery Science. XVI, 400 pages. 2005.

Vol. 3734: S. Jain, H.U. Simon, E. Tomita (Eds.), Algorithmic Learning Theory. XII, 490 pages. 2005.

Vol. 3721: A.M. Jorge, L. Torgo, P.B. Brazdil, R. Camacho, J. Gama (Eds.), Knowledge Discovery in Databases: PKDD 2005. XXIII, 719 pages. 2005.

Vol. 3720: J. Gama, R. Camacho, P.B. Brazdil, A.M. Jorge, L. Torgo (Eds.), Machine Learning: ECML 2005. XXIII, 769 pages. 2005.

Vol. 3717: B. Gramlich (Ed.), Frontiers of Combining Systems. X, 321 pages. 2005.

Vol. 3702: B. Beckert (Ed.), Automated Reasoning with Analytic Tableaux and Related Methods. XIII, 343 pages. 2005.

Vol. 3698: U. Furbach (Ed.), KI 2005: Advances in Artificial Intelligence. XIII, 409 pages. 2005.

Vol. 3690: M. Pěchouček, P. Petta, L.Z. Varga (Eds.), Multi-Agent Systems and Applications IV. XVII, 667 pages. 2005.

Vol. 3684: R. Khosla, R.J. Howlett, L.C. Jain (Eds.), Knowledge-Based Intelligent Information and Engineering Systems, Part IV. LXXIX, 933 pages. 2005.

Vol. 3683: R. Khosla, R.J. Howlett, L.C. Jain (Eds.), Knowledge-Based Intelligent Information and Engineering Systems, Part III. LXXX, 1397 pages. 2005.

Vol. 3682: R. Khosla, R.J. Howlett, L.C. Jain (Eds.), Knowledge-Based Intelligent Information and Engineering Systems, Part II. LXXIX, 1371 pages. 2005.

Vol. 3681: R. Khosla, R.J. Howlett, L.C. Jain (Eds.), Knowledge-Based Intelligent Information and Engineering Systems, Part I. LXXX, 1319 pages. 2005.

Vol. 3673: S. Bandini, S. Manzoni (Eds.), AI*IA 2005: Advances in Artificial Intelligence. XIV, 614 pages. 2005.

Vol. 3662: C. Baral, G. Greco, N. Leone, G. Terracina (Eds.), Logic Programming and Nonmonotonic Reasoning. XIII, 454 pages. 2005.

Vol. 3661: T. Panayiotopoulos, J. Gratch, R. Aylett, D. Ballin, P. Olivier, T. Rist (Eds.), Intelligent Virtual Agents. XIII, 506 pages. 2005.

Vol. 3658: V. Matoušek, P. Mautner, T. Pavelka (Eds.), Text, Speech and Dialogue. XV, 460 pages. 2005.

Vol. 3651: R. Dale, K.-F. Wong, J. Su, O.Y. Kwong (Eds.), Natural Language Processing – IJCNLP 2005. XXI, 1031 pages. 2005.

Vol. 3642: D. Ślęzak, J. Yao, J.F. Peters, W. Ziarko, X. Hu (Eds.), Rough Sets, Fuzzy Sets, Data Mining, and Granular Computing, Part II. XXIII, 738 pages. 2005.

Vol. 3641: D. Ślęzak, G. Wang, M. Szczuka, I. Düntsch, Y. Yao (Eds.), Rough Sets, Fuzzy Sets, Data Mining, and Granular Computing, Part I. XXIV, 742 pages. 2005.

Vol. 3635: J.R. Winkler, M. Niranjan, N.D. Lawrence (Eds.), Deterministic and Statistical Methods in Machine Learning. VIII, 341 pages. 2005.

Vol. 3632: R. Nieuwenhuis (Ed.), Automated Deduction – CADE-20. XIII, 459 pages. 2005.

Vol. 3630: M.S. Capcarrère, A.A. Freitas, P.J. Bentley, C.G. Johnson, J. Timmis (Eds.), Advances in Artificial Life. XIX, 949 pages. 2005.

Vol. 3626: B. Ganter, G. Stumme, R. Wille (Eds.), Formal Concept Analysis. X, 349 pages. 2005.

Vol. 3625: S. Kramer, B. Pfahringer (Eds.), Inductive Logic Programming. XIII, 427 pages. 2005.

Vol. 3620: H. Muñoz-Ávila, F. Ricci (Eds.), Case-Based Reasoning Research and Development. XV, 654 pages. 2005.

Vol. 3614: L. Wang, Y. Jin (Eds.), Fuzzy Systems and Knowledge Discovery, Part II. XLI, 1314 pages. 2005.

Vol. 3613: L. Wang, Y. Jin (Eds.), Fuzzy Systems and Knowledge Discovery, Part I. XLI, 1334 pages. 2005.

Vol. 3607: J.-D. Zucker, L. Saitta (Eds.), Abstraction, Reformulation and Approximation. XII, 376 pages. 2005.

Vol. 3601: G. Moro, S. Bergamaschi, K. Aberer (Eds.), Agents and Peer-to-Peer Computing. XII, 245 pages. 2005.

Vol. 3600: F. Wiedijk (Ed.), The Seventeen Provers of the World. XVI, 159 pages. 2006.

Vol. 3596: F. Dau, M.-L. Mugnier, G. Stumme (Eds.), Conceptual Structures: Common Semantics for Sharing Knowledge. XI, 467 pages. 2005.

Vol. 3593: V. Mařík, R. W. Brennan, M. Pěchouček (Eds.), Holonic and Multi-Agent Systems for Manufacturing. XI, 269 pages. 2005.

Vol. 3587: P. Perner, A. Imiya (Eds.), Machine Learning and Data Mining in Pattern Recognition. XVII, 695 pages. 2005.

Vol. 3584: X. Li, S. Wang, Z.Y. Dong (Eds.), Advanced Data Mining and Applications. XIX, 835 pages. 2005.

Vol. 3581: S. Miksch, J. Hunter, E.T. Keravnou (Eds.), Artificial Intelligence in Medicine. XVII, 547 pages. 2005.

Vol. 3577: R. Falcone, S. Barber, J. Sabater-Mir, M.P. Singh (Eds.), Trusting Agents for Trusting Electronic Societies. VIII, 235 pages. 2005.

Vol. 3575: S. Wermter, G. Palm, M. Elshaw (Eds.), Biomimetic Neural Learning for Intelligent Robots. IX, 383 pages. 2005.

Vol. 3571: L. Godo (Ed.), Symbolic and Quantitative Approaches to Reasoning with Uncertainty. XVI, 1028 pages. 2005.

Vol. 3559: P. Auer, R. Meir (Eds.), Learning Theory. XI, 692 pages. 2005.

Vol. 3558: V. Torra, Y. Narukawa, S. Miyamoto (Eds.), Modeling Decisions for Artificial Intelligence. XII, 470 pages. 2005.

Vol. 3554: A.K. Dey, B. Kokinov, D.B. Leake, R. Turner (Eds.), Modeling and Using Context. XIV, 572 pages. 2005.

Vol. 3550: T. Eymann, F. Klügl, W. Lamersdorf, M. Klusch, M.N. Huhns (Eds.), Multiagent System Technologies. XI, 246 pages. 2005.

Vol. 3539: K. Morik, J.-F. Boulicaut, A. Siebes (Eds.), Local Pattern Detection. XI, 233 pages. 2005.

Vol. 3538: L. Ardissono, P. Brna, A. Mitrović (Eds.), User Modeling 2005. XVI, 533 pages. 2005.

Vol. 3533: M. Ali, F. Esposito (Eds.), Innovations in Applied Artificial Intelligence. XX, 858 pages. 2005.

Vol. 3528: P.S. Szczepaniak, J. Kacprzyk, A. Niewiadomski (Eds.), Advances in Web Intelligence. XVII, 513 pages. 2005.

Vol. 3518: T.-B. Ho, D. Cheung, H. Liu (Eds.), Advances in Knowledge Discovery and Data Mining. XXI, 864 pages. 2005.

Vol. 3508: P. Bresciani, P. Giorgini, B. Henderson-Sellers, G. Low, M. Winikoff (Eds.), Agent-Oriented Information Systems II. X, 227 pages. 2005.